*Charlotte and [...]
you will find this in-
teresting.    Fritz*

*A*dventure Guide

# Hungary

Dante Mena

HUNTER

HUNTER PUBLISHING, INC.
130 Campus Drive, Edison NJ 08818
732-225-1900, 800-255-0343, fax 732-417-0482
comments@hunterpublishing.com

4176 Saint-Denis, Montréal, Québec
Canada H2W 2M5
514-843-9447; fax 515-843-9448; info@ulysses.com

The Boundary, Wheatley Road, Garsington
Oxford, OX44 9EJ England
01865-361122; fax 01865-361133
windsorbooks@compuserve.com

ISBN 978-1-58843-576-7
1-58843-576-8
© 2007 Hunter Publishing, Inc.

Maps © 2007 Hunter Publishing, Inc.

Cover photograph: *Taking a break at the riding show in Puszta*
(© FAN travelstock/Alamy)
Interior photos courtesy of Hungarian National Tourist Board, Hungarian Friends of Nature Association and other sources as indicted.

For complete information about the hundreds of other travel guides offered by Hunter Publishing, visit our Web site at:
**www.hunterpublishing.com**

4 3 2 1

# Contents

# Introduction

A mystery shrouds the true origins of man in the regions of Hungary. When men appeared in the shadows of the Danube valleys and the plains, they inhabited the caves. They spread out at first, gathering fruits, nuts and wild vegetables, and then they began to hunt. They tracked roe deer, bison and giant mammoths. When they came home, they

painted their memories under the flickering light of the cave walls of the region, some of which you can see today. That was back around 50,000 BC. It was the age of Paleolithic man.

But Paleolithic man's dominance ended 20,000 years ago as the cold glaciers of the last ice age retreated. The ambitious and highly intelligent Neolithic man succeeded his cousin somewhere between 5,000 and 4,000 BC. He developed stable communities and introduced farming and social structure, then established territories and separated into specific areas in the region. It was the basis upon which men would build cities and for which they would make war.

## ■ The Land

The land called Hungary today, though teaming with wildlife, natural fruits, vegetables and grains, was a natural bridge between Europe and Asia. The Great and Little Alföld (pronounced Allfurld), or Hungarian plains, are a natural gateway to Europe, leading to the Moravian Gate in the north, a low-lying passage along the Danube River that offers passage into Western Europe. History would see the land absorb the incursions of war-like tribes. These tribes often left settlements behind and mingled their strains into the local cultures. But the mystery of Hungary is that no one knows exactly where the Hungarians came from. It is the land of the Magyars (Hungarians), who speak a tongue that is similar to Finnish. The Huns who flowed across the land in later years, were an Asian stock, not Hungarian. The rapacious Turks followed the Huns, and in the 20th century, the Nazi Germans, and communist Russians, each of whom left their own marks. This extraordinary mix has created one of the most varied and unusual cultural blends in the world.

It is a land of medicinal baths, mineral springs, health spas, and public pools, for, owing to the volcanic mountain chains that surround the country, beneath its soil unique mixtures of life-giving waters that bubble to the surface in literally hundreds of locations throughout the nation.

Hungary is dominated by the Great Carpathian Basin (historically one of the best horseback riding areas of the world), comprised of the Little and Great Alföld (Plains) of Hungary. In fact 84% of Hungary is less than 650 feet above sea level because of this special geography. These two low-lying plains are separated by the modest trans-Danubian mountains, only recently formed in geological history. However, both the Little and Great Alföld are alluvial plains, formed in considerable part by the Danube and the Tisza rivers. Geologists hold that the basin formed during the Tertiary period as the Alpine (to the west), Carpathian (to the north and east), and Dinaric (to the south) mountain chains rose up to fold it in. Gradually a marine trough formed, and in the Mesozoic era massive deposits of limestone and dolomite accumulated on the floor of this prehistoric sea. Today they form the bottom of the Carpathian Basin.

During the Pliocene era the massif in the center of the basin began to subside, yielding to the inundation of the prehistoric Pannonian Sea. (The name Pannonia is at times used in literature and advertising in this region.) The Pannonian Sea added huge quantities of sand and claylike sediment, in some areas as much as 3,000 feet deep. It gradually transformed into a series of freshwater lakes. Subsidence and uplift changed the physiology, drying up some parts and eventually forming the river systems of today. The Danube and the Tisza rivers and their tributaries have, as a result, not only incised the geography, they have brought down great quantities of fluvial sediment which has added hundreds of feet of river deposit on top of the old Pannonian deposits. Because of this, these are generally excellent agricultural areas, accounting for the fact that today 54% of Hungarian soil is under cultivation.

As the Danube river gradually migrated southward, the soil dried, giving birth to fertile expanses of sandy soil interspersed with dunes. It turned the Great Alföld into a grazing paradise, with expanses of flat grassy land, such as the Tisza floodplain and some areas along the winding Danube. This area has often been compared to the Plains States of America, complete with its own cowboys, the Csikós, whose horseback riding skills are legendary.

After the Danube enters the Little Alföld at the Moravian Gate, the low-lying passageway near Bratislava, she meanders and then carves a narrow gorge near Visegrád. Known as the Danube bend, it is the site of a famous castle, and a historic center of knighthood and chivalry centuries ago. Here, great vistas and picturesque views allow one to view the river's course from the heights of the surrounding mountains. On the west bank are the Carpathian Mountains, and on the East Bank are the Transdanubian Mountains, a recently formed low-lying extension, the only fence left to the Great Alföld in the Carpathian Basin. From here, the river takes on its romantic, flowing character, sailing through Budapest, which it divides into two cities (Pest and Buda). To the southwest stretch the plains of the Carpathian basin, the Great Alföld.

The Danube and its tributaries, throughout their winding path, harbor numerous bird sanctuaries, wildlife preserves, castles and outposts of days gone by. But in the north a narrow band of hills commune with the lower Carpathians. To this area, going from northwestern to northeastern Hungary, are the Börzsöny, Cserhát, Mátra, Bükk (home of the famous Bükk National Park), and the Zemplén mountains. Just north of these mountains, in the table lands of the lower Carpathians, a hump sticks up toward Slovakia. This area is primarily Mesozoic limestone formed about 150 million years ago. It is home to numerous caves such as the Domica-Aggtelek Cave on the Slovak-Hungarian border, which extends for 21 km/13 miles beneath the earth.

## Lake Balaton

Standing on the hills overlooking Lake Balaton on a hot afternoon, I will never forget watching a ferry cross the water, from my point of view, scarcely larger than an ant in the midst of the blue expanse. As the Danube is the dominating river and drainage system of Central Europe, so is Lake Balaton without a doubt, the dominating lake of Eastern and Central Europe. Draining into the Danube by means of the Sió-canal, it is the largest freshwater lake in Europe. From some points on its shores you get the inescapable impression that you are looking out on a sea. On its banks, there are numerous beaches, old monastaries, restaurants and hotels. Formed by tectonic forces about 10,000 years ago, it has a surface area of 593 square km/229 square miles. Incredibly, its mean depth is only 3.2 m/10½ feet. Although it is covered by ice in the winter (perfect for ice sailing), in the summer its average water temperature is 23°C/73°F, thus making it both a summer and winter vacation paradise. That accounts for its 2,000,000 visitors each year. The southern shore is sandy beach while the northern shore is marked by older mountains of volcanic origin with numerous old forts on their tops, picturesque vineyards on their slopes and plenty of hiking and riding trails.

## ■ Climate

Hungary is considered one of the breadbasket nations of the world, owing in large measure to its mild weather. Summers can be hot, but are generally quite tolerable. Only occasionally do temperatures range into the nineties. Most of the time summer weather hovers in the 70s to 80s F. Although the rainy season is in the spring, summer squalls can also occur from June through September. The noticeable increase in precipitation in the summer months on the chart below is due to those occasional thunderstorms. This makes for a few interspersed days with sticky humidity, although the weather is generally dry and pleasant. Fall and spring hover around 10-15°C/50-60°F. During some chilly mornings temperatures may occasionally drop as much as 20°, so I would recommend packing a jacket and a sweater. Winters are on the cold side, but tolerable, and often pleasant. They are generally dry, although there can be some heavy snows in the midst of winter. Temperatures hover around 0-10°C/32-50°F, except in January and February when they dip to minus 4-1°C/25-35°F. If you are into winter travel, definitely take a hat or parka. Spring and summer are, however, shirt-sleeve weather and quite nice.

# ■ Wildlife

Protected wetlands predominate along parts of the Danube drainage and the Hungarian plains, which is a home for herons, cormorants, egrets, swans, storks, hundreds of water fowl, and numerous song birds, hawks and eagles as well.

*Black stork*

The Tisza River subdrainage into the Danube, the Puszta (pronounced Phoostah), a unique saliferous grassy desert bordered by wetlands and forest, contains the Hortobágy National Park, the oldest national park in Hungary. Pronounced, "hortobawdyi," this unique area is a nesting place for over 300 observed species of birds. The forests also contain many rare species, including the reclusive black stork and white-tailed eagle.

As you travel the interior areas of the country, you may see stork nests on the rooftops of houses, and sometimes on telephone poles.

Otters (lutra lutra), the highly intelligent and inquisitve comedian of the forest, may be seen along creeks and rivers in some locations. Its dark silky black fur, prized for trapping, shines when it's wet. Its webbed feet give it superb aquatic skills and it navigates the depths of ponds and streams with ease. However, like other species, it is in danger from man. Its primary food is fish, but it can eat any small prey, such as small birds, frogs, squirrels, mice, and rats. Found primarily in Northern Hungary, otters live on the Tisza River system southward as well.

*Red deer*

Red deer are the largest grass eaters of the Carpathians and live along border areas of the hills as well. The stags bear majestic antlers. The last three world champion red deer stag trophies came out of the Carpathians. Though the red deer is elusive, their numbers make it probable that you'll see one or more during your journey. They frequent forest glades and can sometimes be seen in open fields or by streams and lake beds. They have been found south as far as the mountains around Balaton.

Roe deer are more abundant than the red deer, especially in the lower elevations. It is a small almost tailless deer. Reddish brown in summer and grayish with a noticeable white patch around the rump in winter, the male usually has three -pronged bony antlers, which he sheds and grows anew each year. The antlers are used to slash territorial markings on trees, for self defense, and for mating combat. He barks like a dog when alarmed. Once a year the female bears one to three young. Although solitary animals in the summer, they congregate in herds from October to April. They have been found in all areas of Hungary and, in fact, they are the most frequently bagged animal by hunters.

Wild boar, also known as wild pig, range across northern and eastern Hungary. Except for the old males, they travel in groups of five to 15, so

*Wild boar*

where you see one, you are likely to see others as well. Grizzly-haired, brownish or blackish, they stand up to four feet high at the shoulder and males can weigh as much as 550 lbs. Females reach three feet at the shoulder, and 290 lbs. They produce a bevy of young every four months. Nocturnal, good swimmers, with extraodinary hearing, they have been known to hear a match break 100 feet away. But they have poor eyesight. They can be lethally dangerous and, though they are not carnivores, their sharp tusks can be significant weapons. With their swiftness, great strength and ferocity, they are animals to admire at a distance.

The red fox inhabits most of Europe, as well as Hungary. Its rusty brown coat and black tail usually blend well against the forest soil. It reaches only two to three feet in height, so it prefers rodents and smaller animals for dinner. Its tail can be as long as two feet, creating the illusion of a much larger size.

*Buzzard*

The buzzard (common or Eurasian) is one of the most common birds of prey. He is often seen in the Hortobagy National Park or in Northern Hungary. Usually 1½-2½ feet in length, their wingspan of 3¾ to four feet belies their relatively light frame. They weigh less than 20 pounds. Buzzards have rusty brown to variegated gray plummage, with barred tail feathers, and hunt for rabbit, rodents, small birds, or occasionally, carion.

The great bustard. There are an estimated 40,000 of these birds left, which is not much because they have a high mortality rate (70%) in the first year. Hungary is one of the few areas in the world where you will see this bird nesting as it has done for centuries. It is the heaviest bird in the world. Weighing in at up to 30 lbs and with a wing span of over three feet, this bird stands as tall as a roe deer's shoulder, about the size of a large turkey. Its brilliant plumage is a variegated brown and white, and it is crowned with a white neck and moderately brown head. A meaty delight with delicate flesh, it was once almost hunted almost out of existence. Efforts have been made to save it, but still its population has dwindled so drastically that it is listed as a vulnerable species. Although you might see it in some areas of northern Hungary, it is most visible in Hortobágy National Park.

*Great bustard, by Hungarian painter Szabolcs Kókay (www.kokay.hu)*

In addition to the wild breeds and rare species, there are a number of domestic breeds of animals that exist nowhere else in the world. Some of these are in danger of dying out as well, such as the curly-haired red mangalica pig, twisted-horned racka sheep, and Hungarian grey cattle.

Hungary is a unique area for wildlife, inhabited by numerous endangered and protected species, only a few of which we have mentioned. It is for this reason that it is wise to try to be careful of your impact on the environment. Be careful not to leave your mark behind.

Your best chances for seeing wildlife are at the national parks and the zoos. See the *Appendix* for further information on zoos and parks.

# ■ Flora

 When forests begin in the north, they are characterized by the evergreen conifers, gradually mixing with decidous trees, usually spruce, giving way eventually to beech and beech-conifer mixed forest. This is the home of the red deer, the lynx, and the roe deer.

**Decidous forest:** The lowest lying forest areas and the lower basin areas are home to willows, poplars, oak, ash, and elm, and are often bordered by fields of tall grasses and variegated flowers that cover the rolling open terrain. A number of protected sights, national forests and parks cradle these areas also.

**Marshes and wetlands:** Along the Duna and several of the major rivers it is common to find localized marsh vegetation growing profusely on the river banks and mud flats. These too are unique in their flowering plant life. Some of these areas are protected sites.

**The Puszta:** On the flood plain of the Tisza River is a unique terrain in Europe, similar to marsh areas of Central Africa and some parts of South America. Parts also resemble the Great Plains of America. Its unique characteristics have caused Hungary, the EU, and UNESCO to designate almost the entire area a National Park and a World Protected Site. Its salty soil has made it home to hundreds of hardy grassy plants and unique flowers, as well as hundreds of nesting birds, both local and migrating. This is where you will find the Hortobágy National Park and, inside its northwestern border, the fabulous Tisza River and Tisza Lake.

# ■ When to Go

Hungary is a good place to visit any season, although summer is the most common preference. Yet, although in Budapest and the main cities accommodations are available year-round, many hostels and hotels may close down completely in the country-side outside the main tourist seasons. So it's wise to check ahead. In addition, you must always consider when the local festivals and events are taking place. See our website, www. hunterpublishing.com (click on Adventure Guides, then Hungary) for a list of all the festivals and when they take place. At times, these may be so popular that, unless you are booked well ahead, finding a place to stay could be almost impossible. In Budapest and its surroundings, for instance, during the annual Formula 1 race almost every hotel is booked for up to a year in advance. Consequently, hotel rates double, if you can find a room!

Hungary has an excellent tourist support system through their Tourinform offices (see *Appendix* for offices throughout the country). These offices almost always have at least one good English speaker. They can help in bookings, travel arrangements, directions, and sometimes in emergencies as well. However, even at that, it is wise to check directly with the hotel, restaurant or whatever you want to book.

## Best Months

High season is vacation time, the prime travel months of June and July. Rates are high then, and sometimes accommodations may be hard to find. On the other hand, August is beautiful in Hungary, and also extremely crowded. The annual Formula 1 race will keep you out of quality Budapest lodging if you book too late. If you are planning an August excursion, book at least 16 weeks in advance in Budapest or you may well be forced into an unwanted choice.

April-May and September-October are the best bargain months for travelers, and the weather is still good enough to be comfortable throughout your stay. May brings flowers, a chance to see the full bloom of the countryside before the hordes arrive in mid-summer. And, while September is the opposite of May, it means the end of summer and the beginning of autumn. So, you may often see the first of the autumn blooms, and watch the changes in the forest with its musky odors and wild variations of colors. By mid-September the student crowd has gone back to school and most people on summer vacation have gone home, so it can also be a bargain month.

# ■ Travel Documents

 Travelers from abroad must carry passports. A visa is not required from the USA. However, you may be asked for your ID at any time while traveling, so you should definitely carry your passport with you. I was asked for my ID, for instance, on a train between Bratislava and Budapest. There is an increased sensitivity to illegal immigration, as Hungary's exploding prosperity (and entrance into the EU) has made it a target for increasing numbers of people seeking a better life. Your passport may kept at the front desk of your hotel, where its information is logged overnight. So if you leave on an outing in the morning, don't forget to take it with you.

Passports are also not infrequently asked for by bus companies, trains, and, of course, airlines. However, they are also used for identification and tracking with car rental agencies, and sometimes with long-term riverboat cruises.

# ■ How to Get There

 **Budapest's Ferihegy Airport** is the primary gateway to Hungary. Most major carriers offer flights to and from Ferihegy via connecting flights. Direct flights are most often not really direct, but include a stopover at some other European city such as Paris, Rome or Milan. Once you get to these gateway cities, you can book inter-regional flights at exceptionally low rates. So, you can book a direct flight, stay several days in the gateway city you picked, and then take a flight or rent a car to your other destination.

Check with Crossair/Swiss (formerly Swiss Air) and KLM, or Delta, whose rates can often be quite competitive. Since the travel industry has been in a state of flux recently, be sure you check several carriers for their round-trip and return flights. There can be wide variations in pricing.

A not infrequent route to Budapest is to fly via Vienna. You can spend a few nights in this famous city, the former center of the Austro-Hungarian Empire, and then connect to Budapest a few days later, by train or by air. In addition, England has numerous direct flights to Budapest from any one of several airports, frequently at discount prices.

Hungarian carrier MALÉV has an agreement with Delta that allows convenient non-stop flights to Ferihegy Airport 2, which is approximately 10 miles out of Budapest. There is an airport taxi service run by a consortiom of hotels that will take you into town, so check with your hotel to make sure they have a seat for you. It is wise to compare rates with several airlines. Book your flights several weeks in advance. Delay in booking can cost you substantial sums of money, as the price goes up the closer you get to flight time.

# ■ Getting Around

- **Tip 1:** Have your documents with you. While travel in the EU is much easier than in most countries of the world, certain laws regarding international child abduction and illegal immigration are enforced at a number of border points. You should have not just your driver's license, but your passport, as well as documents substantiating that you are insured for foreign travel (see Tip 3 below), and also a copy of your birth certificates and/or adoption papers when traveling with family.

■ **Tip 2:** As in all countries, you must be careful of petty criminals. Make sure your purse and/or wallet is secure. Try to store your credit cards, important documents and large bills in buttoned inner coat pockets. Don't leave personal articles unattended, and make sure they are draped around your neck (not your shoulder) in crowded areas. Never leave valuables in a car. Tourists in every part of the world are a target, but, if you take precautions, it is not likely you will be one of the victims.

■ **Tip 3:** No one wants to think about medical emergencies, but, when planning a foreign trip, that can be a crucial factor. Make sure your medical insurance covers you for overseas travel. If it does not, then you can get supplemental coverage for the trip through several good international companies. This way you can rest assured that you will always be taken care of if you need medical help. If you can afford the extra premium, always make sure the insurance covers you for transport back home if necessary.

■ **4th Tip:** Unfortunately, some people try to take advantage of the natural good will of many travelers. So, if you see someone that seems to need help on the side of a road, don't stop. There have been many scams on unsuspecting tourists. That does not mean you have to leave someone stranded. If you have a cell phone you can call the police for help or, at your next stop, you can try to get help.

## Driving

Without a doubt, a private car is the best way to get around in Hungary. Most American car rental companies have offices in Budapest. Driving on the left side of the road may take some getting used to, but US driver's licenses are accepted in lieu of an international driver's licenses. The main roads are modern and generally well kept, and there are road rests with restaurants and sometimes a few rooms to rent throughout the country. Keep in mind that it may be illegal to cross the border to other countries from Hungary if your rental contract does not stipulate that you are allowed to do so, despite EU allowances. You can reserve a car ahead of time. Most major US and European car rental agencies have offices in the area.

In most cases, a first aid kit, emergency triangle, and registration are provided in the rental, but be sure to check as registration is required by law. In addition, make sure you have chains if you are traveling in the winter months. Tell your rental agency where you are going. They may have some tips for driving in the area, plus they will notify the destination branch office of your itinerary.

## Driver's Tips

Rules of the road are standardized throughout Europe and they do not differ terribly from those of the United States. Crosswalks in Europe are generally painted "zebra" sections on the pavement, or separated by stripes running across the road. While driving, avoid turning right at an intersection corner against the light, as is common in many American cities. In Europe, this could land you a ticket, depending on local enforcement. Make sure your glove compartment contains the car registration and insurance papers. When on the road always carry your passport and your driver's license.

Expect traffic delays (sometimes considerable) during the high points of the tourist season. You can also be sure of some delay at border crossings that still exist between Hungary and Slovakia or between Hungary and Austria (where they do routine border checks of non-EU drivers). Most European travelers take the delays in stride, so be patient.

Cars are powered by unleaded or diesel fuel. Be sure you know what your vehicle is using. And be prepared for gasoline that normally runs two to three times US prices. Fuel is priced by the litre, not by the gallon.

## Parking

Parking is not to be taken for granted. Most tourist spots are fully occupied most of the time and getting a parking spot can be a challenge. Generally, there are no public parking spaces. Your car may have a time placard, to be placed on the window and spun to the time of your arrival. You would use this in some short-term parking spots. However, it is increasingly frequent to find public meters. You park and go to a meter that gives a ticket for a set time period. You pay and punch in for the amount of time you want and the meter issues a ticket, which you place on your dash (make sure the stamped side is visible). Garages, where available, are usually metered as well, although in that case you take a ticket as you enter and pay when you leave.

Toll roads are well maintained and modern, but the cost is off-set by the tolls charged. It is generally better to try to have enough change to pay for tolls exactly. Make sure that you have an the equivalent of an extra $15 in euros just for tolls.

## By Train

Rail lines are one of the more pleasant aspects of European travel. However, in the Central European countries, some of the rail cars are not yet up to the rest of Europe. Nevertheless, travel is quite open and efficient. Most of the trains run on time. In all cases there are second- or first-class coaches to choose from. In most cases the first-class coaches are worth it, as second-class is usually crowded. Second-class coaches may, in fact, have standing room only. The coaches are also old, and can be uncomfortable. Check with the ticket agent to be sure. Also watch for smoking and non-smoking coaches. The smokers' coaches are generally filled with a musty cloud of nicotine-filled fog, and are to be avoided if you are a non-smoker. In addition, there is the "Intercity" train, as opposed to the cross-country train system. The Intercity cars are relatively new and comfortable, with cushioned seats and clean, well lighted accommodations. However, if you have a bicycle, you will be be forced to use separate trains and/or coaches, as there are certain trains in which bicycles are allowed and others in which they are prohibited. So, you must check the train schedules to be sure. In most cases you must carry the bicycle on and off yourself, unless you pay for a special service to carry it for you (which may be unreasonably expensive). The

Hungarian Railway link for booking and information is with
MAV, at www.elvira.hu

## By Bus

Buses will take you just about anywhere, as the bus
system in the Central European countries is
extraordinary. Buses are generally well maintained and comfortable, and often refreshements
are offered in transit (although these tend to be pricey). You
can bring your own refreshments and a lunch on board.
Almost every city has a connecting link with a bus system if
not a train system, and all train stops are integrated with a
local bus system. If you are not into biking, you can construct
a comfortable and satisfactory tour by bus. In addition, the
Hungarian bus company, Volan Busz (Volan Bus) has its own
travel agency, which can help in planning itineraries. I found,
however, that sometimes a local Volan Bus office may not
have English speakers. So it is better to plan this ahead of
time, using their website, which is also in English – www.
volanbusz.hu. Tickets are normally quite inexpensive. However, rural stations may be simply bus stops. You should have
maps, know where you want to go and determine exactly
where to get on and off in advance. These can be confirmed
ahead of time by making contact with their main office in
Budapest, and confirming your travel arraingements, or
alternatively, use Tourinform, which will help in communication (see *Appendix* for Tourinform offices).

## ■ Accommodations

This guide offers a selection of hotels based on location and comfort level. By no means is it all-inclusive. In general the higher-end accommodations in
Budapest are consistently good. As you leave the
main cities, the standards of accommodation become less reliable and the same can be said of anything less than four-star
accommodations. Booking places by phone or e-mail with ratings under four stars can be risky. You can expect the quality
of rooms to be lower than American standards. There may be
a limited television with few stations, or no television at all.
However, breakfast is usually included – in most cases includ-

ing cheeses, meats, breads and coffee or tea and possibly some juices. Rarely do you find ready-made breakfast cereals, American-style pancakes, or ham and eggs, except in four-stars.

You can book accommodations through Tourinform (see page 577 for contacts), which will assure you of adequate facilities, as they know the terrain and are anxious for foreign travelers to have a good time.

🌶 **Star ratings** are explained on page 577.

If you are opting for lower-budget travel, then you should consider that many chalets and cabins are often shared, and that rooms may often come without a shower or bath. You must stipulate that you want a bathroom with your room. In any event, if you are budget traveling, it is wise to carry exra toilet paper, a wash towel, and bath towel, in addition to slippers and robe. It may be handy for the man to carry a battery-powered electric razor (with spare batteries). An electric blow dryer is often stocked as a matter of course in most hotels, but it is still not a bad idea to pack one. Keep in mind that European electric systems are 220 volts, not 110 volts as with American systems. You should have a dryer that will match the European system, or have an adapter for your appliance(s).

If you walk into a city without prior reservations, search out the local tourist information center. I do not recommend this in any but the major cities, as outlying towns may leave you stranded without enough linguistic knowledge to negotiate. However, if you work with Tourinform in advance, this problem is solved.

# ■ Dining

Some tourists may be astonished to find that pancakes or other sweet foods can be served as the main course at lunches and dinners. On the other hand, salads are not so common except in the large cities. But often, when a salad is served, it is a combination of cucumbers, tomatoes, cabbage, and peppers. Vegetables are most commonly served pickled, although in restaurants you may of course find fresh salads as well.

In the 1996 World Chef's Olympics, the Hungarian chefs won the overall silver medal, as well as numerous individual medals. This only underscores the incredible variety and taste of Hungarian cuisine. It is a historical mixture of the Alföld herders' food spiced with the influences of Italian, German, Turkish, Czech, Slovakian, Tarter, Serb, and Croation cooking. Ranging across the plain, much like American cowboys, they developed their own style of cooking in the "bogrács," a deep pot that hung over the fire suspended on a makeshift tripod. That it was a pot and not a pan probably accounts for the emphasis on sauces and soups that we see today, including the famous Hungarian goulash and its less-known cousin, pörkölt (per-kerlt). Inside the bogrács, tasty red Hungarian paprika, flatlands onion, tender plains beef and mutton were stewed with spices and condiments. To this day, Hungarians hold annual bogrács cookouts all over the country, and the best pörkölt wins the day.

A cuisine specialty often served in restaurants is hortobágyi húsos palacsinta (hortobágy meat pancakes). Chicken, beef, or mutton lumps cooked in paprika are submerged in sour cream, wrapped in slightly salty pancakes with a tomato and paprika and spices.

Traditional Hungarian meals start with a soup. Try újházi tyúkhúsleves (újházi chicken soup). Green peas and sliced mushrooms are mixed in with turnips, celery root, kohlrabi, carrots cut into julien strips, and cooked with healthy slices of meaty chicken.

Bakony gomba leves is a mushroom soup named after Bakony mountain, which borders Lake Balaton. Mushrooms are cooked in a thick aromatic mixture including smoked sausage, bacon, sour cream, bay leaves, and kholrabi. A traditional soup at New Year's is the korhelyleves (the drunkard's soup), a mixture of pork, kolbász (sausage), garlic, paprika, thick tomato sauce, sour cream, and spices, guaranteed to set the palate thirsting for more courses.

In hot weather Hungarians often start the meal with a fruit soup, especially hideg (he-degg) meggy (meddy), leves (cold cherry soup), or other fruits that may generally be called hideg gyümölcs leves (cold fruit soup). Fruit is lightly cooked in water with sugar, cinnamon, cloves and/or lemon peel, and then thickened with a mixture of sour cream and flour, then chilled. On a hot day this cold cuisine is delightfully refreshing.

Soups are followed by the meal, of which gulyás is the most famous, a blend of paprika, choice beef, garlic, potatoes, tomatoes, and spices. Gulyás, although classified as a stew, is actually a very thick soup in Hungary. It is guaranteed to keep you eating with its mouth-watering flavor. Or perhaps paprikás csirke (paprika chicken) may stimulate your palate with its blend of mild plains paprika, sour cream spiced with garlic, tomatoes, chicken and spices mixed together in a delightfully aromatic sauce. It is served with the thick rolled noodles so typical of Slavic dishes.

A common dish is sonkás kocka (ham with noodles). Long, flat noodles are cooked and then a mixture of egg yolk, sour cream, ground smoked ham, and whipped egg whites are mixed in and baked. Another Hungarian favorite is káposztás kocka (pasta with cabbage) or túrós csusza (pasta with cottage cheese). Don't forget to try the goose liver, a famous and uniquely flavored Hungarian specialty.

Since Balaton Lake and the Danube and its tributaries make up such a large part of Hungary, you are sure to find some unique fresh water fish dishes. Dorozsmai molnárponty is filleted carp, slit to make room for a stuffing of strips of bacon, and fried, and then drenched in pörkölt sauce, and served with potatoes. Pörkölt is basically paprika, onions, and stewed meat, sometimes prepared with sour cream. It serves as a base for numerous Hungarian dishes. You might also try halászlé (fish soup), which is basically carp with several types of paprika, onions, tomatoes and spices. Some say you have not tasted Hungary without trying this. Halászlé is a tradition at Christmas in many Hungarian homes.

Pusztapörkölt is named after the sheep- and cattle-grazing flatlands of the Alföld, and particularly the arid areas called the Puszta, near the Tisza River. Made from tender beef, it combines the typical pörkölt with tomatoes and garlic. Lecsó (pronounced lech-o) is a sauce base for numerous courses, made from paprika, tomatoes, green peppers, onions, and spices. Its thick, creamy substance adds a unique taste to the menu and you can often get chicken, potatoes, or noodles prepared with lecsó.

Desserts clearly show the Austrian and German influence. Try gundel palacsinta (gundel-style chocolate pancakes), meggyes rétes (morello cherry strudel) or somlói galuska cake with chocolate sauce and cream.

## Dining Customs & Tipping

On the road, in most lower-end restaurants, you generally seat yourself. However, keep in mind, that while tables in the mountains may be shared, in the quality city restaurants the waiter will seat you.

Meals are not served to the entire table at once, but when each dish is ready and hot. So be prepared to watch others receive their plates before you. It depends entirely on the preparation time for each dish.

Tips are the custom, from 10% to 15% of the tab.

In quality restaurants, the waiter will usually provide you with a plate upon which the bill is discretely placed. In the more common establishments, you have to call the waiter for the bill. Do not leave the tip on the table. It is preferable to give it directly to the waiter. VISA and MasterCard are generally accepted throughout the region. If you pay with a card, however, it is better to give the waiter his tip in cash.

## Wine Country

Hungarian wine has been produced for thousands of years, today ranking only behind France and Italy in overall reputation, but outstripping both in certain superior vintages almost every year. In fact, the amount of Hungarian soil devoted to vineyards is around 500,000 acres, only a little less than the vineyards of the entire United States! Hungarian cuisine, understandably, should be complemented with Hungarian wine, and is offered in all good restaurants.

Hungary is home to 20 wine producing regions, producing Cabernet Sauvignon, Pinot Gris, Merlot, Riesling, Chardonnay, sparkling Rosé, and many others. Grape varieties unique to Hungary and excellent for wine include Kadarka, Kékfrankos, Juhfark, and Furmint.

The first international recognition of Hungarian wine came at the council of Trident in 1562 when Pope Pius IV received a gift of Tokaji Aszu wine (the most famous dessert wine of Hungary, originating in the Tokaji region) from Gyögy Draskovich, Bishop of Zagrev. After tasting the wine the Pope remarked, "Summum pontificem talia vina decent" (Such wines befit the supreme pontiff). By the middle of the 18th century, the Hungarian vineyards were indisputably the "wine region of the world," and so it was that in the gold-plated luxury of the palace of Versailles, the illustrious Sun King, King Louis the XIV, offered a bottle of Tokaji wine to Madame Pompadour, saying, "C'est le roi des vins et le vin de rois." (This is the wine of kings and the king of wines). Legend has it that Tokaj wines help produce male offspring. For just that reason more than one royal family seeking to insure an heir to the throne tasted its smooth sweet texture. With such a heritage it is no wonder that UNESCO ranks Tokaji as a World Heritage Region and that Tokaji wines are celebrated in the area at the end of every May with symphonies, local festivities, and an abundance of food and flowing beverage.

There are literally thousands of small vineyards and hundreds of thousands of gardens with grape arbors. I visited one Hungarian man at his country home. He invited me to see his wine cellar. I expected it would match the modest configuration of the house. But I was astonished to walk down deep stairs to a cellar that was larger than his home! He had thermometers and temperature-regulating pipes running around the walls. He was making his own wine, as thousands of others do in Hungary, and aging his own vintage to perfection. Some of the casks had been filled by his grandfather.

The volcanic soils along the Carpathians, near the Tisza drainage, and the mild climate, coupled with the warm sunshine of the basin, make Hungary one of the supreme wine-producing regions of the world. As you walk the streets of most cities, wine shops, Borkimérés, usually at sub-basement level, offer wines directly from kegs. You purchase the wine, and they fill a plastic bottle for you from the keg. But, as a caution, taste and compare.

Although Tokaji Aszu may indeed be considered the king of wines, many other Hungarian wines vie for top honors every year. A good red wine is Egri Bikavér (or bulls blood), because of its rich red color, and because it is from Eger, where a famous bloody resistance to Turk invaders occurred centuries ago. Egri Bikavér was first made in 896. It is aged in native oak barrels for 18 months plus an additional six months in the bottle.

Less pricey than the Tokaji wines but brimming with quality nevertheless are wines from Oremus winery. Their 1972 vintage was recently voted the best dessert wine in the world. Keep your eye out also for wines from Disznókő Winery, which has won several gold medals in recent years. Wines from vintner István Szepsy seem to sell out quickly, as well. Overlooking Lake Balaton like a jewel over the Mediterranean, from the heights of Tihany mountain, the site of a famous Benedictine monastary is also the home of a famous winery. However, its reputation is outstripped by Badacsony, the most famous wine center of Balaton, a broad valley ringed by ancient extinct volcanoes and home to a rich soil that produces world-class vintage from the local wineries. The area is particularly known for its Rieslings. Try vintner Huba Szeremly's Badacsonyi Szent Orán. Of course, your taste in the end must rule.

 Tokaji wine is even mentioned in Hungary's national anthem: "On Tokaj's vine stalks you have dripped nectar." The oldest bottle of wine ever sold at auction was an imperial Tokaji wine from vintage 1646. The bottle was bought by John A. Chunko from Princeton, New Jersey and Jay Walker of Ridgefield, Connecticut for 1,250 franks at Sotheby's in Geneva on Nov 16, 1984. At the time it was equal to 405 British Pounds (Guinness Book of World Records).

If you are a wine buff, try to get to the Hungarian Wine Festival in September. Wineries all over the country open up in a sharing mood and a truly pleasant wine-tasting tour is easy to arrange.

# ■ Connections

## Language

 English as one of the official languages of the EU, and Hungary is a member of the EU. At travel spots, restaraunts, and information centers English is understood, or you can usually find someone to help translate. Often you will see English posted along with the native tongue on important information signs. So, for the English-speaking traveler, language need not be a barrier. The most important travel language aside from English is German. The farther you get from the main cities, the more Hungarian rules. And, although the general rule regarding English still holds, you'll perhaps draw some favorable service if you say a highly appreciated hello in their own language. See the *Appendix* section on Language for common communications in Hungarian.

## Telephones

 Pay phones throughout Hungary are either card or coin. All coin public phones accept only the currency of Hungary. So, do not try euro coins or you will lose them. Telephone booths that require a credit card will not have coin slots. However, telephone instructions are in English and in Hungarian. Pre-paid cards are far more convenient to use, because the local currency can weigh you down with the small change. They may be purchased at tobacconists, convenience stores, grocery stores, post offices, and often at hotels as well.

Dialing outside the country, you use (00) as the prefix, and then the country code. Calling to the United States, whose country code is 1, for instance, you would dial, 00-1 then the area code and number. However, for all calls inside the country you would dial the regular number, preceded by the area code for that region. Unless calling a cell phone, calling outside of Budapest, you would dial 06 first, and then the selected number. If you have a number to dial, make sure you understand how to dial the full number from the location you are at. For example, you might also need to dial the prefix 26, and then the number. Of course, dialing from out of the country in to Hungary is simple. You dial 00 for the international operator, then 36 for the country code, and then the number.

Mobile phones are the rage of Central Europe, with over half of the population using some type of cell phone provider. If you exchange telephone numbers with someone, their number is as likely to be a cell number as a standard one. The mobile telephone prefix is either two or three additional digits. So, the mobile telephone will be a longer number. Also keep in mind that mobile telephone calls are generally more expensive, unless you are under a special plan. If you will be making many phone calls, bring your own cell phone, or purchase an inexpensive prepaid one at a local mobile telephone outlet. It is also a question of telephone etiquette that you not use the mobiles for extensive conversation. It is considered somewhat rude to talk at great length on a cell phone, so keep it confined to finding out essential information.

**Emergency Calls Europe-wide:** 112

# Electricity

We have already mentioned that it is probably wise to leave any plug-in electrical appliances at home, as the European system is 220 volts, not 110 volts, as in the American system. An adapter (transformer) for the voltage requirements can be purchased, but at a high price. Even at that, there may be variations on the plugs themselves, and this would require still another adapter for the sockets. I recommend battery-operated razors instead of plug-in, and in the case of hair dryers, call ahead to the hotel to make sure that one will be available for you. Most hotels do stock hair dryers. If you cannot live without it, then purchase a dual-voltage hair dryer, but be sure to carry plug adapters.

## Internet

 Internet cafés are increasingly evident in every major city. In addition, many of the central libraries and universities are now connected to the Internet. When connecting, simply conduct your search by clicking on English and connecting to your favorite provider.

# ■ Time Zone

 Central European time is GMT + 1 hour. From the last weekend in March to the last weekend in October it is GMT + 2 hours. Rule of thumb is that it is plus six hours from Eastern Standard Time.

# ■ Health & Safety

 Travel in any foreign country should always be hedged with adequate extra insurance in case of an accident. While Hungarian medical systems are adequate, they may not measure up to what American travelers are used to. However, there are some clinics and good hospitals and most have at least one or two people who speak English. At the same time, make sure that your health insurance is up to date, and that you are covered overseas. Medical policies should also include coverage if you have to be moved to another facility, and/or be flown back home.

Are you heading out on a mountain hike or biking on trails? Then let someone know where you are going and when you expect to be back. And, while on your way, stay away from animals. Look, but do not touch. It is better for them, and it is also better for you. Never attempt to feed any of the animals. It is not likely you will have to worry about close contact, but discretion is the first aspect of safety.

As in America, there have been cases of Lyme disease in forested areas. And, as deer are so plentiful, you could expect that the ubiquitous tick, the prime carrier of Lyme and some other diseases, would also be present. Before venturing into the woods dab yourself with insect repellent. Wear pants if possible. Check your head and the heads of your children after a hike, as well as their general physical condition.

Never try to pull a tick out of the skin, as the head may break off and end up giving you blood poisoning. If you happen to find one, the best way to deal with it is to dab the area with alcohol first, and then touch the exposed end of the tick with a cigarette butt or another very hot instrument. It will immediately loosen itself.

# ■ Currency

Although Hungary has been a part of the EU for several years now, she still has not incorporated the euro (€) into her economic structure, although it is an on-going process. Due to currency fluctuations, most Hungarians will not change their currency immediately, because it could obviously cause severe hardship in some sectors of their economy. As a result, local merchants and smaller establishments, as well as a significant number of larger companies, quote in their native currency (forints, abbreviated HUF). There is, however, a gradually evolving effort to quote everything in both € and in HUF. The larger hotels and more upscale travel locations quote in €, because their prices are high enough to protect them from currency fluctuations. Eventually, the € will replace local currency, but it is being done gradually. In this book, we generally quote prices in HUF where the merchant, hotel or restaurant does so, and in € where that is the primary currency used.

| EXCHANGE RATES | |
|---|---|
| 1 US$ | 218 HUF |
| 1 Can$ | 192 HUF |
| €1 | 276 HUF |
| £1 | 405 HUF |

# ■ More Information

The following websites are official state websites that can give you with further information:

- www.hungarytourism.hu
- www.gotohungary.com

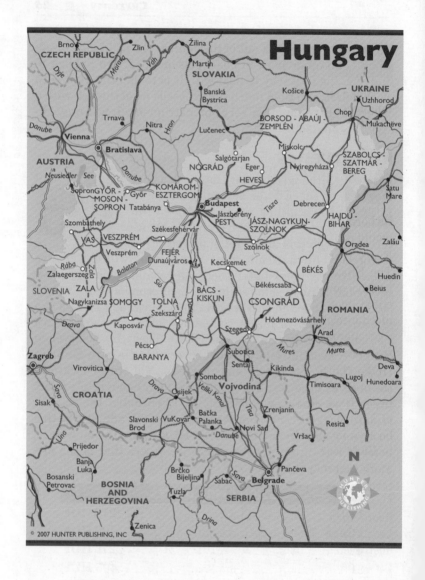

# Hungary

© 2007 HUNTER PUBLISHING, INC

# History

Make strangers welcome in this land, let them keep their languages and customs, for weak and fragile is the realm which is based on a single language or on a single set of customs.

King St. Stephen, 1036 AD

 Through the centuries Hungary has provided haven, in the north to Ruthenians, in the east, to Wallachians and Saxons, in the south, Serbs, and even today, immigrants both legal and illegal cross its borders, seeking a new life. Eventually 14 distinct cultures would contribute to the Magyar nation.

Every Hungarian child knows about it. The battle was lost. The Khazars and Parthenegs exulted over their dead. They had no power to resist any further. Desperately, their seven tribal chieftains slit their arms with their knives, drained their blood into a bowl and drank their mutual mingled life fluids in a covenant of death. It was 889 AD, on the Ural steppes of Central Asia and it marked the beginning of Hungary.

Under their elected leader, Árpád (Are Paahd), they escaped the one foe, to subdue another in the rich, fertile Carpathian basin. It would play a pivotal role in the politics and the power of Europe for the rest of history. A tribute to these leaders can be seen in the famous statues of Hõsök tere (Heroes' Square), in Budapest.

Their language was unlike that of their Slavic neighbors. Historians have traced it to Finno-Ugric (a language of central Ural origin), and others, astonishingly, find roots in Sumerian from ancient Mesopotamia. It stamped the tumultuous Carpathian Basin, the home of a rich Bronze Age culture, destroyed by warlike Central Asian horsemen in the 13th century, challenged by the Celts, then Romans, who divided it into Pannonia and Dacia. Attila the Hun savaged the Romans and encamped the Carpathian basin, but the Avars drove him out, succeeded by Bulgars and then Germans, in turn followed by Slavs.

Árpád and the Magyars conquered the Slavs and carved the Carpathian basin into tribal areas, retained even today.

The greatest historical painting of Hungary is a gigantic circle 120 m/400 feet long, by Árpád Feszty. A section of it is shown above. It depicts the dramatic conquest in the battle of Munkács, at the National Memorial Park of Ópusztaszer.

The different embroidery patterns and colors of the various regions of the country identify tribal ancestries, which controlled the land. Even today, Hungarians use their last (tribal) name first!

The Magyars terrified Europe, making raids as far as Germany and Italy, defeating foes with their Hun fighting tactics. King Otto I finally defeated them in 955. Later, Duke Géza fathered Stephen, the first Catholic king of Hungary. Stephen so rigorously sought Christianity that Pope Sylvester II granted him the title of Apostle at his coronation in Esztergom. Under the crown, at left (seen inside a glass cage in the tour of Parliament today), which bore the cross as part of its seal, Stephen organized Hungary into a nation with a brilliantly efficient centralized administration, which functioned for four hundred years. Yet, time weakened the king's authority. When King Andrew tried to raise taxes in 1222, the nobles rebelled and forced through the Golden Bull, which limited the king's power.

But history would not allow Hungary to live as freely as the spirit of her people. In a pattern that would be repeated throughout history, Hungary absorbed incursions from the east, over and over again. Magyar resistance spilled the invader's blood and blunted their offensives, enabling Europe to resist and survive, but at the price of Hungarian lives. Andrew's son, Béla IV, suffered the Mongolian invasion. Half the population of the Carpathian basin was wiped out. But the Mongols paid a heavy price to hold Magyar land, so, when their Great Khan Ogotai died in 1242, they withdrew. However, it was the end of the Árpád dynasty. The nobles sought a stronger leadership to restore order to a devastated nation. The last Árpád, Andrew III died in 1301.

Louis the Great (1342-82) reinstiuted the monarchy, widened the territory, encouraged science, trade, and industry, and · turned Hungary into the premier power of Central Europe. Yet, the Ottoman Turks disastrously routed Louis' successor, Sigismund, in 1396. A long, fierce struggle culminated in the hero János Hunyadi defeating the Turks at Nándorfehérvár (Belgrade). Though many have forgotten why, Catholic churches throughout the world follow a papal decree to ring the bells at noon in honor of that victory, for it halted the Turkish advance into Europe. Hunyadi's son, Matthias Corvinus, successfully finished off the Turks, conquered Austria, Moravia, and other territories, and made Hungary once again the premier power of the entire region. After his death however, Hungary declined. The Hungarian army was smashed by the returning Ottoman Turks in the famous Battle of Mohács in 1526, resulting in a 150-year struggle with the Hapsburgs of Austria. Hungary was divided into Hapsburg-controlled Royal Hungary along the Austrian border; central and southern Hungary, controlled by the Ottoman's; and a semi-autonomous Transylvanian state ruled by nobles neutral to the Ottomans. Hungarians themselves were split by the Protestant Revolution into Lutherans, Calvinists, and Catholics. Nevertheless, over time, the Ottomans weakened. In 1699 the Sultan surrendered most of the territory back to Austria. Austrian domination ignited a series of peasant and noble uprisings, most memorialized in the celebrations dedicated to Ferenc Rákóczi (Revolution of 1703-1711).

The early 19th century saw the Reform Age of Hungary led by Count István Széchenyi, shown at left. A surge of national pride fostered the construction of Lánc Híd (the Chain Bridge) in Budapest, the national anthem, and the Hungarian National Academy of Sciences, culminating in an uprising on March 15, 1848 led by Petőfi Sándor, the famous Hungarian poet, and by Kossuth Lajos (a national holiday). Yet, despite the desperate desire of the people, Austria, with the help of the Russian Imperial Army, defeated the Hungarians on October 6, 1849, a day of memorium. The widespread Hungarian resistance made Austria realize that Hungary needed attention, crowning Franz Joseph King of Hungary with a dual Austro-Hungarian crown in 1867. But this did not allay tensions. Immigrants and various historical frictions fueled latent pro- and anti-Hungarian feelings in Hungary and surrounding nations. Finally, when Archduke Ferdinand, heir to the throne, was assassinated in Serbia on June 28, 1914, Hungary joined Germany and declared war, igniting a chain of alliances that led to World War I. Germany and Hungary lost.

The treaty of Trianon (known as the Treaty of Versailles) forced Hungary to cede 58% of its land, 68% of its population, and 90% of its mineral resources, including Transylvania, Croatia, and Slovakia. Some 3,000,000 Hungarians, families and land, once united by over a thousand years of history, culture, and language, were split apart by artificial borders made with the cooperation of former enemies and the international community. Although Amer-

*Archduke Ferdninand*

ica refused to sign, the treaty was enforced by Europe. You will find Hungarians on both sides of the border in many areas. Some Eastern European nations still enforce ethnically charged laws. Such laws fueled the fires for WWII.

Hungary dreamed of restoration when she joined Germany in WWII, but, again, Germany lost, and so did Hungary. In 1944, the victorious Russians swept in.

Never fully communized under the Communist Dictatorship of the Proletariat, true to their historical character, Hungarians rose up in revolution October 23, 1956, in the first revolution against Stalinist communism, a national freedom day. People fought against the mechanized Communist military with Molotov cocktails and bare hands so fiercely that they drove them out of Budapest. Even today, some buildings are pockmarked with bullet holes, and the Citadel, overlooking the blue Danube, sports the bomb blast scars from one of the last stands of young Hungarian freedom fighters. The Russians re-entered the city with massive reinforcements from all the Soviet Bloc countries.

Though subdued, the Hungarian parliament continued to push for liberty until the Russians left (1989-1990). She instituted democratic reforms and a free market. In 1999 she joined NATO, in 2004, the EU, and as a growing democracy she recalls a glorious past and promising future, filled with treasures of discovery for the traveler.

## JOSEPH PULITZER

Joseph Pulitzer was a Hungarian-born journalist and newspaper reporter who made a reputation for himself by taking investigative journalism to new levels. He is considered by some to be the founder of modern investigative reporting. He emigrated to America and at the end of his self-made career, willed his legacy to Columbia University in 1904. Columbia was given the responsibility for administering annual awards in literature and journalism. Famous winners have included Earnest Hemingway, John Updike, Norman Mailer and William Faulkner.

# Hungarian Culture

On the floor of the ornate Neo-Gothic Hungarian Parliament today, they puzzle about the aging population. Life expectancy is 72¼ years. With an average age of 38.4 years, the national population is declining by .25% each year. There is a net increase in the number of aged each year, however. At the same time, Magyarország (Nation of the Magyars, as Hungarians call themselves), although it has absorbed many immigrants, has remained substantially Magyar, with 89.9% Hungarians, 4% Italians, 2.6% Germans, 2% Serbians, 0.8% Slovakians, and 0.7% Romanians. There are another estimated 3,000,000 Hungarians living just across the borders in surrounding nations, due to the Treaty of Trianon, still a sore point with many Hungarians. However, there seems to be an acceptance of something that cannot be changed.

Magyarország is a Parliamentary Democracy. There are several political parties and a substantially western outlook. Americans are liked. American fads are popular among the young. Universal suffrage at the age of 18 extends to a population which is 67.7% Roman Catholic, yet buttressed with an astonishing 20% Calvinists, followed by Lutherans, atheists and others. Religious conflict has also played in its history. Church spires dot the nation. The national anthem is a prayer asking God for forgiveness and mercy on the nation, which has suffered. The average Hungarian does not come from a nuclear family so family values are still significant, although divorce and modernization have changed attitudes.

Hungary continues to make gigantic democratic strides. 80% of its GDP is private. Inflation has declined substantially, from 14% in 1998, to 4.7% in recent years and remains today very low compared to most nations of the world. Unemployment has hovered at around 6% for the last few years. Some homeless beggars ply the streets, openly tolerated by the population. Many are alcoholics, a problem since the beginning of communism, but swelled by the shock of democratization. Many lost jobs once guaranteed by the state for life. Today alcoholism afflicts 10% of the population. Generally, however, Hungary has a rising middle class and ever-increasing prosperity. A tribute toward its growing economic muscle is demonstrated by the Hungarian dollar, called the Hungarian Forint (HUF). In 2001 it was at a high point of a little over 300 HUF to the dollar. However, in three years it dropped a third and, as of 2004, hovered around 200 HUF to one. It has recently risen to about 260 HUF.

This is a bargain country to visit. Costs are low. In 2005 its average per capita income was still only one half of the top four EU economies. Yet the modernized telephone fiber optic system connects 3,666,200 domestic phone lines supplemented with 6,862,800 mobiles. Add to this 194,503 Internet hosts, and 1.6 million Internet users, and it is not backward. Modern farms and combines sit next to less mechanized villages. Remodeled buildings spring up next to modern gas stations. Automobiles are everywhere. Compared to the USA, where there are 487 automobiles per 1000, Hungary has 238 cars per 1000, and gaining, 7,875 km of railroad, 81,680 km of paved highways (including 438 km of expressways), and added to that another 106,523 km of unpaved country roads.

Hungary receives 14,402,000 tourists each year, or almost 1.5 times its population, one of the highest ratios in the world. An astonishing 99.4% of those over 15 can read and write, outstripping the United States. All children learn at least two languages: Hungarian and English or German. All children learn Hungarian folk traditions and history (and all can dance the basic folk dances), in addition to a strong dose of mathematics and language.

Language (notoriously difficult), combined with their folk traditions and history, gives Hungarians a strong cultural sense. Sore points include the Gabcivkovo-Nagymaros dam dispute on the Danube, a once joint project of Hungary and Slovakia. Hungary has pulled out of the construction claiming it may alter borders and affect the flow of the Danube. Lawsuits by the nations are in the International Court of Justice. Ethnic problems still cause some concern. Hungary recently extended special citizen rights and privileges to ethnic Hungarians just across her borders. Hungary, however, has carefully kept herself out of the disputes in neighboring Yugoslavia, Serbia, and Bosnia. The average Hungarian is educated, with a European outlook, and generally tolerant and helpful.

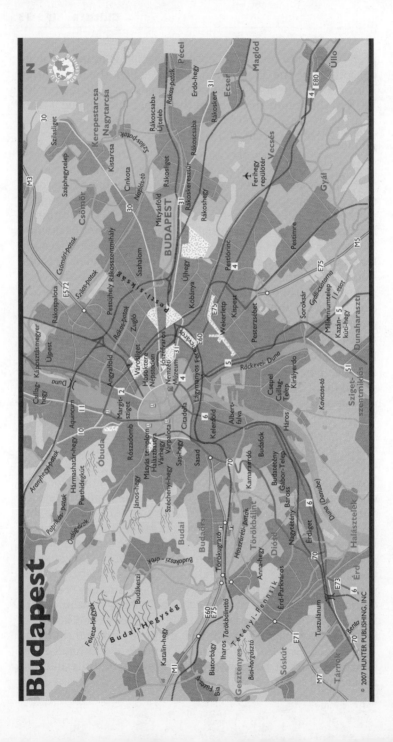

# Budapest

# Budapest

## ■ History

Rose-tinted sunsets and shadowed romance reflect on the Danube, mirroring this city which has been called Paris of Eastern Europe and The Pearl of the Danube.

The home of two million of the nation's 10 million people, it is the center of Hungary's culture, science, industry and

government. Consisting of 27 districts, it consists of three basic areas: **Buda** (including Gellért Hill and Castle Hill), **Pest** (including District 5 – also known as the Belváros, and City Park), and **Óbuda** (Roman ruins). Before Christ, fearsome Celts occupied Gellért Hill, the central mountain that rises from the Buda shores of the city on the Danube (site of the Citadel, Freedom Statue, lookout points, winding paths and bathhouses).

Late in the first century AD the Romans marched in to establish Aquincum, the capital of the province of Pannonia. North of Gellért Hill, later called Óbuda, it is the site of extensive Roman ruins. Later generations would contend with the Goths and the Huns.

In the 13th century construction spread in earnest to the other side of the river, Pest, but the invasion of the Tartars revealed an urgent need for a more defensible position, and so the terraced Castle Hill was built and named Buda. Castle hill rises like a jeweled jade above the city, home to the green-domed palace, museums, shops, restaurants,

*Buda Castle*

monuments, cobble stone streets and ancient ruins. However, after the Battle of Mohács, it was sacked and burned by the Ottoman Turks. (Some say Budapest has survived a thousand sieges.) The Turks constructed exquisite bath houses, and influenced Budapest for the rest of history, evidenced by numerous buildings with onion-curved Turkish roofs. However, the Turks finally surrendered the city in 1699 to the Austrian crown.

After the formation of the Austro-Hungarian dynasty, Buda, Óbuda, and Pest united as Budapest in 1873. The union sparked extraordinary activity. Grand boulevards, Parliament, St. Matthias Church, the first electric subway in Europe (the yellow line), Andrássy út above it. Many structures date from that time. Though WWII devastated Buda, and the Russians forced Soviet-style block monotony, the Hungarian revolution of 1956 put an end to that. Although many of the older structures were not remodelled, neither were they destroyed. So, in spite of her tumultuous history, building and rebuilding, Budapest developed an exciting character unlike any in Europe, combining Victorian, Gothic, medieval, and modern influences, mixed in with Turkish, Macedonian, Slavic, Magyar, German, and Russian. Amidst it all, the gusto of its people wove gypsy violins, love, and the romantic Danube into the cultural mecca it is today.

## THE YELLOW LINE

★★★The subway yellow line, or metro, was the first electric subway in Europe. Built in 1896 and recently restored, its forest-green steel-riveted columns, bright yellow coaches, wood-encased ticket booths, tiled walls and decor take you back to the Victorian era. At every stop, large glass-encased posters celebrate the history of the city. Its stops are a good cross-section of the city, from Hősök tere (Heroes' Square) to the Deák tér to Vörösmarty tér, which connects you to historical hotels, Váci út, great restaurants, and the Danube sidewalk. Tickets are at any entrance to the metro (Pénsztár) or ticket machines (with optional English instructions). Punch them at the metro entrance. The **Budapest Card** will provide entrance for three days. Don't board the public transportation system without stamped tickets or the Budapest Card, or you may land a hefty fine. Tickets may also be purchased in booklets of 10 or 20 (at this writing, 2,500 HUF or about $12.50. Always make sure that you do not remove the tickets from the book, as the book itself is required for validation by roving transport police, who may demand your ticket and ID any time. Budapest's transportation company (BKV) website is www.bkv.hu/angol/home.

## ■ Places to Stay

The number just before the street address refers to the district. Example: V. Apáczai Csere János u. 4, ☎ 36-1-266-7000. The Roman number V in this case is the district of the city. (In Hungarian addresses this is usually where the zip code is placed.)

## EXCHANGE RATES

| | |
|---|---|
| 1 US$ | 218 HUF |
| 1 Can$ | 192 HUF |
| €1 | 276 HUF |
| £1 | 405 HUF |

Long river cruise boats with swimming pools anchor on either side of the Erzsébet Bridge. They come from Germany, Austria, Czech, Romania, and from as far away as Russia. It is the Belváros district of Budapest, center of riverboat slips, night life, restaurants and hotels. Our effort here is to locate accommodations that allow an easy walk or bus ride to the Belváros.

## HUNGARIAN TERMS FOR STREETS

| | |
|---|---|
| utca | street |
| út | avenue, boulevard) |
| ... útja | avenue of ... |
| tér | square |
| ... tere | square of .... |
| körtér | round square |
| krt (körút) | round, avenue |
| köz | little street |
| sgt (sugárút) | radiating road, boulevard, avenue |
| fasor | street with trees along the sides |

# Five Star

★★**Marriott**, €€€€, V. Apáczai Csere János u. 4, ☎ 36-1-266-7000, fax 36-1-266-5000, Marriott Customer Service, 800-932-2198 in the US), www.marriott.com. The Marriott is cozy, with deep dark leather chairs and sofas in a comfortable and expansive lobby large enough to give each seating area a sense of privacy, a piano bar with soft music and a good international restaurant. Nightly entertainment often includes Hungarian gypsy violinists.

There are English-speaking waiters, a terrace barbecue, and a mix of excellent ice-cream from the Marriott La Cremeria. The lobby glass wall reveals the flowing Danube river traffic. Large French windows and a balcony terrace in each room

| HOTEL PRICE CHART | |
|---|---|
| Double room without tax | |
| € | Under €80 |
| €€ | €81-€150 |
| €€€ | €151-€250 |
| €€€€ | Over €250 |

offer picture-postcard views. Nightclubs and concerts, the Danube shore, and Váci street (shops and restaurants, night clubs and theaters) are a stroll away. The front desk is great and the larger part of the staff speak English.

**Sofitel Atrium Budapest**, €€€€, V. Roosevelt tér 2, ☎ 36-1-266-1234, fax 36-1-266-9101, www.sofitel.hu, H3229-RE@accor.com. With a lobby large enough to sport a suspended full-scale aircraft for décor, and with dining tables set on different platform elevations ensconced with palm trees and

plants. The hotel restaurants, Terrace Café and Clarke Brasserie, complement the setting. Glass elevators soar with a wonderful view of the atrium. Each room opens to an inside balcony view as well. Not all rooms, however, view the Danube, and none have outside balconies. But there is an indoor swimming pool, solarium, and two Finnish saunas, as well as a massage parlor and gymnasium. There is a casino next door. Everything is within walking distance.

★**Hilton**, €€€€, I. Hess András tér 1-3, ☎ 36-1-889-6600, fax 36-1-889-6644, US 800-445-8667, www.budapest.hilton.com. Standard double is €160, but a surcharge of €30 and breakfast for an additional €25 throws the hotel into a higher range of cost. For a view, location, and amenities, on the Castle Hill, with panoramic rooms overlooking the Danube, the Hilton is hard to beat. It is not at the Belváros, but across the river in the old city Buda, right in the heart of the Castle District, only a stroll to the Hapsburg palace. The back door

opens out to the breastworks of the Fisherman's bastion. The crowning cathedral of Hungary, the Gothic-spired St. Matthias church, sits next door. The back of the Hilton is a site for weddings, a glass-walled room that overlooks Budapest, framed around the remains of a 13h-century Dominicán monastery which was carefully incorporated into the building. The Hilton staff are delightfully helpful and most speak English as well. A walk down the front of the hill takes you to Lánchíd (the chain bridge) and across the river to the Belváros. Or walk to the stepped hillside tram and cog down from the palace, then walk the Lánchíd.

★★★**Four Seasons Gresham Hotel**, €€€€, Roosevelt tér 5-6, ☎ 36-1-268-6000, fax 36-1-268-5000, www.fourseasons.com. The Gresham lives up to the Four Seasons' reputation with probably the best English-speaking staff in Budapest. Elegance and romance have kept people at the Gresham since it was built in 1906. Its exclusive status evokes the last days of the Austro-Hungarian nobility. Yet the spa on the roof is equipped with the latest cardio machines, free weights, steam rooms, sauna, lap pool and incredible views. The rooms are spacious, superbly decorated, with all amenities, 24-hour room service, underground garage parking, and a superior location fronting the historic chain bridge. Superb cuisine is offered in the Pava Restaurant and the Gresham Kávéház; in addition there is the Bar and Lobby lounge, with evening piano, and Thursday, Friday and Saturday night jazz from 7 pm until around 11-12 pm. Afterwards you can stroll the shore of the Danube and the Belvaros district.

# Four Star

★**Grand Hotel Margitsziget**, Margitsziget (Margaret Island), €€€€, ☎ 36-1-889-4700, fax 36-1-889-4939, resind@margitsziget.danubiusgroup.com, www.danubiushotels.com/grandhotel. Stay at this spa (with two different hotels) on romantic Margitsziget (Margaret Island). Although prices are a bit high, you get what you pay for.

The **Danubius Grand Margitsziget Hotel**, €€€, sits next to the spa hotel and costs about €162 per night for a double room (€81 per person) in high season. The spa hotel, the **Danubius Thermal Hotel Margitsziget**, €€€, is €180 per night for a double or €90 per person. ☎ 36-1-889-4700, www.danubiushotels.com. The two hotels are connected by an underground tunnel. Both have spa facilities and sit in the middle of the Danube on the island! Between the two there are three fine restaurants (special diets, vegetarian, fish and kosher in addition to a Hungarian and international

menu), and nightly entertainment. Their mineral springs are supplemented by massages, saunas, weight rooms, mud baths, doctors and health directors, medicinal and non-medicinal pools, and about anything you might require to be pampered (including cosmetic surgery and dentistry). It is the best buy in this price range.

The island is a protected botanical preserve, providing jogging, bicycling, horseback riding, electric carts, open-air theaters, a Japanese garden, various rose and flower gardens, tennis courts and playgrounds, swimming pools and baths, picnic tables and lots of room to run or stroll. The Belváros is a

Budapest

15-minute walk and Parliament is only 10 minutes. Aside from that it's just plain fun to be in the middle of the Duna, jog its graveled path until you arrive at concrete steps, and meander down to the water to dip your bare toes in the Danube!

**Art'otel**, €€€€, I. Bem rakpart 16-19, H-1011 Budapest, ☎ 36-1-487-9487, fax 36-1-487-9488, www.artotel.hu, aobuinfo@artotels.de and budapest@artolel.hu. €188 per person per room, €€€€ €198 to €319. On the Buda side of the Danube, don't miss the Art'otel, with the funky feel of the 50s and 60s and paintings and design by the American artist, Donald Sultan. It is set in four remodeled 18th-century Baroque houses. Its Chelsea Restaurant is top-rated. Every room has a view at night of the lights of Parliament reflecting on the shimmering Duna. A walk up the back streets takes you up Castle Hill, or walk to the restored Victorian funicular, a stepped cog tram, at Clark Ádám tér and go directly up to the Hapsburg palace. At the same time, bus connections from the front of the hotel put you in touch with the entire city.

**The Hotel Gellért**, €€€-€€€€, XI. Szent Gellért tér 1, ☎ 36-1-889-5500, fax 36-1-889-5505, Gellert.reservation@danubiusgroup.com, www.danubiushotels.com/gellert. €162 to €188 per double room. This aging structure has hosted prime ministers and several presidents of the United States. Built in 1918 at the foot of Gellért Hill and restored in 1973, although some rooms are being updated, on the whole they are small and filled with older furniture. So, why list it? In its time this was considered one of the Grand Hotels of Europe, and it has hosted virtually every dignitary that has ever visited Hungary. The Art Nouveau interior of the lobby and main dining areas is spectacular. The staff is reasonably helpful and internationally seasoned. The Gellért baths, Rococo marble swimming pools framed in tall, rose marble Roman columns soaring to support glass cathedral ceilings, are really special. For this alone you may find the Gellért worth it, although you can enter the baths for a fee without being a hotel guest. The restaurant is first-class (perhaps a legacy of the famous chef

Gundel, who once worked his culinary magic from the Gellert kitchen). Behind the hotel are the many scenic pathways of Gellért Hill. Cross the square in front of the hotel and the Danube shore invites; cross it to the Nagycsarnok, the city market at Váci utca, or access the Belvaros by bus or tram, or stroll the Danube shoreline.

> **The Belvaros** is the downtown shoreline area on the Pest side of the Danube, where many historic sights, restaurants, government buildings, and riverboat docks are concentrated.

## Three Star

★★★**Best Western Hotel Hungaria**, €€, VII. Rákóczi út 90, ☎ 36-1-889-4400, fax 36-1-889-4411, hungaria@best-western.at. €117 in high season. Centrally located, it is the largest hotel in Hungary, on the Pest side. For the money it is probably the best value in the city, although it is not the best location. The rooms are upgraded with western-style amenities and the hotel itself sports restaurants, shops, a beautician, and massage services. It is next to Baross tér, which hosts the Keleti pályaudvar, a Victorian train station opened in 1884 and renovated in 1999 – still sporting the original vaulted, ornate glass ceiling, dramatic oversize statues at the entrance, and decorative yellow tile roof. From there, you can reach all points east in Hungary and the metro connection takes you to all points in the city. Gypsy music rings out in the evenings from the restaurant and there is a full medley of support services. English is excellent at the front desk. From the hotel you take the metro (the red line) to Ferenciek tere, in the city center. Alternatively, you can take the 78 bus or the 7 bus, and with just one transfer reach all main sites.

Budapest

**Erzsébet Hotel**, €€€, V. Károlyi Mihály utca 11-15, ☎ 36-1-889-3700, fax 36-1-3763, ezserbet.reservation@danubiusgroup.com, www.danubiushotels.com/erzsebet. €134 per double. At the center of the Belváros, it's a good stopover. Recently taken over by the Danubius Hotel chain of Hungary, all the rooms are air-conditioned and all have a bathroom and shower, plus satellite TV, but not all have a tub. Right off Vaci út, so restaurants and shopping are everywhere.

★**Hotel Liget**, €€€, VI. Dózsa György út 106, ☎ 36-1-269-5300, fax 36-1-5329, www.taverna.hu, reservation@liget.hu, €90-120 per room breakfast included. Rates are higher during Grand Prix. A heartbeat away from Heroes' Square and Városliget (City Park), you can see the back of the Szépmûvészeti múzeum (Fine Art Museum) and overlook the lower end of the Zoo from its windows. Room service ends at 6 pm, forcing you to go out or dine downstairs in the late evenings. However, it is the only three star I have ever seen that has a television-monitored garage and 24-hour security. If you're driving on a budget and want worry-free parking, here it is supplemented with laundry service, in-room telephones, and restaurant, open till 11 pm (four-star quality). The sauna is small but offers massage services, with a solarium, and it's a short walk to the zoo, city circus, amusement park, playgrounds and museums, the Széchenyi Thermal Spa and restaurants, or a metro ticket to all other points of the city. You can also rent a bicycle from the hotel.

**Hotel Charles**, €, I. Hegyalja út 23, ☎ 36-1-212-9169. On the Buda side, buses 112 and 8 connect to Ferenciek tere and thus all points. It is also a healthy walk if you are so inclined. There is enclosed parking in the back. While not a family hotel per se, it has what a family on a budget needs. From Nov 1 to March 15 there are discounts for five or more. Csider Gábor, the director, has established a help-with-all-questions staff policy. The Tabán, a wide city park, and Gellért Hill are one block away going east, and several parks and the MOM Park shopping mall (which includes a cinema that plays English-language movies) are within a few blocks going west; alternatively, walk or take the bus to Castle Hill. You can also rent their stock of always

new bicycles with luggage racks. The business center has Internet and all rooms have TV and are relatively large. Each unit comes with kitchenette, refrigerator and bath. Do not look for atmosphere and it lacks air-conditioning, but you can buy groceries and fix a home-cooked meal. Their János restaurant, minus the glitz of more famous spots, serves top-notch Hungarian cuisine, with real Hungarian wines. Its primary customers are Hungarians!

★**Hotel Benczúr**, €€, Benczúr utca 35, H-1068 Budapest, ☎ 36-1-479-5650, 479-5662, and fax 342-1558, info@hotelbenczur.hu, www.hotelbenczur.hu/eng. €72 in high season for a double room. Set in the quiet diplomatic

quarter of Budapest, and only a short walk to Heroes' Square, metro station and buses, this place also ranks as a good value. Its guests have included Pope John Paul II, The Prime Minister of Hungary, the British Council, and Queen Zsofia of Spain. Room service, in-house souvenir shop, beautician, excellent restaurant (average entrée runs $10 to $15). The garden and western amenities make it a singular value.

**Hotel Burg**, €€, Szentháromság tér 7-8, H-1014 Budapest. Doubles start at €65. Children under 14 are free and the service is three-star, including room service and restaurant. Right across from the Mattias Cathedral in the Szentháromság tér in the Castle District, it's in the same area as the

Hilton, without a Budapest panorama, but in the heart of the action and the romance. Bus 16 runs through the Castle District and will take you to and from Deák tér, on the Pest side of the Danube. All rooms sport mini-bar, A/C, SAT/TV, in-room bath/WC, and phone. Plus you're on Castle Hill.

## Under Three Stars

Booking accommodations in this category is always risky. However, you can find the best views in Budapest at the ★★**Citadella Hotel**, €, I. Citadel, ☎ 36-1-466-5794, at the top of Gellért Hill, and yes, it is in the Citadel. Be forewarned, this is for adventure more than comfort. Bring your hair dryer and your own towels. The rooms are old but six of them do have en-suite bathroom and shower; four are with shower only and you must use the common bathroom (old). If you want to know about the Soviet Cold War era, here it is. There is no air-conditioning, no in-room phones, and the desk clerk speaks passable English. But, there is a coin lobby phone and every room offers a great view, although only the room with six bedrooms has a view of the Danube. Guests can have their breakfast of choice in the fine Citadel restaurant (four- to five-star, see *Places to Eat*), for just €4. The Disco rocks on weekends.

**Marco Polo Hotel and Hostel**, €, VII. Nyár utca 6, ☎ 36-1-413-2555, fax 36-1-413-6058, www.marcopolohostel.com, is one block from Rákóczi út. Though unrated, its guest roster includes students and occasional families on a budget. It offers bright, simple but well kept individual rooms (and doubles and quads) with en-suite bathroom/shower, hot water, and small televisions. Bedding is changed every three days in all occupied quarters. Coin washers and dryers are available for guests, as are front desk hair-driers, irons and ironing boards. The front desk also provides a wake-up service. Storage and safes are offered as well. There is a lobby coin telephone, two candy vending machines, and they will book car rentals and sights from the front desk. Dining includes the restaurant/bar (open 24 hours), karaoke and live entertainment three nights a week. Everything is accessible by bus or metro (1½ blocks to Rákóczi út). It's a long walk to the Danube. Families can borrow baby beds, high chairs, and cribs from the front desk. Excellent English! Make sure you book well in advance.

Minus the restaurant but offering all the same amenities as the above, is the newly renovated ★**Mellow Mood**, €, V, Bécsi utca 2, ☎ 36-1-411-1310, www.mellowmoodhostel.com. The bright blue paint had just dried when we got there and it had been open for only two days, but it was already 80% occupied. They offer A/C, lockers, en-suite showers and baths, hostel beds with reading lamps, and bright white curtains. Váci út is 50 steps from the front door. The Belváros McDonalds' is around the corner but who needs it when you have an unlimited choice of kávéházak (coffee houses) and éttermek (restaurants). They have concierge services of a higher-rated establishment (including all rentals) so you need to book well in advance.

Budapest

## ■ Places to Dine

McDonalds', Burger Kings, and Pizza Huts and Chinese restaurants have staked out Budapest. They are classier than their American cousins, but the food and prices are comparable. Don't hesitate to try the shopping malls. For example, the largest indoor shopping mall in Europe, the ★★**West End City Center Shopping Mall** (Nyugati stop on the blue line) hosts a number of high-quality restaurants.

| DINING PRICE CHART | |
|---|---|
| Price for an entrée, with tax | |
| € | Under $10 |
| €€ | $10-$25 |
| €€€ | Over $25 |

### DINING GLOSSARY

■ As the Hungarians traditionally say before a meal, Jó étvágyat! (YO ATE-va-dyat), which means bon appetit!

■ Étterem (ATE-eh-rem). If you can manage it, the *r* is slightly rolled. This means a restaurant with full dinners, lunches, and house wines. Locals apply the term loosely. Burger King and McDonald's sometimes receive the label. Generally any eatery labeled as an étterem is a restaurant.

■ Vendéglõ (VEND-aee-glow). The *a* is long, as in *ate*. Literally meaning guest house, it once was the term for a family-run inn. You were the family guest, which meant you got the best of everything. Although generally less luxurious than an étterem, many compete with equal or better quality and somewhat lower prices.

■ Csárda (CHAR-duh). Descended from country inns, they serve country-style Hungarian food. As in a vendéglõ, pricing can range from low to high.

■ Étkezde (ATE-kez-de). The *e* is pronounced as in *end*. A cafeteria buffet, open at lunchtime, it serves common modern Hungarian food (without trimmings). Usually good and also cheap. Take a tray, make your selection, then pay at the cashier.

■ Söröző (SHER-er-zerr). The *r* is slightly rolled, and the *e* is spoken with rounded lips. This is a pub with a fairly good selection of dishes. The waiter serves Hungarian food with more care in preparation than in an étkezde. Do not expect wine.

■ Borozó (BORE-oh-zho). The *o* at the end sounds like *oh!* A wine bar (usually Hungarian), with little or no food. Some serve or specialize in imports from certain foreign countries. Borozós may offer world-class wines, as well as some cheaper selections. Ask the desk clerk for a recommendation.

■ Kávéház (KAH-vaee-hahhzz). The *a's* sound like the *a* of *Genghis Khan*, and the *e* like *a* in *ate*. A coffee house offering strong Hungarian espressos, coffees, and mouth-watering pastries and cakes, sometimes with evening entertainment.

■ Cukrászda (TZUU-krahh-z-duh). The first syllable has a sound like *Sue* but with a *t*, the second syllable sounds like the *a* in *Khan*. They serve pastries and cakes, sometimes with an ice cream bar, either standing or with tables and chairs. Some offer coffee.

■ Gyors Büfé (GYOOR-sh buffet). The *o* is pronounced like the *o* in *door*. It means, literally, fast buffet. They are in train stations and high-traffic areas, serving Hungarian-style fast food, as well as Hungarian versions of foreign foods, including Greek gyros and American hamburgers and hot dogs, soft drinks and packaged chips or candies.

■ Hentes (HEN-tesh. The *e's* are pronounced like the *e* in *hen*. These are butcher shops serving a limited selection of cooked foods and at fairly decent prices, usually a few basic meats, occasionally soft drinks. These are very common around the main train stations.

■ Look under *Languages* in the *Appendix* for simple ordering phrases.

Budapest is a gastronomical paradise. To make it simple, we follow basic streets and locations along underground metro routes, so they are easy to find. At every metro stop there are restaurants in the immediate vicinity. So you can follow the streets and/or metro routes and get a very good cross-section of the city restaurants. Of course, there are other locations, but you can follow city transport routes and locate these eateries easily. Out of the thousands of eateries in town, the website below presents some of the best, which are generally concentrated within a few blocks of the Danube. For more information in English check www.travelport.hu/impressum/objlists/rest_en_116.html.

## Pest

If you feel hesitant about exploring on your own, then the best recommendation for any English speaker in Hungary is to use **Absolute Walking Tours**, www.absolutetours.com, bookings@absolutetours.com. Outside Hungary, ☎ 36-20-211-8861, fax 266-8777; inside Hungary, ☎ 06-30-211-8861. The owner, Ben, is from Oregon and has accumulated a staff of top English-speaking guides. His experience and savvy complement his natural Northwest American openness, and he'll

Budapest

often volunteer a helping hand beyond the call of duty. His services cannot be duplicated elsewhere in the region.

Start at ★★★**Erzsébet híd** (Elizabeth Bridge) on the Pest side (country flags of visiting dignitaries are always alternated with Hungarian flags the entire length of the bridge).

| EXCHANGE RATES | |
| --- | --- |
| 1 US$ | 218 HUF |
| 1 Can$ | 192 HUF |
| €1 | 276 HUF |
| £1 | 405 HUF |

# Ferenciek tere

The first street on your right, facing Pest from Elizabeth Bridge is Vaci út. Take it to the right, and it turns s sharp corner and returns to the shore as Duna ut. There is a small bus station there. Continuing to bear to the right, you will leave Duna út before you arrive at the shoreline road. You must pass through the commercial parking lot behind the bus station. This inevitably leads you under the bridge, to come out on the other side to a small square called **Március 15 tér** (March 15 Square, in honor of the March 15 Revolution). The City Hotel Mátyás (not the City Panzio, next door) overlooks the ★★**Mátyás Pince Étterem** (Literally, Matthias Cellar

*Mátyás Pince Étterem*

Restaurant), €€€, V. Március 15. tér 7-8, ☎ 36-1-266-8008, fax 36-1-318-1650, etterem@matyas-pince.hu, www.taverna. hu (click on Restaurants). Open 11 am-1 am daily. Average entrée is 3,800 HUF. All major credit cards are accepted. Opened in 1904, the staff speaks English and wears period costumes, with décor from the 15th century. Noon and night gypsy violinists play famous Hungarian melodies. It is full of tourists and pricey, but if you want assured quality, and an enchanting atmosphere, you will find it here.

There are dozens of other fine restaurants nearby. Walk one block east to **Ferenciek tere**. Hapsburg, 19th-century Neo-Gothic buildings enclose the square with six-story ornate balcony façades, capped by Gothic spires high above. Cross under the street to the north side of the tér. (The underground metro connects to Deák tér which will take you to all metro points of the city.) The northwest corner streetside windows have 19th-century gold-painted window trim with the famous name of ★★ **Jégbüfé**, € V. Ferenciek tere 10, 7 am-9 pm Mon-Sat, 8 am-9:30 pm Sun. ☎ 36-1-318-6205 or 36-1-318-3271. Cash only. They average 250 HUF per entrée. A small streetside window serves Americai palacsinta, Hungarian waffles wrapped into a cone and smothered in a vanilla or chocolate cream. They are aromatic, not overly sweet, popular, and salivatingly delicious. Inside, ice cream (fagyi) is offered as a complement to the fine pastries, continental coffee and espresso. Pay first and then get your order at the counter. The English is halting, but this eatery is famous. It is a classic standing gyors büfé or fast buffet.

Don't leave Ferenciek tere without returning to the ★★ **Kárpátia**, €€-€€€, Ferenciek tere 7-8, 11 am-11:30 pm daily, ☎ 36-1-317-3596, fax 36-1-318-0591, restaurant@ karpatia.hu, www. karpatia.hu. Average entrée about 3,800 HUF. All major credit cards accepted. The terrace is open dining, but evenings require reservations. It is only

*Kárpátia*

a few doors down from the ★★★ancient yellow Franciscan monastery on the corner (first built in 1250), plainly visible across the street. Memories of centuries ago when Transylvania and the Carpathians were part of Hungary are

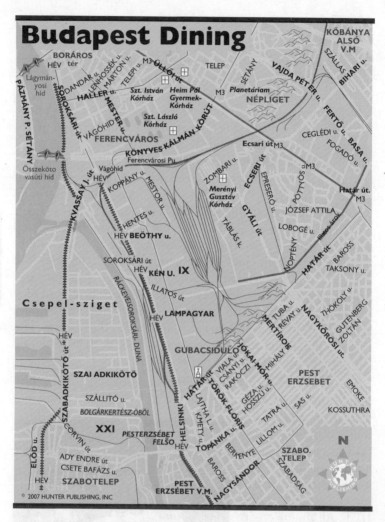

stirred up by gypsy musicians stringing mournful notes in a
Neo-Gothic setting, with dark wood cubicles, ornate quasi-
medieval and Renaissance motifs decorating the walls and
ceiling. A photograph on the wall of the brassiere, shows the
same room in the 1920s. It hasn't changed at all! It's hard to
choose, but this is one place outside of eastern Hungary where
you can bet on the Hortobágyi pancakes and hearty stuffed
Transylvanian cabbage.

After Ferenciek tere, the street changes its name to **Kossuth Lajos utca**. Bustling with cars and people, its atmosphere mirrors the fast-paced working character of Budapest. The once-crumbling gray façades are being freshly painted and restored. Victorian mixes with Renaissance, Turkish, and modern building styles, punctuated with medieval churches. Shiny glass-lined offices and stores compete with györs büfés (fast buffets), sidewalk vendors, restaurants and cafés, touching the street with fingers of cultural change and energy. People walk fast in Budapest. Amidst all of this, lounge in the deeply upholstered leather chairs from the Hapsburg era in the **Empire Étterem** in the Hotel Astoria, €€, V. Kossuth

Lajos u. 19. 7 am-10 am, 12 pm-3 pm, 6:30-11 pm daily, ☎ 36-1-889-6000, fax 36-1-889-6091, www.danubius-hotels.com/astoria. Reserve your place in the evenings. Although on the decline, the building at the intersec-

*Empire Étterem*

tion of the Erzsébet körút (Elizabeth Circle street) breathes history. Its interior is opulent, with Art Nouveau décor and prime service from waiters in tuxedos with green satin lapels. There are red satin drapes, marbled columns and gilt crystal chandeliers. The menu features Hungarian wild game, wild duck, wild boar, and pheasant. Empire has a fabulous vegetarian menu as well. The **Café Astoria**, €, out of the same kitchen, serves a delightfully tasty balance of Hungarian and international pastry, coffees and ice creams.

Continuing past Erzsébet körút, the street changes its name again to the famous **Rákóczi út**. Any number of restaurants and pubs here will give you a good sampling of Hungarian and international delicacies. The street comes to an end at the intersection with Baross tér. Baross tér is dominated by the

impressive turn-of-the-century Keleti train station. Just
before you enter the square, on your left is the Hotel Best
Western Grand Hungaria. On the ground floor is **Beatrix
Restaurant,** €, VII. Rákóczi út 90. Open 11 am-midnight
daily, it features both Hungarian and international cuisine,
as well as vegetarian, and it is spiced with live gypsy music
every night. Next to the restaurant, **The Fiaker Brasserie,**
€ is decorated with replicas of four-wheel wagons (fiaker are
country horse-drawn wagons) and graced with a live
accordianist. Having gone the length from Erzsébet híd to the
**Keleti** (the train station), you may want a change. The Keleti
fronts **Baross tér**. Walk around Baross tér. It is a kaleidoscope of gyors büfés, sidewalk shops, vendors, bars and hotels,
including a Kentucky Fried Chicken, shops and people. The
large below-street-level terrace is graced with the aromatic
smoke of grilling hamburgers and baking pizzas; and Chinese
and Hungarian fresh pastry odors stir in the open air. Sidewalk fruit and vegetable vendors hassle with customers while
people converse under the large umbrella of the Chinese bufé.
But bring your hat, as stone pedestals provide seating in the
center plaza, but they have no shade. Or walk through the
underground connection to the inside foyer of the train station. You'll pass beggars and vendors, backpackers, travelers
and visitors, middle class and low class, train men and taxi
drivers and children, scarcely aware of the splendor of the
building they are in, as you marvel at the glass and steel ornamentation. It could not be built today for the expense, and
perhaps for want of the craftsmen as well. Everywhere there
are small eateries in this slice of modern-day Hungary.

## Blaha Lujza tér

From Baross tér head back down to the intersection of
Erzsébet körút at the Blaha Lujza tér. Turn north. Walk or
tram to the **Oktogon** (the buildings and street form an octagon). Again, dozens of eateries mingle with shops, cafés, theaters and night spots all along the way. Your first stop should
be without a doubt, the ★★★**New York Kávéház**, $-$$$,

# Budapest Metro

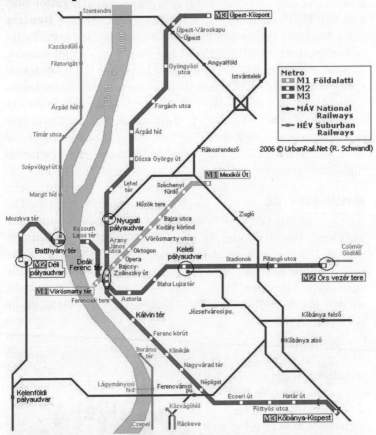

VII. Erzsébet körút 9-11, ☎ 36-1-413-1400 (this number may change). This has been a landmark in Budapest since the turn of the 19th century. Set in a small square, as the street bends, its soaring spires and six-story façade dominate the scene. I was taken aback by the splendor and opulence of the glittering Neo-Baroque interior, with gold columns soaring cathedral-like over the tables. Chefs apprenticed in the old Hungarian style of the Gundel restaurant offer up the famous Hungarian Somloi Galuska (cake in chocolate sauce and cream) and capuccino. Don't miss it.

**Caffé Mozart**, €, VII. Erzsébet körút 36, open every day 9 am-11 pm, ☎ 36-1-352-0664; cakes and coffee between 300 and 600 HUF; cash only. It is adorned with mural paintings from Mozart's life on the walls, and service with period costumed waitresses, although the big plate glass windows mollify the ambience. Mozart was never here, but the tradition of great composers or musicians who have either been influenced by or graced the streets of the city, including Franz Josef Haydn, Franz Liszt, Béla Bartók and Eugene Ormandy, is a strong one. The **Liszt Ference Zene Académia** is the next street north, and down one block west, the venue for numerous concerts.

## Andrássy út

Arriving at the Oktogon, we will head east on the Andrássy út. There are many stately offices and foreign embassies in this diplomatic section of Budapest. Take the underground metro yellow line and go to **Hõsök tere** (Heroes' Square). At each stop of the metro you will find a restaurant nearby, but we will get off at Hõsök tere. Just behind the tér is **Városliget** park (City Park).

On the northwest corner of the Városliget, just down from the city circus and zoo, is the ★★**Gundel Restaurant**, €€€, XIV. Állakerti út 2, open Mon-Fri noon to 3 pm and 7 pm to midnight. ☎ 36-1-468-4040 or ☎/ fax 36-1-363-1917, info@gundel.hu, www.

*Gundel Restaurant*

gundel.hu/etterem. Prices range from 5,000 to 8,000 HUF per entrée. Café entrées run about 1,500 HUF. Presidents, prime ministers, movie stars, royalty, and the jet set have all dined at its tables. Jacket and tie with a reservation are needed for dinner. The famed Gundel palacsinta (Hungarian pancake,

Gundel style), first created by Károly Gundel in the early 1900s, is a heady adventure for the palate, enriched with rum, raisins, lime rinds, and walnuts, basted in a creamy chocolate sauce, then mildly oven-fried. Some say this place is pricey, but there is no doubt you get the best.

Come out of Gundel's and turn around the corner back away from Heroes' Square, and walk half a block to a white stuccoed restaurant on your right with a medieval round tower window on the face and a dark wood trim and

*Bagolyvár*

Budapest

shingled wood roof in Transylvanian style. This is the **Bagolyvár** (The Owl's Castle), €-€€€, Budapest IVX Állatkerti út 2, ☎ 36-1-468-3110, noon-11 pm daily. Average entrée is 2,500 to 3,000 HUF, and it's family-friendly. Started in a partnership between Gundel and American-Hungarian George Lang, it has a different atmosphere than the elegant Gundel's, attempting to recapture mother's cooking and the homespun hospitality of Hungary in days gone by. It even has its own pantry, where you can buy preserves. Although the menu has a basic Hungarian selection, there is a daily menu and the chef will change the food with the season and daily buys of the kitchen (deliciously prepared). The restaurant is run by and staffed entirely by women, from Sándor Zsuzsanna in PR/management to Németh Andrea, the head chef. The feeling is relaxed, with a quiet elegance in the tables and chairs. The dining room has open wood beamed ceilings and there is a shaded outside patio for afternoon and evening conversation over the good food.

## ÁRPÁD

Árpád was the greatest hero of Hungary's foundation, credited with uniting the various tribes into the Magyar nation. His statue crowns the tallest pillar in Hero's Square.

At Hösök tere, in front of the tall spire with Árpád at the top, look west down **Andrássy út**. Walk down about two blocks till you come to the **Russian Cultural Center**. For a taste of Russia, try **Russky Buffet**, VI. Andrássy út 120, €, ☎ 36-1-332-2154 (they do not speak English). This is the bufé on the top floor of the Russian Cultural Center. It's open from noon to 6 pm Mon-Fri. The menu is in Hungarian and Russian, but the food is authentic Russian. Each floor of the Cultural Center features a different event from Russian history, as you climb the stairs framed in rich black marble to the top floor. The room at the top has dramatic Russian murals with onion-spired churches, and kossaks galloping across the steppes. Six tables sit beside a large counter. Russian delicacies are the fare. Try the pelmeny (spicy meat-filled pasta), or pirozhki (small pies filled with mushrooms, meat, or cheese). The menu on the wall verifies its authenticity. Gin and tonic and Russian vodka are offered along with the coffee, cappucino, and tea.

Back to the Oktogon. When you get off the metro, continue west on Andrássy út, past Erzsébet körút, for one block to **Liszt Ferenc tér**. From here, continuing down Andrássy út, there are numerous cafés and small restaurants as well as many theaters, playhouses, and concert halls. You have arrived at the Broadway district of Hungary, frequented by visiting American as well as Hungarian stars. Although not the focus of this book, here a real dining adventure begins in continental style! List Ferenc tér itself is a panorama of low-slung umbrellas and sidewalk cafés, capped by the Liszt Ference Zene Académia evening concerts.

**Buena Vista Étterem Kávézó**, €-€€, List Frenec tér 4-5, ☎ 36-1-344-6303, fax 36-1-413-0226, buenavista@axelero.hu, www.buena-vista.hu, charges on average 2,500 HUF for a meal. Open noon to 4 pm and 6 pm to midnight, it was created by the organizers of the famous Hungarian Woodstock, the annual Sziget Festival on Óbuda Island in northern Budapest. Three levels give feature different restaurants, the upper level a fine restaurant with mahogony tables, low lights and fine wines, including a mini-wine museum, serving Italian, French, and Hungarian cuisine. The second level which spills out into the street is the café and offers dozens of coffees and teas balanced with fresh French pastries and desserts. The cellar is a söröző (a pub). Every table has its own tap dispensing Heineken beer. You can, of course, order food as well. This place is filled Thurs, Fri, and Sat, when there is live entertainment. The waiters use halting English, but at least one is usually fairly fluent.

*Café Vian*

**Café Vian**, €, VI List Ference tér 9, 10 am-midnight daily, ☎ 36-1-268-1154, fax 479-0428, cafévian@axelero.hu. Named after French writer Boris Vian, this is a spacious place, with comfortable sofas and artsy chairs during the days, but it's often packed at night. Bay windows let in summer breezes from the square. Different art work is featured on display monthly. Ambience is informal 1950s avant garde. Try the sandwiches, salads, and finely prepared coffee. Plenty of outside table space on Sat afternoon. I found the sandwiches huge, well prepared, and fresh. They don't skimp on the quality. Generally pretty good English makes the evening that much better.

Cross Andrássy, north toward **Jokái Mór tér**. The **Art Café Alhambrá**, €-€€€, VI Jokai tér 3, ☎ 36-1-354-1068, www. alhambra-restaurant.com. Average entrée is 2,100 HUF. The ambiance is Spanish and Moroccan, with tapas, flat home-baked breads with mutton dishes, Moorish arches, red clay and tile, and frankincense that pervades the air. The change from Hungarian is a welcome break.

## Andrássy út

Back to Liszt Ferenc tér and Andrássy út. Head west down Andrássy út, passing innumerable shops, restaurants and cafés, theaters and movie houses, past the magnificent 19th-century Opera House. Notable eateries include:

**Mûvész Kávéház**, €, VI, Andrássy út 29, 9 am-12 pm, ☎ 36-1-352-1337, €, cash only. Celebrated by locals and visitors, serving cakes, ice creams, and fine coffees.

*Belcanto étterem*

**Belcanto étterem**, €€, VI, Dalszínház utca 8, ☎ 36-1-269-3101, noon to 3 pm and 6 pm to 12 pm daily, www.belcanto.hu. Just off Andrássy. Although pricey, they are often fully booked, so reservations are advisable, although jacket and tie are not necessary. Average 4,500 HUF per entrée. At 8 every night the waiters put down their serving trays and burst into song, with renditions from the classical repertoire of the 19th century. This is only fitting, since the restaurant is right across from the Opera House. Evening meals also include an operatic performance by professionals, accompanied by a salon orchestra. Although the balcony view is less delightful than that of the main floor, during the song hour at least you can hear each other's conversation there. The food comes labeled with the appropriate themes, i.e., Tournedas à la Rossini, Opera Steak, and the like. Basic English is understood.

One block over from Andrássy út near the Opera is **Paulay Ede u**. The **Bohemtanya**, €, Paulay Ede u. 6, noon to 1 am, ☎ 36-1-267-3504, is a cozy homestyle Hungarian restaurant with large servings and low prices. Try the bab leves (bean soup) served Hungarian-style with sausage, ham and sour cream. It will leave you wishing for more.

## Váci út

One block after Deak ter, turn left to **Dorottya út**, an extension of Váci út. Restaurants, nightclubs and shops all along the way lead into Vörösmarty tér and beyond into Váci út. Vörösmarty tér hosts the famous café, **Gerbeaud**, €-€€€, V

Vörösmarty tér 7, ☎ 36-1-429-9000, ☎/ fax 36-1-429-9009, open 9 am to 9 pm daily, gerbeaud@ gerbeaud.hu, www. gerbeaud.hu. This internationally known coffee house (since 1870 at this location, in astonishingly beautiful Victorian splendor) will be

*Gerbeaud*

on your left as you enter the northeast corner of the square on Dorrotya street. There, from the Dorrotya side, there is also an entrance that takes you down a staircase to the cellar. There a **pub** dispenses beer from Gerbeaud's own brewery (Gerbeaud Világos, pale lager and Gerbeaud Barna, dark lager). Then go upstairs to the **restaurant**, €€, where you can sample the cakes at street level, inside, or outside in the umbrella-sheltered terrace. Get one of their famous in-house chocolate bars. The many decorative items include the piano that was originally intended for the *Titanic*, but, as the fates would have it, didn't make it on board, only to end up here. Average entrée 3,000 HUF ☎ 36-1-429-9023, sales@gerbeaud.hu.

**Adriatic Grill**, €€, Apaczai Cs. J.utca, 13 (runs parallel between Váci út and Belgrád Rakpart), open 11 am to midnight. ☎/fax 36-1-266-2919. Cash only. Average entrée 3,000 HUF. This spacious new restaurant includes several Balkan specialties, including prsut (smoked beef ham), kaymak (sheep's milk cottage cheese), djuvech (vegetable dish). Adriatic seafood salad and fish is also offered, as is pleskavica (Balkan-style burger. The Adriatic hosts live entertainment every night.

**Club Verne**, €€, V Váci út 60, ☎ 36-1-318-6274, fax 36-1-485-0773. Open noon to 2 am. Average 2,000 HUF per entrée, cash. Set below ground, the theme is à la Jules Verne, with good food and live music. You'll spot it by the old deep-sea diving suit model spread out with a map held in one hand at the front entrance. Pipes go nowhere, and metallic floors with knobs in a dimly lit cellar bar are supposed to create the feel of being in Captain Nemo's vessel. The fare is standard American with some seafood entrées and yes, country pop in the background! This is one for variety.

For something different try the **1000 Tea**, €, Váci utca 65, ☎ 36-1-337-8217, www.1000tea.hu, contact@1000tea.hu. Open noon- 9 pm Mon-Sat. To get away from it all, in a quiet corner of Váci út, this is the place. In addition to multitudinous teas from China, India, and Japan, try the samosa (vegetable pastry) or biscuits and mixed nuts, in the summer patio or on the soft cushions in the drinking room. A pot of tea will set you back only a few dollars, and serves at least two. Pay cash in forints.

**Restorante Giardino**, €€-€€€, Kempinski Hotel Corvinus, Erszébet tér 7-8, ☎ 36-1-429-3576, fax 36-1-429-4777. Although one block over from Váci út, there is no doubt that only top notch Italian and continental cuisine will come out of this restaurant. The ambiance is smart-casual and expect higher price tags, but you get the best in wines and international cuisine.

Walking back on Váci út will take you to Ferenc Ter, where you started. However, at this point, cross the street (underground crossing) and continue on **Váci út** toward the grand city market, Nagycsarnok, once again, passing restaurants and shops all along the way. At the cross-street **Iranyi utca**, you will find **Central Kavezo**, € (cash only), Iranyi utca 29, open 7 am-11 pm daily. ☎ 36-1-266-2110. A haunt of intellectuals and writers from the time it opened in 1887, the tables are marble blocks and the chairs are utilitarian. But the well prepared salads, seafoods, chicken and pasta dishes are supplemented by divine varieties of house pastry and coffees. Try the Mother Teresa coffee, a blend of Cointreau, whipped cream and espresso guaranteed to knock you off your marble.

*Nagycsarnok*

The most hidden secret of Budapest has got to be the **Nagycsarnok** (big market). Nowhere will you find a greater variety of Hungarian and international goods than in this sprawling market. The second-floor terrace, surrounded with green steel ornamentation, overshadowed by the soaring cathedral, adds an extraordinary sense of space and grandeur. And it overflows with different eateries. This is a not-to-be-missed taste of Victorian Budapest.

## Belgrád rakpart

The Danube shoreline has a special enchantment. Belgrád rakpart runs parallel to Váci út, between the Lánchíd (Chain Bridge) and Erzsébethid (Elizabeth Bridge), a shoreline stroll under the Budapest evening lights. Hotel restaurants compete with boat restaurants and casinos anchored along the shore. To reach the boats floating on the river, you must cross below the tramlines through one of the several mini-passes and then cross a street at a pedestrian light. Many boats and restaurants along this route feature live gypsy music and violins.

**Vénhajó Restaurant** (river boat) on the *Kossuth* steam ship, €-€€, V Belgrád rakpart, Vigado Square, 3rd pontoon, ☎ 36-1-411-0942, fax 36-1-411-0943, www.europahajo.hu/venhajo, venhajo@europahajo.hu, is open seven days from 11 am until the last customer leaves. Situated on the Danube itself, it is actually a part of the *Kossuth* Múzeumhajó (*Kossuth* Museum Boat), a real steamship built in 1913. The restaurant serves genuine Hungarian foods buffet-style, and at great prices.

After dining at the Vénhajó, you may want to walk to pier 7 for more evening fare, and take the *Legend* boat tour, €€, ☎/fax 36-1-317-2203, www. legenda.hu legenda@ matavnet.hu. The cost is 4,200 HUF, or 3,600 HUF for a daylight cruise. You watch Budapest turn on its nightly display of lighting on the historic buildings, with the reflection shimmering across the Danube. The tour is one hour. Suspended television screens show the kings and queens, poets and great leaders Hungary's history, as well as the fascinating background of some of the buildings you can see lit up at night. Two drinks (soft drinks, beer or champagne) are offered during the cruise. Cruises leave from pier 7, right by the Vigado, the concert hall. See the website for all departure schedules.

A great alternative at the Vigadó landing stage, take **Mahartpassnave's** dinner/tour of Budapest by boat, €€, ☎ 36-1-484-4015 or 484-4016, www.mahartpassnave.hu, catering@mahart-

passnave.hu. From May 1 through September 29 it offers up an evening dinner cruise every Wed and Sat night, from 8 pm. It lasts about two hours. You are greeted with a glass of wine, followed by a three-

*Mahartpassnave*

course meal which includes the Hungarian basics, pancakes Hortobágy-style, turkey Jóassony-style, mixed salad, mixed strudels and drinks. A Hungarian dance group and musicians entertain with whistles, shouts and whirling skirts of the Csárdás (a country folk dance) dance, after which guests are invited to join in. The lit-up Hapsburg domes, Gothic spires, and many evening spots on the river edge shimmer on the Danube's surface, creating river views that rival those of Paris. Mahartpassnave has cruises and riverboat connections throughout central Europe. Their connections work well with the destinations of this guide, so research their website if you plan to travel across Central Europe and try the river-cruise options.

**Trattoria Toscana**, €-€€, V Belgrád rakpart, €-€€, 13, ☎ 36-1-327-0045, open midday-midnight daily, info@toscana.hu, www.toscana.hu. Average entrée is about 2,000 to 2,500 HUF. The real Italian, away from the glitz. The head chef is

Italian. Fresh salads, al dente pastas, and quick service. They even offer classes in Italian cuisine.

**Dionysus**, €-€€€, V Belgrád Rakpart 16, ☎ 36-1-318-1222, open midday to midnight daily. In spite of its fabulous view of Gellert Hill and the Freedom statue, it really does evoke the Aegean. The outside sun-drenched terrace requires your hat. White stucco and blue and white checkered tablecloths cover thick wood tables and its hanging green plants evoke Greek tradition. The real moussaka is here, and try the octopus starter for the adventuresome, or the shrimp, sole, or veal.

## The Nyugati

Enter the metro system at **Deák tér**, by walking down the stairs from the street entrance or, alternatively, take any metro subway to Deák tér, as they all interconnect here. This is the central hub of the metro system of Budapest; the color of your line will always keep you somewhat oriented. Look for the blue line to go to the Nyugati. The various stops of the metro are shown on the walls opposite every station. The blue metro line has a stop at Bajcsy-Szilinszky út, a great street for restaurants, cafés and sidewalk evenings. However, we are going on to the Nyugati metro stop, the location of the Victorian steel and glass Nyugati train station, gateway to the gigantic **West End City Shopping Center**, nexus of numerous restaurants, hotels, shops, and night spots.

*Becketts*

**Becketts**, €-€€, for a drink and social hour, V Bajcsy-Zsilinszky út 72, ☎ 36-1-311-1033, fax 36-1-311-0134, www.budapest-sun.com/becketts, beckettskft@axelero.hu, €-€€. Open noon to 2 am daily. Average entrée is 2,600 HUF. Of the many Irish pubs, this is one of the more popular among expats. While its basic international food selection is tasty (try the fried bananas), its primary draw is as a pleasant hangout for the live-in foreign crowd of Budapest. With green awnings and candlelit tables on the sidewalk, as well as live entertainment, the ambience is there.

## Buda Side

Crossing Erzsébet Bridge toward Gellert Hill, the road turns north and splits into two one way causeways going in opposite directions. Heading North you are on Attila út. Running south in the opposite direction is **Krisztina Körút**. On the left rises Tabán park, below Gellert Hill and a favorite spot of summer concerts. Just visible from the street are the yellow gilded Rác fürdő, or Rác baths. On the right Castle Hill dominates. The numerous pubs and restaurants along this route are less pricey than in the more commercial Pest. Originally built in the early 18th century, the **Aranyszarva** (golden stag), €€-€€€, Szarvaz tér 1, ☎/fax 36-1-375-6451, has average entrées at about 2,000 to 3,000 HUF. Open from noon-11 pm daily. The traditional Hungarian heavy and hearty dishes, wild fowl and meat and fabulous sauces are rounded out with Hungarian red wines. I think the eating terrace is a bit too close to the street, which is pretty busy with automobile traffic, but it is elevated and airy, and one side glimpses the Danube. A plus here is that, if you walk around the corner, you are a stone's throw from the back entrance of the Buda Castle walls that surround the Castle District. Climb up the walkway and you can enter, no doubt the way invading Moors once did.

Across the street, southward, the corner of Apród út and Döbrentei út is graced with the outside terrace of the **Tabáni Terasz**, I, €€, Apród utca 10, ☎ 36-1-201-1086, www.tabaniterasz.hu/eng, infor@tabaniterasz.hu. Average entrée is 2,000-2,500 HUF. The poet, historical writer and classical translator, Virag Benedek, once lived in the house that now bears his name, the **Virag Benedek House**. This protected historical site, built in the last half of the 1700s is now the home of this first-class söröző, or pub, that tries to duplicate the spirit of the old world Tabán district of Buda (white plastered two-story houses fronting narrow cobblestone streets, hiding lovely enclosed garden terrace patio areas). Originally built as an inn, it contains four eateries. The outdoor terrace commands a view of the lower Castle District, invisible from the Aranyszarva. Here they serve Hungarian or international cuisine, coffee and cakes. The 250-year-old inner café has an old world ambience, leading you into the garden terrace under a 200-year-old walnut tree. There you can munch on cold crisp salads and grilled meats, then go down to the wine cellar, where over 40 varieties of Hungarian wines are complemented by cheese and salami platters with fresh bread.

The eateries are to the right as you return to Attila út, toward Krisztina tér. To your left will be a continuous park-like island, a divider between the two one-way streets (the other street going back toward Erzsébet bridge is the Krisztina körút). You will arrive eventually at the intersection with Alagút utca, a busy extension of the Lánchíd. To your left, the Krisztina park ends, and on the left corner rises a tall building with an OTP Bank office at street level. Turn left one block, and then turn right. The street becomes two-way. The northwest corner is dominated by the bright yellow **Krisztina**, an unheralded 18th-century church with statues at the entrance and Turkish onion steeples on the roof. Go past the cukrászda (sweet shop), on the right to the **Horváth Gösser Étterem**, $-$$, (Krisztina tér 3), ☎ 36-1-375-7573, 11 am-9 pm, Mon thru Sat and Sun 11-7 pm. Pay cash for German and Hungarian fare and a good quality bar. The food is in healthy as well as tasty portions. Soccer memorabilia from Puskás Öcsi, the most famous Hungarian soccer player, decorate the walls. It's a bit crowded, but it's a place for the locals. Because they don't cultivate the tourist crowd, here you will find the true modern Hungarian food and drink, at reasonable prices

Traveling farther lands you at the Déli train station on the left, and once again, many eateries surround this nexus. On your right is the **Vérmező park** (its name means Blood Meadow).

## BLOOD MEADOW

This may seem a strange name for a park. It is named for a famous incident in Hungarian history. Ignác Martinovics, left, a Franciscan frier, and his compatriots, leaders of the historical Jacobin movement in Hungary, were writers and intellecutals desiring a free Hungary. The French Revolution inspired them to write and influence public opinion toward its ideals of freedom and democracy. The Hapsburgs would have none of that. The Jacobins were executed by the Hapsburg monarch, Francis I, in 1795. The park is the actual location of their execution, which is set off by a marker in the park. However, Ignác Martinovics did not want to be memorialized. As a true monk, he wanted an unmarked grave. Today, on the opposite side of the city, in the Varosliget (The City Park), you can visit the site of this hero of freedom. True to his wishes, he is buried without a headstone.

Within two blocks of the Déli train station are numerous popular restaurants and gyors büfés (fast buffets). One on the park side is in a renovated train diner, **The Orient Express**, € (cash only), I Krisztina Körút, 1012 Vérmező park, ☎ 36-1-213-0122, open 11 am-1 am daily. It is across from the Déli "bullring," so-called because it is a metro entrance below street level that is surrounded by a circular railing above. The Orient Express can be easily distinguished because it is the only structure on the parkside, an aging green diner train car, sitting on the streetside border of Vérmező park. Someone told me this once a part of the Orient Express, but, I am not sure if this is true. Looking as though it could hardly hold a couple, let alone a full complement of customers, inside it is fairly roomy and it is often filled with local people. The Victorian décor is faded and or gone, and its wood-trimmed tables are clearly replacements of the originals. But the service is good and the specialty is lighter Hungarian fare, soups, basic grilled meats, salads, and lighter drinks. A wooden terrace is tucked away in the back, overlooking the park. The food is good and great value.

## Castle District

Always the center of tourist activity, the Castle District condenses not just history, but a healthy variety of cuisines in one leisurely stroll from the north to the south. Though the atmosphere is great, expect prices to be fairly high, geared for tourists.

**Hilton's Dominican**, €€-€€€, ☎ 36-1-488-6600, and also the **Corvina**, €-€€€, Hes András tér 1-3, in the heart of the Castle District, are fine quality. They serve goose liver and other Hungarian specialties in addition to the international menu. Smart-casual is advisable here. I have never known a Hilton not to serve top cuisine, and the Dominican spices their selection with an excellent wine list accompanied by music from the piano. The views over the city from the Dominican wide-panel windows give a special ambiance to a meal here.

**Ruszwurm**, €-€€, I Szentháromshág utca 7, ☎ 36-1-375-5284, www.ruszwurm.hu, ruszwurm@ruszwurm.hu. In the heart of the Castle District, historic coffee house and patisserie open since 1827. Founded by Franz Schwable and later bought by Wilhelm Ruszworm in 1884, it is a tiny medieval enclave with two rooms. In one corner is a glass case with pastries and cakes for your selection and in the second room, light green upholstered chairs evoking Hapsburg memories.

**Rivalda Restaurant**, €€€, Színház utca 5-9, next to the National Dance Theater, ☎ 36-1-489-0236, ☎/fax 36-1-489-0235, www.rivalda.net, rivalda@nextra.hu, is an elegant historic reconstituted Carmelite monastery, going back centuries. Average entrée costs 6,000 to 8,000 HUF. Reservations are advisable. Open 11:30 am to 11:30 pm. Entertainment here is top-grade international and Hungarian music, easy listening and jazz. The chic atmosphere is complemented by a superb menu, including delightful grilled goat cheese and fennel, or filet mignon with caramelized garlic and leeks. Less formal is the 18th-century courtyard café in the back, serving light snacks and coffees.

## The Citadella

The highest restaurant within stone's throw of the Danube is the most historic, at the top of Gellert Hill. The famous Citadel harbors the ★★★**Citadella Restaurant**, €€-€€€, ☎ 36-1-166-7736, www.citadellarestaurant.com, about 20 yards down from the main gate entrance and up the stairs to the side entrance door. It encapsulates Hungarian atmosphere, rough elegance, and history. There are numerous rooms, some bearing boar skins and trophies on the walls, others with turn-of-the-century guns and swords. Then, there are the knights' dining areas. The coat of arms of St. Mattias is draped across the ceiling, and knights' regalia and coats of arms decorate the walls. Spears, swords, pikes and axes from long ago are mounted against the blocks of Hapsburg granite carved by masons from a more romantic period. Examples of Hungarian horsemen's riding gear and various Magyar smoker's pipes and drinking flasks from the puszta, the wild

*Citadella Restaurant*
*(Nannette Vinson)*

Budapest

flatlands of Hungary, are mounted in some corners. Count on being served Hungarian... and that goes for the wines as well, with a fine selection from every corner of Hungary. There is a nightly Hungarian gypsy band and the view over Budapest is breathtaking.

## The Bottomless Lake, A Special Place

*Hemingway*

★★**Hemingway**, €€-€€€, XI, Kosztolányi Dezső tér 2, ☎ 36-1-381-0522, fax 381-0523, hemingway.club@axelero.hu, www.hemingway-etterem.huopen. Open Mon-Fri 11 am to 3 pm, Sat-Sun 11 am to 5 pm, closed Sun Nov to March. Average entrée 2,500-3,000 HUF. Lake Feneketlen (Bottomless Lake), is located in the park of the same name. A long wood terrace stretches over the water, yet from the shore-side entrance an unimposing building hides the restaurant. If you're not careful, this place could be missed, and it shouldn't be. And, if you're a family, with smaller children, here is one place to dine and entertain the kids at the same time. In a separate room of this large restaurant they have set up toys, plus a full movie screen for children's movies and cartoons. Babysitters are supplied by the restaurant so the parents can dine in relaxed African/South American elegance in another section of the restaurant (not so far away that a parent can't make a quick check). On the sprawling wood terrace overlooking the lake, DJs play (including Latin rhythms). Sections of the restaurant thematically open out in Latin, Mediterranean, and African motifs. A corner fireplace with sofas and heavy upholstered chairs sits off from the main Mediterranean dining area, only a few yards from the piano, and you can dine there by the fireplace as well. The cuisine is the rave, prepared by chefs who formerly worked shoulder-to-shoulder with the famous Gundel (see page **). Almost every major star of Hungary has come to this place, and many American stars. The restaurant album includes a smiling photo of Arnold Schwarzenegger, and a note from him – "thank you very much for the great food and the wonderful time.... I'll be back."

## Buda Hills

**Aranymokus Kertvendeglo** (Golden Squirrel Garden Restaurant), €-€€€, 2,000 to 2,500 HUF, Istenhegyi út 25, ☎ 36-1-355-6728, started in 1886. It has been in the same family through four generations. After a period of closure, István and Zsuszanna Verhanovits celebrated 100 years of the family ownership by reopening in 1996. A green leafy bower takes you away from the street. Pots flower with grape plants and the atmosphere of a 19th-century Hungarian house. The summer garden contains 12 booths seating up to six diners each. Traditional lamps hang from a glass ceiling that shields the guests from the patter of the rain and the sun. The inner room is called the winter garden and is notable for the tables separated by green lattice woodwork, decorated with flowers, wooden wild ducks and candles. Here is one place where, aside from the fine quality general fare, the fish platters are truly worth the price. Try the roasted pike-perch Carpathian-style, served with basil. On the other hand, the chicken stuffed with bananas has a delicious juiciness that can't be beat.

## Shopping Center Restaurants & Shops

Hungary has taken to the western styles in hundreds of ways, and nowhere is that more evident than in the main shopping centers that dot the city. They are modern, and in every case they offer not only food courts, but some very good restaurants.

Budapest

**West End City Center**, www.westend.hu, open 10 am to 9 pm daily. It's at the Nyugati palyaudvar. Take trams 4 and 6, or the metro blue line (no 3 line) to the Nyugati. There is a direct entrance into the shopping center from the underground Nyugati plaza center metro entrance. Walk by the artificial waterfall to enter. This largest shopping center in Europe, it must be visited to be believed. Don't think you've seen it all from the entrance for it ranges over a lot of territory, and the best food courts are deep on the inside, surrounded by open glass-faced shops rising five stories high on all sides. Escalators move up and down, and the noise of people, shops, restaurants and theaters fills the air. Almost any menu can be found.

Don't forget the balloon ride, which elevates a helium balloon high over the city for a view from above the roofs of the city (see *Adventures*).

The red metro also lands you at the **Moszkva tér**. It is also at the end of the Krisztina Körút, after the Déli train station. If you are driving, turn right just after the Déli, and then make a left at the intersection of Attila út, which is just at the border of the park on your right. Continuing through several intersections you will finally come to a large intersection at the Szilagyi Erzsébet fasor, and there you make a right to Moszkva tér. A transportation hub, it is also one of the major eating centers of the city, but it caters to the Hungarians and not to the tourists. One block down from Moszkva tér on Margit körút is the **Mammut shopping center**, guarded by a bronze wooly mammoth at the front entrance. It's a glitzy shopping center with numerous restaurants, bars, shops, bowling alley and movie theater. As a bonus, on the north face of the Mammut is an outside three-story market center, where butchers, grocery sellers and sometimes farmers sell fresh vegetables, honey, and other local products. Gyors büfés (fast buffets) intermingle with voices, the smell of freshly cooked pastries and foods, and provide food and drink in this mini-slice of Hungarian city life. All around this area, between the Mammut and Moszkva tér there are numerous small Hungarian restaurants, sörözõs (pubs), and büfés.

**The MOM** (www.mompark.hu): Going western is the style here and the main draw here for the traveler hankering to find something to understand is that they do have English movies in the **MOM Színház** (MOM Movie House). Although it is not as large as the other shopping centers, several restaurants, büfés and cafés fill in space on two of the four floors, and, as would be expected, generally supermarket foods Hungarian-style. Prices are equally low and practical compared to the more glitzy restaurants. It is adjacent to a new office complex and across from the hotel Novotel (Congress Hotel) and park grounds. The Novotel is a good four-star hotel, with pool and family attractions, although it is rather far from the city center. However, the park is a leisurely walk and this shopping center and the movie house score high in terms of modern facilities. In addition, most of the ushers in the movie house speak some English. The carpeted lobby is wide and spacious, including couches, lounge chairs, small dining tables, and occasionally displays the works of local artists. So, it is great for relaxing before or after. This is a good place for a family movie, popcorn, and Cokes in an unrushed atmosphere.

**Eurocenter Óbuda** is on Uj Udvar út. It opened in 1998 in district III. The nearest trams are 86 and 6. A seven-screen multiplex theater sometimes has an English film with Hungarian subtitles. There are 45 shops and restaurants, decidedly western-style. Parking is free and the cool whisp of centralized air-conditioning greets you as you enter in the middle of summer heat.

# ■ Family Places

## Margit Island

Desperation fueled King Béla's prayer for deliverance from the threatening hordes of the Tartars, and, as he turned his eyes to heaven, he said that if God would grant a victory he would devote his daughter to religion. So the defeat of the Tartars was a sign to King Béla I, and in 1245, his daughter, Princess Margaret, entered the convent at Veszprém. She was invested  with the habit at the age of four. She was later transferred to a convent her parents had built on an island, which they dubbed, Margitsziget, or Margit Island.

Since the 18th century the island has been a playground. Gardens, arbors, fields, statues, trees, and flowers are everywhere. Today you can jog, bicycle, swim, play tennis, throw frisbees, relax in thermal pools, walk along park pathways, sit on park benches and enjoy the day, eat at its restaurants, get cold ice cream from vendors, or rent a bringóhintó cycle car (covered bicycle carriages for two to four people) and cycle around the island. Automobiles are forbidden, except for guests of its hotels.

★The **Palatinus Strandfürdő** (Palatinus Baths)

It will cost you €12-20, including food and drink, for a day at the largest outdoor swimming pool complex in Budapest, Margitsziget, ☎ 36-1-340-4505. Reach it via Bus 26, with a stop at Palatinus Strand. Open 8 am-7pm May-Aug, 10 am-6 pm Sept to April. Five fun pools and a thermal bath constructed around a natural spring, three 9% grade water slides for young kids and one 45% grade for brave teenagers and adults. The bell rings every hour to bring a throng of several hundred to the large waves of the Wave Pool. The Adventure Pool is a water maze starting ankle-deep and progressing to chest-high, with low-lying walls, turns and twists, underground jets of water, or with showers that spring out suddenly.

Once every day, inside a causeway in the middle of the pool, a powerful river-like current attracts swimmers to glide along its swift and powerful stream. The thermal bath has only a very slight, almost undetectable odor of sulphur. A sitting shelf runs the entire length of the bath for a lazy dangle at chest level. Bring a blanket (there's plenty of green lawn), slippers, picnic basket, and enough money (cash only) for the restaurant or the many food and drink bars around the water, but get there early, as this is one of the most popular summer spots for Budapestens!

One caution is that there can be nudity here, although rare, because all-body sunbathing is usually on the all-woman terrace, away from the crowds. For families, I urge you to get the low-cost locked and secure family cabins, which are monitored by two friendly ladies, clean, and functional. The cabin and entrance fee combined will cost about €4. The ladies lock the cabins when you leave and keep tabs on everything, so you can retrieve your money when you need it if you leave it in the cabin. Instructions at the main entrance are posted in English as well as in several other languages.

### Hajos Alfred Sportuszoda

This is the first swimming park, as you enter the Island from Margit Híd (Margaret Bridge). ☎ 36-1-340-4946. While families can enjoy themselves, this is where serious watersports enthusiasts will find a home. It is open from 6 am to 5 pm Mon to Fri, 6 am-6 pm Sat and Sun. The complex includes tracks, weight room, and six swimming pools (three specifically for neophytes), high diving and Olympic training. Plaques of past Hungarian Olympic champions who have trained here adorn the walls. This is where the European Water Polo Championships were hosted in 2001.

Budapest

## Város Liget (City Park)

Once the haunt of willows and wolves, time has given it over to history. Here, in 1241, Mongolian soldiers lured Hungarian knights protecting Pest to their last desperate battle. In 1514 it was the assembly point for a peasant revolt of

Hungarians seeking their freedom. It was here, in 1838, that a beleaguered population gathered when raging floods overflowed the lower elevations along the Danube river basin, and it was here too that Hungarian freedom fighters in the revolution of 1849 sought refuge from the emperor's canons. Today it is a playground with restaurants, monuments, and picnic hideaways.

**Zoo and Botanical Gardens** (Állat- és Növénykert), Állatkerti krt. 6-12, ☎ 36-1-273-4900 and 36-1-363-3790, www.zoobudapest.com. Admission for adults is 1,300 HUF (€5) and children two-14 are 900 HUF (€2.50). A family ticket for two adults and two-three children is 4,100 HUF (€20). The zoo is open 9 am to 5 pm daily, and the ticket window is open 9 am to 4 pm. In between dining and museums, you can spend days or weeks with the kids unwinding Hungarian-style. More than 100 years old, the Zoo is a natural environment for both people and animals. The new butterfly garden offers a kaleidoscope of fluttering species as you walk through. The indoor botanical garden houses plants from every major environment of the world, from the cool north to the scorching desert. Underground glass walls let you see some of the more popular polar animals and seals while they swim in their water pens. Walk through the gigantic wired-in primate area, where smaller monkeys inhabit a jungle and swing through the trees within a breath of the pathway. They are not always visible, as they frequently hide from people. There is a camel ride and petting zoo for smaller children, as well as remarkably natural elephant and large animal reserves, plus eateries and souvenir shops.

★★★**Metropolitan Circus** (the only indoor circus in Europe!), City Park at XIV Állatkerti körút 7, Ticket Office, ☎ 36-1-343-8300, fax 36-1-322-4426, www.maciva.hu, circus2@datanet.hu. The metro stop is at Széchenyi Fürdő (Széchenyi Baths), just up from the city zoo. On the website click *információk* for hours and telephone numbers, or click *jegyrendelés* for tickets (classified by colors that are shown on the map of the circus ring). Get the blue tickets at a minimum (1,700 HUF per adult). Children under 14 are discounted 20%. Their regular shows are interspersed with closed periods, especially in Sept. The shows are set in a circle, as in a big time tent circus, and virtually every seat offers an excellent view, although the green and yellow tickets are pretty far away, or set next to the band, almost unbearably loud. A band plays from a bandstand for some shows. The lower ring ticket seats (red) place you within touching distance of the clowns, trapeze artists and gymnasts or the animals as they run around the ring! Advance tickets are sold at the circus windows inside the main entrance and selected outlets (see website). The Budapest Metropolitan Circus started in 1891, one of the oldest circuses and the only indoor circus in all of Europe. Every two years a Circus Festival is held. See www. hunterpublishing.com (click on Adventure Guides, then Hungary) for a link with details on this and all other festivals.

★★**Budapest Amusement Park** (Vidámpark), City Park at XIV Állatkerti körút 14-16, ☎ 36-1-343-1810 or 343-1810, fax 36-1-478-0874, titkarsag@vidampark.hu, www.vidampark.hu. Children under four feet tall and wheelchair patrons are free of entrance fees. Entrance is 300 HUF per person and a pack of 20 tickets costs 5,000 HUF. Most rides require two tickets, so a pack of 20 tickets will last 10 rides. It can get expensive, but history and fun combine in this prize-winning amusement park. Summer hours are generally from 10 am and 7 pm, but weekdays and cooler months usually start at 11 or 12 am and run to 6 pm. Check ahead of time. Although open all year, the winter hours may be limited. Eateries and souvenirs abound.

Europe's longest wood-framed roller coaster ride, and still the most popular ride in the park, dates back to 1922. The entrance has been rebuilt in its original wood and stone motif (and houses a museum of the park's history). The merry-go-round is fabulously ornamental with its gold-leaved angel chariots and steeds, and it is another listed historical monument, originally built in 1906. It received the European Nostra Prize (1998). This is not Disneyland, but is still suitable for children and adults of all ages.

**Vajdahunyad Castle** (Vajdahunyad Várva). Assembled for the 1896 millennial celebrations, its four dungeon towers, assault passages, knight's chamber, statue ornamented church gate, abbey cloister and unique mix of Romanesque, Gothic, Renaissance, and Baroque were brought from their original locations to make a conglomerate of Hungarian history. Children are magnetized by its moat, draw bridge, and soaring front castle walls. The medieval guard towers overlook the excellent Budapest Agricultural Museum, which includes steam harvesters, ancient cotton gins and, in some places, wax figurines and pastoral Hungarian historical scenes. The bronze Anonymus, unknown chronicler of Magyar history, sits opposite in the inner court. Folk wisdom holds that a touch of his quill gives writers inspiration.

**Városliget Lake** and **Ice Skating Rink**, depending on the season, rents boats from its south-side service building to row along the weeping willow-draped shore. Ice skating in the winter requires that you bring your own skates

**Csodak Palotája** (Palace of Miracles), ☎/fax 36-1-336-4044, 1024 Budapest, Fény Utca 20-22 (II District), info@ sodapalota.hu, www.csodapalota.hu. Open Mon-Fri 9 am to 6 pm, Sat and Sun 10 am to 7 pm. Tickets are 800 HUF for adults and 700 HUF for children. Alternatively, a family ticket is 2,300 HUF. Parking is best on the street side of the museum. Metro travelers take the blue metro to Moszkva tér. Turn right and out the metro entrance (away from the hill). Walk east, cross the street to Fillér utca. A short block down is the back of the Mammut, where you continue on Fény utca. The park fronts a set of warehouses that were turned into a community center and park. The Palace of Miracles is inside. The open Hungarian market which you pass on the corner on your right, in the back of the Mammut, offer shops, büfés and street-side foods. The museum is an interactive compendium of science exhibits and educational adventure for the kids (not to leave out the adults). Try the high wire bicycle! Designed with a low slung center of gravity, it stays upright without effort as you bicycle across the wire. It looks perilous, but it is quite safe! The hair-raising electrical games, flotation games and action/reaction thrills may not last an afternoon, but the Mammut shopping center and Moskva tér will keep you entertained with shops, restaurants, and theaters.

## Outside City Center

**Tropicarium Ocean-arium**, 1222 Budapest, Nagytétényi út 37-45, Campona Shopping Center, ☎ 36-1-424-3053, www.tropicarium.hu matrai@tropicarium.hu. Open year-round 10 am to 8 pm. Adult tickets are 1,700 HUF and children between four-14 are 1,000 HUF. The largest aquarium in Central Europe (416,000 gallons of sea water) sits next to other fresh water tanks harboring the native species of Hungary, tropical tanks, and a mini-wonderland of exotic animals. In the arboretum area, tropical macaws and red-billed tocos fly almost at head level, and in some cases can be hand-fed. Alligators, slithering boas and crawling iguanas, sharks and tiny marmosets are but a few of the sights visible in the eight halls of this exhibit. Located in a major shopping center of Budapest, it is a good place to combine shopping, eating (at the food courts) and educational fun for the family. The largest tank includes some good-sized sharks. It is tunneled through by a glass hallway that lets you get inside the giant sea aquarium. Onlookers can touch the fish in the large ray pond (giant stingrays), or help feed them.

**Aquaréna Mogyoródi Vízipark** (The Aquaréna Waterpark in Mogyoród), 2146 Mogyoród, Mogyoródi vízipark út 1 (next to Hungaroring), ☎ 36-28-541-100, www.aquarena.hu. Open 9 am to 7 pm, May 26 to Sept 3, Mon to Fri, and weekends, 9 am to 8 pm. 4,600 HUF for adults, 2,300 HUF for children less than four feet tall. A family ticket (two adults plus two children or students) is 13,000 HUF. Children under three are free. Food and drink are extra. Tickets give access to all facilities the entire day.

Near the Formula 1 Hungaroring Racetrack of Hungary, this waterpark has gigantic slides, pools, Jacuzzis, waterfalls and artificial rivers. The Vacond csúszdák (the Mole Chutes) wind and twist, and in one section toward the end, for a brief few seconds you glide underground, only to emerge in a big splash at the bottom! The Blue Cave Pool (Kék Barlang) is always a hit. Büfés, souvenirs and a delightful children's pool with toys fill out a day or more. Shade is sparse, so make sure everyone is lotioned down, and bring some hats and T-shirts. Fixed umbrellas are sparse and it's a matter of luck if you get one.

★**Cog Wheel Railway** (Fogaskerekû), Szilágyi Erzsébet fasor, District II, Budapest 1028. Take tram 58 and get off at the stop directly across from the cylindrical sky-scraper Budapest Hotel (on the right). Get off on the side facing away from the hotel and  toward the park, then walk into the entrance of the cog wheel station. Metro tickets are valid. Although crowded in the summer, the cabin seating is roomy and picturesque. First built in 1874 by the Swiss, it operates on a cog system that pulls the train up Svab hill to Széchenyi hill. At the top there are a few büfés and a picnic area. However, the better choice is the terrace restaurant at the Budapest Hotel, across the street from the station at the bottom of the hill.

★ ★ **Children's Railway** (MÁV Rt. Széchenyi-hegyi Gyermekvasút), Golfpalya út, District XII, 1121, ☎ 36-1-397-5392, ☎/fax 36-1-397-5396, www. gyermekvasut.com, info@gyermekvasut. hu. Budapest tickets are 800 HUF per person round-trip and children are 300 HUF. At the top of the cog-wheel railway you can get off and walk up Golfpalya út to the children's railway station. The train operates from 8 am to 5 pm Tues through Sun. Although the trains are normally diesel, on weekends a steam locomotive is harnessed for an adventuresome journey.

Begun in 1948 and completed in 1950, it was one of the communist projects to teach children the glory of comraderie, cooperation, and the pride of the proletariat. It was built by children, and then later staffed and run by children (with some adult supervision), who were the top Pioneers of the old Socialist era, the equivalent of Boy Scouts in the west. It was an honor to wear a bright red bandana on the Gyermekvasút (Children's Train), one of the greatest Pioneer accomplishments. Even today, flagmen, conductors, switchmen and cashiers are all bright school kids between 10 and 15 years old, who get one day off for every 15 days of school (the engineer is an adult).

The train rides through the Buda hills and forest. It's part of the Danube-Ipoly National Park, with plants and animals protected, so make sure the kids don't pick or touch! The forest is mostly oak, ash and beech with thick undergrowth. Occasionally you may see deer. The train stops at a number of points where Budapestens get off and/or get on to explore the

Budapest

woods of Buda. The Normafa Stop (first stop after leaving
Széchenyi-hegy) and the Virágvölgyi Station (second stop
after leaving Széchenyi-hegy) put you next to the most popular winter skiing area of Budapest, the Normafa. A pathway
at the Virágvölgyi Station winds up to the Christian (Catholic) pilgrimage sight, the Makkósmária.

At Janos Hegy, take the pathway up the hill to the highest
point of Budapest and a Neo-Gothic lookout tower (see *János-
hegy* below). From the station at Szépjuhászné, stop at the
étterem (restaurant) or the bufé if you like; the food is good.
After eating you may want to take the pathway to the ruins of
the medieval monastery. Also, from the same station walk the
pathway or take Bus 22 to the Budakesi Game Preserve, the
closest such preserve to the city of Budapest. Here you can get
guided tours. Several lookout stands may give views of larger
game, and there is a zoo here as well. The pathway going
straight north from Szépjuhászné leads upward to the Nagy-
Hárs-hegy and the lookout towers of Kaán-Károly Kíláto,
1,300 feet above the Budapest skyline. Eventually your trip
on the railway will take you to Hûvösvölgy, the last stop, a
miniature full-fledged train station. Walk down the stairs
from the station and continue down the hill to Hûvösvölgy
street. The Tram 56 going south will take you back to
Moszkva ter.

The train cars are well kept, but in an old European style and
at three-quarter scale. They are so popular that if you do not
have a seat at the start, you will find yourself standing
through the entire journey.

**János-hegy and Chair Lift** (Libegö), at Zugligeti út 97.
Last stop of Bus 158 at Zugliget út. A campground is directly
across from the Libegö base station at the bottom of the hill.
☎ 36-1-394-3764, www.libego.hu. Open 9 am to 5 pm mid-May
to mid-Sept; 9 to 4 in the off-season. 450 HUF adults,
300 HUF children. Walk a bit farther up from the bus stop
and you will pass the American Ambassador's residence on
the right. The lower stop of the chair lift is just after that.
Ticket services are up the stairs and inside if you want to take
the chair lift to the highest lookout point in Budapest. It's a
fun and not too taxing combination of rides and walking. The
walk up the hill at the top may not suitable for toddlers. At

the top of the partly paved walkway is a Neo-Gothic lookout tower, the Erzsébet Kilátó (named for the Austro-Hungarian queen of the 19th century). Take your picnic basket, or buy your meal at the büfé at the top of the funicular. It tends to be crowded, but there are plenty of tables and space on the ground for blankets. A candy shop at the lower station entrance supplies potato chips, sodas, and candy bars. Usually a crowd is walking up and/or down the slope, so it is easy to simply follow them up to the tower, which costs 300 HUF at the ticket booth.

## Movies

At any one time there are over 20 theaters in Budapest that may be showing English-language movies. While many are dubbed, some are merely subtitled. The best way to find out about them is to check with the newspaper the *Budapest Sun* (www.budapestsun.com). They carry a weekly listing of all movies in the city. Most Budapest theaters can be fairly classy, some offering tables and benches for use at intermission, and some even providing büfé-style cuisine. The seats are often ergonomic and the isles in the newer theaters have a pleasing terraced design that allows each row to be almost a separate seating area of its own.

**Corvin Budapest Film Palota**, Budapest 1081, Corvin köz 1, ☎ 36-459-5050 fax 459-5040, www.corvin.hu; for information about films (can answer questions in English), ☎ 459-5059. Take M3 to Üllői út exit, or take Tram 4 or 6. This recently renovated movie complex in the splendid architectural setting of the circular Corvin Koz Apartment complex, shows American films on Wednesdays. Tickets at this writing are 750 to 1,500 HUF per adult and 600 to 800 HUF for children.

**Palace Cinemas** plays many English-language movies, with Hungarian subtitles. They operate out of three movie theaters, at the West End City Center, The Mammut, and the Campona. Reservations: ☎ 1-345-8160; www.palacecinemas. hu. The Mammut shopping center theater (two theaters, the Mozitermek 1-8 and the Mozitermek 9-13) and the neighboring restaurants are sure to please. There is also a bowling alley. It is located one block off of Moskva tér at Lövöház utcá 2-6. In addition to the MOM shopping center Palace Theater outlet, Budapest XII, Alkotás út 65, there are other theaters. such as the West End Mall (Váci út 1-3) movie theater, at the Nugati Pályaudvar mentioned earlier, and the Campona, XXII Budapest, Nagytétényi út 37-45.

# ■ Nightlife

## Concerts, Opera, Theater

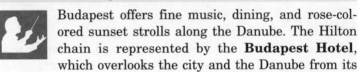 Budapest offers fine music, dining, and rose-colored sunset strolls along the Danube. The Hilton chain is represented by the **Budapest Hotel**, which overlooks the city and the Danube from its dominican ruins, incorporated into the hotel, with brickwork almost a thousand years old, where lookout points view the lights of Budapest as they start to dot the cityscape in the evening. Dining is accompanied by classical and contemporary music, and the soft sounds of the piano bar add to the quiet elegance. Ten yards across from the hotel, **Matthias Cathedral**, the coronation cathedral of Hungary, hosts Friday and Saturday concerts. From its gold Baroque chapel, the ringing music of Vivaldi, Mozart, Bach, Liszt, or Verdi may end with a stroll out to the Trinity Square and along the ramparts of the castle walls. The **Military Museum**, on the north of the castle complex, with its spectacular wall and ceiling paintings and gold-trimmed marble columns, offers a similar venue. In the evenings musicians from Budapest music schools perform their recitals in its acoustically superb ballroom, after which strollers enjoy the romance of castle walks and picture-perfect views overlooking the city at night.

**Opera Dinner Cruise**. The Operetta Ship (☎ 36-1-402-0063, fax 402-0064, www.operetthajo.hu, operettaship@kulturinfo. hu, €€€, costs €52 with dinner and €35 with no dinner; children under five are free and ages five to 14 are charged a reduced rate. (I do not recommend that you take this cruise without the dinner. Standing and watching others eat ruins the enjoyment.) Singers and dancers of the Hungarian State Opera House and the Hungarian Operetta Theater make for superb singing, both popular and operatic, accompanied by exciting dance routines, in period costume. The top-notch cuisine is based on famous Hungarian composers' favorite dishes. Romantic night views of Budapest from the deck add to the enjoyment.

★★★ **Opera House**, 1061 Budapest, Andrássy út 22, ☎ 36-1-353-0170, www.opera.hu. Opera season is from Sept through April, Tickets start at about only €5, incredibly inexpensive. Built between 1875 and 1884, the opera house combines neo-Renaissance and Baroque styles by the seminal architect of the time Miklós Ybl. In the front, curving staircases lead on either side to the tripartite portico and driveway. On either side are the porticos with statues of Franz Liszt and Ferenc Erkel by the great Hungarian artist Alajos Stróbl. Entering the building your gaze is drawn to the buffet in the foyer, and the richly designed grand staircase. One of the most beautiful in all of Europe, a night performance in this fabulous structure takes

one back immediately to the turn of the century when The Palace of Andrássy Street hosted the Hapsburgs in artistic opulence. Book your seat in an opera booth among the five stories of balconies and join those who likewise view from the royal viewing box, amid richly gilded boxes, red velvet banquettes, damask-covered walls, and rich Baroque chandeliers. Daily tours at about 800 HUF can give you a sample without the concert.

*Opera entrance*
*(Nannette Vinson)*

**Duna Palotta** (Danube Palace), 1051 Budapest, Zrinyi utca 5, ☎/fax36-1-

317-1377. Average price 5,000 to 6,000 HUF. Concerts and/or performances are from late May through early Nov. Built in 1895 in Neo-Baroque, it is almost on the bank of the Danube, in District V, close to the Lánchíd (Chain Bridge). Béla Bartók, and Antonin Dvorak are among the many famous names in music who have played out of this richly ornamented structure. Today it is the home of the Danube Symphony Orchestra, and the Danube Folklore Ensemble. Concerts play out in three different venues, folk, opera, and classical favorites, all emphasizing Hungarian composers and music.

**Franz Liszt Music Academy**, 1061 Budapest, Liszt Ferenc tér 8 (a small street between Andrássy and Kiraly utca, just before the Octagon off Andrássy út), ☎ 6-1-462-4679, www.lfze. hu, www.Koncertkalendarium. hu. This is one of the best places for small concerts in the city. It was built in Secession Style and the acoustics are marvelous. Tickets can be had for less than five dollars for most programs, but season ticket sell-outs keep at-the door purchases going.

Get seats early, first-come, first-served, as it's very popular with the locals. Franz Liszt founded the academy. Its small museum displays three of the original pianos that Liszt used to write some of his great compositions, a lock of his hair, his personal prayer book, and a bronze replica of his right hand, not to mention many other items. Cafés or restaurants are steps from the front entrance.

**Organ concerts**, St. Stephen's Cathedral, 1051 Budapest, Szt István tér 1, ☎ 36-1-311-0839 (Hungarian and sometimes English), take place every Monday evening, May through Sept, and more frequently in the summer. St Anna's 1011 Budapest, Batthyanyi tér 7, ☎ 36-1-201-3404 (Hungarian) has a soft white blue interior, also weekly concerts, as does nearby St. Francis Wounds Church, 1011 Budapest, Fo út 43, ☎ 36-1-201-8091 (Hungarian).

**Corvin Hall** in Buda Castle (Royal Palace), Szentháromság tér 6, ☎ 36-1-222-2111, occasionally plays host to operettas from Strauss and Mozart as well as concerts by the Hungarian State Folk Ensemble. Castle strolls can take you to several fine restaurants as well as to romantic panoramas.

**Capital Operetta Theater** (Budapest Operetta Theater, or Operettszínház), 1065 Budapest, Nagymezo utca 19, ☎ 36-1-312-4866 and 36-1-353-2172, built in 1898, still hosts works by the now internationally recognized Budapest Operetta Theater Company. Budapest rivals Vienna as a home for the operetta. Nowhere is it more evident. The Hungarian composers Kálmán and Lehár are performed, along with Strauss and Mozart. There is ballroom dancing in the grand ballroom and costume balls take place as well.

**Erkel Theater**, 1081 Budapest, Köztársaság tér 30, ☎ 36-1-333-0108, with a ticket office at 22 Andrássy út, ☎ 36-1-353-0170, hosts various performances throughout the year. Romantic ticket packages can include a taxi transfer to the theater from your hotel, a bottle of champagne, a dessert and an evening of *Faust*, or perhaps *The Magic Flute*, by world-class performers. The work most popular with Hungarians is *Hunyadi László* (a 15th-century soldier and politician who opposed the Austrians), composed in 1844 by Ference Erkel, founder of the Hungarian State Opera and composer of the Hungarian National anthem.

**Intimate chamber concerts** are held at the Béla Bartók Memorial House, 1025 Budapest, Csalán út 29, ☎/fax 36-1-394-4472, ☎ 36-1-394-2100, www.bartokmuseum.hu, Bartok-1981@axelero.hu. Most are on Friday nights, from mid-March

**Budapest**

to June, and again from Sept to the middle of Dec. The recital room is very small and charming and the quality of the playing is always high. This was the last residence of the great composer (1932-1940). The museum itself is open during the day, Tue-Sun from 10 am to 5 pm.

Hungry for English? Try the **Merlin Theater**, 1052 Budapest, Gerlóczy út 4, ☎ 36-1-317-9338, fax 36-1-266-0904, www.merlinszinhaz.hu. Tickets, 12 pm to 7 pm daily, 2 pm-6 pm weekends. It hosts visiting English-speaking troupes and also has a local expat English-speaking theater company. It is quite popular and is especially patronized by English-speaking residents of Budapest.

If you prefer a simple night with some soft jazz, a piano bar or just plain conversation, try the **Incognito**, VI Liszt Ferenc tér 3, ☎ 36-1-342-1471 or 36-1-351-9428, Hotel Mercure Budapest Korona. Its restaurant Rubin offers Hungarian piano and violin music in the evening. Such evening entertainment is also found at the **Kempinski Corvinus bar** in the evening, the **Hilton restaurants**, the **Corinthia Aquincum**, III fejedelem utca 94, ☎ 36-1-436-4100, the **Meridian**, and the **Astoria** (see *Places to Stay* and *Places to Dine*).

# Nightclubs & Discos

As with any cosmopolitan city you can find what you want in Budapest. Bars, cocktail lounges, casinos, and strip clubs can sometimes be tourist traps. Use caution in these kinds of spots. Váci út, in particular, tends to become a parasite paradise in the evening after the shops close. I once walked with a friend from America and we were accosted by streetwalkers at least two or three times in every block. My son visited a night club at the foot of Gellert Hill on Hegyalja út, and later showed me pictures of its women in different states of undress. I had warned him, but, nevertheless, one evening I got a call asking that I come down to help him. It seems that the women had surrounded him, pressuring him to order several rounds of drinks. When the time came to pay the piper, he was faced with a bill of almost $200 dollars. I have heard of some of these tabs multiplying into the thousands. Of course, he didn't have the money and, as he told me over the phone, two huge burly guys were watching over him. A small beer and a sack of peanuts can set you back a fortune.

**Petõfi Csarnok** in the northeastern end of the Városliget, Budapest XIV, 1146, Zichy Mihály út 14, ☎ 36-1-363-3730, fax 36-1-3729, www.petoficsarnok.hu, is a huge meeting place for dancing (after all the park is here), for events, and as a place to learn different folk dances. Check with their office for the monthly programs. In addition, well-known bands and an active disco crowd join together in summer concerts.

**E-Klub** in Budapest X, next to the Planetarium, ☎ 36-1-263-1614 or 36-20-414-5025, www.e-klub.hu, office@e-klub.hu, is open on Fridays and Saturdays and filled to the brim with local students from the Budapest Technical University. Cover is 800 HUF for men and 600 HUF for women.

**Janis Joplin Bar** (known as Janis' Pub), V, Király Pal utca 8, ☎ 36-1-266-2619, info@janispub.hu, www.janispub.hu, www.restaurantguide.hu/janis, has loads of eats, music and dance. More laid-back but longer lasting than many places in this district.

**Becketts** is more home-grown, with live entertainment, and is visited by many expats (see *Places to Eat*).

**Alcatraz**, H-1072 Budapest, Nyár út 1, ☎ 36-1-478-6010 or ☎/fax 36-1-478-0581, www.alcatraz.hu, info@alcatraz.hu. This is an Internet café during the day, serving teas, coffees and light fare; it rocks at night with live entertainment and good food.

**Fél 10 Jazz Club**, VIII, Baross út 30, has jazz and dancing nightly. Open Mon-Fri noon-4 am and Sat and Sun 7 pm to 4 am. English is spoken here.

**Club Seven**, Akácfa utca 7, ☎ 36-1-478-9030, fax 36-1-478-9035, www.clubseven.hu, info@clubseven.hu, is a classy café, bar, and music club. This is one of the hottest scenes in Budapest for single men, with good-looking topless dancers, and an upscale young crowd. Most credit cards and English are welcome at this disco, plus casino, plus pizzeria, bar, and cocktail lounge. Be careful of your tab and your money here.

**Budapest**

**Morrisons**, Révay utca 25, District VII, ☎ 36-1-269-4060, has been described as a cool place to hang out. Enter to a long counter with a red British phone box (the trademark of the place), and other British memorabilia. Order your drink from the bartenders, a congenial group, and then walk into the next room, where several tables beckon before you hit the dance floor. The third room provides a television retreat (nine TVs stacked on top of each other).

**Nincs Pardon**, Almássy tér 11, District VII, ☎ 36-1-351-4351, is a landmark for night-clubbers, with a bohemian type of cellar bar that attracts many locals and expats. Not exactly a modern facility, but trendy, with speakers hanging from the ceiling above the dance floor. It usually rocks after midnight. There is live music on weekends.

**Liszt Ference ter** is good for a walk in the evening, and at selected clubs, for cocktails, dancing, and late night and early morning strolls.

**Piaf**, VI, Nagymezõ utca 25, ☎ 36-1-312-3823, near the Octagon (Oktogon). Known as a hangout for artists, this wild little place attracts writers, actresses, and a bagatelle of characters to its lively dance venue.

**Trocadero**, V, Szent István körút 13, ☎ 36-1-311-4691, near Margit Bridge. Latin dancing and mixing with an earthy crowd. The dance floor is large.

**Dokk Jazz Bistro**, III, Hajógyári sziget 122 (Hajógyár Island), emphasizes jazz and western culture. It is classy, but on the expensive side.

**Fat Mo's**, V, Nyári Pál utca 11, www.fatmo.hu, ☎ 36-1-267-3199, fax 328-0706, is a popular hangout for the expats of the city as well as locals, middle aged and middle class, with a relaxed and sometimes wild atmosphere... all in fun. Live music fills the place before midnight on most occasions.

**Old Man's Pub**, VII, 1072 Budapest, Akácfa utca 13, www.oldmans.hu, oldmans@mail.matav.hu, ☎ 36-1-322-7645, features live music and various dance styles almost every night of the week, plus a separate room for smooth jazz. But here it is mandatory to get a reservation if you want to be assured of a decent table, the place is packed, popular, and sure to please.

Goldman György tér is a center for dancing, food, and live entertainment between May and October. Most of the square is cordoned off and used by the Zöld Pardon and the Café Del Rio (see below). Music every night varies between DJs and live entertainment. Expect a young crowd, and bring a 100 HUF coin for the entry fee.

**Zöld Pardon**, XI, 1111 Budapest, Mûegyetem Rakpart, Petõfi híd budai hídfõ (at the foot of Petõfi Bridge), www.zp. hu, info@zp.hu, ☎ 36-1-279-1880.

**Café Del Rio**, XI, Goldmann György tér 1, www.rio.hu, ☎ 36-30-297-2158, a backstop to Zöld Pardon, it too has a large garden dance area and two massive bars, one specializing in cocktails.

**Vizimozi Cinetrip**, at the Rudas Bath House, Döbrentei tér 9, district 1. Take Tram 18 from Moszkva tér or take Bus 7 from Ferenciek tér to the Rudas Baths. Every couple of months at the Rudas Baths there is an all-night swim party, with bath, movie, dancing, drinking, and DJs. Silent films can be viewed from the main pool, or the belly dancers may offer a better eyefull in the domed Turkish baths. This is a touch of heathen Budapest, with pools, partying, and music. While the Rudas are normally for men only, on these nights it is open to the fair sex as well. These celebrations are more frequent in the summer.

If you are looking for the edge of the outrageous then you might try the fetish parties at **Heaven 51**, a private club at Ó utca 51, district 6. From Pest you take the blue metro M3 to Arany János utca or the yellow metro M1 to the Opera. Admission is 969 HUF and the preferred dress code is fetish, that is leather, rubber, etc. If you didn't bring yours on vacation, you can rent a costume for about 1,500 HUF.

**Made Inn**, ☎ 36-1-311-3437 (on Andrássy út 112), north of the Oktogon, has a patio and music with an accumulation of expats and locals.

When any international rock group comes to town, they usually play at the **Népstadion** (Sun Stadium), which has the largest seating capacity in the city for this type of event.

## Casinos

 Except for the Las Vegas Casino (smart-casual), normal attire in the casinos of Budapest is evening dress. Roulette, black jack and poker are available at any of the casinos. Drinks and some eats are served at all. The more well known are:

**Las Vegas**, next to the front street entrance of the Sofitel Hotel Roosevelt, tér 2, ☎ 36-1-317-6022, fax 266-2082, www.lasvegascasino.hu.

**Casino Vigadó** (also known as Tropicana Casino), Vigadó utca 2, ☎ 36-1-266-3062, fax 327-7285, www.tropicanacasino.hu.

**Varkert Casino**, Ybl Miklos tér 9, ☎ 36-1-202-4244, by the Danube, down the street from the Golden Stag toward Groza Péter Rakpart.

# ■ Itineraries

 **Absolute Walking Tours**, outside Hungary, ☎ 36-20-211-8861, fax 266-8777, inside Hungary, ☎ 06-30-211-8861, www.absolutetours.com, bookings@absolutetours.com, has a series of walking tours. Their knowledgeable Hungarian/English-speaking guides are tops in the city. Following are tours that you can also do on your own.

Start at ★★★**Erzsébet híd** (Elizabeth Bridge) on the Pest side. You may notice flags flapping from the ramparts of Erzsébet híd. The country flags of visiting dignitaries are always colorfully alternated with Hungarian flags the entire length of Elizabeth Bridge.

## ★★★Gellért Hegy (Gellert Hill)

From Móricz Zsigmond körtér take bus 27 or 107. You must get off at the top stop, and walk up the hill on Sirtes út. Alternatively, you can do it on foot in 20 to 30 minutes from the Buda end of the Elizabeth Bridge or the Freedom Bridge by following any of the footpaths to the top. Although there are parking spaces at the foot of the Citadel, you must still walk up about 50 yards to its walls.

Gellért hegy rises 430 ft above the Danube atop steep dolomite cliffs. Before the turn of the century it was the limit of

Buda, and the foremost outpost of the Castle. While there are villas on the lower slopes, the upper slopes are laced with woods, trails and spectacular views.

*Gellért Hill (HNTB)*

Reaching the foot of Gellérthegy, stairs rise before you to the huge ★**statue of St. Gellért** defiantly raising a cross. Made by the sculptor Gyula Jankovics in 1904, the statue reputedly stands at the very spot where St.Gellert, then an Italian missionary, was stuffed in a spiked barrel by pagans and rolled down the hill to plunge into the Danube in 1046. Just to the right of the stairs is a monumental retaining wall made of huge granite blocks, laced at the top with stone handrails and balustrades from the turn of the century. It forms a heavy stone border that reaches around the hill going up the Hegyalja út. A large chiseled stone plaque reads in giant letters that the wall was built in 1902, in the final days of the Hapsburgs. Below St. Gellért's statue, an artificial waterfall, Ferenc Medgyessy's creation, called St. Gerard's (Gellért's) Fountain, refreshes the walking trail.

Now walk back the way you came, but gradually take the higher trails. You will shortly come to the ★★★**Citadel**. This imposing fortress, visible from the entire waterfront of

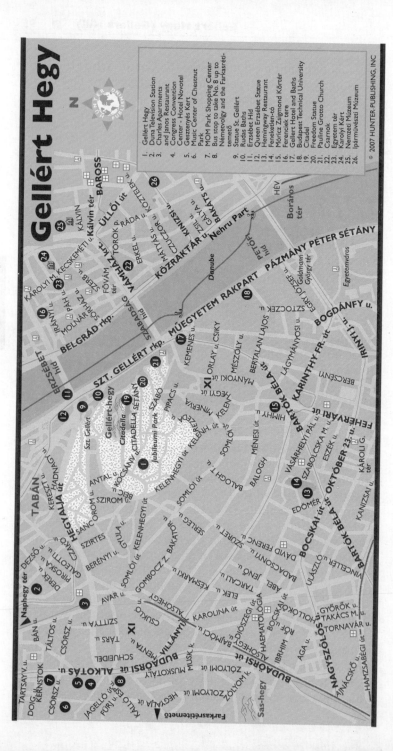

# Gellért Hegy

N

1. Gellért Hegy
2. Duna Television Station
3. Charles Apartments and Janos Apartments
4. Congress Convention Center – Hotel Novotel
5. Gesztenyés Kert
6. Music Center of Chestnut Park
7. MOM Park Shopping Center
8. Bus stop to take No. 8 up to Németvölgy and the Farkasréti-temető
9. Statue St. Gellért
10. Rudas Baths
11. Erzsébet Híd
12. Queen Erzsébet Statue
13. Hemingway Restaurant
14. Feneketlen-tó
15. Móricz Zsigmond Körtér
16. Ferenciek tere
17. Gellért Hotel and Baths
18. Budapest Technical University
19. Citadel
20. Freedom Statue
21. Pauline Grotto Church
22. Csarnok
23. Egyetem tér
24. Károlyi Kert
25. Nemzeti Múzeum
26. Iparművészeti Múzeum

© 2007 HUNTER PUBLISHING, INC

the Danube at City Center, was built between 1850 and 1854 by the Hapsburgs to keep Budapest under heel after the war of Independence. The city bought the fortress from Austria in 1899, after the Austrian troops had left. The walls were symbolically destroyed, but partially rebuilt to house Hungarian and German troops in WWII. Today, inside the Citadel, you can tour the remains of a German bunker below ground that housed the German air command during WW II, complete with wax figures and a WWII battle film. It's not spectacular, and is cheesy in parts, but interesting for its neutral treatment of the German army, as well as its favoritism toward the Hungarian soldiers. Young Hungarian Freedom fighters made their last stand against the Russians here in 1956. Bomb blast scars and bullet holes are still there. Various examples of artillery pieces are on display. We earlier noted the fine Citadel restaurant and the unrated hotel that occupy the structure (see *Places to Dine*, above). There is also an outside büfé.

Once inside, walk as far as you can to the north wall. On the left side of the Danube is **Buda**, and in the far distance, **Óbuda**. To your left and to the north are the **Buda Hills**. In the far distance on your left are the **Pilis mountains**. Closer to home in the same direction, you will see below you the **Castle District**, marked by the spires of **St. Matthias Cathedral** and the grand **Hapsburg Palace**, and from this direction the medieval guard towers on the southern flank stand out visibly. Closer in, the green area between Gellert Hill and the foot of the Castle District is the **Tabán** (see the following section). Looking north the closest bridge, just below and just to the right at the foot of Gellérthegy, is **Erzsébet híd** (Elizabeth Bridge). It is the newest bridge in the city center.

*The Chain Bridge*

Looking north, the next bridge is the famous **Lánchíd** (Chain Bridge), the first bridge to unite

*Chain Bridge, with Margaret Bridge & Margit Island
in the distance (Nannette Vinson)*

Buda and Pest, and a historical landmark. Farther north, the bridges are, in order, **Margaret Bridge** (it runs across the southern tip of Margit Island), **Árpád Bridge**, and the **Northern Railway Bridge**. On the Pest side of the river, from this vantage, **Parliament's** Gothic spires are plainly visible on the eastern bank of the Danube, in the distance.

★★**The Statue of Liberty** rises high above, just across the south wall, within throwing distance. You can get to the foot of it by walking out of the Citadel and around to the base of the statue, which is another lookout point. In the evening it is dramatically flooded with lights. It's a female figure 132 feet high, holding the palm of victory. She was once adorned with the communist red star, and had soldiers at her base; they were removed when the Russian occupation ended.

*Statue of Liberty*

Stripped of its communist markings, the Statue of Liberty has become a symbol of Hungarian defiance and freedom.

On the south side, hidden below, are the **Gellert Hotel** and baths. Unseen against the hill, the grotto church constructed by the Paulines in 1932 is evidence of their resurgence after Joseph II dissolved their order in 1786. Beyond, the Buda shoreline stretches to include the campus of **Budapest Uni-**

**versity of Technology** and, beyond, the housing districts of the Lágymányos and the Kelenföld, then the smokestacks from the **Csepel Works**, Hungary's largest factory.

## ★ The Tabán

From the summit of Hegyalja út and the lighted intersection at Sánc út, there is a striptease joint on the corner, where my son learned a lesson about the world's enticements. Walk across

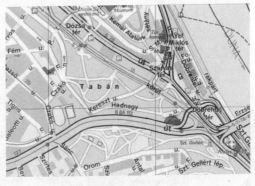

Hegyalja, and continue north past the athletic field, which you will see on your right. Turn right at the next street, Cáko út. Walk down to the end of the street. You are at the lower summit of the Tabán. Different views along this crest reveal not just the palace, but some incredible views of the southern flank medieval battlements. While you may be tempted to run to the Castle District from here, I urge you instead to take your time and walk down the street to your right. It will take you around and through the Tabán Park, with small children's swings, a tennis club, and extensive pathways and stairs. It is a favorite for winter sledding with local families.

But its peaceful repose has reminders of Hungary's past as well, and to a certain extent her haunted present.

This low-lying hill was once a Turkish suburb. In the 19th century it was home to Serbs, Greeks, and Gypsies, and a den of

*The Tabán*

Budapest

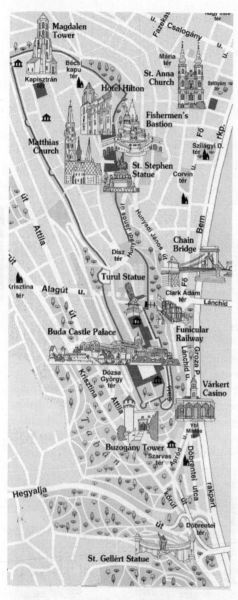

brothels and gambling dens. Most of the housing was cleared away at the turn of the century due to plagues, and wars took their toll as well. Three prominent structures of the old Tabán remain: the 18th-century **Aranyszarvas** (Golden Stag Restaurant), the bright yellow **Church of St. Christines** (1790) and the **Benedek House** (1730), across the street from the Aranyszarvas. It is now a restaurant, called The Tabán. Hidden away, but almost directly across the street from the Aranyszarvas and to your right as you gradually descend are the golden yellow façades of the 15th-century **Rác Fürdő** (Rác Baths), fed by a thermal spring that was used as early as the 14th century. Exploited by the Turks, it was turned into one of their famed baths, still used today (at this writing under reconstruction).

From the Middle Ages through the 1930s the Tabán was a densely populated, lively area of small houses, ferry-men, coach-men, vineyard workers and tradesmen, and in later years, by prostitutes and brothels as

well. The name Tabán comes from a Turkish word which identified the area as the place of the tanners. Later, a Serbian
word meaning literally tanners was modified and used in
Hungarian for the Tabán. Plagues, wars and ethnic tensions
each helped to destroy this once-prosperous town. Rising in
its place is a ★ **statue dedicated to freedom fighters** who
died in the 1956 revolution, put together and financed by survivors. It is not widely discussed, but many in the government
today actually participated in crushing that revolution, and
that significant fact alone perhaps accounts for the official
silence that accompanied the construction of this monument.
There are still old memories and old wounds. A wide bleached
white obelisk, it rises 18 feet from its square base, with the
faces of young Hungarian freedom fighters chiseled on its
front, facing the Danube. At the top, an eagle with out-
stretched wings, symbolizing freedom, looks down on the
wreaths that sometimes decorate the foot of the obelisk, while
around it children play on the slopes, scarcely aware of its
presence.

Walk farther down the hill, along the street, and just to your
left is another monument. It is a large stone cross, about 12
feet high. A religious painting marks the top. A plaque is
emblazoned on its face just below eye level with an insightful
inscription. It says that here in 1865 a cross was first erected
by the Eastern Greek-Serbian church, and it was demolished
in 1880 (what stories the stones might tell). The inscription
continues that here in 1987, a similar stone cross was erected
in its memory. These two statues are themselves stories,
glimpses into the tortured heart of Budapest and Hungary,
political upheaval and subdued regional ethnic tensions, yet
resting in the peaceful outward setting of the park. Despite it
all, life goes on, and Hungary continues to build toward her
future.

Farther down at the intersection of Krisztina Krt, cross the
street, across the divider, and over to the corner of the
Aranyszarva (Golden Stag Restaurant). You are at the corner
of a small intersecting street called Apród utca. Cross the
street to the yellow house at No.10 Apród utca. A statue of a
woman rises in front toward the lower corner of the restaurant's outside terrace and you will note an inscription at the
base dedicated to **Virag Benedek** (1754-1830). A famous
Hungarian poet, this building was his home, which today

houses the fine restaurant, the Tabán, and a museum. The original 18th-century house is still intact. Around the corner from this building is the **Church of St. Christines** (1736), bright yellow and with a green four-sided onion-dome roof.

Back across the street, walk to the Aranyszarva (Golden Stag Restaurant), and go down Apros utca about 40 feet to the bust of Andrássy, for whom Andrássy út was named. Continuing around toward the Duna, the aging façade of a former part of the palace is on your left. At 1-3 Apród utca, is the ★★**Semmelweis Museum of Medical History**, ☎ 36-1-375-3533, open 10:30 to 5 daily except Sat and Sun. This museum is home to the largest medical archive in Europe, outside of London. Ancient petri dishes and pharmaceutical grinding bowls line the entranceway. Upstairs, there are Egyptian medical tools, papers and articles from medieval times up through the early 1900s, medical tools, mannequins, microscopes, doctors kits (including bleeder instruments), chastity belts, displays of anatomical studies, and a full-size turn-of-the-century apothecary. An 1800s still at the very end of the exhibit hall was used for pharmaceutical manufacturing as well as for making liquor. Just about every apothecary had one in those days, a medicinal necessity. Paintings show doctoring methods, plagues, and living conditions from the 15th century to the 18th century.

The museum is dedicated to Ignác Semmelweis (1818-1865), one of the greatest medical pioneers of Hungary. A hundred years before the germ theory of disease, he pioneered clinical sterility techniques in surgery and child birth that led to his being celebrated as the savior of mothers. His eclectic ways earned him the animosity of Vienna however.

*Várkert Casino*

Across the street is the **Várkert Casino** (Castle Garden Casino). The building was designed by Miklos Ybl, one of the more famous Hungarian architects and built in 1897. This small intersection of streets is now called Miklos Ybl, for the architect's namesake. Now, walk back to the back street of the Aranyszarva and look toward the southern battlements of the Buda Castle. They are easily accessible.

## ★★★ The Castle District

The Castle District, rising 165 to 200 ft, is Hungarian history. You can get there by car, or by bus 16 from Clarke Adam tér. The bus starts at the Buda end of the Chain Bridge and goes directly to the national gallery (Palace). The Vár bus starts at Moszkva tér (its station is up the stairs on the side of the hill to the west of the metro entrance) and then winds through the Castle District. Aside from Apór út at the Tabán, you can approach from any of the sur-

*Fountain at Buda Castle*

rounding streets, Fö utca, Batthyány utca, or Attila utca, and from most side streets.

## History of Buda Castle District

The Castle District is a monument to desperation, a saga of the unique turbulence that history brought upon Budapest. The Mongols swept down from the plains of the Alföld like demons from hell. Pest did not survive. It was 1241 AD. The hordes, known wherever they went for the merciless destruction of their enemies, annihilated the peaceful city on the shores of the Danube. Not content to claim victory, they raped and plundered until there was nothing left. They burned every structure to the ground, and in a bloody work of extermination, every single man, woman, and child was run through with a sword. The terror of that day lived on.

From the Buda side of the Danube they watched the carnage in horror, and swore that they would build a stronghold against the next storm from the east.. They moved their

Budapest

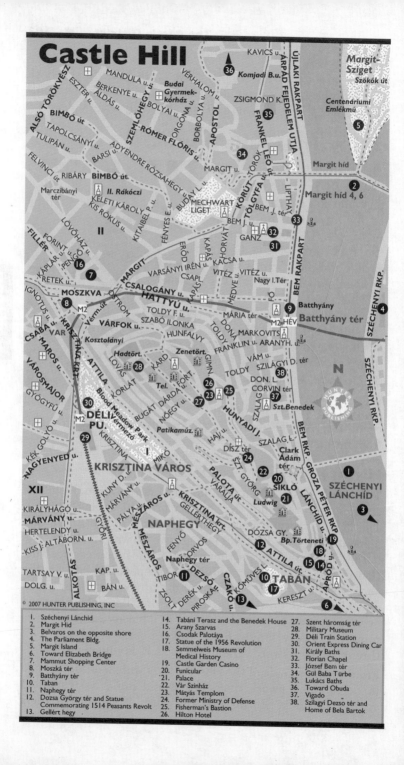

# Castle Hill

1. Széchenyi Lánchid
2. Margit Hid
3. Belvaros on the opposite shore
4. The Parliament Bldg.
5. Margit Island
6. Toward Elizabeth Bridge
7. Mammut Shopping Center
8. Moszká tér
9. Batthyány tér
10. Taban
11. Naphegy tér
12. Dozsa György tér and Statue Commemorating 1514 Peasants Revolt
13. Gellért hegy
14. Tabáni Terasz and the Benedek House
15. Arany Szarvas
16. Csodak Palotáya
17. Statue of the 1956 Revolution
18. Semmelweis Museum of Medical History
19. Castle Garden Casino
20. Funicular
21. Palace
22. Vár Szinház
23. Mátyás Templom
24. Former Ministry of Defense
25. Fisherman's Bastion
26. Hilton Hotel
27. Szent háromság tér
28. Military Museum
29. Déli Train Station
30. Orient Express Dining Car
31. Király Baths
32. Florian Chapel
33. József Bem tér
34. Gul Baba Türbe
35. Lukács Baths
36. Toward Obuda
37. Vigado
38. Szilagyi Dezso tér and Home of Bela Bartok

© 2007 HUNTER PUBLISHING, INC

houses to the top of the steep castle hill, keeping the outsides windowless for defense, and then put fences in between the gaps to develop an outside wall. Gradually powerful defensive ramparts were added until, by the 16th century, it became a stronghold. Inside, the Royal Palace occupied the south and residences the north. The defensive position was so strong that the Turks had to take it by trickery, not by force, in the siege of 1541. It was only after repeated sieges that the united Christian armies retook Buda Castle in 1686. Rebuilt in Baroque style, it was again besieged in the 1849 revolution. After the Hapsburg victory in 1867, the castle became the center of the new Hungary. Within two generations the Germans came, made a last desperate stand against the Red Army from December 1944 to February 1945 and, by their bitter resistance, brought the total devastation of Castle Hill. In reconstruction, medieval structures were uncovered. Rehabilitation remained faithful to history. The result has turned this district into an internationally recognized World Heritage Site.

## Walking the Castle District

The back entrance of the Castle District almost hides the first evidence of the Turkish defeat of 1686. To the right, before you pass the outside bastion walls, you will see small mushroom-shaped pillars clustered beneath the shade of the trees. The tops are actually turbans. You guessed it! It is a Turkish graveyard dating from 1686. As you enter the castle under the circular Mace tower, it will lead you through the Ferdinand Gate. Passing the southern bastion you enter the lower garden, and then, through the door you enter the palace. However, at this point you may find yourself redirected to the front entrance. So we can go to the traditional access for the Castle District, aside from walking trails and bus or car, and that is via the funicular at Adam Clarke tér (7:30 am to 10 pm daily). It was opened in 1870 for workers. But it has also suffered from the wars and was rebuilt after WWII using an electrical cable system instead of the old steam power. The coaches glide up the hill and take only a little over a minute. At the top, go to the palace at your left first. Head for the black wrought iron gates with the dramatic spread-winged Turul, a

*The Palace Museums*

mythical bird that is said to have fathered Árpád, the great Hungarian chieftain. Follow the steps down and note the proud statue of Eugene of Savoy mounted on his steed, one of the great leaders of the Christian armies that took Buda Castle back from the Turks in 1686. From there enter ★★★ the **Palace**, today housing three different museums. Exploring it and the museums can easily take an entire day and is not suitable for small children.

The **Hungarian National Art Gallery**, which you enter at first, occupies the B, C and D wings of the Castle, a huge and magnificent compendium of Hungarian art stretching back centuries. Some of the more prominent Hungarian artists include Mihály Munkácsy (famous in 19th-century Europe), Károly Lotz, whose breathtaking fresco, *Olympus, Home of the Gods*, decorates the fabulous opera house, Bertalan Székely, one of the greatest masters of Hungarian historical painting, whose murals decorate Matthias Church, among others, Jozsef Rippl-Ronai, for earthy depictions of Hungarian life, romantic lovers husking corn, and saucy women, and Tivadar Csontváry-Kosztka for subtle symbolism, almost on the verge of new-age Impressionism. The ground floor is for medieval altar art and the top floor displays the work of modern artists.

The inner courtyard to the right leads to the **Museum of Contemporary History**, housing the Ludwig collection of post-WWII art and a substantial exhibit of communist memorabilia. The fountain in the corner of the courtyard is a masterpiece by the Hungarian sculptor, Alajos Stróbl. It is based on a ballad by Mihály Vörösmarty, with King Mátyás meeting the commoner Ilonka while on a hunt. Erected in 1904, at the same time as the courtyard lions, the realism is vivid and compelling. To the left are the Baroque residences of Empress Maria Theresa (1715-1738). At the back of the courtyard begins the **Budapest History Museum** (Vármúzeum), www.btm.hu.

The colorful courtyard colors bricked into the ground actually trace the outline of the palace structure of the Anjou kings, though they do not necessarily lie directly over it. Archeologists are still working that one out. At the same time, somewhere below us, the palace of the Anjou kings, starting with Lajos the Great, was built over the first palace-fortress constructed by King Béla IV in 1243 to defend Buda from the Tartar hordes.

The archeological exploration of the old palaces is an important project of the History Museum. But the medieval is still there. Upon entering the museum from ground level, you can take the tour that explores the medieval castle. Much of this area was not destroyed. From a smoke-stained stairway you enter into a cavernous, dark dungeon. King László V imprisoned Mátyás Corvinus here in 1457. But, in 1458 Mátyás ascended the throne, and promptly used the cellar dungeons to imprison Vlad Tepes, the Impaler, better known as Dracula. However, the brighter rooms of the museum recall the religious idealism of an age that believed in the supernatural. The Gothic hall is from Sigismond's Palace in the early 15th century. The tiny Royal Chapel is a miracle. It has survived almost intact through sieges and wars since the 14th century, though at times buried by rubble, only to be rediscovered in the 20th century. The stones upon which the Anjou kings kneeled and the altar where they prayed are the same. It was re-conse-

crated as an ecumenical chapel in
1990. The doors opposite the main
entrance lead to the Ferdinand
Gate and the Mace tower. We will
not go there, but will turn back and
walk out of the palace.

Heading north from the Royal Palace, you are at St. György tér. On
your right is the entrance from the
funicular and then, after a set of
buildings, is the **Sándor Palace**. It is now only open to the
public on the National Heritage Day, the third weekend of
Sept. Count Vince Sándor had the palace built in 1803 as his
personal residence. It remained in the Sándor family until
1831 when it was sold to Pallavicini Marquis. After the Hapsburg treaty of 1867, he sold it to the state. It has been a house
of state ever since. Until the end of WWII, 19 Hungarian
Prime Ministers had worked and lived here. It was here that
Admiral Horthy's Prime Minister, Pál Teleki, shot himself in
April 1941 as a protest against Hungary's decision to join Germany in an attack on Yugoslavia, less than four months after
signing the Treaty of Eternal Friendship with Yugoslavia.
After being gutted and bombed in WWII, the building collapsed. It was rebuilt with meticulous attention to historical
detail after 2002. Photo archives, antique furniture, memorabilia were brought to the project. By January 2003, the
Sándor Palace was reopened as the office of the President of
Hungary. Official receptions, the greeting of foreign dignitaries and state business are conducted here.

Next to the Sándor Palace is the ★★**VárSzínház** (Castle
Theater), Színház utca 1-3, www.szinhaz.hu/varszinhaz. It
was originally built as a church for the Carmelite order in
1736, but Joseph II dissolved the order in 1784. After that it
was used by a German theater company up until 1790, and
then was taken over by Hungarians. Surprisingly, the front
Baroque façade has stayed intact through the wars. Performances are still given at the theater.

The next structure cannot be missed, sitting in the middle of
the district, commanding your immediate attention as you
enter from either the east or the west roads. It is the former
★★**Ministry Of Defense Building**, a bomb-blasted and
bullet-ridden skeleton from the war-torn past. It still sits

there, and controversy rages over what to do with it. There are those that want to preserve it as a war memorial, to which its blackened hulk is certainly testimony. Its appearance is a stark reminder of how the Buda district looked after the Red Army's siege of 1945 and, for some, a grim memory of the 1956 standoff of the Hungarians against the Russians as well. Ironically, it was on this same site where, in the Middle Ages, the executioner's gallows were erected, and many a head rolled onto the stone pavement.

After the Ministry Of Defense, going north, you enter **Dísz tér**, the main market center of the Middle Ages. Jews, Germans, and Hungarians each had their own market days. At this point we will turn toward the left and walk past the gigantic **statue of a Hussar**, created by the great military artist and sculptor Zsigmond Kisfaludi Stróbl in 1932. Turn right at the outside street, which runs along the perimiter wall. This is **Tóth Árpád Sétány** (Tóth Árpád walkway). From here you can look at the Buda hills and, in closer view, the Déli rail station (Western railway station), or northward, at the foot of the Castle District, Blood Meadow Park. This section of the walls actually dates from Turkish times. It is known as the **Long Wall** of the Castle District's Bastion Promenade. It was once bolstered with several round cannon outposts. Farther north, the ★**War History Museum** is also called the Esztergom Bastion. The cannons are from ancient Hungarian and European foundries.

At Szentháromság utca, turn right until you come to the statue of András Hadik, the commander of the castle under Empress Maria Theresa. You may note that the horse's testicles shine. For some reason, lost in time, it is said that rubbing the horse's testicles brings good luck! As you

*Old Buda Town Hall*

continue, you will pass the Ruszwurm Coffee-House at No. 7 (see *Places to Eat*). If you look directly across from it you will see the former **Buda Town Hall**, 2 Szentháromság utca (built in 1692), today the Collegium Budapest Research Institute. The Pallas Athene statue stands on the corner holding the coat of arms of the city of Buda. Houses no. 5 and no. 7 both have medieval doors and Gothic niches (with seats). The reason for these niches with seats, an extraordinary rarity in dwellings, is a subject of speculation. No one knows exactly why they were built.

As you continue, you arrive at ★**Szentháromság tér** (Holy Trinity Square). The middle is dominated by the richly adorned Baroque ★**Trinity Column**, which is famous throughout Central Europe. The fabulous beauty of this monument may overwhelm your understanding of its somber meaning. It was commissioned by Buda's city council in 1713, a memorial to those who died in the devastating plague of 1691, hoping that dedication would ward off further bouts of the horrible pestilence. King David from the Bible is depicted at the foot of the monument, praying to heaven for an end

*Trinity Column*

to the terrible blight. Various saints and cherubs are seen ascending up toward the Holy Trinity, Father, Son, and Holy Ghost, sitting on clouds with cherubs astride them. To the left of the square you will see a building which is now a hostel. Formerly the Ministry of Finance, it was built in 1906 with tiled roof and spiked towers.

★★★**St. Mátyás Church** dominates the square. Built and rebuilt as often as the Palace, it has been the place of coronations and worship over many centuries. It is said that the first king of Hungary, King István, built a church on this site as an offering to the German settlers in 1015. It was destroyed in the Tartar invasion of 1240-41. Nevertheless, King Béla IV rebuilt the edifice in Romanesque style and dedicated it to the

Virgin Mary. Characteris-
tically independent, the
Magyars asserted themselves
when the St. Mátyás congregation, after the Árpád
dynasty died out in 1301,
refused to accept the Vatican-
supported Charles Robert. A
mini-religious war ensued (to
be repeated many times over),
which culminated in a Magyar tour-de-force, when the
congregation of Buda formally
excommunicated Pope
Boniface VIII along with his
entire supporting priesthood
of cardinals, bishops, priests,

*St. Mátyás Church*

and deacons. Of course, with power and persuasion, the Vati-
can eventually reigned victorious.

Charles Robert was crowned in the cathedral in 1309. His
son, Lajos the Great, who had built up a Gothic bastion at the
palace, rebuilt Mátyás Cathedral in contemporary Gothic
style. It was basically the same as what you see today, complete with rising Gothic pillars. But this too was covered over.
Subsequent monarchies wanted something better. The popular Mattias Corvinus was crowned King here in 1458 at the
age of 14, and was married twice here as well. His first wife,
the Bohemian princess Catherine of Podebrad, died as his
queen, and was succeeded by his new wife, Beatrix, princess
of Naples, who influenced his Renaissance tastes and the subsequent refurbishment. This was again changed, however,
when the Turks conquered Buda in 1541. On the night of their
victory, they occupied the church and turned it into a mosque
for thanksgiving prayers to Allah. For the next 145 years the
art and treasure of the church was systematically effaced
from the walls and replaced by whitewash and inscriptions
from the Koran. The recapture of Buda by Christendom under
the Hapsburg banners in 1686 saw the Jesuits energetically
put a seminary and a monastery on either side of the church.
With equal vigor they not only removed the Koran, they also

Budapest

removed the Gothic and replaced it with Counter-Reformation Baroque façades and dark interiors with candlelight.

After the 1867 compromise with Austria, Emperor Franz Joseph married Queen Elizabeth, to the tune of Franz Liszt's Coronation Mass in its chapel. After the wedding he lost no time in ordering the removal of the Jesuit embellishments. He wanted the Gothic, and so restoration and refurbishment began again. While the siege of the occupying Germans in 1945 did a lot of damage, enough was there to maintain the integrity of the original. Old pictures and plans rendered the work that much more accurate, remaking the authentic original in most senses. This fact is reinforced by the inside, which has remained substantially the same. As you enter, to the left is a small chapel where stands a red marble statue of the **Madonna and Child**. It was donated by King Ulászlo II in 1515. When the Turks came, this statue was bricked behind a wall by the people of Buda. The Turks were none the wiser. However, in 1686, during the final assault of the Christian armies, a store of gunpowder behind the wall exploded, and out popped the statue. The fear of God fell upon the Turkish defenders. At dawn the next day they surrendered. This is the legend, in any case.

Above the baptismal font is a spiral window showing the Lamb of God. Four waterfalls flow down from the window, depicting the Danube, Drava, Tisza, and Sava rivers, the four main rivers of Hungary. These are depicted on the Hungarian coat of arms by four silver stripes. Moving to the left and just below the window is a chiseled stone relic from the 13th century, two apostles holding the Bible.

The **St. Imre Chapel** is the next inward, followed by the chapel containing the sarcophagi of King Béla III (1172-1196) and his wife Anna Chatillon. Franz Joseph had them taken from their original resting place in Székesfehérvár and brought to this chapel in the 19th century. By all means enter to the basement where you will get a real feel for the medieval past.

After St. Matthias Church, walk out and toward the panoramic views of the ★★★**Fisherman's Bastion**. The ambience is here, and one can almost imagine what it was like to be a pike man looking down from the walls of its round Neo-Gothic

*Fishermen's Bastion*

and Neo-Romanesque towers. But, surprise, it is indeed, not actually a bastion, and was built to give a worthy backdrop to the St Matthias Church by the architect, Frigyes Shulek, circa 1901-1903. However, stones of the original castle wall were used in construction. The Fisherman's Guild was responsible for these defensive walls in the Middle Ages. Their quarter was just below. Looking down from the battlements to where the road turns just below at the foot of the bastion, you can see the statue of János Hunyadi (father of King Matthias), who repulsed the Turkish advance into Europe in 1456. Not far from him is the statue of Saint George

(the original, done in 1373, is in Prague). In the courtyard of the Basilica is the statue of Saint Stephen I, the first King of Hungary from 1001-1038. (1906 by Alajos Stróbl). Bring your camera.

Now walk back to Hess András tér, and walk to the front entrance of the ★★**Hilton Hotel**. The western façade of this

*Hilton Hotel (at water level)*

building has preserved the Baroque and Louis XVI style from what was once a school building of the 18th century. The charm may lead you to the concierge who can provide information about the concerts they hold in the courtyard. Walk out of the hotel. Go to **Hess András tér 3**. This house was built in the 18th century on foundations from the 13th century. The carved stone sign above the gate indicates the **Red Hedgeho (Vörös Sün) Inn**, which is a legacy from 1760. The first theatrical performances of Buda were held here in the 18th century. Now, as you look at ★**No. 4**, which faces the hotel, note that it was formed by joining three 14th-century houses. The *Chronica Hungarorum*, the first book printed in Hungary, was made here in 1473 by András Hess. Today it houses the Fortuna Restaurant, where you can dine amidst the authentic medieval, probably made by the same masons who built the palace. The statue in the middle of the square is Pope Innocent XI, in memory of his call to all Christian nations to unite in a Christian league to liberate Buda in 1686.

Everywhere, the ambience of another time charms the visitor. Head for Táncsics Mihály utca. I call this street Baroque alley. **No. 9 Táncsics Mihály utca** was once the Hungarian mint. Only a stone's throw from the Hilton Hotel, in the 19th century, the famous revolutionary, Kossuth Lajos and a group of his fellow freedom activists were jailed here. While he was behind bars in that building, Kossuth translated *Macbeth* into Hungarian. We also know that next door at No. 7, the curly-haired musical revolutionary Ludwig van Beethoven lived while he visited Budapest in the year 1800. Today it is a

*Vienna Gate*

small museum displaying the works of the famous Hungarian composer Bartók. Now, just a bit farther, on the map it is called the Bécsi Kapu, but we know it as the ★**Vienna Gate**. It is the only original standing medieval gate, although it, like so many other things in this European city, has received a Neo-Classical remodel. The plaque commemorates the recapture of Buda by the Christian army in 1686. Up from the gate, at No. 7 Bécsi Kapu, his home, Baron Lajos Hatvany once extended his hospitality to Thomas Mann.

From 7 Bécsi Kapu, walk back up and turn to Kapisztrán út, where the rising memorial tower seems disjointedly out of place amidst the ruins from which it rises. It is a dedication to the Mary Magdalene Church, used by both Protestants and Catholics during the Turkish occupation as it was the only church still left standing after their siege on the city. Later centuries would see it fall, but in that time and place they looked on it as a miracle. It is listed in documents from the year 1276.

Before leaving the Castle District, sweeten the memory with a wine tour at Szentháromság tér 6 (the House of Hungarian Culture houses the **House of Hungarian Wines**). Their labyrinth holds 450 different types of quality wine from 22 historic wine regions in Hungary. Visitors get a tasting cup at the entrance and are allowed to wander around and taste up to 70-80 different wines. Open 12 to 8 pm. That should give you the courage for the next suggestion before you leave the Castle District. Go on the **cave tour** at No. 9 Úri utca (see *Caves*).

The limestone base of Buda is interlaced with caves and passages from the action of underground springs and thermal water. What you see on these tours is but a small vestige of a huge three-story 10-km/six-mile network. They have served as wine cellars, refuge during siege, storage warehouses and other things. Two floors beneath the Ruszwurm café, after the tunnels were lit up for the first time in 200 years, explorers found the tortured skeleton of a man in chains.

## ★Buda Hills

From the hills to the western shore are the Buda Hills. The Gellérthegy, the Tabán, the Castle District, are all the better known areas of the Buda Hills. But, they are part of a complex of hills. Rozsadomb, Naphegy, Gellérthegy, Várhegy (Castle Hill) and, on the outskirts, Sashegy, fragment the area and give it a unique reputation for beauty going back beyond the

*St Matthias church*

Middle Ages. As one old 16th-century Italian saying went, there are three pearls in the world, Venice on the water, Florence in the plain, and Buda in the hills. Indeed, woods meet city in many areas bordering the city, and often a short hop on a tram or bus will take you to the woodlands that border the city on this side of the river. Small parks interlace the streets, and often benches and small shops nearby can provide a short lunch or snack.

The entire area is home to wildlife, barely noticed as it blends in. In the backyard of my home in Budapest, I have a visiting porcupine, woodpeckers and doves and the Hungarian blackbird called the rigo, which returns every year. Geese fly over-head as winter approaches. Also in the Buda Hills is the Budapest Game Reserve. The Buda Hills, in conjunction with the Pilis Hills and the Danube Bend, harbor an astonishing variety of wildlife and birds, which you may miss if you don't look for them.

Starting at the foot of Gellérthegy and working our way north, pass the baths and the Gellert Hotel, and continue on Bartók Béla út to ★★**Moricz Zsigmond Körtér**. Numerous small eateries and shops dot the way, and at the Körtér itself there are bakeries and restaurants all around. This has been called the second transportation hub of Buda, with numerous trams and an underground metro. Strut over to Villany út, right off of the square, and you will see numerous examples of the attempt by Hungarian architects to develop a unique Hungarian style of architecture in the wooden gabled apart-ment houses. On your right is a showcase of communism, a 50s multi-story building now used for public offices and, as you continue, the Catholic church and school originally con-structed in 1723 and an imposing statue of Béla Bartók, the

great Hungarian composer. The ★**Szent Imre Church** with its fabulous gold altar and statues retains the original façade and Baroque interior. Across the street from the church is a park and the ★**Feneketlen to** (Bot-tomless Lake), overlooked by the Hemingway Restaurant. (These waters are not for chil-dren.) It's a protected reserve, with ducks, ringed snakes, rep-tiles and tortoises, accompa-nied by a significant carp population. Member's of the Budapest Angler's Association maintain the lake along with

*Bottomless Lake*

the Parks Department, in exchange for certain controlled fishing rights. Around the park winding paths and picnic benches connect in a playground. This lake is a monument to the Victorian era of Budapest. Built in the 1870s by the famous Hungarian hydro-biologist Elek Wojnárovits, it incorporates a clay-lined basin, a design well ahead of its time.

★**Naphegy tér** is a short walk up from the Tabán. Its most distinguishing feature is the tall communications tower piercing the sky. Quite visible from Castle Hill, the spire is like the flagpole of the international news communication center of Hungary. Broadcasts from all over the world are received there and, because of that, it is the home of many foreign language speakers. Although entrance to the structure is restricted, its transparent glass façade and stairwell offer an unusual contemporary design contrast to the Victorian styles in other parts of the city. Fronting the building is Naphegy tér (Sun Hill terrace, last stop of the 78 bus), a small, pleasant park with slides for children and park benches and trees. There are an astonishing variety of buildings here. Some are clearly pre-WWII Victorian mansions, and others a mixture of Soviet-era luxury apartments and modern buildings with designs ranging from Turkish curves to thatched roofs. A walk around the neighborhood takes you through a cross-section of modern middle class and upper middle class Hungary.

From the square, go south on Dezso út until you pass the playing field on the left. You will reach an L intersection which intersects from the right. Just beyond this mini-intersection, separated by a small island, Hegyalja út rushes by with its traffic. While there is a street entrance from Hegyalja út, you are not allowed to enter Hegyala from that intersection. It is one-way, coming into the neighborhood, and you are going out of the neighborhood. If you are driving, you must follow the L, turn right, and follow the street down, then find the first left to get to Hegyalja. However, if you are walking, there is a bus stop on Hegyala út, to the right. It is visible from the L intersection.

Take the number 8 bus up the hill to the intersection of Németvölgyi út. You can reach the same intersection on the

59 tram from Moszkva tér. There are several flower shops in the area, and a chapel. This intersection is in front of the extensive ★★**Farkasréti temetõ** (Wolf Meadow Cemetery). This is a cemetery whose origins date back to a distant time. Hungarians traditionally take care of their own ancestors' graves. And, it is here that rich and poor alike lie side-by-side. There are fabulous crypts, statues and carved marble, interspersed with humble grottos where jars filled with ashes hide stories from the past. It is here that Béla Bartók, the famous composer, is buried. The conductor Sir George Solti is interred in the same soil where revolutionaries and heroes, villains and pirates have been laid. The bones of Mátyás Rákosi, the Stalinist dictator up to the 1956 Revolution (he incarcerated over 100,000 Hungarians and executed some 2,000) are buried at this spot.

But, increasingly, Hungarians come to a special place here. Its extraordinary mortuary chapel, a vaulted wooden sacrum modeled after the human torso, leaves room for the resting place of the coffins where the heart of the human being would normally be. This was built in total defiance of the Soviet state boxed architecture under the design and supervision of **Imre Makovecz**, called the Robin Hood of Hungarian architecture by Hungarian radio. Born in 1935 and also sentenced to death after 1956, he survived to see Hungary resurrected as a free nation. Banned from working in the cities and from teaching, he made his creative statements in the countryside and in the mountain communities of the country, while architectural disciples spread his work on coffee shop napkins and through discussions on the trains and meeting spots of the country. Across the street from the cemetery there are several restaurants. Farther up on the tram the unique tram stop and turn-around is dominated by another restaurant with a Hungarian soldier's statue proudly mounted over the entrance and several small flower shops.

Budapest

# ★★★Viziváros

Start the next day at Adam Clarke tér, at the head of the Chain Bridge. Northward, the narrow strip between the Castle District above and the low-lying border of the Duna below is called the Viziváros, or Water Town. It is just underneath the ramparts of the Fishermen's Bastion (hence the namesake, for this was the fishermen's district in ancient times). Today it is the habitation of upscale apartments and homes, with cast iron gates and carved wooden doors, many of them more than 100 years old. This entire town, with its grey 19th-century buildings and Roccoco residences, has retained the exact street layout of the medieval city, which makes it a fascinating place to walk. The main street is Fő utca, which runs from Clark Ádám tér to the Király Baths. After years of flooding, the quay was constructed at the shore, and the street level was raised by over three feet, which explains why the pavement suddenly drops down at the entrance to most of the 18th-century buildings.

Heading north on Fő utca you will come to Corvín tér, and its large eclectic building the ★Buda Vigadó, I Corvin tér 8, ☎ 36-1-201-3766, a concert hall built between 1898 and 1900. Its statues of famous monarchs and dancers set it apart. Inside, there is a café (ground floor) and restaurant (first floor), which are set in Art Nouveau surroundings, with marble columns, a winding staircase and a 300-seat theater. This is the home of the 90-member Hungarian State Music Ensemble, and performances are inexpensive and high quality.

Next stop at Szilágy dezsó tér the Neo-Gothic red-brick Calvinist Church and, across the street, the gray apartment block at Szilágyi Dezső tér 4, built circa 1911, is also a former home of Béla Bartók (1922-1928). So many places in Budapest hold haunting memories. The ★Danube embankments here are where the Arrow Cross (Nyilas) Hungarians, the Hungarian branch of the Nazi party, systematically massacred thousands of Jews in the last cold winter of the war, between 1944-1945. Many were tied together in groups – men, women, old people, children and babies – then thrown into the deadly, cold Danube River.

Continuing down Fő utca takes us to the tri-sided Batthyány tér, whose open face on the Danube is a painter's picture of

Parliament across the water. Anchoring the square on the south side are the rising spires of St. Anne's Church, a last reminder of the Italian Baroque style that was once the rage of Europe, but which made little imprint in Budapest, except in isolated spots such as this one. It was built in 1740-46. During the dark years of Stalinism the Hungarian Prime Minister Mátyás Rákosi, known as Stalin's most loyal disciple, was worried that Stalin might visit Parliament. From across the river he could see the soaring symbols of Budapest's religiosity. Plans were made to remove the church, with the excuse that the Batthyanyi tér metro construction required it. However, before the plans were executed, providentially, Stalin died in 1953, thus saving the church.

Next door is the **Angelika Cukrászda**, Batthyanyi tér 7, Watertown's most famous café, one of the first private businesses in Hungary after the communist dictatorship. It is also the former presbytery of the church (remodeled, of course). While here, make sure you stop by Nagymama Palacsintázója, where nothing but pancakes are served in an astonishing variety, and superbly tasty!

**Batthyány tér** was once the market center of Watertown, and hence you will find the iron and glass market hall (Vásárcsarnok) built in 1897 by Samuel Pecz, on the same spot where a market has continuously operated since the Middle Ages (you can still shop here!). Two doors farther down is a building dating from 1776, the **White Cross Inn**. Its old ballroom was once used for theater and carnivals from its dominant position over the main façade. Emperor Joseph II is rumored to have stayed here in the 18th century, and the notorious Casanova de Seingalt, the namesake of the neon sign that points to the Casanova Piano Bar here. The **Hikisch House** comes after the White Cross, and it dates from 1795, notable for its bas reliefs of cherubs on the façade

*White Cross Inn*

# Vizivaros

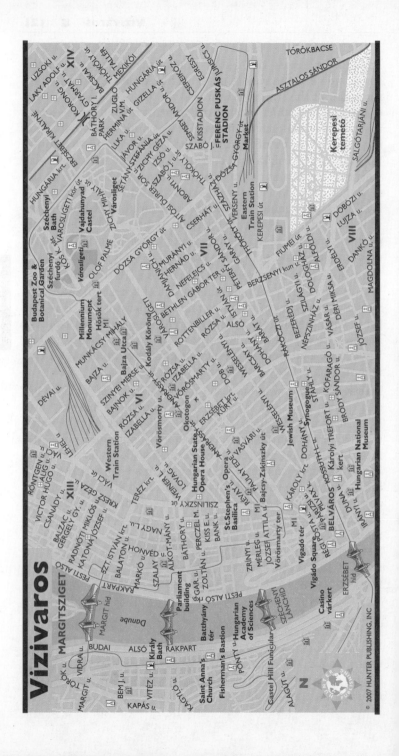

© 2007 HUNTER PUBLISHING, INC

doing various tasks and because the owner was an architect who also added his work to the church across the square.

Moving on to the next block you will find the bright red-bricked **Military Court of Justice**. It was built in 1915. From March to the end of December 1944 the Gestapo used the building as their administrative headquarters. For them, it doubled as a military prison. No one knows how many Budapestens may have died here. But, the modern era has brought a different despair. Imre Nagy, the erstwhile leader of the 1956 revolution against the Russians, was imprisoned here until 1958, when he was secretly executed. His exhumation and official funeral in 1989 was a symbol of the rebirth of Hungary and the final rejection of the communist dictatorship. In deference to public pressure, the square was renamed Nagy Imre tér. On the back corner of the building there are three plaques. One commemorates the victims of the Nazis. One commemorates the victims of communist terror. One commemorates Nagy Imre, a lingering reminder of the historical independent spirit of the Hungarian people.

The next stop is the ★★**Király Baths**, with crescent-topped Turkish domes and a neo-classical exterior. But the baths themselves substantially pre-date the Victorian façade. Built in 1570 by Pasha Sokoli Mustafa, of all the Turkish baths in Budapest, this is perhaps the most romantic. Tiny windows stud the dome walls, allowing streams of light to penetrate into the rising steam from the mineral water of the main pool. The entrance to the baths is in the green extension that was built in 1727, embellished with round windows and a stone balcony. The baths are open for men and women on different days.

In the eclectic nature of the city, from the Turkish domes we walk to Baroque, next door. At No. 90 you will come upon the **Florian Chapel**, built in the 1700s on behalf of the Greek Catholic Church. You are now at the corner of Ganz utca and Fõ utca. From here, turn up toward Ganz utca on your left, and at the end of the street you will find the **Foundry**

**Museum** (Öntödei Muszeum). This was the location of the Abraham Ganz Foundry (1865) originally. Today it contains a display on its history and cast iron stoves from the era of its glory.

Back down to Fő utca, continue on to the turn at József Bem utca to József Bem tér and the statue of the famous Polish general who fought with the Hungarians in the failed revolution of 1849. Bem never returned to Poland. The Turkish influence in Budapest was enough to take his heart elsewhere. As the Austrian and Russian troops closed in on Hungary, Bem escaped to Turkey. He converted to Islam, became the Pasha of Aleppo and reorganized the Turkish army before his death in 1854. More recent history marks this spot, however. On the fateful day of March 23, 1956, a rally to support reforms in communist-occupied Poland turned into a massive march of Hungarians who poured out of their homes and the side streets, accumulating into an ocean of people that, from here, marched across Margit hid (Margaret Bridge), just up the road and over to Parliament. The stubborn Hungarian cry for freedom would not be silenced. It was the beginning of the 1956 Revolution.

However, for the moment, we will walk up to Mártírok utca, better known as Margit Körút, and, instead of heading across the bridge, for now turn left and walk straight up the hill to Margit út, following it around toward Margit ter. Once again, history tells us of the peril of the people. This street is named after the martyrs killed while held in a military prison established here during the White Terror of Admiral Horthy's inter-war regime. And, ironically, Margit út itself is bordered by another symbol of ancient occupation. You will shortly come to Mecset út, which will take you to a Muslim shrine, the **tomb of Gül Baba II**, Mecset utca 14, www.btm.hu (click on Gül Baba Türbe at the bottom of he screen), ☎ 36-1-326-0062 or 326-0928. Open 10 am to 6 pm daily; Oct 10 am to 5 pm. Closed Mon. 400 HUF adults. The bellicose and dynamic dervish was a member of the proclaimed Bektashi order. A life of distinguished command finally led to his service in the takeover of Buda by the Turks in 1541. The victory of the Turks led to the transformation of Mátyás Church in one night, to serve as a Mosque for thanksgiving the next day. Providentially, Gül Baba suffered a stroke during the ceremony. Pasha

Mohammed ordered a magnificent burial for the great hero of the Turks, and built this octagonal structure surrounded by roses.

Now, to know the rest of the story, Gül Baba means Father of the Roses in Turkish. Legends say he was responsible for the great harvest of roses that adorned the hill behind him, which in Hungarian is called Roszadom (Rose Hill). The reality is that he was quite bloodthirsty, and could very well have painted many roses red with blood, but it is hardly conceivable that he could have planted any!

*Ttomb of Gül Baba II*

Back toward Fő utca, however, bearing north, you are on the other side of Margit Körút. Now, at Bécsi út turn left and head north to Frankel Leó út. While the Turks have not left a great deal behind to show for their 145-year occupation, on this street is one of their more famous inheritances. ★★**The Lukács Baths** (see *Adventures*). Although 19th-century decadent opulence breaths from the style of the building, the baths date back well before the Turks to medieval times and the Knights Hospitalers of St. John. While once in ancient times known only for medicinal

*Entrance to the Lukács Baths*

therapy (and still so used today), the Turks introduced pleasure and leisure into the undertaking. In 1884 a Grand Hotel was built around the baths and they attracted an international clientele, especially catering to those with rheumatism. The **Ivócsarnok** (Drinking Hall), is the dispensing center for

**Budapest**

*Thermal pool at Lukács Baths*

the sulphurous healing water. There is also a 40° thermal bath and pungent herbal steam room, adorned with plaques of gratitude from past patrons, in languages from all over the world, going back over a hundred years. Linked to the Lukács Baths are the Császár baths, predating even the Lukács.

Go past the small passageway on the left where the modern structures seem to connect, and it takes you to another set of Turkish domes pitted with tiny windows. This is the location of the bath's origins. Pasha of Buda, Mustafa Sokoli, known as Veli Beg, ordered its construction in 1571. Meandering out of the baths, across the street, another Turkish domed roof topped with a spire awaits future renovation. Next to it there is a pond where water bubbles out of the earth. It was once used as a mill, but the Turks used it to drive a gunpowder mill. The houses on this street were originally built by József Hild as spa hotels for the baths and all recall the turn-of-the-century grandeur that was Budapest.

Before leaving the area, take a short side-trip to number 49. Here you will find a six-storey Neo-Gothic synagogue... inside the apartment building! It is a remnant of Budapest's Jewish heritage, built by Sándor Fellner in 1888. Originally this area was a small park. The apartment block was built around it in 1928. The façade was decorated with the Star of David and a seven-candlestick menorah to signify what lies in the heart of the property. Jews have at times been persecuted, at times reviled, at times accepted and at times befriended. Perhaps in some mysterious way, the hidden parts of Budapest tell a thousand stories we have yet to learn.

# ★★Óbuda

Continuing northward, we arrive at the origin of Budapest. In 15-11 BC the Romans conquered Western Hungary and named it Pannonia. A Roman Legion camp was established in the heart of Óbuda and, just to the north of it, a residential community, Aquincum. In 106 AD the emperor Trajan made it the capital of Lower Pannonia. Although prosperous, the decline of the empire eventually led to the decline of Aquincum, and it was finally destroyed by 350 AD. The year 409 brought the Huns, and Attila found the remains of the Roman camp area suitable for his headquarters. Subsequent generations saw successive waves of conquerors until finally the Magyars settled property rights permanently about 896. The Árpad Kings lived in Óbuda during the rapacious invasions of the Turks, up until about 1240-41 when they finally decided to move to the more defensible Castle Hill. Though there was a temporary revival of the area in medieval times, the Turkish occupation of the 16th century resulted in the destruction of almost all its old grandeur. Salvation came in the 1700s when the wealthy Zichy family transformed the ruins of the once demolished city to a new Baroque splendor. Palaces and churches rose up with the new residences.

Once again, however, waves of conquest and destruction destroyed even this vestige. Communist doctrine aimed to eliminate the bourgeois past. In that strange rationale of doctrine and fanaticism, it meant that art and craftsmanship were the greatest evils, to be replaced by concrete block residences and rigid conformity to the new social values of the proletariat. Gray, anonymous, faceless structures replaced the old order. Yet, whether for utility, or from a desire to preserve Hungary's singular identity, pieces of its glory remained, and elements of the history and uniqueness of the area survive, often blended in odd ways with current construction. Pieces of a Roman wall or Dominican monastery may coincide with the entryway of an office building. Pillars and columns remain in odd places. Baroque palaces may still be found astride a temple-like synagogue. Pieces of history salt and pepper the area. The best way to explore it is to take

Budapest

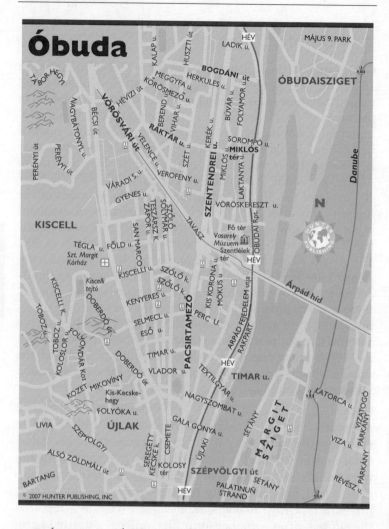

the HÉV train to Árpad hid (Árpad Bridge). As you leave the
train, it opens out on Szentlélek tér. At the northeast corner,
at Szenlélek tér No. 1, the large, beautiful white Baroque
building was part of the **Zichy Palace** complex of the 1750s.
The **Vasarely Museum** melds with it at Szenlélek tér 6. Victor Vasarely, Hungarian-born French artist, donated 400 of
his works for this famous museum. His colorful art from the
1960s was the avant-garde of Cubism, with numerous examples of the geometric genre. His work makes a clear progres-

sion from dynamic symbolism into textile designs and abstract subjects.

Around the corner of the building and through the gate is a small courtyard. **Miklos Zichy's Palace** looms up above, so well preserved that you can almost imagine the man himself looking down from its Rococo stone balcony. Zichy's favorite sculptor was Károly Bébo; creator of the statues that now stand forlornly at the back of the garden. This palace is also home to the **Kassak Museum**. Lajos Kassak was a constructivist from the 1920s and the 1930s. At first rejected, he was resurrected in the 1950s by the communist government as a representa-

*Frey Krisztián,
Mehitabel, 1966*

tive of the rise and spiritual energy of the working class. His fascinating works are complemented by temporary exhibitions on the Cubism and Dadaism of artists from another era. Other popular exhibits include full rooms, furniture and personal effects taken from the Békasmegyer district (the district of the nobles), arranged in their original settings, as well as a toy exhibit spanning 1860 to 1960.

The avant-garde is left behind, however, as we enter Fő tér and 18th-century Óbuda. This is one area not touched by the zealous 60s proletariat designers. During Roman times it was the center of the legion's encampment, reborn again in the 17th century and then, after several invasions and wars, it was again resurrected at the turn of the 19th century. The rather imposing **Town Hall** was built in 1903. The two facing sculpted figures used as pillars are typical of attempts to mold a Hungarian style. To the right of the square, Laktanya utca is home to the remarkable work, ★*Strollers in the Rain*. This great piece of art, in sun or rain, powerfully depicts human figures with their umbrellas standing in the rain, by

Budapest

*Strollers in the Rain*

Imre Várga. His museum is the building marked number 7. Still active today, the intense realism and form of his pieces is unforgettable. Born in 1927, Várga's artistry graces not only Hungary, but all of Europe, and has established him as one of the prominent realists of our time. He draws heavily on Hungarian culture and history for his inspiration.

Back to Fõ utca and its intersection with Hídfõ utca, we are reminded again of the damage of social planning Soviet-style. Around us traffic and auto horns blair. Nevertheless, look to the right as you pass the vaulted split of the bridge road above, and you will find steps leading to the underground ★**Flórián tér**, the center of today's Óbuda. Roman ruins were first discovered here when they excavated for a house in 1778. It is at the intersection of Vörösvári út and Pacsiertamezo út. At the bottom of the steps you will stand on the site of the **Árpad Castle** of the 12th century. To your right is the **Roman Baths Museum**. Shell-shaped pools were adorned with heated mosaic floors. Beyond, in the orange corridors, scarred by graffiti, you will find remnants of the ancient Roman past, such as columns set against a background of stone blocks.

Leaving the passage you can hike to the right on Kiscelli út after crossing Pachirtamezö út. This will start you on a climb of what is known as **Remetehegy** (Hermit's Hill). It rises above Óbuda, with a clear view of Pest and Buda. The Romans built a watchtower here. But, legend has it that Roman soldiers hated duty on the ridge, as they repeatedly disappeared while manning their post. The Roman ruins remain, but no Romans, and tales persist that the hill is haunted.

At the top of the street you will come directly to **Kiscelli Kastely** (Kiscelli's Castle, called Kiscelli's Museum today), Kiscelli út 108, ☎ 36-1-388-7817, fax 36-1-368-7917, www.btmfk.iif.hu, fovarosikeptar@mail.btm.hu. Built between 1744 and 1760 as a Trinitarian monastery, it is the depository of various paintings and artifacts from the history of Budapest. Included in the variety is the printing press upon which Sándor Petöfi first printed his *Nemzeti Dal* (National Song), which played a significant role in inspiring the national uprising against the Hapsburgs in 1848-1849.

Walk back to Pacsirtamezõ út and then head south to Nagyszombat út. The old ★★**Roman Amphitheater** is now surrounded by a steel fence, but open at the gates. It is greened over with grass, but the stone abutments and circular motif sink down noticeably from the surrounding streets. Known as the Round House, it once held 16,000 people, the largest amphitheater in the empire outside of Rome. In later years, after the Romans left, dwellings rose on top of the circular raised walls of the old Roman ampitheater. They were cynically dubbed "The Round House." Scarcely could the new occupants have dreamed of the old glory. The ampitheater once held 16,000 people, the largest ampitheater outside of Rome. The ampitheater still has its tunnels and hidden entrances. Lighted by torches, they once led to dungeons where both prisoners and animals awaited their moment in the ring. I found an unpleasant pile of trash flowing out of one of the tunnels, so keep on eye on the kids here. Aside from that, this is a real adventure and an interesting exploration. Now surrounded by post-1950s construction and traffic, only the ghosts of the Romans and the stones of their history remain. I could walk up the stone entry stairs, scale what was left of the heights and sit on a stone bench where Marcus Aurelius himself might have looked down on the games (from the first through the third centuries most of the Roman Emperors visited Aquincum).

From this point it is probably wise to take the 86 bus back to Raktár út, head east a few yards to Miklos út, make a right, and go back toward the HEV station. From there, we board the HEV again and head to the next stop, also in Óbuda. This is ★★★**Aquincum**, the official capital of ancient Pannonia, where Roman centurions and their families made their homes. The ruins of Aquincum are revealing enough to get a feel for Roman life in Pannonia. Marble sewer drains bear testimony to the advanced engineering of Rome. The gymnasium was unearthed complete with a central heating system.

*Aquincum ruins*

Two shrines and a temple to Mithras, the Persian god of light, adorned a thriving community of tradesmen and artisans. The wide variety of discoveries here have led to the establishment of the ★★**Aquincum Museum**, ☎ 36-1-250-1650, fax 430-1083, www.aquincum.hu, csepanyi.andrea@iif.hu, just down the road on Szentendrei út 139. For opening hours and fees see the website. The stone and cement archways of the town are still waterproof, even after the centuries. A Roman aqueduct once transported water to

*Aquincum from above*

Aquincum, and parts of it serve as a median divider for the city streets. The museum structure itself dates from 1896 and was copied from a Roman temple.

You may want to stop by the **Kehli Restaurant**, III Mókus utca 22, ☎ 36-1-368-0613, 250-4241, fax 387-6049, www.kehli.hu. Average entrée costs 3,000 to 4,500 HUF. In the suburb of Óbuda, it was the favorite of actress, Rachel Weisz. Reservations are often necessary. Diners enjoy authentic gypsy music and Hungarian cuisine, featuring the house specialty, bone marrow on toast. While it sounds like a dish made for the rough Hungarian palate alone, it is actually rather tasty.

*Aquincum Museum*

Budapest

## ★★★Pest

### The Bridges

The stirring history of the union of Buda and Pest actually begins with its bridges, straining across the wide river to join two different worlds into one city and one nation. Before they were built, the two sisters were strangers, even

*Lánchíd bridge*

into Roman times, when the Romans also had a lesser though still significant outpost on the Pest side of the river. As with Hungary, so with Buda and Pest, the bridges have been built and torn down over and over again.

No greater symbolism of Budapest exists than the romantically draping supports of the **Lánchíd suspension bridge**. It encapsulates both the struggle and the union of Buda with Pest. From the Buda side of the Danube, at Clarke Adam tér, facing the lions that guard the entrance to the Lánchíd, you

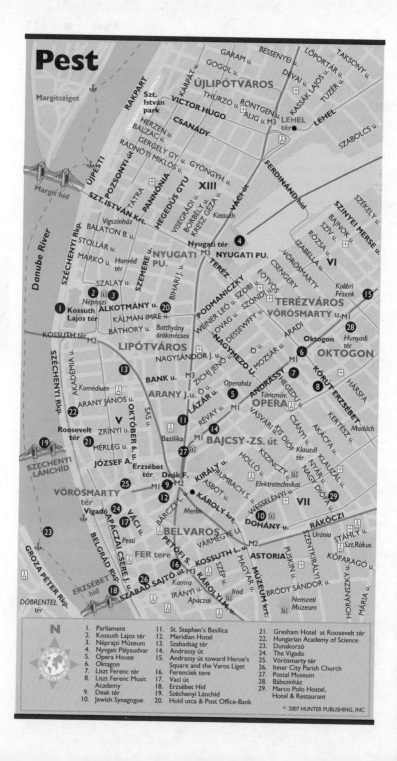

# Pest

Margitsziget

Margit híd

Danube River

GARAM u.   BESSENYEI u.   LŐPORTÁR u.   TAKSONY u.

GOGOL u.   DEVAI u.   KASSÁK LAJOS u.   TÜZÉR u.

**ÚJLIPÓTVÁROS**

KÁRPÁT u.   THURZÓ u.   RÖNTGEN u.   ALIG u. M3   LEHEL tér   LEHEL

Szt. István park   VICTOR HUGO   CSANADY

HERZEN u.   BALZAC u.

GERGELY GY. u.   SZABOLCS u.

RADNÓTI MIKLÓS u.   GYÖNGYH. u.   FERDINÁND híd

ÚJPESTI   TÁTRA   PANNONIA   HEGEDŰS GYU   **XIII**   VÁCI u.

SZT. ISTVÁN Krt.   VISEGRÁDI u.   BORBÉLY u.   KRESZ GÉZA u.   Kossuth

Vigszinház   BALATON B. u.

STOLLÁR u.   **Nyugati tér**   4

MARKÓ u.   Honvéd tér   **NYUGATI** M3   **NYUGATI PU.**   TERÉZ   CSENGERY   VÖRÖSMARTY

SZÉCHENYI Rkp.   SZEMERE u.   **PU.**   BIHARI J. u.   EÖTVÖS   SZINYEI MERSE u.

SZALAY u.   PODMANICZKY   SZÖBI u.   SZOND   BAJNOK   SZÉKELY u.

2   Néprajzi   3   **ALKOTMÁNY u.**   WEINER LEÓ u.   OVAG u.   DESSEWFFY u.   **TERÉZVÁROS**   SZIV u.   RÓZSA u.   IZABELLA u.   **VI**

1   Kossuth Lajos tér   KÁLMÁN IMRE u.   ARADI   **VÖRÖSMARTY u.** M1   Kolibri Fészek   15

BÁTHORY u.   Batthyány örökmécses   20   Ő u.   MOZSÁR u.   Oktogon   Hunyadi tér   28

KOSSUTH tér   M2   **LIPÓTVÁROS**   NAGYSÁNDOR J. u.   NAGYMEZŐ u.   6   **OKTOGON**

AKADÉMIA u.   13   **BANK u.** M3   ZICHJ JENŐ u.   M1   7   KÖRÚT ERZSÉBET   8

Komédium   **ARANY J. u.** Ő u.   Operaház   5   HEGEDŰ   HÁRSFA

ARANY JÁNOS u.   LÁZÁR u.   Táncműv.   **OPERA**   CSÁNYI u.   KERTÉSZ u.   Madách

22   SAS u.   RÉVAY u.   M1   VASVÁRI KIS DIÓF.   AKÁCFA u.

Roosevelt tér   ZRÍNYI u.   11   14   **BAJCSY-ZS. út**   Klauzál tér   NAGY DIÓFA u.

21   MÉRLEG u.   Bazilika   M1   KSZINCZY.   NYÁRI u.   29

19   JÓZSEF A.   27   KIRÁLY u.   HOLLÓ u.   Elektrotechnikai   **VII**

SZÉCHENYI LÁNCHÍD   Erzsébet tér   Deák F.   TRUMBACH S. u.   WESSELÉNYI u.

25   M1   9 M2   ASBOT u.   10   Bábszinház   28

VÖRÖSMARTY tér   12   **KÁROLY krt.**   **DOHÁNY u.**   **RÁKÓCZI**

Vigadó   24   BARCZY u.   Merlin   Uránia   STÁHLY u.   Szt. Rókus

23   17   VÁCI u.   **BELVAROS**   VÁRMEGYE u.   M2   **ASTORIA**   KŐFARAGÓ u.

APÁCZAI CSERE J.   Pesti   **FER tere**   **KOSSUTH L. út**   PUSKIN u.   BRÓDY SÁNDOR

GROZA PÉTER Rkp.   BELGRÁD Rkp.   **PETŐFI S.**   16   M3   MAGYAR u.   MÚZEUM krt.   SZENTKIRÁLYI u.   HORÁNSZKY u.   MÁRIA u.

ERZSÉBET híd   18   **SZABAD SAJTÓ út**   KÁROLYI M. u.   Kamra   Irod   Nemzeti Múzeum

DÖBRENTEI tér   26   IRÁNYI u.   Apáczai

---

**N**

HUNTER PUBLISHING

1. Parliament
2. Kossuth Lajos tér
3. Néprajzi Múzeum
4. Nyvgati Pályaudvar
5. Opera House
6. Oktogon
7. Liszt Ferenc tér
8. Liszt Ferenc Music Academy
9. Deak tér
10. Jewish Synagogue

11. St. Stephen's Basilica
12. Meridian Hotel
13. Szabadsag tér
14. Andrassy út
15. Andrassy út toward Heroe's Square and the Varos Liget
16. Ferenciek tere
17. Vaci út
18. Erzsébet Hid
19. Széchenyi Lánchíd
20. Hold utca & Post Office-Bank

21. Gresham Hotel  at Roosevelt tér
22. Hungarian Academy of Science
23. Dunakorzó
24. The Vigado
25. Vörösmarty tér
26. Inner City Parish Church
27. Postal Museum
28. Bábszinház
29. Marco Polo Hostel, Hotel & Restaurant

face a history of nearly 200 years. In the 1820s there was no towering causeway. Instead, a long narrow pontoon bridge bobbed perilously on the surface of the Danube current. Pest was bursting at its seams, filled with tanners, craftsmen and travelers, Baroque houses and huts, narrow alleys and dust-filled roads. Wood-framed stables and huts competed for space and odiferous dominion over the rising sea of humanity. Beyond Pest stretched the Alföld, a wasteland wiped clean by the dominating Turks and Tartars, and crowned with the ravages of the Austrian mercenaries. Fields, and only a few farms, and mansions and marshes stretched across the flat fertile lands to the distant Transylvanian mountains. There the borderlands of the Hungarians abutted the principalities of Balkan, Slavic, and Romanian nobles amidst the crumbling Ottoman

Empire. However, on the Buda side, nobles and bishops and craftsmen intermingled in the Watertown and the Buda Hills. At the toes of the Buda Hills, the shoreline strip of flatland along the Danube stretched north from the Watertown to Obuda. There a new class of merchants bartered for wealth amidst the shadows of the once-great empire, the Roman ruins. The roads that snaked through these once separate towns joined, and then stretched out to Vienna, the new golden imperial city, and the Austrian crown lands. The link would tie the future of Hungary and Budapest to the rise of the Holy Roman Empire, as her kings and queens played pivotal roles in the future of Europe. But, just as that future was foretold by the roads that linked Buda and Vienna, that greatness depended on the joined hands of Buda on the west, and Pest on the east of the Danube shore.

In 1810 a Russian naval officer named Vladimir Bronyevsky wrote that the populations of the two cities live at constant variance with each other, representing two entirely different societies, life-styles and outlooks. But, times were changing. Feudal dominions were crumbling and nobles competed ever more with merchants and the middle class for road space. Pest grew to rival its neighbor and then to surpass it. After the Turks were driven out, the population of Buda and Óbuda was jointly 9,600 and Pest a meager 2,600. By the time our Czarist officer wrote his memoir, the population of Pest was at 35,000, while the Buda banks sheltered 25,000. By 1870, Pest dwarfed Buda, with a population of 200,000 against 70,000 for Buda and Óbuda combined. The growth was almost geometric. By 1901, scarcely 30 years later, Budapest was at 734,000 people, one of the most populous and advanced cities in the world. Much of that growth sprouted from the flat, fertile plains of the Alföld on the banks of Pest.

Before bridges, the river was a barrier, to be forded by barge and ferry alone. Nevertheless, cold winters sometimes froze the Danube and makeshift straw-covered roadways would string across the ice. It is not insignificant that Matthias Corvinus, the son of János Hunyadi, the great Christian hero who stopped the Turkish advance, was chosen to be king while standing in the middle of the frozen Danube. A chronicler wrote about this event in 1848, "on this night, the

Almighty who dwells in Heaven did freeze the water of the Danube to its very depths, and such a thick, stable mass of ice was formed thereby, that next morning every man could cross the Danube without a boat, as if he were indeed walking across a most flat field, no manner of water obstructing the traffic."

But the same frozen roadway had been a catastrophe in the winter of 1241 when, as the smoke of burning Pest rose up behind them, the fierce Mongol armies of Batu Khan tried the ice with their horses, warriors astride. Then, while desperate prayers and chants arose from the churches and monasteries on the Buda shore, men laced ropes around the most prominent juts of the ice flows and pulled, trying to break the ice apart before the hordes could cross the river on its frozen surface.

The pressure of time and growth created a different situation in 1820. After many years, a pontoon bridge had finally been built that strained against the current, and held. The Pest-Buda pontoon bridge was pulled out of the water at noon and in the evening to allow for barges and ships traveling the Danube, and also for the horse-drawn barges moving up and down the river. Long lines of wagons and carriages accumulated on both shores, horseflesh and leather mingling in the wind across the river, while they waited their turn on the pontoon roadway. But winter's bite ended the lifeline. The 46 pontoons were dismantled and huddled in Pest for fear of ice flows. In such times, either side may as well have been a completely different world, as most often the river did not freeze. It became a vicious, impassable barrier with a relentless current pushing jagged-edged blocks of ice that would pierce the hull of a ship. In December of 1820, Count István Széchenyi, then a Hussar captain, was on his way to his father's funeral. He spent an entire week trying to find a way across the Danube ice, when he wrote, "I would give a year's income if a permanent bridge could be built between Buda and Pest."

Though bridges had been standing for centuries on the Moldau, the Thames, and the Seine rivers, their structures of wood and stone were simply unsuitable for the powerful current and the severe winters of the Buda-Pest Danube basin. But, time and the Industrial Revolution added a new terminology, steel suspension bridge. Széchenyi brought back the technology and a British architect and engineer, Adam Clarke, to build a bridge. A joint stock company was formed in 1837, and the debate for approval began in parliament.

Only commoners paid a toll on the old pontoon bridge across the Danube. The anecdote of a traveling Frenchman was repeated throughout Hungary. How do the toll takers know who should pay and who should not? 'Whoever looks as though he has money pays no money. Whoever looks as though he has no money, pays. But, the construction of the Lánchíd was politically charged because everyone would have to pay! In the debate in Parliament, one noble said he would rather travel for days to ferries at other parts of the river than be taxed. Nevertheless, rising expectations led to the laying of the first foundation stones in 1848. Kossuth Lajos, the leader of the Hungarian Revolution of 1849 wrote in his newspaper, *Hirlap*, that the foundation of civil equality was laid.

It was opened at the high point of the Revolution, and it was joked that the bridge should be tested with Hapsburg loyalists, and if it held, then they knew it would be good; if it collapsed, well, all the better!

The bridge did not wait to become a part of history. Hungarian and Austrian forces, armed to the teeth, marched over it in the see-saw movements of the 1849 Revolution. Finally, the Hapsburg Emperor's Austrian army was trapped in the castle. A plan was hatched to destroy the bridge. It would stop further incursions from Pest and isolate the army surrounding the castle from re-supply. The commander of the risky sabotage was an infantry colonel. A massive quantity of gunpowder was providentially misplaced under the bridge, under the carriage way instead of at the anchors. To those involved, fate would seem to have sealed the bridge's end. However, the colonel's soldiers refused to ignite the charge beneath this symbol of Hungarian equality. So, in imperial fashion, he took the cigar out of his mouth and set the burning edge to the black powder trail. Incredibly, the explosion did no damage, except that is for the colonel, who failed to outrun the explosion and blew himself out of existence!

## BRIDGE FABLES

The bridge served as the focus of anecdotes, even before it was finished. A children's fable holds that the tunnel under the castle hill was made to house the Lánchíd bridge so that it could be moved to a location where it wouldn't rust in rainy weather. And then there is the common fable, even told by some tour guides, that a cobbler discovered the lions guarding the bridge had no tongues and the despairing sculptor threw himself into the Danube over the discovered mistake. This suicide, however, never happened. Marschaikó, the sculptor, who died a natural death in his old age, laughingly exclaimed, "Just let your wife have a tongue like my lions. Then we'll see who'll have the last laugh."

Lánchíd spanned the river to drive the spirits of Buda and Pest together across the water. Bridge followed bridge, until finally, at every possible spot of communion, a bridge reached across the two shores.

**Margit Bridge** was inaugurated in 1873, a conglomerate, with iron from France, granite from Bavaria, and statues by the Parisian sculptor Thabard. Tragically, it was the first of the Danube bridges to be victimized at the end  of WWII. The Germans were busy preparing their charges, around the pillars and beneath the spans. The bridge was jammed, overflowing with screaming people, blaring trucks and cars, horse-driven wagons, and trams desperately struggling and pushing across in a panic, fleeing from the fast-approaching front lines. In the middle of the day, suddenly, a thunderous explosion ripped through the shrieking humanity and steel and concrete. "I shall not forget it as long as I live. A tram crowded with passengers was thrown into the air and I saw men, women, and children sinking into the water," wrote an eyewitness. How many lives were snuffed out on the river that day will never be known and not one man from the German platoon lived to tell what happened. So has tragedy multiplied across the Danube. January 1945 saw this, the last bridge designed by a foreign engineer and constructed with foreign materials, disappear.

**Frances Joseph Bridge**, built in 1894, was dedicated by Emperor Franz Joseph I. Today, reconstructed after the war, it is called Freedom Bridge, with its legendary Hungarian bird, the turul, adorning the topmost pillars with wings outspread, a testimony to the millennial celebrations of the Magyar conquest. It has come to symbolize the Hungarian fight for independence.

Then there was **Elizabeth Bridge**, which at the time it was opened in 1903, was the longest chain bridge in the world, at 870 feet. It always was and is today the symbol of the modern world, somehow joining the old world of Hungary with the new.

The Germans did a thorough job in 1945. After they were through, the Danube again divided Buda and Pest, and it would have seemed that the heart of the city and of the nation had been dealt a lasting blow. But the cement holding the Magyar people together was stronger than the river's current. In the spring of 1945 Budapestens were crossing the Danube on pontoon bridges again, laying plans to reconstruct the bridges in their old glory. That post-war pontoon link, called The Ugly Duckling, is commemorated by plaques where the floating causeway once linked the opposite shores. It reached from

Batthyanyi tér across to the south end of Parliament, following approximately the line of the metro's underwater link today. Of the reconstructed bridges, only Elizabeth Bridge was completely redesigned. The others (all visible from the Citadel) are faithful to the spirit in which they were built – Szabadság híd (Freedom Bridge), just across from Gellert Hotel, Lánchíd (Chain Bridge), at city center, Margit híd (Margaret Bridge) at the southern end of Margit Island, Árpád híd (Árpád Bridge), at the northern end of Margit Island. They therefore link not just the two cities, but the history and the culture of Budapest and Hungary, a statement of the will to survive.

### ★★★Parliament

In 1848 Míhaly Vörösmarty, one of the greatest Hungarian poets, wrote, "The motherland does not have a home." Indeed, for thousands of years, Hungary had no need of a home. The nobles and the kings and queens

took the law with them wherever they went. A national home was aristocratically epitomized by the palace, or by the fortress walls of the citadel. But, this was not to match the rising tide of the Hungarian people, and the social changes of the industrial revolution saw the nobility gradually join with the millions of the lower classes to make a nation, concentrated in the spirit of the Revolution of 1849 against Hapsburg dominance. In the aftermath of the revolution, the convening Diet finally legislated a Parliament building, to encompass the spirit of Hungary, the noble and the peasant, the tradesman and the cleric, but all of them free. Parliament would rise in Pest, symbolizing the rising democracy of the middle and lower classes, free from the yokes of the royalty looking down from the palace in Buda.

Budapest

Ground was broken on October 12, 1885, on the quay at Tömõ in the Lipót district. Over 17 years an average of 1,000 workers labored on it daily. Some materials were dragged clear across the country to supply the project. Entire industries blossomed to supply construction. Enormous amounts of earth were moved to make way for 40 million bricks and over half a million ornamental stones that were carved into decorations for the building. Unfortunately a soft limestone was often used, which needs constant restoration or replacement.

Parliament itself encroaches on the Danube, with a foundation wall seven feet thick. It is 300 yards long and as much as 140 yards wide. Inside are 10 courts, 27 gates, 29 staircases and endless hallways. The graceful, thin white Gothic pinnacles that crown its shape are known throughout Europe. There are 88 statues depicting great Hungarian leaders adorning the exterior. But the exterior is totally eclipsed by the gilded and marbled interior, filled with extraordinary murals, paintings, statues, and ornately crafted floors, walls, and windows. The focus of the building is the Hungarian crown, inside a glass case, which lies beneath the 82-foot cathedral-like dome. Statues of kings surround it.

The spectacular entry stairs, bordered with imported marble columns, run nearly the full width of the hallway. They could not find the proper stone in Hungary, so the rose-colored pillars were excavated from a mountain in Sweden. Each one soars 18 feet and weighs four tons. The elegance and grandeur are heightened by the nearly 88 lbs of 22 to 26 karat gold used in adornment.

### ★★★Kossuth Lajos tér

The front steps of Parliament spill onto Kossuth Lajos tér, probably the most famous square in Hungary. In 1996 one of several eternal flames was erected in front of Parliament. Dedicated to those who died in the 1956 revolution, it is overlooked by the statue of

Imre Nagy at a modest distance, the former leader who tried to liberalize communism. Imre Nagy took refuge in the Yugoslav embassy following the crushing invasion of the Soviet Army into Budapest. He was lured out on the promise that he would be given free passage, but he was promptly arrested the moment he left embassy grounds. Kossuth Lajos tér itself is named after the famous revolutionary war leader, whose statue is prominent in the square, the work of the great Zsigmond Kisfaludi Stróbl.

Farther north in a small park stands the drooping figure of Mihály Károly under a broken arch, a memory to his brief leadership in that brief moment of history when there was a democratic parliament before WWI. In the see-saw of war and politics, he escaped to Paris when Béla Kun's Council Republic took power in 1919. Although he was named as Hungarian ambassador to France, his criticism of the Stalinist show trials led to his rejection and he was buried in disrepute. The communists exhumed him in 1962, however, to rebury him in Kerepesi cemetery. Attila József, the great Hungarian poet, broods farther south, his eyes looking out over the Danube. At age 32 he threw himself in front of an oncoming train. His ignominious death in 1937 was a political protest against the evolving authoritarian rule that was laying the groundwork for Nazism in pre-WWII Hungary. He despaired to see Hungary turn from her vision of a free country. At the opposite end of the square an equestrian statue of Ferenc Rákóczi II, the Prince of Transylvania looks down on the square. Rákóczi led the heroic war for Independence from 1703 to 1711, and ever since the uprising has been called the Rákóczi Revolution. Ballads and songs have honored its memory as one of the most glorious periods of Hungarian history. The famous Rákóczi March has two variations, one by Liszt and one by Berlioz, both written in his honor and in the name of the revolution.

## ★★Néprajzi Múzeum (Ethnographic Museum)

The Néprajzi Múzeum (Ethnographic Museum) stands across from Parliament, once the home of the Palace of Justice. A careful eye may notice the resemblance to the Berlin

Reichstag. The building was the second-place finisher in the design for Parliament in 1888. It is notably topped by the statue of Justice riding her carriage drawn by three straining steeds. Designed by Alajos Hauszmann, its breathtaking interior with red and black marble pillars, topped by gold Corinthian leaves, white stairways, stained glass windows, and Károly Lotz's extraordinary ceiling painting, blend to make a delightful tour on its own. Across from this building is the Agriculture Ministry, the third-place runner up in the competition of 1888, which, however, is now strictly for official administrative offices.

From Lajos tér, take a stroll up Alkotmány utca to Hold utca and make a right turn. At the juncture of Báthory utca, in the middle of the square is the eternal flame, in memory of Lajos Batthyány, Prime Minister of the short-lived government of 1848-49. After the Hapsburgs finally suppressed the brief cry of freedom in Hungary, they took Lajos Batthyány to this very spot and executed him by firing squad. At the time it was the corner of a sprawling Hapsburg military barracks, a symbol of Austrian dominance, built by the orders of Emperor Joseph II in 1786, a symbol of the centralization of Hapsburg power. It was known then as The New Building. However it was torn down and buried with its old memories in 1897. The small series of streets and buildings between here and Szabadság tér were all erected over its ruins. It might be said that Batthyány's spirit lives on, and so does Hungary's.

## ★★Szabadság tér

In that fiercely defiant spirit that so characterizes Hungary, Szabadság tér, or Freedom Square, one block farther down, was purpose-fully chosen to be laid over what once was the New Building, replacing the dust and concrete of mon-archism with the free rang-ing spirit of an open park. As with Lajos tér, the significance of the spot remains central to an understanding of this nation, for it has become a symbol of national mourning, as well as resurrection and rebirth. During the Horthy era, it was the focus of public grief over the tragic treaty of Trianon, which carved Hungary's heart with the knife of European politics. The four tiny lawns at the top of the square were once each occupied with a statue, representing the land lost to Slovakia, Romania, Yugoslavia, and Austria. A Hungarian flag flew at half-mast permanently in their midst, expressing Hungarian refusal to accept the conditions of that treaty. The Russians took the flag away and replaced it with their typically massive proletariat sculpture, and although an element of the occupation, this one has remained. It symbolized for many the Russians who died liberating Budapest from Nazi occupation. Now, look for the statue dedicated to Harry Hill Bandholz. He was an American general whose efforts saved the crown jewels of Hungary from falling into Romanian hands in 1919. The plaque notes that the statue was first erected in 1939, then removed by the Russians in 1949, but replaced again in its rightful spot in 1989!

Szabadság tér is surrounded by buildings expressing Hungary's spirit and history, eclecticism and Art Nouveau, egalitarianism and tradition.

## ★★★Post Office Bank on Hold utca

Back on Hold utca, this was completed in 1901 in another attempt to create a unique Hungarian style. None did it with quite the splendor or style of Ödön Lechner's fabulously ornate structure. The façade experiments with shapes and ornamentation, combining ceramic, brick, tile, iron and glass. Look for the bees that seem to climb up toward the yellow ceramic beehives, symbolic of the flowers and the bee ranches of the flat Alföld plains. The entire structure is a work of art, encapsulated by the fabulous curvature and riotous colors of the roof. When asked why he focused so much effort on the roof details, which no one could see, Lechner remarked, "The birds will see them." Unfortunately, he built only three such public structures, succumbing to the tide of criticism from his colleagues.

### ★★★St. Stephen's Basilica

From Lechner we enter the world of the church and Hungary's medieval history. From Szabadság út go to Bank út, and walk one short block east to Hercegprimás út, make a right and walk to St. Stephen tér and the imposing St. Stephen's Basilica. Three generations of architects spent a good portion of their energies on this marvelous structure. It was started in 1851 by the aging József Jild. He died in 1886, after which the famous Miklós Ybl took on the work. Ybl was not to see its completion. He died in 1891, to be succeeded by Jozsef Kauser, who completed it in 1906, over half a century from when the first foundation stones were laid. The white statue of King István I stands resolute behind the altar. A small chapel in the back holds a gold and glass casket ornamented in fine jewels, home of the Holy Dexter, the actual preserved right hand of St. István, clenched in a fist. Befitting its sacred character, the hand has been shuffled back and forth in the former crown lands since it first was severed from King István's arm in 1038. It was canonized in 1083. Don't leave the Basilica until you have gone up to its cupola, which is accessible by elevator and stairs. Its 360° view of Budapest from a height of 65 m/195 feet will provide lifetime camera shots. www.basilica.hu. Basilica tours, in English and Hungarian, cost 1,600 HUF at this writing, Mon through Fri, 9:30 am and 11 am, 2 and 3:30 pm, and 9:30 and 11 pm.

### ★★★Roosevelt tér

Leaving the basilica, we walk down Zrínyi utca west, to Roosevelt tér. At the intersection of the Lánchíd with the Pest side of the Danube, Roosevelt tér was formerly known as Ferenc József tér, and it was in this square where the Austrian Emperor, for whom it was then named, made his agreement with Hungary in 1867. While seated on his horse, the Hungarian crown with its crooked cross draped across his forehead, he took his coronation sword and pointed it to the four points of the compass, swearing that he would protect the nation from its enemies in all directions.

The imposing Art Nouveau structure that directly faces the Lánchíd is the ★★★**Four Seasons Hotel Gresham Palace**, formerly the Gresham Palace, Roosevelt tér 5-6. Considered one of the outstanding examples of Art Nouveau in the world, it was built in 1905 by Zsigmond Quittner for the Gresham Life Assurance Company of London, on the same site where earlier the Nako house had stood since 1827. The Nako

house was a much smaller Neo-Classic palace built by the merchant Antal Deron. Lord Gresham, the founder of the London Stock Exchange, and president of the Gresham Life Assurance Company, originally built the structure for the aristocracy. It fulfilled its purpose as one of the most exclusive hotels in Europe, up until WWII. Painstaking restoration and reconstruction remained faithful to the original design, using the best artisans in the nation. The result is once again a supreme example of turn-of-the century Art Nouveau, from

the original iron ornamental peacock gates, which open out with a panoramic view of the Danube, up through the beautifully restored ceramics and staircases.

To the northern side of Elizabeth Square, No. 9,

*Hungarian Academy of Science*

the famed **Hungarian**

**Academy of Science** reigns. It was built at the instigation of Széchenyi, who sacrificed a year's salary to spur fund raising. When asked how he would live for a year on nothing he replied, "I have friends."

It was the first Neo-Renaissance building in Budapest when it was completed in 1864, another symbol of rising Hungarian independence. Across from the Academy, István Széchenyi's statue stands in the center round overlooking the Chain Bridge (Lánchíd). Opposite him is the seated Ferenc Deák, architect of the 1867 compromise. From Erzsébet square southward between the Lánchíd and the Erzsébet Bridge is the famous Dunakorzó (promenade).

## ★★★Dunakorzó (Promenade)

This walkway on the Danube shore was once known throughout Europe, a rival to Paris, Vienna and London, a center of world culture. An effort to revive some of the spirit of that time is seen in the Buchwald chairs that now grace the walkway. These rows of light blond wood and wrought iron frames once cost a small fortune to rent on the promenade. It turned the industrious Buchwald into a millionaire. The first historic pontoon bridge that was once the singular link between Buda and Pest once anchored where the promenade opens up to the Vigadó tér.

The same spot that is now a meeting point for riverboat riding and for afternoon walks, is also the front lawn of the ★★★**Vigadó concert hall**, www.vigado.hu ☎/fax 36-1-266-6177, a structure whose glory also defines the constant struggle with history that has so characterized the Magyar nation. Vigadó tér once to serve as redoubt. It turned into a national statement with the construction of the famous white marble concert hall that faced the rolling waters of the Danube. At its opening ceremony in

1833, 2,600 candles burned in the great hall, and 160 mirrors reflected the candlelight. It was the year in which Johann Strauss Sr. hosted concerts, and then, in later years, the master composer and conductor Franz Liszt, whose benefit performances for the flood victims of 1838 drew the kings, queens, and nobility of all Europe. But they would have been none to happy had they known that only 10 years later its purpose was turned against them. The First National Assembly of Hungary gathered there in 1848, and voted to organize a revolutionary army against the Hapsburg monarchy.

From the opposite side of the river, as the war for independence raged forward, Buda castle was under siege, but, not without protest. The Hapsburg garrison of the palace tried to blow up the Lánchíd (Chain Bridge), and then they turned their long range cannons toward the Vigadó, not just a redoubt any longer, but a symbol of the independence of the Hungarian people. Its hundreds of thousands of hours of labor and art, its sculptures and Corinthian pillars were turned to shattered concrete. The Hungarians did not know that the Hapsburgs were even then hiring Russian armies and German Hessians. It was with myopic vision, an illusion of independence, that Arther Görgey, the leader of the Hungarian forces at the siege of the castle wrote, "...in the midst of the columns of smoke, the burning grenades, like showers of falling stars, crashed down upon the city with a terrifying roar... it seemed to be a grand waving of lighted torches in the death march of the Austrian dynasty."

The Hungarian spirit continue to burn, even after the revolution was crushed. Even after the bombardment from the castle and the absolute destruction of the early 19th-century Vigadó, it was reborn in a new palace-like building, in the Romantic style of the new period, the work of architect Frigyes Feszt. Its inauguration was on January 15, 1865, with a splendid public ball. Once again, Pest made a statement to the world. But, it too would fall. It was burned to the ground in 1944-45.

The back wall that remained was supported using the office building you see today at Vörösmarty Square; then, with painstaking efforts, architects restored the main façade once again.

## ★★Vörösmarty Square

To the left of the Vigadó is Vigadó utca which leads into Vörösmarty Square. One short block up, in the center of the square, is the statue of **Mihály Vörösmarty**, reciting the lines from one of his works, "Be faithful to your land forever, Oh Hungarians."

Sculpted in vulnerable Carrara marble, it is draped with plastic in the winter. This square is one of the liveliest in Buda-

*Vörösmarty Square*

pest, with wandering minstrels, artists, and frequent booth exhibits and happenings during the summer months. The Art Nouveau **Luxus Department Store** looks down from the east side of the square. Built in 1911 by Kálmán Giergl and Floris Korb, it still has shops on the ground floor. In this square is also the entrance for the historic yellow line metro (see page 37). At the northeast corner of the square, a small street branching east takes you to the British Embassy (about 20 yards, on your left), and to a cross-street. Cross the street, and continue east. On your right are hotels, and on the left, Erzsébet tér.

Walk a bit farther to Deák tér, the nexus of another metro entrance and the intersection of buses and trams. From the islands in the middle of Károly Körút, you can take any of the trams going south. Seat yourself on the left side and look out. Get off at the Doboi út, two stops later, where the magnificent ★★★**Budapest Synagogue** (Dohány u. 2, Mon-Fri 10 am to 3 pm, Sun 10 am to 1 pm) dominates the street with its multi-story mosque-like structure towering with gilded onion-shaped domes. The tours, worth every penny, recall the wealth and tradition of a culture that links back to the ancient Middle East. It is a venue for concerts as well as church services. But the Jewish cemetery is on

*Budapest Synagogue*

the shadowed north side of the building, facing Germany, and the names on the headstones convey the rape of a people, writers, doctors, lawyers, butchers, musicians, artists, mingled with the women, children and babies, in the years 1944 and 1945. Surrounded by iron bars, it is almost isolated in a hidden corner, while the new/old Budapest enters the European Union. This is the largest synagogue in the world, outside of Israel.

## Váci út

But now we turn back toward Deak tér, and walk to Vörösmarty tér, then veer southward and down Váci út. On the left you will find Martinelli tér, and down the street the 1906 **Török Banking House**, another classic example of Art Nouveau, crowned with its magnificent top cornice work.

Back to Váci út and continue to **Petőfi tér**, a sliver of a park huddled next to the Danube, running parallel to the river. Nestled among the houses is the wounded **Greek Orthodox Church**, somehow still standing after the war. The statue of Petőfi Sándor calls out. Raising the scroll in his hand he is proclaiming the stirring words that sparked the revolution of March 15, 1848, "Arise Magyars. Your fatherland calls/this is the time, it's now or never/Do we want to be captives or free men? This is the question, answer it!" Out of the café that birthed the stirring words, Café Pilvax, the early leaders roused the streets of Budapest. Lajos Kossuth sent a delegation to Vienna, with 12 demands. The emperor duplicitously agreed, while he laid plans to crush the Hungarian spirit.

Budapest

Petőfi was the victim of their counterattack in Transylvania, and was killed at age 26. Kossuth ended up in exile for the rest of his life in Torino. Of the leaders, 16 Hungarian generals were executed and the rest were interred in the New Building jails.

Next to Petőfi tér, is the **Marcius 15 tér**. Hungarians have not infrequently gathered in memory and in protest at this spot to express the frustrations of the people. It was here on March 15, 1942 that free democrats and opponents of Admiral Horthy's Nazi-oriented regime gathered to hold a gigantic anti-war protest. A little over 10 years later, on October 23, 1956, students gathered here in unison with a like gathering across the river. After listening to a reading of Petőfi's famous words, they made revolutionary demands for free elections, the withdrawal of party chief Mátyás Rákosi, and the withdrawal of Soviet troops. Hundreds of thousands joined these students, and then melded into a sea of Hungarians that marched across Margit hid (Margaret Bridge) from the other side of the river, the spirits of Pest and Buda linking arms and hearts to make their demands heard.

For a time it did look as though the revolution might succeed. Rákosi escaped to Moscow, and the new reformist communist leader Imre Nagy became prime minister. For a brief time the people sensed the fresh wind of freedom. But, the communists would have none of it and on November 4, the Soviets entered Hungary again, with troops, tanks, artillery, and armies from virtually every nation of the Warsaw pact... a combined force that was as fiercely resisted as it was large. The hands, picks, and Molotov cocktails of the Hungarians fought desperately, but hopelessly, against the cold steel of Soviet armor. The erstwhile leaders of freedom were soon arrested and executed. János Kádár was forced upon the Hungarians as the new prime minister. Ironically, Marcius 15 tér hides a sunken garden which reveals the few remains of Contras Aquincum, the Roman outpost whose construction this side of the river was meant to send a message of Rome's imperial presence. Although what is left lacks the powerful thick walls of the original, it was at this spot that both Emperor Constantine and Julien the Apostate visited this territory.

# ★Inner City Parish Church

On the inward southern side of Marcius 15 tér stands Inner City Parish Church (Belvárosi Plébania templom). This is the oldest building in Pest. Ignoring the painted yellow Baroque façade, a close examination will reveal the pattern of the ages in its variegated structure. The foundation level hides the burial spot of **Bishop Gellert** (1046), who was martyred at the hands of the pagans in his terrible plunge to the Danube from Gellert Hill. A Romanesque church eventually rose up,

financed by the victorious kings of Christendom. The stones of that church are still there, though they may be hard to define. However, after the Tartar invasion, there was a Gothic rebuilding, clearly discernible in the character of the stones. At the side of the church, note the Baroque façade, added circa 1739, after the Turks had occupied it and used it as a mosque. The façade, however, is quite distinct from the darker medieval stone and Gothic windows and buttresses. Inside, the bright interior will reveal two rose-colored tabernacles from 1507 at the end of the aisles. Nineteen Gothic figures peer out from behind the altar, but a mihrab (prayer niche) is set apart by its Arabic calligraphy, spelling out the name of Allah, a reminder of the Turkish occu[ation (1541-1686). The eye can discern two different styles. On the left is the Baroque, of later construction, while on the right is the 15th-century Gothic, spiraling to meet in the arches. The Parish Church was once the center of the fortified town of Pest, and also at the heart of the most expensive district, surrounded by 18th-century mansions. However, these were gradually taken down, caused as much by city expansion as by the wars and the flood of 1838.

On the east side of the church, face away fron the Danube. A small street leads us under a connecting archway between what used to be the monastery behind the church, and the 18th-century Old City Hall of Pest. On the other side of the archway, we intersect with Váci út. Make a short right, and then a left at the next street, Kigyo utca.

## ★★Ferenciek tere

We arrive at what was once called Liberation Square (Felszabadulás tér). It is known as Ferenciek tere today, lined with Neo-Gothic and turn-of-the-century structures evoking the glory of the past, and, as the street opens out, we walk inside the gates of the Paris Arcade on the left.

*Paris Arcade Ceiling*
*(Nannette Vinson)*

On the left, the entryway to the ★★**Paris Arcade** places you immediately in the time when the Eiffel tower was built and the Hapsburgs ruled in one of the grandest examples of architecture from this period, mixing Gothic and Art Nouveau in balance. Black wrought iron gates and trimmings stand out against the stained glass and Venetian balconies. The building is the legacy of Henrik Schmahl, circa 1911. This is one structure untouched by the two world wars. Intricate ironwork mingles with stained glass and ornamented concrete.

Part of it is now occupied by the Ibusz tourist offices, as well as the Jégbufe at the narrow entrance corner (*See Places to Eat*).

Across the street to the right, the **Franciscan Church** invites another look, though we mentioned it earlier. On its side you will also see the relief (repeated often in Pest) of Wesselényi's heroics in the flood of 1838, and note the high-water mark of the flood.

*Franciscan Church (Nannette Vinson)*

Heading once again back up Váci út, we arrive at the Central Market Hall, dominating the east end of the Freedom Bridge (Szabadság híd).

## ★The Covered Market

*The Covered Market*

The 1890s saw the Budapest City Council concerned with public health. The stench of the plague exuded from open markets, and therefore, in the zeal for new construction, they commissioned Samu Pecz to design and build five glass-covered halls to serve as the city markets. All five opened for business on the same day in 1897. This one is the largest of the five, originally with 1,100 stalls, and designed to receive goods directly inside the hall, by interior side rails, or

*Interior of Covered Market*

by barge through a specially constructed canal. The fabulous iron work is still there, reminding one of the Eiffel Tower. Refurbished and retiled, the market today houses almost every type of international food shopping possibility in the myriad shops that fill its space.

## Serbian Orthodox Church

Back onto Váci út, head right on Szerb utca, to the Serbian Orthodox Church. Sitting contemplatively amidst graves and trees, it symbolizes the strong historical tie to Serbia. Eugene of Savoy received significant aid from the Serbs in his fight against the Turks. The reward came to 40,000 Serbs who were offered refuge in Budapest in 1717, when the Turkish surged again upon European soil. The Serbian church was originally dedicated to St. George, but in the famous battle of 1686, when the Christian armies recaptured Budapest, it was seriously damaged. Rebuilding efforts included a wooden tower, a new nave, and restoration of its huge variety of icons. These were basically completed in 1752. The small entrance fee introduces a church with cubicles and benches, balanced by oriental yellows, gold, and reds, spread over with Gothic arches. Photography is not permitted inside.

At the top of the street, at Király Pál utca, another tribute to the trauma of the 1838 flood is emblazoned on the wall. Erected in 1938, the flood centenary, the red marble shows the reach of the flood waters against the white relief of a stone map.

## University Church

Arriving at Egyetem tér, the Neo-Baroque Law and Political Science Faculties of the University stand out in the square.

Open for a look-see, it is but the introduction for what lies behind the building. Around the corner is the University Church. This church symbolizes another aspect of Budapest history, also remembered in the cathedral cave at Gellert Hill. The counter-reformation is symbolized in a Baroque church built by the Hungarian-born Pauline order. Its extraordinary interior is a contrast of colors and marble, balanced with wood pulpits, pews, and doors that were the work of the monks themselves. The Paulines were founded in Hungary in the 13th century, and constructed their first house of worship in a country town. Their inheritance of the relics of St. Paul, acquired by King Lajos the Great (1342-82), helped to define the order. Turks demolished their small church in the country during the occupation. They say revenge is sweet. After the Turks were driven out, the Paulines demolished the former mosque and built another church in its place. (It is no wonder that the chancel does not face eastward!). It was consecrated in 1742. The Paulines did not continue undisturbed. In 1786 Emperor Joseph II abolished the order, which is linked to the construction of the church in the cave at the side of Gellert Hill. It is today, however, a functioning order of the Catholic Church.

## Káolyi kért

*Magyar Nemzeti Múzeum*

Making our way up Ferenczy István út to Múzeum Körút (Museum Circle), take a right and go to the great courtyard and the ★★**Magyar Nemzeti Múzeum**, 14-16 Múzeum krt, ☎ 36-1-338-2122, fax 317-7806, hnm@hnm.hu, www.hnm.hu . Open Nov 30-Mar 15 10 am-5 pm; Mar 16-Nov 1 10 am-6 pm. The eight-column Greek Corinthian façade marks the structure with the Neo-Classical design of Mihály Pollack, who was commissioned to construct it in 1836. The original collection in this building was donated by Ferenc Széchenyi in 1802. Before there was a structure to accept it, it was protected in the monastery of the Paulines, next to the University Church. After construction commenced, it became one of the flood's victims. But, again, construction resumed and was finished in time for the revolution of 1848. From the front steps, on Mar 15, 1848, Petőfi Sándor stood up and recited his famous national poem, which he had completed only hours before.

Hungarian history is revealed in the busts, statues, and artifacts here. In the garden, the bust of Alexander Monti, the Italian general who led an Italian force during the Hungarian revolution, shares space with Giuseppe Garibaldi's statue. Hungary's struggle for freedom extended to Italy, where Hungarians also took part in the struggle for independence against Hapsburg rule. Mussolini donated a column from the Roman Forum to Hungary in recognition. Out in the back garden, Liszt Ferenc once held benefit concerts.

Leading past that garden, we are confronted with the **National Radio Station**, site of bitter fighting in the 1956 Revolution. I was told by a Hungarian that their last broadcast words were "America, where are you?" and then the radio went silent.

A brief walk to Kalvin tér takes us to the intersection with Üllői út where we take the metro toward Kőbánya one stop to Ferenc Körút. At the intersection we walk down Üllői út.

## Museum of Applied Arts

At 33-7 Üllői út, the Museum of Applied Arts (Ipár-müvészeti Múzeum), ☎ 36-1-217-5222, open 10 am to 6 pm daily, closed Mon, is a masterpiece from the architect Ödön Lechner, who designed this building for the Millenial Celebrations. Built in 1896, its goal was to establish a separate Hungarian style of architecture. The blend of styles adds almost a Turkish aspect to the rich curvature in the porticos and balconies. But these are hidden by the bright colors that surround the pink marble steps and Byzantine light yellow pillars. Stained glass ceilings grace a pure white almost ethereal hall. The museum is for carpets, jewelry, handcrafts, and ceramics

from the faed Hungarian Herend
works and other ceramics houses all
over the world. There are fabrics
and hand-worked objects from down
through the centuries, along with
some interesting old-world musical
instruments. From here you can
walk to the Ferenc Körút metro
stop, and take it back to Deak Ter.
We are ready to embark on our
exploration of Andrássy út. Take the
metro back toward Újpest, and get
off at Deák tér.

*Museum of Applied Arts*

## ★★Andrássy Boulevard

Andrássy Boulevard splits off from the huge intersection at
Deák tér and heads east, into what we might say is the heart
of cosmopolitan Budapest. It is the home of sophisticated
shops, restaurants and coffee houses, concert halls and offices
mingling with the extraordinary energy of the modern Hungarian culture. In 1868, one year after the new order was
established, Prime Minister Gyula Andrássy returned from
Paris, harboring in his mind a Hungarian Champs Elysées!
Though buildings were in the way and Pest seemed to be
growing in a different way, Andrássy pushed through his plan
for the grand boulevard. In 1872 the single-story residences,
from the small ring road past the outer ring road to the park,
were demolished and residents were relocated. In an extraor-

*Corner of Andrássy at Deak tér, with Bajcsy-Zsilinszky at left*
*(Nannette Vinson)*

*Portal on Andrássy (Nannette Vinson)*

dinary example of focused energy, within 15 years, the entire length, two km, was rebuilt and lined with upscale Victorian apartment houses, fabulous villas, sophisticated shops and restaurants, and department stores. It has never since lost that air of energy and class. Many an unknown Hungarian artist has graced Budapest with masterpieces adorning front door porticoes and balconies on Andrássy. For that reason alone, it is worth a walk up this classic street. However, as an alternative, you can take the yellow metro line. It runs under Andrássy street the entire way, since 1896, from Deák tér to Mexikoi út.

## A SUCCESSION OF NAMES

What you see as Andrássy út was originally called Sugár út (Radial Avenue). At the death of the visionary leader Andrássy in 1890, it was named, naturally, Andrássy út. History would not be satisfied with stability for such a notable street, however, and when the communists took over in 1947, its name was officially changed to Stalin Avenue. Ten years later, during the rise of freedom in 1956, the people renamed it Avenue of Hungarian Youth. After the Russians reinvaded Budapest, in deference to the Hungarians, who had bruised the iron curtain of Russian hegemony, the Russians allowed it to be renamed Népköztársaság (People's Republic) in 1957. Such artificial socialist identity was not to survive Hungarian self-awareness. After the Russians' were ejected in 1990, the street signs were replaced with Andrássy út once again. The Hungarians had never forgotten their prime minister from the 1880s.

At Elizabeth tér (which adjoins the smaller Deák tér), the northeast corner intersects with Andrássy út, which heads east. The northeast corner building is marked by a plaque dedicated to Count Andrássy, whose

*Sculpture on Andrássy (Nannette Vinson)*

ingenuous character led Franz Joseph to appoint him as foreign minister of the Austro-Hungarian empire. Franz Joseph also funneled money from the empire's treasury to build "Andrassy" street, and the plaque commemorates that partnership. The more recent plaque from 1989, recalls the historic friendship between Austria and Hungary.

Across the street at No. 3 is the **Postal Museum**, open 10 am to 6 pm daily. There are turn-of-the-century telephone booths, postal counters, vehicles, maps and furniture are balanced with some notable historical documents (a letter from the hand of 18th-century Empress Maria Theresa) and other postal memorabilia. We now take the metro yellow line again to the Opera.

★★★**Operaház** (Opera House). At 1061 Budapest, Andrássy út 22, ☎ 36-1-353-0170, www.opera.hu. Count Andrássy persuaded Franz Joseph to finance the construction

of this fabulous structure, and over 10 years were spent in its construction (1873-1884). Lit up at night, the graceful front leads to a scaled-down entry, which however opens out into a

*Opera House*

Budapest

breathtaking structure built for the upper class of Hapsburg Europe. Gold and scarlet glitter amidst the rich frescoes of Károly Lotz and Mór Thán. The elegant passages of paneled oak are draped in blue and gold silk, complemented by the sweeping marble staircase. Franz Joseph was present at the grand opening in 1884.

The building across the street from the opera house is appropriately the home of the National Ballet School, formerly the Drecshler House, built in 1884 by Ödön Lechner before he developed his unique Hungarian style of architecture.

Next door, the **Goethe Institute** occupies what was the notorious **Three Raven's Inn**. The haunt of 20th-century poet Endre Ady, a forum of intellectuals once met there, including Béla Bartók, Ady, and Ödön Lechner, all of them interested in developing a fusion of Hungarian folk culture with the growing influence of western art and culture.

Now, walk farther up Andrássy to Nagymezö utca. To the left, theaters and cafés will immediately meet your eye in this mini-Broadway of Hungary. The **Thália Theater**, VI, is at Nagymezö utca 22-24, ☎ 36-1-311-1874, www.thalia.hu, hunglerzsuzsa@thalia.hu. Box office is open 10 am to 6 pm daily. Newly renovated, it has a 522-seat auditorium and is air-conditioned.

Within the same block is the **Budapesti Operettszínház**, Nagymezö u. 19, ☎ 36-1-353-2172, www.szinhaz.hu/operett, operett@operett.hu, ☎/fax 36-1-269-0118. With a newly restored interior, it duplicates the Art Nouveau of ages past, with statues serving for the light stands and adorned with marble, parquet, velvet, and chandeliers.

Next door to the Operetta House is the **Moulin Rouge**, Nagymezö u. 17, ☎ 36-1-332-9000, a garish Baroque spot draped in rich reds with golden

*Budapesti Operettszínház*

cherubsd. They serve dinner starting at 7:15, followed at 9 by a 60-minute cabaret. A late evening cabaret at 11:45 is followed by a live band and dancing.

Across the street is a house built by **Mai Manó**, one of the premier photographers of Hungarian history, winner of the Gold Medal in The Paris Exhibition of 1900, the imperial court photographer of the Hapsburgs and founder of the National Hungarian Photographer's Association. Now it is **The Hungarian House of Photography Mai**, Nagymezõ u. 20, ☎ 36-1-473-2666, fax 473-2662, maimano@maimano.hu, www.maimano.hu. Built in 1894, it was bought by Sándor Rozsnyai and his wife Mici Rozsnyai (Miss Arizona in 1930!) They built the Arizona club in the yard, which remained open until 1944. Speculation is that they were killed by Nazis in 1944. After the war it went through different occupants, until finally the Hungarian Photographers' Association bought the building.

## THE ADMIRAL WITH NO NAVY

A country without an ocean and an admiral without a navy defeated President Roosevelt! Hungary is over 166 km/100 miles from the nearest ocean, landlocked by skyscraping mountains and hills. It has never had a sea-going navy. Nevertheless, when Captain Horthy signed on with Austro-Hungarian forces, he commanded a warship with such distinction that he was made Admiral of the Austro-Hungarian fleet in the Mediterranean. During WWI President Woodrow Wilson assigned the up-and-coming Franklin Delano Roosevelt, himself a former navy man, to urge the Italians to make a more aggressive use of their superior navy. FDR was anxious to succeed. It was his first assignment in the Department of State. But it was to no avail. In an exhausting session with the Italian cabinet, FDR exhorted the Italian allies to take the offensive and attack at the first opportunity. But, finally, after long discussions and desperate diplomatic maneuvering, Admiral Thaon de Revel, the minister of the Italian Navy, drew a deep breath and rose from his chair. "Yes," he admitted, "the Austro-Hungarians are weaker. But, the Dalmation Islands hold hidden coves and inlets invisible from the sea where enemy ships could hide, and furthermore it is the perfect setting for the Austro-Hungarians because they have a daredevil commander, Admiral Horthy, who will swoop out and attack on the most unexpected occasions. No, we cannot expose our fleet to that risk." Roosevelt had never heard of Horthy before, and he could say nothing in reply. Later he admitted, "That was my first diplomatic defeat, and I owed it to Admiral Horthy."

*Music Academy*

Our next major intersection is at Liszt Ferenc tér, but instead of visiting the coffee houses, we turn right and walk to the ★★**Zene-akadémia** (Music Academy), at the corner of Király utca and Liszt Ference tér. The imposing seated statue of Liszt Ferenc by Aljos Stróbl dominates the second-floor façade, introducing this perfectly preserved Art Nouveau building. During the day enter through the Király út entrance and, after you walk up the richly tiled and brown marble staircase, you will enter the concert hall, with its hanging chandeliers and an atmosphere of luxury and subdued artistry.

> Liszt is considered one of the greats of the musical world, and his famed Hungarian dances have been popular since the late 1800s. However, Liszt himself was a German speaker who claimed he had a lamentable ignorance of the Hungarian language!

Returning to Andrássy út, we head north only a block to the **Oktogon**, lined with modern food stores. Although currently bearing its original name, for 40 years, during the long Russian occupation, it was known as November 7 tér (in honor of the Russian Revolution), and intersected with Lenin körút (today known as Teréz körút). As if that wasn't enough, before that the Oktogon bore Mussolini's name for 10 years!

Both the German occupation and the Russian occupation were periods of terror, which is well documented at our next stop.

Farther up, at ★★**Andrássy út 60**, was a center of repression and unspeakably terrifying screams in the night. It is today called the House of Terror, www.terrorhaza.hu, open 10-6 daily except Mon, 1,500 HUF admission. From 1939 to 1945 it was the headquarters of the Arrowcross, the notorious Hungarian Nazis Party and it was known as the House of Terror. Of course, they were driven out by the Russians, but the Russian communist methods found an equally suitable home in this building. From 1949, its turn-of-the-century style was forgot-

*House of Terror*

ten in favor of dark cell rooms, and it gained a new name, the House of Horrors. Today it is a museum, flanked by barbed wire, and sober insights into the recent past. It provides a glimpse into the grim inhumanity of man to man. The Stalinist secret police occupied it from 1953. Many people were muscled and dragged in and never came out. No one is exactly sure of the numbers. But, down the hallway from the director's office, a small room with various instruments of torture on the wall leaves an uncomfortable reminder of the screams that must have issued from this room. It is a suffocatingly small room, and there is a drain on the floor (one might speculate as to why you would need a drain in such a place). The elevators will take you upstairs to where Nazis and communists dined, while in the basement, the dark, dank walls enclose bare cells with a few wood planks for beds. Prisoners were not allowed to leave the cells and their waste accumulated. After the 1956 Revolution, the Russians, showing their innate sensitivity, turned the basement into a clubhouse for communist youth. From the Oktogon we continue our walk, or take the metro at the Oktogon to Kodály Körönd.

**Kodály Körönd** is at this writing still in need of renovation, but the glimpse into the glory of the past still shines through. A close inspection will reveal four buildings, with Victorian cupolas and towers, gold paintwork, chiseled façades and balconies and, were it not for the press of traffic and modern dress, you would be thrown back into the early 19th century. Zoltán Kodály, who worked with Béla Bartók to research the folk history of Hungary for his music, used to live at No. 87-89 Kodály Körönd

Farther up at 69 Andrássy út is the ★**National Puppet Theater** (Bábszínház), www.babszinhaz.hu, bubob@hdsnet. hu, ☎ 36-1-322-5051, fax 342-4765. This listed building, built between 1875 and 1877, contains a 350-seat auditorium that hosts performances by the Rajko Folk Ensemble and the Budapest Gypsy Orchestra. Performances here are not in English, but they are world-class. Puppet shows are generally at 3 pm Mon to Thurs, and 10:30 am to 4 pm Fri to Sun. The puppet theater itself is closed during the summer, although Hungarian folk music is performed all year.

As we continue up Andrássy út, we now pass sophisticated 19th-century mansions, villas, and offices, eventually ending at Hősök tere. Or you can take the metro.

## ★★★Hősök tere

The triumphal colonnade and center column of Hősök tere were originally designed for the Millennium celebrations of 1896 to commemorate 1,000 years since the Magyar tribes took over the land. The Millennial Monument was to have glorified the dual monarchy, but subsequent events stalled the project. The angel Gabriel perches atop the column (1910). According to Hungarian legend, Gabriel appeared to Pope Sylvester II and urged him to recognize István as king. Accordingly, the apostolic double cross and the Hungarian crown, it is said, represent the unity of Hungary and the Christian west. At the base of the pillar, rounding its form, are the fiercely determined seven mounted Magyar chieftains

*Heroes' Square*

who elected Árpád as the first king of Hungary. Árpád is the foremost figure facing the square. These tribesmen took the oath of blood. In the center top of the colonnade, to the left, the figure of war drives his frenzied horses with a whip. To the right, by contrast, is peace, holding out the palm in her hand. On each side of these mythical figures is a historical depiction of famous figures from Hungary's past. However, as with all things in Hungary, it has changed more than once. In the original, which was completed circa 1914, the five figures to the right were Hapsburg monarchs. The collapse of the Austro-Hungarian empire in 1918, followed by the defeat of WWI, settled forever the fate of those figures, more so as the communists took power under the notorious Béla Khun. His revolutionary council lasted only from March to August 1919, but managed to destroy the Hapsburg figures, smash Franz Joseph to pieces, and judiciously deface everything else with graffiti, proclaiming, "Long live the Council Republic!" A comeback came with Admiral Horthy, but more as a protest to history than a statement.

After the Treaty of Trianon in 1920, in protest, Franz Josef and the Hapsburgs were recast in bronze, representing a snub to the allies.

Budapest

In 1929, Heroes' Square received its official name. A plaque commemorating the fallen heroes of the war of 1914-1918 was placed at the foot of the column of the angel Gabriel. The Hungarian words echo with a defiant ring, "To the thousand year boundaries!"

 The borders of Hungary had been established a thousand years ago, and her culture and history had been closely identified with those borders. But the treaty of Trianon after WW I redrew the national boundaries and drastically reduced the size of the nation. It is still a sore point, and its impact is reflected on this plaque at the foot of the angel. According to Hungarian folklore, the angel Gabriel helped form the crown lands of ancient Hungary. It is a story told and retold to every Hungarian child.

*Heroes' Square monument*

But history would not leave the monument alone in this state either. After the defeat of WWII, the monarchs were once again taken down, in deference to the new communist era. The original Heroes' memorial plaque disappeared, replaced with a simple memorial plaque in 1956, which has since been dedicated to the unknown soldier killed during the Hungarian Revolution.

The various statues in the square depict events from the life of each leader. St. István is on the far left, circa 1000 AD, being crowned as the first Christian king of Hungary. Béla IV overlooks the devastation of the Tartar invasion in 1241, while Janós Hunyádi, on the other side, defeats the Turks in the Battle of Belgrade in 1456. Hunyádi's son, the famed Mattias, has around him a covey of humanist scholars. Hungary's greater territorial history is encompassed in the statue of Gábor Bethlen, the remarkable Calvinist leader from Transylvania. In this depiction he is in the midst of negotiations with the Bohemian lords against the Hapsburgs in the Thirty Years War. And, in the last relief, Kossuth Lajos dramatically calls the peasants to revolt in the revolution of 1848-9.

Our attention should now turn to the ★★★**Museum of Fine Arts** (Szépmûvészeti Múzeum), www.szepmuveszeti.hu or www. museum.hu, open 10 to 5:30 except Mon, Dózsa Györgyi út 41, ☎ 36-1-469-7100. Sitting inside a replica of the Greek

Parthenon is one of the finest art collections in Europe with a catalogue of works by Rafael, Rembrandt, a fine Spanish Collection, including several marvelous El Grecos and Goyas, Italian works by Giorgione, Bassano, and Corregio. Other paintings and sculpture date from the fourth century through the 18th century. German and Flemish works include a Dürer portrait and Bruegel's characteristic human situational portraits. At the museum entrance are a group of powerful statues and busts by Rodin. In the back, one of the finest graphics collections in the world (over 10,000 drawings and 100,000 etchings) includes work by Da Vinci, Dürer, Cezanne, and Manet. This section is not always open, as many of these works are sensitive to light. The Egyptian gallery is not to be missed, and includes thousands of works of Egyptian art, including ancient coffins.

Opposite, on the southern side of the square, the ★★★**Palace of Fine Arts** (Mucsarnok) displays contemporary art. It's open Mar 16 to Sept 30 from 10 to 5 ; Oct 1 to Mar 15, Fri, Sat, and Sun, 10:30 am to 4:30 pm. ☎ 36-1-460-7000, info@ mucsarnok.hu, www.mucsarnok.hu. Once again, the soaring Greek columns hold up the portico and give an air of grandeur befitting Imperial Rome. Inside sits the unusual three-dimensional display developed by Hungarian László Magyar, the only one of its kind in Europe. It covers all of Hungary, using infrared controlled headphones to present information on the architecture, culture, and society. You can hear the narration in English, German, Italian, Spanish, or French, in addition to Hungarian.

## Városliget (City Park) & the Zoo

Leaving Heroes' Square we will go to the Városiget, or City Park, and head north past Gundel's on the left, a short walk up Állatkerti út (Animal garden street). Even if you don't have children, the zoo is worth a visit for its world-class variety of animals. Built in 1866, it was far ahead of its time, integrating habitat environments for the animals with Budapest architectural styles from the 19th century. Zolnay majolica (made in the Zolnay factory in Hungary) tiles the roof of the elephant house, which recently won the Europa Nostra prize for architecture. It is one of dozens of buildings by Hungarian architects from the same era, using Art Nouveau in combination with an outdoor display.

To avoid redundancy, we will pass over most of the Városliget (City Park), which we discussed in the *Family Places* and *Nightlife* sections above, and will spotlight the ★**Széchenyi baths** once again. When they were built in 1879, it was con-

*Széchenyi baths (HNTB)*

sidered a technological breakthrough to reach the hot steaming waters 3,000 feet below the earth's surface. It still is no mean feat. No expense was spared in building baths equal to the technology. The largest in Europe, their warm waters soothe in summer or winter, bubbling with currents, whirlpools, and underground jets. Chess tables are laid out at surface level, at the foot of Neo-Classical statues, a Roman patrician's leisure occupation. City park water adventures can be matched by a round-trip to Margaret Island, but not with the grandeur of the Széchenyi.

## Statue Park

The remains of the Soviet Empire did not die! They still live on in Statue Park in Budafok, where gigantic Soviet-era statues and public edifices, as well as many items of historical interest, have been collected in an expansive outdoor museum. It can be reached by car out of Deak tér, although it is wiser to take the daily bus from Deák tér. Full information can be found on their website at www.szoborpark.hu/en.

# ■ Adventures

## In the Air

### Hot Air Ballooning

Although not in Budapest proper (free flight hot air ballooning is restricted over the city), the office is in Budapest. Hot air balloon flights over the nearby Hungarian countryside start at several points, depending on the wind. Fly over castles and villages of Hungary in the clean refreshing air of the country, landing to a bottle champagne (the custom for all who take their first balloon flight), a certificate of accomplishment, and a lifetime adventure memory. **Sup-Air**, Hársfa u 1, open Mon through Fri, 9 to 4. ☎ 36-1-322-0015. The company is actually the outlet for the national Hungarian Balloon Pilots Association. Accordingly, its licensed pilots meet some of the most rigorous standards in Europe, explaining its virtually accident-free safety record since it was organized in the 1970s. The pilots are participants in international balloon expos and competitions (including the United States). Almost all speak at least some English. You will be picked up, and taken by mini-van to the launching area from a pre-arranged spot. Generally, you will just begin to see the sun rise as the balloon reaches its filled-out form, and you climb into the balloon. The drift into the sky reveals the land of the Huns below, stretching to limitless horizons. The total time is about four hours, from the time preparation begins until the flight ends and you are driven back to your pre-arranged drop-off point. The cost is about US$120 per person, with a three-person minimum, although flights can be arranged for up to 24 people (with appropriate discounts)! For extra kicks you can arrange for special balloons, such as a Budweiser balloon, or others.

## Tethered Ballooning

Hot air ballooning over the West End City Center is becoming one of the more popular tourist attractions. It costs 5,000 HUF for adults, 3,000 HUF for children, day and night, and offers an unexcelled 360° panorama of the entire city. Its popularity means there is a waiting list. It is a completely safe captive flight, soaring 500 feet over the city. Lit up by flood lights at night, the balloons are visible from great distances. Each flight is about 20 minutes, with 25 passengers per flight maximum, flown by licensed balloon pilots (they will not fly in questionable weather). Peak season, 10 am to midnight; off-season, 10 am to 6 pm. The **Balloon Club Café**, on the Nyugati tér side of the Millennium Roof Garden, opens out on to the launch platform. ☎ 36-1-238-7623.

## Sightseeing by Plane

**Indicator Inc.** covers a lot of territory in their 20-minute sightseeing adventure over Hungary (or longer by pre-arrangement) and there are discounts for two or more persons. Join the birds over the Danube Bend, and then make a high flyover across the Jewel of the Danube, Budapest. Indicator is a member of European Regional Airliners Association, and possesses the high-standard Air Operators Certificate (AOC). American and Swiss aircraft are chartered for established regional routes with licensed pilots in Europe. Indicator Inc, H-1122 Budapest, Városmajor u 30, ☎/fax 36-1-202-6284, 214-2749, or 2750, mail@indicator.hu, www.indicator.hu.

## Helicopter

As unlikely as it seems, the French travel agency, **French Adventures**, provides lots of air and sightseeing adventures for Hungary. Budapest can be viewed by a spectacular helicopter ride. Although a bit pricey, the ride seems all too short at 20 minutes for €300 per person. But, with five or more persons, the price is reduced to €160. For the money, you may as well go for the historic Danube bend. The long river canyon of the famous river can be viewed by helicopter for €400 per person. If you have five people, the drop in cost is dramatic to €250. www.frenchadventures.com/eurohungary.html.

## Caving

### ★Labyrinth

Castle District (Budapest I or 1st District), Uri utca 9 (M2 Moszkva tér to Várbusz 16, info@ labirintus.com, www. labirintus.com, ☎ 36-1-212-0207, fax 489-3282. Open daily 9:30

am-7:30 pm; summer hours June 16-Aug 31, 9:30 am-9:30 pm. Entrance fee 900 HUF. Wander through at your own leisure; you'll find dark corners, cave paintings, a fountain with soft music and dripping wine! There are mysterious statues and a tongue-in-cheek effort to provoke mellow thoughts about homo sapiens' future at the end... I'll leave you to discover what I mean. You can always eat at the restaurant in the cave entrance, below the surface, but be sure to wear tennis shoes, not sandals, and a long-sleeved shirt or sweater, as some parts can be a bit damp and cool. Don't panic if you feel that you're lost – that's why it's called the Labyrinth. It's easy to retrace your steps, or to find the hidden door that leads out (which you can find by a clue!).

Budapest

# Pálvölgyi Stalactite Cave

Szépvölgyi út 162, ☎ 36-1-325-9505, fax 336-0760, palvolgy@axelero.hu, www.showcaves.com. On the website click on Hungary and then Pálvölgyi Barlang. There are additional links on the site. Deak tér M2 metro to Batthyanyi ter. Take bus 86 to Kolosy ter, and then the 65 bus to Pálvölgyi Barlang stop. It stops across the street from the entrance trail (where there is also parking).

There is a small buffet restaurant, restroom, tables, and picnic-like grounds around the entrance. Open April to Oct, Tue-Sat, 10 am to 6 pm. 1,500 HUF (costs vary depending on the type of tour). There are several levels of adventure. The rigor of the tour is your choice. If you choose the climbing tour you will be provided with a caving overalls and headlamp. The ticket office is next to the entrance, which you reach down a pathway to a small valley area. A little over a third of a mile, the moderate tour and the climbing tour are both far less rigorous than the Mátyás Cave adventure (see below). The hitch here is that the guides may be familiar with English, but it can be halting. The ticket window people speak perfect English however. As you enter, the moderate tour will lead you past various formations in well-lighted surroundings. Some parts of the tour require that you climb up ladders. Leaflets and brochures are available in English. The air of the cave is supposed to be therapeutic for respiratory disorders.

# Szemlö-Hegy Cave

H-1025 Pusztszeri út 35, ☎ 36-1-150-842, 843. Open daily 9-4. Adults 300 HUF, children 200 HUF. Take Bus 29 to Barlang utca (Cave Walk). Try the same website as for the previous cave, but click on Szemlö-Hegy barlang. It belongs to the Danube-Ipoly recreation area. Discovered in 1930 by a local gardener, today it has a proper reception area with seating, refreshment dispensers in the lobby, a small mineral sample shop, where you can buy souvenirs and samples of various minerals (up the stairs to the right as you enter), and a fairly interesting museum of minerals, with samples, photographs of speleology, geology, and mining. Films are offered in a projection room for waiting guests. The 40-minute tour leads down a walkway that is partially paved in concrete and has handrails at all suitable locations. The guide here speaks both English and Hungarian.

## ★★Mátyás Cave

For those in basically good health, this cave is safe but you'll be happy when you come out alive! One of the largest in Hungary is the Mátyás Cave. It is one of the few in the world formed by thermal action from within the cave, rather than from outside. Limestone openings and caverns were formed over thousands of years, creating a labyrinth for the adventuresome. It extends from about 600 feet above sea level all the way down to the level of the Danube river and is closed to the public. But it is open to specialist caving tour guides who can be booked through **www.absolutetours.com**. Ben, who runs the tours, is from Oregon, a laid-back and efficient businessman who has accumulated a staff of professionals to help. Photos of this and other adventures as well as contact information are on the website.

The entire trip lasts three hours – 1½ hours down and 1½ hours up. You are provided with a special caving suit and a helmet with a lamp. The temperature remains at an even 50° all year and, while that may seem cool, the physical activity works up a sweat, so it is advisable to wear light clothing, such as shorts, a T-shirt and old sneakers. If you are the least bit claustrophobic, or if you are overweight or have health problems, you may not want to try this. As you get deeper down, various passages open up, while others narrow down. The Sandwich of Death is a narrow passage that you have to literally crawl through, belly flat and head down, a slit in the earth just big enough for a prostrate struggle... about 30 yards long. It is completely safe, but, skinned knees and shins may be the norm, so you should be prepared for stretching, bending and, of course, a little sweat in the bargain.

Budapest

## On Horseback

 Decimated by two world wars and a half-century of Soviet mismanagement, the great Hungarian horse tradition is being reborn today. Inns with stables dot the country. Olympic courses spring up next to stables where Hungarians practice ancient horseback bow-shooting, and where tourists may train and do the same thing! Cross-country horseback riding tours make use of the multiplying country inns that stable horses and turning Hungary into a mecca for horsemanship and equine tourism. Stables are not located directly in the city centers, although you can entertain yourself at the racetrack in Budapest, just beside the Expo Center. As of this printing, the racetrack has been updated to one of the most modern in Europe. There are some parts of the grounds that still leave the impression of the past Soviet era, but, as you enter, the nice new track will be a pleasant surprise. The race horses increasingly come from all over Europe.

While a lot of riding in Hungary is the follow-the-leader type, or a coach ride through open fields, you will usually be asked to ride inside a corral until they are sure of your experience. After that you may be strung along, be given lessons (for a fee), or you may be allowed to range the land. Superb cross-country rides take you across open fields, through forests, past fields of grain and sunflowers, forging streams and following the horse tracks of the Magyars 1,000 years ago. You must have experience to go on one of these rides, usually backed up with lessons in English-style riding. Although there are a few stables in Hungary that offer western-style, (see below), generally the horses in this country are used to the English style, which requires that you sit high in the saddle, and use little body pressure on the saddle. However, many schools also offer beginner lessons and there are several tours that will start you off learning the English methods. Bring your own English regalia, for formal instructions. Or, enjoy the Hungarian equine culture. It is risky in high season to show up at a riding center without booking in advance. The best way to assure a good quality stable, aside from those listed here, is to check with the Hungarian **Hungarian**

**Equestrian Tourism Association**, Radáy u. 8, Budapest IX listed below, ☎ 36-1-456-0444, fax 36-1-456-0445, mltsz@axelero.hu, www.equi.hu.

Because there can be such variety of services and quality in the treatment of and the services of animals, we have chosen to follow the standards of the Hungarian Equestrian Tourism Association (MLTKSZ). The main purpose of the organization is to establish uniform quality levels of instruction, facilities, and care of animals. Hungary has one of the highest standards of equestrian tradition in the world. It is one of the few countries in the world where you can have a free-ranging equestrian tour, across valleys and mountains, without fences or signs to stop your sightseeing, and with a complement of boarding hotels with stables that can allow you to ride from castle to castle and sight to sight in great portions of the country. Facilities are rated based on a horseshoe system. Five horseshoes are the highest, while one is the lowest. The standards are high, so even lower-rated facilities may provide you with a wonderful and safe adventure. As with the hotels, we start with the highest-rated. These are a sure bet, but you are also sure to pay for it. Should price be a consideration, call first. Most of these facilities have someone who handles phone calls in English as well as Hungarian, and often other languages.

| Horseshoe Ratings | | | | | |
|---|---|---|---|---|---|
| Horseshoes | Average Score | Horses | Services | Language Skill | Total Score |
| 5 | 4 | 10 | 3 | + | 22-25 |
| 4 | 3.8 | 8 | 3 | + | 19-21 |
| 3 | 3.4 | 8 | 2 | - | 17-18 |
| 2 | 3 | 6 | 2 | - | 15-16 |
| 1 | 2.4 | 5 | 1 | - | 12-14 |

**Average Score** is based on the five criteria: (1) Environmental; style and condition of stables and buildings, suitability of ranch for equestrian purposes, hygiene. (2) Technical aspects; condition, quantity, cleanliness, safety and comfort of equipment and veterinary concerns. (3) Suitability of the horses for service in tourism; controllability, temperament, and level of training. (4) Range of and standard of equestrian services; marketing activity (such as brochures), value for the money, accident prevention and safety, and other related items. (5) Aptitude and qualifications of the manager and staff; professional and personal qualifications, such as awards, years working with horses, certifications, etc. In order to qualify for a five-horseshoe rating, the average score for each criterion must be above four. The scores shown on the chart are the minimum average score for the five criteria on a scale of one to five. All four-horseshoe rated stables must score four in criterion 3 above.

**Horses** means the number of horses available for the service provided. The actual number of horses stabled is usually higher.

**Services** indicates the number of services provided; cross-country riding, carriage riding, teaching, training, horse shows, breeding, riding therapy, mounted hunting, etc.

**Language Skill**. Four- and five-horseshoe rated stables must have some staff members who can communicate in foreign languages (usually German and/or English). In addition, at least one member of the staff must be fluent enough to offer instruction (usually German and/or English). The lower horseshoe ratings do not have such a compulsory requirement for their staff members, although they may have equal or even greater language facility than some higher-rated stables.

**Total Score** reflects, in the case of one-, two- and three-horseshoe stables, an average score of three or more in criteria 3, 2, and 1.

Note that a one-horseshoe stable may still provide excellent service and that some stables may increase, while some may decline in their ratings over time.

The website, **www.gotohungary.com/whattodo/horse-riding.html**, is also helpful, but it recommends only Pegasus Tours for riding. There is more than one horse tour company in Hungary (check with the Equestrian Tourist Association mentioned earlier). When I called Pegasus to get help and information, the assistant manager indicated he was a close relation to the owner and was almost insultingly short and rude, and not quite cooperative. I asked to have an appointment and he said he would call back, and never did! Investigation found some inconsistencies in what people said about their service. I would recommend booking through **Equus Tours** in Northern Hungary (they also book tours throughout the country), which also works out of Budapest. The owner is the President of the Hungarian Equestrian Tourism Association. Their liaison, Marta Jokaim, is based in Budapest and will hand-hold visitors (with a smiling personality and excellent English). Contact her at jokaim@hu.inter.net, mobile ☎ 36-20-911-8275.

## Sóskút

**Sóskút Equestrian Club**, 2038 Sóskút, Bajcsy-Zsilinszky út 61, ☎ 36- 23-347-579 or 36-1-23-348-479. Or contact Szucs Gaspar Kinga, ☎ 36-30-460-1395, lovassport@lovassport.hu. Rated five horseshoes. Lying in a protected natural environmental area, it is an easily accessible 22 km/13 miles from Budapest, with full accommodations, restaurant, and with added insurance as required by the guests. Highly rated by European championship standards, it is the only one in Hungary that has facilities for every all possible equestrian events, for English-style riding for moderately experienced riders and up.

**Petneházy Lovasiskola** (Riding School), at II. Feketefej u. 2, ☎ 1-36-397-5048. Also contact Vrabel Ilona, ☎ 36-20-483-2160, www.petnehazy-lovascentrum.hu, petnehazy@vnet.hu. Rated four horseshoes. On the outskirts of the city limits, in the Buda Hills, the area is laced with trails and covered with trees. Riding can vary from cross-country to riding inside the enclosed corrals and grounds.

## Gödöllõ

**Lázár Equestrian Park**, 2182 Domony-völgy, ☎ 36-28-576-510, fax 36-28-576-511, ☎/fax 36-1-322-8124, www.lazarteam.hu/en and www.lazarlova-spark.hu, lazarteam@hu.inter.hu. A top show facility. The Lázár brothers are both car-riage-driving world champions and their ranch is only five km/three miles from Rassalkovich Palace in Gödöllõ. Their specialty is foreign tourism as well as company and social functions. Guests can also participate in horse competitions (with appropriate experience and guides). Horse shows, team driving races, horseback archery, carriage riding in the forest, carriage driving competitions, and Hungarian-style catering are offered. There is also gypsy music and a folk dancing and art program, plus cross-country riding. Riders and horses also prepare for international competitions, so you need to confirm in advance.

**Árpád's Blood Riding School**, Árpád Vére Lovasiskola, 2100 Gödöllő, Szárítópuszta, ☎ 36-20-973-0474, www. horseridingshow.hu. Contact János Harangozó. Rated three horseshoes. English speakers can also call ☎ 36-30-526-9391 for Victoria. An additional website for the stables is www. arpadvere.hu. Set amidst trees and forest in the Gödöllő nature preserve. Visitors are greeted by twisted-horned racka sheep, curly-haired pigs, and horses, ranging freely over the grounds, as well as several small ranch buildings, stables, and yurts. From absolute beginners to pros, aside from cross-country horseback riding, various instructional programs can take you through jumping, hunting horseback, stunts (for the properly experienced), and competitive jumping.

Weekly horse shows feature some of the top riders of the nation, and entire groups of Hungarian horsemen staging battles out of the pages of Magyar history. Knights hold their lances aloft and Magyars shoot their short-range bows from horseback, dressed in authentic clothing and gear from the first Magyar settlements, all of it handmade using the ancient techniques. This is real! After the wild shows, when arrows whiz through the air from their galloping steeds, and charging hosts of warriors let loose their battle cries, there are falconry shows from horseback, and demonstrations of historical arts. Evening finds the campfires lit. Everyone settles down for night-time cookouts in authentic Hungarian bokacs style, home-made sausages and the genuine goulash, fire dancing, and stories of ancient lore. During the day you learn to groom and care for your horse, shoot bow and arrow, and make ancient Hungarian instruments, tools, and clothing, or perhaps your own bow and arrow. It has been said that this place is a living history lesson from the age of the Magyar settlements. This is not a tour. It is an adventure, requiring that you stay in the yurt campground for a period. Yurts were the traditional Hungarian tent habitations – slightly modified here for modern sensibilities. In a separate building there are, showers, and WC although they are bare-bone, and designed to maintain the rough, country atmosphere. Cooking is out of the camp kitchen.

The camps are often booked solid with young people. However, during certain periods they book families and groups. This requires advance planning, and reservations. The camp has included visitors from as far away as Japan. Janos and his family have helped to train stuntmen who have worked with Arnold Schwarzenegger, Harrison Ford, and a number of other Hollywood stars, played in movies, and held exhibitions at Disneyland. He has been in business since the 1980s. They have also trained students in horseback archery since the 1990s. Janos holds the Guinness world record for shooting six arrows from 18 feet accurately in 11 seconds, using the ancient Magyar bows – all on horseback while riding at a gallop! It had to be done within a gallop length of 60 yards. The targets were thrown randomly in the air by participants. They were 9¾ inches in diameter.

## Galgamácsa

**Galga Lovas Klub** (Galga Riding Club), 2183 Galgamácsa Külterület, Fehér u. 1, ☎ 36-30-949-2806. Contact Dr. Réka Horváth. Rated three horseshoes The club is on a 14-acre wooded area about 45 km/27 miles from Budapest and five km/three miles outside of Galgamácsa. In addition to cross-country, there is room and board, full training, with qualified instructors for show jumping, dressage, and cross-country riding. There is a 20-box stable and a roofed riding hall as well.

## Monor

**Hotel Hegyessy Nyerges** (Hotel Nyerges and Riding School), 2200 Monor, Hegyessy tanya 57, Pf. 2/12, ☎ 36-29-410-758, kafkazs@monornet.hu. Contact Zsuzsa Csoltkó Kafka. Rated three horseshoes. It features the largest thatched roof hotel in Central Europe, built like the meeting huts of the Hungarian plains! Located 18 km/11 miles from Budapest on Highway 4, it has a full complement of services. Although there is no cross-country horseback riding from this location, they do have room for three guest horses, and provide instruction for individuals as well as groups, from beginners to moderately advanced. Carriage rides and dressage instruction are enhanced by a pool, 33 guest rooms, meeting rooms, receptions, dances, poolside parties, and top notch cuisine.

## Zsámbék

**Pegazus Lovaiskola**, Pegazus Riding School, 2072 Zsámbék, Dozsa György u. 30, ☎ 36-220-331-3755. Contact Ilus Maus, mausilus@axelero.hu. Rated three horseshoes. Pegazus specializes in training novice to intermediate level riders. It operates out of the backyard of what appears to be a nicely maintained peasants house. Guests who are training use the 20x40-yard riding arena. There is a small eight-horse stable, and they do not take in guest horses, but they do offer cross-country riding for intermediate and advanced riders in the scenic Zsámbék Basin. And, if desired, there are sleeping accommodations and board for up to eight people.

## Tök

**Tök Horseshoe Stables**, Patkó kft, 2073 Tök, Fö u. 1, ☎ 36-23-341-381. A top show facility. Tök is a small village in the Zámbék Basin, 30 km/18 miles from Budapest, the home of the Tök Stud farm and Tök Stud and Inn. Bed down for the night, enjoy a good  meal from their Hungarian chefs and ride horses all day. The 140-stud farm includes the prized Lipizaner and race trotters. Many of these same horses also participate in horse shows and mock horse drives, complete with whistles and whips. Horses can be rented for cross-country here too. Also offered are carriage rides, training for beginners, as well as instruction in saddling horses, jumping and team competitions. From leisure to competition, anyone who likes horses will find a full range of equestrian programs to suit every taste.

**V&S Lovasmajor** (V&S Farm Stables), 2073 Tök, Anyácsapuszta, ☎ 36-30-942-3926, rated four horseshoes. Contact Lajos Végh. Wooded hills surround this riding school, which is located about 30 km/18 miles west of Budapest. Leisure riding, pony trekking, and some competition-level riding begs to be tried in the newly built roofed riding hall (with expert instructors, of course). Although there are guest facilities, there is no restaurant, so be prepared to picnic for breakfast.

## Pusztazámor

**Ikertorony Kft. Öreg Tölgy Kastélyfogadó** (Old Oak Mansion Inn), 2039 Pusztazámor, Kossuth Lajos u. 22, ☎ 36-23-347-744. Contact János Krajcsovics, ☎ 36-30-964-9533. Rated two horseshoes. In a listed historic building, it has been refurbished with an eye to historical detail, including period furniture, a huge dining room, English drawing room, and a restaurant. The mansion is in an eight-acre historical park with trees hundreds of years old and a pond as well.

## Kisoroszi

**Pej Kft.** (Bay Horse Riding School), 2024 Kisoroszi, Szérú u. 2, ☎ 36-26-392-102. Contact Csilla Eőry, ☎ 36-30-560-3614. Rated two horseshoes. Actually in the town of Kisoroszi, they offer show-jumping, dressage, day-treks, and a package of several one-day cross-country treks (star tours), as well as livery.

## Budapest

**Favorit Riding School**, 1162 Budapest, Mókus u. 23, ☎ 36-31-966-9992, favoritlovarda@freemail.hu. Rated one horseshoe. They offer riding instruction, a children's camp, summer riding camps, and during the summer cross-coun-

try pony trekking is organized every month. The well-trained horses out of this stable often appear in movies and are frequently featured in horse shows.

### Galgamácsa-Megyerke

**Rózsakúti Vadászház és Lovaspanzió** (Rózsakúti Hunting Lodge and Riding Center), 2183 Galgamácsa-Megyerke, ☎ 36-28-579-510, galgamacsa@vnet.hu, www.galga.hu. Rated three horseshoes. Contact Antal Turóczi. Indoor and outdoor riding can include instruction in eventing, carriage riding and driving, a children's camp, riding therapy, and visits to the stud farm. Full range of services here includes board and meals, as well as cross-country, single, carriage, and group riding.

The following stables have been added on recommendation of the Hungarian Equestrian Tourism Association, with five horseshoe ratings:

## Budapest Surroundings

**Bélápa Farm**, 8088 Tabajd, Bélápuszta, ☎ 36-20-955-0546, info@belapa.hu www.belapa.hu. Contact Dr. Jármy Miklós, mobile 36-20-955-0546.

## Western Hungary, West of Budapest

**Bábolna National Stud Farm**, 2943 Bábolna, Mészáros u. 1, ☎ 36-34-569-28, 36-34-569-204, fax 36-34-569-294, 36-34-569-101, turizmus@babolnamenes.hu, menesbirtok@babolna-menes.hu, www.babolnamenes.hu.

**Szelle Farm Stables**, 9226 Dunasziget, Sérfenyő u. 99, ☎ 36-96-233-515, fax 36-96-216-521, szelle@axelero.hu, www.go.to/szelle. Contact Szelle Kornél, mobile 36-20-953-3223.

The following stables have been added on recommendation of the Hungarian Equestrian Tourism Association at a four horseshoe rating:

### Budapest Area

Tiborcz Riding Club, 2060 Csabdi, Tükröspuszta, ☎ 36-22-704-093 info@tiborcz.hu www.tiborcz.hu. Contact Tiborcz Péter, mobile 36-30-267-7344.

### Far West of Budapest

**Vadon Riding Club**, 9423 Ágfalva, Magyar u. 35, ☎ 36-99-505-780, fax 36-99-505-789, lovasklub@vadongroup.hu. Contact Fedor Ferenc, mobile 36-30-640-3863.

The following has been recommended without a rating by the Hungarian Equestrian Tourist Association:

**Stampok Park**, 2023 Dunabogdány, P.O. Box 21, stampokpark@stampokpark.hu, www.stampokpark.hu, ☎ 36-26-390-704. Contact Bodnár Irén, ☎ 36-20-454-6407.

## Hiking & Biking

## Hiking/Cycling Tips

There are really no challenging high mountains in Hungary, although some areas of Northern Hungary are a challenge. The terrain is often well-suited to the leisurely walker as well as the more serious hiker. If you do not feel comfortable enough in the language and/or culture, then, it is probably best if you use a tour guide (see **www.absolutetours.com**. Ask for Ben).

Hungary is, without reservation, one of the great hiking and biking countries. Budapest is laced with trails. There is a preponderance of easy trails. Homes and small hostels accommodate the thousands of people that walk the country annually. Even if you don't speak the language, they are often quite accommodating, and I have not met any that did not communicate enough to settle on an agreement for an overnight stay. **Tourinform** (see pages 571 ff) is a big help here, and they will book homes and hostels ahead for you. Some of the trails have been traveled for thousands of years. Many cross old royal hunting lands, pass caves, and meander by friendly villages. The trails are almost always a short walk from a hotel, or from a train station or parking lot.

 Many Hungarian children learn orienteering in school. They learn how to read a map and how to follow different signs, how to find their way using markers and the position of the sun and the stars. So, usually a Hungarian child will be able to find their way just about anywhere and all they need is a landmark and the sun!

## Trail Marks & What They Mean

Trail marks can be almost anywhere, so keep your eyes peeled. They may be on a tree trunk, a stone, a pole, or a post. Stones, posts or poles are usually used in open fields, but marks can be on anything that might seem to be obvious, or sometimes not so obvious. They are supposed to be located at turns. I have seen some instances on longer trails when they were not. They are painted with four possible alternate colors on a 4.8-inch-square white background. The trail maps and the markings on the trails themselves will be in matching colors. Blue trails will be marked with blue signs, yellow with yellow, green with green, and red with red. The colors signify the importance of the trail. In other words, a main trail will usually be blue, and it will always lead you directly to a village and/or primary sight. The national blue route traverses the entire country in a ring by which one can see all of Hungary on foot, including a large number of its greatest natural wonders.

### Shapes of Signs

- **Horizontal stripes** indicate starting points of major trails.
- **Blue horizontal stripes** lead to a starting point, but these are usually distant points, such as a city or major regional center. Blue routes always traverse several regions.
- **Red stripes** indicate long-range trails across one or two regions. While they are not as long as blue trails, they can still be a long walk, and often can take several days if you traverse the entire trail.

- **Yellow stripes** indicate trails within a single region, usually set at a county line.
- **Green stripes** mark local trails, within walking distance of a village in most cases.

### Sign Symbols and What They Mean

These are always in the same color as the trail mark.

A **standing cross** is located at all trail interconnections. It may not always be major trails. Some connections off a main trail may lead to a prominent lookout point, or to a site of interest such as a castle. To decipher that aspect, look to the other symbols.

**Triangles** lead to a hilltop, a peak, or some type of a high outlook.

**Squares** take you to accommodations and facilities, usually in populated areas.

Circles lead to springs, wells and sources of drinking water.

Omega ('Ω) marks a cave location on the trail.

The letter L as a marker leads to ruins and monuments or an archeological excavation.

A **circle with an arrow** indicates a short trail around popular locations or parking and rest areas.

An **arrow with a white background** marks a trail with significant forks or bends, and shows that you need to follow the direction of the arrow.

An **X** across an existing trail sign, usually in black or gray, indicates that you should not follow this trail. It has been cancelled. You should turn and go back, or go via an alternate route.

## Maps

Take a map with you and, if you are planning on doing any significant walking, I highly recommend that you get a good map with the hiking trails marked. Absolutely the best map for these excursions is the **Budapest Atlas**, published by Freytag & Berndt, 1165 Budapest, Szemlékes út 25, ☎ 36-1-258-5848. A wire-bound book, its mapping is excellent and clearly marked; all bicycle and hiking paths, bus routes and stops, MAV routes and stops and railroad stations are clearly marked. In addition, there is a list of helpful phone numbers.

The pages are referenced to each other so that a route can be followed page by page.

Supplement this with tour maps. All maps follow the color scheme and symbols we discussed in the earlier paragraphs. Most trails are marked with the Hungarian symbols, and few trails have English instructions. The maps, if in color, will usually show the trail marked with its appropriate letters, or in some cases, with lines. On some tourist maps, the difficult trails are marked with a dotted red line. Maps with all of the above markings are available from the **Hungarian Association of Friends of Nature**, in the VI district, at H-1061 Budapest, Bajcsy-Zsilinszky út 37, ☎ 36-1-311-9289, 36-1-311-2467, fax 36-1-353-1930, www.fsz.bme.hu, www.fsz.bme.hu/mtsz. This is located just north of Bosniak tér, across Bajcsy-Zsilinszky út from the metro station. They are on the third floor. There is usually someone there who can speak at least a little English. They have a variety of both hiking and biking maps, but especially interesting is their compendium of hiker's souvenir maps. These show local trails (usually black and white with appropriate markings), and a location where you get a stamp at the beginning of the trail (at an eatery, shop, or hotel) and another at the end. Since the stamps are given only by the authorized locations, and these are usually at hotels and often at eateries, they are good places to end or start a day's excursion. The bonus is a lasting souvenir with a direct connection to your adventure memories.

You can also get a variety of tourist maps and hiking and biking maps at the **map store** just a few doors down from their headquarters. In fact, when you see the map store, you will know that the entrance of the Association is just a few doors down.

## Rules

The 10 commandments for hikers in Europe, as accepted by the Nature and Hikers Association of Hungary:

- Be thoroughly prepared, with maps, clothing, insect repellant, some drinking water, and know where you are going.
- Use the marked trails, and avoid closed or forbidden areas.
- Avoid damaging flowers and plants; respect and take care of wild animals and birds; walk quietly.

- Protect the cleanliness of the forests, waterways, meadows, and mountains.
- Observe fire regulations. Don't leave open camp fires, don't throw away cigarette buts or matches unless they are completely out and then put them into a trash container.
- Treat all hiking and forest monuments and buildings with respect.
- Never leave a companion alone or in trouble.
- Observe the rules of the community.
- Respect the interests of foresters, hunters, and anglers.
- Love nature and encourage others to love it.

 **Nature Conservation:** Hungary is an extremely nature-conscious country. Its laws are designed to protect its natural treasures, its landscape, its monuments and historic locations and its breathtaking variety of habitats. Be conscious of your role in the environment and be aware of the protected species, so that you can do your part in protecting the harmony and glory of our planet.

## Absolute Walking Tours

In Budapest, look for **Yellow Zebra Tours** and/or **Absolute Walking Tours**. They are both owned by the same company, ☎ 36-1-266-8777, www.absolutetours.com and www. yellowzebra.com, Sütő ut 2, near McDonald's at Deak Tér, behind the Meridian Hotel. Absolute and Yellow Zebra are specialists in walking and biking, and if you don't want to get lost, and would like some advice and help getting around, this is the best in Budapest. In addition, their Internet café and attendants will help you keep in touch with home. They use licensed tour guides, which means that the guides must have passed language and Hungarian history examinations. They'll show you the primary sights, how to get around the city, aspects of your stay that may save you money, including what you might want to avoid, as well as what you might want to see. No tours Dec 25-26, 31 or Jan 1.

 The owner, Ben, who is from Oregon, says that if you mention this guidebook, you will get 500 HUF off any of the tours you take.

**Absolute Walk:** A 3½-hr walk that includes Inner Pest, Heroes' Square, City Park, and Castle Hill in Buda; 9:30 am & 1:30 pm daily April to Oct; 10:30 am daily Nov to Mar. Cost 3,500 HUF students, 4,000 ft adults.

**Hammer & Sickle Tour:** Go back to the communist days. See their exhibition room with relics and artifacts. Visit a communist apartment, talk with people who lived through the times of double passports, ration lines, Trabants and Socialist society. Includes a tour through the famous Statue Park, where communist statues and monuments have been collected to preserve the historical memory of that fateful period. Apr-Dec, 10:30 am Mon, Wed, Fri, Sat and Sun; Jan-Mar, Sat only. Cost 5,000 HUF students, 6,000 adults.

**Absolute Pub Crawl:** If your hedonistic sensibilities won't leave you, get inside information on where to drink, and where not to in Budapest's undiscovered bars, pubs, wine cellars, and hidden hallways. The first pub always accents the locals. It is all the wine and/or beer you can drink during the first hour. Following that will be a visit to the second pub/eatery, where you can fill up on food. The third pub will give you a free shot. And, if you are still standing and want more, there is a fourth, fifth, sixth.... The tour is reputed to be about three hours, but the owner reserves the right to extend it to six+ hours, depending on the group! Of course, it's not all drink. The guide imparts folklore, street wisdom, and a healthy understanding of alcohol and food, Hungarian-style. 8 pm Mon, Wed, Thur, Fri and Sat; Jan to Mar, Fri and Sat only. Cost 4,500 HUF students, 5,000 adults.

**Absolute Hungaro Gastro:** The real Hungarian food and wine experience tour is on Wed, Thur, Fri and Sat at 4 pm; Jan to Mar, Fri, Sat only. Student 5,000 HUF, adult 6,000.

**Absolute Night Stroll:** Legends, wines and illuminated sights. From May 1st to Sept 30th, every Wed, Thur, Fri, Sat, Sun at 8 pm. Student 3,500 HUF, adult 4,000.

All regularly scheduled tours above meet at Deák Square in front of the Church, in all weather conditions. No booking needed, just show up.

## Yellow Zebra Bikes & Internet Point

 www.YellowZebraBikes.com. Two locations in the city: **Deák Store**, Budapest, Hungary 1052, Sütő St. 2 in the courtyard behind McDonald's and the

National Tourist Office, with an entrance just to the right, ☎/fax 36-1-266-8777; **Opera Store**, Budapest, Hungary 1065, Lazar St. 16 (just behind the Opera House back side), ☎/fax 36-1-269-3843. Services, in addition to bike tours, include cheap Internet, basic travel info for Budapest and Europe, apartment and tour booking.

**Daily Bike Tours of Budapest:** 3½ hrs, including Inner Pest, Heroe's Square, City Park, and the Castle Hill in Buda. It's a good way to make friends and to get to know the city safely and sensibly. April to Oct daily at 11 am; July-Aug at 11 am and 4 pm; cost 4,500 HUF students, 5,000 adults. Tours meet at Deák Sq. in front of the Church.

**Bike Rentals:** All year from either location at 500 HUF per hour to 3,000 for the whole day; €50 deposit required.

**City Segway Tours:** www.CitySegwayTours.com, Budapest, Hungary 1065, Lázár St. 16, ☎/fax 36-1-269-3843. Segway daily tours of Pest downtown areas for 2½-3 hours plus 30 minutes training on how to ride a Segway. 10:30 am year-round plus 6:30 pm April to Oct. Advanced booking required via telephone or Web. Cost 12,500 HUF. Meet at our store on Lázár u. 16 behind the back of the Opera House.

Other tours with the same high standards incorporate certain surrounding areas. Private tours are also available. Standard area tours include the Absolute Eger Wine and Town Tour, Absolute Szentendre and visits to the artist's colony, and the Absolute Danube Bend Tour, Szentendre, Visegrad, and Esztergom.

In line with its walking tours, Zebra also hosts a series of bicycle tours, ponchos and helmets provided as needed, and they can give you excellent insight on what you need to do for longer bicycle excursions (see bicycle tours, below). Absolute Tours and Zebra tours have been written about in major newspapers, and they are well-known in Hungary.

## Hiking Trails

 Around Budapest, we have already mentioned the trails at **Gellérthegy** (Gellert Hill), which is at the end of the Erzsébet Bridge. **City Park** (at the end of Andrássy ut) offers excellent small trails. A full day's excursion can take you to **Margit** (Margaret Island), including a picnic lunch, or **Janos Hill**, with its three-terrace tower overlooking the Buda Hills and Budapest. However, try

**Hármsatár Hill**, just above the hills of Óbuda. In the early evening the Danube shines like a ribbon against the plains of the Alföld. Numerous paths stripe the hillside from the towns of Pilis and Hûvösvölgy. Take the 65 bus to the end. Follow **Hamashatát hegy út** to the top. The **Normafa** is one of the most popular ski resorts of Budapest. While it can get crowded during special events, it's a part of an interconnected network of trails that lace the Buda hills, and has places of repose and beauty as well as wildlife and picnic areas. Take the 21 bus from Moszkva tér, all the way to the end. The Széchenyi lookout point is also interconnected to the same trail system.

The **National Blue Trail** offers the finest walking/hiking in the nation. From the Austrian border, at Velem, it extends 11,400 km/6,835 miles through aromatic forests and over flowing streams, alongside mountains and through fields blooming with flowers, by villages and cities, and into the hills and peaks of the Bukk and Aggetelk National Forests. It then goes down through the wine country of Tokai, across the Tisza River and the plains of the Hortobagy where sheep and cattle graze. Follow the map for this trail, or connect to it at any number of points throughout the nation, as we detail in the following pages. The local **Tourinform** (see *Appendix* for Tourinform offices nationwide) or local hikers and nature associations can probably act as your best consultant on which part of the trail is suitable for you in any particular area. **Hungarian Friends of Nature**, in the VI district, H-1061 Budapest, Bajcsy-Zsilinszky út 37, ☎ 36-1-311-9289, 36-1-311-2467, fax 36-1-353-1930, www.fsz.bme.hu, and **Zebra Tours**, Sütö út 2, near McDonald's at Deak tér, behind the Meridian Hotel, www.yellowzebra.com.

## Bicycling

 Bicycle rentals, once rare, are now in vogue, and almost every major hotel will arrange them for you. We noted several of them under hotels in this section. There are also an ever-growing number of bicycle maintenance shops. Check with the local bicycle associations, or Zebra Tours (see above).

Wherever there are hiking trails, you can almost always find bicycle paths as well. In most areas of the country, bicycle paths are marked. Mountain biking is common, and numerous trails criss-cross the area. However, biking on some main roads may be illegal, and all expressways are illegal. But, as long as the road is posted, there are no restrictions on where you may bicycle. No special license is required to ride a bicycle in Hungary.

The national tourist office publishes a booklet called *Cycling Tours in Hungary*. It describes 38 recommended routes in Hungarian, German and English. The book called *Budapest Kerképárútjai* (from the Hungarian Bicycle Association, Budapest XIV, Szabó J. u. 3, ☎ 36-1-468-3511) details the bike lanes that thread through the city and around it in this commonly stocked classic. 32 routes are described by Viktor Csodás and György Fehér.

All bikes must have proper safety equipment – properly maintained breaks and gears, plus front and rear lights and reflectors. Bikes may not be taken on board buses or trams in the city. The extra city Mav (Hungarian Railway) has compartments that will allow bicycles, and you must make arrangements to transport them on special cars if you take the train. Some boats and ferries will allow bicycles on the Danube between Budapest and Bratislava or Vienna, and to some points in between. Balaton's ferry's also allow bicyclists to board for cross-lake transfers.

## Spas & Baths

Luxuriate in Hungary's thermal spas, but, more than that, the curative effects of many of the spas in this country are famous the world over. Bathing and fun often go hand-in-hand with wellness and recovery. Over 400 thermal batmh springs make it internationally famous.

Most springs are thermal, and the great majority are medicinal. They carry combinations of minerals and trace elements that have been shown to have curative affects on people with certain types of ailments. The water compositions vary, some thermal baths are reputed to have affects on certain conditions (such as arthritis), while others do not. But, though wonderfully regenerative and relaxing, they are not for everyone. Medicinal baths are not recommended if you suffer from pyretic conditions (fever), tuberculosis, hyperthyroidism, high blood pressure that is not responsive to medication, acute phlebitis, anemia, post myocardial infarction (for six months following a heart attack), infectious diseases of any sort, heart and circulatory disorders, epilepsy, mental illness, incapacity, incontinence and/or malignant tumors, and they are not recommended in pregnancy. That being said, most people use the spas for (a) recreation and. I believe, (b) to cure hangovers. But, whatever your preference, leisure or adventure, it's here.

The high-end spas, and many lower-scale, will give you everything from physicals and heart examinations to pedicures. All have rich thermal properties and gentle lounging pools, separated from the more active pools. Many have caves and currents, slides and waterfalls, and a variety of imaginative adornments. Almost universally, they have restaurants and cafés that open out for munchies as well. Generally, you pay at the front pénztár (cashier), and you will have a choice of a cabin or a locker. I always pick a cabin because it provides a convenient storage and sense of privacy for the whole family. Some of the spas are old, but there are state standards, and the water is changed and recirculated every day. Every facility I have seen has been clean and basically well-maintained. Sometimes in Budapest you will be given a number, and you have to wait for your number to come up before you can enter the pool. They are usually displayed on an electronic board, and in some cases they call out the number (in Hungarian), so review the numbers in the language appendix at the end of the book. Attendants usually expect a tip, averaging 100 to 300 HUF, depending on the size and quality of the establishment.

## A Few Definitions

**Medicinal water** – Any mineral water with medically-proven curative affects. Official certification as a medicinal water is preceded by a series of tests, inspections, analysis of data, and case studies that take several years to complete. Only after that is complete is the certification allowed to be posted by the establishment.

**Thermal water** – Any naturally occurring water in which the temperature exceeds 30°C/86°F.

**Medicinal bath** – A bathing establishment that either has its own source of recognized medicinal water or, lacking this, can offer a full range of medical treatments and facilities (hydrotherapy, mechanotherapy, electrotherapy, etc.).

> **Tip:** An excellent website to search for spas in Budapest is: www.spasbudapest.com/tartalom. php?idx=1.

★**Gellért Medicinal Spa** (St. Gellért Spa, at the Hotel Gellért, see *Places to Stay*). Records dating from the 15th century speak of the wondrous waters bubbling up from the earth here. It became the Turks' favorite site due to the abundance and superior warmth of the water. In the 17th century it was called Muddy Bath (Sárosfürdő). The marvelous Art Nouveau style has been retained and the feeling of opulence and luxury remains. In addition, newly fitted with modern filtration and circulating equipment, it provides virtually every type of service for a medicinal bath, including outpatient hospital and inhalatorium. Yes, a doctor and nurse are there as well. Mud packs, massages, and underwater traction are offered. See *Places to Stay*.

★**Budapest-Király Baths**, H-1027 Budapest, Fő utca 84, ☎ 36-1-202-3688. Bathe in the same place where the Turkish Pashas relaxed. This unique facility was started by Arsian, the Pasha of Buda in 1565, and completed by Pasha Sokoli Mustapha, his successor. The Király Medicinal Bath has never had its own source of thermal springs. The Turks built it here, within the outer walls of defense of the old Buda, and then connected underground piping to the Lukács baths, because they wanted to have their all precious baths in times of siege. Following the recapture of Buda, the König family came to possess the baths in 1796, and they rebuilt them

**Budapest**

blending the old and new in the form we see today. After WWII it was restored. The interior and exterior front entrance are exactly like the original, with bright amber lights and roof skylights that send streams of light onto the steaming water. Today, aside from the pools, you can avail yourself of pedicures, hairdresser, massage, and sauna, as well as the mini-buffet. 1½ hours costs 4,100 HUF. Days for men are Tues, Thurs, 9 am to 9 pm; Sat, 9 am to 1 pm. Days for women are Mon, Wed, Fri, 7 am to 7 pm.

**Rudas Thermal Bath**, Rudas Gyógyfürdő és Uszoda, H-1013 Budapest, Döbrentei tér 9, ☎ 36-1-356-1322, fax 36-1-375-8373, www.spasbudapest.com (click on all-year baths, and follow the links), info@ budapestgyogyfurdoi.hu. Established in the 15th century, it is only open to men, except on the once a month party night... where your basest thoughts can take flight amidst the hot coed cli-

mate when there is dancing, a movie to watch poolside, and service from the staff.

★★**Széchenyi Spa**, Széchenyi Gyógyfürdő és Uszoda, H-1146 Budapest, Állatkerti krt. 11. ☎ 36-1-363-3210, fax 36-1-363-3210 or 3123, info@budapestgyogyfurdoi.hu, www. spasbudapest.com (click on all-year baths, and follow the links). It is one of Europe's largest bathing complexes and one of the top medicinal baths in Hungary, more for ambience and size than specialization. These extensive waters are fun, with warm underwater jet streams and currents. You would never know that its medicinal aspects are famed going back to 1881, when it was known as Artesian Bath. A communal thermal department and outpatients' hospital (physiotherapy section) were officially added in the 1960s. A water chute, underwater aeration bubbling up between your legs, neck

*Széchenyi Spa*

massage, water-jet massage points fitted on the submerged benches can be supplemented with hand massages and special pampering services.

**St. Lukács Spa**, Frankel Leó út 25-29 in Budapest, ☎ 36-1-326-1695, fax 326-1696. You can also reach them on www.lukacsfurdo. hu. In the 12th century the Knights of St. John and the Knights of St. Rhodes/Malta settled near the present site of the Lukács Medicinal Bath. Their avowed mission was to look after the sick and so they built these baths next to their monasteries as an aspect of their treatments. The pump room was completed in 1937. The first full-service medicinal bath section (outpatient hospital) in Budapest was created in the Lukács in 1979.

★★**Aquaréna Mogyoród**, in Mogyoród at Vízipark utca 1, ☎ 36-28-541-100, fax 541-101, www.aquarena.hu, info@ aquarena.hu (in the suburbs; see *Central Danubia* and *Family Places*). Hotels abound with springs and thermal waters in Hungary, but in Budapest, every one of them has Finnish saunas, steam baths, and often pampering amenities such as mud baths, cosmetic and dental care, hydro-massage and Jacuzzis. In many cases you can also use the facilities as a paying visitor and not a hotel guest.

**Corinthia Aquincum Hotel**, located in Óbuda, 1036 Budapest, Árpád fejedelem útja 94, ☎ 36-1-436-4100, fax 436-4156, www.corinthiahotels.com, reservations@aqu.hu, is a five-star hotel that offers perfumed aroma baths, as well as scrub and brush massages and lava baths.

**Danubius Thermal and Conference Hotel Helia**, 1133 Budapest, Kárpát u. 62-64, ☎ 36-1-889-5800, www. danubiushotels.com. The hotel is on the Pest side of the Danube, looking across to Margaret Island. It is three km/1.8 miles from city center, 25 km/15 miles from Ferihegy Airport, and only 6.6 km/four miles from the Kelleti (Eastern) train station. Aside from the thermal baths, they have complete gymnastics and exercise facilities.

**Best Western Lido Hotel & Active Wellness Centrum**, 1031 Budapest, Nánási út 67, ☎ 36-1-436-0980, fax 436-0982, www.bestwestern.com (click on search by region, and then follow to Hungary). A four-star facility, while they do not offer a hot spring, they do combine hot bath treatments with a superior sporting program. Indoor swimming pool, Jacuzzi, solarium, massage salon, sauna, squash court, bowling, tennis court, gymnastics club, motorbaot, rowing boat, kayak, canoe, cycle rental and transfer services make this a base for adventure excursions. When you get back, the beauty parlor offers a hairdresser, cosmeticiain, manicurist, and a pedicurist.

**Danubius Thermal Hotel Margitsziget**, 1138 Budapest, Margaret Island, ☎ 36-1-889-4700, www.danubiushotels.com, is a four-star thermal facility brimming with extras, all the way from doctors (including a cardiologist) to dance aerobics. Since this is one of the centers for sports rehabilitation and relaxation, you may rub shoulders with a European sporting star while you lounge in the thermal waters, or jog on Margaret Island. A number of different thermal pools provide a relaxing ambience quite set apart from the screaming and jumping at some of the more active pools in the area.

**Csepeli Strand Fürdö**, Hollandi út 14, Budapest H-1213, Bus 71 and 71A, ☎ 36-1-277-6576, info@budapest-gyogyfurdoi.hu, www. spasbudapest.com (click on all seasonal baths, and follow the links). This huge park and playground is a favorite of families since kids take to this place like a duck takes to water! It has two swimming pools, a thermal pool, and a children's pool and slides. The separate thermal pools are a

pleasant 38°C/100°F. Open 8 am to 7 pm, May-Aug, and 10 am to 6 pm, Sept-May.

**Dagály Gyógyfürdö**, Népfürdö utca 36, District XIII, Budapest 1138, Tram 1/Bus 133, ☎ 36-452-4500, info@budapestgyogy-furdoi.hu, www.spasbudapest. com (click on all seasonal baths, and follow the links). One of the city's largest complexes, it recently added four new pools. Thermal water is pumped in from the nearby Széchenyi baths for the three thermal pools, which range from 33° to 38°C or 91° to 100°F. Playground, slides, sports fields, restaurant, and free table tennis round out the all-day fun and relaxation Open 6 am to 7 pm, May to Oct, and 6 am to 6 pm, Oct-April. It's at the head of Árpad bridge, in Pest.

**Pestszenterzsébeti Jódos-sós Gyógyfürdö**, Strandfurdo, Viziport út 2, Budapest 1203, open 7 am to 4 pm, Mon-Fri, and 7 am to 3 pm, Sat, ☎ 36-1-283-0874 or 36-1-283-1097, info@

budapestgyogyfurdoi.hu, www.spasbudapest.com (click on all seasonal baths, and follow the links). A small pool for children is paired with a wave pool for bigger fun. However, thermal is the specialty here, and the three thermal pools rovide a range from 28° to 39° (82° to 102°F). Near Gubachi bridge, it is on the suburban bus route for 48 and 51 and it's a HÉV connection.

   The **HÉV** (pronounced Hayv) is Budapest's suburban commuter train. It is part of the urban BKV, or bus system, although it extends beyond the city boundaries. Go to www.bkv.hu and click on hév menetrend.

**Palatinus Strandfürdõ**, Budapest H-1138 (take bus 26 to the Palatinus Strand stop on Margaret Island), ☎ 36-1-340-4505, info@budapestgyogyfurdoi.hu, www.spasbudapest.com (click on all seasonal baths, and follow the links). Open 8 am to 7 pm, May through Aug, and 10 am to 6 pm, Sept through April. We mentioned this sprawling park and pool in the *Family Places* section above; be aware that its thermal pool is set aside from the large recreation pools and so offers like-minded bathers a segregated place in the sun. The park, in the middle of the Danube River, surrounds you with eateries and things to do and see as well.

## On the Waterway

   Hungary has had private water services and tours for over 150 years. We will review the boat tours, then go on to other more personal and sporting water adventures.

## Hydrofoil the Rivers of Central Europe!

Hydrofoil your way between Budapest, Vienna, and Bratislava and many other destinations on one of the most successful hydrofoil cruises in the world. They have a fleet of nine hydrofoils that carry an average of 25,000 passengers each year. From Budapest to Bratislava one way is €68 and roundtrip is €99. Children six-16 are half-price, and those under six are free if they don't take a seat. You can transport baggage and bicycles (add €18 for bicycles) on your trip as well, so it is a great way to combine this adventure with a transfer to Bratislava for your stay in Slovakia.

## Dining & Danube Sightseeing

Folk music and lazy river currents seem hardly compatible, but mix in wine, dining, and a healthy dose of pampering, then join in the dancing and add to that the shoreline of the Danube... you will have a lifetime memory. That's what you get on the **MAHART PassNave Kft.**, 1056 Budapest, Belgrád rakpart, ☎ 36-1-48-44-013, 48-44-025 or fax 266-4201, www.mahartpassnave.hu, www.szemelyhajovas. hu, hydrofoil@mahartpassnave.hu. The cost is 9,500 HUF. From May 1st through Sept 29 this cruise departs from the Vigadó Square Landing Stage every Wed and Sat at 8. Another option is their Wine Districts of Hungary program. While you cruise the Danube in the early evening, from June 17 through Sept 9, the three-hour program includes wine presentations from the best vineyards in different regions of Hungary. Wine connoisseurs from all regions of Hungary take part. Departures are from the Vigadó landing stage, every second Thurs at 7 pm. 5,900 HUF.

Daytime cruises may run between Margit Island Bridge and the Hotel Gellert and include a complimentary drink. These operate from March 27th through Sept 27th, 11 am, 1, 2, 3, 4,

5 pm. And from the first of May through Sept 26th there are cruises at 6, 7, 8:30 and 9:30. 2,400 HUF, with children under 12 given 50% off.

A longer cruise under more luxurious circumstances is the dining cruise on the Danube. These may be on any one of several boats, but if you want to combine Hungarian dining with sightseeing, and you don't want to hire a guide, then study this book and watch the shoreline as you cruise and dine. The base price is 1,600 HUF, and the buffet dining is an added 2,800 HUF (3,200 HUF in the high season, June 15-Sept 5). The afternoon cruise departs at 12 and returns at 1:30, while the evening cruise leaves at 7:30 and returns at 9. Another dining cruise can be taken with music and dance as well, but at a low price of 3,200 HUF for the buffet added to the base cruise price of 1600 HUF. It operates from June 19 to Sept 5. The afternoon cruise leaves at 12 and returns at 1:30, while the evening cruise departs at 7:30 and returns at 9.

The famous castle fortresses of Visegrád (1,050 HUF one-way, 1,680 HUF round-trip), Szentendre (950 one-way, 1,520 HUF round-trip) and Esztergom (1,200 HUF one-way, 1,920 round-trip) are set at the romantic Danube Bend, where the mountains on both sides of the Danube have harbored citadels and fortresses of medieval empires and kingdoms. It is thrilling to see the castles and ancient churches come into view from the deck of the ship. You can also take your bicycle (add 600 HUF).

## Canoeing

Try a canoe... tour the river of history! Use a bona fide licensed canoe agency, such as what we recommend here, or check with the local Tourinform (see *Appendix*). There are numerous river routes open for canoeing, the more famous being the **Danube** from Rajka to Mohács (366 km/220 miles) or the **Tisza River** from Tiszabecs to Szeged (570 km/342 miles). However, there are also many less congested waterways, running through forests and seemingly isolated as you travel by villages where time seems to have stood still for hundreds of years. From Békés to Szeged the **Körös River** offers a 208-km/125-mile stretch, or try the 205-km/123 miles of the **Rába River** from

Szentgotthárd to Győr. Many travel tours will also organize water excursions for anywhere from one day to much longer excursions lasting into weeks.

Canoeing the Danube is one adventure that can be had at an extremely moderate price... but, you must be ready to camp and that means in a tent, and to fix your own meals. However, that said, there is a lot of help and a lot of savvy, and, many of the campgrounds are along the Danube, on private property, secluded, safe and ready for your tent. Under a competent guide you are assured an eco-friendly view of the country-side of Hungary. Canoeing and/or kayaking can be serene, and at once, breathtaking, riding the waves of river traffic, brushing past castle walls or surrounded by forests and reed banks as you hear the cry of the loon in the morning mists. These are for beginners as well as advanced and so the whole family can go. And, the price is extraordinarily inexpensive. Of course, it means that no one is serving you Hortobagy pancakes either. But, then, you can always include the restaurants after or before the river ride. Try a $60 weekend (€43) from Ecotours, ☎ 36-1-361-0438, www.ecotours.hu, ecotours@matavnet.hu. The tour includes a canoe and all necessary equipment except tent (tents are extra), kitchenware for cookouts, water barrels and bottles, first aid kits, trip materials, brochures and maps of the specific regions if available.

The **Danube Bend excursion** begins at Esztergom, the famous religious capital of Hungary, dominated by the famous **Basilica of Esztergom**, which overlooks the plains and the river like a mythical castle, and the medieval **Royal Castle**. You paddle from there downstream, through the Dan-

ube Ipoly National Park, passing the hidden nests of egrets and herons, listening to haunting bird songs and the sweep of the water as it brushes the shore. Optional here is to visit the great for-

tress castle of **Visegrád**, imposing from the river, sitting high above the Danube basin, a monarch of her medieval past, or optionally, you can also include **Szentendre**, which will charm you with her Hungarian folk past. You will also visit Danube Islands and pass by volcanic formations and glens scarcely seen any other way. The tour ends at Budapest.

This is one of many well planned adventure tours from Ecotours. You may also want to consider their once-in-a-lifetime, once-a-year, 240-mile marathon canoe adventure along the Danube and its tributaries. This one, however, is for experienced paddlers.

The Hungarian Tourist board publishes a small magazine, *Water Tours in Hungary*, which is a substantial aid to finding information, learning the rules and knowing who to contact. It is a given in most cases that you should use a tour guide if you are not familiar with the country, and they can also recommend specialists that can make your canoe excursion eventful and safe. The **Hungarian Friends of Nature Federation** (MTSZ), in Budapest district VI at Bajcsy-Zsilinszky u. 31, 2nd Flr. 3, ☎ 36-1-311-9289, publishes a series of maps for water tours, Vizitúrázók térképei (water tour maps).

**Fröccs Vadvízi klub**, H-111 Budapest, Lágymániosi u. 7, ☎/ fax 36-365-1595, www.froccs.hu, froccs@froccs.hu (in Hungarian only) organizes white-water rafting tours out of Budapest to the Soca River in Slovenia and, depending on the number of people in your group, may also work in Hungary or Slovakia. Their home base is Budapest. Instruction, equipment, food, special clothing, and camping are all included. There will be a stop riverside to fix a meal, as the riverhands once did in ancient times. Half speak English. Tours take place in March or April to Oct, depending on seasonal variations in weather.

Aside from the tour guides, you may be one of those who seeks adventure on your own, a confident soul ready to pioneer. Well, there is indeed a safe way to satisfy that wanderlust in Central Europe, just a bit out of Budapest. Hungarian waters have only a few places where there is white water rating other than 1. On the international scale for white water rapids, class 1 means moving water with few riffles, small waves, and few or no obstructions. So this can be a safe and exciting way to see the great cities of Central Europe, for the whole family, while you learn how to handle a canoe in virtually all kinds of rivers and streams.

★**The Great Amber Trail Adventure**, along the Slovakian border, down to Budapest. Although this starts on the northern border, along the Ipoly River, its villages and forest glades, its misty riverbanks and its varied currents give any paddler a feel of Slovakia and Hungary, of mystery and adventure.

The Ipoly River Reserve is one of those rare untouched areas of Hungarian-Slovakian forest, interspersed with dams, roads, trails and villages. Check with The Friends of Nature under *Hiking & Biking* above.

From Budapest, head to Ipel'ské Predmostie in Slovakia. As recommended by the association, it is better to start there than in Drégelypalánk for reasons having to do with border-crossing complications. By car from Budapest take Route 2/A to Route 2 to the Parassapuszta-Sahy border crossing. Then take Route 527 to Ipel'ské Predmostie. Depending on conditions, the trip will take 2½ to three hours. If the canoes and the participants are getting to the starting point separately, take the train from Budapest toward Vác with connection through to Drégelypalánk rail station. From there it is a 10-minute ride by bus to Parassapuszta border station. From the border station you must walk about half an hour farther to Sahy. In the main square of Sahy a waiting area sits astride the stop for the bus that departs for Ipel'ské Predmostie. It will arrive at one end of the town. Walk through the town and continue about 300 yards; just before a small bridge there will be a road that leads off to the right, down to the riverbank. This is your starting point.

The Ipoly springs from the Vepor Mountains in Slovakia and flows 253 km/152 miles to the Danube. It starts at a height of about 3,000 feet above sea level, dropping in stages to 500 feet at Ipolytarnóc. When it reaches Drégelypalánk it is 385 feet. The Lower Ipoly Valley refers to the 80-km/48-mile stretch between Drégelypalánk and Szob.

This is the first stretch of the Amber Trail. On this part, the Korpona and Selomec streams enter from Slovakia, and the Kemence and Böszöny tributaries from Hungary. Due to a relatively small drainage and generally low rainfall, the Ipoly's water flow is relatively small. However, heavy rains can affect the river dramatically, and this must be considered in your trip. Do not plan trips following or during heavy rains. Low water levels (8-10% fullness of the riverbed) and the relatively low decline means a current of about 1-2 mph and a depth between 1½ and 4½ feet. Before a dam, the river current noticeably slows, even though it deepens to six and 15 feet. This same phenomenon is often experienced at curves as well.

The river width is on the whole between 30 and 45 feet. Some gaps are as small as 12 feet, and it widens considerably before dams to between 60 and 75 feet. Summer temperatures range from 22-23°C (71-73°F). In very hot weather it is not uncommon to have water temperatures between 25-28°C (77-82°F).

Going through the Tesa area or the pass at Ipolydamásd, just before it enters the Danube, are the low grade white water stretches. There are also other small stretches of low grade rapids along the river. These offer no problem for the practiced canoeist. For any beginner they will grow your whiskers real fast! There are four dams below Drégelypalánk. You can moor at stairs by each dam, on both shores. You will have to carry the boats to the lower level. Since this requires some packing and unpacking, previous canoeists recommend that you simply camp out at the dams. Since the water is warm, its good for a swim and you'll be fresh for the next day's excursion. However, it is difficult to find firewood around the dams. So, this may be a consideration in what you bring with you (log stove, etc.). Occasionally there are floating wood jams, and sometimes there is a mixture of trash. You may have to get out and gingerly navigate across the logs while you tow the canoe through.

Some of the equipment you may need: Plastic tarps and sheets, waterproof barrels to store personal valuables and essentials necessary to keep dry, water canisters or canteens, sponges, a scoop for water in the boat (a cut-in-half plastic bottle), axe, saw, a good sturdy knife, cord and/or rope for the front and bottom of the boat, string, canned heat, a spray deck, pillow, cellular phone, sandpaper, synthetic resin and fiberglass repair for the boat. You can restock provisions along the way.

Once loaded, from Ipel'ské Predmostie (Ipolyhídvég in Hungarian) you will pass an old stone bridge from the 1800s on the right bank after about a mile. The end of the unpaved road leading to Drégelypalánk is on the opposite shore. For the next 17 km/10 miles haunting bird sounds from rare species echo across the water... this is great on a misty morning. Most cross-river obstacles are in this stretch because it is unimproved and it is not dammed. As you approach the Šahy dam (as you approach all dams, the water deepens and slows) 58 km/35 miles downstream, navigate to the dam stairs, and transfer to the lower level. Don't camp here, but go just a bit farther downstream. You will shortly see the steeple of the church at Šahy, followed shortly by your approach to the bridge for E77 (the first upstream bridge of the city). You can temporarily moor near Šahy and pick up supplies in the main square. The language here is primarily Hungarian, and some English is spoken. Currency is easily exchangeable.

You are two bridges away from a good campsite. The next bridge will be a railroad bridge, where you must be careful of underwater obstructions, as here there are the remains of an ancient wooden bridge, some of which is under water. However, the Presel'any nad Ipl'am (Pereszlény in Hungarian) pedestrian and roadway bridge follows. About 300 yards later on the right bank is an excellent camping site. The national boundaries between Hungary and Slovakia are reached again when you come to the railway bridge at Tésa, passing to the right of the island. If the water is low this may not be so apparent, so be careful to watch your bearings here. But from here on, the left bank belongs to Hungary and the right belongs to Slovakia.

*Letkés*

Anglers fish below Malé Kosihy dam. Dark deep holes along the river banks, interspersed with plant roots are the hiding places of bullheads, barbels, and sometimes pikes weighing five to

**Budapest**

10 lbs. Your arrival at the bridge at Letkés requires a stop to register with customs and the border police, and to re-supply. The Hungarian village of Letkés is on the left and the Slovak village of Salka is on the right bank.

*Visegrád*

Farther downstream, just after the next large bend, mountains veer up on both sides of the Ipolyadamásd pass. Watch for the village of Lelédhídmajor. Excellent camping sites are on the left bank near the island. After the pass, the river flows through a flatland, and you may notice some stands of shriveled trees. It means the colony of herons is nearby, for their acidic droppings damage on the plant life. Not long afterward is a powerful right curve, followed by the rooftops of the village of Szob, and then, after a railway bridge, the mouth to the Danube. Rowing the Danube from here is spectacular, although this deep (at places up to 3,000 feet) and wide river is sometimes choppy due to boat wakes and the ebb and flow from dams. From here, on your way downriver to Budapest, stop off at Visegrád, the famous castle of medieval Hungary, with a spectacular view of the Danube Bend, and, farther down, at the marvelous castle ruins in Vác.

# Central Danubia

Following the slow, winding blue Danube River, just 40 km/24 miles north of Budapest, the world-famous Danube Bend turns sharply from its southeasterly course to flow south through

a gracious and panoramic S shape that has been a favorite viewpoint of photographers from all over Europe. The surrounding valleys and mountains are dotted with medieval castles and villages, a wealth of folklore, artistic treasures and breathtaking natural scenery. It was the home of the early dynasty of Árpád whose strategic defensive positions were at the same time in easy striking distance of the flat plains of the puszta. Fresh bubbling springs and natural resources provided sources of water and materials for weapons and shields. So abundant was the game that it would later be designated a royal hunting reserve by King Mátyás. The regional capitals that encompass this area, **Esztergom**, **Visegrad**, and **Szentendre**, would at one time or another in the turbulent history of Hungary serve as shelters for royal families and be sites of siege from the Turks, Ottomans, and waves of invaders from both directions.

*Danube Bend*

The melding currents of the Danube Bend and the Ipoly River, its primary tributary, form the heart of this region. Set amidst the **Pilis Mountains** and the **hills of Visegrad** on

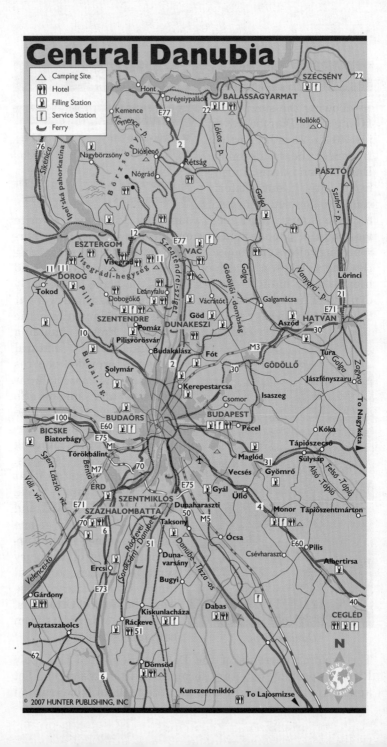

# Central Danubia

*Science Library*

the western shore, and the **Börzsöny Mountains** on the eastern shore, it is but a day's excursion from Budapest, but you cannot possibly encompass its sights and do it justice in one day. Hungarian wines and the rich medieval legacy of castles and villages, serfs and knights and the royal households that once held sway over its panoramic vistas, could fill your calendar for months.

So we have described some hotels for the area as you travel through. And the wealth of trails here make accommodations a must if you want to do some adventuresome exploring.

The Danube-Ipoly National Park, which encompasses both shores, is a combination of scenic valleys and mountains and plains and climate variations that have spawned unique plant life that are today protected species. The Hungarian husang plant is a remnant of the Ice Age, and it grows only in the Carpathian basin. The Pilis flax, which tempts any romantic excursion with its perfumed aroma, is a denizen of the Pilis Hills, and it is one of the Park's protected species.

The primary auto routes are **Route 11** heading northeast, which will take you along the Danube to Esztergom, through Dorog, to **Route 10**, and then back to Budapest. On the eastern shore, you would take **Route 12** along the Danube, between the rising mountains on both sides, through Dunakeszi and Vác until you arrive at Szoba, near the border with Slovakia. You can also drive the western shore, then cross over to the eastern shore via the Island of Szentendre, which is bridged to both sides of the Danube.

We will start our journey on the western shore, and as a favor for those biking or walking, from Budapest, you can take the 45-minute ride on the green coaches of the **HÉV** (on which you can transport bicycles) from Batthyány tér to Szentendre (268 HUF). They run every half-hour from 2:50 am to 1:40 pm. ☎ 36-1-368-8814 (only Hungarian). Remember to order your ticket for Oda-Visa (round-trip). If you have a bicycle, specify *beetseeklee* (bicycle).

Another option is a 30-minute trip, minus bicycles, by bus from Árpád Hid Bus Station to Szentendre. Contact **Volánbusz** in Szentendre, ☎ 36-26-311-996. The buses travel with varying frequency, at 20-minute to one-hour intervals from 6:30 am to 10:40 pm each day. They arrive at Platform 5 of the Szentendre Bus Station, which sits next to the HÉV suburban railway station. From Szentendre you can reach most of the hiking villages in the Pilis Mountains of Central Danubia and buses commute to all main cities in the area (see *Szentendre*, page 229).

From spring to autumn, the colors of the banks change, and so does the feel of the Danube Bend. Bring your camera. Romance and scenery combine on the boat cruises, to Szentendre, Visegrád, and Esztergom. The boat leaves the V. Vigadó tér at 9 every morning, and arrives at Szentendre at 10:40. The afternoon boat leaves at 2. Although it's a bit pricey, snacks and drinks are available on board. Return boats leave Szentendre at 11:45 am and arrive in Budapest at 1 pm, or the evening boat leaves at 5:55 pm and docks at the Vigadó at 7 pm. The cost is 760 HUF one-way, or 1,200 HUF round-trip, payable at the Vigadó boat ticket office. Contact **MAHART**, in Budapest (see *On the Waterway*, in Budapest, pages 200 ff). Another option is the hydrofoil but it is limited to trips between Bratislava and Budapest, Bratislava and Prague, or Vienna and Budapest.

The Pilis and Visegrád mountains are to a great extent part of the **Duna-Ipoly National Park**. The canoe adventure that ends in Budapest begins in these hills (see *On the Waterway*, Budapest, pages 200 ff)). The limestone peaks of Pilis harbor caves and hot springs. The tallest peak is 2,200 feet. In the Visegrád Mountains, water has carved its way through and left huge deposits of andesite to form numerous valleys. The highest point in the range is Dobogókő, which rises 2,100 feet. It marks the start and finish of numerous interconnecting trails, most of which are an easy walk. On the other hand, they can lead to many more strenuous adventures. Dobogókő provides access to Oszoly rock for climbers, to Pilis peak for paragliders, and to Dera Canyon, Vaskapu Pass, and Holdvilág Valley for hikers and mountainbikers. It is also home to a regional museum of tourist history. From this point you can reach the Danube by trails

Central Danubia

that take you through steep rocky canyons, or streams and gentle valleys if you prefer.

Most of the Danube riverbank area has been built up, and not much is left of the floodplain forest that once made the embankment a nature paradise. Yet, there is hope if you take a boat to the Szentendre Island, or cross over to it on the Tahi Bridge from the town of Tahitótfalu. The island, created by the alluvial deposits of the Danube, is 21 miles long and varies from .6 to 2.4 miles wide. It appears almost like the opposite shore of the Danube as you travel Route 11, but it is not. It is easy to understand why the island was the core of the royal hunting lands in ancient times. Willows nod from the shoreline of the floodplain, while in the spring the inner sandy areas sprout needle grass and flowers. Ducks and other waterfowl swim idyllically by the shore, nesting in banks and resting for longer journeys. Fish abound, and it is consequently one of the favorite places for patient casters to snatch bream and pike.

The island is also home to villages that recall Hungary as she once was, as well as some newly constructed areas: Kisoroszi (home to a modern golf course), Tahitótfalu, Pócsmegyer and Szigetmonostor. Farther up, Route 11 opens out to the steppes that take you to Austria and the borderlands of Slovakia and Czech. At the nexus, the glorious city of Esztergom where the magnificent green cathedral dome reaches upward. Kings were crowned in the cavernous sky-scraping basilica and from its gigantic structure cardinals of ancient Hungary delivered the admonishments of papal power in the Middle Ages. Across the river, the steppes of Slovakia reach into the distant hills.

# ■ Places to Stay

## Pomáz

### Two Stars

In the suburbs of Budapest as you head north, for those seeking penny-pinching savings, here's the place.

The **Kara Hotel**, €, about $45 for a double, at Benicsky utca 63, ☎ 36-26-325-355, fax 36-26-525-366, www.karahotel.hu, karahotel@axelero.hu. This is 10 minutes up the road from the Plague Cross and has both pension and private rooms.

| HOTEL PRICE CHART | |
|---|---|
| Double room without tax | |
| € | Under €80 |
| €€ | €81-€150 |
| €€€ | €151-€250 |
| €€€€ | Over €250 |

It's a student's or very low-budget traveler's lodging but don't let that fool you or put you off. Its cellar restaurant is probably the best eatery in town and, for the money, an incredible deal (3,000-6,000 HUF). But it may fool you as you look outside and walk into the main dining area, as there is no hint of the lower cellar. Eat in the cellar and you'll experience the ambience of medieval Hungary, but there is one hitch... no live music. Nevertheless, both price and quality are a bonus here and, in addition to the Hungarian, they have a substantial Swabian (early German-Hungarian) menu. This place is popular with the locals!

## Szentendre

### Three Stars

**Duna Club**, Duna Korzo 5, €-€€, single rooms $41 to $82, doubles $49 to $95. Breakfast included. ☎ 36-26-314-102. This hotel has full facilities, including swimming pool, sauna, massage, gym, satellite TV in all rooms, private phones, tennis court, mini-bar in the rooms, safes, parking, bar, and air-conditioning. The restaurant is also good, averaging 3,000 HUF per entrée.

★★**Ister Kft. Danubius Szalloda Hotel**, Ade Endre utca 28, ☎ 36-26-312-511, ☎/fax 36-26-312-497, www.hotels.hu/

danubius_szentendre, €€, €55 for a double. A three-star hotel, but they are trying hard to make it four. It includes a restaurant (with entertainment), pool, television and private phone, mini-bar and hair dryer connection in every room. 24-hour room service, good English from the staff, and all front desk services, including car rentals and bookings for special trips make this a good value. Good for the money, and it is only a five-minute walk to the town square.

## Two Stars

**Kentaur Hotel**, Marx tér 3, ☎ 36-20-940-6018, fax 36-1-2512-301, €-€€, http://roomservice. hu/hu/hotel/181/ kentaur.html, klau@ roomservice.hu. At €53 for a double, this is a good value. Breakfast is included but because the lack of facilities, keeps it from being a three-star hotel. It's a small family-run hotel with spacious rooms, comfortable bedding, and well-maintained facilities. Satellite television and mini-bar as well as hair dryer and individual bathrooms in each room. But the house bar is open late, so don't expect total silence at 1 am. There is parking in the front and the desk clerk and some of the staff speak English well.

## Visegrad

## Four Stars

★**Hotel Beta Duna Silvanus**, Rt. 2025 Visegrad, PF 24, ☎/ fax 36-26-398-311, www.hotelsilvanus.hu, info@ hotelsilvanus.hu, €€€, €140 for a double. Above the Citadel, on Fekete-hegy (Black Mountain). Part of the well-known Danubius chain, it offers full traveler's services and activities, from summer bobsled to horseback riding. All the amenities, beauty treatments, baths, and various medicinal skin and body therapies seem even better while you sip Tokai wine and watch the sun set on the Danube from your terrace. Both the individual rooms and the terrace restaurant have postcard views. The swimming pool is enclosed with glass walls, allowing you to feel

the glory of the area while you soothe your muscles in the warm water. Medicinal thermal pools, one of 90° and one of 106°F, rise from a natural spring 3,900 feet below the earth. The hotel offers wellness stays and medical staff as well. The rates are actually quite inexpensive, considering the ambience and amenities. Babysitting services, pool, sauna, excellent restaurant, and good-quality rooms are enhanced by the marvelous location.

## Three Stars

**Mátyás Tánya**, Fõ u. 47 ☎ 36-26-398-309, fax 36-26-397-122, €-€€, www.hotels.hu/matyas_tanya. Reasonable and good-quality, although not all amenities are available. The price can shoot up to €70 for a single in the Christmas season, though prices usually range

from €40 for singles to about €60 for a double. All rooms have satellite TV, shower, in-room telephone, and mini-bar. The vegetarian option kitchen is complemented with its own quality wine cellar. Great outdoor ambience and terrace for the summer. Parking is inside the hotel parking grounds.

## Two Stars

★**Hotel Honti**, Fö út 66, ☎ 36-26-398-120, fax 36-26-397-274, www.hotels.hu/honti, hotelhon@axelero.hu. €16 to €24 per person. Although this is rated three-star in Hungary, it is on the low end. Still, it sits in the forest next to the Akátputi stream, about 100 yards from the shoreline and is probably the best deal in Visegrad for quality and price. It combines a small lodge ambience with full services and access to all sports activities, but minus a swimming pool. Air-conditioning and a TV in each room. The restaurant is decent and the service good. Rooms come in singles, or two-, three-, and four-bed options. They all have showers and TV (Hungarian stations). It may be possible to negotiate a favorable rate if you have a large family.There are locked facilities for bicycle storage here as well.

# Leányfalu

## Two Stars

**Hotel Székely Villa**, Mókus út 5, Leányfalu, 2016, ☎ 36-26-383-098, €. Three stars, but I would rate it two stars for lack of a pool. But, there is a sauna, steam bath, restaurant and bar, TV, telephone and parking.

# Dobogókő

## Three Stars

**Pilis Udolohotel**, Tery Odon út 1, ☎ 36-26-347-522, fax 36-26-347-557, €-€€, €20-55, hotel@pilishotel.hu, www.hotels.hu/pilis_hotel. This is a traditional European lodge atmosphere, with amenities. The views are great, and forest and mountains  surround you. Telephone in every room, bar (with live music), restaurant, in-room TV, indoor swimming pool, sauna, tennis court, massage, bowling, billiards, souvenir shop, and parking. The restaurant here is a real bargain, offering good traditional cuisine, from only 1,000 up to about 4,000 HUF.

**Manreza Konferenciaközpont**, Feny u. 1, ☎ 36-26-347-681, fax 36-26-347-633, manreza@manreza.hu, www.manreza.hu. Pricing here has gone to €56 per double for guests who are not part of a conference, with all taxes and fees included. €€. Open year-round. Surrounded by woods, it's a  winter wonderland from its hotel windows. Although the furniture is not new, nevertheless, at this writing the hotel is making an effort to upgrade. Billiards, laundry, wheelchair access, table tennis, and equipment rental for all sports. From here you can explore on horseback (rented through the hotel), hike, ski, or hunt. Bar, restaurant (they also serve vegetarian), parking, phone, television, tennis court. Computer connections in each room.

**Nimród Hotel**, H-2099 Dobogókõ, Eötvös Sétány 4-6. €€-€€€, ☎ 36-26-547-003 or 36-70-455-2153, fax 36-26-348-008, nimrodhotel@axelero.hu, www.nimrodhotel.fw.hu. First- and second-floor rooms, 10,000 HUF for single to 14,000 for double. The third floor is reserved for higher-end apartment accommodations, ranging from 17,000 to 20,000 HUF. Pool, billiards, tennis courts, weight room, and sauna are included. Room service and vegetarian kitchen round out the full kitchen service. Although breakfast is included, for ages 17 to 70 there is an additional charge for the use of the other facilities. There are two indoor swimming pools, saunas, solarium, gymnasium, outside tennis court, ski track, sled run, and the ski run includes a marked cross-country run. The restaurant here is good, and the food a bit pricey. This hotel sits on the highest peak in the Pilis hills and offers unparalleled skiing for this area, though this is not Slovakian or Alpine sking.

## Leanyfalu

### Less Than Three Stars

**Beta Hotel**, Móricz Zsigmond u. 30, ☎ 36-26-381-315, €€, singles to doubles. Rooms have refrigerators, private bath, shower and TV. Built in 1993. A pool makes up for the lack of standard AC, though you can pay extra for AC. You can rent bicycles and they have an indoor pool, laundry dry-cleaning service and at least minimal room service. Although you might get better for the money, it is still not a bad deal.

**Platan Panzió Dobogókõ**, Dobogókõ 2099, Téry Ödön u. 15, www.platanpanzio.hu or www.hotels.hu/platan_dobogoko, platanpanzio@axelero.hu, is about a half-mile walk down the hill from the Nimród. ☎/fax 36-26-347-680. 5,040 HUF per person. The rooms are clean, but bare bones, and you pay cash only in forints. Bar, parking, color television, restaurant.

# ■ Hotels East of Danube & in Börzsöny Hills

## Göd

### Five Star

★**Pólus Thermal Palace Golf Club Hotel**, H-2132 Göd, Kádár u 49, Göd, €€€-€€€€, www.poluspalace.hu, ☎ 36-27-530-500, fax 36-27-530-510, reservations ☎ 36-27-530-520, fax 36-27-530-521, sales@poluspalace.hu. All amenities, spa and wellness resort, golf course, horseback riding, everything needed for pampering... but, expensive. Full 18-hole golf course, where the hills meet the plains between Vác and Dunakeszi. For golf information, golf@poluspalace.hu, ☎ 36-30-400-5611.

## Nagybörzsöny

**Szent Orbán Erdei Hotel**, 2625 Kóspalag-Nagyírtáspuszta, www.szentorban.hu, szentorban@szentorban.hu, ☎ 36-27-378-047 or 36-27-378-034, fax 36-27-378-045. On Highway 12 after Verocé, turn right at the railroad tracks on the road that leads to Kóspallag. Once at Kóspallag, follow the signs. This is a European mountain log cabin lodge. Without balcony, 17,900 for double, with balcony, 21,900. SAT/TV, phones, mini-bar, sauna, pool, and the restaurant serves wild boar and venison, grilled at the covered terrace in summer, with 30 different wines. A separate lower-rated inn has kitchenettes at 35,000 HUF per night, with two or three beds and a shared bathroom. Bonus here is that they provide training in rafting and horseback riding, as wellas sledding and horse-drawn wagon excursions. There is also swimming in the outdoor Olympic pool, tennis courts, an adventure obstacle course, mountain bike trails, walking trails and a variety of other activities. Sçandinavian sauna and a cold pool are supplemented with a beautician and masseuse. It is in an isolated part of the forest, away from crowds.

 **Note:** Nagybörzsöny listings here are for convenience, for travelers not looking for the amenities of star-rated hotels and who want to be in the woods and mountains.

**The Butella Söröző or Borozó**, Hunyadi tér 29, Nagybörzsöny, ☎ 36-27-378-035, with rates from 3,000 to 5,000 HUF per night, is just above the main road next to the Romanesque church. It offers relatively clean accommodations, although the bathrooms are shared. Ten minutes farther on the same track will bring you to the lake, and to the **Nagybörzsöny Kőszeg Vendégház**, ☎ 36-27-377-450. This is 3,000 to 5,000 HUF per night. In the village some people speak English. While it is possible that one of the local villagers may also rent a room to you, your best bet is to book through Tourinform (see *Appendix*) for this area.

## Kemence

As with the above listings, because you are near the border and in the mountains, you may want to stay a night or two. That being said, Kemence has one place worth considering.

**Feketevölgy Panzió** (Fekete Pension), H-2638 Kemence, Pf.5, ☎/ fax 1-36-27-365-153, ☎ 1-36-587-110, fax 1-36-27-587-140, www.feketevolgy.hu info@feketevolgy.hu. It is recommended that you fax or e-mail first if you do not speak enough Hungarian to communicate. It is an excellent value. The basic room rate for a double, per person, is 4,600 HUF, which includes breakfast. But full board is an extraordinary value, including breakfast, lunch, and dinner, at 7,000 HUF per adult and 4,300 HUF for a child. Their facilites include a restaurant, pool, in-room phones and TV, and sauna. There are 18 double bedrooms. The bathrooms and douche are shared. Horseback riding, hiking, fishing, and hunting are all possible out of the lodge. A nearby lake is open for fishing. It is five km/three miles outside of town in the Fekete Völgy Valley off good quality side-roads. They are German, but you can get by on English. Were it not for the bathroom situation, this would be a solid two star. It is clean and a good place for sportsmen or those on a low budget. The food is good.

## Cegléd

★★**Hug Görög Olasz Étterem és Pánzió**, €, 2700 Cegléd, Szolnoki út 15/a. Doubles 7,500 HUF, three-person room 11,500, four-person room 15,000 HUF. Rate two stars and friendly. ☎ 36-53-318-645. Open 11 am to 11 pm daily. Greek-Italian with good Greek cuisine. Breakfast included, heavy wood furniture, parquet floors, cable TV and mini-bar, Internet connection and all rooms have bathrooms and showers, but noise from the restaurant can keep you up.

## Monor

**Hotel Hegyessy Nyerges**, 2200 Monor, Hegyessy tanya 57, pf 2/12, ☎ 36-29-410-758, fax 36-29-414-640, kafkazs@monornet.hu or contact Zsu Zsa Csoltkó Kafka at mobile ☎ 36-30-986-8988. This is the largest thatched-roof hotel in Central Europe. I don't know if there are even any others like it anywhere in Europe. It is only 18 km/11 miles from Budapest along Highway 4. There are 33 rooms, plus meeting rooms, reception area and poolside terrace. Dances and parties are held here, as well as frequent weddings. It's especially popular with Hungarians because of the unusual roof!

# ■ Hotels Southwest of Budapest

## Százhalombatta

**The Hotel Training**, 2440 Százhalombatta, Augusztus 20 u. 6, ☎ 36-23-354-688, fax 36-23-354-985, www.hoteltraining.hu, hoteltraining@hotel-training.hu. €-€€. Just off of the M6 motorway, it has been recently updated and has modern singles and doubles in its standard hotel. There is a separate hostel hotel with shared bathrooms, which are in good condition. Now billing itself as a spa, it offers plenty of amenities, including Jacuzzi and sauna, but there is no pool and it is rather far from the Archeology Park. Neverthteless, they try to please, will help book tours, provide spa services, and some of the staff speaks English. Prices vary from 8,000 HUF for a bare-bones single to 20,000 HUF for a double bed with double bath.

# ■ Places to Dine

## Pomáz

**Kara Hotel**, €, at Benicsky utca 63, ☎ 36-26-325-355, fax 36-26-525-366, www.karahotel.hu, karahotel@axelero.hu, is 10 minutes up the road from the Plague Cross and has both pension and private rooms. This is a very low-budget hotel, but don't let that you off. Its cellar restaurant is probably the best eatery in town and, for the money, an incredible deal (3,000-6,000 HUF). But, as you enter the main dining area, there is no hint of the lower cellar. You need to ask. In addition to the Hungarian food, they have a Swabian (early German-Hungarian) menu. This place is popular with the locals.

| DINING PRICE CHART | |
|---|---|
| Price for an entrée, with tax | |
| € | Under $10 |
| €€ | $10-$25 |
| €€€ | Over $25 |

## Szentendre

**Golden Dragon** (Aránysárkány Restaurant), Alkotmány út 1, ☎ 36-26-301-470, €-€€€, Despite the name, this is not a Chinese restaurant. It is on this narrow side-street ascending from the main square and has been here since 1977. Any restaurant lasting that long has done something right. They serve Hungarian food and, although it is on the pricey side, the food is excellent. Laura Bush and other notables have eaten at this place on the Danube. Every year it is also the site of an artistic extravaganza. Local artists are invited to submit their creations, inspired by the meals of the house. The artworks must be created from cooking utensils. The Rotary Club of Szentendre meets here every Thursday night between 6 and 8 pm. I highly recommend the sour cherry soup Villány-style (spiced sour cherry juice mixed in sour cream, with an added sparkle of red wine from the Villány region). The garlic soup is another treat. Its full-bodied flavor will not son be forgotten (garlic gloves are steamed, taking out most of the acid but retaining flavor, then creamed in butter, mixed in cream and walnuts and ewe cheese). The famous Hungarian goulash is seved here, but, if you are looking for something exotic, try the Dragon's bullion soup, a throwback to Árpád, made with quail eggs and beef marrow, or the steak in Roquefort sauce and walnuts. For the latter, pickled joint of beef is prepared to taste, and then combined with an abundant variety of roast vegetables and potatoes. Walnuts in thick Roquefort sauce are served separately, as a mouth-watering complement.

**Angyal Borozó**, at Alkotmány út, ☎ 36-26-301-255, will not disappoint you. €-€€. The food is good, down-to-earth Hungarian, and the servers are English-speaking. This has the feeling of the country. But Szentendre, like Budapest, is filled with shops and restaurants on almost every street.

Sandwich and a drink? Try **Dixie**, Csirke és Salátbár, 2000 Szentendre, Dumtsa u.16, open 8 am to 8 pm daily, Fri and Sat till 9 pm. €. This will only set you back about 1,000 HUF per person. Yes, they try to be like the southern US here, with decorations to match. Good quality salad bar, cold cuts and bread, with soft drinks or coffee. Low prices keep a body and budget healthy.

★**Visegrad Renaissance Restaurant**, H-2025 Visegrád, Fő út 11, across the street from the Mahart boat landing. Open 12 pm to 10 pm daily. €€-€€€, ☎ 36-26-398-081, renrest@ visegradtours.hu. This is one place where you won't find paprika on the menu. The reason? It wasn't around in the Middle Ages. The menu here replicates what a family in Visegrad might have eaten at the time of King Mátyás. You get a crown to wear (paper). The medieval ambience is helped along by music being played on a lyre. Come for dinner on Thurs nights. This is when knights square off in a duel, with their steel ringing in the hallways, while you eat out of clay crockery with wooden spoons. Reserve well in advance.

**Gulyás Csárda**, Nagy Lajos Kir. U. 4, €-€€, ☎ 36-26-398-329, serves large portion in country style, so be careful of how many servings and side-dishes you order.

**Nagyvillám**, Vadászcsárda Fekete-hegy. This is up on the hill overlooking Visegrad, ☎ 36-26-398-070. Open March-October 12-9, with live music and good Hungarian food. €-€€.

## Dobogókõ

Although Dobogókõ is a town for nature lovers, and the restaurants do not have the glitz of the Budapest five-star restaurants, the food is good, plentiful, and meant to please locals as well as tourists. So, your table values are good.

**Bohem Tanya**, €-€€, is by the parking lot at the bus terminus. Open Mon-Sat, noon to 10 pm; Sun, noon to 6.

Down by the ski lift, past the Nimrod about 1,000 feet and you come to the **Zindelyes Csárda**, €-€€, serving country-inn food inside a wooden cabin.

**Izek Haza** is across from the Nimrod (Fri-Sun. noon-8 pm), €. Plain and simple Hungarian food for the locals.

## Cegléd

**Hug Görög Olasz Étterem és Pánzió**, €-€€, 2700 Cegléd, Szolnoki út 15/a, ☎ 53-318-645, 11 am to 11 pm daily. Greek-Italian cuisine, caviar on ice, meat, fish or vegetarian Mediterranean-style. The staff speaks English. On weekends there is live entertainment, gypsy and contemporary, until closing hours in the semi-covered outdoor terrace.

## ■ Nightlife

The place to be is on the Danube, and no more romantic interlude can be imagined than wining and dining over the picturesque Danube Bend as the sun sets. The **Silvanus Panorama Étterem** is situated in the Hotel Silvanus, and, if evening music and fine wines over the Danube suit your taste, this is the place to be. It is complemented with fabulous views of the valley and a wonderful set of spa pools where you can laze away the night hours. We can say the same of the **Danubius Spa and Conference Hotel**. The range of services through the hotel is astonishing, including horseback riding and hunting, but ending in the evenings with the piano bar, soft music, dancing and, once again, a dip in the hot waters of the spa to cap the night. Sensual, pampered, and delightful.

# ■ Itineraries

## Western Bank of the Danube

### Pomáz

Taking Route 11 or the HÉV, stop on the eastern edge of the town of Pomáz. Mon through Fri regular buses leave the bus station every two hours (on weekends, every hour) headed to the Pilis mountains and the hiking drop-off point at Dobogókõ, an 18-km/11-mile trip. That this is a town with an ancient heritage is attested to by the Roman sarcophagus that graces the outside front entrance of the town hall. Serbians who were fleeing the Turks arrived in the late 17th century. Added to that was the influx of Germans, by the 19th century, and each in turn mixed with the Magyar cultural base.

#### Places to See in Pomáz

**Magyar Neprjzi Gyujtmeny**, Tues 2-6 pm, Sat and Sun 10 am to noon, and 1 to 6 pm. Entrance is 100 HUF. This is an ethnographic collection of folk costumes and embroidery from the last several hundred years. Behind the Transylvanian gate at Jozsef Attila utca 28/b, it was put together by the private collector János Hamar, and covers four regions of Hungarian-speaking communities.

The **Community History Collection** at Kossuth Lajos utca 49 (Kõszeg Történeti Gyûjtemény), daily 10 am to 6 pm, closed Dec and Jan. 150 HUF entrance fee. This is a 10-minute walk up the road past Hõsök tere, on the left of the main road. It re-creates a 19th-century German commoner's kitchen and main room, as well as a Serbian commoner's kitchen and main room. The attendant speaks a little English. The ancient enamel stoves served double duty as boilers, and they each have a hot water tap on the side. Some archeological finds from the area are to the left of the entrance. The Swabian community (German) that was once here was mostly deported back to Germany after WWII. (Once again the specter of history rears its head, touching all the lives of Hungary in that hectic mix of Magyar and German and Serbian and Slav.) It is only in the last 10 years that the community has overcome the painful memories, and reaches out to family connections once again.

The substantial Serb community here is well integrated into Hungary, but has still retained its Serbian identity. Their dance troupe has traveled to Belgrade every year and has garnered prizes for their Serbian folk dancing. Street-corner chatter still rings with old ladies speaking Serbian to each other. Ten minutes farther up Szabadság tér is the **Plague Cross**, which was erected in 1702, and only five minutes off from there, up Szerb utca, is the **Church of St. George**, which holds masses for the community at 10 am on the second and fourth Sun of the month. This monument, as with the famous fountain in the Castle District, was erected both in honor of those who died in the plague, and in hope that God would protect the community from its return. Behind the church is a public square, **Vujicsics tér**, named for Serbian composer Tihamer Vujicsics (1929-75) who was born in a home marked by a plaque on Plegania utca, just beyond. The Vujicsics Ensemble preserves his name in memorium. Though it is now based in Szentendre, it was originally formed in Pomáz, and still plays here frequently.

## Szentendre

**Tourinform Office**, Dumtsa Jenő u. 22, Mon-Fri 9:30 am-4:30 pm and Sat 10 am-2 pm, closed Sun. ☎/fax 36-26-317-965.

Farther up the bend from Pomáz, the "Jewel of the Danube Bend," Szentendre rises into view, dotted with multicolored and multi-textured village homes, crowned with ancient church steeples. It is home to one of the greatest ethnographic outdoor museums in Hungary, an entire village of homes from different areas and different centuries, demonstrations and exhibits in which you can participate, and numerous folk fes-

tivals throughout the year. Check the website, www.sznm.hu. Excellent support data for Szentendre is at http://web.axelero.hu/rozsasand/szentendre/Tortenelem/index_en.html.

Due to its strategic and outstanding natural endowments the place has existed since the New Stone Age. It has been home to Illyrians, the Celtic Eraviscus tribe, Roman legions, Lombards, Avars, and Magyars. The 17th century brought a wave of Serbians fleeing the relentless advance of the Turks. It was here that they settled and built, laying the foundation for the town's unique cultural heritage.

Although the Serbs were the primary settlers in the post-medieval period, the early 19th century brought crop disease and floods that eventually led many to abandon the city. Ironically, that helped preserve the city because the dwindling labor pool discouraged industrialization. As a result, the Baroque heritage is still visible here, as is the Serbian-Mediterranean ambience, with ancient churches and Cyrillic-inscribed monuments. The intellectual and artistic community discovered this place in the 1920s, followed by a surge of tourists in the 1960s and 1970s. Tourism has grown every year since. Today, tourists often outnumber the native population of 20,000, sometimes by as much as 3 to 1 in the high season. And with good reason.

The proximity to Austria and Slovakia, as well as its relative distance from Budapest has led to German, Slavic, and Serb influences, from conquerors and refugees. These have melded with the Magyar heritage, and have led to a unique folkloric tradition.

During the reign of Caesar Augustus the site of Szentendre was occupied by the Roman garrison called Ulcisia Castra (Wolf Camp). Thanks to the Romans, population centers sprang up around Szentendre. These became villages as Szentendre turned into a regional center over time. Today these are a paradise for those who enjoy outdoor activities and medieval discovery. In the fourth century Wolf Camp changed its name to Castra Constantia. The ruins of this ancient city are hidden by a hill located between the S bend of Highway 11 and Bükkös Creek. Today, the **Roman Museum of Stonework** is on the southernmost side of the uncovered town, housing an exhibition of relics found from the Roman era.

As Rome declined, the system of Roman camps and watchtowers was swept away by the onslaught of migrating tribes in the fifth century. Now, only the Roman ruins are left, barely making an impact along the banks of the Danube and in a few places on Szentendre Island.

In later years Szentendre became a regional center for the Lombards, and then for the Avars, who made it their tribal center. Each in turn fortified the place and lived off of its abundant wildlife and fertile soil.

But history would not rest with these precursors. Prince Kurszán and his Magyars stormed through, conquering the Avars and permanently occupying the land. The first documents that mention the town are dated 1009. Then, the settlement was built around Church Hill, the geographic center of Saint Andrew's church, for which the town, at that time, named itself. After the 14th century and a sudden influx of Serbs, its importance increased. It turned into a fortified, walled city, situated midway between the royal castle of Visegrad and the palace of Budapest. Then, during the wars of the Reformation, Calvinists saw that they could retreat to the island in a strongly defensive position and so they moved their villages on to Szentendre Island. Parts of their settlements are still there.

In 1690 Nándofehérvár (Belgrade) was overrun by the Turks. The Serbs, loyal allies of the Hapsburg dynasty, fled for their lives. Listening to the pleas of his defeated allies, Kaiser Leopold granted special rights to 6,000 of these loyalists and settled them in Szentendre. As a result Szentendre remained loyal to the Hapsburg monarchy and never joined the war of independence in 1848-49. However, Szentendre garnered ever more refugees with the passage of time. Greeks joined

the influx, later followed by Catholic Dalmations, and then Bosnians.

Many hoped they would someday return home, so they built temporary houses from wood. Generation after generation, they stubbornly clung to their dream. Perhaps it was the Duna River itself that kept their hopes alive. The Danube always has had a way of preserving memories, and all the communities around it are as much under its enchantment as are visitors. But time brought bitter reality to the fore. The Karlóca Peace Treaty in January 26, 1699 marked the end of Ottoman domination, but that domination merely passed to the Austro-Hungarian crown. The communities that had once hoped they might return to an independent homeland realized that hope would not be realized.

But, once the reality set in, the community that had settled here, and whose children had been born and died here, set about to make its roots permanent. The 18th century witnessed the rise of permanent dwellings and beautiful Baroque churches. As the local population applied itself, the town became known as a home of skilled craftsmen, excellent wines, and industrious merchants. The warehouses and homes of many of these rich tradesmen still stand within the area bordered by Péter Pál, Dumtsa Jenõ, and Bercsényi streets. On the other hand, the narrow houses of the ordinary townsfolk, laced with alley-like streets, are located around Fõ tér. These houses typically have a shop at ground level, living quarters in the second floor, and storage in the attic.

The 19th century saw variations of disease and disaster, until eventually the Serbian community, which had been at 42% in 1815, dropped to only 19% in 1890. An influx of other nationalities, and Magyar citizens, had changed the population mix, not to mention the emigration of older Serbs, still trying to get back to their homelands. The result was that the once-proud

Serbian churches turned into Catholic and/or Calvinist worship centers. Nevertheless, the Serb Orthodox Church has works of gold and silver, as well as fabulous icons. There are two Catholic churches, including the 13th- to 14th-century Catholic Parish Church on Church Hill (with the prominent sundial clock on its face).

In 1888 the Budapest Szentendre rail line was built to usher in the 20th century, but it did not change the character of the place. Then, in 1926, the Art Foundation began to influence construction and preserve the city's character. It has remained a tourist town because of that, maintaining its Baroque ambience while the rest of Hungary aggressively tackles the future.

## Places to See in Szentendre

Szentendre is itself a museum, but, given that, it is also home to over 20 museums and art galleries, with work by some of the most famous artists in Hungarian history, among them Jenö Barcsay, Margit Kovács, János Kmetty, and Károly Ferenczy. A visit to the recently opened **Art Mill** (Mûvészet-Malom) reveals an old mill with the medieval flour maker's trade creating an ambience that oozes around the different exhibits and cultural activities. But of all aspects of your visit here, do not miss what is most famous to Hungarians. Szentendre has the most visited ethnographic museum outside of Budapest in the entire nation, the fabulous ★★★**Open-Air Folk Museum**. Entrance fees run from 400 HUF per person to about 800 HUF per person. It is constructed at the foot of the hills, on 140 green acres of fertile Duna

*Houses from Botpalád and Kispalád in the Open-Air Folk Museum (Péter Deim)*

Central Danubia

*On the grounds of the Open-Air Museum*

land. If you want a real taste of the real Hungary of the past the reconstructed villages and homes are built exactly according to the period and the style of their respective originals, from every period and every part of Hungary. The extraordinarily revealing descriptions from the life of each region are also written in English. Every year, more exhibits are added and new artifacts are brought in. Its grounds are surrounded with shops and eateries, and there is a playground in the back. In addition, tours are offered in English. Numerous festivals held on the museum grounds attract people from throughout the region, not just tourists. Book more than a day if you are interested in history, culture and adventuresome activities. At this museum you can try your hand at the handicrafts as many of the exhibits have interactive demonstrations. Turn the ancient potter's wheel and make your own cookware, bake Hungarian brioche (kalács) and participate in everyday peasant activities of medieval times. Try to arrange your stay in conjunction with one of the folk festivals held on the museum grounds (especially the summer festival), when dancing and music is done in authentic dress, accompanied by skilled musicians playing genuine folk instruments. The website, http://www.sznm.hu/eng/index_eng.html, has descriptions of events, hours and costs. Or call ☎ 36-26-502-511 or 36-26-502-516 (in English), fax 36-26-502-500; sznm@sznm.hu.

The museum has brought other attractions here as well, turning the town into one of the most highly concentrated historical centers in Hungary outside of Budapest.

The following museums and galleries are also based in Szentendre:

*Gate of Kovács Margit Ceramic-Collection*

**Anna Margit-Ámos Imre Collection**, Bogdányi u. 12, ☎ 36-26-310-244, Tue-Sun 10 am-4 pm, Mar 15-Oct 31, Fri-Sun 10 am-4 pm, Nov 1-Mar 14.

**Doll Museum**, Sas u., Wed-Sun 10 am-4 pm.

**Barcsay Collection**, Dumtsa J. u. 10, ☎ 36-26-310-244, Tue-Sun 10 am-4 pm, Mar 15-Oct 31, Fri-Sun 10 am-4 pm, Nov 1-Mar 14.

**Wine Museum**, Bogdányi u. 12, daily, 10 am-11 pm.

**Boromisza Tibor Museum**, Somogyi-Bacsó part 4, ☎ 36-26-310-244.

**Czóbel Museum**, Templom tér 1, ☎ 36-26-312-721, Tue-Sun 10 am-4 pm, Mar 15-Oct 31, Fri-Sun 10 am-4 pm, Nov 1-Mar 14.

**Ferenczy Museum**, Fô tér 6, ☎ 36-26-310-244, fax 36-26-310-790, Tue-Sun 10 am-4 pm, Mar 15-Oct 31, Fri-Sun 10 am-4 pm, Nov 1-Mar 14.

**Kerényi Jenõ Museum**, Ady E. u. 5, ☎ 36-26-310-244, Wed-Sun 10 am-4 pm, closed Nov 1-Mar 14.

**Kmetty János Museum**, Fô tér 21, ☎ 36-26-310-244, Wed-Sun 10 am-6 pm, Mar 15-Oct 31, Fri-Sun 10 am-4 pm, Nov 1-Mar 14.

**Kovács Margit Ceramic-Collection**, Vastagh Gy. u. 1, ☎ 36-26-310-244, Tue-Sun 10 am-6 pm.

**Marzipan Museum**, Dumtsa J u., Mon-Sun 10 am-6 pm.

**Mûvésztelepi Gallery**, Bogdányi út 51, Mar 15-Oct 31, open Wed-Sun 10 am-4 pm.

**Népmûvészetek Háza**, Bogdányi út 51, Tue-Sun 10 am-4 pm, Mar 15-Oct 31, Fri-Sun 10 am-4 pm, Nov 1-Mar 14.

**Roman Museum of Stonework Finds**, Dunakanyar körút, Mar 15-Oct 31, Tue-Fri 10 am-4 pm.

**Open-Air Village Museum**, Sztaravodai út, Pf. 63, ☎ 36-26-312-304, or 36-26-310-686, fax 36-26-310-183, Tue-Sun 9 am-5 pm, closed Nov 1-Mar 14.

**Szentendrei Képtár**, Fô tér 4, Tue-Sun 10 am-4 pm, Mar 15-Oct 31, Fri-Sun 10 am-4 pm, Nov 1-Mar 14.

**Serbian Ecclesiastical History Collection**, Pátriárka u. 5, ☎ 36-26-312-399, Mar 15-Oct 31, Wed-Sun 10 am-4 pm, Nov 1-Mar 14, Fri-Sun 10 am-4 pm.

**Vajda Lajos Museum**, Hunyadi u. 1, ☎ 36-26-310-244, Tue-Sun 10 am-4 pm, Mar 15-Oct 31, Fri-Sun 10 am-4 pm, Nov 1-Mar 14.

**Railroad Museum**, at the Hév Station, Tue-Sun 9 am-5 pm, closed Nov 1-Mar 14.

## Art Galleries

**Aktív Art Gallery**, Pátriárka u. 7.

**Artéria Gallery**, Városház tér 1, ☎ 36-26-310-111.

**Erdész Gallery**, Bercsényi u. 4, ☎ 36-26-317-925.

**Ipszilon Gallery**, Dalmát u. 9, ☎ 36-26-314-332.

**Metszet Gallery**, Fô tér 14, ☎ 36-26-312-577.

**Mûhely Gallery**, Fô tér 20, ☎ 36-26-310-139.

**Palmetta Design Gallery**, Bogdányi u. 14, ☎/fax 36-26-313-649, open 10 am-6 pm daily. Closed Tues.

**Péter-Pál Gallery**, Péter-Pál u. 1, ☎ 36-26-311-182.

**Tasi Gallery**, Mester u. 6.

**Surprise:** In the middle of Szentendre, surrounded by thousands of years of Central European history, amidst the peasant dances, the knights, the legends of battles and glory from the Middle Ages – there stands, in a corner of the Marzipan Museum, a life-size statue of Michael Jackson. Perhaps this makes up for the fact that there is no McDonald's in Szentendre?

## Leányfalu, Tahitótfalu & Dunabogdány

The Pilis Mountains roll steeply down to the meandering Danube waters. They leave little room for habitation on the shore. Yet, only a few miles away lie the villages of Leányfalu, Tahitótfalu and Dunabogdány. Farther up the Danube embankment is the community of Tahitótfalu, the town split in two, half on the shore, and the other half on Szentendre island, connected by a bridge. On the island ancient memories weave the village history of Kisoroszi, Pócsmegyer, and Szigetmonostor, challenged by the newer villages of Surány and Horány, with their weekend cottages. Heading north on the shoreline through the small village of Dunabogdány we arrive at the historic Visegrad.

Leányfalu harbors several hotels and it is no accident because a hiking trail through the town leads to Visegrad, thus making it a perfect hikers' (and mountain bikers') stop after Szentendre (see Places to Stay).

### ★★★Visegrad

Visegrad is not Hungarian, even though it is in Hungary. Actually, Visegrad is a Slavic name. Visegrad means "high castle" in Slav, and it got its name from the Slavic settlement that inhabited the area in the ninth century. The name was never changed, and it has become a part of Hun-

Central Danubia

garian history as a home of Hungarian kings and medieval glory.

As the river turns out of the Danube Bend and comes to Szentendre Island, it branches into a Y around the island. This point is the apex of a 30° angle from the island, looking up to a castle fortress whose towers pierce the sky from its mountain-side position. As though ready for siege today, defensive walls lace the hillside, finally winding down to banks of the river where, under the castle's dominating shadow, the village of Visegrad sleeps, itself decorated with old defensive walls and an ancient lookout tower. Here was the glory of chivalry, the home of the famous King Matthias and the knights of Visegrad. Although the Romans built an advance outpost here, and the citadel itself was standing before the construction of the palace (1245-1255), its true fame began after Charles Robert (1301-1342), constructed the palace high on the side of the hills overlooking the town and the river.

## NAPLES COULD HAVE BEEN HUNGARIAN

Charles Robert (Charles Anjou) was born in Naples, but laid claim to the Hungarian throne through his grandmother. He was given the name King Károly I of Hungary at his coronation in 1308. His reign brought prosperity for the nobles and protection for the church, and, as the power of Hungary under King Charles grew, so did its influence. The Hungarian court became famous throughout Europe. Charles laid plans to marry his son, Andre, to Joanna of Anjou, thus linking Naples to his royal line, and allowing Hungary to lay a legitimate royal claim to this part of Italy.

At the age of six, Andrew, his son, was betrothed to Joanna of Anjou, who was seven and a descendent of the former King Robert of Naples. However, King Charles died before his son came of age. Both Andrew and Joanna were potential successors to the throne of Naples, but she was one year older, and she had a blood line from the previous king. So, in a historic coup de grace, the pope crowned Joanna Queen of Naples, thus circumventing the rights of her husband. This was possible because they were so young. But it could still end with young Andre as a future successor. We will never know exactly what happened, but it was rumored that Queen Joanna hated Andre. "I was sacrificed to a man whom I can never love," she confessed to her lifelong chambermaid and friend Dona Cancha. She later also said "I am troubled by his look, his voice makes me tremble: I fear him." The growing hatred festered until she hatched a plot to assassinate Andre on a hunting trip. The plot was discovered, although she was not implicated. But Andre was surprised and overcome one night in his bed, then hung by a silk cord from a castle window, strangling to death. She claimed she was sleeping at the time and was not involved in the murder, but an official inquiry was launched by the Pope. The leaders of Naples, the Pope, and the royal house of Hungary were enraged. King Lajos (Louis the Great) had succeeded Charles. He was the brother of Andre and vowed to bring anyone involved to justice... including, should it go there, Joanna herself. Her guilt was eventually revealed by the guards on that fateful night, who were imprisoned and tortured, until they gave full confession. Eventually, an enraged mob broke through and ripped her to pieces before she could be taken to the gallows. Over the next 20 years, wars and counter-wars loomed over the city from the powerful Hungarian royal forces, even leading to the sacking of Naples... but the claim of the Hungarian throne over Naples by a legitimate royal blood line was ended.

Visegrad would reign as a famous city of the Middle Ages. King Mátyás (Matthias) lavished his treasure to expand and upgrade the palace whose panoramic views over the romantic Danube are without peer. In 1488, in the height

*King Mátyás & Queen Beatrice*

of its glory, when King Mátyás and Queen Beatrice reigned here, János Thuroczy wrote of the place that its upper walls were stretching to the clouds floating in the sky, and the lower bastions were reaching down as far as the river. It was the protected enclave for the Hungarian crown, with the cross of the Holy Roman Empire kept in a locked and guarded room inside the east wing of the upper castle walls. In the early 1440s Alzbeta, daughter of King Sigismund, stole the crown jewels and surreptitiously (one wonders which of the castle guards were paid off, or which lost their heads as a result) took them to Székesfehérvár to crown her baby son Laszlo as the king.

So it was that the castle and the court of Visegrad were centers of power and intrigue.

Unfortunately, much of the glory is gone, but a hint of it can be seen in the **King Matthias Museum**, Fö út 29. This is about five minutes farther on Fö útca after it joins the highway once again. Continue on and you will come to Salamon torony utca. Go through the Budapest gate of the old castle fortifications. The museum,

*Well in the Museum from the era of King Sigismund*

which is a part of the restored Solomon's Tower, houses portions of the restored palace. It is a marvelous five-story, 13th-century edifice and has most of its original fountains and statues. The Tower was built on top of an even older Roman look-

*Solomon's Tower*

out. It is considered one of the best preserved and largest of the Romanesque Towers surviving in all of Eastern and Central Europe. The tower is part of the 13th-century water bastion defensive system for the castle. Before the construction of the palace, in 1316, it was the defensive center and residence of the royal house, which was forced to flee Buda when the Turks invaded.

The towering **Castle Citadel** is itself a tourist attraction, of course. Today it houses a museum of the history of Hungary and its knights and heroes, where you can range across the moat and visit the embattlements, walk in the knights' hall

*The Citadel*

and kings' throne room, visit the kitchen and the residences as well as see an eye-opening exhibit of ancient torture equipment.

Although most local activity is centered around the ferry and the church at the shoreline, the three main historical sites lie to the north of the city center. All the city sites are easily accessible by walking, but it is a steep hike to the Castle walls above and, if your time is short, consider the bus instead. If you walk, get off the bus at the Hajoalomas (the boat stop, or dock) near the Solomon Tower, and take the trail to the castle. It will take an hour to two hours. Otherwise, the steep hills are definitely for hardy hikers, for all-day treks, or pony trekking.

Three sites are worth considering in the surrounding hills:

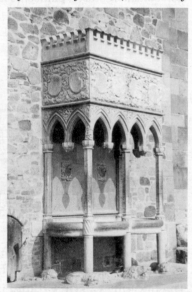

1) The site of an ancient Roman camp, **Sibrik hegy** (Sibrik Hill) from 330 AD, a triangle-shaped fortress north of Visegrad. After Prince Géza moved the capital to Esztergom, he renovated the walls of the ancient fortress and turned it into one of the first county seats of Hungary. It was the headquarters for the bailiff of the region, and consequently held stables, housing for troops, workshops, storage rooms and a prison. A stone building was erected

*Portico from original palace built by King Károly Róbert in 1320-23 (Magyar Természetbarátok Szövetség, Muskovics András)*

for the bailiff and for high-ranking guests. King St. Ladislas held king Salamon prisoner here in 1083. The seat declined in importance with subsequent reigns, and in 1083 it was destroyed in the Mongolian invasion.

2) **Feket hegy** (Black Hill) is a few minutes farther up, southwest from the castle to the adjoining summit (it is also the location of the Hotel Silvanus), and it is crowned by the Nagyvillám (big lightning) lookout. The Nagyvillám melds into Mogyoró

*Restaurant at Hotel Silvanus on Black Hill*

hegy (Hazelnut Hill). Sometimes the Nagyvillám is identified with Mogyoró hegy (Hazelnut Hill), so don't get confused.

3) **Mogyoró hegy** (Hazelnut Hill) has a bobsled run, restaurants, camping, and a year-round game preserve.

Alternatively, you can drive or bike by following our route around Esztergom, and back down on the other side of the Pilis mountains to the same spot, a lengthy and circuitous but beautiful route. Trails lace the area and interconnect at the Nagyvillám and Mogyoró hegy.

If this were a hiking book, we might dwell more on the trails, but there are so many, and the area covered is so vast in some aspects, that we can only suggest you doublecheck with the Magyar Természetbarát Szövetség (Hungarian Friends of Nature Society) listed under adventures, or at your hotel desk. Trails wind everywhere in this area, and so it is a favorite for strollers, walkers, hikers and, on some trails, mountain bikers. It is impossible to get lost up here, because the trail markings are fairly good, and the castle and the Danube easily determine your bearings.

In season, raspberries abound... but they don't last a long time because they are not a protected species. A few trails to inquire about, if you are so inclined, are the **Dera Stream**

**Gorge**, from Pilisszentereszt, and the **Moonlight (Holdvilág) Rill**, a place of ancient rites and worship. They can be reached by hiking trails out of Pomáz, Rám-Szakadék, Hóldvirág (Moonflower Pit), and the Lajosforrás (Lajos Spring).

## THE INTERNATIONAL PALACE GAMES

In early July of each year in this wonderful medieval town they bring back the past with a glorious festival. The International Palace Games in Visegrad are gaining international recognition, and attract people from all over the world to participate. They begin with a medieval parade, complete with a royal couple and knights of the castle. This is followed by several days of jousting tournaments, archery, and swordplay. Minstrels and songs enliven the area, along with street-side booths and many exhibits that may invite you to try your hand at the medieval arts and crafts. Games and exhibits from the Middle Ages abound. Tickets are 1400 HUF for adults and 1000 HUF for children.

## The Eastern Bank of the Danube Bend

As we head north on the banks of the Danube, staying on the Pest side, we enter the rolling hills and the backwater area of the Danube River. It is fed by several streams and rivers, and leads us eventually to the foothills and then the mountains of Börzsöny. We have something of everything here. If you are so inclined, almost every city or village on the shoreline has docking facilities. Göd and Szödliget play host to yachts and pleasure craft on their Duna shores. For Hungarians, skiing is a starved sport in this land of little snow; so they have developed grass ski slopes at Szokolya. The natural wonders, the former volcano (Dél-Börzsöny Csõvár), the Limestone quarry at Naszályu, the Somlyó mountains of Fót, made famous by their grapes, and the Danube's wonderful arteries and byways are intermixed with castles and villages that still retain medieval ways.

Moving east, we reach the northern rolling lowlands of Pest, which is a part of the Great Alföld. It is easily accessible by auto or by bicycle, and there are numerous walking trails. Byways interconnect all points as well. Take Route 12 north, or by train make connection on the oldest railroad in Hungary, via Budapest – the Vác line. On the way, the real character of the countryside can be sampled. However, if you are traveling by car and are looking for top-quality accommodations, stop at the **Polus Thermal Palace Golf Club Hotel** in Göd (see *Places to Stay*).

## Dunakeszi to Fót

The city of Dunakeszi is often called the gate to the Danube Bend. The first written document dating the town was written in 1125. The first census in 1715 counted 18 families. The strength of the region was its agriculture, and by 1870 it was one of the prime tomato producing areas in Europe. But still it remained a backwater hamlet of Budapest until the 19th century, when it was noted that the smooth riding terrain was good, not just for tomatoes, but for horse racing as well. By the beginning of the 20th century, the population had exploded as racing stables and estates began to cover the countryside and swallow up the tomato patches. In the Alag district of Dunakeszi, where horse breeders and racing tracks established the neighborhood, wealth exploded, so much so that the Jockey Club paid all the taxes of the district. Stablemen arrived, not just from Hungary, from Tiszaszolos and Tata, but from other countries of Europe. From as far away as England, jockeys, horses and trainees arrived in Dunakeszi. Wealth led to further industrialization, but also a social

*Fót Parish Church (Magyar Természetbarátok Szövetség, Muskovics András)*

Central Danubia

*Parish church from the air*

imbalance. As always, the stark contrast of great wealth against dire poverty brought its own twisted reconciliation. The area became a center of leftist movements and, as the Russians drew near toward the end of WWII, the citizens of Dunakeszi prevented the dismantling of the railroad and industrial equipment. After the war, going into the 1950s, the area was restored. Today the Hungarian Horse Racing Company cares for it. Throughbreds and trotters are trained, stabled and raced on the hundreds of acres at Dunadkeszi stables, and many have won numerous Austrian and Bavarian derbies. But further inland from the Duna shore, heading east on Kossuth Lajos street takes us to the next community, **Fót**. Here, the income from horses financed the beautiful four-tower Romantic-style **Cathedral** (at Vörösmarty út 2), which was built by Count István Károlyi according to the designs of Miklós Ybl between 1845 and 1855. The count was a great patron of horses and of the arts.

The Károly (Charles) Castle was also expanded using the designs of Miklós Ybl and now this castle's park, ceremonial hall, church and the Vörösmarty wine cellar, can be visited on Somlyó Mountain. Locals in the same vicinity celebrate the **Fót Autumn Festival** (check with Tourinform (see *Appendix*).

## THE TURUL & ATTILA THE HUN

A Hungarian legend recalls Emese, wife of Ügyek, the descendant of Attila the Hun, who once dreamed that the legendary Turul bird appeared to her. The Turul is emblazoned on the gates of the palace, guarding its Danube entrance. She dreamt that a pure clear stream began to flow from her, westward, and that it grew and grew until it became a mighty river.

The Turul told her that she would give birth to a mighty line of rulers, and that they would flow west. The legend bore fruit in fact. Emese bore Álmos, the father of Árpád, the great Magyar chieftain, who led his people westward and founded Hungary. The legend itself justifies the folk wisdom of Hungary, that the Hungarian Alföld and surrounding hills were a rightful inheritance bequeathed by Attila the Hun, and rightfully belonging to them as descendents of the Hun. In actuality, no one knows exactly where the Magyars came from... and there is no cultural or racial proof that they had anything to do with the Huns of Attila's day. Nevertheless, the legend of the Turul persisted, a mythical bird that represented God's power and will. The Turul has been considered by folk legends as the ancestor of Attila and the symbol of the Hun nation. In many reliefs, the Turul is depicted with the flaming sword of God, harking back to the legend that Attila the Hun bore the sword and dominated the world with its power.

## THE SON OF ATTILA

Following the assassination of Attila, the great Hun warrior, the German tribes rose up in rebellion. Many bloody battles ensued, as Teutons battled Huns. In the Carpathian Mountains, the outnumbered Huns were forced to seek reinforcements. Alone, with only a small group of warriors, Csaba, the youngest son of Attila and leader of the Székely tribe, left the scene. He took a group of his greatest warriors and body guards, and fought his way out of the enemy encirclement. He then rode east to raise another army and return to their settled homeland. He made good on his promise, more than once. As time passed, legends grew up around the returning chief and his Hun warriors. Today, over campfires, as the legends are recounted, children look up to the starry milky way and see its river of stars, the Hadak útja (Warriors Avenue), and know that Attila and their ancient ancestors will return with their mighty armies of courageous warriors from the stars, to protect their homeland, and the Carpathians, the heart of the empire of the Huns.

# ★ Göd

The town of Göd sounds like Gerd, as in herd. If you pro-
nounce it like the English God, that will confuse a Hungarian
completely. However, there is an ancient Scythian legend
about the sword of God. According to this legend, those who
possessed the sword were invincible and destined to rule the
world. Based on Hungarian legend, the Isten Kardja (Sword
of God) was acquired by Attila the Hun, a sign that he would
be the most powerful ruler on earth. Afterward, he conquered
the barbarian tribes, and the Roman Empire, uniting his
namesake Huns in the most powerful empire in the world.
The legend identifies the wielder of this sword as the scourge
of God, sent to punish evil and destroy its roots. So now you
know why Attila the Hun was often referred to as the scourge
of God and, all things considered, there may have been some
truth to this.

Göd is one of the most favored weekend resort areas on the
west bank. From spring to autumn the golf course here is full.
From here we next come to Vác, the historical, cultural and
administrative center of the countryside on the left side of the
Danube.

# Vác

What Esztergom is
on the right bank
of the Danube, Vác
is on the left bank.
Vac is younger. As
with many of the
leading cities of the
Middle Ages, the
church was the
reason for the city,
not industry and
not trade. And,
though it is a mere
bishopric, not an

*Vác Franciscan Church & Friary (Magyar*
*Természetbarátok Szövetség, Muskovics András)*

archbishopric, it began with a royal edict from the great St.
Stephen, the first king of Hungary. The Cathedral (at Marcius
15 tér) was therefore built with all the wealth and splendor of

the church at that time, rising over 150 feet, with 12 gigantic Corinthian pillars and magnificent Renaissance balustrades with frescoes and artistic treasures gracing the walls and ceilings.

Other sites include the **Upper Town Parish Church** and the Baroque **Bishop's Residence** (1699-1755), as well as the **Town Council Hall** (1764). All three were the work of F.A. Maulbertsch, probably the greatest exponent of the Baroque-Classical style in the 18th century.

*Vác Cathedral*

The historic center of Vác stretches between Konstantin tér, overlooked by the Constantine Cathedral, and along Köztársaság út, stretches to Március 15 tér (March 15th Square) to the north, which is dominated by the Franciscan Cathedral. The route is lined by 18th- and 19th-century patricians' houses as well as most of the town monuments.

In the ornate chambers of the **Vác Cathedral**, at Konstantin tér (Constantine Square) the **Mori Memento Exhibition**, a medieval burial site, is home to the coffins of adults and children, artifacts, and mementos, from the time when the Dracula legend supposedly was born.

Vác, being a respectable town, would not be without its **Holy Trinity Statue**. It's on Szentháromság tér (Trinity Square), and it is today considered one of the finest monuments in the country (1750-1755).

Another world-class monument is the classical Baroque **Stone Gate**, a triumphal arch erected for the visit of Maria Theresa in 1764. It was built by Bishop Migatti on Köztársaság út. Only a few years before that the Baroque **stone bridge** (1753-1757) was built over the Gombás Stream. Today it's a protected monument dominated by six large stone statues. But since you are on the Danube shore, going north out of town, stop and take a walk along the Danube embankment, gaze across the river to Szentendre on the opposite bank, and cast your eye over the natural flatlands of the Danube shore, home to herons, grey herons and cormorants. Often you can watch them take flight, gracing the sky with the liberty of their wide-spread wings.

Try the **Spring Festival** here, which is an extravaganza attracting regional and national talent, and the **Vác World Festivities**, or the **International Gregorian Festival** which brings echoes of heaven into cathedral concerts. Then there is the more hedonistic, Magyar cultural statement, the **Vác Wine Festival**. As with many other events, information about these events is available through Tourinform (see pages 571 ff).

## Vácrátót

From Vác we can turn away from the Danube to discover inland sights as well. One of Hungary's richest plant collections is in the nearby **Vácrátót Botanical Garden**, open daily 8 am to 6 pm, Oct-Mar 8 am-4 pm.

*Photo by János Scheffer (www.schefferj.ps.hu)*

Entry is 160 HUF. The botanical garden is gigantic, at almost one square mile. Count Vigyazo founded it in the 1870s. He bequeathed the garden to the Hungarian Academy of Sciences. Waterfalls, artificial stone hills and mountains, mock ruins, forest-like glades and the garden itself will take anywhere from two to three hours to walk. The lake, overshad-

*Photo by János Scheffer (www.schefferj.ps.hu)*

owed with willows and brush, is a romantic delight. Over 12,000 species make this the largest collection in Hungary. Coordinate the visit with one of their summer concerts in the garden. Tickets are at the Philharmonia ticket office in Budapest. Turn east off Route 2, north of Szõdliget (five km/three miles before Vác) or by bus from the Nyugati train station (1½ hr) or by bus from the northern end of the blue line metro (Újpest).

## Route 12 – the Unknown Danube Bend

The rolling hills of Verõce, Kismaros, Nagymaros, Zebegény and Szob sprouted vineyards, next to chestnut orchards, in the 15th century. The wine produced here joined other renowned Hungarian wines in the Middle Ages. These were called Ezerjó, Mézes fehér and Budai zöld. Today the wines produced are varieties of Italian Riesling and Cabernet Sauvignon. In the 19th century an infestation of phylloxera, a serious vine pest, wiped out the grapes. The disaster was less serious than in some areas of the world, where the climate and soil were not so resilient. The local farmers turned to raspberries and currants, while they worked to bring the vineyards back. Today, raspberries and currants are still significant crops here.

### Verõce

Continuing above Vác, the next community to catch our attention is Verõce. At the beginning of the 20th century, the town was filled with writers, poets, and musicians. Many of the villas that look out on the Danube from the

shoreline were built then. The house of **Géza Gorka**, Verõce 2621, Szamos út 22, one of Hungary's most significant ceramic artists in the 20th century has been made a museum, where the collected works of Géza and his daughter are on display, joined by other contemporary exhibits from the area. At this writing hours and fees have not been settled yet.

## Kismaros

Kismaros is almost a part of Verőce, and among its highly regarded historical buildings are the Roman Catholic Church and a village museum, which has recordings from the old Swabian era. The town also preserves and nurtures its tradition through its **Marus Days**. These are a celebration of rural farming and culture that now emphasizes preservation of the ecology and history of the Danube Bend as well.

## Szokolya

From Kismaros, walking toward Szokolya, the onion-shaped steeple of the **Calvinist Church** rises up in the distance. Ádám Mányoki, one of the most important painters of the 18th century and court painter to Ferenc Rákóczi II and to Ágost Erős, Saxon Prince-elect, was born here in the Calvinist rectory.

## Nagymaros

In 1709 a plague practically wiped out the population of Nagymaros. The population today is made up in part of Germans who were relocated here in 1715. The **Roman Catholic Church** is a reconstructed edifice from its days of glory, but the tower has retained its 13th-century Gothic form to this day. The town also celebrates the memory of Kálmán Kittenberger, the great African hunter and writer (See *Gödöllő*). Every year they hold a two-day **Kittenberger, Kálmán Days** festival, which features African booths and contests, and workshops, taking place at Nagymaros 2626, Nagymaros város Önkormányzat, Fö tér út 5.

## Zebegény

The railroad and the road hardly leave enough space along the riverbank for the lovely town of Zebegény. The picturesque **Parish Church** in the village was built in the Hungarian Art Nouveau style. The two renowned architects, the Transylvanian Károly Kós and Béla

Jánsky, designed it in 1908. The Art Nouveau wall paintings in the church were done by students under the direction of Aladár Körösfői-Kriesch, the founder of the Gödöllő Art Community (see *Gödöllő*, page 185). The church has concerts every summer. Nearby, the Nine Stations of the Cross lead up Calvary Hill to the classical **Calvary Chapel** (1853). The **Trianon Memorial** (mid-1930s), designed by Géza Maróty, sits next to the chapel. A lookout with a wide-ranging panoramic view of the Danube Valley sits near it.

*1918 work by István Szőnyi*

One of Hungary's most notable figures of modern art, **István Szőnyi**, immortalizes the landscape and the people of Zebegény in his works. Although he was born in Budapest in 1894, he later settled in Zebegény. He exhibited the resistance to oppression that has been so much a part of Hungarian culture. During WWII, he put his talents to work, and in partnership with his son, forged documents for those seeking to escape the Third Reich. He was awarded the Bronze Medal of Liberty in 1946. His memorabilia, paintings and etchings are preserved in the house where he once lived (now a museum).

Ironically, here in the mountains, far from the sea, the **Shipping History Collection** features the lifework of retired Captain Vince Farkas. The old **windmill**, built in the 18th century, brings you closer to the transition into the mechanical age, highlighted by the historic **seven-arch railway viaduct** (1851). Marked **hiking trails** lead from Zebegény to a series of interconnected trails that will take you to the more distant peaks of the Börzsöny. The annual **Dunakanyar Art Week**, 2627, Zebegény, Dunakanya Kulturális Alapitvány, Dózsa György út 26, attracts classical music groups, singers and folk dancers, and has exhibits from throughout the region.

## Szob

Szob is on the border between Slovakia and Hungary, but forget about crossing here, as it is not open to cross-border traffic. For that reason, few tourists venture this far north on the Danube routes. As a result, the area gives you a taste of untainted Hungary. If you want a quick tour without visiting villages, try **The Börzsöny Museum**, Haman utca 14, Mar-Oct, Tues-Sun 10 am to 6 pm, Nov to Feb, Fri-Sun 10 am to 4 pm, 300 HUF entry. Folk costumes and tombstones are displayed here, as well as samples of petrified trees from the region. But don't come only for this museum. Here in the mountains and lower hills of the northern Danube Bend, you will find treasures, both geological and man-made. And Szob, like Zebegény, offers a number of programs, including the **Danube Bend Art Days**, where the villages of the area, with their extraordinary wealth of folk culture, join with the artists who come here.

## ★★The Ipoly River & the Duna-Ipoly National Park

The Ipoly River meanders along the northern border of Hungary, a dividing line between the mountains of Slovakia and Hungary. Its waters also define the borderline of the Börzsöny Mountains, which range west to end in their plunge to the romantic Danube. A jagged surface and volcanic rock, pillars and peaks, steep causeways and canyons characterize the range. The highest peaks are Csólvanyos (2,700 feet) and Nagy-Hideg Mountain (2,600 feet). One can scarcely discern that they line the perimeter of an ancient volcanic crater. They are thick with forests of Austrian oak and blue beech. Nevertheless, while some parts of the protected Danube-Ipoly National Park allow you to wander freely, other parts require you to stay on the designated hiking trails. Their rugged isolation has preserved one of the most fascinating areas of Hungarian folk culture, going back thousands of years.

The villages and surroundings are the home of the **Palóc people**, whose origins pre-date even the arrival of Árpád. On the border between Slovakia and Hungary, the Hungarian ethnic influence has not totally overridden their regional identity and, as noted by Ferenc Bako in his monumental work, *The Palóc People*, they are a transitional group. You will find most of their villages remain as they were a thousand years ago, even down to the costumes. The folk tradition is so strong that individual towns and villages have retained their own special dress since before the advent of the steam engine... and the women can be seen in their famous bonnets and, if you're in the know, you can still identify the village origins of a denizen by the blend of colors and patterns in their dress. A number of the villages have retained language characteristics that completely set them apart from the Slavs to the north, and from the rest of Hungary. As such, driving through, hiking, biking, or busing from village to village in this region, is a rich adventure in cultural and ethnic history.

*Palóc*

The there are the flora and fauna of the Börzsöny Mountains, home of 70 protected species of plants and more than 100 protected species of birds, deer and boar and smaller mammals. In winter, snow stays a long time on the former volcanic caps and in the enclosed valleys. This is ideal cross-country skiing territory, but minus the challenge of the Alps or the Slovakian peaks. At the same time, an abundance of trails and bike pathways are interspersed with rest areas at lookouts and glades.

## Márianosztra

The medieval religious imprint persists today, no more evident than in this out-of-the-way area as we one trail heading inland away from the river. From Szob we can follow the footsteps of the Pauline monks, who started here and headed into the middle of the forest in the 14th century, where they built a monastery that still stands today in Márianosztra. It is a nine-km/5½-mile walk or, if you prefer, drive or take the hourly bus. Márianosztra is one of Hungary's best known pilgrimage destinations. Built on medieval remains, the inner sanctuary of the Baroque parish church contains an 18th-cen-

tury copy of the famo*us* **Black
Czestochowa Madonna** (the
original was taken to Poland in
1382 by Hungarian monks). The
believers who make the pilgrimage in July, September, or December can see the **Calvary Chapel**
and **Stations of the Cross**, built
in 1772, on the eastern edge of the
village. The interconnections
across the countries of Europe are
at times astonishing.

## The Borderline Trail from Szob to Nagybörszöny

The road winds out of Szob, heading up the Ipoly River valley.
Willows and alders along the riverbank give shade for those
who come to fish. The forest shimmers in virtually every
shade of green. Birds and animals hide, but you feel their
presence and sometimes you see them. At Letkés the bridge
spans the Ipoly to Slovakia, but offers entrance only for locals.
However, we are going farther up the river. Romantic fairytale hollows dot the riverbank. As you go through Letkés and
Ipolytölgyes, there are also walking trails, which eventually
lead you to a road marked for Nagybörszöny. Alternatively,
you can drive, bicycle, or bus from Szob directly to
Nagybörszöny.

### Nagybörszöny

Nagybörszöny is among the oldest towns in the Ipoly Valley.
Up through the 18th century, it was a prosperous gold, copper,
and iron mining town. But eventually the ore gave out. Now,
it is a minor logging town, home to four churches of unusual
historic value. The **Bányász (Mining) Church** was built in
Gothic style, replete with mining symbols and decorations
carved with hammer and chisel on the wall. Just below it is
the **Mining Museum**, open Tue through Sun, 10 am to 4 pm,
Petőfi utca 19. Explanations are in German or Hungarian, not
English, although much of it is self-explanatory. 200 HUF
admission.

But what is a Gothic village without its **water mill**? In Europe, there are few water mills still in operation from 200 or more years ago, but the mill at Nagybörszöny is still going strong, and it is an open museum, Tue-Sun 10 am-4pm. 100 HUF admission. The gigantic carved wooden wheels and stone grist still work as they did centuries ago.

One of the most beautiful monuments of the Árpád era, the **Nagybörzsöny Saint István (Stephen) Church** has been

here since the 13th century, on the left as you enter the village. It was basically abandoned after the 15th century and left as a cemetery chapel. If either one or both of these buildings are closed, it is almost an adventure in itself to get inside. Go to Petőfi utca 17 and ask for the key – "Kérek a templom kulch, Szabad latni?" They are monstrous medieval keys.

Having experienced this village, you may want to walk, drive or bike to the nearby towns of **Ipolytölgyes**, **Vámos-mikola**, **Bernecebaráti** and **Perőcsény**. They are

*Nagybörzsöny Saint István Church (Hungarian Institute for Culture)*

all are within walking distance, and all have their own Baroque monuments and churches, thatched-roof buildings, and the hospitable Palóc people. However, there is one place in the Ipoly National Park – Szent Orbán Erdei Hotel – where you can choose a wide variety of accommodations, and be greeted in English (See *Places to Stay*).

## Kemence

The 12th-century Kemence is a walk back in time, amidst archaic houses and crooked streets. This is also a Palóc town. There is a small village museum, and much of the town retains its turn-of-the-century ambiance. The town is favorite starting point for hunters and ramblers heading into the Börzsöny Mountains, and many of them start by riding on a piece of history – the Kemence Forestry Museum Railway, a restored line that was originally built in 1910. It still takes passengers into the forests and mountains of the region. Though a series of floods in the 1990s wiped out bridges and substantial parts of the rail line, it was subsequently restored with a combination of new technologies. The line is what remains of the once-active gravity run mining train. Horses pulled it uphill to the mines, and then gravity was allowed to bring it down again. Today, the class MD-40 locomotive is working again, and it pulls restored open-air coaches up and down the line about 20 km/12 miles. The ride is beautiful and there is a chance to see wildlife along the tracks.

## Down the South Side of the Börzsöny

Leaving the eastern peaks of the Börzsöny, we turn and head down the mountain range, once again facing Hungary, and heading southeast. The slopes are gentler here as we leave the volcanic remains of the Ipoly Valley and wander instead down gentler slopes. The highest peak, the 2,800-foot Csóványos, is easily scaled via mountain trails. The forest here is full of blue beech and Austrian oak. The alder forest of Drégelypalánk or the red pine forest of Diósjenő seem almost mystical, at times wrapped in fog and filled with ferns and dew-dropped plants. The area is rich in pheasants, rabbits, and deer and more than 100 protected species of birds. The variety of plant life and the many shades of green in the spring are astounding.

### Hont

Farther north, we arrive at Hont gorge. About 30 minutes' walk from Drégelypalánk, the canyon here is reputed to be the ancient riverbed of the Ipoly River. Pleistocene fossils fill the soil, testimony to a time that was as rich in flora and fauna as today. The town of Hont shows the influence of Slovakia, with a village memorial to the divisions of a tortured land. It was once part of the larger county of Hont in Slovakia. But, in the treaty of Trianon, the Ipoly River was used as a dividing line between Czechoslovakia and Hungary, and so Hont, and its sister Slovakian community of Bánk, south of the Ipoly River, fell into the territory of Hungary and have been Hungarian since. The **Slovakian Regional House**, with its open chimneys, has displays on Slovakian peasant clothing and lifestyles. The 20-acre lake remains the major attraction of the town. It is a center for boating, swimming and fishing. But for anything lively you'll have to wait for the **Bánk Summer Festival**, when they hold concerts, folk music, and dancing at the waterfront stage and booths spring up with souvenirs and cultural exhibits.

## Drégelypalánk

Drégelypalánk stands under the shadow of a famous medieval **castle** of the same name, whose battlements rise atop a 1,300-foot-high volcanic cone. Though the castle of Nogrod is much larger, this one is beyond doubt the most famous of all in the area, and its histori-

cal legend has echoed all across Europe. Inside the walls of the 13th-century structure that once stood here, 146 Magyars under the command of György Szondi, watched with swords, bows and arrows and catapults at the ready, as an army of 12,000 Turks surrounded their beleaguered garrison. It was 1552, at the height of the Turkish advance, and castles had fallen everywhere to the merciless attackers. But at Drégelypalánk, the Magyars resolved they would die fighting, sword in hand, to the last man. For 4 days they beat back attack after attack, and, true to their oaths, the castle was only taken after an overwhelming crowd of Turkish pike men finally thrust through the very last defender. Today, only the ruins remain atop the volcanic mound, but you can still imagine the hordes below, and the heroic stand of the Hungarian knights. The Magyars had blunted the offensive. The Turks never advanced beyond this point. And, in open acknowledge-

**Central Danubia**

of the defenders' heroism, the Turks themselves erected memorial graves to the valiant few whose bravery had stopped their entire army.

## FALLING IN THE WELL

 Because medieval villages were often isolated from each other, and because entertainment was difficult to find, young boys and girls felt a wanderlust. As a result, local cultures not only created types of dress and manner, but often tried to provide variety and excitement for the local youth to keep them from departing. This led to village playhouses or, as we call them today, youth centers, where young people could meet for fun and games. This was no better demonstrated than in the village of Ormansag, where they played "falling in the well." A young girl or boy had to be pulled out of a well, but at the price of giving a kiss to the rescuer – one kiss for each meter of the well's depth. It was said that Ormansag had the deepest wells in Hungary, and the smallest number of teenagers leaving to seek marriage elsewhere.

## Diósjenő

Diósjenő is the eastern Börzsöny's most important excursion center. Numerous trails lead off into the Duna-Ipoly National Park. Its 75-acre lake is one of the favorite spots in this part of Hungary for watersports.

## Nógrád

The famous writer whom no one knows, "Anonymous," whose statue graces the city park in Budapest, wrote about Nógrád in his chronicles. The **castle** remains at Nógrád are testimony to an ancient past, some of the oldest castle ruins in Europe, built between the 11th and 12th centuries. Árpád gave Nógrád and its surrounding lands to some of his top chieftains. The villages Jenō, Keszi, and Tárjan, in Nógrád County, still retain the names of the chieftains who once occupied them. At Nógrád they promptly built up the earthen ramparts that were already there, and then built this castle. The effort was not isolated – the entire Nógrád county area was dotted with defensive citadels. The proximity of this area to Buda, however, made it a prime target for the invading Turks. Between 1553 and 1554 every Nógrád county stronghold fell to their merciless armies, who retained a stranglehold on the region until the 16th and 17th centuries. The returning Christian armies under the Hapsburgs swarmed across the land, driving the Turks out of Buda and then marching forward to rid the land of the invaders. But Nógrád never came under siege. Legend has it that the castle was taken without firing a single cannon. On the 19th of August, 1685, the castle was struck by lightning in a storm as the crusaders advanced. While parts of the walls crumbled around them, the Turkish garrison, sure that the forces of heaven had intervened, panicked. Casting fearful looks to heaven, they either fled or surrendered without firing a single arrow or striking a single blow.

## Rétság

The Baroque **Roman Catholic Church** with a single nave was consecrated in honor of Saint Andrew in 1729. The geographic location of the town and its excellent connections via train and bus to Budapest and to the river make it a great starting point for exploring the surrounding area. The **Penny Cup Horse Race** and the **Nógrád County International Festival** make a longer stay in the town worthwhile.

## Bánk

Just a little town, connected to Nógrád, although it does house the **Slovak Minority Exhibit** in an old peasant house. 2653 Bánk, Petōfi út 94, ☎ 36-35-300-168. Open May 1 to Oct 31, Tue-Sun 10 am to 2 pm. Free of charge.

**Central Danubia**

## CONSIDER THE CONSEQUENCES

If you have ever complained about a rickety plastic chair, consider what could happen if it were a stone throne, Hungarian that is. King Béla I, of Hungary had been ruling Hungary for three years, reigning from Dömös, when one day, as he sat on the massive stone throne, it began to sway, then toppled over and killed him.

## ★★Gödöllõ

A walking tour of this large community must start at its heart, the Grassalkovich Palace. It is within easy driving distance of Budapest, or a short day's bicycle excursion. From the Keleti Train station you can also get to the same destination by what is called a local train, as well as the more conventional long distance trains. The local train makes numerous stops to connect the towns and villages in outlying areas, including Gödöllo.

The trip takes you through hills and rolling landscape with tall grassland and deciduous forest. The average height of the terrain is 750-900 feet, and it extends from the eastern edge of Budapest to the western part of the Mátra Mountains, and from the northern part of the Alföld to the Nógrád Hills. Between Fót and Mogyoród, flatlands predominate, like the Plains States of America. Gradually the landscape changes around the city of Gödöllõ, where we find rolling hills interspersed with sand dunes, and hills covered with loess (windblown silt). It is today a protected natural environment and can be reached by taking the M3 route, or alternatively, the HÉV or normal train from Budapest from the Keleti station.

Here, gleaming white in the summer sun and surrounded by green park-like grounds and a game preserve, **Grassalkovich Palace**, the summer palace of the onetime Hapsburg King Franz Josef and his wife Elizabeth (Sisi), stands like a fairytale edifice, one of the prime examples of

Baroque in the entire nation. It is open year-round except Dec and certain holidays, 10 am to 6 pm, Tues to Sun, ☎ 36-28-418-124, www.kiraly-kastely.hu. From Budapest it's about 50 minutes. If coming by train, get off at the Szabadság tér station of the HÉV suburban railway. It leaves from Ösz Vezére tere in Budapest. At the Szabadság tér station there is a small museum dedicated to the royal couple (this was once the reception house for the summer palace). You must walk southeast and cross Ady Endre út to

*Grassalkovich Palace (Magyar Termés-zetbarátok Szövetség, Muskovics András)*

get to the palace grounds and museum. The bus stop for the VOLAN coach line from the Népstadion in Budapest is farther to the northwest. Walk back from the bus stop along Szabadság tér to the intersection of Ady Endre and turn left; or, if you are adventurous, you can walk through the park in the same direction. Alternatively, take the train from the Keleti train station to Gödöllõ and get off at Szabadság tér station.

As you would expect, the communists used the palace as a military barracks during the Soviet occupation. Built in 1741, it is named after its original owner, prince Antal Grassalkovich, the former friend and confidante of empress Maria Theresa. Hungary bequeathed it to Franz Josef in 1867 after his coronation as the emperor of the Austro-Hungarian Empire. From 1867 to 1916 the Hapsburgs lived and entertained in its glorious grandeur. The living quarters of the royal couple, comprising 26 of the rooms, have been meticulously restored and filled with period furniture. Queen Elizabeth's memoirs are displayed, along with mementoes of the Grassalkovich family, who originally built the palace.

While on the grounds, you can pick up an espresso at the café, purchase a memento at the gift shop, or make use of the local photographer for a life-long memory. Each of the seasons brings an event, often accompanied by evening festivities in the ballroom or in the courtyard of the palace. The **Liszt Ferenc Piano Festival** (end of Oct) and the annual **Harps Festival** (second week of Oct) are gaining recognition as international musical events. More regional but just as musical and entertaining are Gödöllő's **Spring Festival** (the last two weeks of Mar), **Baroque Palace Days** (first week of Aug) and the **Palace Concerts Chamber Music Festival** (last half of June through the first week of July).

The 78 acres of its surrounding parkland shelter rare species of plants and aromatic blossoms in season. Following the standards of most dynastic palaces, the gardens were landscaped in traditional French style, with a center circle and radiating rows similar to the gardens of Versailles. In later years, after the wars, the English style was incorporated into the design. Cypress trees and flowers and an abundance of green shrubs set a relaxed country mood that was the preference of Queen Elizabeth. On the other hand, it is a unique experience to sit for a summer concert in the southern wing Baroque theater. You can be sure that you are sitting where a duke, a prince, or perhaps a queen once sat. It seats only 100 and remains exactly as it was when the Hapsburgs entertained the royalty of Europe with operas and performances the prince's 24-man orchestra.

Gödöllő is today the center of the Agricultural University of Hungary, and accordingly, the **Agricultural Museum**, Péter Károly utca 1, ☎ 36-28-410-210, open Tue to Sun 8 am-4 pm, Sat 8 am-2 pm. It has a complete collection of historical artifacts and exhibits on food production and cultivation in the county, including various ancient wood implements.

★**The Town Museum**, 2100 Gödöllő, Szabadság tér 5, ☎ 36-28-421-997, across from the train station, offers a unique tour of the town, the Secessionist Tour. Call ahead, and they will provide an English-speaking guide. The Secessionist Period was at the turn of the 20th century, when Hungarians pursued their own unique style of art and architecture. The tour includes the Nagy Sándor House, 36 Körösfői út (his stained glass work titled *Sisters*, with its angular forms and contrasting motifs, is on display

*Nagy Sándor House*

at the museum), Belmonte Leo's house (34 Körösfői ut), the Körösfői-Kreisch house (28 Körösfői út), which bears a signed memorial plaque, Remsey Jenő's residence, 6 Körösfői út, the Weaving School, 47 Körösfői út, and the cemetery.

The Art Colony that flourished here was less than a mile from the museum and became famous for its Art Nouveau creations. Founded by Aladár Körösfői-Kreisch, the Colony's artists incorporated elements of the peasant culture and of everyday life into their art. It revolutionized Hungarian artistic history. Starting in 1904, they established their School of Weaving, where they spun and wove their own clothes and used natural vegetable dyes from the plants of the country. But it was much more than clothing that they brought to their enterprise. Their long, loosely fitting clothes, with Grecian sandals that duplicated the simplicity of peasant wear, were an attempt to incorporate the natural elements of the world around them. Furniture, clothing, glasswork, ceramics, leatherwork, pottery, their homes, their gardens, were considered art. Their lifestyle included vegetarianism, exercise, and cleanliness of body and mind. The Colony also emphasized education, producing numerous children's books and toys modeled after folk traditions, for which they made regular study trips into the country. Their combined efforts were recognized in international exhibits in Milan, St. Louis, and Turin. Commissions to work on buildings of national importance followed. As individuals and/or in groups they have worked on the Parliament Building and the Music Academy in Budapest and on numerous churches and public buildings.

The Colony was home to some of the great artists of Hungary from 1901-1920. Their works are still studied today.

## Máriabesnyő

The town of Máriabesnyő, now basically a suburb of Gödöllő, hosts tens of thousands of pilgrims each year to visit the miraculous 13th-century ivory figurine of Mother Mary and Baby Jesus at the **Capuchin Abbey of Máriabesnyő**. This is also the location of the tomb of the Grassalkovich family dynasty.

## Száritópuszta

From the intersection of Szabadsag út and Ady Endre sétány, at the eastern end of the Grassalkovich Palace Park, follow Ady Endre until it intersects with Allomás út. There, make a right, and you will be heading south to the first major street on your left, Kösztársaság. Take Kösztársaság past the suburban village of Marikatelep, to the next major ranch-village, Száritópuszta. Here, dramatic staged battle scenes on horseback are held in period costume. Check with Tourinform for the schedules. The ranch is the site of frequent equine events, races, jousts, and carriage races.

## Domonyvölgy

From Gödöllő you can also reach Domonyvölgy (Route 30 east) where the world champion carriage riders, the Lázár brothers, demonstrate feats of skill and supreme horsemanship, a rebirth of Hungary's galloping past. The **Lázár Equestrian Park** hosts many magnificent animals and stables (see *Adventures on Horseback*, page 285).

## Mogyoród

The exit for Mogyoród on Route 3 (Expressway 71) comes as you head toward Gödöllő.

We have talked about kings, queens and medieval Hungary, here is the present, the home of the **Hungaroring**, the only Formula One racetrack in Central Europe, where the annual Budapest Formula 1 races are held in July and/or August (www.formula1.com and www.hungaroring.hu). The great racecar drivers of the world compete here every summer. But there is more than just watching. You can try your own hand at the track. They offer special driving courses and training for individuals, including controlled sliding and obstacle courses. Unfortunately, this does require that you bring your own vehicle. On the other hand, not exactly Formula 1,

but a thrill for some, and certainly the kids, is the indoor **Hungarokart Center** (1 Ipar, 2146 Mogyoród, Tue-Fri 4 pm to midnight, Sat noon to midnight, Sun noon to 10 pm. ☎ 36-28-540-140, gocart@hungarokart.hu). This is go-cart heaven. Although they are closed on Mon, during the rest of the week they are open year-round. The snack bar tables look out on the racetrack through glass walls, so, if you are not so inclined, but you want to watch your kids racing, that is always an option here, while you sip on a cool drink.

## ★★Aszód

Heading east, the Galga River Valley comes into view. Aszód sits in the midst of the valley, home to the museum of Petõfi Sándor. The museum is housed in a former high school, the *gimnazium* where Petõfi Sándor

studied from 1835-1838. Originally a one-story school building constructed by János Pdmanicazky in 1769-1771, the second story was added in 1872. Up until 1958 it was a school, then a high school (*gimnazium*) and then a Lutheran boys home. However, since then, it has gone from a local museum of Aszód to become a regional museum center for museums of the communities of Dany, Galgamácsa, Iklad, Tura, Verseg, and Zsámbok. As such, it has become a major regional histori-

cal archive, hence its name as the **Galga Valley Exhibit**.
Starting from remains of Neolithic communities and settlements in the nearby hills, in the entry room, burial customs
and ancient rites of the once-thriving Lengel Neolithic culture, you will view the progressive development of the area,
century by century. Although the dig is occasionally suspended due to financial difficulties, nevertheless, the
museum has accumulated a fine collection. Walking past the
Neanderthal exhibit, you enter the Bronze Age room on the
first floor, and view Avar jewelry and unique metal diadems of
an ancient tribal chief. The fourth room displays the history of
agriculture through the 18th and 19th centuries, and an
exhibit on the main events of the 1848-49 Revolution. The second floor includes reproductions of a blacksmith shop and
another of a shoemaker from Aszód, along with many turn-of-
the-century farming and industrial instruments. The next
room leads to dress and costume from past centuries. Village
differences are compared. The last room is an exhibit on
Petõfi Sándor's life, including a school book in which his
school grades were recorded. Outside is an excellent
ethnographic display.

## ★Isaszeg

Every Hungarian child knows about Isaszeg, for it was here
that one of the most famous battles in Hungarian history was
fought. At the beginning of the Hungarian Revolution of
1848-49, the Austro-Hungarian forces, some of the best of
Europe, seemed to dominate the battlefield, and it appeared
that the seekers of freedom had been put to flight, so much so
that the Emperor Franz-Joseph proclaimed, "The Hungarian
state has ceased to exist." But in only a few months, things
changed. The Hungarian peasants and tradesmen had been
trained and the Hungarian Hussar regiments had been
formed. Relying on the ancient horseback riding history of
their ancestors, they honed their skills for quick cavalry
maneuvering and hand-to-hand fighting, together with a
newly disciplined and intensely patriotic infantry and artillery. Hungarians attacked. A contemporary account noted,
"The Hungarian Hussars, the best cavalryman in the world,

overrode the enemy like a wild boar trampling on corn, and drove the imperial forces back." Then, in a move to wipe out the insurgents, the Austro-Hungarian army closed around the Hungarian forces. It looked as though the Hungarian army of independence would be strangled to death. But, to the astonishment of all Europe, the Hungarian Hussars cut a swath through the Imperial armies. The Hungarians defeated the Imperial

armies, and effectively drove them out of the country. The Austro-Hungarian empire was saved only by the intercession of the armies of the Czar, who marched into Hungary with overwhelming force months later. During the **Turning Points in History** days here, you can watch a reenactment of the battle and see the Hussars parade, with their polished metal helmets glittering in the sun as their horses dance to the music of the bands.

**The Ethnographic Museum**, 2117 Isaszeg, Madách utca 15, ☎ 36-28-582-280, open Wed to Sun 10 am-6 pm, contains a regional historical collection, as well as artifacts from the days of the Hussars. A well in the yard dates from the same period.

## ★ Csömör

Scarcely distinguishable from Budapest, Csömör lies off of Highway 3, just beyond district XVI of Budapest. It attracts people from all over Hungary and from abroad. The **Csömör Corpus Christi** procession starts by covering all the churches and surrounding streets with carpets of flowers. Every year a joyful parade and celebrations are connected to the **Pentecost Festival** and **Wedding Party**. In this exuberant festival, the traditions of Slovakia are preserved and nurtured. Original Tót (Slovakian) wedding dresses and traditions from different parts of Hungary and towns outside the borders are brought here by villagers to show their traditional dress, celebrations, and music. Parades, colorful costumes, songs, dancing and many real weddings, are joined with street vendors and open bars, flowing wine and glowing faces. Check with Tourinform (see pages 571 ff) for the specific day, as it varies from year to year.

# Southeastern Budapest

This area is one of the biking centers of Hungary, as the flat roads allow easy cycling in all kinds of traffic and weather. It is reachable on the M5 and by trains. This is the gateway to Budapest, and the center of the wholesale market, where villagers come from near and far to sell their vegetables, which eventually end up in Budapest kitchens. It was itself a fertile area of agriculture, although now it is largely overrun by the city. This geological region was formed when the mountains shaped the Danube. The undulating lowland scenery was sculpted into its smooth terrain as the tributaries of the Danube carved out their channels and, at the same time, deposited rich silt and sand, loess and gravel. What remains in these lowlands is marshland and bog, another national protected environmental asset.

## Vecsés

This starts where Budapest ends. The town has a reputation throughout Hungary as the source of the best sauerkraut in the world. But you won't find it sold in stores. It is made in barrels. During the time of the Turks the town was depopulated and was repopulated at the end of the 18th century with Germans. They domesticated various vegetables and developed a unique sauerkraut. It passed down from generation to generation within the Klan families, much to the benefit of Hungarian cuisine, which offers sauerkraut from Vecsés on many a restaurant plate. The center boulevard into town takes you to the city covered market (*piac*), where you can buy some of this famous product. In the same market, hundreds of stalls sell everything that traditional Hungary eats, and also wears... you can sample various wines and Hungarian fast foods at the different standing eateries and stands. Not many speak English here, but the slice of Hungarian life, with people pushing and walking, carrying shopping bags and arguing with vendors, is not duplicated in the states. As with any crowd, pack your wallet inside a vest coat pocket, and keep your handbag on the shoulder, zipped shut.

# Õcsa

Õcsa stands out as a community that received the European Nostra Prize in 1996 for its work on preserving the **Calvinist church**, one of the country's most significant Romanesque monuments. You can mark the church immediately by its cemetery, set apart by its unique 500 ancient wooden grave markers, known in Hungary as the kojafas of Õcsa. The inner sanctum is adorned with medieval frescoes, the prime reason for the European preservation award. An ancient organ rings with its deep-piped wood tones to accompany the choristers that give

*Õcsa's 13th-century Romanesque Protestant Church (photo Hungarian Friends of Nature, Muskovics András)*

concerts here frequently. However, the town's efforts to preserve its heritage are no more clearly demonstrated than by a walk up Öreg mountain, where beer and wine making cellars abound, and the preserved 100-150-year-old thatched roof peasant houses dot the countryside.

Õcsa is also home to one of the least known but most important works of conservation in the world today. The ancient European bog-forest still can be found here, blanketed in

*Fresco from the Roman-esque Church*

morning and evening mists, tapestried ghost-like with ferns and thick hanging moss. The **Õcsa Landscape Protection Reserve**, listed by the United Nations as a Protected Wetlands Site of international importance, requires that you usually walk through in the silent fog with a guide, but always with permission. At the same time, its unique swampy combination of hills and flatland makes it a huge migratory stopover for songbirds. Migratory songbird populations are declining in Europe, but scientists lack the data to determine why. Is it during the breeding season, or is it during the winter migration south that the losses are occuring? So, at least a portion of the estimated 500 million songbirds that migrate between Europe and sub-Saharan Africa are banded at three stations... the Mwea National Reserve in Kenya, the Lago di Lesina in southern Italy, and the Õcsa wetland in Hungary. The birds fly on fat reserves, often crossing the last 2,100 miles of their journey across the Mediterranean and the hot sands of the sub-Sahara nonstop, without eating. Eco tours allow you to participate in the work, learn about all aspects of caring for, capturing, tagging, and studying the migrations and habits of these birds. You work from 6 am until dark tending nets, extracting birds from the nets, and making field and vegetation studies. Contact **Ecotours Hungary**, H-1113 Budapest, Villany út 62, ☎/fax 36-1-361-0438, www.ecotours. hu, ecotours@axelero.hu.

## HUNGARY'S GEESE

Hungary has raised geese since antiquity. Every year, 45,000 tons of goose meat leaves the country – or one sixth of the 300,000 tons of poultry processed in the nation. Even the by-products, feet, tongues, and wings, have a market. Some 2,000 tons of such by-products sell to China annually. But goose liver is king. Throughout the world, $225 million worth of

Hungarian goose liver was sold between 1989 and 1994. France (French find Hungarian goose liver lighter than the domestic version), Switzerland, Germany, Holland, and Japan all buy it, and Hungary beats out its top competitors, Israel and Poland, every year in this highly selective market.

## Monor

Follow Route 4 southeast from Budapest and you come to Monor, where the flat plains of Hungary have begun to mingle with the hills and the landscape is broken by interspersed plains woodlands. Grape-growing and wine-making have been practiced here for centuries. And, although the locals organized a defense force to watch the Turks from the slopes of Strásza (Sentry) Mountain, the mountain and the surrounding area have always been primarily dedicated to vineyards. The 900 buildings on the sides of this mountain are a naturally preserved cellar village. The surrounding forest is home to deer, pheasants, partridges and rabbits. The area caters to hunters, cyclists, hikers, and walkers, as well as those touring by car. This is a place to visit during the **Orbán Days** festivities, with its wine and song.

Alternatively you can hone your golf skills at **Paplapos Golf & Academy**, 35 km/21 miles from Budapest and only about six km/10 miles from Ferihegy Airport. There is a six-hole course that meets international standards (four par-3 holes, one par-4, and one par-5). There is also a driving range with 8 tees and a 25-yard chipping and putting green. If you need instruction, it is here. For a fee, pros teach the basics. To get here from Budapest, take Highway 4 toward Debrecen. At 35 km you will come to the turn-off for the Monor town center. Take the turn-off and then follow the signs to Gomba. Pass through Gomba and, as you come out of town, at the crucifix on the right, turn right. The Academy is about two km farther on the road.

Just outside of Monor there is also a high-quality **riding school**, and the largest thatched roof hotel in Europe. I don't know if there are any others in existence quite like this (see *Places to Stay*, page 223).

**Central Danubia**

## Csévharaszt

Most notable for its forested environs, the juniper grove on the south edge of town has been a protected reserve since 1939. Hiking trails lace their way through town from the surrounding Csévharaszt forest. The Csévharaszt forest was discovered by one of Hungary's famous botanists, Paul Kitaibel. Next to the village are the remains of a 15th-century church, and the park is open to visitors. This almost uninterrupted stretch of forest extends between M4 and M5 clear down to Nyáregyháza. Abundant large and small game make it a hunter's paradise. At the same time, acacia, aspen, and pine forest interlaced with the thicker growth make it an excellent area for horseback riding in the forest mists. Bicycling, hiking and riding are highly popular in this area... yet its primitive atmosphere has been preserved.

## Pilis

Continuing past Monor on Highway 4, we come to the village of Pilis, the source of one of Hungary's rare flatland springs, the Gerje, whose waters feed the Tisza River. At the edge of town there is a 25-acre park with a three-lake system, The **Millecentenárium Memorial Park**, with artificial islands, is home to storks, ducks, wild geese, migrating birds, and wild geese. Hungary's largest standing cross, over 36 feet tall, rises in the middle of the park. The 18th-century evangelical church is one of the largest in the country, rising like a monarch over the village. The serenity of the town may be deceiving, however. Music blares and thousands of young people come here every year for the **Pilis Pop Music Festival** (check with Tourinform for the schedule).

## Nagykáta

The history of Nagykáta dates back to the 12th century, when the Káta family settled in the region. On the outskirts of the town at Kenderhalom are the remains of the old town dating back to the days of Árpád. The Registrum of Várad, the castle register of the king, first mentions the village of Káta in 1221. Over the years it grew, but it too was subject to the frequent foreign incursions, and so for a time in the 17th century it even disappeared from the map and from all official documents, only to be revived in 1696, when an official record of deaths and births was started in the restored town. Although only home to 13,000, it is nevertheless the center of the Tápió Region, which includes about 20 villages around the Tápió River. The region's 70,000 people sit in one of the richest nature reserves of Europe, containing 70 protected plant species and 180 protected animal species. The International Bird Protection Committee has named the Tápió-Hajta as one of Europe's most important bird sanctuaries, centered especially around the Reed Lake in the community of Famous, so grab your binoculars and go to one of the many bird stands that surround this park.

## Tápióbicske

For a time this small town shone brightly in Hungary. On April 4, 1849 it was the headquarters of the revolutionary general György, during the battle of Tápióbicske, when an imperial army engaged the Hungarian army for

*The Battle of Tápióbicske*

independence in a fierce battle. The Hungarians won. In the village park, a tall statue by Gyula Jankovics marks the burial spot of the men who died there. A statue of György stands at the head of a large memorial grave where many of the fallen were buried in a collective grave. The Iron Cross marks another burial ground of the fallen. The White Cross, marks a third burial site. Every year, since 1882, children in the village of Tápióbicske receive a gift known as the patriotic bun, or Hazafias bukta, on the memorial day of the battle. On the same day, crowds gather in the village from surrounding communities to watch the re-enactment of the Battle of the Hid, one of the major confrontations of the war.

**Central Danubia**

# Tápiószentmárton

Have you ever ridden 12 horses at one time? Victor Buck of Tápiószentmárton set a new world record in multi-riding at the Pair Driving Equestrian World Championships, on August 1999 in Kecskemét, Hungary. He rides 12 horses while standing on the hindquarters of two of the horses. Using reigns, he takes them through walking, galloping, turning, maneuvering, in circles and zig zags. Aside from the challenge of keeping all those horses in line without their being hitched together, consider what a feat of balance this is. The previous record holder was another Hungarian, Gábor Szegedi of Kiskunhalas, Hungary, who rode 11 horses.

However, at a farm on the outskirts of town, where some believe that Attila the Hun is buried, on the 2,800-acre farm of János Kocsi, people are drawn to something completely different. János bought his farm after the fall of communism, and soon became aware of a strange type of energy from the soil. His property lies exactly over Attila's Hill. But over time, as he worked on the property, he sensed a feeling of rejuvenation working around it. Somehow, a girl recovered from her myopia on the property as well, and then several others experienced cures from a variety of different ailments. János himself doesn't know where this comes from, or how it happens, but now he charges 500 HUF, either to see his horses or to experience the apparently curative electro-magnetic effects on the property. Many people now come here from throughout Europe simply to sit on the low-lying hillside, some wrapped in blankets, from morning to evening, hoping to get healed. Most people say that they feel much more relaxed after visiting the site.

## MY TREASURE

Kincsem (My Treasure) is among the greatest race horses in history. But this treasure started as a young chestnut-colored filly who could not be sold because she was too common-looking; she was a household name in Europe before she died. Her 54 races without defeat included all the great races in England, France, Germany, Austria, and Poland, as well as Hungary. She most often won her races by over a length. Ten times she won by 10 lengths. Twice she distanced the field. Although she died in 1887 at 13 years after a bout of colic, her legacy has lived on. Her female line has continued to produce a remarkable record, winning the Hungarian Two Thousand Guineas five times, the Austrian Two Thousand five times, two derbies in Hungary, three in Austria, one in Germany, Italy, and Romania, twice in Poland, five Hungarian St. Legers, one German St. Leger, and the French Prix Royal Oak St. Leger. Robert Hesp, her trainer, as if somehow connected, died 39 days after his famous charge. Kincsem was not buried underground; her skeleton can be seen at the Hungarian Agricultural Museum in Budapest.

Pets are named by people, but in Hungary, a person was named after a pet. The famous Kinscem developed a fondness for a particular boy named Frankie and his cat. No one knows who Frankie's parents were, and he came to be known as Frankie Kinscem, but they were inseparable. The owner of Kinscem, Ernest de Blascovich saw that it was better to keep them together, so they traveled everywhere as a group. Frankie later registered in the military under the name of Frankie Kincsem. When he died, his wish was carried out. His horse-given name was chiseled on his tombstone.

**Central Danubia**

# Cegled

Cegled, we might
say, is a glimpse into
the heart of Hun-
gary. Much of it, as
with much of the
nation, was rebuilt
again and again, but
its reconstruction
has retained a spirit
of the past. The
**Town Hall** was
erected in 1891-93.

Through the main entrance, you enter an apparent palace,
where a walk through the hall of columns leads to the grand
staircase, and upstairs to the ceremonial hall, gallery and
conference rooms. Tourinform is located in the town hall, so
this is an excellent place to get your bearings and find out
about events and anything new in the town, as well as other
accommodations. From the front entrance of the town hall,
walk out to Kossuth tér (Kossuth Square), and across the
square to the Neo-Classical **Holy Cross Church**. In 1368 a
chapel dedicated to St. Anne was built on this spot, at the
behest of Queen Elizabeth, who bestowed the town of Cegléd
on the Clarissa nuns of Óbuda. The Turkish wars, however,
had their effect upon this religious town, and so the Gothic
church that had been ravaged by war was finally torn down
and another erected in its place. It was designed by Erenc
Homályossy (Tunkel), a master builder from Szolnok, and
was consecrated in August 31, 1827. The main altar is the
work of Lôrinc Dunaiszky (1830) and the Calvary scene was
completed in the same year by Jószef Schöfft, an artist from
Pest. The church is open to visitors every day of the week, and
may be called for a tour (☎ 36-53-311-144).

At the corner of Kossuth tér and Eötvös tér stands the historic
**Old Catholic Parish Church**. Look for the plaques on the
walls. One commemorates Lôrinc Mészáros, the second in
command of the peasant revolt of 1514, and a former priest of
this parish. The leader of that rebellion was György Dozsa
and he was often accompanied by Father Lôrinc who, like

Moses of the Old Testament, distinguished himself by carrying a big stick as he marched forward with the armies of the Hungarian peasantry.

Just beyond this intersection at Kossuth tér 4 is the **municipal market**, where farmers and vendors from the surrounding area ply their wares on Tues, Fri, and Sun. You will not find folk costumes here, but it is a place to pick up some freshly grown produce from the farming countryside.

Next stop in our walk is the unmistakable **Kossuth Cultural Center**. This grand structure was once hailed as the Palace of Culture. Built in 1927, after WWI, its style evokes a Neo-Classical eclecticism with modern influences, so characteristic of that time in Hungarian history. Inside is the **Cegléd Gallery of Art**, with the work of Hungarian artists, as well as works by artists from all areas of Europe and the USA. Continuing past the Cultural Center, we come to the statue of György Dózsa (unveiled June 26, 1972) the leader of the Peasants Revolt of 1514. This statue was created by one of the great sculptors of modern Hungarian art, Jószef Somogyi.

Our walk takes us to one of the events that shook Europe, every bit as much as Patrick Henry's speech shook the colonies in the American Revolution. The plaque commemorates the great speech of Kossuth Lajos, who made his powerful recruiting speech on September 24, 1848, in Cegléd Market, which is today Kossuth tér. The speech was so powerful that its reprints in Vienna sparked the revolt against the Hapsburgs in Austria, and forced the resignation of Mettersmitch, the Austro-Hungarian monarchy's foreign minister, and one of the most powerful men in Europe.

At Szabadság tér on the opposite side of the Town Hall is the **Calvinist Church Garden**, in the back of the largest Calvinist Church of Central Europe, the **Cegléd Calvinist Great Church** (the foundation stone was laid in 1835 and the church was consecrated in 1871; it seats 2,400). The balcony mounted on the back, almost as an afterthought, is marked by several descriptive historical boards. It was from this balcony, taken from the former Zöldfa (Green Tree Inn), in the town of Poszony, that Kossuth Lajos introduced the

*Cegléd's Calvinist Church*

first freely elected Prime Minister, in the revolution of 1848-49.

Turning toward the walkways in the garden, the wooden belfry is over the ceramic sculpture of Gábor Varga, unveiled on October 23, 1989, in memory of the revolution of October 23, 1956. It marks the year when Hungary became officially separated from the old Soviet Block as an independent nation once again. Also at Szabadság tér is the slim-towered **Lutheran Church**. Consecrated on November 31, 1896, it is meant to recall the words of Luther's famous hymn, *A Mighty Fortress Is Our God*, hence its fortress-like appearance.

Down from the Lutheran Church is the **Drum Museum**, which was opened in December 2000. Formed around a fabulous collection by the drum collector Sándor Kárman, there are percussion instruments from symphony orchestras to modern jazz ensembles, and exhibits on the history of the drum from ancient times. Lectures and concerts are held in its small 30-person auditorium. One building beyond is the **Cegléd Municipal Library**, where you are welcome to sit down in the quiet interior and read a good book or magazine in English.

Turning to the center of the square is the dominating statue of Kossuth Lajos, made by János Horvay, and unveiled in 1902. Kossuth's own son, Ferenc Kossuth, worked with the sculptor to fashion the head of the statue. A copy of this statue was erected in New York in 1928.

Returning along Széchenyi út we reach Rákóczi út. The Art Nouveau **Lajos Kossuth Secondary School** (Kossuth

Gimnazium) was designed by Gyula Pártos and opened in 1903; the carved wooden pillar in the front garden is a tribute to past teachers and students of the school. Directly across the main street from the school are the **Municipal Sports Hall**, and the **Municipal Open Air Baths** (medicinal, at 96.8°F and rich in iodine, they are recommended for therapeutic cures). You may want to take a dip. But even better are the **Cegléd Thermal Baths Kft.**, 2700 Cegléd, Fürdő út 27. They have a relaxing thermal adult pool, as well as adventure pools and slides for the young, a children's pool and large family bathing areas, plus a male-female meeting area (see *Spas & Swimming*, pages 292 ff).

On the way to the railroad station on Rákóczi út we stop by **Gubody Garden Park**. First known as People's Park (in honor of the proletariat revolution of the 1940s and 50s), it was renamed for Ferenc Gubody, a former mayor of the town, in 1907. The center fountain is bordered by a bust of the former mayor by the sculptor János Hovay, while on the opposite side stands a modern work by the Japanese sculptor, Hidetoshi Yakahama.

Not to be missed by nature lovers is the **Arboretum** of the Fruit Research Institute. Between the Park and the Arboretum (both municipally protected natural preserves) there are 750 species of trees and numerous extremely rare flowering plants. The Csíkosszéi bee orchid meadow contains 5,000 early spider orchids, each worth (I have been told) an estimated 100,000 HUF, or about $500 per flower. Don't pick from this garden. It could be construed as more than petty theft. These are complemented by bug orchids, loose flowered orchids, and burnt orchids.

Recall the *Sound of Music*, and the magical voices that came down from the Austrian Alps? The **Girls Chorus** of the Lajos Kossuth Secondary School is internationally known, as are the younger farm choruses, the Nightingale Children's Chorus, and the Puella Chorus. Both of these farm choruses have won, between them, both gold and silver medals at the Choral Olympics in Lynz, Austria. These young people are not to be missed.

The **Cegléd Wind Orchestra** traditionally gives performances at the town hall, and in various festivals all year

**Central Danubia**

round. But jazz fans may find it more to their liking to come for the **Cegléd International Jazz Festival** in the Municipal Sports Hall. And, where you have jazz, you also have percussion. The best drummers from throughout Europe come here for its **Jubilee International Drum and Percussion Gala Concert**. This is supplemented by the summer music camps, which bring jazz musicians from Budapest to join with budding young musicians in exploring the intricacies of soft jazz. There is also the **Cegléd Music Camp**, held every September. Crafts, market stands, a military band parade, stage performances, horse shows and a wine extravaganza to boot, attract people to the Szabadság tér and its surrounding streets. The Cegléd and District László Unghváry Wine Order holds festivals and parades, initiation ceremonies, and wine-tasting competitions throughout the year, celebrating the superb wines of this region.

We eventually arrive at the train station, again, built over what was previously destroyed. The original line between Szolnok and Pest opened up here in September 1, 1847. With the wars, however, came its demise, until it was reconstructed in 1909.

## Southwest Budapest

We will now go to Route 70, which heads southward, and meet up with Route 6 southwest of the city. Here we will take the exit for one of the wonders of modern archaeology.

### ★★Százhalombatta

One of a kind, loaded with adventures and things to do, is a sprawling archeological dig and excellent museum, the **Matrica Museum and Archeological Park**, 1-3 Gesztenyés út, ☎ 36-23-354-591, fax 36-23-540-069. Open April 1st to Oct 31st, every day except Mon, 10 am to 6 pm; Nov 1st to Mar

31st, Tue to Fri 10 am to 5 pm, and Sat-Sun 1 to 5 pm. The Archeological Park is a must for any who are at all interested in history. Tickets range from 2500 to 3000 HUF, depending on the tour you take and whether adult or child. It is part of an international research project and, at the same time, one of the most entertaining sites I have ever visited. An important Middle Bronze Age Vatya settle-

ment on the river Danube, it has yielded extensive numbers of artifacts, and the museum and Archeological Park were constructed to house them. But this place is much more than that. Depending on the tour, you can participate in the making of pottery or weaving and spinning as they did in the Bronze Age, and you can take what you make home with you. A variety of films demonstrate different aspects of Paleolithic history, and the exhibits include a bevy of activities that provide interactive enjoyment, for adults as well as children. The findings include large gravesites. The southernmost grave in the cemetery, tumulus 115, has been restored and should not be missed. The 2,700-year-old oak burial chamber was preserved intact partly due to the funeral pyre ashes which were taken inside the grave mound and scattered all over the funnel-shaped passage that leads to the grave chamber. Inside the tumulus, a multi-media show explores the world of the prehistoric burial rites. The museum exhibits span 4,000 years, through prehistoric, Bronze age, Celtic, Roman, medieval, and up to the pre-WWII period. Iron Age ramparts are across from the Bronze Age earth fort, the Roman bath and camp of Matrica, the early medieval village of Baté, and mysterious mounds and gravesites literally fill the area. Take the half-day tour with a meal to sample prehistoric pie made from the local plants, made in the ovens and cooked in the same way as they did thousands of years ago. If you are in the mood, after learning about the recipes, enjoy one of the full meals, prepared as in prehistoric times. Tours can take more than one day, and can also encompass packages offered by the Museum – such as lodging and horseback riding at the riding stables directly across from the site. These usually range in cost from 8,000 HUF on up, depending on the package. Contact the museum for information. Every third Sunday from May to Sept, Family Day provides special programs and food tasting.

Leaving Százhalombatta we head back on Route 70 north to the Budaörs exit, unless you choose to stay a day at the **Hotel Training**, 2440 Százhalombatta, Augusztus 20 u. 6, ☎ 36-23-354-688, fax 36-23-354-985, €-€€. Prices vary from 8,000 HUF for a bare-bones single to 20,000 for a double bed double bath (see *Places to Stay*, page 224).

## Budaörs/Wudersch

Budaörs is an old settlement, mentioned as early as 1282 in some documents as the Villa Kech Kekvurs, a center for nuns. But as with so much else in Hungary, it was wiped out in the Turkish invasions. Its restoration in 1707 was named for a village beauty who used to attract men from the Buda hills for good times. So much for the heritage of the nuns. But at that time, it nevertheless became staunchly Catholic, for it was one of those villages deliberately settled by Germans at the behest of the Catholic Hapsburg monarchy.

> ### WHAT'S IN A NAME?
>
> The town of Törökbálint near Budaors has a mountain on its border called Türkensprung, which means "Turk's jump." Folk wisdom holds that when the Christian armies returned to Hungary, the Turk chief fled here with the revenge-seeking Christian knights in hot pursuit. Rather than be taken alive, he leapt to his death, both horse and rider. Another similar German named hill in the nearby mountains is called Vierundzwanzig Ochsenberg, which means

"Mount of 24 Oxen." Don't believe that it has anything to do with farming. Again, the local legend says that the last Turk gun pulled up the hill required 24 oxen to do the job.

German traditions still live in this town, but the main attraction is the airport, which was opened in 1937. It is home to planes from all over the world on **Aviation Day**, a time for acrobatics, early planes, with parachutists jumping. Food, booths, and aerial buffs abound, with many speaking English.

There are several places to stay in this town, at lower than Budapest rates.

# ■ Adventures

## On Horseback

 Because this area is an international center for horses, check with Tourinform (see pages 571 ff) on the latest schedules for competitions. Pony cart competitions are held at Nagykõrös and Kocsér, while the two-hand and four-hand horse competitions take place at Tápiószentmárton, Tápiógyörgy, Újszilvás, Jászkarajeno and numerous other shows and exhibitions are held throughout the summer months.

## Monor

Also in this area is the **Hotel Hegyessy Nyerges** (Hotel Nyerges and Riding School), 2200 Monor, Hegyessy Tanya 57, pf 2/12, ☎ 36-29-410-758, fax 36-29-414-640, kafkazs@ monornet.hu. Or contact Zsu Zsa Csoltkó Kafka at ☎/Mobile 36-30-986-8988. This is the largest thatched hotel in Central Europe. Yes, I said hotel, and yes, I said thatched roof. I don't know if there are any others like it anywhere. It is 18 km/11 miles from Budapest along Highway 4. The 33 rooms are supplemented by meeting rooms, a reception area, poolside terrace, dances and parties. They arrange weddings here frequently.

# Döbrönte

**Hasik Hotel**, 8597 Döbrönte Fõ u. 4, ☎ 36-89-569-990, fax 36-89-569-991, hasik@hasik.hu. Rated five horseshoes. In the center of the small Swabian village of Döbrönte, at the foot of the Bakony Mountains, with pool, sauna and tennis courts, it is also a well-known stable. Learn how to ride English-style or, if you are an experienced rider, take your cross-country horseback tour from here.

# Gödöllõ

★★**Árpád Vére Lovasiskola** (Árpád's Blood Riding Stables/ School), 2100 Gödöllo, Szárítópuszta; contact János Harangozó, ☎/mobile 36-20-973-0474, or Victoria at 36-30-526-9391, www.horseridingshow.hu, arpadvere@freemail.hu. Rated four horseshoes. Set in the most beautiful part of the Gödöllo Hills nature reserve. Live in the hand-made yurt huts while Hungarian Racka sheep graze around you. An archery range is set up near a jousting field. János Harangozó here holds the Guinness world record for number of arrows shot into their target from a galloping horse. Stuntmen per-form dramatically staged war games, mounted archery, fire jumping, disc shooting, sword fighting, and jousting. They have come from around the world to stay at these camps. Without TV or heating (not necessary in the warm months), you sleep in yurt huts among pelts and wool spun by the ancient methods, as the Magyars did in the days of Árpád. Learn Hun techniques of bow and arrow shooting with Hun equip-

ment. If you have sufficient riding skill, you can even learn mounted archery. Join in evening song sessions by the campfire as well, accompanied by flute and guitar. And, most of all, learn about the care, feeding, and riding of horses. János Harangozó and his stunt riders here have worked with Hollywood greats.

**Lazar Equestrian Park**, 2182 Domonvölgy ☎ 36-28-576-510, fax 36-28-576-511, lazarteam@ elender.hu, www.lazarlovaspark. hu. This world-class ranch of the world champion team driving Lazar brothers is only a few km outside of Gödöllő. They frequently hold shows, dazzling the crowds with feats of horsemanship and team driving. They also have competitions, carriage riding in the forest, Hungarian-style catering extravaganzas with gypsy music, and horse riding in the surrounding area.

## Gilgamácsa

**Galga Riding Club**, 2183 Gilgamácsa Külterület, Fehér u. 1, whoisreka@hotmail.com. Rated three horseshoes. Dressage and cross-country riding, show jumping, with a roofed riding hall and a 14-acre ranch, including a restaurant, hotel, overnight boarding facilities and camping as well.

## Hiking & Biking

Biking and hiking tours and events are held all over the country, but you can try:

**The Hungarian Cycle Tourist Associaton** (MKTSZ), ☎/ fax 36-1-311-2457 or 36-1-353-1930, mktsz@dpg.hu.

**The Friends of City Cycling**, ☎/fax 36-30-922-7064 or 36-1- 317-1307, info@vbb.hu or www.vbb.hu. They organize one- to four-day tours, such as the thermal bath tour, etc. with branches in Szeged, Debrecen, Szekesfehervar, Gyor, Zalaegerszeg, Tatabanya, Pecs, and Siofok. The main office is in Budapest, H-1053 Budapest, Curia út 3. II. em. 1 (second floor, room 1). They organize two-, three-, and four-day tours, and can provide information or contacts for your cycling through their other branches as well. They also maintain a public bookstore with maps, guidebooks, information on cycling and helpful contact information for cyclists throughout the nation: FRIGORIA Könyvkiadó, 1119 Budapest, Pajkos u. 66, ☎/fax 36-1-203-0915, www.frigoriakiado.hu.

**Hungarian Mountain Bike Association**, ☎/fax 36-1-339- 9289, mtbszov@matav.net, www.mountainbikesport.hu.

The climbing clubs most active for the Borsony Mountains are:

**Climbing Club**, FTSK Exelsior S.E. XI Budapest, Bartók B. U. 19, ☎ 36-1-385-3601, lazartr@elender.hu.

**Hegyisport Climbing Club**, II Budapest, Dénes u. 1, 36-1- 376-1007 hsc@dpg.hu.

**Black Rock Climbing Club**, 2081 Piliscsaba, Béla király út 98-102, ☎ 36-26-373-857.

Maps and information are available in the Czech Republic, Bratislava, and also in Budapest about the **Danube Bicycle Trail**, which starts in the Black Forest and winds its way south with only a few minor breaks to finally end in Budapest. The plans are that eventually this bicycle route will traverse the entire region to end at the Black Sea. But, as it stands now, this is a fine long-distance bicycle adventure. You should check with the bicycle associations and the Tourinform offices in Hungary.

**Bicycling Szentendre Island and the Danube Bend**, western shore (right bank). Head out from Budapest along Route 11, on the bicycle path toward Szentendre, and on to Visegrad. The path ends at Leányfalu. And, because of heavy traffic, it is probably best to cross over to the island at

Leányfalu via ferry, then head north to Kisoroszi and cross back over to the shoreline by ferry. After Leányfalu, traffic is heavy all the way through to Visegrad and you are on the shoulder of the road for numerous stretches. So although you could cross over to the island at Tahitótfalu on the bridge, because of the traffic and for safety, it is probably better to use the ferries, and so much more romantic. The island can take up nearly a day with its 78 km/47 miles of roads. Add 50 km/ 30 miles for the shoreline roads. You can find any number of places to stay on the way. The next day, bicycle back, but cross at the north end at Tahitótfalu, and follow the road around the island, across unsurfaced dikes and surfaced road. Incredibly, on the Island there is hardly any traffic as compared to the banks of the Danube. Allow three days for this adventure.

**Bicycling the east side of the Danube Bend** (left bank) all the way to Szob. The entire stretch has bicycle pathways that parallel Route 2, from Budapest to Dunakeszi, Göd, Szõdliget, Vác, Verõce, Kismaros, Nagymaros, Sebegény, and finally Szob. It is about 70 km/42 miles, and can take two to three days if you want to see all the sights. There is lodging along the way. The bicycle paths are generally well marked throughout this area. It is very difficult to get lost. Take the tour book, *Kerékpártúrák* and the *Magyarország Autóatlasza* (see *Budapest, Adventures, Bicycling,* page 192).

Footpaths cover the hills of these areas, and some well-paved and carefully maintained bicycle trails offer the cycle enthusiast a wealth of places to go in safety and at any level of comfort or challenge one may desire.

From about seven km/ four miles northwest of Visegrad is the Danube Bend village of **Dömös**, reachable by walking trails, or by roads on the other side of the Pilis range. It is a stop-off point for buses, which makes it easy to reach. In the center of the village are a series of signposts. They point to different trails that you can take into the surrounding mountains, which abound with raspberries in the summer. Follow the trail to Malom about 2½ km/1½ miles, and you will come to a fork. To the right is the famous Rám precipice, about three hours farther. This one can get difficult. It should not be attempted when the weather is wet. Beyond, the trail leads on to Dobogókõ (altogether about five hours). A left turn will take you to the equally famous Vadallo rocks, and the Pulpit Seat, which towers overhead. This trail is quite steep and requires handle holds embedded along the trail. In parts it follows a 641-m/1,923-foot crag, which I do not recommended for those with no stomach for such risky ventures.

## Favorite Hike

Try the hike from Dobogókõ to Dömös, down the Rám precipice. This four-hour walk will offer spectacular views of the Danube Bend, but you need to be in good condition. Don't attempt it in foul weather, as the rocks can get slippery. However, you can walk just about everywhere up here in safety. The trails are fairly well marked, although occasionally you will stumble on a sign that is worn, or a spot where the waymarks are not quite clear. A good map is necessary, and you should have some map reading and locating skill.

Stock up on eats and a canteen of fresh water may not be a bad idea. Remember that, although they are making progress on cleaning the water, it is still not safe to drink stream water.

The interconnecting trails will take you all over the Pilis range, and they offer the best views of the Danube, plus a rich forest hiking experience of this side of the Danube, without strain. But, because of that, the trails in this area may be crowded in the peak summer season.

To start this hike, in Dobogókõ, facing Eötvös Loránd menedékház, walk down the road to the television station/tower. Off to the right of the fence take the downward trail until you come to the way-marked crossroads where you take the red triangle trail, then left, down a steep grade to the asphalt road. Go right, but cross the road and walk it to the next rough trail on the left. This will take you to the hunter's shack. Don't be alarmed that you have lost the trail. It actually gets rather narrow and descends dramatically to a small running stream at the bottom. Cross the stream and scale the opposite bank to the pathway. Turn right and then make a sharp left, then up again to another forest road. Cross it, and keep your eyes open for the red triangle that takes you uphill. At the top, a fence blocks the way and is the intersection of the red cross walking path. Here, walk to the left to pick up the red triangle again.

Now you must stick to the main path, keeping an eye out for the triangle at a fork that heads uphill. From here, the trail climbs the forested hill until you come to Prédikálószék (the Preaching Chair), aptly named, for it has a wonderful view of the Danube Bend. There is an implanted wooden cross in the rock outcrop, as though set for a preacher to make his sermon before the echoing majesty of the hills.

Veering down to the left, you'll pick up the red triangle path again and it will take you to Vadálló-kövek ridge. Here, across the rock face, you descend a narrow path, through a stretch of woods. At the bottom, turn left to find the green waymarks, and continue, through a young people's camp ground and cabins, and across a small shallow stream (this may be dry, depending on the season), and then, after the stream a fork in the path. Here you stay with the green waymarks, veering right, and then continue, crossing the road that you will find, continue to veer right on the path and across another stream, staying with the green waymarks. This will take you to Rámszakadék, which requires a steep climb up the side, taking hold of grab chains.

 Be forewarned, this particular part of the trail is borderline mountain climbing. It is not for the inexperienced or the frail.

Once at the top of the gorge, your walk will take you past a picnic area. After the picnic area is a road. On the other side of the road go left for several paces to a pathway that climbs to the right through the forest and which takes you to a forest road. Cross it and find the small path that transverses the scrub area. Continue the climb, until you reach a trail junction at the top of the ridge. Intersecting it is the red way-marked path. Turn left, go past the television tower, and you will see Dobogókõ to the right. You can find your own way down (but stick to the paths).

## Spas & Swimming

 Aside from the canoe and boat excursions in this area, which we have already basically covered in the section on Budapest, there are also numerous thermal baths, with bubbling thermal waters from beneath the earth, children's pools and other options. Many are located next to or even in hotels.

Read the section on thermal pools in the Budapest chapter, pages 193 ff, for warnings and advice.

 **Danubius Spa and Conference Hotel**, 2025 Visegrád, Lepencevölgy, ☎ 36-26-801-900, fax 36-26-801-914. info@thv.hu, www.danubiushotels. com/visegrad, €€-€€€, four star, but approaching five star. €-€€€. A part of the Danubius group, it offers its spa, spring, and mineral water at a constant 102°F, bubbling up with calcium, magnesium and hydrogen-carbonate ingredients. The water has been shown to have astringent, anti-inflammatory and antiseptic qualities, and some anti-allergic effects as well. Next door to the Lepence thermal bath, it taps the same waters, but adds its top-quality restaurants, swimming pools (indoor and outdoor), sauna, aromatherapy, steam bath, solarium, salt chamber, doctors and therapists on staff, and a variety of physio, electro, oxygen and hydrotherapy treatments. You can't avoid the sense of pampering here, from the poolside lounge bar, or while eating dinner at one of the restaurants as you listen to the evening music. Trails are everywhere, and all the sites of the area are in easy walking, or driving, distance.

**Pólus Palace Thermal Golf Club Hotel**, 2132 Göd, Kádár u. 49, ☎ 36-30-400-5611, fax 36-27-532-515. golf@hu.inter.net, www.poluspalace.hu, €€-€€€.

This thermal wellness hotel features everything necessary to be pampered, with the added bonus of its own golf course – par 72, 18 holes, in a protected natural area. The 6,208-yard course has a day and night driving range, and professional golfers who will offer instruction to help sharpen the swing (for a fee, of course). The wellness pool has a 12-function thermal adventure adjustment to set it to the level you like the best, with bubbling waters and currents. Then, there is the steak house, the restaurant, and bar; all feature top entertainment and there are international-quality chefs on staff. All adventures are arranged from the front desk, from horseback riding or flying to boating on Balaton or the Danube. When you get back, try one of the three restaurants.

**Aquaréna Mogyoród**, in Mogyoród at Vízipark utca 1, ☎ 36-28-541-100, www.aquarena.hu. Aquaréna Mogyoród is rated as Hungary's most attractive aquapark, with plenty of excitement and great fun for all ages. It is set in 32 acres of parkland 18 km/11 miles from the center of Budapest. Besides the 26 slides, one of the park's key attractions, a slow-flow chute winds 900 feet into the Blue Cave, a reconstructed facsimile of Capri's Blue Grotto. The adventure pool includes mysterious counter-currents, a waterfall, and mushroom showers. The round Jacuzzi is away from the adventure and children's paddling pools, a good choice for relaxation. And then, the umbrellad terraces, eateries, and showers all balance the fun with a leisurely, Mediterranean ambiance.

**Thermal Hotel Liget**, 2030 Erd, Római u. 9, ☎ 23-366-010, fax 23-366-075, hotelerd@axelero.hu, www.hotelerd.hu, €-

€€. Basic two-star services but with three-star quality. Only 15 km/nine miles outside of Budapest, through Budaors on M7 south to the Erd exit. This is what Hungarians classify as another wellness hotel, with its medical staff and treatments, in addition to the fun aspects, and it is well priced for families on a budget. Singles run €60-64, doubles €70-82, and a family apartment €82-95. However, their hotel stay packages may be 20% cheaper and include medical and/or fitness packages that combine massages, treatments, use of bicycles and tours of Budapest and the surrounding area. This is one to reserve in advance, which can earn free use of the baths and sauna, plus breakfast included. The hotel was built on a medicinal thermal spring that rises from the depths of the earth, carrying with it a host of trace elements that are supposed to induce healing. Of its 27 rooms, three are specifically designed to accommodate families. The nearby strand incorporates two indoor and three outdoor pools, in addition to the hotel's restaurant, brasserie, bowling, billiard room, etc. The restaurant has a relaxed elegance, but the tab is modest, about 3,000 to 4,000 HUF for a full-course meal with wine complement.

**Cegléd Thermal Baths Kft.**, 2700 Cegléd, Fürdő út 27, ☎ 36-53–505-000, fax 36-53-505-009, www.cegleditermal.hu, info@cegleditermal.hu. It is a three-story complexa. The large picnic and recreation area has a low cost entry fee (1,000 HUF all day, although amenities, such as massage, will add up). It has something for everyone in the family, with entertainment, restaurant, access to local boating on a quiet lake, strolling on park-like grounds, diving into current-driven waters, soaking in healing thermal springs, manicures, massages, pedicures, cellulite treatments, or just plain fun. In fact, this place is attracting thousands of people just for the enjoyment, let alone the growing number coming here for therapy and medical treatments. The waters are medicinal, rich in sodium chloride and hydrogen carbonate; the quiet adult pools are separated from the adventure children's pools. The main indoor gallery has a wave pool, a mineral bath pool and a children's pool. The outside pools range over much larger territory. Since this is a wellness center, there is a range of services that include massages, therapeutic baths, remedial gymnastics pool, and a gym and weight bath, dry and wet sauna, and solarium. A year-round restaurant (1,000 HUF up to 3,000 HUF) has terraced open space to look out on the pool area. This is set in a large park, off of Route 40 on the outskirts of town, where you can walk and relax, have a picnic, or rent a rowboat for leisure on the lake.

## Canoeing & Boating

The primary adventures up the Danube were already noted in the Budapest section. However, due to the possiblity of other types of cannoe trips, and or fishing and hunting, we have added the appropriate organizations to contact. Now, you can also contact Tourinform for more general information. Most of the naitonal organization offices are located in Budapest, and accordingly, there is some duplication on addresses and phone numbers here. The national headquarters of these organizations can refer you to local help, and on occasion may also set you up with a specific tour.

**Rómaifürdõ Leisure and Student Sport Association**, János Rátkai, 1031 Budapest, Petúr u. 22, ☎ 36-20-436-521.

**Hungarian Friends of Nature Association**, in Budapest, ☎ 36-1-331-2467, fax 36-1-353-1930, although primarily for hiking, also has a branch that deals in water tours, canoeing and kayaking.

**Hydrofoil cruises** allow you to bring your bicycle and gear, and they leave the Vigadó in Budapest throughout the day. Since the primary cities of the Danube Bend are reachable this way, this is an exciting option, but not the only one, as the same hydrofoils will carry you to Vienna, or to Prague or Bratislava, as well as Szentendre, Visegrad, and Esztergom, among other points. While it is a bit noisy, you feel the boat gain speed and rise up out of the water as you head out in a cloud of spray. The alternative, is a **boat cruise**, not nearly so short, and certainly, depending on the hour and the intention, it can be romantic. Contact the **Vigadó Boat Ticket Office**, or MAHART, the national boat company, ☎ 36-1-318-1223. Although a bit pricey for some, snacks and drinks are available on all cruises. The boat cruises in the evenings are the most beautiful in Europe, and you'll never forget the return, as you pass Visegrad, with its fortress castle visible on the hillside, or Budapest, whose Gothic towers and castle gleam like the jewel of Europe on the shimmering waters of the Danube.

## Golf, Tennis & Other Sports

 Golfers were once a rare breed in Hungary. But since the advent of privatization, and since the country has been making some astonishing strides economically, a growing class of people are taking to the greens. More information is available at:

**Budapest Golf Park Country Club**, Szentendre Sziget, zone 2024, ☎ 36-26-392-463/5.

**Pannon Golf and Country Club**, Máriavölgy, zone 8087, ☎ 36-22-353-000.

If you are a squash or cricket fan, try **Griff Squash and Fitness Club**, XI Budapest Bartók Béla út 152 ☎ 36-1-206-4065

And, should tennis be your field, contact **Városmajori Teiszakadémia**, XII Budapest Városmajor utca 63-69, ☎ 36-1-202-5337.

For hunting, on foot or on horseback. Licenses and controls are required, but once the paperwork is complete, there are large areas where you can hunt European-style. Contact:

**Széchenyi Zsigmond Vadásztársaság**, Széchenyi Zsigmond Hunting Society, Malom utca 3, Budapest, ☎ 36-30-948-8776.

**Vadász Hunting Club**, Kender utca 9, Budapest, ☎ 36-30-948-8776.

For fishing, try:

 **National Federation of Hungarian Anglers**, Magyar Országos Horgász Szövetség (MOHOSZ), H-1124 Budapest, Korompai u. 17, or their second office at H-1511 Budapest Pf.: 7. www.mohosz.hu.

**Angling Association of Cegléd**, Kölcsey tér 9, Cegléd, ☎ 36-53-320-651.

**Barátság Horgászegyesület** (Friends of Angling Association), Sorház utca 55, Cegléd, ☎ 36-53-310-378.

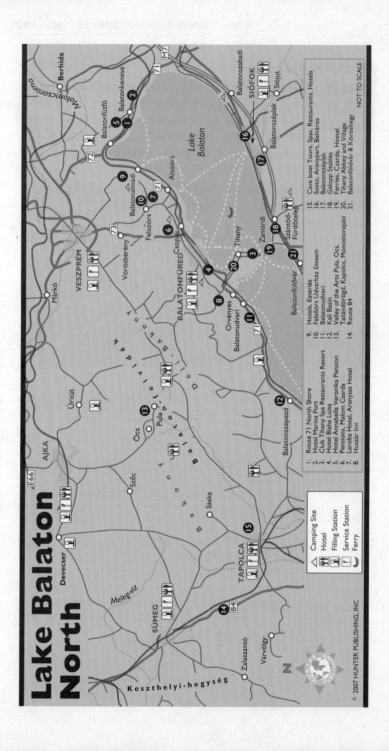

# Lake Balaton
# North

© 2007 HUNTER PUBLISHING, INC

NOT TO SCALE

**Keszthelyi-hegység**

N

Legend:
- △ Camping Site
- 🏨 Hotel
- ⛽ Filling Station
- 🔧 Service Station
- ⚓ Ferry

1. Route 71 North Shore
2. Hotel Marina Port
3. Club Tihany Spa Restaurants Resort
4. Hotel Blaha Luisa
5. Hotel Annabella Veronika Pension
6. Pensions, Malom Csarda
7. Laroba Hotel, Arany895 Hotel
8. Huszár Inn
9. Hotels, Exteriés
10. Felsőors Udvarház Etteeem
11. Balatonudvari
12. Kali Basin
13. Valley of the Arts Pula, Ocs.
14. Route 84

15. Cave boat Tours, Spas, Restaurants, Hotels
16. Sosto, Aranypart, Belváros
17. Balatonszéplak
18. Galopp Stables
19. Ferries, Csarda, Hostel
20. Tihany Abbey and Village
21. Balatonföldvár & Köröshegy

Talándörögd, Kapolcs, Monostorapáti

# Lake Balaton

Lake Balaton shimmers with its playful waves as the warm wind of summer brushes its surface, splashing the sun's rays against the surface and, from some

vantage points, stretching out like an ocean to infinity.

This is one of the great tourist centers of Europe. Often called Europe's Inland Sea, it is the largest lake in all of Eastern Europe, 232 square miles of silky smooth water and 197 km/ 118 miles of shoreline with harbors, playlands, and vacation homes. It is large enough to have formed a part of the front line between the Hapsburg and the Ottoman empires in the 16th century, justifying a naval presence from each. The Ottoman fleet was based at Siófok, and the Hapsburg fleet was anchored at Balatonfüred. It attracts retirees, as well as families with children, as well as the young crowd.

Incredibly, as vast as this great reservoir of water seems, its average depth is only nine to 12 feet; its deepest point, at the the Tihany Well, is a mere 37 feet. This results in a deception. Looking over the blue waters on

a warm summer day may lull a person into a sense of complacency. Children and families play and swim, some far from the shore. Usually the water is above 68°F, but it may rise to around 81° in a heat wave. However, occasionally winds comb the water, stretching down from the Bakony Mountains on the north and west sides. They whip up the waves to form crests as high as 20 to 30 feet. It is not a common condition, but you should keep it in mind. Fortunately Hungary has an excellent storm warning system. Wherever you are boating, or swimming, if you see a buoy or tower flashing (the warning

lights flash 30 times a minute), then leave the water or put to shore. If you don't see the light flashing but you see everyone leaving the water, get out. Like any ocean storm, it is nothing to be played with.

But Balaton's beaches and surroundings are a mini-Mediterranean, minus the rough surf and salt water at most times.

In early May, sails dot the lake in a picturesque, almost dreamy water scape, making it a favorite area for painters. Sailing tops all sports. Boats can be rented almost anywhere, but the main ports are Keszthely, Badacsony, Tihany, Balatonfüred, Balatonalmádi, Siófok, and Balatonföldvár. Wind surfing is popular. Swimming, not to be outdone, is most pleasant on the southern shore, which slopes gently for several hundred yards before you even get waist deep, so it is a favorite of families with smaller children. The northern shore on the other hand, in some places drops rather steeply, and so it is less attractive to some. A swim competition attracts competitors from around Europe (check with Tourinform for the schedule) every summer. Meandering shoreline trails and gentle walkways are just as popular as some of the more rigorous hiking excursions.

Camping sites are centers for fishing in the lake or hunting for boar and stag in the mountains. Don't expect a Hilton at camping sites, but accommodations are generally clean and quite reasonable. Campsites are frequently booked up well in advance. Some also offer cabins, tourist support, rentals and maps.

In winter Lake Balaton frequently freezes, with ice eight to 11 inches thick, ideal for winter skating and wind sailing. Check with your hotel to make sure that it has been okayed for such activity during your stay. In cold winters the ice may penetrate much deeper. In 1927 it reached a thickness of about two feet.

Unless you are on a hiking tour of the country, it is best to navigate the perimeter of the lake by car, or cycle its bicycle paths.

# ■ Getting to the Balaton Region

**Volan Bus** has regular buses to and from the region.

If going by **train**, buy your tickets at the **Déli train station**. The **személy** (semayee) train stops at all local train stations, and the **gyors** (dyorsh) train is an express direct route. The **Balaton Express** is really a slow train, but it may be your best bet. It circles the lake, making regular stops at all the main towns, and it probably is the easiest way to travel during high season, which finds many of the roads crowded near the larger towns. A small caution. Do not expect first-class seating. Most of the coaches are old. But it is indeed a way to get a feel for the country. Students and retirees, young vacationers and occasionally business people, all use the trains. It is not uncommon for a group to break out a lunch or a snack and eat on the train. The trains have small swing-out tables just for that purpose.

> **Tip:** When you purchase your ticket, make sure you also book a seat, or you could wind up standing during the journey.

**Passenger boats** across the Lake offer any number of cruises. Contact ★★ **Balatoni Hajózási Rt.**, H-8600 Siófok, Krúdy sétány 2, ☎/fax 36-84-310-050 . On the other hand, it's always great fun to ride your car or bicycle onto the cross-lake **ferryboat** that travels from Tihany to the opposite shore at Szántód – the quickest way across the lake between the northern and southern shores. Children under three travel free and under 13 are half-price. From mid-April through autumn (Sept or Oct, depending on the weather) regular ferries ply the waters from Siófok to Balatonfüred. From there they head to Tihany, and then back across to Balatonföldvár. The high point of summer brings service across the full length of the water, from Balatonkenese to Keszthely, a journey lasting about six hours, with stops on both banks along the way.

Between Tihany-rév and Szántód-rév car ferries operate April through Nov. From Révfülöp to Balatonboglár and from Badacsony to Fonyód car ferries operate from mid-April to mid-Oct.

# ■ Balaton Northern Shore

## Getting There

 By car, after you have followed Route M7 out of Budapest, take the turn-off for 71 to the North Shore. From Budapest it is a two- to three-hour drive, with road stops and eateries along the way.

From the Déli train station in Budapest, Kesthely (Kest-hey-ee), on the far southeastern end, is four hours and costs about 2,000 HUF (€8). To reach the famous wine region of Tihany, on the other hand, book the train to Balatonfüred, which costs about 1,200 HUF (€5), and from there take a bus to Tihany. Harbors dot the shore, and one can travel by ferry from one end of the lake to the other (See *Getting to the Balaton Region*, above).

Once at the lake you will find hundreds of small hostels and villas, as well as hotels. The villages along the route vary from quaint to modern. Signs frequently border the road saying Szoba Kiadó or Zimmer Frei ("Room for Rent" in Hungarian and German). Booking rooms directly without a tourist agency can sometimes result in a lower price, but not always. Expect to pay anywhere from 5,000 to 6,000 HUF. But if you are looking for all-around packages with amenities and support services, probably the best bet is one of the local hotels, at a higher price. Since the area is tourist-oriented, and internationally seasoned, almost any hotel in any of the major towns will offer fairly decent accommodations. If you are on a budget, book away from the shore, but within striking range of a public beach or of one of the many public baths and swimming pools. As a bonus, some hotels and cottages have private beachfronts.

# Places to Stay

 Balaton has literally hundreds of private establishments, weekend cottages and individual and family lodgings available. Often these can more than compete on price with some of the finest hotels. Go

| HOTEL PRICE CHART | |
| --- | --- |
| Double room without tax | |
| € | Under €80 |
| €€ | €81-€150 |
| €€€ | €151-€250 |
| €€€€ | Over €250 |

through Tourinform, which has an up-to-date listing, and can often make short-term, short-notice arrangements as well as long-term arrangements. Some homes and cabins have every convenience, including satellite television and pools. Some may not be so luxurious, but the locals are on the whole extremely helpful, and often have a passable knowledge of English. We have not listed cottages as there are so many and such a wide variety.

## Five Star

Five-star locations for Hungary are all in Budapest except for a few notable ones that we have listed in other sections. However, some of the four-star hotels listed here, though often somewhat older, compete with the finer hotels in Budapest, so they are not to be ignored.

## Four Star
### Balatonkenese

★★**Hotel Marina Port**, 8174 Balatonkenese, Kikötő u. 2-4 ☎ 36-88-492-369, fax 36-88-492-370, info@yacht.hu, www.yacht.hu. From June 1 to Aug 31 the cost is 26,500 HUF (€106) for a standard double in high season. €€-€€€.

The restaurant cuisine, with an average entrée of about 3000

HUF (€12), is pricey, but the food is good. Room service ends at 10 pm. Satellite English television, A/C, Internet connections. The waiters and the front desk are very good in English. Most of the staff speaks some. They have a modern dock and boats (sail only, a few with electric motors) are rentable. A bonus is that you can get sailing lessons too (see *Water Adventures*, pages 353 ff). Yacht club members receive a substantial discount, but you must dock a boat at the marina for that. Every room has an extraordinary view, great for sunrise and sunset. There is a pleasant indoor pool and sauna along with wellness programs, a gym, massage, sauna, special diets or shakes, and weight reduction and conditioning programs.

## Hévíz

★**Hotel Europa Fit**, 8380 Hévíz, Jókai u. 3 ☎ 36-83-501-100, fax 36-83-505-101. They offer a welcome cocktail and a host of extras. €€€. While the room rate is on the high side here, many extras are included, such as weekly beauty consultations, full use of all baths and saunas, free conditioning and exercise programs, excursions, tennis, billiards, children's pool, and open-air adventure pool, steam bath, sauna and aroma chamber. For children, there is baby sitting, a children's pool, animation/cartoon room, and playground. For the rest of us, there are quiet thermal pools, plus excellent restaurants. There is a poolside restaurant and bar. A piano is played nightly in the Gallery Café. Numerous packages cover everything from weight loss to treatments for specific ailments.

## Tihany

★★**Club Tihany Holiday Center**, H-8237 Tihany, Rév 3, pf. 31, ☎ 36-87-538-500, fax 36-87-448-083, €-€€, www. clubtihany.hu/english. Though rated as a four-star, it is not quite up there due to its age and the fact that not all rooms have A/C. But total amenities make the rates extraordinary

bargains. Doubles come with a balcony view of the lake for romantic evenings, A/C and half-board (dinner and breakfast are included). This does qualify as a true resort, with several restaurants (including a disco, a separate brasserie and a nightclub), sports facilities, pools (with poolside restaurant service). There are organized programs for all ages, plus instruction from beginner to advanced in sailing, wind surfing, boating, horseback riding, tennis and archery. Badacsony Hills hiking excursions with guides can be added on. The rooms have movies in English, as well as other languages, and most of the staff speaks passable English. The staff is superb. There are beauticians, cosmeticians, and massage therapists. Wellness and medical facilities are staffed with doctors, nurses, and health specialists, who design programs for losing weight, combating fatigue or physical conditioning. Packages include accommodations and full board, plus doctors' examinations, spa and pool therapy, massages and other treatments. They are widely known for treating arthritis, and a host of degenerative diseases using medicinal baths, indoor and outdoor pools, salt treatments, saunas and hydrotherapy tanks. For that reason the Tihany

attracts virtually every segment of society from every part of Europe. Open all year, but they are often booked up as much as a year in advance. It is advisable to contact and reserve well before your arrival.

# Three Star
## Balatonfüred

**Hotel Blaha Lujza**, 8230 Balatonfüred, Blaha Lujza út 4, ☎ 36-87-581-210, €€. Open from Mar through Dec. This was once owned by "The Nightingale of the Nation," Lujza Blaha, singer and actress at the turn of the century. Although the two-story hotel fronts Blaha Lujza út, the back joins with the Borcsa Étterem (Borcsa Restaurant). In summer it's open April 1 to Oct 31, 10 am to 11 pm, Nov 1 to Mar 31, 11 am to 10 pm (*see Places To Eat*). Although rooms are small, all have color cable TV, mini bar, telephone, safe, and shower/bath, plus there is a fitness room, solarium, sauna, tennis court, and enclosed parking lot.

★**Hotel Annabella**, Balatonfüred, 8230 Balatonfüred, Deák Ferenc u. 25, ☎ 36-87-889-400, reservations 36-87-889-431, fax 36-87-889-435, sales.balatonfured@danubiusgroup.com, www.danubiushotels.com/annabella, €€-€€€, It's a hotel with a Mediterranean feel and the staff is excellent in English. They have five air-conditioned suites, among other options. This is part of the Danubius group of hotels, the largest and probably the best Hungarian hotel chain, in business since the 1950s. Extras include everything from a pampering pedicure followed by aromatherapy bath, to sailing and horseback riding, all booked from the desk. Many of the rooms are not air-conditioned, but they are well-insulated so there really is not much concern about weather variables. On the other hand, the views are terrific from every room, and if you don't like the Balaton shore, you can compensate with a dip in the indoor or the outdoor pool. Evenings feature a live piano bar every night. A folklore program on Thursday evenings caps it for the indoor-outdoor restaurant café. If you've had enough walking, you can rent a car here as well and keep it parked in their free parking lot.

**Hotel Marina**, 8230 Balatonfüred, Széchenyi u. 26, reservations ☎ 36-87-889-536, fax 36-87-
889-535, marina.reservation@
danubiusgroup.com, www.
danubiushotels.com/marina. €€.
Up a notch on the scale from the
Hotel Annabella, one double with
bath runs about €42/10,500 HUF
in low season to about €70 in high
season. Suites are wonderful,

from €92 in low season to about €120 in summer high season,
breakfast included. You can expect an additional charge of
about €4 for window views of Balaton. The cuisine and variety of dining here is a welcome addition. Although they only
serve buffet for breakfast, the dinners are excellent; there is
also the hotel coffee shop and the bar and terrace on the roof.
The Beach Pálmakert Bar and nightclub hosts good entertainment and rocks until 2 am. Kids are welcome. There is a
babysitter, a children's room with special programs to keep
them occupied, as well as a playground. There is also a beauty
salon and a private beach on the shore, where you can rent
pedal boats, rowing craft, and sail boats, or try the swimming
pool, sauna and massage. Table tennis, badminton and billiards are available and a complete set of tours and activities
can be booked from the front desk.

## Below Three Star

### Balatonfüzfő

**Veronika Pension**, Balaton Körút 129, Felsővilla sor,
Balatonfüzfő, €. Rate this a two-star. It is directly opposite
the beach. They have a good website at www.zimmerinfo.hu/
fuzfo/veronika. Showers, toilet, small refrigerator and TV in
each room make for a well-rounded budget facility. Balcony
views overlook a yard large enough for barbecues and soccer.
They also have table tennis and billiards inside, and enclosed
parking. They offer doubles, triples, up to five bedrooms, but
it is advisable to book several months in advance. Try www.
hostelz.com for that. The 24-hour reception will rent bicycles
and boats. Meals can come from the kitchen, and a hot break-

fast with all the trimmings is €3. Cuisine is modern Hungarian and some international. €9 per bed can't be duplicated for the location and what you get, particularly for low-budget singles, or families.

★★**CASTRUM campsites**, €, are a chain that is well known for quality and, considering all factors, come close to a three-star hotel for the amenities offered. It's north of Kesthely on the promontory called the Szépkilátó (beautiful view), right off of Route 71, where many a painter has painted a brilliant sunrise over the silky waters of the lake. Look for the sign that says CASTRUM Balatongyörök camping park. Bungalows are available July 16-Aug 31 for €60 per night (15,000 HUF) and Sept 1 to Oct 15 for €36 (9,000 HUF). An additional bed is €6 (1,500 HUF) per night, and breakfast is an additional €4 (1,000 HUF) per person. There is a café, grocery store, confectionery, game room, buffet and restaurant (the Beach Pub), and a neatly numbered camping layout for tents and campers with electric hook-ups and privacy, as each is surrounded by a brush hedge. 48 apartment bungalows are equipped with kitchen, bathroom, bedroom, satellite hookup for TV (you have to bring your own, or you can rent one), and daily housekeeping, changing of linens, and towels included. Each apartment has a roofed terrace with garden furniture and a front space parking area. As with some hotels, there are tennis courts, and professional instruction, with changing rooms, showers, and toilets. The sandy beach is shallow enough to allow the young ones to play in the water and a bar as well as a volleyball court border it. The small dock here has sailing facilities, with sailboats, boards for windsailing, and rowboats. A private fishing platform in the reeds awaits the patient angler and the rental shop includes table tennis, bicycles, and watersports accoutrements.

## Csopak

★**TheYouth Resort**, Ifjúsági Üdülö, ☎ 36-87-446-505, €, 3,000 to 7,000 HUF. One Star. This is on Sport utca 9 just east of the strand. It has rooms with showers and offers sports facilities. Next to it, appearing a bit run down, is the **Hotel Piroska**, ☎ 36-87-446-576, 7,000 to 10,000 HUF, on Sport utca 5-7. As is common in Europe, these rooms have a common bathroom, but everything is clean and the balcony view over the garden is good for open windows in summer. No air-conditioning.

**Rozmaring Panzió**, Ifjúság sétány 4, ☎/fax 36-87-446-583, €. The camping and buildings are set in park-like grounds by the strand . It is open May to Sept. 5,000 to 7,000 HUF per person. Do not expect a picnic here. No air-conditioning. No showers in any rooms. Public toilets.

## Alsóörs

**Laroba Hotel**, 8226 Alsóörs, Füredi u. 42, ☎ 36-87-575-210, €. Newly renovated and rebuilt in 2002, rooms are modern and clean, and equipped with minibar, TV, Internet connection and telephone. The restaurant, known as the Halásztanya (Fisherman's Farm), has been serving Hungarian dishes, and especially those centering around fish from Lake Balaton, for almost 100 years.

**Aranysas Hotel és Bungaló Alsóörs**, Sedfû út 13/A, ☎ 36-87-447-124, €-€€. 14,900 HUF for a double in high season (July-Aug), 11,500 HUF the rest of the year. Only a couple of minutes walk to the beach, it is located in a tree covered park. Large rooms are equipped with shower and TV, telephone and mini-bar. The traditional Hungarian restaurant is well-known. But there is a bonus here as well – private, well-maintained bungalows in the back. Although lacking kitchens, you can use the hotel and restaurant facilities (open 8 to midnight), indoor parking, sauna, fitness room, table tennis, billiards, an outdoor garden and indoor grill.

## Örvényes

**Huszár Inn**, H-8242 Örvényes, Malom u. 2, ☎ 36-87-449-072, fax 36-87-549-003, huszar@tourinform.info. Open April 1st to June 30th every day 9 am to 10 pm. July 1st to Aug 31st 9 am to 12 am. Closed Nov 15 through April 1st. €-€€. With superb cuisine, it's not a bad place for an overnighter, though there are no support facilities. Three double-room cottages and one full apartment. Includes cable TV and a parking enclosure. Each cottage has a bathroom.

Lake Balaton

# Places to Dine

## Balatonfüzfő

**Susogó Étterem**, 8715 Balatonfüzfő, József Attila u. 9, ☎ 36-88-450-760, €, susogo@freemail.hu. Good Hungarian food at a good price, and the menu is in English as well as Hun-

| DINING PRICE CHART | |
|---|---|
| Price for an entrée, with tax | |
| € | Under $10 |
| €€ | $10-$25 |
| €€€ | Over $25 |

garian. The waiters do not speak English, but the owner does speak a little and is quite helpful. Expect to pay around 1,500 to 3,000 HUF.

## Balatonalmádi

**Arany Korona Vendéglő**, H-8230 Balatonalmádi, Kossuth Lajos út 11, €-€€. You will pay about 4,000 to 7,000 HUF. Just above the Calvinist Church, it has been dubbed by some as the most authentically Hungarian place in Balaton. Enter a csárda (country inn) atmosphere, with gypsy music and fine wines. Try the goulash here; it's paprika hot, but authentic.

As you walk the shore at the park, try a cup of espresso and pastry at the **Coffeehouse Liget**, on the sidewalks in the park, built in 1928, and still serving delightful Magyar sweets.

## Felsőörs

**Udvarház étterem**, 8227 Felsőörs, Fő u. 22, ☎ 36-87-477-521 or 36-87-577-021, €-€€, open noon-midnight, www.udvarhaz.hu. Expect to pay about 2,000 HUF at a minimum. It is a small Hungarian 19th-century-style restaurant, in a country house built in 1862. Try the sirloin with green pepper and sautéed potatoes. The selection of wines here reflects the best in Hungarian viniculture, exquisite when sipped while the gypsy violin group plays every evening.

# Alsóörs

In a country atmosphere, you cannot appreciate the essence of the country unless you try at least one or two family house/ tasting cellars. Commercialized, but a sure value, visit the **Simon Cellar**, 8226 Alsóörs, ☎ 36-87-477-270, mobile 36-20-945-2121 or 36-30-277-7467, €-€€. At the end of Barátság road, it is only a few minutes away from the cycle road, and an easy walk from downtown. There is an inside restaurant/tasting lounge and an outside covered patio area. There is no gypsy music (except on summer weekends), but their own vineyard and wines pleasantly complement a menu of home-style Hungarian cuisine. Their specialty is growing, tasting and selling wine. Olaszrizling, Chardonnay, Tramini, Sárgamuskotály, Zenit, Szürkebarát, Jégbor, and others, all can be sampled while children are kept busy with a separate program. It is sold by the liter and two or more liters earn a discount. They have organized horseback riding and carriage rides. Open daily June 1 to Aug 31st, 11-7. Off 71, make a right at May János út, go four blocks and then left on Barátság and drive to the end.

**Laroba Hotel**, Halásztanya (Fisherman's Ranch) étterem, the 8226 Alsóörs, Füredi u. 42, ☎ 36-87-575-210, €€-€€€, It has a 100-year tradition of superb Hungarian dishes, especially centered around fresh-caught fish from Lake Balaton. You can't make a mistake here. A bit pricey, but it's the real thing. The menus are Magyar, from the times of Árpád forward. As throughout this region, the wine list is supreme.

# Balatonfüred

**Cimbora Grill Garden**, 8230 Balatonfüred, Széchenyi u. 23. ☎ 36-87-482-512, €-€€. Open noon-11 pm. It is only five minutes from the RR station and right next to Highway 71. The pier and the promenade add appeal to its own vine-shaded terrace. Aromas from the chef's grill drift in the Balaton air. Turkey, spare ribs, pork chops, split roast, sirloin, leg of chicken and the indomitable Hungarian specialties of goose are complemented by 10 salad delights at the salad bar. I found the salad fresh, and well prepared. With beer, bottled or tap, and fine Hungarian wines, or soft drinks, this is a relaxed and relaxing place.

The **Stefánia Vitorlás Restaurant Guest-House**, 8230 Balatonfüred, Tagore sétány 1, ☎ 36-87-343-407, vitorlas. étterem@axelero.hu, www.vitorlasetterem.hu. €. You will pay 1,600 HUF (€6.4) to 2,000 HUF (€8), and you can sit and dine where perhaps a duke or the Hapsburg emperor once came to dine and cruise at the first yacht club of Lake Balaton. Walk to the end of the promenade, and then over to the dock. Today it is a confectionary, restaurant, pub, and guesthouse, right next to the yachts and the fresh smell of the lake. You will pay 1,600-2,000 HUF for a meal with everything.

 **Koloska Csárda**, Sándor József 8230, Balatonfüred, Koloska Völgy. Open 11 am-11 pm daily, April 1 to Oct 31. €-€€. A true Hungarian Balaton-style country csárda or country inn. Not just food and wine are offered, but optional stabling and horseback riding as well. Beginners are also welcome in its Koloska Lovasiskola (Koloska Riding School). Cuisine is Hungarian, with specialties of the house including jack-knife roast from Arács, spit-roasted pork, and kettle goulash. The wines are from Tihany, Balatonfüred, and other Balaton areas. Gypsy music and dance accompany some meals.

**Borcsa Étterem Summer** (see *Places to Stay*) is open April 1 to Oct 31, 10 am to 11 pm, Nov 1 to Mar 31, 11 am to 10 pm. €-€€. A good meal rounded out with a glass of wine can run you 3,000 to 6,000 HUF. The restaurant with roofed open-air terrace, white tented roof and white outdoor furniture, is supplemented by a pizza parlor and a terraced brasserie (great panorama), which opens out to the Tagore Promenade.

# Tihany

**Club Tihany Old Captain's Restaurant**, H-8237 Tihany, Rév u 3 Pf: 31, ☎ 36-87-538-564, fax 87-448-083, €€-€€€. Although the hotel housing the restaurant is old, it certainly keeps up a European sense of elegance. The meals here are top-notch Hungarian and international cuisine, accompanied by music and sometimes song. There is a fine international as well as Hungarian wine list. As an added bonus, visit its Balaton Wine Tavern, which has an excellent cross-section of Hungarian vintages, especially from the Balaton region. Open 6 pm to 11 pm daily, except Sun, May 12 to Oct 12. They also serve cold foods, and they have summer barbecues.

## Keszthely

**Oázis Reform Restaurant**, Rákóczi tér 3, €, is a salad bar pure and simple. It is open from 11 am to 4 pm and is best in the earlier hours when the salads are crisp.

## Balatonfenyves

Hubertus Riding School (see *Adventures On Horseback*, pages 357 ff) is home to the **Hubertus-Hof Restaurant**, 8646 Balatonfenyves, Nimród u. 1, ☎ 36-85-560-930, hubertus@hubertus.hu, www. hubertus.hu/english, €€. Open daily from 11 am to 10 pm. Although the hotel is not  the best, there is something entirely unique about this restaurant. The Hubertus-Hof restaurant has numerous game dishes, all of them fresh, which means the game was taken that same day, often only hours before it is served on the table. For starters, order the pancakes with game ragout filling in Eger sauce, cranberries and tangerine pieces. What a beginning! The flavor will not leave you, even when you start in on the exquisite dinner. Pick the game dishes from Nagyberek, which are freshly dressed from the game farm. Try grilled breast of pheasant with blackberry sauce and potato croquettes. The chefs here can compete with chefs anywhere. No entertainment, but then the food more than compensates. In summer there are two outside terraces, each with its own ambience, quiet Mediterranean or country relaxed. Inside dining offers country elegance Hungarian-style, with a fireplace to warm you in winter while you admire the beauty of the snow in the woods outside the window, or as you watch the green unfurl in spring.

**Csiga Kisvendéglõ** (Little Snail Guest House) Tessedik u. 30, €. Open Mon-Fri 11 am to 9 pm. This is about 20 minutes from Fõ tér on a quiet side of town. They serve authentic modern Hungarian meat and fish dishes at a great price, 800 to about 1,600 HUF for main dishes.

## Örvényes

**Huszár Inn**, H-8242 Örvényes, Malom u. 2, ☎ 36-87-449-072, fax 36-87-549-003, huszar@tourinform.info, www.huszar. info. €. Open April 1 to June 30 every day, 9 am to 10 pm, July 1 to Aug 31, 9 am to 12 am. Menu will run anywhere from about 1,500 up to 3,000 HUF and it's all typical Hungarian, with a bonus – the wines are the finest in the area.

## Csopak

The **Malom Csárda** (Mill Inn) shouldn't be missed here. €-€€. It is situated over Nosztori Creek, a 10-minute walk up Veszprém út to No. 3, at the northern end of the village. Open 11 am to 11 pm daily. The surviving open-chimney stove of a 19th-century inn has been incorporated in the csárda. Cuisine is Hungarian and will cost you from 1,500 up to 5,000 HUF; here, as in many other places in Balaton, it's half what you would pay in Budapest for the same.

## Family Places

**Club Tihany Holiday Center** (see above, page 304) has something for everyone, from toddlers to adults who want a taste of a vacation club scene. But the range of activities and the low cost attract families from all over Europe. On a different order, catering to adults but offering a lot of kid fun is the **Zalakaros spa** on the shores of the protected Kis Balaton, approximately 40 km/24 miles from the shoreline of the bigger Balaton. http://zalakaros.ohb.hu/index.en.html.

Also, review the *Itineraries* section, where many family beaches and locations are discussed.

ZALAKAROS

This is an 800-year-old town where they discovered medicinal spring thermal waters in 1961. See www. zalakaros.hu. The waters were found to speed recovery from some gynecological and locomotor diseases, including arthritis, and were also found to speed recovery in orthopedic and some post-operative nerve conditions. But the rejuvenative quality of the waters was so popular that they turned the town into a family spa as well as medicinal Mecca. Located south of "Kis Balaton" (Little Balaton), a protected international reserve filled with thousands of birds and wildlife, take Route 7 west (Route 71) along the southern shore, and continue toward Nagykanizsa, but get off in the town of Galambok. From Galambok, head north toward Zalakaros and Kis Balaton. It is approximately 40 km/24 miles south from the larger Lake Balaton. The **Hotel Karos Spa**, shown above, H-8749 Zalakaros, Alma út 1, ☎ 36-93-542-500, www.karos-spa.com, is about the best for medicinal recovery, and offers a family-friendly atmosphere, but its five-star accommodations and programs are expensive. However the

Lake Balaton

town website lists a number of other hotels, hostels and camping sites, or ask the local tourist office for information. It also includes prices and open hours for the huge public bathing complex, the **Gránit Gyódfürdõ Részvénytársaság**, H-8749 Zalakoros, Termál út 4, www.furdo-zalakaros.hu, which offers pool-side eateries and programs for both fun and recovery.

# Nightlife

## Balatonfüred

The **Beach Pálmakert Bar and Nightclub** at the Hotel Marina, €-€€, hosts good entertainment and rocks until 2 am (see *Places to Stay*, page 303).

**Butterfly Nightclub** at Club Tihany Holiday Center, H-8237 Rév út. 3, pf 31, ☎ 36-87-538-564, fax 36-87-448-083, is open 9 pm to 3 am daily. Disco music (sometimes live), with dancing and cocktails. €-€€.

**Stefánia Vitorlás Étterem**, 8230 Balatonfüred, Tagore S. u. 1, ☎/fax 36-87-343-407. Open 8 am-12 pm summer season and 10 am-10 pm off-season. i. Not a disco, but great ambience out on the dockside of Lake Balaton, and a good dance spot, 1950s-1970s style. There is a shoreline atmosphere on the famous Tagore Walkway, dance music and live musicianst. It's also a favorite spot with the locals. Prices are very reasonable here.

# Itineraries

We have purposely hugged close to the Balaton shores, but those reaching out for adventure can head north past Veszprém, and hug the Austrian border, or go south by the Balkans. The roads in both directions are good and sprinkled with gas stations and stopovers.

## Balatonkenese

Coming to the Balaton shore on M 7, this is the first major town you will pass. Houses line the shoreline and the entire coast seems hemmed in by private property. Indeed, we won't stop here, just for that reason, so don't be discouraged. But it is

worthwhile noting one of the native plants, whose discovery, somewhere in this vicinity, dates back to the 16th century. Today it is a protected species whose primary home is here. It is called the tátorján colewort, shown above. The Tartars taught the Hungarians how to use this plant centuries ago. Its most remarkable characteristic is its huge carrot-shaped rootstock, sometimes as thick as a man's thigh, which stretches down a yard or more into the soil. During periods of hard poverty Hungarians would dig up the roots, and roast them in place of bread. There are a variety of ways to prepare it, Tartar-style, of course.

## Balatonfüzfő

You have an option here to carry through to Veszprém, north of Balaton (see Central Transdanubia). Like so much of Hungary, this is one of those towns whose modern texture belies a strange mystery from its stormy past. Archeological evidence suggests that it existed in Roman times. However, it is first mentioned in historical documents under the name of Máma. This town may have been destroyed by subsequent invasion, but apparently it predates the Magyar conquest. Documents show the first king of Hungary, King Stephen I, bequeathed Máma to the Greek nuns of Veszprém Valley. They built a church, which was demolished in the Tartar invasion of 1242. Thus the church ruins today are dated to the 13th century, but here begins a mystery. For documents indicate that it was rebuilt in honor of King St. Leslie, and that it was still standing in 1292. According to the records, this town and its church was evidently obliterated in the Rákóczi war of independence.

Lake Balaton

But the record of a visitor dated 1761 says "There is a hermit and a home for him on the field next to the village. He is far away from people, however, he lives next to the church that was built in honor of St. Leslie with the permission of the archbishop of Esztergom." So, this record says that the church dating from the late 13th century was still standing. Since then, of course, there have been world wars. But there is absolutely no record of the destruction of this church anywhere. There is no evidence of a fire, no evidence of a conqueror, no evidence of a war that may have taken it down, and there are no church records anywhere as to its fate. A photo from 1928-29 shows only the ruins. Only one western gable remains today of the church that was. It was not here when the Germans came in during WWII. So, what happened to it?

If you decide to stay here a night and don't want to shop the villas by the shore, go the **Veronika Pension**, Balaton Körút 129, Felsővilla sor, Balatonfüzfő, Hungary, which is directly opposite the beach (see *Places to Stay*, page 307).

Balatonfüzfő boasts one of the largest beaches on the North Shore, called **Föveny Beach**. The water starts ankle-high, and very gradually deepens, but does drop rather sharply farther out. Yet this is a great place to control the younger ones in the water. There is a free changing room, plus beachside büfé and éttermek (restaurants), and a waterslide. Don't expect to be alone; these beaches are popular. Get there early, and bring an umbrella and blanket.

**Tobruk Beach**, on the other hand, is the smaller of the two, but offers a lot more for the money. This beach is for active types and young families, with a mini-soccer court, beach volleyball, crazy golf/mini-golf field, a climbing wall, different types of jumping games, pedal boats, children's canoes (called snuki), and table tennis. The beach is half-grass (with some trees) and half-sand. Singing, dancing, and different types of programs take place on Fri and Sat nights during the summer on the open-air stage, free of charge. At this writing, entry costs children 180 HUF, adults 280; a weekly ticket is 1,000 HUF for children and 1,500 HUF for adults. Parking is about 500 HUF, but if you stay in an apartment or room within walking distance, that is not relevant. After 4 pm, all tickets are discounted.

# Balatonalmádi/Vörösberény

**Tourinform Office**,
8220 Balatonalmádi
and Vörösháza tér 4,
☎/fax 36-88-549-081,
balatonalmadi@
tourinform.hu.

Farther down Route
71 from Balaton-
füzfő, Balatonalmádi
is actually an inte-
gration of three villages, Balatonalmádi, Vörösberény, and
Káptalanfüred. Balatonalmádi was originally known as
Almádi. A charter of land mentions it in 1493, the year after
Columbus discovered America. It was called the region of
Almádi, famous for its wine production. The devastating
phylloxera epidemic in the 1880s effectively destroyed a good
portion of the vineyards of Hungary. Almádi was wiped out.
The recovery entailed not only replanting vineyards and restoration of the wine cellars; it also transformed the local econ-
omy. Although wine is still important, Balantonalmádi today
caters to tourists as well and is loaded with fine hotels (see
*Places to Stay*, pages 303 ff).

The fame of its
smaller cousin,
Vörösberény,
relates to con-
struction, not
wine or travel. In
fact, Vörösberény
means red sand-
stone, named for
the quarries that
once burst with
activity on the
outskirts. The high oxidized iron content of the soil has dyed
the stone red. Red sandstone marks the Óvári lookout tower,
high above the town, as it does the statue of Pannónia Aqua in
the middle of Városház tér, the village square. As you walk

Lake Balaton

320 ■ Balaton Northern Shore

through the town, in addition to the red sandstone, you will
see the hand-sawn wooden balconies of many a house in the
area.

There are lots of restaurants and wine cellars in the area, as
well as plenty of music and dance. The music pavilion promenade, hosts bands playing across the open water every week.
In the summer, almost every day there is some type of activity
or event in the town and classical music concerts in the
Vörösbény Szent Ignác Catholic Church. Famous European
musicians as well as top young Hungarian talent come here to
play music, from early folk, to ecclesiastical, classical and
Baroque. Seven piers and docks along the shore offer sailboat
rentals, wind surfing and, in some cases, lessons. Every pier
has facilities. And just about every hotel can make arrangements for you.

## What to See in Balatonalmádi/Vörösberény

Most of these places are covered in Hiking & Biking, pages
348 ff).

The **Christian Reformed Fortified Church**, Veszprém u.

107, is the oldest monu-
ment in the city, men-
tioned in early records
of King St. Stephen as a
gift to the Greek nuns in
1297. Built in Roman-
esque style, Gothic nev-
ertheless exudes from
its design as well. The
Turks ravaged it and it
had to be rebuilt, this time with a wall for defense, in the 15th
to 16th centuries.

### Balatonalmádi-Vörösmarty Templom Square

**St Ignatius Roman Catholic Church and Monastery**,
Veszprémi út 83. Built between 1770 and 1779, the frescoes,
the pulpit and the altar are considered architectural masterpieces. Sitting on a hill that dominates the surroundings, the
former cloister was considered a palace of the Jesuits of Győr
in Berény as early as 1758. It was converted into a hotel, but
then in 2005 that closed its doors, but the church and monastery remain.

**St Imre Roman Catholic Church**, Balatonalmádi dr. Óvári F. u. 47. This parish church in the middle of the town was built by architect István Medgyasszay and, unlike the Hungarian folk style, this building is distinctively influenced by Transylvania, but equally incorporates the red sandstone of the area to give it a distinctive style all of its own. Built in 1930, it stands next to the **Holy Right Hand Chapel**, itself moved here from Buda castle in 1956. Its rich gold mosaic is by Miksa Róth. It depicts King St. Stephen, and his famous right hand, which lies permanently in state in the basilica in Budapest. Some of his remains are reputedly here as well.

**Városház tér** (City Hall Square) is bordered by churches, the town hall and marked by several statues. Most notable is the **Pannonia Aqua**, made entirely of the red sandstone.

### Öregpark (The Old Park)

Its sycamore, maple, and willows have had a chance to grow for almost 100 years, shading the green grass with broad, leafy branches and the draping sorrows of the willows. Statues decorate the area, including the great poet Petőfi Sándor, the revolutionary Kossuth Lajos, and the famous rebel of the nobility, Rákóczi. Time your stroll in summer to the Mozart quartets or the strains of Bartók, or any number of great composers whose notes ring from the music pavilion, a turn-of-the-19th-century structure in the park which hosts concerts throughout the summer and spring. If you do not buy from one of the vendors that ply the park grounds, enhance your walk with a cup of espresso and Hungarian pastry at the Coffeehouse Liget.

### Beaches of Balatonalmádi

These all have very low entry costs. Adults average about 500 HUF and children 300 HUF.

**Budatava Beach** and **Neptun Beach** are open from 8:30 am to about 7 pm. Grassy lawn and trees make it for comfortable sitting, but many beachgoers come early just to get the shade of a tree, so plan on renting an umbrella if you're late. There are various catering and eating places, along with sun beds, sports equipment rentals, umbrellas, and newspapers and magazines in a number of different languages.

**Wesselényi Beach** is open 8:30 am to 7 pm The largest beach in town, it has a giant waterslide, boating, hydro cycles, and inflatable castles. A playground even spills over into the water. Various entertainment programs are held here. There are anywhere from 20 to 30 different caterers and restaurants and the longest water chute on Lake Balaton. Interactive programs sometimes incorporate guests and onlookers into folklore dances and other events.

**Káptalanfüredi**, open 8:30 to 7 pm, 240 HUF adults, 120 HUF children. Restaurants front the long, newly planted grass ways, which are shaded by some trees. Here too, you can swim, but it is quieter and more for cozy couples or seniors than some of the more active beaches. The shore is relatively undisturbed.

## Felsőörs

Located on the road four miles southwest of Balatonalmádi, the village dates from the 11th century. The main church was built in Romanesque style with an unusual Baroque rectory. Its five-register organ was carved in 1745 and can be heard in summer organ concerts.

From Felsőörs there are several rural trails branching out from the west and south end of the village. Follow the yellow and red signs for the **Malom-Valley**, **Miske Peak** and **Szabadság lookouts**. The 45-minute to three-hour walks are favorites. The forrás hegyi study trail recounts the tertiary period of the earths' history, but all the information boards are in Hungarian.

And, as with all areas around Balaton, you cannot escape the wine. There are numerous cellars to pick from here too. However, this one especially merits a visit: **Rásky Pince**, H-8227 Felsőörs. Call Tourinform to arrange the meeting beforehand; the owner will arrange for a translator for a tasting session.

## Alsóörs

Once a Roman settlement and outpost, it graces the slopes of Somlyo Hill. The town is a bona fide relic of the Árpád dynasty. Magyars built on top of the Roman remains. Chartered in 1200, it has remained Magyar since, and its quarries and red standstone made it famous in the Middle Ages. The oldest house (7 Petőfi Alley), from the 15th century, called the **Turkish House**, was the home of a minor nobleman and still stands. Its nickname comes from the fact that the chimney reminds people of a turbaned head. The local 13th-century church retains the Gothic and Baroque features incorporated over the ages. The Old Town is still dotted with thatched roof cottages. Often a building sits on top of Roman ruins that were incorporated into the structure. The town's greatest charm is that it has tried to preserve the medieval tradition. It is the birthplace of Sándor Endrődi (1850-1920) one of the great poets of Hungary.

But there is something special here that attracted the Harley Davidson National Congress of 2005. The theme of the Congress, hardly to be expected in this little part of the Hungarian countryside, Ladies on Bikes. What a small world we live in.

## Csopak

The village of Csopak (www. csopak.hu), about nine km/5.4 miles farther down from Balatonfüred, has only one real reason for a visit... wine. From the train station, walk up Kossuth utca to the old village, but don't hesitate to branch off. There are numerous wine cellars around the old village, and many have well-advertised dens, inviting you to drop in. Csopak's claim to fame is its white wines (not excluding reds), of which the best-known is probably Olaszrizling. Here, you buy it out of the barrel.

This small community of 1,800 maintains its own tourist office, the Csopaktourist office, Veszprémi út 33 (Route 73 to Vesprém), ☎ 36-87-455-025, www.csopaktourist.hu. A list of the various Csopak programs and celebrations is on their website. It is famous for the wine produced from its fine red soil, and it also has its share of smooth, sandy beach. The train station is on Löcedombi utca, right next to the intersection of Löcedombi utca and Kossuth Lajos utca. Route 71 passes through town and intersects with Kossuth Lajos utca

Lake Balaton

just across the railroad tracks from the train station. You can easily get your bearings from the train station. Kossuth Lajos utca is lined with restaurants and shops. From the train station, head north, away from the shore, on Kossuth Lajos utca. You will pass Fehérvizi utca on the right. At the next intersection, make a left and follow the street that enters the intersection at a right angle. This runs parallel to the shore. Do not take Patakvölgy ut toward the shore. It is going in the wrong direction. Stay parallel to the shore. This street turns into Berekháti út. About 15 minutes from the intersection with Kossuth Lajos utca, the road will turn away from the shore again, and you will  come to 34 Berekháti út. Combine your wine with Hungarian cuisine at **Linczy Pince Vendéglő-Borozó**, above, H-8229 Csopak, Berekháti út 34, ☎ 36-87-446-294, fax 36-87-446-250, linczy-pince@freemail.hu, www.linczmayertamas.fw.hu.

There is one place here that shouldn't be missed for a meal. **The Malom Csárda** (Mill Inn) is situated over Nosztori Creek. The Malom Csárda, ☎ 36-87-446-063, www.balaton.hu (click on Malom Csárda in the search box) is about a mile from the train station. Walk up Veszprém ut (Route 73) to no. 3, on the outskirts of the town heading away from the shore. A gypsy violinist plays Hungarian songs to accompany the meal and the wine every evening.

## Balatonfüred

Balatonfüred has attracted tens of thousands for years. Vestiges of an ancient Roman encampment remain. However, the earliest document that mentions it is dated 1211. The medicinal waters that effervesce their way to the surface are mentioned in 17th-century documents. Mátyás Béla, a Hungarian scholar circa 1730, wrote, "The village has two mineral springs; one is beneficial for drinking purposes, the other for bathing." In the small building attached to this latter spring, the mineral water was heated for bathing. The reputation of the water attracted many people, particularly in May. Since there was no shelter against rain or sun nearby, the visitors stayed in tents pitched at random. Why would people be so attracted to a spring that they would rough it so? Wonder water. Drinking the water had a marvelous curative power on kidney, bowel and stomach problems, very common in those days. The news spread to Tihany Abbey, which soon rented and then later purchased the spring. Then, in 1743, Ágoston Lécs, abbot of Tihany, established the first officially recognized spring. The curative powers of the waters became famous far and wide. By 1772 an official analysis of the waters (there are seven springs altogether) resulted in their certification as a health and medicinal resort. By 1785 the influx of people from virtually every part of Europe prompted Joseph II to order the appointment of a resident doctor and surgeon.

The main well is in the town center at Gyógytér (Healing Square), with the **Lajos Kossuth Drinking Hall** (built in 1800; renovated in 1853). The Heart Hospital for Heart Diseases, with its open balconies, dominates the square from the east. It has gained fame through its use of these medicinal waters in successful treatments for heart disease, gastro-intestinal problems, vascular, and pulmonary problems (incorporating modern methods as well, supervised by doctors).

But all is not medicine. The **Trade Union's Sanatorium** (erected in 1802) marks the spot where the first permanent theater in Transdanubia performed in Hungarian. At the the time that was revolutionary, as public performances were in Italian or in German. Today, the Great Hall leading to the building, is lined with plaques of famous writers, scientists, artists, and notable personalities who have successfully

Lake Balaton

taken curative treatments. It is also the Cultural Center with a seating capacity of 400.

The **Anna Ball** selects the annual Ball Queen, famed in Hungary. It is held here every year. But the origin of the annual event is actually in the **Horváth House** (1825), the other structure fronting the square. In 1825 the Szentgyörgy-Horváth family arranged the first Anna Ball in honor of their daughter, Anna. Held on the last Saturday of July, is a tradition that now dates back over 170 years.

## WHO DRANK THIS WATER?

Of seven local springs, six funnel their water into the baths in Balatonfüred. However, the Kossuth Lajos spring stands apart from the six in that it is open to the public and sits in a colonnaded veranda of its own, where you can sample the water. But don't expect a mountain spring taste. It is called sour water, but consider the benefit. It gains its fame from the balance of minerals in combination with slight amounts of radon that have beneficial affects upon the body. Emperors, kings, queens, princesses, princes, lawyers, great scientists and composers all have joined ranks here. And when Emperor Joseph personally visited the site, although the sour water disgusted him, he drank more than one glass, and pronounced an official sanction to make it a health center. You might be standing on the same spot as Emperor Joseph did in 1753, when he sampled exactly the same well water.

But it was at the turn of the 19th century that it became an internationally famous resort. This was reinforced after WW I, when a rebuilding process incorporated large curative facilities. That was, ironically, matched by the opening of dozens of places selling aromatic wines that were grown in the surrounding hills. Balatonfüred was awarded the title of

International Town of Viticulture and Wine Growing by The International Office of Wine Growing and Viticulture in Paris, in 1987, recognizing it as one of the great wine culture regions of the world.

Balatonfüred was the home of the first Lake Balaton steamship, the *Kisfaludy*, and the first yacht club on the lake (dating to 1867). Numerous villas of famous personalities have been situated around its surroundings. The home of the great novelist Mór Jókai (1825-1904) is today a memorial museum with original furnishings and writings. The Lakeshore promenade, named after the Nobel-prize-winning Indian poet, Rabindranath Tagore, gained its name when out of gratefulness at being healed from his heart ailment, he planted a lime tree here in memorium. He established a precedent that has been followed by a number of famous people who have benefited from the life-giving waters. The tree-lined walk of a little over half a mile looks out across the lake. While the lazy waters lap the shore you will see busts and statues of famous figures of Hungarian and international history. At the end of the promenade on the edge of the Rose Garden stand the statues of The Fisherman and The Ferryman, which represent the ancient trades of the lake. From this point the pier leads to the port, with rowboats and sailboats on both sides of the pier, as well as a restaurant on the landing stage. You may want to see the ceremony of **Unfurling the Sails**, a grand parade of yachts and sail boats, with music, food and festivities, the hallmark of the

start of the Balaton season in May.

Lake Balaton

## Walking the Blaha

Another center of the town is Blaha Lujza Utca, where the summer home of Lujza Blaha, a famous Hungarian singer and actress, looked over the lake in 1867, but which today has only memorial columns. The nearby **Pharmacy** (1782), the **Vasutas Üdülő** (Railway Employees' Holiday Home) and the **postal building** were up and functioning when America had

the War of 1812. But don't stop at that, go into the **Kedves Cukrászda** (Confectioner's and Coffee Shop) to have a coffee and sweets. It was established in 1782.

## Lóczy Cave

The twin-towered Catholic church, built of red stone, is at the begining of Kossuth Lajos utca, where a footpath with green and blue waymarks leads to Lóczy Cave (at the end of Öreg-hegy út). The cave itself opens out of a quarry. It is one of the more interesting cave sights of Balaton, with aragonite peastones sparkling in the stratified walls stretching to a length of about 120 yards. Discovered in 1894 during a mining operation, it was not excavated until 1934 by the son of Lajos Lóczy, one of the great speleologists of Hungary. The cave has two large halls and a gallery 22 yards long. However, the larger part of the cave still remains unexplored, and is blocked off from tourists. The temperature is a stable 50°F year-round. It is open from May to Oct.

From Lóczy Cave a footpath waymarked with green triangles runs to Tamás hegy where you will find the **Jókai Kilátó** (Jókai's lookout tower). About 480 feet tall, it gives an enchanting panorama of the lake, the boats and sails plying on the horizon, the wooded mountains of the Balaton Uplands and the Tihany Peninsula. If you walk this pathway in the autumn, you will notice the fiery red leafed bushes along the way. These are the Hungarian fustic, characteristic of this hillside in particular.

From the cave you will also find the red waymarks for another path that leads to the wooded, rocky ravine called the **Koloska Völgy** (Koloska Valley). Pressing farther on the same path will take us to the **Recsek-hegy** with a lookout tower on the peak. This is a higher climb (1,300 feet), but it gives an even better view from the lookout tower, which is named after Gáspár Noszlopy, a hero of the 1848-1849 War of Independence.

Balatonfüred rocks with the annual **Balaton Wine Festival,** usually between Aug 5 and Aug 20. Check with Tourinform. At the same time, don't overlook the **Cimora Grill Garden**, on Széchenyi u 23, or the **Stefánia Vitorlás Restaurant Guest-House**, 8230 Balatonfüred, Tagore sétány, or the **Koloska Csárda**, in the nearby Koloska Völgy (Koloska Valley), where you can combine meals with a stay and horseback riding (see *Places to Dine*, page 312).

## Tihany

Tihany is not serviced by the rail line that circles Balaton, although from the rail station at Aszófö, five km/three miles distance, or from Balatonfüred, a bus to Tihany synchronizes its schedule with the train schedules. Bus fees are around 200 HUF. You can also go by ferry from Szántód or from Balatonföldvár. There are also train and boat connections from Balatonfüred to Tihany. Since only cottages and residences are available due to restrictions on building, Tourinform is about the best source for booking rooms. They are at Tihany Village, Kossuth u. 20 (☎/fax 87-448-519). The Tourinform office is only open between May and Oct, Mon-Fri, 8:30 am to 7 pm and on weekends 8:30 am to 12:30 pm.

Demand for rooms is high, so prices will be on high side. Many of the proprietors speak at least a little English and German, and often are well traveled. There are some excellent accommodations for singles, seniors and families (see Club Tihany in *Places to Stay*, page 304). Tihany's small number of restaurants and cafés vie as well with those overlooking Balaton Lake.

Tihany is the site of the oldest Bronze Age fortified ditch system in Europe, above the crater lakes. The two lakes create an oasis of unusual beauty and singularity. The first inner lake is an average of 75 feet above the level of Lake Balaton. There are geyser cones along its Southern Shore. Hot steaming water regularly spurts out from the tops of some them, creating unearthly travertine and hydroquartzite formations, testimony to the still-active earth beneath our toes. The Golden House geyser cone, covered with yellow lichen, sits like a monarch amidst the rising forms. The mild micro-climate has spawned over 1,000 insect species within the cone environs. There are 800 different butterfly species in the surrounding forests and hills, home also to the breathtaking, bright and rare ruby tiger and red underwing. Cicadas and balm crickets singing in the early evening, and perhaps the call of the rare horned sparrow owl accompany the setting sun.

★★Tihany's 18th-century **Benedictine Monastery** (open 9 am to 5:30 pm daily), a World Heritage Site, is accessible for a single fee of 300 HUF. It sits atop the hill, at the end of the road overlooking Lake Balaton and clearly commercialized, with  books and pamphlets and mementoes in the souvenir shop. These scarcely affect its old-world ambience. The medieval cloister exudes an astonishing primitive beauty, with an exquisite wooden altar, carved by an 18th-century resident monk, the magnificent gold work of the nave, and the frescoes. These all belie the fact that it was re-built between 1719-1754 from the stones of the earlier Tihany Fortress Castle. The frescoes were done by three of Hungary's celebrated 19th-century painters, Károly Lotz, Bertalan Székely, and Lajos

*Organ in Tihany Abbey*

Deák-Ébner. Parts of the Abbey, a work of many hands, are nevertheless clear surviving relics of the Middle Ages. The Monastery was established by the order of King Andrew I in 1055. The undercroft of the abbey is carved into the hill and houses the king's marble tomb, in the basement crypt of the abbey. He died in 1060. The document contains the earliest known writing in the Hungarian language. One wonders what stories of intrigue and courage took place here, hidden by the picture-postcard views. For it is a curiosity of history and Hungary, that the Turks, so rapacious and fierce, failed to mount the walls of this high redoubt of Christianity during their entire 150 years of occupation.

Try one of the summer choir or instrumental concerts. The abbey has incredible acoustics that take you back in time. Then walk down the east side steps to the café, order an espresso or eat one of their delicious ice creams while you sit at an outside terrace table and look out at the long view of blue Lake Balaton.

The adjoining former monastic residence is now the **Tihany Museum**. It covers the history of the region from the Iron Age onward.

Óvár Hill, 660 feet high, adjoins Tihany, with a walking trail leading up to it (check with Tourinform, as they are re-marking the trails here). This is the site of the oldest and best preserved Iron Age earthworks in Hungary. Three concentric mounds, built up and then set with a single gateway, are clearly evident. The defensive perimeter was so successful that the Romans later used the same works to defend their camp. On the same hill facing the lake, caves served as homes for the Benedictine monks in the early medieval period. History holds that they did not come from Rome, but from Kiev, and formed the unique St. Nicholas Hermitage of Oroszkō.

Lake Balaton

# Örvényes

This is not a spectacular location, but it is a place to relax and get to know the locals. The beach deepens a trifle too quickly for children, but it is free. A cross-section of young adult, middle aged and older tourists as well as Hungarians are attracted to it.

There is an interesting historical sidelight to this town of 174 residents. The **watermill** of the town, whose old wooden wheel is turned by the flowing waters of the Pécsely stream, has been operating in its present form since the 18th century, but is actually much older. It attracts people from all over Europe. Open from 10 am to 4 pm daily, except Mon, it can be visited from the 1st of May to the end of Oct. While we don't know exactly when it was built, we do know that it was operating in 1211 according to the records of Tihany Abbey. The miller's dwelling house, next to it, is a folk museum, itself an 18th-century monument. The double-arch bridge adjoining was built in Baroque style in the 17th century. The statue dominating its arches is St. John of Nepomuk.

On the eastern edge of the village, on the hill above the mill, the single-aisle, square-ended church is a faithful reconstruction of the one that stood there in the 13th century. Just about every home has its own vineyard and the surrounding gently sloping hills produce some of the finest Hungarian wines. The ancient Balaton grapes in this village produce a special sweet base and it is perfected with recipes from the cellars on the hillsides. Italian (olasz) rizling, rizling szilvani (bases of white vines), with the Örvényes label, are special fruity wines with a rich full-bodied flavor. While in town stop by the **Huszár Inn**, H-8242 Örvényes, Malom u. Their restaurant should not be missed (see *Places to Dine* and *Places to Stay*, pages 314 and 309).

# Balatonudvari

Balatonudvari was another one of those sleepy towns that belonged to the abbots of Tihany. It made its living by fishing, reed cutting, animal breeding and viniculture. The local public bathing concession opened in the 1920s. But the attraction here is not the Balaton shore. Go to the cemetery, spotlighted with its 13th-century **Roman Catholic Church**. Opposite the church, on the other side of the longer road, the Baroque 18th-century **Calvinist Church** sits at the western end of the village, joined to its graveyard where dozens of grave stones are shaped into hearts. The majority were made by stone masons in the 1800s. I have always wondered, who carved that first heart tombstone? A lost lover, a grieving husband? We will never know. Similar art has been found in other areas of Balaton as well, but nowhere in such a concentration. The Catholic Church attracts some of the finest artists and chamber ensembles in Hungary during the summer months and throughout the year on weekends.

In addition, there are two ports on the lake, mooring small craft and offering rentals. A walk through town takes you through the formerly separate communities of Balaton and Udvari. The balance of the restaurants, cafés, and wine cellars, however, seem to be in the old community of Udvari. As the evening wears on, sometimes as you walk by the half-opened door of a csárda or borozó (country restaurant or wine drinking bar) you will hear the men singing, or perhaps a violin or gypsy orchestra.

A walk on the green waymarked pathway leads to **Hideg-hegy**, and a view of the lake that requires a camera. But you can also take the yellow waymarks and step into a place that time forgot They take you to **Kû-Völgy**, a geological remnant of a time when strange precipices and limestone gorges were shaped into twisted canyons and tortured forms. This too may require your camera. Both hikes take about three hours.

## ★Káli Basin

Traveling west, uphill from the lake, woods and vineyards intermingle. A sweet scent can be detected in the wind during summer. Winepress houses and wine cellars hug the land, barely visible above the miles of ripening fruited vines. The land and the vines have been married for centuries. The Romans liked the climate, so similar to that of their grape arbored hills in Italy, and planted their own vineyards, naming the area Tusculanum, which means holiday resort. During the Austro-Hungarian Empire, white wines from the Káli basin and environs were delivered to the Royal Court in Vienna.

It is the heart of the Balaton-Uplands National Park, uniting six protected areas of 160,000 acres, the heart of Balaton's viniculture: Small-Balaton, the Peninsula of Tihany, Pécsely, Tapolca, the Káli-basin, Keszthely-hill, High-Bakony and the protected area of Somló. Marked, well-maintained, easy hiking paths lace the area. Pinot Noir, Merlot, Cabernet Franc, Cabernet Sauvignon, Muscatel, and Riesling vines grow here, along with Grey Monk, Irsai, Olivér, Tramini and red grapes that produce fiery red wines with a characteristically sweet fragrance.

## ★Balaton Uplands National Park

The fertile sediment, which filled the Kali Basin from ancient prehistoric volcanic emissions, contributed to a fabulously productive farming industry. The medieval forests shrank as viticulture flowered and as the locals reached out to trade with villages on the shores of Lake Balaton.

*Chapel on St George Hill*

But, inland, the torturous testimony of nature's past could not be avoided. Volcanoes, submerged beneath the water, gushed fountains of hot pressurized lava. The water battled to cool the crusty basalt as it came up in the Pannonian sea. As the struggle continued, pillars and pipes of hardened lava cones formed into eerie monuments, some of them rising 30 m/100 ft into the air. Their bizarre wind-eroded shapes are part of the panorama at Kõvágóörs, Szentbékkála, and Salföld, while on Mount Hegyes-tû, the prehistoric crater Lake Kornyi gives testimony to the chaos of prehistory. The lingering effects of that age have brought an effusion of healing waters, filled with minerals and trace elements. They have healed and laid claim to recreation and rejuvenation since before Roman times. So has come the great complex of healing and wellness resort hotels surrounding Hévíz. Perhaps this is the secret of

*Csobánc Hill*

the wonderful water called Theodora, which is packaged and shipped to all points east and west. Originating from the wells of Kékkút, it was known even in Roman times.

At Salföld, grey cattle, Hungarian Racka sheep and buffaloes of the Alföld graze in the nature protection reserve. Walk the path up to Csobánc hegy (Csobánc Hill), a panoramic 375-m/ 1,230-foot outlook that lays open the Káli basin to the north, a vista of Balaton to the south, and touches the ruins of the castle fortress of Csobánc hill. It was here in 1561 that the Ottomans encountered another stubborn resistance from the Magyars. The leaders of the two sides, with the united support of their armies, decided to fight it out between themselves... may the best man win, and the loser would abide by the victory. Later, in 1707, 60 Hungarians, in the rising spirit of the Rákóczi revolution, took over the garrison and withstood the repeated assaults of 1,500 Hapsburg troops.

From the same hill you can look in the distance toward the flat-topped Badacsony Mountain, whose picture-perfect form adorns so many postcards. Stripped of its basalt to feed the building needs of that booming metropolis to the north, Budapest, the 19th century saw it robbed of a substantial portion of its basalt pillars and forest. The quarrymen who lived on Badacsony Mountain's eastern slope in the town of

*On Badacsony Mountain*

Felsőkolónia, barely heard the cry of the environmentalists. It was not until the 1950s that the sound of the jackhammer finally ceased because the rape of the land was becoming so plain. What you see of forest now, on the hill and at the quarries, is the result of reforestation. Somehow, as with Hungary as a whole, there is revival after destruction.

The flora and fauna of the Western Balkans join here with the steppes and, in parts, with the dense woods of the Balaton National Park, where the Mediterranean fern grows on St. George Hill.

The area should be visited in the summer, during the Káli Festival, when wine mingles with the numerous artists and visitors who display their wares and share their wine in Salföld and other local areas. Check with Tourinform.

## Valley of the Arts

After the communists left this land in 1989, its villages and much of its once-prosperous culture seemed doomed to extinction. No one had jobs. The viniculture that once prospered here was devastated by mismanagement. In that time of turmoil and reassessment, the Hungarian composer István Márta joined with a number of local people to form the Association for Culture and Nature Protection in Kapolcs, the first non-governmental organization after the fall of the Iron Curtain. Out of it came an extraordinary event of communal cooperation.

Desperate to find solutions to the local employment crisis, the villages of Kapolcs, Monostorapáti, Öcs, Pula, Taliándörög, and Vigántpetend, all within walking distance of each other, decided to join hands with the new organization, and take advantage of an area that had always attracted artists and the romantically inclined. Gradually, they built it up, and step-by-step began inviting artists to their area. Homes and hospitality were freely offered. Artist talked to artist, and word spread, first to the creative talents from Hungary, then to adjoining countries, and then, as tourists also talked with tourists and the crowds began to grow, it spread to Europe, and thence, throughout the globe. Cultural exhibits sprang up, evenings with poets and readers of literature, musical groups, theater and folk concerts, and finally, jazz and classical mixed their strains in the wine-scented romantic air. The Valley of the Arts is a testimony to the resurgence of the human spirit after communism. Centered near Kapolcs, on the north side of the Káli Basin, it has hosted the international community in growing numbers. In 1989 there were 1,500 guests; in 1999, 60,000; in 2000, 100,000; in 2001, more than 200,000. In 2002 the creative arts exploded with 2,500 participating artists, 250 festival programs, 75 exhibitions, 15 stage performances, 60 classical music concerts, children's programs, jazz, movies, dances, and puppet and minstrel performances. Numerous opportunities exist to learn folk crafts, take rides in horse-drawn wagons, and even live-in for short periods with villagers.

## Badacsony

*Badacsony Mountain*
*(www.zimmerinfo.hu)*

Man's footsteps have worn trails on Badacsony Mountain for thousands of years. Amidst its basalt formations the rich volcanic soil carpeting the lower slopes produced the famous Grey Monk (Szürkebarát) wine. It has been the site of vineyards since before the Romans, when the Avars buried grape seeds with their dead to assure that they would have enough of the vine to produce plenty of wine. The tradition bears fruit today in the wines named Badacsony Kéknyelû, Zöldszilváni, and Olaszrizling.

Come during the harvest festival in the second week of September. Of the towns around the big mountain, the town of Badacsony itself gets the brunt of the tourists and the ferries from the towns of Boglárlelle, Fonyód, and Szigliget arrive here. Badacsony is also reachable by train or by car.

The town of Badacsony is named after the mountain, and sits at its base. You can take a jeep-taxi (800 HUF) from the front of the post office on Park utca, a fun, bumpy three km/1.8 miles up the hill, through vineyards, to the **Kisfaludy House** (also called the Rózsa Szegedi House) and the **Rózsa Szegedi Museum** (Tue-Sun 10 am to 5 pm). The house, built out of the

*Rose Rock*

basalt of the mountain, is the former residence of Sándor Kisfaludy. He is among the many poets who have celebrated the romance of Balaton. The museum bears the name of his wife. A short walk up the trail from Kisfaludy's house brings us to **Rose Rock** (Rózsakő). This great monolith of a rock has spawned its own romance. Folk wisdom holds that, if a man and a woman sit back to back upon the rock and think about each other, they will marry within a year!

About an hour farther on the trail will take you to **Kisfaludy Lookout Tower**. Overlooking Balaton from its elevation of 437 m (1,433 feet), the views over the blue inland sea are spectacular. Continue on the same trail to the **Stone Gate** (Kōkapu), the site of a magnificent drop decorated with gigantic basalt pillars unique to Balaton.

There are many wine tours in the town of Badacsony. Stop by the **Egry Museum**, named for

the painter Jószef Egry (1883-1951). He was born into a poor family. Circumstances forced him into the trades of locksmithing and roofing. But he eventually won a scholarship to the Academy of Fine Arts where he honed his natural talents. His works capture the sunsets and the moods of this

*Kisfaludy Lookout Tower*

beautiful shimmering lake as few artists have been able to do. The museum is up Egri sétány, just across the rails. It is open May through Sept, Tues-Sun, 10 am to 6 pm.

A number of hikes and tennis shoe excursions can be taken from the town. The waymarks are posted for the trails to the perfectly conical Gulács hegy, the so-called "organ pipes," carved by nature out of basalt at Szent György hegy (see *Hiking & Biking*, page 351).

## Tapolca

Don't miss this place, not for its ubiquitous wine cellars, but for its caves and springs! The caves are open to anyone (see *Cave Adventures*, page 355 ff). Tapolca is only a stone's throw from the western tip of Lake Balaton. It is easily reachable from Badacsony Mountain (follow the signs), by car, bicycle, or on foot. Settled in Roman

times, it later became a popular royal and episcopal estate. The town lies at the foot of the formerly volcanic Saint George Hill (Szent György hegy).

The **Tapolca Lake Cave** is one of a few public lake caves in the whole of Europe. Also known as the Tavas Barlang, at 3 Kisfaludy út, it is a short walk from the heart of the city (follow the signs). The limestone cave lake system is toured by "cave boat," across mysterious emerald green waters.

Lake Balaton

The town of Tapolca gets its name, however, from its bubbling hot springs. The water, pressurized and heated from the bowels of the earth, led the locals to form a dammed lake called Malom tó (Mill Lake). A mill was constructed on the water's edge in the 18th century. It utilized the heat and water pressure for energy. The mill was recently turned into a hotel. The historic center of the town is the **Templomdomb** (Church Hill). First inhabited in the Neolithic age, it is also the site of one of the oldest grammar schools in Central Europe. Yet, the wine culture permeates this town as well, evidenced by **Fõ utca** (High Street). The Tapolca wine merchants built many of their cellars along this street. It is lined today with cafés and restaurants, some hiding the cellars inside.

## Szigliget

Driving on Route 71 toward this town you cannot help but feel a rise of excitement as the remains of the 13th-century **Szigliget Castle** come into view from the top of Castle Hill (info@szigligetvar. hu, www.szigliget.hu, open from March 15 to
October 31, 9 am to 6 pm, adults 300 HUF, children 150 HUF). At the foot of the hill, the village houses still look as they did nearly 700 years ago. Both the town and the hill so dominate this area that it was certain to be a site for sieges and battles. Yet, in its entire history as a frontier fortress in the Turkish wars, the Turks never took the castle. Like Tihany to the north, Szigliget remained a bastion of Christian resistance.

Evidence has confirmed that the site was inhabited in the Stone Age. Neolithic man was succeeded by the Celts, then the Romans. Later came the Avars and, after them, the Magyars. When the Tartars advanced into Hungary, leaving destruction and murder in their wake, the Abbey of Pannonhalma constructed the castle for self-defense. As it rose skyward, its strategic importance increased. In 1262 it

*Church ruins*

became a royal property. With the years, however, it changed ownership frequently. Each time it changed hands it was modified and improved, until it became an impregnable citadel. It withstood every Turkish assault ever thrown against it. Ironically, its strength led to its destruction. In 1702 the emperor of Austria ordered it blown apart so that it could not be used by the freedom fighters in the Rákóczi War of Independence. Unfortunately, it has largely been neglected since that time.

However, you can walk up to the castle by taking the path behind the white 18th-century church that sits up on top of the steep hill off Route 71. On the same pathway the Baroque **Lengyel mansion** (built in 1787) has preserved its iron gate, emblazoned with the Lengyel coat of arms, a unicorn. Today a restaurant named the **Vár Vendéglő**, it invites a rest with its casual umbrella-covered outdoor tables. It is open from 11 am to 11 pm and serves Hungarian food at 800 to about 1,500 HUF. As you continue up the hill, you will pass an entryway for the castle, and then you will arrive at the lower castle battlements, which curve round and the straighten as they lead up a steeper pathway. The higher battlements open out to spectacular views of Badacsony, the beautiful Lake Balaton, Tapolca Bay, and the Keszthely Mountains.

From the church you can also take the six-km (3.6-mile) tourist path, which is posted with information boards in Hungarian and in English. It will take you by the Old Village (local expression for the oldest part of the town), where thatched roofs and bleached white village houses evoke the atmosphere of the Middle Ages. The pathway also skirts all the main sites of the area.

Before leaving, you may want to visit the town square. The **Eszterházy Palace**, today a writer's colony, sits across from the mayor's office in the town square. Its 26-acre grounds are an open botanical reserve with 150 different species of pine,

**Lake Balaton**

*Eszterházy Palace*

now carefully cultivated and preserved. Also, from the town square, walk southeast to the **Lido** (public beach and swimming pool). Ice cream vendors, fast food stands, and miscellaneous peddlers service hundreds of locals from the surrounding area who come here in the summer. Entrance fees for the Lido run from 300 to 500 HUF. Opposite the Lido and up a cone-shaped hill, called the Skirt of the Queen by the locals, excavations are ongoing. Apparently there are ruins of another castle here, but no one knows exactly when it was built. A series of small mountains shelter the town from climate extremes and give it a Mediterranean sub-climate (they even grow figs here). Next, we leave Szigliget and head farther south on 71 to Balatonederics.

## Balatonederics

No one would ever expect an African safari park in Central Europe, but it's here. It is a tribute to the astonishingly mild climate of Balaton. Endre von Nagy, a Hungarian hunter and explorer, established the **Africa Museum and Safari Park** at Vajda major, ☎ 87-466-105. It is open from May 1 to Oct 31, 9 am to 5:30

pm. Entrance fees are 450 HUF for children under 12, 550 HUF for seniors, and 800 HUF for adults. The park also has children's pony and camel rides, a bufe/restaurant, and souvenir shops. The founder established the museum in 1913.

Because of his marriage with Alexandra Hatvany (the Hatvany family was involved in WWII) he was imprisoned in 1944. In 1950 he was released by a new regime. But, as communism took deeper hold, he fled to Tanzania with his wife, where he established another zoo and animal park. His writings were published internationally, and so influential had he become that four different hunting organizations took on his name after his death. In Tanzania, several schools and a lake were renamed in his honor.

## Keszthely

This is the most densely populated city in the Balaton region and it could justify a tour book of its own. Its history is astonishing. Keszthely sits at a nexus of roads that have been there for thousands of years. A natural transportation center, it has been the confluence of invasions and settlements that have permanently marked the city. Through the ages, up through the Iron Age, Celts, Avars, Romans, Huns, Magyars, Goths, Lombards and Turks have followed the same roads in its tumultuous history. The footpaths settled into the soil, and the city built up around them, so that today, the main streets follow exactly the same paths that were trod upon by Stone-Age men. The north-south axis along Sopron út, Kossuth út, Festetics út, and Fenékpuszta út follows the ancient trails. The Roman road, built before Christ, and used for transporting heavy stones, follows Bem út, Vásártér út and Zsidi út. On the other hand, Georgikon út and Tapolcai út are the newcomers. They were constructed in the seventh and eighth centuries.

Today however, office buildings, shopping malls, and a spreading urban blanket have appeared. But, the best way to explore the town is to start in the old town square, **Fõ tér**. The **Town Hall**, at the corner of Fõ tér and Kossuth út (28 Kossuth út) was built in 1768.

*Town Hall*

Today it is the home of the **Goldmark Károly Community Center** and the **Tourinform** office. The **Holy Trinity**

*Parish Church*

**Statue** marks the center of the square. The more modern **Theater of Keszthely** (many concerts and performances are held here) is an add-on to the 19th-century grammar school. It sits next to the **Parish Church**, which was originally built in 1386. The church used stones from the nearby castle of Fenékpuszta. In time it was converted to a fort, and then again rebuilt into a church after its destruction in one of the many battles that have marked the area. A 15th-century Renaissance fresco was uncovered on its walls in the 1970s. The northern part of the square, leading to Kossuth Lajos utca, has been converted into a pedestrian walkway. It is lined with eateries, shops, and plenty of sidewalk umbrella tables.

*Fresco in Parish Church*

Continue your walk up Kossuth Lajos utca. At 21 Kossuth Lajos utca is the **Károly Goldmark House** (sometimes referred to as the Pethõ House). The composer was born here in 1830. Farther up the street, look for the quaint sign hanging over the door at Kossuth Lajos utca 11. The sign says Baba and Puppe, marked in bold letters over a couple of Victorian costumed ladies. They claim this is the largest doll collection in Europe. But, actually, it is a **museum of wax figures** of famous people, clothed in authentic period costumes. Incongruous at best, the **Parliament of Snails** is composed of 4½ million snail remains from the ancient Pannonian sea.

Kossuth Lajos utca changes to Kastély utca, lined with peasant's Baroque houses each having trapezoidal roofs and bright plastered walls with white trim. These are the **Dongó-Ház dwellings**. The employees of the Festetics Palace lived in these homes, in relative luxury for their time. Every morning they took the same route to work that we are walking. We pass the Párizsi udvar (Parisian Court), then farther north we cross the main street of town, which is also Route 71, and walk to the **Festetics Palace**, an outstanding example of Baroque Hungary. The museum entrance fee is 700

*Dongó-Ház dwelling*

HUF. Evening concerts start at 8 pm and are 1,200 HUF at the door, or at the museum desk.

*Festetics Palace*

One of the few perfectly preserved palaces of Central Europe, the Palace contains 100 rooms. The wing facing the town was built in 1750. The other wings were added between 1883 and 1887, in the glory days of the Austro-Hungarian Empire.

The exquisite empire oak woodwork of the Helikon Library stores 86,000 volumes. Many are original leather-bound books, still in their places from the 18th and 19th centuries. A superb collection of porcelain from Japan, China, France, and Germany, necklaces and gold work from the Árpád kings, memorabilia from the Huns, Turks, Ostrogoths and some magnificent Byzantine finds grace the galleries. One of the largest collections of armor and weapons from the Middle Ages gleams beneath the crystal

*Festetics Palace interior*

Lake Balaton

chandeliers. Gold trim and artistry remind a visitor of the palace of Versailles.

Concerts are held throughout the year, and are weekly in the summer. Indoor performances are usually held in the magnificent gilded Hall of Mirrors. Outside summer concerts are held in the English and French gardens.

From the Palace, walk up Fenékpuszta út, away from town. It will take you to the **Fenékpuszta Castle Fortress** on the outskirts of town. Originally the site of the Roman fortress of Valcum in the second through the fourth centuries, it sits next to one of the ancient strategic spots of the area, controlling access to the road to Rome. The Huns overran it, but it was retaken by Rome. In later years the Goths defeated the Romans here and burned down the Roman fortifications, then rebuilt them as an imposing citadel. It became the seat of their king Thiudimer, who fathered Theodoric the Great of the Ostrogoths. This fortress also held out against the Turks for a time, but was finally overrun. The **Orthodox Christian Basilica**, just down from the fortress, was erected in the fourth century. Archeologists believe it replaced a Roman building that apparently used central heating. The southern entrance of the ancient Roman fort has been reconstructed, guarded by four inner gate towers and two barbicans.

## Other Sights in Keszthely

**Georgikon Farm Museum** (also called the Majormúzeum), Bercsény út 67, ☎ 36-83-311-563, was the first institute for advanced agricultural studies in Hungary. Founded in 1787 by György Festetics, its exhibits include viticulture, farming, and rural crafts, enlivened by dioramas. The museum is

marked by an old steam-powered plow sitting in the front. It is open May through Oct, Mon-Fri, 10 am to 5 pm, and weekends until 6. Entry is 300 HUF.

The **Balatoni Múzeum**, 8350 Keszthely, Múzeum út 2, is open Tue-Sun 10 am to 5 pm. Entry is 240 HUF. It is

*Balatoni Múzeum*

on the opposite side of town from the Festetics Mansion. Its exhibits cover the geological and archeological history and the flora and fauna of Balaton through the ages.

A walk from the town center on Erzsébet út (Elizabeth Street) will take you to **Helikon Park** and its memorial. The Hullám and Balaton Hotels in the park are still standing and functioning. They were built in the 19th century. Off the park, lakeside docks welcome boats. Boat rentals are available here as well. Guides are available for fishing or for boat cruises. Check with the Tourinform office in the town square.

The shoreline beach, called the **Libás**, is free of charge at this writing.

Down the hill from Fõ tér, the **open-air market** operates from early in the morning to the early afternoon. It attracts vendors from the entire country to buy, sell and trade everything, from clothing to appliances, honey and wine.

## ★★Héviz

No trip to this area would be complete without a visit to this healing resort. It is loaded with hotels, cottages and numerous places to eat. Follow Route 71 until it changes to Route 75 and then follow the signs for Héviz. Situated only six km/3.6 miles from Lake Balaton's shore, the

*Héviz Lake*

Héviz is the second-largest warm-water lake in the world. Its 4½ acres of silky surface exude vapors that create dreamy misty mornings. The surrealistic waterscape is heightened by a carpet of water lilies that float on its serene surface. Its temperature is an astonishingly consistent 98°F. Winter water temperatures may drop considerably, but are still quite warm. But its secret involves much more than warm water. Its natural circulation system brings up 109 gallons of water every second from the depths of the earth, laden with very slight amounts of radon, sulphur, and trace minerals that kill many types of bacteria. People suffering from rheumatism, arthrititis, and others inflammatory diseases have found relief in its waters since 1795. Walk the causeway that leads to the building in the center of the lake. There you will find lockers, massage services, and floats that can be rented to lounge in the water. A bufe can provide light foods, and in true Hungarian style, palinka or coffee.

For those taking a bus from other towns in Balaton, all buses to Héviz stop opposite the entrance to the thermal baths. Follow the signs for the *Fürdõ & Oacute* (Bathing Lake). Tickets are about 800 HUF for three hours or, alternatively (definitely a better deal), 1,200 HUF for the entire day. Summer hours are 8 am to 5 pm daily. Winter hours are 9 am to 4:30 pm. The ticket will give you a locker. You insert the ticket into a slot on the locker and the key will pop out. You have to keep the ticket until you leave because it is used to monitor the time of your stay. Be forewarned that there are no wading areas. It is not for children, although there is a playground on the shore. The best option for those with children is to find lodging in one of the better hotels, where the hotel pools may be more child-friendly. Almost all of the local hotels have packages that include the thermal pool amenities as well.

## Adventures

### Hiking & Biking
### Walking the Red Sandstone from Town Hall Square in Balatonalmádi

 This is an easy walk of six km/3.6 miles. The trail is marked by blue triangles and will take anywhere from three to four hours. It leads us by the red sandstone quarries for which Balatonalmádi is known, and up to the Óvári Lookout Tower.

Start in the village square at the **statue of Pannonia Aqua**, by the sculpture Gábor Mihály, next to the railway underpass. The foundation of the statue is red sandstone from the Almádi quarry, historically owned by the Gyõry-Fülöp and Toscani families. In the middle of the square is the **Pannónia Cultural Center and Library**, and on the east end the **Town Hall** with its **Loft Gallery** of artistic treasures. From the square, facing away from Balaton, walk to your right up József Attila út. You will come to **Szent István Park** on your left. Széchenyi sétány (Széchenyi Promenade) borders the far side of the park, on your right as you face away from Balaton. Walk up Széchenyi sétány and, when you come to the divide, stay to the right. (Going left will put you on Széchenyi Park út, which is the wrong street.) You will soon find yourself at Szent Imre Herceg utca, which climbs the hill.

The plants include oak and ash trees and acidic soil shrubs and flowers, such as rowan, privat, may-bush, juniper, and sloe. Due to the mild climate in Balaton, the parks are green most of the year.

Farther up, we intersect with Kilátóhegy út, joined by a steep slope and steps. We can take a welcome rest at the park bench. Kilátóhegy út walks us into **Banya Park** where stairs will lead down to the red sandstone quarry. The lookout in Banya Park is the **Óvári Belvedere**, named after the attorney and parliamentarian, Dr. Ferenc Óvári (1858-1938), one of the great contributors to the town's history. The lookout was erected at the turn of the 19th century. Although faithfully restored, the roof is now tile. Before us is Füzfő Bay. The village of Vörösberény is marked by the Romanesque church (tallest tower) and by the Catholic church and former Jesuit monastery, now the hotel Kolostor (second-tallest tower). Boat quays and docks are in the near distance.

From this vantage point over the lake, the evening is romantic, with blue hues and the reflection of the orange sunset giving way to night shadows and pinpoints of light across the basin. To your right is the **Kenese Escarpment**, a monolith of sand and clay that is 4 to 5 million years old. It is part of the Upper Pannonian Tihany Formation. Covered with patches of loess, it passes over to the River Sió, where the Pannonian mountains of the outer Somogy continue to form the geographic history of Hungary. Some 12-14,000 years ago, at the end of the last Ice Age, several basins subsided, joined, and were then flooded by the melting glaciers to form Lake Balaton.

Below our feet is the **Balatonfelvidék**, made of the sandstone of the Late Paleozoic (Permian) age. Here, exposed

grains of sand were deposited 250 million years ago. The unique purplish and reddish hue is from the iron forms of hematite and limonite that encrusted grains of quartz, and oxidized.

As we walk back down in a circuitous route, first to Lomb utca, and then wind around to Batthyány utca, we pass through the same grounds as the old quarry. Here, the Romans chiseled their building materials for their Pannonian empire. Through them, the stonemasons of the village inherited the skills of their craft. A 13th-century document mentions that Italian masters also came to work here. The secrets of the ancient art of quarrying were thus preserved, learned, jealously guarded, and passed down from father to son. As you continue the descent, from Batthyány utca down Dr. Lenkei Vilmos utca, you pass through a vaulted passage that hides an old steam locomotive. No. 375 was one of the first in the world that integrated water and coal tanks internally. Farther down in our descent, the stair, Csikász, is named after Imre Csikász, the painter of Almádi. We saunter past the wheeled well, Söreny, with the inscription S.L. 1907 @ 28 m. Both well and drinking trough in front of it are 100 years old. The descent takes us inescapably down to Ferenc Óvári út. Here we find the Chapel of the Holy Dexter, at Ferenc Óvári út 47. Built in 1930, to the design of István Megyaszay, the chapel to the left of the main nave, since August 20, 2001, has preserved fragments of St. Stephen's Holy Dexter (from his right hand). The gold mosaic is by Miksa Róth, not a local artist. It was actually saved from the destruction of the Royal Castle in Buda by Vicar Sándor Pintér in 1957, brought here, and restored by local artists.

Now we head down the sloping Twin Promenade, which is divided by trees, and cross the Highway 71 and the railroad. We have come to the **Old Park**, nestled against the shore. We have a choice here, to follow the rows of young platens that lead to the entrance of Wesselény Beach, or follow the parkway sidewalk. Let's follow the parkway. The park was created in 1890, a mix of white and black poplars, white willows, and marsh cypresses. These were supplemented with rare species from exotic locations. The yaw gum trees and the pungent junipers are accompanied by orange mulberries, evergreens, birches, and a double row of orange twigged willows. Our walk continues past numerous busts of the nation's famous, until we arrive at the **Remete Brook Bridge**. A bench sits silently, yet it speaks of the church history that underlies everything Hungarian. It is dedicated to the once Vice-Prefect of Vezprém County, Desző Véghely, who founded the park. Along the shoreline pathway near the railroad underpass, is a testimony to Balaton's extraordinary climate – a gingko tree, directly from Asia.

## The Tapolca Escarpments

From Tapolca, walk toward Raposka village, and follow the blue waymarks. These lead to **Szentvölgy hegy** (Holy Valley Hill), which rises 415 m/1,361 feet, a great spot for photographing the scene. Continuing to the far side of the hill, the blue waymarks lead to the **Lion's Head Well**, near the Baroque Catholic Chapel, and near the **Taranyi Wine Press House**. Eventually the blue waymarks take us to **Szigliget**, where the castle fortress invites a look. Now, we continue, up the blue trail through vineyards to Badacsony mountain's heights at 438 m/1,437 feet.

## Lóczy-Geyser Nature Trail at Tihany

The first modern nature trail in the nation, it was established 50 years ago. Its concentric 18 km/11¼ miles connect just outside the monastery grounds at Tihany.

## Stone Gate to Gulács hegy

This four-km/2½-mile walk takes us to the perfectly conical hill near the village of Nemesgulács. At the train station, cross the tracks and follow the trail toward Szent György hegy (Saint George Hill), which rises to 415 m/1,362

*Szent György hegy*

Lake Balaton

feet. The hill is home to some of the finest vineyards in Hungary, and to Szürkebarát (Grey Monk) wine. Only a few km east we can see the **Castle of Csobánc hegy**, where the women joined with the men to battle the Turks.

## Bicycling

Bicycle rentals are ubiquitous at the hotels, but usually require a hefty deposit. Although it is possible to rent them at other locations, good shops are few and far between. For information and support, contact **Tempo 21**, Balatonfüred, Ady Andre út 54, Mon to Fri 9 am to 5 pm and Sat 9 am to 12 pm, ☎ 36-87-480-671 or 36-20-9243-672.

### A Day of Cycling from Balatonfüred

A nice single-day tour by bicycle starts in Balatonfüred. Look for the cycle path signs, and use the map suggestions provided by Tourinform (see *Appendix*). From Balatonfüred, cycle through Balatonszőlős, to Pécsely, then on to Vászoly, Dörgicse, Menschely, Nagyvászony, Nemesvámos, Veszprém, Szentkirályszabadja, Vörösberény, and ending in Balatonalmádi – for a total of about 68 km/42½ miles. This covers pleasant terrain with a few moderately difficult but not over-challenging grades for a person in good physical condition.

### Cycling the Balaton Ring Road

Cycling the Balaton Ring Road will give you the flexibility to branch off, where otherwise by car you could not. It circles the entire shore, basically on the old M7 and old Route 71 (visible on any road map of the lake). Although the road can get significantly congested, it is peppered with numerous signs for cottages and hostels for rent, and exploring them is easy when you are cycling.

## Wine Adventures

Wine tours here are confusingly ubiquitous and of high quality. Tourinform (see *Appendix*) straightens it out. Balaton has hundreds of cooperating establishments taking part in nine basic tours with hundreds of variations. Tourinform will make arrangements, book accommodations (luxury or budget), and can even fit in a translator as necessary.

Badacsony, Csopak, Balatonfüred, Szigliget, and Balatonboglár have established reputations for wine production. There are other areas as well. And consider that, while the volcanic soil and climate of the Northern Shore is best for white wines, there are many wonderful fiery reds in the same area. For instance, Csopak and Balatonfüred are well known for Füred Riesling and Cabernet Sauvignon. The slopes of the Tihany peninsula produce Merlot. Farther southwest, around Badacsony, look for Szürkebarát (Grey Monk).

## Water Adventures

### Sailing

 Balaton ports usually have at least one or more rental outlets for sailboats, rowboats, and sometimes, pedal boats and, in the winter, windsailing equipment. However, this business is volatile, so check with Tourinform (see *Appendix*). Most hotels have contacts for rentals. The following have proven reliable in the past:

**Hotel Marina Port**, 8174 Balatonkenese, Kikötkő út 2-4, ☎ 36-88-492-369, fax 36-88-492-370, info@yacht.hu, www.yacht.hu. This is not only a fine hotel, but its modern dock and rentable sailboats may include lessons. For the truly ambitious, in one program, a full three days and two nights are incorporated into an internationally recognized skipper's license training session (63,000 HUF). Previous sailing experience and a passing grade on appropriate examinations is required. Sessions for basic international sailing licenses (72,000 HUF), for small motor and sail craft, also use the Danube for the motor craft training sessions.

**Club Tihany** (see *Places to Stay*), ☎ 36-30-22-789-27, fax 36-87-44-88-17. Their full dock facilities and internationally seasoned staff make things easy. They have lessons for sailor's and skipper's licenses as well. Rentals include sailboats, wind surfing craft, rowboats and, for kicks, pedal boats.

**Vega Yachtsport Lt.**, Balatonfüred, H-8230, Tihany út 1, ☎ 36-20-9350-198, fax 36-20-9350-198, vegayacht@vegayacht.hu, www.vegayacht.hu. Vega will give you private yacht rentals with or without a skipper (you must be licensed to have a yacht without a skipper). They also support rentals with skippers, planned excursions, and/or training.

**Balaton Yacht Charter**, contact Mr. Andreas Novotny, ☎ 36-30-22-789-27 (Nov through April), ☎ 36-87-448-817 (May 1 through Oct 31), office@wind99.com, www.wind99.com. They have been offering lessons and operating a fleet of sailing ships at Balaton for years. You can choose your charter with this company, but you must have proof of licensure before you are allowed to sail a ship on the lake without supervision.

**The Balaton Shipping Company** (BH - see *Southern Shore*), 2 Krúdy Walkway, H-8600 Siófok, ☎ 36-84-312-144, fax 36-84-312-907, ☎/fax 36-84-310-050, info@balatonihajozas.hu, www.balatonihajozas.hu. The shipping lanes of Lake Balaton are managed by this company, with its fleet of ships and ferries. While their headquarters is on the Southern Shore, check their website for phone numbers, shipping schedules and fees for the Balaton cruises from ports on both the Northern and Southern Shores, many including refreshments or meals and, in some cases, entertainment.

## Water Skiing

 The only ski tow on Balaton Lake operates out of Balatonfüred. Although motorboats are prohibited on the lake, your water skiing adventure is still available for 1,500 HUF per tow.

# Ice & Snow Adventures

Winter ice sailing is a unique sport. It is only possible where wide-open smooth-frozen surfaces combine with the wind. There is no place like Balaton for this combination in all of Europe, leading to its fame as a host for world ice sailing championships. Check with the hotels and the sailing centers we have listed. In addition, Tourinform coordinates information about competitions, rentals, ice sailing support information, and translation services as agreed (see *Appendix*).

## Bobsledding

 Bobsledding in Balaton is not what you think. Probably the longest dry bobsled in Central Europe is at Balatonfûzfõ, at Uszoda út 2, ☎ 36-88-586-170, fax 36-88-439-058, mail@balatonibob.hu, www.

balatonibob.hu. They are open from 10 am to the evening in summer (they close at 5 pm in the winter). The track is 800 m/ 2,400 feet, where you can attain speeds of up to 40 km/hr (25 mph), and floodlights make it possible to use the run after nightfall. Four speeds and a full braking system allow you to control the sled to a certain extent, but it still evokes a hot rush because many parts of the run are open on all sides, although it is quite safe for youngsters. Many parents ride down with their young children. In addition, the bobsled park offers wall climbing, a rope slide, and a rope bridge.

## Air Adventures

A number of hot air balloon flights are available in Balaton, and Tourinform (see *Appendix*) can make arrangements. Costs will vary, but usually average around €100, which means at least an hour or two, a toast of champagne, and a flight certificate. Hungary has an extraordinary pilot license requirement, resulting in an astonishing safety record, with no accidents for over 80 years! The balloon drifts softly in the air. You do not feel the wind, and people, animals, village houses, and barns can be observed from the balloon. Hot air balloon flights over Balaton will give you once in a lifetime pictures that cannot be duplicated, especially in the morning or in the evening, when the sun's rays play across the countryside and the waters of Balaton in exotic colors.

## Cave Adventures

★**Pond Cave in Tapolca**, H-8300 Kisfaludy, Sándor út 3, ☎ 36-87-412-579 or 36-87-411-644, is open from 9 am to 6 pm, June to August, and from 10 am to 5 pm the rest of the year. It was a hard task that led to this discovery. Pál Tóth, a successful baker had secured all the money and equipment, and he set about to build his house. It was 1902. Ference Németh, the bricklayer, and his men, were helping. After they had dug several feet

they encountered unusually hard rock and were forced to use
dynamite to chisel through. But, it was not long after they finished the last charge, and the men started to shovel away the
debris, that Tóth jumped back and screamed at his men to
move away. A gaping hole had opened up before him. Once
over his astonishment, he crept in on his knees and worked
his way down, but found nothing unusual to stop the work. So,
they began to dig again, when suddenly the cave collapsed
into a gigantic cavernous black hole. This time Ferenc
Németh took the lead in exploring this new find. As he went
down he felt strangely warm and the humidity increased. He
began to sweat. The slope seemed to level out a bit, but it was
getting too dark and deep to move any farther. He returned
later, equipped with lamps, ropes and gear. Cave led to cave
and, in some places, underground pools. Finally, they came to
a large lake. On the other side they could see a continuation of
the cave system. With growing excitement they returned
again with floats and barrels and paddled to the other side.
Amazingly, the system did not end, but continued into an
incredible spreading labyrinth below the earth. Eventually,
experts came.

In ancient times, lukewarm water
rising from the depths of the earth
had interceded with the cold waters
left from the Pannonian sea. As they
mixed and brushed against the limestone rocks, an acidic chemistry
formed cavities, then hollows, and
eventually, the Miocene-age limestone gave way to a huge maze of cre-
vasses, caverns, caves, and grottos,
some bearing the waters of the
prehistoric sea that once was there.

The villagers soon formed a cave
company, improved the entrances
and constructed steps, lights, and safety cables. Today you
can follow the same trail that Ferenc followed and cross one of
the largest underground lakes in the world in a boat. The labyrinth sometimes requires that you duck your head to avoid
scraping the roof of the cave. At times gaping dark holes going

deeper into the earth blot out part of the cave water surface with a mysterious blackness. In parts of the cave the emerald green water gives the ambience of another world, only heightened by the warm air, which is said to carry health benefits. Take this tour into the underworld, for there are few like it in the world.

## On Horseback

 The following facilities are based upon the recommendation of the Hungarian Equestrian Tourism Association. They are rated based upon the horseshoe system developed by the association (see Budapest, *On Horseback*, pages 176 ff ). Open cross-country riding is available from many stables, as are lessons, and sometimes carriage rides, as well as horse shows for groups. Hungary's horseback riding tradition is one of the greatest in the world. It goes back before the Huns, to the days of the Magyars.

These are rated five horseshoes:

**Szentmihàlypuszta Farm Stables**, 8788 Zalaszentlàszló, Szentmihàlypuszta, ☎ 36-20-268-0832, fax 36-83-334-116, reithof@t-email.hu, www.reithof.hu. Contact Dr. Nagy Judit, mobile 36-30-957-8832.

**Kabal Ménes Kft. (Hotel Kabal)**, 8951 Gutorfölde, Rádiháza,☎/fax 36-92-375-003. Contact Mármarosi Brigit, mobile ☎ 00-36-30-416, radihaza@axelero.hu or info@radihaza.hu, www.radihaza.hu.

These are rated four horseshoes:

**Gyula Vezér Lovasbirodalma** (Chief Gyula Riding Empire), 8286 Gyulakeszi, Czobánc hegy, Hrsz. 050/4,☎ 36-87-709-701, fax 36-88-580 691, gyulavezer@vazsonykom.hu, www.equi.hu/gyulavezer. Contact Németh Gyula or Mézáros Zsu Zsana, mobile 36-20-931-7446.

**Hévízi Lovaspanzió** (Szabó Horse Guest House), 8380 Hévíz, Lótusvirág út, ☎/fax 36-83-340-851, reiterpa@axelero.hu, www.reiterpansion.fx3.hu. Contact Szabó Ferenc, owner, but Somogy Krisztina speaks some English, mobile 36-30-560-1332.

**Hétkúti Wellness Hotel Es Lovas Park** (and Riding Park), 8060 Mór, Dózsa György út 111, ☎ 36-22-563-080, fax 36-22-563-092 (The Horse Guest House, ☎ 36-22-562-296), hetkut@hetkut.hu, www.hetkut.hu. Contact Kerekes Krisztina, mobile 36-30-997-2405. This four-star wellness hotel, with pools, saunas, and beauty services, also has fine riding stables with a full range of guest and riding programs for beginning up through advanced riders.

**Sümeg Castle Stables**, 8330 Sümeg, Városoldal u. 5, ☎ 36-87-550-087, fax 36-87-550-088, varistallo@lovasiskola.axelero.net, www.sumeg.hu/capari. Contact Capári Róbert, mobile 36-20-439-1846.

**Sárkány Eco Guest House**, 8999 Csöde, Erdész út 9, ☎/fax 36-92-371-064, sarkanybio@axelero.hu, www.hotels.hu/sarkany_bio. Contact Doszpot Éva. This facility is rated three horseshoes.

*Siófok, on Balaton's Southern Shore*

# ■ Balaton Southern Shore

## Getting There

The signs may be confusing as you enter the Lake Balaton region from Budapest on M7. But just remember to stay on M7 westbound, which will take you along Balaton's South Shore. It is a two- to three-hour drive from Budapest, with road stops and eateries along the way.

Along the sun-baked shoreline sometimes you can see people hundreds of yards out, wading in what appears to be deep water, specks in the inland sea. But this vision is deceptive. In most cases, they are only chest deep. In many places you can wade out for 10 or 20 yards and the water will only be ankle deep. Often, to get to swimming depth, you have to move out at least another hundred yards. Yet, the sand is so silky that it was once used for blotting ink in the Middle Ages, so it is a natural favorite of families with children.

By the same token, it is the party favorite of the young crowd, and in the summer, nightclubs and discos open up along the shore (especially at Siófok).

Yet, the South Shore is more than a playland. Inland villages and cottages are just as rich in history and charm as any other part of the country. The shoreline was the border of Turkish territory on more than one occasion; many towns have their stories of glory, and everywhere wine. Maps of self-made tours, wine cellar locations, directions for vineyards are available through Tourinform (see *Appendix*). Tourinform will also pre-set appointments. Literally hundreds of weekend cottages, hostels, and hotels vie for the tourist dollar. However, there are some cautions (see below).

## Places to Stay

Before you book in Southern or Northern Balaton consider that it slows down in the winter. While there is some nightlife and recreation, it is not like peak season. You can get great rates and you don't have to compete for beach-front towel space, but the water

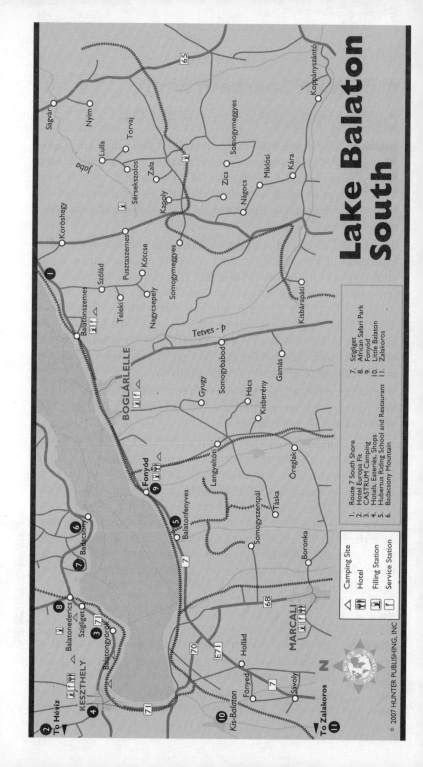

# Lake Balaton South

1. Route 7 South Shore
2. Hotel Europa Fit
3. CASTRUM Camping
4. Hotels, Eateries, Shops
5. Huberus Riding School and Restaurant
6. Badacsony Mountain
7. Szigliget
8. African Safari Park
9. Fonyód
10. Little Balaton
11. Zalakoros

△ Camping Site
🏨 Hotel
⛽ Filling Station
🔧 Service Station

© 2007 HUNTER PUBLISHING, INC.

may be too cold to swim in, and perhaps it might even be frozen! Winter is great for wind sailing and ice-skating, but don't plan outdoor swimming excursions. For this reason a number of good hotels are only seasonal. However, a caution applies

| HOTEL PRICE CHART | |
|---|---|
| Double room without tax | |
| € | Under €80 |
| €€ | €81-€150 |
| €€€ | €151-€250 |
| €€€€ | Over €250 |

here as well. Seasonal hotels usually have inadequate heating for the winter months. So when a Balaton hotel advertises rates that are out of season, that can mean just before or just after the high season, usually a period lasting perhaps four to eight weeks, or perhaps something else. Make sure you know what the hotel means when they quote you an off-season (or out-of-season) rate.

Of course, the better hotels (four and five star) have in-room heating and central air. As most hotels are upgrading in the post-Soviet era, it is still wise to check. Larger hotels are well insulated and they have wonderful window views over Balaton. An open window and the evening lake breeze are usually quite comfortable, and even romantic, in hot weather. Don't overlook local realtors or Tourinform, all of whom are also primed to offer summer or weekend cottages as well.

## Four Star

**Azur Hotel**, 8600 Siófok, Erkel Ferenc utca, 2/c Vitorlás út 11, ☎ 36-84-501-400, fax 36-84-501-435, info@hotelazur.hu, www.hotelazur.hu, €€€. The newest addition to the Southern Shore, it takes advantage of the nearby thermal waters of

Nagybereny. The piped-in springs bring recovery, rejuvenation, and recreation. A bubble pool, children's pool, regular indoor-outdoor pools, and a thermal pool are also used by professional trainers to give instruction in physical conditioning,

weight loss, and, in some cases, recovery (the gym includes cardio-vascular equipment). Saunas, salt chambers, aroma therapy rooms, aromatic oil treatments, and a full range of massage services, beauticians and cosmetologists are available, in addition to tennis courts, an outdoor track, and children's programs to keep kids busy. English is spoken throughout, and standard hotel rooms can be upgraded to suites with in-room saunas, Jacuzzis, and sitting rooms. Satellite TV and Internet connections in every guest room keep you in touch with the world. But who wants that!

**Conference & Wellness Hotel Residence**, 8600 Siófok, Erkel Ferenc út 49, ☎ 36-84-505-900, fax 36-84-340-387, info@hotel-residence.hu, www.hotel-residence.hu, €€-€€€. The high level of services at the Hotel Residence include an indoor and an adventure pool, sauna, children's pool, a "bubble bath," massages, a cellulite room, thermal baths, gymnasium, and a medical staff to supplement all of that. The children's play room is supervised by play-coordinators who speak English, while beauticians and cosmeticians pamper the guests. The excellent restaurant, with its royal burgundy upholstered chairs, and superb wine list, serves Hungarian and international cuisine. Packages cater to all age groups, and a special program for seniors includes doctor's examinations, a lab test with 26 parameters, electrocardiogram, sonogram, and beauty treatments with full room and board at about €300 for three full days, as of publication date.

**Best Western János Atrium Hotel**, 8600 Siófok, Fõ út 93-95, ☎ 36-84-312-546, fax 36-84-312-432, janus@janushotel.hu, www.janushotel.hu, €€. Doubles are €100 (25,000 HUF) in low season and €111 (27,750 HUF) in high season. A bargain, two-story townhouse suites are €139 (34,750  HUF) in low season and €155 (38,750 HUF) in high season. Although it seems sparse on support services compared to some other hotels, don't be fooled. Its wellness and beauty staff do everything they can to please and the huge underground pool, sauna, whirlpool, and gym room compensate for the lack of beachfront. The front desk is excellent in English. Internet in every room requires your own PC. A rail line runs across the back of the hotel (infrequently), but it is about a football field away and the windows and walls are acousti-

 cally double-insulated. It's hard to notice any train. Color TVs, SAT, minibar, phone, private bathroom/shower and good housekeeping make it comfortable. The restaurant and café are first class (see *Places to Eat*). And you are in easy walking distance from the beach.

## Three Star

These are usually seasonal with no air-conditioning on the South Shore. Some do have portable room air-conditioners, and most have fans. Check with the hotel.

**EUROPA Hotel**, 8600 Siófok, Petõfi Sandor sétány 17, ☎ 36-84-313-411, fax 36-84-310-626, balaton@accor-hotels.com,

www.pannoniahotels. hu, €€. Doubles are €78 (19,500 HUF) in high season and €60 (15,000 HUF) in low season. Four-star amenities and a staff that speaks excellent English make this a true value hotel. Babysitting services include a children's pool, movies, playground, and excellent support staff. The café and restaurant on the bottom floor are supplemented by the nightclub Europa on the top floor, with spectacular window views over Balaton. Wellness programs are available in addition to the standard guest activities, which include minigolf, horseback riding, watersports, boating, or just lounging pool-

side. The water off the private beach is shallow for 100 yards or more. Videos, hotel cable channels (primarily Hungarian), telephone, and desk/chair in every room keep you comfortable. One downside is that parking is a block away.

**Hunguest Hotel Ezüstpart**, 8600 Siófok, Liszt Ferenc sétány 2-4, ☎ 36-84-350-622, fax 36-84-351-096, reserve@ balaton.hunguesthotels.hu, www.hunguesthotels.hu, €€-€€€.Even though this hotel has been rated four stars, because it is without air-conditioning in this location, we are forced to give it three. However, services and consideration by the staff are good. Doubles in the off-season are €125

(31,250 HUF), and in high season are €153 (38,250 HUF). They have five different buildings and a range of room packages for almost every budget. Every room in the three-star building has a balcony view. In-room telephone, video,

SAT TV, and mini-bar are standard. And the hotel also has a fine bar, Olympic-sized pool for adults, a children's pool, sauna, Jacuzzi, gym, solarium, infra cabin and beauticians. Rentals for watersports add to a range of beachside fun as well.

★**Hotel Aranypart**, 8600 Siófok, Beszédes József sétány 82, ☎ 36-84-519-450, fax 36-84-312-049, hotel@aranypart.hu, www.aranypart.hu, €€. As of publication, a balcony room for two in peak season, breakfast included, is €59 (14,750 HUF), making it a highly competitive hotel. Apartments are only €10 more, at €69 (17,250 HUF). Their packages are extraordinary. In high season, between June and July, the price is €198 (49,500 HUF) per person for a couple, covering seven days and six nights, half-board, with a buffet dinner, a welcome drink at the first dinner, unlimited use of sauna and fitness room, and, of course, the beach. The add-ons at this writing are at Hungarian rates, not tourist rates, making it one of the best bargain hotels in Central Europe. The hotel

has had to struggle out of Soviet mismanagement and is well on the road in a free market. The staff, once Russian, German, and Hungarian, has now been broadened to include English. The children's programs (with English/Hungarian and German/Hungarian "animators," who entertain the children) include instruction in such fun activities as archery, a children's disco, and swims and excursions purposely designed to give parents long breaks. While the carpeted ambience of a four star is not here, beauty parlor/salon, pedicures, massages and a gym and sauna, in-room SAT/TV, minibar, computer connections, and on-premises dry cleaning ease the difference. The hotel's beach extends for hundreds of yards before you are waist-deep, leading to games and inflatable castles for lakeside fun. Add a superb kitchen that can compete with any of the finer restaurants, and their wine list includes fine imported wines as well as Hungarian classics. Give it to the Hungarians on this one.

**Hotel Fonyód**, H-8460 Fonyód, József utca 21/a, ☎ 36-85-561-500, fax 36-85-561-904, dotel.fonyod@enternet.hu, www.hotel-fonyod.hu, €-€€. At €44 (11,000 HUF) low season and €65 (16,250 HUF) in high season for a double, it is for lower budgets, but adequate in amenities. Located on the only real hill in southern Lake Balaton, it is close to mountain trails, and you are five minutes from the lake shore and the harbor. The train and bus station are only a few minutes away. The terrace served by the hotel cafeteria looks out over Balaton for a wonderful ambience. The inside restaurant tables are small and not in the best atmosphere, but the cuisine is Hungarian to be sure, and the kitchen offers room service. In-room TV (small TVs and Hungarian stations), in-room phones, a fitness room, sauna, small indoor pool, masseuse, a bar and closed parking, are all managed by a 24-hour front desk. There are park-like grounds, plus a converted high school gymnasium complete with varnished hardwood, benches, and an outdoor soccer field. Away from the beach crowd, Hotel Fonyód is for the hiking crowd and those who do not need every amenity.

# Places to Eat

## Siófok

The **Janos Café-
ház** is located in
the Best Western
János Atrium
Hotel, 8600 Siófok, Fõ út 93-
95, ☎ 36-84-312-546, fax 36-
84-312-432, janus@janus-
hotel.hu, www.janushotel.hu,
€. You feel as if you're on a

Caribbean Island here. Light streams in through wall-sized
windows and a cathedral glass ceiling filters the sunlight to
stream in shades of white, green, and bright pastels. They
bathe the interior, with each table set in what feels like a
small private grotto surrounded by green plants. Black iron
glass-topped tables and wicker add to the ambiance. Coffee
cakes, sandwiches, and salads are served, along with free
Internet.

The **János Étterem** is the second restaurant in the Best
Western János Atrium Hotel in Siófok, completely different
from the café in its feeling. Low lights, elegant woodwork, and
turn-of-the-19th-century decorations give the impression of
subdued elegance. The menu is Hungarian with some international dishes. It was a favorite of the composer Kálmán and
his wife, whose photos and comments adorn the entry wall.
Vera Kálmán's favorite dish was said to be Balaton fogás – a
giant pike perch found in Lake Balaton).

**Hintaló Vendéglõ**,
8600 Siófok-Ezüstpart,
Vécsey út 6, ☎ 36-84-
350-494, nitalo@
maildatanet.hu, www.
restaurantguide.hu/
hintalo, €. A short walk
from the rail station on
Vécsey út. Try the eve-
ning bogrács cookouts,

in which the real Hungarian goulash was invented. The food is cooked in a huge pot (the bogrács) suspended over an open fire, in the manner of the Hungarian plains. The children's menu includes baby food and there is a

| DINING PRICE CHART | |
|---|---|
| Price for an entrée, with tax | |
| € | Under $10 |
| €€ | $10-$25 |
| €€€ | Over $25 |

small playground and diaper-changing area. Although you might expect wine, their four beers are European continental, Stella Artoise (Belgian), Borostyán (Hungarian), Staropramen (Czech Pils), and Becks (German). The atmosphere is Hungarian country csárda, family-friendly and at a reasonable price.

## Zamárdi

**Kocsi Csárda** is part of the Galopp Lovas Üdülõfalu (Galopp Horseback Riding Holiday Village) at 8621 Zamárdi-Felsõ, on Siófoki út, ☎/fax 36-84-349-010 or 36-84-349-020, kocsicsarda@t-online.hu, www.kocsi-csarda.hu, €-€€. Off M7 in Zamárdi, going toward Szántod, the high, dark wood open-beam ceilings contrast with the white walls and country lamps. Their wines are superb. The restaurant comes alive with gypsy music nightly and, on occasion, indoor horse shows (usually while tour groups are there). Good food and good entertainment. Money well spent.

## Szántód

The **Rév Csárda**, H-8622 Szántód, Szent István 152, €, sits at the harbor's edge, where ferries transfer passengers and cars to the Tihany Peninsula, rising in the distance on the opposite shore. It is the narrowest point of the lake, making it a natural crossing point and a natural place for this csárda (country restaurant), which is also a hostel. A favorite of Hun-

garians and returning
European travelers, it is
a combination of pub
and café, with families
congregating for lunch
and dinner. Built in
1840, it is commercial-
ized, but the food is
excellent, explaining
why sometimes there

can be a lengthy wait for the meal. Special attractions are the
dancers and gypsy violins in the frequent evening programs,
and an occasional disco. Evening goulash parties and sum-
mertime barbecues are staged during tourist season. It is a
place to clink glasses and watch the ferry cross the water as
the sun sets.

## Balatonszemes

**Kistücsök Étterem**,
Borpince es Vinotéka,
8636 Balatonszemes,
Bajcsy Zsilinszky út 25,
☎ 36-84-360-133, fax 36-
84-360-883, tucsok@
enternet.hu, www.
kistucsok.hu, €-€€. This
was actually a livery for
postal carriers and coaches ages ago. They would stop, stable
their horses, eat at the "Postakocsi Inn," as it was called then,
and imbibe the famed red wines of the Somogy region. Game
shot in the local mountains was the main course. The restaurant retains the tradition with fish caught fresh out of the
lake, or wild pheasant, venison and boar from the mountain
forests nearby. Try the saddle of deer tenderized in wine, and
served with caramelized prunes. It's impossible to forget its
flavor. But the vegetarian specialties are excellent here as
well. Try the pancakes stuffed with leafy spinach and served
with ricotta sauce. A wine expert can help you toast the 13 different nectars from the vineyards of Somogy. Summers, you
can dine in the garden, with the accordion playing in the
background, or choose the serenading violin in the dining
rooms.

## Nightlife

The Southern Shore is a party animal's haunt at night, as well as a family's retreat during the day. There is plenty of action and fun for young couples and singles. Although we have picked a few places here, don't be afraid to experiment. Balaton is loaded with hidden treasures. Along the shore, most towns have at least one hot night spot. However, typically, they are only open in the summer. The best time for clubbing is during the months of June, July, and August.

 The 24-hour line for party information in Hungary is at ☎ 36-20-333-3303.

**Palace Disco Pizzeria**, 8609 Siófok-Széplak, Deák sétány 2, info@palace.hu, www.palace.hu. The Palace is three floors, an outside garden, a stadium, tons of electronics, and live entertainment (including visiting international stars for special shows). It's a place for strobe lights, laser shows and people, one of the best spots for night action in Hungary. Added to that, the strip along Siófok is one of the liveliest in Europe, with dozens of hot spots.

**Flört Dance Club**, 8600 Siófok, Sió utca, infoflort.hu, www.flort.hu. This is a gigantic two-story party. Once the music, light show, and dancing start, they don't stop. There is a great bar and eats, but who has time for them?

**Locomotion, The Party Bunker, 8600 Siófok Centrum, Fõ út 174-176,** ☎ 36-84-315-717. During peak season, spotlights shine up into the sky to make sure that all party goers can find their way here. Thousands flock here every night in peak season.

**Coca Cola Beach House, on Petõfi sétány,** www.coca-cola.hu (a Hungarian website). On the hottest part of the beach in Siófok, it sets the standard for beachside fun and entertainment. Food, drink, and music meld with people and visiting international bands and singers. (See also *Itineraries* in Siófok.)

**Bacardi Music Café, 8600 Siófok, Petõfi sétány 5, www.**bacardi-music-cafe.hu. This is next to Coca Cola Beach

House. Although its not nearly as large, its always trying to meet the same standard, and sometimes doing it.

**Diner M, 8600 Siófok, Petõfi sétány 3, ☎ 36-84-510-074,** www.dinerm.hu. Dinner M is not as large as some of its competitors, but, for those wanting hot dogs, shakes, and hamburgers, this is the place. The Amerikai Étterem serves up American-style foods, but adds pure American jazz, swing and sometimes Hungarian music. Its American-slanted ambiance keeps it crowded most of the time.

## Itineraries

### ★★ Siófok

The first and largest resort on the Southern Shore is Siófok, www.siofok.hu/terkep/varosterkep.html. It fronts the water with modern "in-crowd" beaches, nightclubs, and restaurants. In the summer, hundreds of thouskands of people flock here, swelling the resort population to five and six times the number of permanent residents. They come to Coca Cola Beach on Petõfi sétány, and to other beaches, where grass lawns and trees border the sand, making it perfect for blanets and picnic baskets. Canoe, raft, and paddleboat rentals vie with the giant water slides, beachside entertainment, discos and eateries to entice the crowd. (See *Free and Fee Beaches* below.)

Such a seething mass of fun-seekers always attracts some lesser elements, so you will see strip bars and seedy hostels as well. But, not to be fooled, there is much more to Siófok, the birthplace of the composer Imre Kálmán. Classical music can be heard in the concert halls. The Golden Cockle International Folklore Festival attracts folk groups from around the world to charm onlookers with their instruments, song, and dance.

On April 12, 1861 the South fired on Fort Sumter in America. It was the same year that, across the Atlantic, the Southern Railway of Hungary connected Siófok to northern Hungary. By the end of the 1800s Siófok had become *the* vacation spot for the upper crust of Hungarian society.

There was a bathing pavilion in the water, as well as "bathing boxes" on the shore. Every winter the bathing pavilion was towed out of the water and set on higher ground to prevent ice damage. It was a necessary precaution. Balaton often froze to a thick, glass-smooth surface in the winter (suitable for wind sailing on the ice).

After WWII the community mushroomed and absorbed nearby towns until it extended 15 km (9¼ miles).

The main town road heading south is Fő utca. It is also part of the old Balaton Route 70 (or Route 7), which bisects the shore/nightclub area from the inland residential community.

 **Information:** Siótour (Shee-oh-tour), the Somogy County Tourist Office (the Southern Shore is in Somogy County), is at the intersection of Szabadság tér and Fő utca. They can help with brochures, maps, and local contacts (see also Tourinform in the *Appendix*). A calendar of events and concerts is available at the Balaton Cultural Center at No. 2, Fő tér.

 Next to the cultural center are the town council building and two turn-of-the-century schools. Schools have changed since the early 1900s however. Today the younger generation studies mathematics and science, as they did then, but English has replaced German as the most popular second language. Teenagers carry their own Walkmen and mobile phones, and many have

computers at home. They wear street clothes just like those of kids in America. But, almost universally, Hungarian kids wear backpacks. They carry the books and supplies they have bought themselves. The schools do not pay for these things. Year-end examinations are done in suits and formal dress. Although the older generation complains about the younger generation (what else is new?), Hungarian children are generally quite focussed and serious. It is the nature of Hungarian culture to emphasize education, a fact that has marked its society for centuries... except during summer playtime, of course, as in Siófok.

Near the intersection of Fő utca and Sió utca, the Sió Bridge and dam, and the **Beszédes József Museum**, reveal a glimpse of Balaton history. The museum is fronted by a bust of its namesake, Beszédes József, the hydro-engineer who drained the marshes and constructed the Sió Canal (between Lake Balaton and the Danube) in the first half of the 1800s. The museum displays a history of hydro-engineering in Hungary, including water control systems for the Danube and Lake Balaton, and many artifacts from the city's history.

Heading toward the beach, Mártírok útja leads off Fő utca toward the lake and Petőfi Sétány, the lakeside shore promenade. On the way, turn right onto Kálmán Imre Sétány and go to No. 5. It is the birthplace (1882) of **Kálmán Imre** (Emmerich Kálmán), the composer of operettas. Now a museum, the house is filled with his personal mementoes.

Continue on Mártírok útja and you eventually come to the **shoreline promenade**. To our left is the port of Siófok, and southwestward, on the other side of it, are the communities of Újhely and Balatonszéplak. Extending past them is the Silver Shore. The Silver Shore is only a little less glitzy than the Golden Shore, with plenty of eateries and shops, and an excellent beach. It probably gets its name from the droves of upper-middle-class customers who once came here to spend their vacation money.

The port is flanked on the western side by two piers and a host of yachts, rowboats, and sailors. The eastern pier is more popular for strollers and fishermen. A walk on the piers toward the promenade and along the canal reveals the genius of Beszédes József. For example, the sluice and locks appear

Lake Balaton

modern, yet they are now almost 200 years old. The National Meteorological Institute owns the 36-foot-tall tower on the far side of the canal. Instruments in the tower provide weather forecasting information. They also form the core for an early storm warning system.

Next to the port, we look northeast to the promenade (Petőfi Sétány), called the Nagy Strand, which stretches out to a grassy beach bordered by a tree-shaded embankment. It eventually leads us to the Golden Shore, which leans out and extends for 1½ km (.9 mile) along the shoreline.

The Golden Shore gets its name from the wealthy people who once spent their vacations here. It is a slight promontory that extends for 1½ km (.9 miles) along the shoreline. Although a concrete walkway stretches the length of it, the beach sand itself is easy to walk on. It is full of bathing houses, lockers, refreshment stands, restaurants, and rental facilities for different water adventures. Beachside fast food aromas mix with blaring music from shops and radios, as rollerskaters weave through crowds of families, couples, tourist groups and bathers. Farther east, hotels claim their own beachside properties, joined by upscale shops, restaurants, a supermarket, sports grounds, and the beachside tourist office.

German is a dominant language here, attesting to the millions of German tourists that come to this area. But don't let that put you off. It is astonishing how many locals speak English, so you can feel quite comfortable in asking directions, even if your Hungarian is terrible.

## Free Beaches

Almost all free beaches have restrooms, watersports rentals, water slides, hundreds of vendors, and plenty of restaurants. The Golden and Silver Shore also have ice-cream vendors. However, during the peak season the free beaches host 50,000 to 70,000 visitors daily. Get there early with a blanket and a beach umbrella.

**Note:** When you see a sign that says "Privat" or "Belépni tilos," it means it is private or restricted. Do not enter an area with such posted signs.

**Latinka Sándor Beach**. On the northeastern end of Siófok, past the Silver Shore, Baross Gábor utca intersects with Vasúti utca (Railway Street). This is the site of Latinka Sándor beach. Baross Gábor utca used to be Latinka Sándor utca, hence the name of the beach is Latinka Sándor Beach. It is about a 100 yards long.

★★ **Nagy strand**. This extends from the port to the Golden Shore, parallel to Petőfi Sétány. There is a small section next to the port, called the Rózsa kert (Rose Garden), which is off-limits to swimmers. However, from there until Petőfi Sétány turns into Deák Ferenc sétány, which is the beginning of Golden Beach (Aranypart), it is open. This is the site of Long Beach, the home of the Coca-Cola Beach House (daily bands and visiting groups throughout the summer, except Sunday). Long Beach itself does require a fee (see *Fee Beaches* below). However, the greater Nagy Strand is also filled with cabins, restaurants, watersports rentals, vendors, and loads of activities for young and old.

★★ **Aranypart (Golden Shore)**. This beach extends out farther into Lake Balaton than Nagy Beach. It starts where Petőfi sétány changes its name to Beszédes József sétány, and continues to about where Baross Gábor utca and Posta utca intersect. It is the biggest free beach, over two miles (four km) long, and it is also loaded with just as much activity and water options as Nagy Beach.

**Szent István Sétány (St. Istvan Lane)** is a solid if small 188 yards long.

**Ezüstpart (Big Silver Shore)**. Extends from the intersection of Csongor Street and Liszt Ferenc Street southwest in Újhely,

**Lake Balaton**

for about 1.6 km (one mile). From the harbor, it extends south-west, after the Újhely beach.

## Fee Beaches

| All Fee Beaches Charge the Same Prices |
| --- |
| Daily children . . . . . . . . . . . . . . . . . . . . . . 100 HUF |
| Daily adults . . . . . . . . . . . . . . . . . . . . . . . 200 HUF |
| Weekly adults . . . . . . . . . . . . . . . . . . . . 1,000 HUF |
| Weekly children. . . . . . . . . . . . . . . . . . . . 500 HUF |
| Daily cabin . . . . . . . . 1,200 HUF (highly advisable) |
| Weekly cabin . . . . . . . . . . . . . . . . . . . . . 6,000 HUF |
| Safe deposit. . . . . . . . . . . . . . . . . 500 HUF per day |

★ **Long Shore** (also called Coca Cola Beach, inside of Nagy Strand). Long Shore is not that long, at 600 yards or about a quarter-mile, but it extends inland to encompass nearly 20 acres, loaded with people, activities, snack bars, restaurants, and vendors. Its Coca Cola Beach House hosts singers, bands, dancing, and a disco. They also organize beachside water games and activities. Its three ticketing entrances open out to a grassy, treed expanse, but get there early to stake a place. A mini bungee jumping tower, water chutes and slides and an "air castle" in the water round out the fun.

**Sóstó.** Distinguished by its artificial peninsula, northeast from the harbor, it is in the suburb of Sóstó, toward the lake from the intersection of Latinka Sándor utca and Pusztatorony tér. Pusztatorony tér is circled with boutiques, shops, snack bars and grocery stores. Slides and rentals abound here, and an Internet café at the entrance will allow you to write CDs, or send pictures home.

**Újhely.** This is the community that borders the western pier of the port of Siófok. The Újhely Shore is lined by Deák Ferenc sétány, a promenade that extends the full shoreline until it turns into Liszt Ferenc sétány (where it becomes the Long Silver Shore – see *Free Beaches* above). However, entrance to the beach is at the end of Betlehen Gábor utca. There are changing rooms, showers, slides, and lockers.

After taking in the beaches for a few days, we leave Siófok for Zamárdi and Szántód, heading farther southwest on Route M7.

## Zamárdi, Szántód

Leaving Siófok on old M7 is like leaving Los Angeles. You know you did, but you are just not quite sure where. We pass the community of Balatonszéplak (a part of Újhely) without noticing, and enter Zamárdi (www.zamardi.hu). Zamárdi stretches for 10 km/six miles and it is home to one of the largest free, grass-covered beaches in Balaton (three km/1.8 miles).

Zamárdi is at least 2,000 years old. Like other villages on the South Shore, it was totally wiped out by the

*Zamárdi Parish Church*
*(www.zamardi.hu)*

Turks in the 16th century. Its rebirth parallels the development of the church in Hungary. Abbots Videbald Grosso and his successor, Ágoston Lécs from Tihany, actively led a resettlement of the devastated area. Historical documents first mention Zamárdi in 1082.

The resort hugs the shore between the rail line and the water. It is a town of shady avenues, flowered gardens, and holiday homes. The primary street, Fő utca, leads to the Baroque **Parish Church** (1771-1774). It replaced a Gothic church that was built using the stones of Roman ruins, but which fell to the Turks. Based upon the remains of charred bones that were found inside the Gothic church's remains, it appears that the villagers fled inside. The Turks then burned the village and the church, with the villagers inside. The altar and pulpit of this church today are historical monuments. Its fabulous organ, built in 1786, was once a marvel of Central Europe, but was destroyed by the Red Army in 1944. They

Lake Balaton

installed an artillery lookout in the tower and used the organ for firewood. Peasant houses face the southwest end of Fő utca. Look for No. 83. It is open to the public.

Since the center of the resort is the train station, you can arrive in the middle of town, without a car, by rail. Near the train station, confectionery shops, a market, and various retailers form a square (Szabadság tér). Szent Istvan út borders the square toward the lakeside. Batthyány Lajos út and Rákóczi út both intersect as they come into Szent Istvan út. Walk to that intersection, and then walk up Batthyány út to the next street, Kossuth Lajos utca. Walk up Kossuth Lajos utca toward the shore. This route will take you to the tourist office, hotel, self-service restaurant, and, eventually, the beach. As in many areas of Siófok, the beach slopes gently into the water and you can wade several hundred yards before you are waist-deep. For that reason, it is popular with families, away from the fast crowd at Siófok. Most hotels have children's programs and "animators," whose job it is to keep the young ones entertained.

*Donkey Stone (www.zamardi.hu)*

For adventurous exploring, take the red way-marked pathway from the railroad station up to Kő hegy (174 m/522 feet).

It will take you to the gigantic, mysterious **Szamárkõ** (Donkey Stone). The was also once known as the Jesus Stone and, before that, The Devil's Stone. We know that the area was a center of paganism, in constant friction with Christianity and Rome. We also know that pagans often chose just such a stone as an altar for sacrifices to their pagan gods. But some historians say it was probably used as a base for light signals to Tihany, on the opposite shore.

Zamárdi has an extraordinarily clean (waste disposals every 10 m/30 feet) and safe beach. It is safe to park at Kiss Ernõ utca in the longest parking lot on the shore, and walk safely along the shore at night, while the serene waters lap the shore. Rental shops, changing cabins, vendors, and sidewalk eateries serve swimmers during the day. On Tuesday, Friday, and Saturday evenings in July and August, on the free beach at the end of Bácskai út, bands entertain the beach crowd and dozens of booths display the goods of local vendors.

This beach is also the frequent site of "interactive" horse drawn amateur coach driving (sometimes you can learn and participate). They also hold Hungarian Puszta horse riding shows and folklore programs. These are at the behest of the Kocsi csárda, which is a part of the Galopp Horse Riding Village on the outskirts of town. A restored ancient mini-village, the Galopp Horse Riding Village has cottages remodeled to 21st-century standards, decorated in period furniture, and rented out to tourists. The well known Kocsi csárda serves supreme Hungarian cuisine, and after you dine and wine, you can ride. If you don't know how, horseback riding lessons are an option. (See *Places to Eat, Places to Stay,* and *Adventures, Horses and Hooves.*)

## Szántód

Four km/2.4 miles farther south-west from Zamárdi, Szántód's triangular peninsula marks the narrowest point of the lake (1.5 km/.9 mile). It is ideal as the base for Balaton's ferry transportation system. The ferry used to be a wood-hulled ves-

sel, powered by sail, then was converted to use the power of
the automobiles to run it. In 1928 it was discarded in favor of
a steel-hulled engine-driven ferry. Today there is an updated
fleet that transports over a million passengers and hundreds
of thousands of vehicles every year, and connects most major
towns of Balaton.

The **Rév Csárda**, built in 1839 in Baroque style (see *Places to
Eat*), is famous throughout Hungary. A popular public beach
stands to one side, while on the opposite side a fee is required.
The tourist hotel is fronted by souvenir shops and street vendors. Campgrounds here supplement others on the road
between Szántód and Zamárdi for those who are backpack-
ing.

About three km/1.8 miles farther southwest on Route 7 you
will see an old car painted bright yellow, elevated on stilts, at
the side of the road. This is the entrance to the
**Szántódpuszta**, an authentic 18th- and 19th-century village. Open daily 9 am to 5 pm, from mid-April to the end of
October, the entrance fee is 550 HUF. In July and Aug it is
open 8:30 am to 7:30 pm. The reed-thatched roofs, furniture,
and layout are genuine Hungarian rural farmstead. An operating blacksmith's shop hammers out horseshoes and plows,
and several restaurants serve the tourist crowd. Horses are
rented for 2,000 HUF and carriage rides are given for 2,600
HUF. It is also the house of the large "Balaton Aquarium," the
only exhibit on the fish life of the lake. Attendants speak only
German or Hungarian, but everything is pretty much self-
explanatory, and the descriptive brochure is also in English.

## Balatonföldvár

Balatonföldvár is only
four km/2½ miles farther
southwest of Szántód. It
is the only resort in
Balaton that was
expressly created as a
resort. Once bordered by
a high loess embankment
built in the Iron Age by
the Celts, it was never

developeda, remaining a wooded wilderness on the outskirts of the village of Köröshegy until the 1890s. Then the famous Count Széchenyi made a deliberate effort to develop it. This explains why it is one of the most beautifully

laid-out resorts on the Southern Shore. The eastern edge of the resort is called Alsótelep (Lower Settlement). The railroad station, constructed in 1928, is in the town center. A well, built in 1974-1975, sits next to the station. North of the railway station are the hotels, camping sites, and beaches.

A concrete breakwater encircles a 22-acre area to form the port. Inside the protected enclave, tiny artificially created Galamb sziget (Pigeon's Island) invites sunbathers to row out from the shore, although there is a path to it on the eastern side. This is one of the busiest places in Lake Balaton for boating. Rentals are available at many shops and most hotels. It is also the site of the annual Balaton triathlon.

The monument in front of the building at the landing stage is dedicated to Jenõ Kvassay, the designer of the port. To find bathing spots, stroll Kvassay sétány (the shoreline promenade), which connects to Bajcsy Zsilinszky utca at the port and heads southwest for about a half-mile, sided by holiday homes and private beaches. Look for signs advertising places to stay. Parallel to Kvassay sétány is Rákóczi Ferenc utca.

Lake Balaton

Next to the intersection of Route 7 and Petőfi Sándor utca is the village square and the mayor's house. For a great excursion, walk up Petőfi Sándor or its parallel street, Jószef Attila utca. It will take you to the steep banks of the Iron-Age earthworks. Keep on the ascent and you will reach the 60-foot tower, built in the 1970s solely to provide a panorama of the lake and its surroundings.

The red waymarks starting at the train station, on the other hand, will also take us up to **Lucs Tető** (Lucs Top), which overlooks the lake at 712 feet. Were we to continue on the red waymarked path for about another 6½ miles, we would come to the remains of **Fejérkővár** (White Stone Castle), on the outskirts of the village of Kereki. Both of these locations provide superb picture possibilities.

## Köröshegy

Balatonföldvár was once merely a suburb of this inland town, famous for wine and horses. Today, it is an inland suburb of Balatonföldvár. The town boasts a listed monument, the 15th-century Gothic **Roman Catholic Church** in town center. Built by Franciscan monks, its squat tower is a hallmark of their order's construction style. The nave has no aisle, and its stark, massive appearance gives the impression of a fort. Its walls rose up when pagans, robbers and Turks ravaged the land. Incredibly, the structure has survived intact, so what you see is substantially what existed when villagers hid inside for safety, and when monks asked for God's protection within its walls. Peasant carvings and Calvary pictographs decorate the walls. The altarpiece, Christ on the Cross, is apparently the work of a Viennese master. Gothic, rose-tinted windows direct the light into an acoustically fabulous interior. For that reason, concerts are held in its sanctum every year.

In those days when the church was filled with peasants and villagers, the fruit of the vine overflowed, as it does today, to make the smooth Balaton wines. Italian Riesling from Köröshegy is considered some of the finest in Hungary. Stop by the **Kishegyi Pince wine cellar**, H-8617 Köröshegy, at Jószef Attila út 5. But make an appointment first through Tourinform, so you don't find the doors closed (check with the Siófok office – see *Appendix*).

# Balatonboglár

The southern Balaton shore has been the home of some of the finest wines in the world, and the center of production has been in Balatonboglár, heralded as an international city of wine since 1987.

Viticulture has blossomed here for over a thousand years, explaining why just about every home in the area is also a wine cellar, producing vintage wine that vies with any in the world. Local inns and restaurants have "secret" recipes that flavor their culinary creations with the local wines. It makes for palate adventures that are as good as in some of the high-end restaurants of Budapest. Try to visit during the three-day **Balaton Vintage Festival**, held every August 20th. Music, dance, romance, food, and whatever else goes with the wine, overflow in a celebration of the harvest season.

The town boasts much more than wine, however. Fourteen international-caliber tennis complexes suitable for competition, with two or more tennis courts each, along with the numerous hotel tennis courts and private clubs, attract competitors from throughout Europe. We now head southwest on M7 to Fonyód.

# Fonyód

Fonyód returns us to castles, battles and redoubts. It stretches for eight km/4.8 miles along the shore, dominated by the double-peaked hill that rolls down to lap the silky water's edge. The two peaks are Vár-hegy (Castle Hill, 233 m/764 feet) and Sípos hegy (Sípos Hill, 207 m/679 feet). As with the basalt ranges on the Northern Shore, they were created by raging volcanic eruptions that consumed the area in a fiery, molten cauldron. But the Fonyód Hills were stripped of their basalt beauty by ambitious Hungarians looking for building materials.

Impassable marshland once surrounded the hills, providing an easily defensible position. Thus, the Romans left their imprint here in the Iron Age. After they left, by the 11th century, a village stretched from the marshlands to the eastern face of Sípos Hill. Of course, a castle went up. The remains of the moat and the castle foundation are on the edge of

Lake Balaton

Nagyberek, which is a walk up Szent István utca, the street that runs through the center of the resort.

But the glory of Fonyód is not in castle walls, but in the village church that once stood near it.

The Magyar Bõ clan, one of the fiercely independent blood covenant tribes of Árpád's era, first settled Fonyód. History does not record all the struggles that united them to the nation, but one of them certainly took place here. The Turks swept into Hungary during the invasion of the 16th century, killing, raping, looting and destroying, threatening Europe and the very existence of Christianity. This small town was one of the villages in its way.

Captain Bálint Magyar called a hasty meeting as the massed Turkish forces approached. We do not know the words that were spoken in that meeting, but the priests, townsmen, tradesmen, soldiers, peasants and villagers gathered at the church, resolved to defend the town rather than flee. What better place to do it than where God had planted his house. So, the church was turned into a fortress and surrounded with hastily built walls. Deep moats and ditches were desperately dug out by exhausted mud-splattered Hungarians, working around the clock without rest. Wood was cut from the swamps and forests and long palings were planted firmly around the redoubt, their sharpened points facing outward to repel charging horses and massed infantry. The year was 1550. It was not until 1573, 23 years later, that a concentrated mass of Turkish armies finally swarmed across the defensive works to eliminate the last of the town's defenders. The tiny town of Fonyód had withstood an empire for over two decades. We do not know how many Turks may have lost their lives at the redoubts of Fonyód, nor how many villagers perished. But it is certain that this town and so many others on the great Alföld and the mountains of Hungary forced the Turks to deal with the Magyars, rather than sweep on in to the heart of Europe.

Though every man, woman, and child had perished, as in all things Hungarian, the spirit would not die. The Magyars came and replanted the soil again. The Turks, depleted by the occupation, were weakened. They were not able to hold off the crusading armies of the Hapsburgs. Hungary, the cross

embedded upon the crown of her rulers, as witnessed in Fonyód, had done her job for Western civilization, but at a horrible price.

Resettlement emphasized wine and fishing. With the advent of the 19th century, however, railroads brought vacationers from Budapest and beyond. The long sandy beach with its shallow water, easily heated in the summer sun, was and is a great attraction. By the time WWII broke out, Fonyód boasted the resorts of Fonyódliget, Sándortelep, Bélatelep, and Alsó-Bélatelep.

M7 runs parallel to the railroad and the shore, called Ady Endre út and Vitorlás utca as it runs through town. The town commercial center is at the shore end of an axis running north and south. It stretches from the eastern side of Castle Hill, at the shore, along Szent István utca. The harbor is on the northern extreme of the axis. Notably, at the harbor, István Kiss's creation, the sculpture called *Double Nude*, holds our attention before we walk the **longest pier** on Lake Balaton, a promontory 1,522 feet long. It was built at the end of the 19th century. Today, in addition to boating, it is the site of an annual Balaton fishing contest. The breakwater dam is joined to an artificial peninsula planted with trees and grass. Go to Larfe Beach, east of the port, for swimming.

As you walk south along Szent István utca, turn off on József utca, a winding street with wonderful old villas. When you arrive at the salmon-colored **Crypt Villa** (Kripta villa) you have come to a love story or, some might say, a twisted obsession. A widower died here and joined his wife. He had interred her in a red

**Lake Balaton**

marble crypt below his house! Even after she died, he never left her side, until he finally joined her in the grave. They still lie there together, overlooking the opal waters of Lake Balaton.

Farther on, some marvelous views of Balaton open out from the street. But, back on Szent István utca, we continue south, past the Balaton travel office and eventually arrive at Fácán park on the right (about 25 minutes). The park holds the remains of the border fortress that existed at the time of the Turkish occupation, and the original location of Fonyód village. Little is left, but it can be seen how the 30-foot-wide moat and a concentric system of ditches worked for their defense. A drawbridge once spanned the moat and a tower looked out for danger. Now, only the memory sees the lake and only the legend recalls it.

The **Fonyód flea market** attracts people from throughout the area on Wednesdays and Saturdays. The **Balaton Triathlon** is in July, which coincides with the **Festival of The Golden Shell**. It is capped by a dance group from Leipzig that comes here to celebrate in Bavarian song and dance. Universally, the town festivities are held in the central park, which features bicycle paths, vendors, an open-air public pool, and plenty of places for picnic baskets and blankets.

## Adventures

## Hiking & Biking
### Cycling Off Old M7 to the Inland City, Nagykanizsa

 Cycling the shoreline M7 will give some wonderful views, and touch upon many opportunities for beachside exploration. But the traffic is heavy, and there are a lot of people. To get away from the crowds and experience the region's plains and mountains, take the road to Balatonbereny off M7. From there, head south to Balatonszentgyörgy. There you veer toward Batyánpuszta. From Batyánpuszta head east following the signs to Tikos. The same road will start to veer south, and cross Route 7 toward Somogysámson, to Somogyzsitfa, and on to Szöcsénypuszta. Be careful here. You want to turn and follow the road southwest toward Nemesvid, then down to Nemesdéd. At Nemesdéd we make another turn toward Miháld and cycle through the town of Varászló, past the Halastó (Fish Lake), through to Pat. From there you push down to Sand, and then to Nagykanizsa. It is about 72 km/43 miles and it takes you through villages and by some of the natural wonders of the lower highlands. There are no severe gradients and you ride through the protected territory of the Little Balaton most of the time, so waterfowl and some smaller wild animals may easily be seen on your trip.

The city of Nagykanizsa was the site of the International Women's Saber Championships in 2003. In a cliffhanger match, the two top contenders battled with their swords for the gold. The USA edged out Hungary, 45-41. Nagykanizsa was also the site of the 2002 European Ultra Light Craft Flying Championships. It is highly advisable to book accommodations through Tourinform (see *Appendix*), before you get there.

## Wine Adventures

As with the Northern Shore, there are hundreds of possibilities to sample the nectars of viticulture on the South Shore of Balaton. As with the North Shore, book one of the many possible tours through Tourinform (see *Appendix*), and with proper arrangements, they might even provide a translator on some occasions, although often it is not necessary.

## Thermal Adventures

In Zalakaros, try the spa called **Granít Gyógyfürdõ Rt.**, 8749 Zalakaros, Thermál út 4, ☎ 36-93-340-721, fax 36-93-340-318, thermalfurdo-zkaros@axelero.hu, www.furdo-zalakaros.hu or www.bad-zalakaros.hu. Zalakaros is south of Lake Balaton, as you follow Route 7. Get a cabin when you enter. For an additional 900 HUF, or about €4; the peace of mind and privacy are worth it. Outside baths run up to 1,000 HUF or €5. The inside adventure pools and bath are 2,000 HUF or €8. As with other places in Hungary, get there early and plan on making it an all-day affair. It is open all year, except Dec 25. It

extends inside and outside amidst pillars and columns, curves and grottos, giant slides, children's pools and wave pools, steam baths and hydro-massage pools. There is a medical staff here for treatment of customers looking for medicinal baths. Restaurants, büfés and cafés line the play areas, with hundreds of lounge chairs and an ample green lawn to lay out a blanket. Pampering can include the beauty salon services, pedicures and manicures.

Also see the Hotels Azure and Conference and Wellness Hotel Residence in *Places to Stay*.

## Water Adventures

★★ **Balatoni Hajózási Rt.**, H-8600 Siófok, Krúdy sétány 2, ☎/fax 36-84-310-050, www.balatonihajozas.hu. Siófok and many of the ports on both the Northern and Southern Shores launch cruise ships that feature disco or soft Balaton evening sunset dinners (bring the camera). Several combined tours include wine tasting and sightseeing trips to the Tihany Peninsula, a miniature train ride back to the docks, and on-board appetizers (peanuts, light foods, soft drinks, and coffee). The Badacsony tour includes a miniature train ride through the

vineyards of Badacsony, culminating at the Borbarátok Inn, where you learn about wine tasting and the wines of the region, engage in a wine-tasting contest, and then back to the ship by miniature train. All cruise ships have refreshments (pricey).

Aside from these cruises, it is great fun to take the ferry that crosses from Szántód to Tihany (about 1,100 HUF/ €4 to €5 per car plus 350 HUF/€2 per person). It takes 20-30 minutes, while the winds of the Balaton "sea" blow through your hair on the open deck.

## On Horseback

 Thre is a special adventure place to stay in Zamárdi-Felső for those on a budget. **Galopp Lovas Üdülőfalu (Galopp Horse Riding Holiday Village)**, 8621 Zamárdi-felső, Siófoki út, ☎/fax  36-84-349-010 or 36-84-349-020, kocsicsarda@t-online.hu, www.kocsicsarda.hu. Galopp is a combination restaurant, cottage, village (see *Places to Stay* and *Places to Eat*), and horseback riding adventure rolled into one. They provide the animals, feed and care, and you ride and live almost like a villager. "Programs" must be coordinated with a group. However, individual family rentals make use of the same facilities and horses, the Hungarian Kabardin, a black and/or brown steed known for its strength, intelligence, and amiability. €30/7,500 HUF a day includes the cottage with modern amenities and, at last writing, three hours riding time per day. They groom, feed, and stable the animals. However, each cottage has a stable, and as an option, depending on management approval, a family can stable a horse on premises and give the children a chance to learn about the care of the animal. Riding lessons are €9/2,250 HUF for a 30-minute session (for beginners up to intermediate level). The adventure of staying in the village, in a cottage that is 200 years old, and working so closely with the villagers and their animals, has a unique attraction.

Lake Balaton

At Balaton's Southern Shore the Hungarian Equestrian Tourism Association has one five-horseshoe farm (see *Budapest Horses & Hooves* for information about the rating system).

**Kabóka Riding Farm** (also known as the Varga Farm), 8130 Enying, Tóth Árpád út 2, ☎/fax 36-22-373-743, peter@kaboka.com, www.kaboka.com. Contact Varga Péter, mobile ☎ 36-30-291-9110. A guest ranch and top-rated stud ranch as well, supported with tours, sightseeing, cross-country horseback riding for the experienced, lessons, excellent private rooms, and horse shows during certain times of the year. The latest quoted rate was €30/7,500 HUF per night per person. Lessons are €12/3,000 HUF per lesson. Aside from the pool, gym, and country kitchen, they also have a heated pool, and a large lake for fishing (€7/1,750 HUF per day).

# Northern Hungary

Every year, hundreds of thousands of people hike, bike, ride, climb, and walk the green valleys and limestone mountains of the Aggtelek National Park, the Bükk National Park, and the Cserhát, Mátra, and Zempléni hills in Northern Hungary. Storks, eagles, wrens, blackbirds, woodpeckers, and flocks of other birds make their home in forests, grasslands, and cliff sides here. Majestic antlered stags and deer range through the forest. Fresh springs and cold clear creeks tumble down from the mountains. Species a hairline from extinction find a home, and thrive.

UNESCO World Heritage Sites dot the terrain. Isolated villages have kept traditions for hundreds of years. The Palóc people amaze onlookers with the intricacies of their embroidery. The bright, colorful Matyó folk dress delights onlooker. Thermal waters spring up out of the earth, sometimes in caves, lighted and modified to be tourist-friendly.

The hub cities are **Gyöngyös**, **Eger**, and **Miskolc**. Aside from the local Tourinform offices, and also the Hungarian Friends of Nature mentioned in the Budapest chapter, you may also get help for travel in this area from the **North Hungary Regional Marketing Directorate**, 3300 Eger, Dobó tér 9, ☎ 36-36-512-440. fax 36-36-512-446. emrmi@ hungarytourism.hu. www.nordur.hu.

# ■ Places to Stay

## Jósvafõ

### Tengerszem

**Tengerszem Szálló és Oktatási Központ**, 3758 Jósvafõ, Tengerszem oldal 2, ☎/fax 36 48 506 005, info.anp@axelero.hu, www. anp.hu, www.1hungary.com/

| HOTEL PRICE CHART | |
|---|---|
| Double room without tax | |
| € | Under €80 |
| €€ | €81-€150 |
| €€€ | €151-€250 |
| €€€€ | Over €250 |

tengerszem_szallo. €-€€. 11,000 HUF (€44) to 13,000 HUF (€52) per night for a double in this chalet includes a minibar, television, telephone, and bath in each room. Although not a Hilton, it is well kept and adequate. It usually caters to student groups but many tourists book a room here as well. The hotel is right at the entrance to the Aggtelek caves. You can buy your tickets for the cave tours at the hotel. Nature trails abound. The restaurant serves Hungarian cuisine at 1,200 HUF (€5) to 2,500 HUF (€10). Dining is in a country atmosphere with nice views out of the windows and an open terrace in the summer.

## Szilvásvárad

**Hotel Lipicai**, 3348 Szilvásvárad, Egri út 12, ☎ /fax 36-36-564-038 or 038, lipicalhotel@axelero.hu www. szilvasvarad-lipicaihotel.hu. €. 3,900 HUF (€15.6) to 7,000 HUF (€28) per person per night in high season make it a bargain small town hostel/hotel. It sits between two running streams in the middle of the woods and it's loaded with extra adventure amenities (including Lipizaner stallions). The hotel rooms (not the hostel) each have a bath, toilet, television and a small terrace. The tasty food costs about 1,500 HUF (€6) to 3,000 HUF (€12), for wild fowl, trout, with a choice of diabetic-friendly, Hungarian and international cuisine. It's only a couple of minutes from the outdoor museum and the entrance to the famous Szalajka Valley, as well as the train station. Horseback riding, sledding in the winter, gliding, rock climbing, archery, hunting, jeep tours, and walking tours may be available to any guest, depending on demand. The proximity of numerous trails makes this an excellent base point for hiking. There is a tennis court, soccer field, bar, and secure parking.

# Northern Hungary

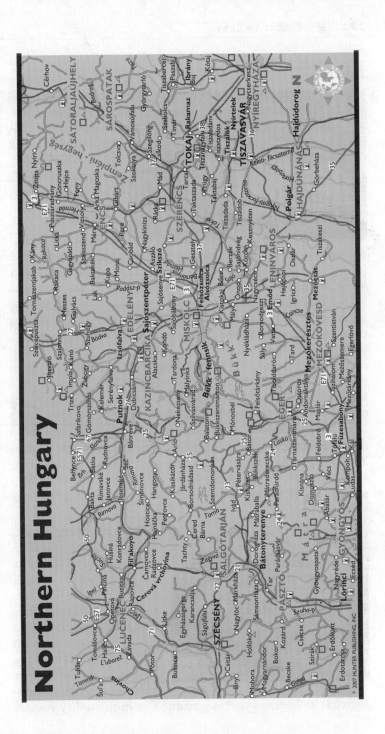

## Eger

**Hotel Korona**, 3300 Eger, Tundérpart 5, ☎ 36-36-313-670, fax 36-36-310-261, koronaho@mail. agria.hu, www. koronahotel.hu. €€-€€€. At €65 to €125 for a high-season double, its unassuming front belies a newly renovated interior (originally built in 1789). The well-known István Wine Cellar sits 40 feet below (also known as the National Wine Museum). As a guest, you can participate in the wine cellar tours. Gypsy music adds to the gastronomic variety of the kitchen. Adventure programs and excursions are organized from the front desk. Over

22 regional wines can be sampled from the restaurant table. You can pamper yourself in the pool, Jacuzzi, gymnasium, sauna and with a massage, while kids play in the children's playground or the sand box. Service is excellent and the English is good.

★★**Hotel Eger-Park**, 3300 Eger, Szálloda út 1-3, ☎ 36-36-522-222, fax 36-36-413-114, hotel-egerpark@axelero.hu, www.hotelegerpark.hu. €€. Doubles run €75 to €85 in high season with cable or SAT television, air-conditioning, indoor swimming pool, sauna, Jacuzzi, and aroma-therapy room. The high-quality restaurant has a luxurious dining room in the old part of two joined buildings where entertainment is provided by a gypsy band. The large park behind the hotel is laced with tree-lined pathways. Add to this the wine cellar, cafés, and the Brasserie, with bowling, billiards, and a pool.

**Senator Ház Hotel**, 3300 Eger, Dobó tér 11, ☎ 36-36-320-466, fax 36-36-320-466, senator@enternet.hu, www.senatorhaz.hu. €€. €62 to €72 for a double in high season. Although not equal in amenities to its upscale cousins in the  area, it is nevertheless filled with ambience from the past (including period furniture and décor). The exception is the restaurant, which feels almost Mediterranean. One of the first houses built after the Turkish occupation, it was sold in 1727 when Serb Simon Szabo sold "his own house for 90 forints to György Boldogi." The Boldogi family retained possession for a century and then sold it to András Szvetics, a municipal "senator," and hence the name. The original owners have long since passed away. The café is passable and offers room service. A television in every room and private bath, laundry, Internet, and 24-hour reception make it a fair price.

★**Hotel Minaret**, 3300 Eger, Knézich Károly út 4, ☎/fax 36-36-410-233, info@hotelminaret.hu, www.hotelminaret.hu. €-€€€ (best buy for the money in Eger). 12,300 to 14,000 HUF for doubles in high season. Under the shadow of the historic Minaret, down from the castle, the restaurant is good-quality, reasonable, and gives 24-hour room service. Minibar, SAT TV, telephone, and bath in each room, plus a children's playground, non-smoking rooms, and a swimming pool, together with beauty services, manicures, a 24-hour concierge, and free parking.

## Miskolc Area

**Lévay-Villa-Panzió**, H-3529 Miskolc, Lévay Jószef út 13, ☎ 36-46-500-890, fax 36-46-500-891, levayvilla@axelero. hu, www.hotels.hu/ levayvilla. €. €40 for a double in high season. It is located in downtown Miskolc, next to  the Népkert (Public Garden). Rooms have a phone, cable TV (with CNN and BBC), minibar, A/C, and are supplemented

 with a fitness room, sauna, indoor lounging cold pool (included in room rate), laundry, 24-hour room service, Internet connection and, if you like, a vegetarian kitchen. Central safe and monitored parking add to the security. For variety, a walk down the street takes you to the Café du Boucher Belgian Pub and Restaurant, an outlet of the European, Belgian Beer Café International chain.

**Hotel Bástya Wellness**, 3519 Miskolc-Tapolca, Miskolctapolcai út 1-3, ☎ 36-46-561-590 or 36-46-561-591, www. bastyawellnesshotel.hu. €€. 55,500 HUF is a bargain for doubles (the rate does not apply from Dec  20 through Jan 3). This is a quality wellness hotel and the rooms are spacious, with in-room telephone, Internet connection, and a 23-station SAT TV with some English stations. It is only 100 yards from the entrance to the Miskolctapolca Cave Bath (see *Cave Adventures*), but the hotel also has its own indoor pool, wellness center, Jacuzzi, sauna, steam cabin, and fitness room (included in price), which are supplemented with other amenities and wellness and fitness programs. Their package offers include some real bargains. The restaurant is a bit on the high side. It averages 1,200 HUF (€5) to 4,000 HUF (€16), but the Hungarian fare is supplemented with selections for vegetarians and diabetics.

★★**Hotel Palota**, 3517 Miskolc Lillafüred, Erzsébet sétány 1, ☎ 36-46-331-411, fax 36-46-533-203, reserve@hotelpalota.hunguesthotels.hu, www.hunguesthotels.hu. €€-€€€. The cost of €97 in low season and €106 in high season for a double is quite reasonable for this 3- to 4-star hotel. The Palota has done well to keep a  16th-century ambience, although it was constructed much later. The room rate includes use of the pool and sauna, whirlpool, fitness room, parking, and HBO on the cable TV. Add to  that the bowling alley, billiards, brasserie, and every adventure you might want, bookable without a hassle from the front desk. Sounds of the waterfall in the back, and the castle-like atmosphere, help make this a good value for the money. The food in the restaurant is absolutely top-notch.

★**Anna Hotel**, 3519 Miskolc-Tapolca, Miskolctapolcai út 7, ☎ 36-46-422-212, fax 36-46-422-400, www.hotels.hu/

annahoteltapolca,
annahotel2@chello.hu. €€.
Doubles run 8,100 HUF for a
"two single-bed" room and
10,600 HUF for a double-bed
room. Anna Hotel sits like a
fairy tale beside the road, complete with rounded towers. If
you enter the cukrászda (a
sweet-shop), its sweet-smell-
ing delights charm visitors.
But it is truly a "fürdő" hotel,
with full access to the Miskolc Tapolca Cave thermal baths
and spa (see *Cave Adventures*). You can arrange boating on
the lake next to the baths or hike the surrounding trails and
amble the park-like grounds. The beds are classic European,
with thick, cozy comforters, not the blankets used by American hotels, and the rooms have SAT TV (with some English
stations), minibar, in-room bath, and room service (usually
from 6 pm to 10 or 11 pm). The pub is good, but the restaurant
is one of the best in the region, serving full-course Hungarian
and international cuisine, with pastries and sweets the specialty. But you will pay accordingly (see *Places to Eat*).

**Fortuna Panzió Hotel**, 3519
Miskolc-Tapolca, Pf. 57, ☎ 36-46-
432-345, fax 36-46-561-266,
mtapolca@fortuna-panzio.hu,
www.fortuna-panzio.hu. €. High-
season accommodations at €22
per person is a bargain, but I
strongly urge taking the half-
board option at an extra €13 per
person per day. The breakfast
may include several varieties of
ham and eggs or Hungarian-style
eggs with peppers and tomatoes
or French toast, as well as several

other options, in their dining rooms on the lower floor. You are
served personally by the owners, and their daughter, and
local college and high school students that are friends of the

family. The service is solicitous and the rooms are clean and adequate, although not five-star. The quality of the food and the concern of the owners, however, rates this panzió at least three star. Summer terrace dining is possible, and every room has a TV, mini-bar, in-room bath, closet, bed stand, and lamps. It's in walking distance of the cave baths. From the corner of the hotel walk down one block past the strand (closed), and on to the brick walkway through the park. Bearing right will eventually take you to the entrance for the cave baths.

## Sárospatak

**Huszár Pension and Restaurant**, Sárospatak, Kazinczy út 3, ☎/fax 36- 47-313-018 or 36-47-511-158, chromath@axelero. hu and huszarpanzio@freemail.hu, www.huszarpanzio.hu. €. Doubles (with two beds) are 9,000 HUF (€36 ) per person, breakfast included, and it's a bargain, with SAT TV (some English stations), minibar, in-room mini-refrigerator, safe, and a shower. The restaurant is widely touted, but reasonably priced. Expect to pay about 1,200 to 3,000 HUF. The wine list includes some top-quality selections from Hungary. Aside from eating, the hotel arranges horseback tours and other excursions for guests. The front desk service is equal to the concierge services of some finer hotels. It's walking distance to everything in town.

## Sátoraljaújhely

★**Hotel Hunor**, 3930 Sátoraljaújhely, Torzsás út 25, ☎ 36-47-521-521, fax 36-47-521-522, hotelhunor@internetker.hu, www.hotelhunor.hu. €-€€. For 13,500 HUF in low season to about 14,200 HUF in high season you will find good English at the front desk, and hotel amenities that include SAT TV, in-room telephone, bathroom, minibar, wireless Internet and

air-conditioning. In addition, there is a safe at the front desk, free enclosed parking, free bowling, billiards, table tennis, an outside tennis court, free whirlpool, swimming pool, Jacuzzi, sauna, and a fitness room. Massages, horseback riding programs, wine tasting, bicycle rentals, local village crafts, and porcelain-making classes based on the methods of the ancient guilds are booked from the front desk. The hotel is a stone's throw from the ski lift for Magas mountain, the longest ski run in Hungary.

## Tokaj

Because of the international wine reputation of Tokaj, it attracts millions of visitors, but I think you are better off checking with the local Tourinform Tokaj office for recommendations (see pages 571 ff) and booking a room at a local guesthouse. What you get for the money at the hotels here is at best mediocre. The locals are known all over the country as friendly and engaging for the most part. They will often have their own wine cellar, and will usually give you personal attention, tips on getting around, and a negotiated room and board that will be quite a bit cheaper than typical hotel rates.

## Mátrafüred

**Füred Hotel**, 3232 Mátrafüred, Kékesi út 1-3, ☎ 36-37-520-030, fax 36-37-520-039, info@ furedhotel.hu, www.furedhotel. hu. €. Doubles cost 9,900 HUF, with cable TV, phone, minibar, and in-room bathroom. The solarium, sauna, and open-air bath are supplemented by a glass enclosed terrace, good for sun-bathing in summer or winter. The restaurant is small but adequate. Darts and an outdoor bowling green are other amenities, as is the use of the indoor heated shooting gallery not far from the hotel. Trained instructors work with you using small and large caliber rifles, telescopic sights, and pistols.

**Hotel Avar**, 3232 Mátrafüred, Paradi út 24, ☎ 36 37 320 134, www.szallasinfo.hu/avar. €-€€. €31 up to €52 for a double gives you SAT TV, minibar and television in every room, gym, sauna, swimming pool, and full support facilities for winter and summer sports. It's a great money-saver, with fairly good accommodations. However, because of the distance from the Mátra Mountain ski slopes, I do not recommend you stay here in the winter. Nevertheless, for summer excursions, this hotel is in the heart of the Mátra Mountains and an excellent base for single-day or longer excursions through the mountain forests here.

**Hunguest Hegyalja Hotel**, 3232 Mátrafüred, Béke út 7, ☎ 36 37 320 027, fax 36 37 320 028, hegyalja.matrafured@axelero.hu, www.hotels.hu/hegyalja. €. This is a straight Hungarian hotel, so expect to speak a bit of Hungarian here, but it is an incredible money-saver. Doubles run from 2,620 to 7,000 HUF. Singles are 1,660 up to 5,000 HUF. There is television in every room, a swimming pool and a restaurant, but if language is an obstacle for you, move on to others.

## Mátraháza

★**Bérc Hotel**, 3233 Mátraháza, ☎ 36-37-374-102, fax 36-37-374-095, berchotel@axelerol.hu, www.hotels.hu/berchotel. €. 13,000 to 15,000 HUF in summer for doubles (two to three times higher in winter and during Christmas-New Year's). It sits atop a hill overlooking a small valley in the forest with camera-ready views of the mountains. Parking lot, souvenir shop, restaurant, pub, indoor swimming pool, sauna, solar-

ium, gym, massage, tennis, bowling, billiards, room service, and a vegetarian kitchen where they will also prepare diabetic meals. Thousands of hikers and skiers are drawn here. The hotel's restaurant is also a dance club and brasserie. Meals are on the high side at about €12 to €15. Many people book well in advance here; you should do the same.

## Parádsasvár

**Castle (Károly) Hotel Sasvár**, 3242 Parádsasvár, Kossuth út 1, ☎ 36 36 444 444, fax 36 36 544 010, sasvar@sasvar.hu, www.sasvar.hu. €€€-€€€€. €120 to €200 and up to stay in the only five-star hotel in the area, and the first castle hotel in Hungary. It is a place for "royal" pampering, from antique period furniture to underground pools, to interconnecting tunnels between the wings that open out on to indoor water pools. Squash, a tennis court, billiards, and a swimming pool, plus adventures on horseback and in jeeps throughout the surrounding hills. Situated amidst manicured lawns and green forest, the palace was once a part of the royal family estates. Since 1990 it has been back in private hands, operating as a five-star hotel, renovated to reflect its former glory. Several top chefs manage the kitchen. Almost any course is open for discussion, although menu specialties emphasize French and Hungarian. But check on their full-board all-inclusive offers. The hotel makes an effort to treat guests like royalty. You are welcomed by the quartermaster, and a valet takes care of your luggage, and there is no "cleaning woman" – rather, the lady's maid takes care of things. Obviously, price is not the issue here, only quality, and the "king's" service. This is a honeymooners' or a princess's getaway, perhaps if you want a special treat for your wife, or if you are simply looking for the best accommodations in the mountains of Northern Hungary.

## ■ Places to Eat

### Tokaj

**Hotel Tokaj**, 3910 Tokaj, Rákóczi u 5, €-€€, €8 to €15, ☎ 36-47-332-344, is a small hotel with a restaurant that is famous for Hungarian fish prepared with recipes that reach back into

| DINING PRICE CHART | |
|---|---|
| Price for an entrée, with tax | |
| € | Under $10 |
| €€ | $10-$25 |
| €€€ | Over $25 |

history. There is nothing fancy here, just a genuine country "csárda" style with the best food of its kind; harcsa or ponty halászlé (catfish or carp fish soup) and túrós csusza (cottage cheese pasta). Be careful of bones. Hungarians typically eat their fish soup expecting to take the bones out as they sip and eat it.

### Miskolc

**Café du Boucher Belgian Pub and Restaurant**, H-3529 Miskolc, Görgey u A. u. 42. €€-€€€. A part of the European restaurant chain, Belgian Beer Café International, this brasserie offers Flemish, Walloon, Hungarian, and international cuisine. The most popular Belgian beers are served, including the famous Stella Artois; Hoegaarden White, the original white beer; Leffe, the beer of the abbeys; and the Belle-Vue Brewery fruit beers. Average meal will be about 1,700 HUF up to about 4,500 HUF. Open noon to midnight every day, and noon to 1 am, Fri and Sat. The menu is in English, French, and German.

## Eger

**Fehér Szarvas Vadasztanya** (White Stag Hunting Inn), Klapka Street 8, €€-€€€, €10 to €30, ☎ 36-36-411-129. Just south of Dobó István tér, this is the place you should go if you want the local "wild" cuisine served as it was to Prince Rákóczi. It is not the cheapest, but it's absolutely the best quality. That means stag and wild grouse, rabbit and mushroom, not to mention paprika-laced stews and gravys. The wild flavor is present even in the sumptuous sour cream dressings. The piano accompanies other instruments nightly in hunting lodge-style surroundings. It is often booked up by the locals as well as by visitors, as you would expect, so reservations are definitely advised.

**Elefanto Pizzeria és Étterem**, Katona István tér 2, H-3300 Eger, €-€€, ☎ 36-36-412-452, www.elefanto. hu and www.hippolit. hu. The average dinner entrée is 2,000 to 3,500 HUF. Although they advertise themselves as a pizzeria, this is a

relaxed restaurant with incredibly tasty Italian pastas and superb Hungarian cuisine. Look up the street north from the northwest corner of Dobó tér. You can see its romantic green, white, red, and wood façade fronted by an elevated terrace, with an overarching roof for outside summer dining. Or if you prefer, dine inside. Their staff is engaging and friendly. A slight downside is that the menu is in Hungarian, but there is usually a waitress with enough English to help you get by.

Nevertheless, make an effort to communicate here. They don't need more business, but they can't keep customers away. It's worth it for the tourist to find out why. Try the csirkemell csíkok tejszínes kukoricával, rizs körettel (chicken in sauce with corn and spiced rice). It creams its way down and massages the palate with flavor. Any of the sauced pastas and desserts are superb.

## Hollókő

**Muskatli Bistro/Cafe**, Kossuth utca 61. €€-€€€ The food is good although a little on the high side. But there is both an indoor and an outdoor dining area, and a full-service bar. Try palacsinta (pancakes) topped with vanilla sauce.

## ■ Nightlife

**Hippolit Club**, Katona István tér 2 (ground floor), H-3300 Eger, ☎ 36-36-412-452, www.hippolit.hu. Open 12 am to 12 pm Mon through Thurs, and until 4 am on Fri and Sat. An air-conditioned disco on weekends, it is a welcome outlet for both younger and older customers.

## ■ Itineraries

## ★★Aggtelek National Park

The Aggtelek National Park was established in 1985 to protect its meandering caves and peculiar surface formations. Deciduous forest blankets 75% of its area. The clearings are a mosaic of rare plants interspersed with rocky outcrops. Of Europe's 400 bird species, 310 either migrate through or live here. In its 56,000 acres there are over 200 caves. The adjoining park in Slovakia adds another 101,000

acres. Jointly between Slovakia and Hungary, this is the most explored karst region of Europe, with 700 documented caves and a breathtaking variety of plant and animal life. Parts of the area are like walking through a fairy tale sequence. It is not uncommon to meet red deer, or an antlered stag, while on a hike. Although certain protected areas are off-limits, well-marked trails make exploring easy. Many caves in the park are restricted and require a professional guide (see below). Nevertheless, a number are well-explored and modified for safe tours and public viewing. The most famous is the fabulous **Aggtelek Cave System** (Baradla-Dominica Cave, comprising Baradla on the Hungarian side and Dominica on the Slovak side).

To get here from Budapest you take Route 3 (E71) to Miskolc, where you switch to Route 26. At Sajószentpéter turn on to Route 27, taking the exit for Aggtelek-Jósvafő.

## SURVIVAL IN A HUNGARIAN CAVE

The Aggtelek National Park is known all over the world to professional cavers as the site of spectacular cave explorations, many open only by permission to professionals or groups with guides. This particularly applies to scuba diving cavers, a unique and at times dangerous hobby. In January 2002, at the Rákóczi Barlang (Rákóczi Cave), the veteran cave diver Zsolt Szilagyi dove with his friends into the dark, mysterious waters of the submerged part of the cave, 6½ miles from the Slovak border. At the end of the dive, his buddies waited, but he did not return. Life depended on a suspended "core rope," hanging from a loosely tied point at the roof of the cave, pulled taught by a lead weight on the other end, hanging in the dark water 60 feet below. All the divers had attached a lifeline, a tethered rope connection, to this cord, and then entered a hole called

"The Gate," the entrance to the completely sub-merged "Devil's Beer garden." Strange and wonderful formations were lit up by the bright underwater lamps. But the way back was through muddy water where the lamps were useless. Their lifeline, attached to the core rope, was essential. So, when returning, each diver disengaged his lifeline and went up "in the blind," hand-over-hand following the core rope through the swirling brown water. They could not see each other and each felt totally alone. Visibility was only about six inches.

Zsolt Szilagyi was the last person. His hand felt the core rope so he disengaged his lifeline, expecting to follow the core rope to the surface. But, as he detached the lifeline, the core rope fell away. He had been inadvertently pulling the lifeline through the gate toward himself and it had dragged the core rope. Unaware of the predicament, Zsolt Szilagyi had pulled the core rope loose from its mooring. When he juggled his lifeline to disengage from the core rope, the core rope came completely undone. It now plunged to the muddy bottom, dragged to the depths by the plummeting lead weight.

Zsolt groped to find the sides of The Gate, to claw his way upward, but he couldn't tell where he was going. It was impossible to trace his path in the dark muddy water, and his oxygen was running low. His buddies searched for two hours, and then called cave rescue, fully expecting to find their friend lifelessly suspended in the cold liquid, when suddenly, at the surface, they heard his voice. Zsolt had found an air pocket where he could keep his head above water. Incredibly, it was connected to the main chamber by an almost microscopic crack – just enough so they could manage a distant muffled voice communication. Rescue efforts were mounted, but the complex of interconnecting caverns and grottos in the Rákóczi Cave is complicated. Rescue teams went into the cloudy water over and over again, but they still couldn't find him. And though they could hear his voice, it was getting weaker. It was certain that he could not last much longer in the cold water. 48

hours later no one heard his voice. Desperately, Slovakian cavers began tunneling a six-foot-wide by 10-foot-high triangular tunnel. Finally, five days later, the rescuers broke through to the tiny hole where Zsolt had survived. 233 people and 143 dives had been necessary for the rescue.

## Szécsény - Hub Village

www.szecseny.hu; Tourinform Office, 3170 Ady Endre út 12, ☎ /fax 36-32-370-777, szecseny@tourinform.hu.

Heading north out of Budapest, skirting the Danube eastern shore, we take E77, by the Duna-Ipoly National Park, which is just to the west. At the intersection of Route 22 we head east, following Route 22 through Balassagyarmat, toward Szécheny.

The leisurely meander of the Ipoly River along the edge of Szécsény, and the tranquil lake in its center, make it hard to believe that some of the most momentous events in Hungarian history have taken place here. The first known reference to Szécsény is from a document dated 1219. A villager sued his neighbors for 10 oxen in damages (a huge price), to be paid in marks. German currency and influence was predominant in this area even then. The priest ruled that God should decide the verdict in a trial by fire (see below). As often happened, the parties negotiated a settlement before the trial (3 marks).

The fortress here was one of the most important of a chain of castles built to contain the Ottoman hordes. It was taken and retaken several times by Turkish armies, who made it the administrative center of 134 villages. Finally, in 1638, Jan Sobieskui, the Polish king who raised the Turkish siege of

Vienna, vanquished the Turks and drove them from the area. In place of the crescent moon, he planted the flag of the Imperial throne of Hapsburg Austria. Later, the Hapsburg Imperial forces were driven out in the peasant revolt of the Rákóczi Revolution. The Hapsburgs took it back again. Then, 20 years later, Gábor Bethlen took it again for the people. Enough was enough and, when the Imperial forces took it again, they razed the castle and burned it to the ground.

Yet, there was something here that would never die. In a green field north of the town, you will find the Philadelphia of Hungary. In 1705, minor nobles, freemen, tradesmen, and the representatives of workers' guilds gathered from throughout the nation. The air was electrified with enthusiasm. They wanted freedom. In Borjúpást, a broad green field north of the town, they voted Ferenc Rákóczi II as their leader and marched on the castle. It was a bold declaration of independence against the powerful Austro-Hungarian monarchy. After the castle was taken, a "National Assembly" convened inside its walls and declared Ferenc Rákóczi the ruling prince of an independent Hungary. The nation rallied to the call and, although the Rákóczi Revolution was defeated, it left a lasting impact on Hungarian history.

## CAPITAL PUNISHMENT AIN'T SO BAD

The villager of Szécsény Hungary was well within his rights in going to the authorities (the priest or local Lord) to demand justice in 1219. But, justice in medieval terms was nothing like the 20th century. Back then trial by ordeal was the most common method of establishing guilt or innocence. It was assumed God would supernaturally intervene on behalf of the innocent. The villager's victory was to gain a trial by fire. The accusers were required to either walk across burning coals or to hold a red hot branding iron and walk slowly for three paces. The burned flesh was then wrapped by the local priest, set in wax, and sealed. After three days, the wrapping was taken off. If the wound was healing on its own, the accused was innocent.

Ordeal by water required the accused to be tied and then taken to a deep lake where he was thrown in. If he floated, he was guilty (in this case innocence was no guarantee of survival).

A noble would undergo trial by combat. While we may think this would be the end of it, in fact, this was only the trial. If you were guilty... well, a woman guilty of murder was strangled and then burned. A thief had his hand chopped off (using an axe on a chopping block). Someone who pilfered in the royal forest would lose an ear. High treason required that you were hung, drawn, and quartered. In 1215 the Pope decreed that priests could not "help out" in a trial any longer, so it became a trial by a jury of village peers. It was an unpopular decree because many villagers felt that neighbors who held a grudge would rule against them. But justice was served in England. In 1275 a new law allowed the accused to be tortured if he refused a trial by his peers.

## Places to See in Town

The **Fire Tower**, Széczényi 86, on Rákóczi út, is Hungary's leaning Tower of Pizza. If you stand back a distance you can see that due to its clay soil, subsidence at the foundation has caused it to visibly lean northward. In 1893 a town fire watch functioned from its then two-story tower. But, when a new town hall was built in 1905, it created a problem. It blocked the view of the tower toward the south. A fire that could destroy the city might easily start unnoticed. So, conceding its necessity, the town fathers added two more floors to the fire tower. Now you know the "rest of the story." No sentinel looks for flames today, but perhaps no one would want to in the leaning structure. Probably the added weight of the two extra floors caused it to lean.

**Forgach Castle (Széczényi Castle)** and **Ference Kubinyi Museum**, Széczényi 7, Ady Endre út, is open Tue-Sun 10-4. It stands where the famous fortress once stood. The museum is named after Ference Kubinyi, who discovered the 23 million-year-old pine tree that rests in the Ipolytarnóc museum. Although the exhibits downstairs depict county his-

tory, upstairs the famous
hunter and writer,
Kalman Kittenberger, as
well as several other big
game hunters, have left
behind memorabilia that
display lifetimes of adventure, including life-size
models of various ani-
mals. The colorful
Kittenberger was a
famous big game hunter
with "Hemingway" bra-
vado. He was sent to East
Africa between 1902 and
1925 to accumulate speci-

mens for the Hungarian National Museum, but soon acquired
international acclaim as a big game hunter and writer. While
collecting, he was once mauled by a lion. Half in jest, he
amputated his own finger, which had been partially chewed
off, bottled it in preservative, and sent it back home as a speci-
men.

Remains of Széczényi Castle at Ady Endre út sit on the old
course of the Ipoly River, on a small ridge in the midst of the
village houses. Although no one knows the exact date of its
construction, it is mentioned in a charter of 1461, 31 years
before Columbus discovered America. The Franciscans added
a monastery and church. After the Ottomans, a reconstruction in the 16th century was followed by its obliteration at the
hands of the Hapsburgs in a later revolution. Nevertheless,
some of its stones were used to build the Forgach Castle, and
there are still some remains of walls and the outer towers.
The north-west bastion (great lookout point) and the 30-ft-
wide northeast bastion (now the Bastion Museum), for example, are reminders of that time.

It is incredible how much the history of the church has played
in the lives of the people. Half of the population, the sweat of
great numbers of nameless artists and the employment of villagers and craftsmen, were devoted to construction done in
the name of or by the church. The **Franciscan Church and**

**Monastery**, Széczényi 9, Haynald Lajos út, is a prime example. Northwest of the castle, it was built by the declaration of the Pope in 1332. Although there were some modifications in the 17th and 18th centuries, the rosettes and carved animal and human figures are 14th century adornments by an unknown sculptor, as is the octagonal pillar in the middle of the sacristy, the keystones, and the corbel blocks. Rákóczi (of the Rákóczi revolution) reputedly prayed in the Gothic oratory above the sacristy. But the Turks were here too. Rather than obliterating the structure, they converted parts of it for their use.

Many undocumented buildings have disappeared from history in Hungary. Next to the Franciscan church and monastery, the mysterious remains of another structure lie at Széczényi 7 (on Somogyi Bela út, which intersects with Ady Endre út). There are no walls left, although you can certainly tell that there once was a wall amidst the rock and mortar, about three feet thick to perhaps six to nine feet in some places. This **church** was discovered in 1976, and we know it is 12th-13th century, but that is all we know.

And don't forget the **Trinity Column**, the ever-present reminder of the devastating affect of the plague, which sits on Rákóczi út, the main street through town (Route 22). It was erected by Zsigmond Forgach to commemorate the passing of the plague in the 18th century.

 Publicity is everything, but it doesn't always work. In the Middle Ages most towns had a "gibbet" at the outskirts of the town for public display. People's bodies were hung on them and allowed to rot for weeks as a warning to wrongdoers. But, even with the severity of the justice, the city of Lincoln in England, for instance, in 1202, had 114 violent murders, 89 violent robberies, and 65 people wounded in fights. But, perhaps the high crime rate was because justice was meted out infrequently. In that same year in Lincoln, England, there were only two executions.

Traveling north, just before we leave town, Rákóczi út turns to the right. The road, however, also continues northward, which we now follow. It turns into Ludányi út, which leads us toward Ladányi-halászi, on through Nógrádszakái, and on to Ipolytárnoc.

## Ipolytarnóc

A gigantic building houses a museum of unusual finds from this chaoticaly jumbled pre-historic area. Fossilized pine and shark teeth join with the imprints of rain-drops and waves on a soil that is over 22 million years old. More than 1,200 footprints of differ-

*Fossilized footprints*

ent animals have been identified. The imprint of stealthy predators sneaking up on rhinos, bisons and other animals are intermingled with birds and plants. A volcano erupted in ancient history, covering and preserving the soft sandstone in which the imprints were made, turning them into a perma-nent memorial. A European diploma of merit has gone to the 29-foot piece of a 23-million-year-old fossilized pine tree here which, by calculation, must have been 285 feet tall.

Now head back to Széchény and, once in town, take the road south, Kossuth út, off Rákóczi út. Kossuth út makes a sharp turn before Varsányi út. Don't take Varsányi út. Keep with the turn and eventually the road will lead to Hollókõ.

## ★★★Hollókõ

Amidst the snow-draped ridges of the Cserhát Mountains this village sits as though the 18th century had never passed away. The Castle once dominated its landscape. Overlooking the village, it determined the life of the village, harboring its own legends and stories in the mortar and stone. The Kacsics family built it in the 13th century. Legend says that a member of the family named Andras (Andrew) kidnapped the daugh-ter of a nobleman from a neighboring manor. He enclosed her

in a room in the Castle (I don't think it was in the highest room in the tallest tower). However, unbeknownst to the young Andras, the girl's nanny was a witch. She made her magic dances and potions and called for the "evils" to come to her aid. They turned into ravens and, stone-by-stone, carried the stones of the Castle away. So now we know that more than the Turks were involved in its destruction. Nevertheless, this may be the origin of the name of the town. Hollókõ means "raven stone."

Hollókõ is an outstanding example of rural life before the agricultural revolution of the 20th century. Small whitewashed cottages sit astride the two main cobblestone village streets. The church, a relic from the 17th century, sits prominently in the middle, symbolizing the inevitable tie of the villagers with religion. Hollókõ women walk by white picket fences facing the streets, in black-pleated skirts, black shawls and black stockings, with colorful decorations and scarves.

Hollókõ is a UNESCO World Heritage Cultural Site. It is easy to see why. Although it was heavily burned in the early 1900s, a rebuilding effort in 1909 was done with the old village in mind. Of the buildings in the village, 58 are listed historical structures, as is the church. The **Post Museum**, on Kossuth út 80, shows the clothes and weapons of postmen 200 years ago, who had to brave bandits and enemies to deliver their packages. At the **Weaving House**, Szovoház (94), there is always an on-going weaving demonstration, and handmade pieces from Hollókõ and other Hungarian towns are sold at bargain prices. A nice handmade fringed shawl was only $10 recently. The **Village Museum** is a peasant house, exactly as it might have been 200 years ago. As houses expanded, they kept the width of their properties, and so, extended toward the back. The center room was a kitchen with stove, centrally heating the house. At either end of the house a bedroom served dual purposes. The nicer of the two was usually for the youngest newlyweds of the house, and it was also used as a living room.

You might want to try the **Muskatli bistro/cafe** at Kossuth utca 61. The food is good although a little bit expensive ($10-20) But there is both an indoor and an outdoor dining area, and a full-service bar. Try palacsinta topped with vanilla sauce.

*Hollókő Castle*

Now head back to the village of Széchény. If it is late and you are not pressed to get to the next town, bed down. Relax and enjoy the pathways through the surrounding area. Get up early to leave for Aggtelek. Or, if it is not too late, press on, keeping in mind that you will be driving mountain terrain now and that the best lodging will be in Aggtelek (make sure you are booked ahead in Aggtelek). Take Rákóczi út north, then a right turn onto Salgótarjáni (22 east). Eventually Route 22 intersects with Route 21. Take 21 south about eight km (five miles) to pick up Route 23 east. Stay on Route 23 as it turns north and navigates the hills.

You will pass through marvelous terrain, low-lying villages and mountains and forest. And, there is no reason not to stop and walkup an inviting pathway or make a picnic. But, remember your goal. Route 23 melds in with 25, and continues north. Don't turn east. Eventually, it meets with Route 26, which comes from the east. Here take 26 about two km/1.2 miles east to the village of Seréynfalva. The main road through this village leads us directly north to our next stop, Kelemér, and Gömörszőlős, and then the world-famous Aggtelek Cave and forest region.

# Kelemér

Kelemér is about seven km/4.2 miles south of Aggtelek. The town's area has many rare plants and insects, leftovers of the "Carpathian Basin" flora and fauna from the Ice Age. It stands apart from the typical "Carpathian Mountain" flora and fauna so characteristic of the rest of the Aggtelek and Bükk Mountains.

Bordering the town, the **Mohosok Nature Reserve** is the home of the Little Mohos Lake or Kis-Mohos tó (tó is pronounced like toe in English). Although the mountains and valleys in this range are generally pine forest, this lake has preserved its character as a peat bog. Yet, it has no inflowing or outflowing streams. Scientific studies have pointed to only one possible answer for its survival. The microclimate of the enclosing valley has fostered a perfect balance between the lake, the bog, and its surroundings. It has made survival possible for rare plants and insects. Eerie early morning mists are punctuated with bird songs, but even the bird songs seem somber. Perhaps this is what led to some of the finest and yet saddest literature in the nation.

Kelemér is the former home of the priest-poet **Mihály Tompa**, 3728 Kelemér, Tompa Mihály út 51 (the white house on the corner). The house, now a museum (300 HUF) contains his papers, personal mementoes and period furniture. (If it is closed knock on the door of the Reformed Church.) Tompa stands alone as the creator of Hungarian allegorical poetic literature. Born into a shoemaker's family in Rimaszombat, after college he went to Gömör as a camp preacher for soldiers during the 1848-1849 Revolution. At the year's end of 1849, he went to Kelemér to marry Emilía Soldos. The hopeful union was marred by failure of the revolution and the loss of his wife's first child. The sorrow led to some of the most melancholy creations in Hungarian poetry, *To the Stork*, and also *To the Sons of the Bird*.

From Kelemér, on the one main road leading west, over the crossroads, and in walking distance, is the town of Gömörszõlõs.

## Gömörszõlõs

Gömörszõlõs sits amidst a green valley, a stand of restored peasant houses and a church from the days of King Istvan. The weaver, the baker, the tanner, the farmers, all use the same methods and the same equipment as they did 100 years ago. The crafts shop sells tasty Hungarian homemade biscuits and sweets, as well as handmade folk craft items. But its attraction goes beyond that. In this small village of just over 100 people, almost everyone is engaged in and willing to help you learn about one of the village trades. In fact, in a sense, you can hire on. From honey-cake baking (no sugar – they used honey in the days of Árpád) to perhaps felt making, or weaving, you can work with the villagers and even board with them, as medieval travelers used to do. Visit in harvest time, to help pick fruit out of the orchards, which are 400 years old, or learn haymaking. English is halting, and you should be making an effort to learn the language. But it can be the experience of a lifetime. This small place won the 1999 "Tourism for Tomorrow" prize from British Airways.

After staying a few days you may have learned the skills of your "guild." Now drive or walk back to the crossroads, but continue north and press on through Zádorfalva to Ragály, where you veer northwest to Aggtelek.

# ★★★Aggtelek Caves

**Tourinform**, Aggtelek H-3759 Aggtelek, Baradla oldal 1, ☎/fax 36-48-343-073, has information and sometimes helpful suggestions. However, for extreme adventures, application is made directly to the park service, **Aggteleki Nemzeti Park Igazgatóság** (Aggtelek National Park Directorate), H-3758 Jósvafő, Tengerszem oldal 1, ☎/fax 36-48-350-006 or info.anp@axelero.hu.

You are about to enter one of the great discoveries of subterranean exploration in the history of the world. It crosses borders. Its history reaches back past the Ice Age to Stone Age man and the dinosaurs. It harbors species that live nowhere else on the planet. It is the longest cave system in Europe. Entering from the Hungarian side, the caves thread their way a little over 19 km/11 miles, to finally join the Slovak side. In Hungary it is known as the Baradla Cave. The two entrances on the Hungarian side, at Aggtelek and Jósvafő (about four miles north), have hotels and restaurants for the thousands of people that come here. These are not five-star accommodations, but adequate.

The Aggtelek entrance to the Baradla-Dominic cave system is by far the most popular because of its spectacular caverns, but, nevertheless, Jósvafő has a wonderful cave tour as well. The one-km cave walk is just one way to explore these caves. You can apply at the park headquarters for everything from canoe excursions across the dark waters of this and other caves, to diving (experienced only) in the depths of their sinkholes (see *Adventures*). Of course, you can also apply for simple cave explorations in caves that are already prequalified, with an experienced caver (i.e., Vass Imre, Béke, or Rákóczi Cave Tours and a number of others.) There are also local guides for hiking, rock climbing, and canoe excursions. Cave lakes abound, but the most significant are the Esztramos, Kossuth and Also caves. The Kossuth is 33 m/53 feet deep, and both it and Also have flowing water. Nevertheless, a simple walking tour is crowned with fantastic perspectives of color and shape, and a breathtaking feel for the gigantic expanse of this cavernous system.

From either Aggtelek or Jósvafő, tours are Apr to Sept, daily 8 am to 5 pm and Oct through Mar 9 am to 3 pm. Short tours will cost about 1,500 HUF and the long tours run 5,000 HUF. The special "Radish Branch tour," recently opened up, is seven hours long and about 7,000 HUF. The long tours (flashlight and hiking boots) and canoe tours may or may not be allowed, with a written application. There are no longer standard boat tours in the caves. It may be necessary to wait a few days for special private bookings.

The long tour begins at the Aggtelek entrance (next to the Barlang Hotel) and it varies from five to seven hours. If you can do it, this is the one to take, by flashlight. Climb ropes and ladders, scale boulder-faced walls and cross water-filled gullies. Jósvafő (next to the Tengerszem Hotel) offers only short one- to two-hour tours, but they are along well-lighted concrete paths. The two-hour Styx stream tour passes by and over the underground river Styx, sparking memories of the Greek river entrance to the world of Hades. You pass The Observatory Stalagmite, rising a massive 19 m/62 feet as you enter the Hall of Giants, where music and lighting dance together in the echoes and shadows of the cave. Hanging from the ceiling, and sometimes flying by, you may see the harmless horseshoe bats, mouse-eared bats, or the often-photographed grey and brown long-eared bats.

By the flowing stream and disappearing into the dark corners of the cave, the endemic small crab, or blind raptor beetle crawls into their hidden spaces. Paleolithic men once underwent their manhood rites while their campfires flickered against the yellow karst cave walls. The rock itself is 230-million-year-old Middle Triassic limestone. The cave is much

younger, formed about two million years ago when waters seamed in from cracks in the limestone, eroding and then dissolving the rock to create various formations. As the water level stabilized, the moist air formed dripping points of water on the cave roof, which over time deposited their lime in a multitude of colors, one drop at a time. The accumulating stalactites and stalagmites decorate the passageways with spectacular formations. The formation of one millimeter/.04 inch of dripstone takes 12 to 20 years. So the 30-m/98-foot long Giant is more than 250,000 years old. Then there are the Dragon's Head, Tiger, the Mother in Law's tongue, the Hall of Columns, The Eagle, and the Butcher's Shop, where giant bacon strips seem to hang from the ceiling. The spectacular size of this monument has enabled Hungary to host marvelous concerts in a gigantic cavern, dubbed The Concert Hall. Listening to the rich tones reflecting from the cave walls is an unforgettable experience. Check with Tourinform for concert dates and details.

## Jósvafő Study Trail

From Aggtelek take the seven-km/4.2-mile walk to Jósvafő (the Baradla study trail), crossing the Jósva stream several times. It is marked in yellow, and it takes about three hours. You can also drive the connecting road between Aggtelek and Jósvafő. Jósvafő has the **Jósvafő Folklore Museum**, a display of typical village interiors and early 20th-century farming implements. Open Apr 1-Sept 30, 10 am to 4 pm, and between Oct 1 and Mar 30, by prior arrangement, 11 am to 1 pm, ☎ 36-48-350-084. The museum often hosts folklore performances on the stage in the granary.

The Jósvafő Cave has a branch called the **Békes Cave**. The air in the Békes Cave has been found to be absolutely pure, germ-free, and without pollens or surface pollutants, making it therapeutic for the cure of respiratory ailments. As a result, a local doctor and a center for respiratory and asthmatic healing are based here. The resort house, hostel, and recovery center, near this entrance, sits beside the Josva Stream, not far from Lake Tengerszem, amidst wooded and tranquil surroundings. Looking for help on a cure, or for recovery from smoking? It is usually recommended to stay about three weeks. Contact **Jósvafõ Idegenforgalmi**, Szolgáltató Kft., 3758 Jósvafõ, Kültelek 1, ☎ 36-20-511-25-09 envira@chello.hu.

In 1987, 10 rare **North Star Hucul horses** were sent to Aggtelek. Today there are over 100. There are only about 2,000 of these horses in the entire world. Hucul breeding in Hungary has followed methods that were established centuries ago in "royal" stables for animals with high intelligence and quick response. The state farm is open for lodging, riding, and sledding in the winter on these legendary horses of the Carpathians. In the town of Josváfõ, **Tancsis M. stables** are located at út 1, ☎ 36-48-350-052, open daily 8 am to 3 pm, 1,000-2,000 HUF per hour.

> **Did you know?** Miklós Pintér, the Hungarian horseman, smashed Buffalo Bill's 1861 riding record of 24 hours and 483 km/290 miles with a succession of horses. Miklós ground out 486 km/292 miles in 23 hours, 55 minutes. Three km/1.8 miles farther in five minutes less time. The record still holds today.

Want the adventure in the woods but looking for a little reassurance? Private guided tours within the park area of Aggtelek are available from **Litkei Krisztina, Gömörszõlõs, Kassai u. 37,** ☎ 36-48-434-181. Her nature walks and tours (advance booking required) include a biologist with some variations, such as herbal identification and herbal tea making and tasting. The standard fee is 5,000 HUF+ VAT (tax), but the cost of souvenirs is not included. The total usually averages an affordable 6,500 to 7,000 HUF.

The **Tohonya-Kuriszlán study trail** is nine km/5.4 miles and is marked with yellow rings. It takes us around Jósvafõ and brushes by the Hucul herd stud farm on an approximately six-hour hike.

Now, leaving Aggtelek, we head for the Bükk National Forest and mountains. Our first stop is Szilvásvárad. We go south, back the way we came, to Route 26. On Route 26, head east. Just before the town of Vadna, turn off south toward Nagybarca and Bánhorváti. Keep pressing southward following the signs toward Szilvásvárad. This will take us by the Bükk National Park.

## Bükk National Park

*"Sitting under a solitary tree*
*for hours I listen to*
*the foliage rustle and whisper fairy tales,*
*into my ears" (Sándor Petőfi)*

The Bükki Nemzeti Park (Bükk National Park) is a place where the air is pure and the trees whisper with an ancient breeze. It is a lofty plateau about a thousand

*Bükk National Park (© Fatér Imre)*

feet above the rest of Hungary's countryside, spreading over 95,775 acres. Small valleys and ridges are interspersed among crags, with some excellent rock climbing, hiking, biking and incredibly beautiful forest. Seasonal creeks and waterfalls tumble down slopes and gulleys in a terrain that is 97% wooded. It is the highest national park in the nation.

But the earth is testimony to ages of turmoil. Garbonian, Permian, and Triassic layers are jumbled amidst the slate, sandstone, basaltic tuff, and volcanic garboro. Sometimes you will stumble on to the bright white stone, rhyolite-tufa. About 20 to 30 million years ago a seam opened and gave out rhyolite powder instead of magma. With time it cemented into the much harder siliceous solfatara, a bright white stone. The surface keeps changing and erosion has destroyed much of the rhyolite powder, but what remains has often formed "rhyolite babes," naturally sculpted figures in stone. They have evoked numerous local legends and folk tales and names. "Stone Lady" near Egerszalók, joins with many cone-like "babes." Mysterious alcoves have been carved out of the rock by human hands, a puzzle to scientists for over a century. At first they were believed to be cultic urn chambers used by a Celtic tribe thousands of years

ago. Others theorized that pagan priests of some ancient tribe had secretly ensconced their gods in these hiding spaces. Fragments from 11th-century pottery led to another theory – that they were used by beekeepers. What is your theory?

The soft rhyolite-tufa made it possible for the citizens of Eger and other surrounding communities to dig interconnecting cellars and tunnels. Near Noszvaj, Szomolya, Cserépfalu and Cserépfalva huge cave apartments have been found, hidden by the brick houses that were subsequently erected in front of them. Many of these old caves were used as cook shacks or storerooms.

In the same manner, natural caves were often used as stables. Even today there is "Stable-Rock Cave," also the site of a Paleolithic cave settlement. The actions of water and wind and the chemicals in the earth have produced hundreds of peculiar formations and laced the area with karst caves (at least 400 of all caves in Hungary are in the Bükk National Park). Paleontologists have found ancient fossils of international importance here. The Szeleta, Istállóskő, Suba-hole, and the Balla-cave, among others, have been the homes of Paleolithic men and a peculiar sub-culture of advanced hunters, as evidenced by the types of arrowheads that they used, called the Szeleta. The Istvan Lápa Cave is the deepest in Hungary and even experienced cavers find the Japer Cave a risky challenge.

**Tip:** *Strange caves, not for the inexperienced, can leave you out of breath. If you find a cave, and it goes for any depth or length, be careful. Many contain mysterious drops, or can collapse. Some lack oxygen, or worse. One famous cave known as the "killer cave" was the home of millions of blue snails. The decomposition of the large number of corpses, in the natural cycle of the colony, led to hydrogen cyanide, a highly poisonous gas that, if inhaled, attacks the pulmonary system and kills. Public caves are safe. But, if you find a strange cave in Hungary, don't explore too deeply; call an expert.*

Bükk's flora and fauna include 90 species of nesting birds, such as hawks, imperial eagles, and Ural owls in the steppe region. The cooler Bükk slopes, rising 1,500 to 2,100 feet, have Austrian oakwood forest, threaded with fresh brooks and streams in season. On the dry, warmer slopes, steppe prairie and scrub forest may form an island with its own characteristic plant life. Above 2,100 feet, look for short-stemmed highland beechwoods. The plateau itself is primarily mountain beech, but sprinkled with Mediterranean, Illyrian and mountain plant species sprouting out of rock beds, due in part to the variations of soil and exposure of shade and sun.

Hundreds of years ago, a chain of castles and fortresses dominated some of the highest mountains and ridges of Bükk. Their remains are a witness to the tortured past of the nation. Almost all were leveled in the Rákóczi War of Independence. And, while you will find various castle remains on your hikes through the area, only two remain more or less intact, both outside of the park boundary. These are **Eger** (see under *Eger*), and **Diósgyõr** (see *Diósgyõr* under *Miskolc*).

Several narrow-gauge rail lines, leftovers from mining at the turn of the 19th century, still operate. The train at Szilvásvárad, and the Miskolc to Farkasgördõ-Örvénykõ shouldn't be missed. And, although we treat some of these separately, the most frequented areas are actually Szalajka Valley, Lillafüred, and Bankut. Bankut is a winter vacation center. There are  no hotels in the park itself; most facilities are in the towns that fringe its boundary. The forest train schedule may vary, from Apr 1 to Oct 31, so call ☎ 36-36-355-197 or 36-30-289-7201.

Ottokar Kadic, a Hungarian archeologist (born in Slovenia in 1876) drew international attention to the caves of the Bükk Mountains with his discovery of prehistoric man's unique habitat and implements. In the spirit of the times, an international scientific controversy ensured, for no one had ever expected such a find in this region. He was slandered and his work was labeled as a grand fake.

So, in a cold November at the turn of the century, Kadic cut a 36- by six-foot trench. Then, he went down 20 feet and found the bones of cave bears and prehistoric relics and an ancient fireplace, which confirmed his dating. Charcoal remains were indisputable proof. The Museum of the Imperial Court in Vienna, which had at first rejected his findings, had to give grudging acknowledgment to the vestiges of an ancient man-made campfire. Kadic's subsequent work unearthed a huge archive. The deeper and wider he went, the more the famous Szeleta cave yielded ancient treasures. Close to 600,000 chipped implements revealed an Ice Age hunting culture of esthetic sophistication that had developed on its own. It was a milestone and established Hungary as one of the centers of this type of study in the world.

Due to the many rare species, travel in the park is controlled. But, you can take tours in Bükk and in Eger with the **Egri Spartacus Orienting and Hiking Club**, 3300 Eger, Faiskola út 2.3/2. They will make arrangements through

their members. English-speaking contacts are Bátor Szilárd,
☎ 36-20-93-69-556, szilard.bator@nokia.com, and Lajozner
Atilla, ☎ 06-30-21-84-736. You can also rent bikes in
Felsőtárkány at the Park Hotel, ☎ 36-36-434-630 or 36-30-
335-2695. E-mail them at parkhoteltaltos@freemail.hu at
least a week before you get there. Their website is www.
parkhotel-taltos.hu.

# Szilvásvárad

Szilvásvárad is the
most popular excursion
destination on the bor-
ders of the Bükk
National Park in the
summer, and with good
reason. It lies at the
head of the Szalajka
Valley, where you will
first encounter the
open-air **Forest
Museum**, at the foot of
Csortos-kõ, a memorial to the charcoal burners who once
piled huge bonfires with logs to make charcoal. The ash from
the bonfires was used as an ingredient in steel making, called
by its original Latin name (from the Romans), sal alcali. This
evolved into its current name, Szalajka, hence the Szalajka
Valley.

From the train station,
walk north and turn
right at Egri út to
where it turns to Park
út, and then up. Or, if
you drive into town,
Egri út is the main
road; as you enter, don't
turn left, but continue
straight ahead to Park
út. Park út makes a 90
degree turn north. At Park út 8 is the **Lippizan History of
Horse Breeding Exhibition**. The museum is open daily 9-
12 and 1-5 pm. It is across from the **Pluto Pánzió**, a place to

eat stay, at Park út 8, ☎ 36-564-400, fax 36-564-401. It uses the same website as the Lovas Étterem, www.lovasetterem.hu.

**Lovas Étterem** (restaurant), Szalajka völgy út, ☎ 36-36-564-057, fax 36-36-355-555, lovasetterem@t-online. hu, www.lovasetterem. fw.hu. There are no address numbers on Szalajka völgy út. However, from the  train station, which is right on the outskirts, you can easily see the village. From the train station walk east, parallel with the main road (Egri út). The road will start to turn left. At that point a smaller rural street intersects from the right. Take that street. It is Szalajka völgy út, and you will see the grandstands and the state exhibition grounds. About 150 feet from the intersection, the Lovas Étterem (restaurant) sits next to the grandstands. The food is delicious.

 The train station, on Egererdő út, is the home of the **Szilvásváradi Erdei Vasút (Szilvásvárad Forest Train)**, 3348 Szilvásvárad, Vasútüzem, ☎ 36-36-355-197 or 36-36-564-004, szilvasvarad@egererdo.hu, www.kisvasut.hu/szilvasvarad, which runs a narrow guage line up the hills and costs about 300 to 600 HUF. The train is operated by the Hungarian National Railway, MAV. The stops in its route up the Szalajka Valley are:

- Szalayka-Fatelep
- Szalajkavölgy-Lovaspálya
- Szalayka-Halastó
- Szalayka-Fátyolvizesés

You can walk, but do take the four-mile narrow guage railway as it winds through the picturesque Szalajka Valley. You will pass the cascading 51-foot-high Fátyol Waterfall, fed by pure spring water bubbling out of a cold cavity in the mountains. After passing through green forests, at the last stop you will reach the foothills of the highest mountain in Hungary, Istállós-kõ, and the source of the Szalajka spring. Another 15 minutes up the path (the red markers) is the Istállós-kõ Cave. Mentioned earlier, it is a prehistoric monument filled with the bones of tundra deer, cave bears, water buffaloes and mammoths, all lying near the vestiges of an ancient caveman's hearth. At this point, pathways may take you up and around the mountain if you like, or return, and head south on Route 25 toward Bélapátfalva, eight km/five miles farther.

## Bélapátfalva

Bélapátfalva is south from Szilvásvárad (see above). Alternatively, north of Eger on Route 25, take a right turn about 14 km/8.4 miles out of Eger, just after the town of Szarvaskõ. The road takes you through Mónosbél and on to Bélapátfalva.

At the bottom of Bélkõ Hill in Bélapátfalva are the remains of the Romanesque **monastery** built in 1250 by the order of the bishop of Eger. It was the home of Benedictine and Cistercian monks. The remains are attached to the village **church**, one of the most beautiful intact Romanesque churches in Hungary. At the same time, adjoining trails take you up to the mountaintop of Hélkõ behind the village. However, we will press on south to Route 25 and Eger.

## Eger

In the old town, its cobblestone streets and ancient structures take you back to the time of knights and castles.

In Dobos tér (square), three dark bronze statues dramatically bend their twisted metal into shapes of tarnished and tortured history, memorializing when this single  town held on for Christian Europe. Above the city, the **castle fortress of Eger** looks down from where on September 1, 1552, farmers and women and children had huddled together. A gigantic army of Turks had overrun the Balkans and were marching across the country. Now, they were closing in on Eger. When the castle gates closed, the total in the garrison was only 2,000 – 1,200 regulars and 800 civilians, including women and children. They were hopelessly outnumbered. As the vast Turkish war machine (some put the number as high as 150,000) closed in, and the thousands of campfires of the enemy flickered in the night, captain Istvan Dobo grimly assembled his knights. His words echo into Hungarian history, "The power of walls is not in the stone, but in the souls of the defenders."

It was the custom then to imbibe the local brew to gain courage, and so they did, which in Eger was the source of Hungary's fame, her wine. As the Turks mounted their attacks, day after day, week after week, and the Christian soldiers died, women mounted the ramparts and replaced them, pouring boiling oil down from the walls. The story of the women of Eger is told and retold in Hungarian legend, as is the heroic defense of the castle, which lasted 38 days. We do not know how many Turks perished, but, it was tens of thousands, so much so that the small garrison had demoralized their entire army. But, inside the castle, they could not know it. They were weakened. Their small force had been depleted. The few left seemed destined for extinction.. The stock of wines was drying up. And, from the castle walls, it could be seen that the Turks were massing their reserves as well as the regular force. The entire Turkish army was going to attack in over-whelming numbers. Captain Dobos knew this was the last stand.

To gain courage one last time, he ordered that the stores be mixed; Blue-Franconian, Merlot, and Cabernet were stirred together, mixed into a rich ruby-red intoxicant, and they drank it. The famous Egri Bickaver wine was born. In the cellar, next to the archer's room, adjacent to the armory, the wine had its desired effect; some, covered from head to toe with the mixture, and others, with its rich red drops still wet on their beards, sallied forth to the ramparts. The sea of attackers charged en masse. But, as they fired their seige weapons and their ladders, ropes and hooks assaulted the walls, the men and women of Eger fought valiantly on. At first by the hundreds, and then by the thousands, man-to-man and woman-to-man, covered with wine, the blood of their own wounds mingling with the blood of the dying, they felled the clambering Turkish warriors. The battle lasted the entire day without let up. Turkish soldier after Turkish soldier climbed the seige ladders only to be felled when he reached the rampart. The catapults fired ceaselessly. The hours passed. The sun rose in the morning, baked the dead and the wounded with its heat through the day, and then started to fall in the afternoon.

As the cool evening brushed the castle, the attackers retired from the walls, climbing over hills of their own dead to make it back to camp. Though they had lost many men and women, the castle defenders of Eger had miraculously held on for another day, the day that should have been their last. Then, the rumor began. The Egri people were covered in red, and the men had red droplets on their beards and faces. They must be drinking the blood of bulls, or even, perhaps the blood of the dead, said the Turks. They must be holding secret rites and they had the aid of demons. Perhaps even some of the defenders themselves were demons. The word spread, and finally reached the Sultan. With that, he looked out on his tired and wounded troops, realizing that, if they lost another battle, he might lose his entire army to discouragement. They could not continue.

The next morning, the remnants of Eger's valiant defenders looked out on a deserted plain. The Turks had left. The castle was saved and so was Hungary, and perhaps Christian Europe. This is the true story of Eger, one of the great stands of history, and it is the true story of the famous Egri Bickaver wine. Ever since, it has been the symbolic drink of Hungarian resistance to

tyranny and foreign invasion, as well as a famous wine in its own right.

Ironically, when the Turks returned again in 1596, non-Magyar castle guards betrayed the city, and the Turks entered unopposed, and remained for 150 years. After the Rákocsi War of Independence, the Austrians blew up the fortifications and Eger's strategic role was ended.

Restored for tourists, the castle's only approach is through Kossuth Lajos utca. Entry to the castle grounds is 300 HUF (8 am to 5 pm, but in summer until 6 or 7 pm). It will require 800 HUF if you want to see the inside castle museums. Heroes Hall and certain underground parts of the castle require a guided tour and will cost extra.

King Stephen founded the first episcopate on the hill over the stream called Eger, circa 1000 AD. It was followed by the first castle in 1241, spurred by the Tartar invasion The castle and vicinity hide the excavated remains of a 13th-century cathedral and the restored parts of a 15th-century bishop's palace. Heroes Hall displays the wax images of famous historical figures, the heroes of Eger and István Dobó's tombstone. The wax figures in the jailhouse and mint are likenesses of people from the 15th century memories, joined with a separate gallery of 16th- to 18th-century paintings.

The **István Dobó Castle Museum** is itself a monument to time. It was established in 1872. The labyrinthian hallways and rooms were used as a barracks and an armory, and can eventually lead you down to the wine cellar (adjoining the archery room), where you can sample a goblet of the famous brew.

Walk out of the castle and head down Kossuth Lajos út. Baroque and Rococo palaces line the walk with wrought iron balconies and entrances. The Deputy Provost's House (4) is followed by Vagner Canon's House (6). Afterward is the County Hall (9) where the incredible wrought iron gates of Fasola Henrik guard the entry, followed by the Baroque Franciscan monastery and church (14) The Buttler house (26) is one of the oldest remaining buildings in the town.

Continue on Kossuth Lajos street to Eszterházy tér and the the **Basilica** (1831-1836). Alternatively, from the train station walk south down Vasut, turn right to Deák Ferenc út, and press north, past the bus stop, until you arrive at Eszterházy tér. If you like classical organ, there are organ concerts here every day from 11:30-12, Mar 15 through Oct 15. Sundays, the concerts are from 12:45-1:15 and cost 400 HUF. The large statues in the main facade are *Belief*, *Hope*, and *Love*; they were carved by Marco Casagrande of Venice, which shows just how far the reach of Hungary went in those days. The main altar is the work of the Viennese master, Danhauser.

Across from the Basilica is a must see, from the stand point of the author. After all, it is the the repository of Dante's *Divine Comedy*, and I mean an early Latin version from 15th century. The **Lyceum Konyvtar** at Eszyterhazy ter 1 is one of the most striking and beautiful libraries I have ever seen, bar none, and it is filled with many original wood carvings. Built between 1765 and 1785 after the style of Louis XVI, it is today a teacher's college. The hall in the western wing is filled with frescoes that symbolize the four university faculties, and the library in the south wing is a spectacular experience, for depicted in wood and fresco across the ceiling is the *Trident Synod* (1545-1563), a glorious depiction in yellow and gold. Entry is 450 HUF. Open Apr-Sept, Tue-Sun, 9:30-3:30 and Oct-Mar, Sat-Sun, 9:30-1, closed Dec 23-Jan 5. Upstairs, Hungary's first

observatory will give you a bird's-eye view of Eger through a unique system of mirrors and lenses devised in the Middle Ages.

Now it is time to head up Széchenyi út. It intersects Kossuth Lajos út just east of Eszyterházy ter. It is lined with fashionable restaurants, brasseries, confectionaires, and small shops. Széchenyi út 1-3 is the **Archepiscopal Palace**. Next door, at Széchenyi út 5, the Hapsburg Empress, Mother Theresa, left behind her 250-year-old coronation cloak.

Keeping in mind where we are, it is a short walk to Dobó Square. The square is marked by the statue of István Dobó, the hero of Eger's stand against the Turks. The statue is by Alajos Strobl. Now over to Dobó ter 4-6 and the inescapably ornate **Minorite Padua Saint Anal Church** (1758-1771), one of the outstanding examples of the pomp of Baroque style in Hungary. Farther down is the **Palóc Folk Museum** (No. 6) and its ethnographic review of the Eger area, dominated by the Palóc culture, art, pottery and embroidery. A somewhat grim sight is the **Tortenit Tarház**, at Dobó út 9, a house of prehistoric arms, open Tue-Sun 9-5. Closed Dec 21- Jan 5 (400 HUF).

Exploring farther afield, you could not have escaped the dominating **minaret** that suspends itself over Eger, at Knézich út 17. This is Europe's northernmost Turkish-era building, and it soars 120 feet. The top is reachable via a very narrow winding staircase. The view from the top is beautiful, but consider that it was here that the Turkish "muzzein" once heralded the glory of Allah at sunrise, sunset and noon, every day, over a "conquered city."

One other sight, the intricate wooden carvings and icons of the **Greek Orthodox Serbian Church**, at Vitkovics út 30 (1784-1786), may astonish you. If the manager is not there and it appears closed, ring the bell. He will come out. The outside is unassuming, but the inside is breathtaking.

Assuming we are now ready for something more earthy, go back to Széchenyi út and stop by the **Dobos Cake Shop** to taste the "Baghdad," a delightfully rich ice cream concoction with expresso. Now we will head back to Eszterházy tér.

From Eszterházy tér, walk across the street south and continue on Deák Ference út south to the next street, Telekesy l. út. Walk west on Telekesy l. út and it will spill out into Bartok tér. Continue in the same direction, but bearing south. Bartok ter is intersected by two streets at the westernmost end. Take the street to the south, which is Király út. Stay on Király út until it opens out and eventually changes to Szépasszony völgy út. Szépasszony völgy út leads directly into the Szépasszony-völgy, the **Valley of Beautiful Women** (the signs say "Nice Ladys Valley"). Some say the namesake came from pagan myths. But, of this there is no doubt, it is the center for the wine-tasting in Eger, overlfowing with Egri Leányka, Medoc-Noir, Egri Bikavér, and dozens of others from small cellars throughout Hungary that have contributed to its growing reputation as one of the great wine centers of the world. So, sampling here is not like taking a liter off the shelf of a wine shop in America. The valley is home to nearly 200 small tufa stone cellars carved into the side of the mountain, themselves relics

of the 13th, 15th, and 16th centuries. For hundreds of years it has been a magnet for visitors for the low prices and profusion of the heady wine made in local cellars (currently about 70). It all works "glass in hand."

Every cellar has its own individual personality. Cellar 22 was rocking to a live gypsy violinist and troupe, and toasting German tourists, while Cellar 2 features wine and spice. Cellar 16 rings with lively music and the younger crowd... and so on. If you buy a liter you can sample for free. If not, pay by the glass. At the end of your day, or evening, it may be wise to book in for the night. That's probably why hotels and guest houses surround the area.

Recover from your festivities in the Szépasszony-völgy at the local **Turkish bath** at Fürdő út 1. Alternatively, the **open-air baths (Strandfürdő)**, at Petőfi tér 2, are in the park. They are open all year, with six outside pools, one indoor pool, a Turkish bath, adventure pool, wave pool, medicinal waters, and food and drink. The entrance is on Klapka street. Open Mon-Fri

6 am-7 pm, May through Sept; 9 am-6 pm Mon-Fri and Sat-Sun 9 am-7 pm, Oct through Apr. The cost is 800 HUF. Now take Route 24 west out of Eger to Sirok.

## Sirok

On Route 24, 12 miles west of Eger, the 1,000-foot mountain overlooking the town of Sirok is capped with the remains of a 700-year-old fortress. Bring a camera for the views. Unusual rock formations dot this area. Can you recognize the difference between the rock formation of "the nun" and "the monk?" Carved rhyolite tufa cave homes are hidden behind many façades along the main street of the village. Sirok is the starting point of the famous 35-mile **Mátrabérc Tour**, a trail designed specifically to scrape the top ridges of the Mátra mountains. Views and wildlife abound. But, you must be prepared to backpack that one.

Now head back to Eger and from there head south to Route 71 (also known as Route 3), which you pick up going east to the next major town on the way to Miskolc, Mezőkövesd.

# Mezökövesd-Tard-Szentistván (Matyóland)

Between Eger and Miskolc on Highway 3 is the town of Mezökövesd, one of a consortium of three villages known as Matyóland. Surrounded by Protestant reformism, through the centuries this one area has remained a Catholic island and the center of a unique folk culture. They embroider floral patterns with silk threads on a black background, on the clothing of both men and women. Their exquisite and unique patterns are considered a folk treasure of Hungary. The greatest example of this folk art is at the home, now museum, of one of its most famous designers, **Bori Kis Kanko** (1876-1954). The house is furnished in Matyó style at Kis Janko Bori út 22.

It is possible to buy photographs, artifacts, examples of dress and artwork, and some home furnishings at the **Matyó Museum**, Szent László tér. The local culture is so strong that even the **Saint László Catholic Church** (Szent László tér 22) has the Virgin Mary depicted wearing Matyó dress in a fresco (unique in the world). You might also wander over to a collection of older agricultural equipment and tools at the **Machine Museum** on Eötvös József Road 32, the yard of an old farmhouse. But, having done so, we press northeast on E 71 (Route 3) to Miskolc.

# Miskolc & Surroundings

Miskolc is the picture of an older, bustling industrial town. It follows a long tradition. The first Ice-Age settlement in Hungary was discovered here. It was followed by habitations in the Copper, Bronze, and Iron Ages. Nearby in Zöldhalom puszta, they have uncovered the grave of an ancient Scythian ruler. Other finds have included ancient Germans, Sarmatians from the sixth century, and Avars from the ninth century. The town gets its name from the Magyar tribe that was called Miskolc. In the late 18th century it became a center of industry for all of northern Hungary. Several large glass works were later joined by Henrik Fazola's foundry in 1770. Westward, another foundry was established in Diósgyõr in 1870.

Entering Miskolc on Route 3 from Matyóland, make a left on to Budai Josef út. It is the street that borders the south side of the Népkert (City Park). Follow it to the end of the park, where you make a right. This puts you on Györgey Artur út. If you were to go left, it would put you on Csabai Kapu út, and would lead you to Miskolc University. As it is, in turning right you will pass the Science and Technical College on the right, and just after the "Y" in the road (bear left at the "Y"), to your left will be the **Mindszenti Church**. A monolithic stone carving of the Virgin Mary fronts this 18th-century Baroque church. There is parking there. Just past the church, at another "Y," we bear left on Mindszent út and, as we continue, it changes its name to Papszer út and starts to curve north. As it starts to curve, to your right is the **Otto Herman Museum** at Papszer utca 28. The oldest part of the building originates in 1453. The museum itself was founded in 1899. Inside is one of the finest archeological exhibits in Hungary, in addition to local, town, theological, ethnographic, coin, and paleontological exhibits of the area. Added to that is a gallery of 200-year-old Hungarian paintings.

Opposite the museum on the left is the **Avasi Church**, whose belfry rings out every 15 minutes. Built in the 13th century, it was modified and extended in the 15th century as a Gothic hall church with three naves. This is one  of the best-preserved in the country. Although the Turks tried to burn it down, substantial elements still remain. The former Gothic tower, never completely reconstructed, was for a time the town archive. In the sanctuary of the church, the inlaid stalls are from 1490.

Heading back to Györgey Artur út, make a left, cross Széchenyi Istvan út. It will change its name twice, and we continue as it changes its name to Kazinczy Ferenc út. We pass Régi Posta út, which enters from the right. On the left is Hősök tér, the site of the famous **Minorite Church and**

**Monastery,** built circa 1729-1740. The next cross-street after Régi Posta út is Deák Ference to your left (Horváth Lajos út on the right). Deák Ference divides the north and south parts of Hősök tér. Cross the street to the north side and walk west on Deák Ferenc toward Deák Ferenc tér, at its westward end. The **Greek Orthodox Church** is on your right at 7 Deák Ferenc tér (1785-1806). The Greek community built it when they fled from the Turks to Miskolc. Its richly ornamented iconostasis, 16 m/48 feet high, is the largest in Central Europe. It holds one of those unique religious symbols that we see scattered in different parts of Europe. The picture of a Black Madonna is in the main nave, donated by Tsarina Catherine II. Next to the richly decorative Greek Orthodox Church stands the **Hungarian Orthodox Ecclesiastical Museum,** home of the largest Greek Orthodox collection in the country.

Now walk back. One street before the intersection with Kazinczy Ferenc út, Déryne út enters from the south. As you walk south on Déryne út, the **Museum of Actors and History of Theater** is at 3 Déryné út. It is the site of the first theater in Hungary dedicated to "Magyarul" (the Hungarian language). It opened in 1823. Today it has a five-stage theater complex and museum, as the National Theater, blessed with the most modern technology. You may be able to get a booking for a good play, but don't expect English. The historical archives, which include wax figures, are worth a walk-through. Having completed this exhibit and booked your tickets, you may want to see one more site in the old town.

We continue to Széchenyi Istvan, where we cross the street, then head right to Rákóczi út, at the next intersection. Here, on our left, inside the restored 17th-century **Rákóczi House,** the **Gallery of Miskolc** contains the greatest works of Miskolc's artists. The town of Miskolc supported Rákóczi in the revolution. This house was his general headquarters in 1704.

The dominating **Avas Hill** is 234 m/767 feet high. It is frequently mentioned as the "Gellert Hill of Miskolc," harking back to Gellert Hill in Budapest. As you would expect, it has its share of caves. And likewise, it is famous for the former wine production from its hillsides. Today, an arboretum sits astride a large swath of land. On top you cannot miss the sky scraping Miskolc Television Tower. Made with an attempt to add creative flair to Soviet-style concrete, the tower pierces the sky 70 m up (210 feet) to give superb views of the area. Try the espresso bar at the middle level, then go to the window viewing stage. The horizon seems to extend forever to the plains of the south. But turn northward, and the 2,000-m/ 6,600-foot Tatra peaks of Slovakia rise snowcapped in the distance (on a clear day). To the west, the Bükk Hills are a green carpet of forest. The western panorama yields a view of the volcanic, solid basalt, Tokai Mountain. Miskolc sits on the border of both mountains and plains, so visible from the tower, in the center of the Borsod-Abaúj-Zemplen counties.

Stop by **Miskolc Plaza** shopping center/mall for McDonalds or restaurants and shopping, at Szentpáli út 2-6. The bonus here is that there is an eight-screen multiplex cinema. Some movies are "szinez felirato" (English with Hungarian subscript).

## Miskolctapolca Thermal Cave Baths

Miskolctapolcai Termál Barlangfürdo, 3525 Miskolctapolca, Pazár István sétány 1, ☎/fax 3 6 - 4 6 - 5 6 0 - 0 3 0, barlangfurdo@miviz.hu, www.barlangfurdo.hu. In Hungary you should experience at least one thermal bath. Head back on Highway 3 south and get off at Miskolctapolca. From there, follow the signs for the Barlangfürdö. You enter through a triangular tower to the open pools, or through a stained glass foyer to the inside baths. This natural thermal cave has been hailed as one of the natural healing centers of Hungary, and it's unique in Europe for its even circulating water through the tunnel cave. There is plenty of room and high ceilings. And it's fun. A rock tunnel (slightly modified to allow for modern swimming and safe wading) follows an artificial current created with water jets, to take you through passages with romantic indirect lighting from beneath the water and above from the cave walls. This

leads you to two lake pools. There are actually seven pools in all. In addition, there are adventure pools, artificial waterfalls, and a constant temperature of 30°C/86°F. Options include mud baths, manicures, and beauty treatments in the salon while the kids jump in the children's pool, or enjoy the grassy lawns and patio. Bring an umbrella and blanket; or eat in the restaurant. The water has been proven effective in the treatment of articular, rheumatic and cardiovascular diseases. At the same time, the extraordinarily germ-free clear air of the cave has a phenomenal effect upon the respiratory tract. But, most people come here for the sheer fun and novelty of it. Several hotels are within walking distance and range in price from about $20 a day to over $100 at some medicinal wellness hotels. After spending a few days in the healing waters, we are ready for the hills. So we head back to Miskolc, and from there to Diósgyõr.

## Diósgyõr

*Diósgyõr Castle*

From Miskolc we go east on Zedényi Béla út about eight km/4.8 miles, into the community of Diósgyõr, today a mere suburb of Miskolc. Diósgyõr is halfway between Buda and Krakow. As a result, when Louis the Great reigned from Poland, it played an important role as a stopover. Serious construction started some time in the 13th century. It is mentioned as a castle outpost for the first time in 1271. Louis the Great held many significant international conferences in the knight's hall of the castle. In later years it lost its significance and was used only

Northern Hungary

as a hunting lodge, but it was often part of a dowry for Hungarian queens. Every August, castle games include mounted knights, medieval games, archery contests, and plenty of food.

## Lillafüred, Hámor (Lower Hámor) and Felsö Hámor (Upper Hámor)

*"...the valley is growing narrower and narrower, finally trapped between rocks, bluff and wild; the road is twisting and turning upwards along the bank of the Szinva, which forms numerous cascades and on top of the hill gathers in a lake. Its water is dark green as it reflects the forests of the surrounding peaks like a mirror."* Travel Letters to Grigyues Kerény, No. 10, by Sándor Petöfi, July 8, 1847.

We continue west through Diósgyő and pass through a scenic valley, then the towns of Lower Hámor and Upper Hámor, home of the once-thriving iron trade that brought prosperity to the area.

*Lake Hámor*

We will pass **Molnár Point**, near the Szeleta Cave, which gets its name from a local legend. It seems that above the green carpeted valley, once a young miller (Molnár means miller), climbed the hill with his young lover. They had pleaded with their families to be united. According to medieval custom, family approval was required for marriage. But neither family would give their permission because the two young lovers were too far apart in social class. At the top of the hill, they clasped hands and, in a last farewell to their valley home, they plunged together over the cliff to their deaths. Thus both romance and tragedy fill the history of this area.

Finally, as you enter Lillafüred, **Lake Hámor** greets the eye and, rising above it, the neo-Renaissance **Palota Palace Hotel** (see *Places to Stay*), romantically overlooking the lake.

*Palota Palace Hotel*

The Szinva stream and its waterfall can be heard from the hotel.

Lillafüred can also be reached from Miskolc by light railway (half an hour). The valley has been associated with dreams and romance from the very beginning. It was turned into a holiday resort at the end of the 19th century, when András Bethlen, then minister of agriculture, named it after his wife as a token of their courtship, so Lilla Vey is remembered today as Lillafüred, which means Lilla's bathing place. The story and the name caught on, and it attracted ever greater numbers with time. Lillafüred's existence is also intimately tied to the mining industry, a vital element here for almost 200 years. The lake was once not nearly so large then as it is now, although the area has always attracted onlookers for its beauty.

Henrik Fassola constructed his iron works at Újmassa in the 1700s and he needed power. Frigyes Fassola, following his father's footsteps enlarged it and finally built a plant in Diósgyōr. By the 1860s there were eight steel plants in the lower valley. Such growth needed energy, which at that time was supplied by water. So, at the intersection of the Szinva and Garadna streams, an earthen and concrete dam raised the level of the small creek. It swelled to a mile wide and 27 feet deep in some places. Hámor Lake, fed by creeks and water falls, reflected the green forest like a mirror on its surface. Word spread rapidly and so did its popularity.

Lillafüred borders Lake Hámor, in the eastern Bükk mountains, in the valley of the Szinva, averaging 900 to 1,050 feet above sea level. St István peak (1,815 feet) is on one side and the double peaks of Fehérkō lápa (1,761 feet) and Jávor Mountain (1,878 feet) are on the other side. The Hotel Palota which borders the lake also abuts the village of Felsö-Hámor. The small village itself does not offer a lot in terms of sightseeing, but it is an excellent base for bicycling, hiking, rock climbing, exploring nature, caving, or boating on the lake.

The area is most notable for three famous caves. The **Szent Istvan Cave**, on the mountain road leading to Eger, is about 1,500 feet up from the Hotel Palota. A one-hour guided tour will lead you through a lighted dripstone cave with the Fairyland, Santa Claus, Jack and Jill, and Eagle formations, stalagmites, stalactites, sink holes, and large chambers. The cave was discovered by a dog. He fell in through the natural shaft at the mouth of the cave. Neighbors heard his pathetic howling, mounted a rescue effort, and he was saved. The area of the cave open for public viewing is only about 150 yards, although it actually winds for about a mile beneath the earth.

The **Petõfi Cave (Anna Cave)**, on the other hand, is below the hotel, with an entry past the hanging gardens. The plants embedded in the limestone 40,000 years ago made lace-like leaves, branches, and grass, in beautiful tufa formations seen nowhere else in the world. A stroll through the cave takes about 30 minutes. The waterfall, which is near the cave at the back of the hotel, is the highest in Hungary, but is more notable for its terraced, step-like descent. It's a favorite for picture takers.

**Szeleta Cave** is about 270 feet above the highroad, the local name for the road back to Miskolc. Take the tourist path with the red squares in back of the hotel, and walk up. This is the site of some of the richest paleo-

*Molnár szikla*

logical finds in Hungary. The skeletal remains of humans, ancient bison, and other animals, as well as pottery shards and hunting weapons are here. The pathway from the cave leads on to the **Molnár szikla** (Miller's Cliff), that site of tragic love that we noted earlier. It is marked by a huge wooden cross.

## Walking the Area

 Leave the Anna Cave, and walk downhill along Felsö-Hámor by following the blue trail waymarks. They take us along Erzsébet sétány (Elizabeth Walkway). Still keeping to the waymarks, cross the Szivna Creek, turn right and walk to the former Chancellery, built at the end of the 18th century. Today it is the **Central Metallurgical Museum** at Palota út 22. It represents the only real museum of early Hungarian foundry history and is open 10 am to 5 pm daily. Continue on the blue path past the statue of King St. István, the work of Dezso Borsodi Bindász (commissioned by Borbálo Fassola in 1806), and we reach the village Roman Catholic Church. The 1806 statue of Nepomuki Szent János (St. Janos Nepomuk) guards the front. Continuing east, we arrive at the lower end of Felsö-Hámor. From here we make a sharp right and cross back across the Szina, continuing to follow the blue waymarks to the southwest, which takes us back somewhat in the direction of Lillafüred.

As you near the **cemetery**, leave the waymarks for the moment, and walk in. Not only do the graves go back more than 200 years, but the cast iron work of Henrik Fassola, with its swirled Gothic letters and the ornamental crosses is inescapable. Yet, though he founded the industry that hammered out weapons for Hungary's Hussars, and created some of the finest ornamental ironwork in Hungarian history, Henrik's grave is unmarked and no one knows where his body lies in this cemetery. In Hungary, the family takes care of the grave and, because of wars and emigration, sometimes you will find graves that have been neglected. But, Henrik's family did not even memorialize the man. No one made the effort to build his grave.

Interestingly, Ottó Herman's ashes were interred here. His notes and letters were what initially created interest in the area during the 18th century. Next to his gravesite is that of István Vásárhelyi (1889-1968), who explored the fauna of the Bükk.

Back to the blue pathway, we continue to the lower end of Felsö Hámor. We have nearly reached the upper entrance to the Hámori pass of the Szivna Creek.

While the lower valley is primarily layered dolomite and clay shale, the cliffs soar above, a hard wall reaching for the sky. The Szivna River, in ages past, when the land was lower, cut a tunnel through, and thus opened and widened out to form Lower-Hármor. As the limestone cliffs rose higher, however, the Szivna continued to cut both a tunnel and the valley floor. Then, the tunnel evidently collapsed some time in the Ice Age. Walking along the highway, up the gorge from Felsö – Hámor, the ver-

tical lines of the upper cliffs are dramatically visible. Climbers are often visible, working their way up toward the summit of Fehérkő (White Stone). The summit is also reachable without climbing if you take the blue route in the opposite direction from where we began at the Anna Cave.

As the gorge is narrow and traffic is usually heavy, it is advisable to walk on the left-hand side of the highway. As we approach the middle of the gorge, across the way on the right-hand cliff wall, a marble slab commemorates Jenö Vadas, Hámor's native son scientist-teacher and forest engineer. Finally, as we approach the lower end of the pass, it narrows further, to its approximate original width (much of it has been widened for the road).

The internal cliff wall of the lower gate is famous for four caves: the Szinva Pass Cave, the Herman Ottó Cavern, the Herman Ottó Cave, and the Puskaporosi Cavern. The Herman Ottó Cave is at the level of the lake, and the Herman Ottó Cavern is 210 feet above. They are connected and have streams of flowing water.

Ottó Herman, himself a hunter, thought that prehistoric men crouched with bows and arrows and chiseled stone axes at the ready, watching silently as game squeezed through the gorge single file. When escape was impossible, they launched their ambush with deadly effect from the shadows of the caves. Later explorations by Ottokar Kadic and Tivadar Kormos between 1910 and 1917 found flint chips, arrow fragments, and the bones of cave bears, hyenas, rhinoceros, and deer, all of which confirmed Ottó's speculations. The Puskaporosi cave alone yielded almost 1,000 arrowhead fragments, fueling speculation that it was also a tool-making workshop. Further explorations have uncovered Early Stone Age (Hallstatt) New Stone Age Bükk, Bronze Age, and La-téne (Celtic) cultures.

Now, to regain our bearings for further exploration in other parts of this area, head back to the Anna Cave, and walk "up" along the blue route. This will take us to the top of the cliff walls of the gorge, 1,761 feet up (bring a camera). Now, we can drive or continue walking on the blue route to Újmassa. It is about 2½ miles.

## Újmassa

One year after America declared Independence, Újmassa hosted the first iron foundry in Hungary, in 1777. But the "golden age" of industry ended when the Diósgyör foundry opened in the 19th century. The less efficient Újmassa foundry was forced to close. The workshops and their equipment were sold. Some of the better structures were turned into restaurants. Erected circa 1820, the Roman Catholic Church, and the Chancellery (late 18th century), remained. Floods in 1812 prompted the villagers to dig a common regulated bed for the formerly separate Szinva and Granada streams. This is what we see here today. We can drive or walk on the forest path through Ómassa to Bánkút.

## Bánkút

On the slopes of Bálvany Hill (2,800 feet), Bánkút (2,640 feet) is the premier ski resort of Hungary. However, it is not a world-class ski area, and some facilities are in need of updating (see *Snow & Ice Adventures*). There are plenty of hiking trails and it is a jumping-off point for numerous hiking excursions. The Hungarian Friends of Nature mentioned in the Budapest section and Tourinform in the *Appendix* can offer support and suggestions, maps, and information about accommodations.

Back to Miskolc, we drive north out of the city on Route 3 (E71). In the suburbs take the turn-off for Felsõzsolca and Route 37. Head north on Route 37 to Sárospatak. We are now entering the Zempléni Mountains.

## Zempléni Mountains

It starts as a volcanic ridge, stretching high above the surrounding country, capped by the **Nagy-Milic mountain** (2,682 feet). It winds down through woods, across ridges, through passes, by dark caves, and then across the breathtaking landscape of a land that at times seems to stretch to infinity, though it is by itself but a small speck on the planet. Many trails were once like this in America, before the land was covered with roads and speckled with industry. But, here in Hungary, the perception of virgin forest is retained on much of the trail called the "**blue tour**." This is a cross-country excursion of 2,000 km/1,250 miles. Pamphlets and information are available from the Hungarian Friends of Nature mentioned in the Budapest chapter.

The blue tour begins at Nagy-Milic mountain. To the north are the beautiful Carpathians, of which the Zempléni Mountains are a lower extension. Averaging 1,800 to 2,400 feet high, they form part of the border between Hungary and Slovakia. The core of these mountains is the **Zemplén Nature Reserve**, a 61,750-acre area of forest criss-crossed by winding trails. Almost 6,000 acres are strictly protected for the rare species living there, the regal golden eagle, the stealthy lynx and the proud wolf. Plants and orchids found nowhere else in the world thrive here. Our next three towns,

Sárospatak, Sátoraljaújhely, and at the southern fringe in the lakelands, Tokaj, skirt the Zemplén Mountains.

## Sárospatak

*Sárospatak Castle*

Tourinform Office, 3950 Sárospatak, Eötvös út 6, ☎ 36-47-315-316, sarospatak@tourinform.hu, www.sarospatak.hu. Heading toward Sárospatak on Route 37 the romantic Zempléni Hills are on the left, and on the right you will eventually be parallel to the River Bodrog. Many a prince and princess rode the royal boat on its waters in the Middle Ages, traveling the route between Tokai and Sárospatak. As we come to Sárospatak we will take

Wessellényi út, make a right-hand turn, cross the railroad, pass the train station, and take Édelyi Janos út at the "Y" and head to Rákóczi út. From there you will see the top of the Castle. The Bodrog River winds behind the Castle remains. We will go there first, and get a bird's eye view of the surroundings. From the ramparts looking northwest you will see the old town center, where most of the places we visit are located. There are also a number of pánziós (small bare-bones places to stay), étterems (restaurants), and cafés, as well as a few sorösös (pubs) and wine cellars in the same area.

This town has been referred to as "The Cambridge of Hungary" or the "Athens on the River Bodrog," for it has been home to poets and thinkers. From its sequestered location in Northern Hungary, the resounding call for freedom has echoed in the Hungarian consciousness. The famous Hungarian poet revolutionary, Sandor Petõfi, wrote of Sárospatak, "This town was the lion's den of the Hungarian revolutions. Here the lions of freedom dwelt."

The remains of the **Castle** are some of the earliest in Hungarian history, dating from the 11th century. As the princes of Transylvannia and the upper nobility of Hungary assumed ownership of the town, the Castle was extended and reinforced in the 15th and 17th centuries. It was the favorite home of Prince Ferenc Rákocsi, the Hungarian revolutionary. The finest Renaissance portion of the Castle is the "Sub-Rosa Hall," in the adjoining Palace. The Pal-

ace was the site of meetings held by Protestants, which Catholics would later call "the anti-Hapsburg-Wesselényi conspiracy" (1666-1671). But a little more than a generation later, at the time of the Rákocsi Revolution in 1708, a "national assembly" of fighting serfs assembled here and passed a rousing declaration that they were free men. After the Hapsburgs defeated the freedom fighters of the Rákocsi Revolution, they blew up all the fortifications, and particularly tried to level this one. However, Hungary set about to restore this treasure with the advent of freedom in the post-Soviet era.

The Castle consists of the Castle proper (Szent Erzsébet út 19) and its Palace Museum (Kádár Data út 21). Rich 11th-century Gothic remains are in the Red Tower of the Castle, while late Renaissance dominates the Palace. The **Palace Museum** is filled with Rákócsi family treasures, information about the ever-present viticulture of the region, a grand library from the 16th-17th century, and a ceramics exhibit. The **Castle Church** has a large carved wooden altar and a magnificent Baroque organ, the finest works in Hungary of this type.

In Hungary you will have noticed many of the streets are named after great Reformist figures. That is especially notable in Sárospatak, such as Wessellényi út as we come into town. Despite the strong Catholic tradition of the nation, the Reformation took hold here in the 1500s almost co-incident with Martin Luther in Germany. Calvinism challenged the Catholic tradition in northern and eastern Hungary, leading to the formation of several Calvinist colleges and universities.

Sárospatak in particular is dominated by its **Calvinist College** (Rákocsi út 1). A fountain of thought and poetry, the great revolutionary, Kossuth Lajos, as well as numerous famous thinkers in Hungarian history all studied here. Established in 1531, its support came secretly, from the purses of Protestant nobles who, if discovered, were harassed, arrested, driven into slavery, and killed. The college was eventually driven into hiding in the mountains of Transylvannia, where the Prince of Transylvannia, an ally undercover, kept the location a secret, revealing it only to would-be students. For a quarter of a century the college continued in hiding until shifting religious and political fortunes allowed it to return. A harbinger of democracy, unique on the European continent, there was a type of autonomy and student representation here, with scholarships for poor students and paid travel studies abroad. Busts and statues of the greats of Hungary dot the school grounds.

Even in modern times the students and faculty have kept its remarkable tradition of freedom. After WWII, communists instituted regulations that forced the students to leave the school and enroll in a state-controlled "theological seminary" in Debrecen. After the official announcement of the restriction, as the school year approached, the 1951-52 seminary class had no enrollments. But, then, suddenly, in the dark of midnight, the students en masse arrived in Sárospatak, ready for their studies. Even the hammer and sickle could not dim their spirit. Many faculty eyes were filled with tears of pride as they began their classes, but those who wondered what would happen next did not have to wait for long. Communist soldiers showed up on October 22, 1951, forcibly closed the school, and evacuated the students. Among the students, to this day, it has been called "The Exodus." This would have been the death knell to many a school, but not this one. In 1988 a foundation was formed to reestablish the College. As freedom dawned in the former communist block, in 1989, the buildings were handed back over to the church, and studies began again. At this point, the College also teaches Hungarian to visiting English students and it is possible to study as a resident and get a degree in English.

From the Castle head north one block to Szent Erzébet út. The tall Gothic spire marks the **Ignatian Monastery** at Szt. Erszébet 15. It was built the same year Colombus discovered America, in 1492.

Occasionally, there are boat trips between Tokaj, Tiszacseged, and Tiszafüred, usually booked with groups (See *Adventures*). If you can, come here in August, when the **Zemplén Art Festival** brings all the surrounding villages in for the festivities.

## Sátoraljaújhely

This is 13 km/7.8 miles north of Sárospatak. the northernmost major town of Hungary, a gateway to Slovakia. It is set like Pompeii beneath the pyramid-shaped volcanic mountains. Made a "town" by King Stephen in 1261, it thrived in the Middle Ages, situated as it was on the primary trade route between Russia, Poland, Transylvannia, and Hungary. Ferenc Rákóczi II was born in nearby Borsi, and Lajos Kossuth launched his illustrious political career from its streets. This and nearby Széphalom were home ground for Ferenc Kazinczy, who led the movement to preserve the Hungarian language. It is also a winter resort, incorporating the nearby Magas-hill ski and sled tracks and an older 1,333-m/ 4,400-foot cable lift (libegõ)

The 13th-century **Paulite-Piarist Monastery and Church** (Barátszer) on Deák Ferenc út 11-14, directly off Kossuth Lajos út or Route 37, is adorned today with Baroque ornamentation from later years. Sitting in the town square, Kossuth tér, the **Catholic Church**, is across from the statue of Kossuth Lajos which fronts the Old Town Hall at Kossuth tér 5. Between the church and the statue of Kossuth is the **Nymph Well**, the former water supply of the town, a fountain of clear water from the Zempléni Mountains. Retaining its original furnishings, the **Kazinczy Ferenc Museum** at Dózsa György út 11, which is directly off Kossuth Lajos út or Route 37, was the center of the literary life of Hungary in the 18th and19th centuries.

The tomb of the miracle-working rabbi, Mózes Teiteblbau, is in the old Jewish cemetery at Kacinsky út 91. The building and the cemetery are mute testimony to the lives and contributions of Jews who were eliminated in WWII. Many of the headstones appear as forlorne as the memory of the men, women and children who went to the ovens from Sátoraljaújhely. While a boy, at death's door due to an incurable illness, the parents of Kossuth Lajos desperately brought him to the rabbi Mózes Teiteblbau, who cured the young man and prophesiėd that Kossuth Lajos would be a "star" among nations and in Hungary.

Satoralhjaujhjely is also a border crossing to the town of Slovenske Nove Mesto in the Republic of Slovakia, one of three crossongs to Slovakia that will give bicyclists easy passage. The other two are the Esztergom-Sturovo ferry, which is open to bicycles, and Komarom (see *Central Danubia*), northwest of Budapest. A bridge over the Danube connects Komaraom and Komarno, Slovakia's counterpart across the Danube. Most border crossings cannot be traversed on a bike because primary motorways and national highways, those with single-digit route numbers, ban cyclists.

Depending on your vacation time, you may want to start heading back toward Budapest, via Miskolc, and on through on Route 3 to Gyöngyös and the Mátras Mountains. However, if you have more time, drive south to Tokai, bearing south, down Highway 37 to the intersection of 38, where you swing east toward Tokaj.

## ★★★ Tokaj

Amidst its laid back sunbaked slopes, Tokaj could not escape the turbulent history of Hungary. Sitting at the confluence of the Tisza and Bodrog rivers, according to 11th-century documents, earthworks of a castle existed in 1074, subsequently reinforced with stone and mortar, circular walls, and battlements in the 15th century. The Turks burned the town and demolished the castle in 1567. It was subsequently rebuilt, then retaken, then taken again, switching possession several times. Imperial troops under the command of General Basta finally burned it to the ground. After the Tartar invasion of 1241, King Béla IV settled Italian winemakers at Tokaj. From then on, fine wines poured from the slopes of Mt. Tokaj and from the Hegyalja region to the north and west.

Had it not been for the threat of Turkish invasion, Tokaj Azu wine, toasted by kings, queens and popes, would never have been discovered. The region has always been known for wines, going back to before the Middle Ages. But Tokai did not stand out remarkably from other wines. A turning point came, however, as the rumor spread that the Turks had begun to invade the region in the middle of the 17th century. It was fall, just as the grape harvest was about to begin. Mate Sepsi-Laczko, a Hungarian Calvinist clergyman and vine grower, who would normally have harvested his grapes, postponed his October harvest and prepared to flee with his family. The word had spread that Turkish hordes might flow over the hill at any minute. Grapes on the vine turn brown and begin to rot in the sun if they are not picked. Mate Sepsi-Laczko's sweet crop began to wither as a fungus shrank them down and thinned their skins. Finding that the Turkish threat was only rumor, he returned to discover that his crop, unlike many, had served as host to a particular fungus that had ripened the grapes to an extremely smooth textured sweetness, unlike anything he had ever tasted! He aged and distilled the vintage, and so Aszu Tokaj wine was born, a dessert wine that would enter history as a toast of royalty. Voltaire once pronounced it a wine that "could only come from the boundless goodness of God." Pope Benedict XIV received Tokaji Aszu (wine from Tokaj) as a gift from Empress Matria Teresa and apparently said, "Blessed be the land that has produced you, blessed be the woman that has sent you, blessed am I who drink you." Beethoven shared his love for the vintage with Goethe. If you are here, and you have not had any original Tokaj Aszu wine, you must at least sample the vintage. Its velvet texture and superb sweetness are unlike any other. You will find some of the finest cellars in the world here, bar none, along with exhibits on the history of the culture that has spawned such a reputation in its vintage. The entire town can be walked, and various cellars and etterems can be visited.

*Rákóczi Cellar*

Try the **Rákóczi Cellar**, 15 Kossuth Lajos tér. ☎ 36-36-352-408 or 36-36-05-352-141. Formerly the Rákóczi family's wine cellar, not only is it a tavern today, but guided tours (English) will walk you through its 24 tunnels and about 1.5 km/.9 mile of aging production in the cave whose walls are lined with the fungus that has made Tokaj famous (500 HUF). The **Szerelmi Pincesor (the Row of Love Cellars)**, may provide free sampling, including the famous Tokai Aszú, and at my visit the szamorodni, furmint and several others mellowed here. The central hall of the cellar once had 24 different galleries.

Processing here is thousands of years old. Today, the cellars hold 20,000 hectoliters of wine. The grand tours can also lead to the volcanic Nagy hegy (big hill/mountain), which, at 1,548 feet, rises in a perfect cone to dominate the landscape.

Visit the **Tokai Museum**, at 7 Bethlen Gábor út, to get a feel for the region, Tue-Sun 10 am to 6 pm. The historical contribution of Greece, whose traders were frequent visitors, is traced at a small community church, turned museum – the **Greek Orthodox Church**, 23 Bethlen Gábor út. Concerts and exhibitions are held there at various times of the year. The **Town Hall** at Rákocsi út 44 (dating from 1790), is a listed art monument. However, for sampling, try the **Himesudvar**

**Press House Museum and Wine Cellar**, Bem út 2, ☎ 36-47-352-416, Mon-Sun 10 am to 4 pm.

You must stay for the **Harvest Procession**, at the end of Sept. Tourinform (see *Appendix*) can arrange for you to stay in homes and vineyards in the surrounding region.

The **Tokaj-Bodogzug Protected Zone** sits astride the confluence of the Bodrog and Tisza rivers, and is a favorite for angling. Pinewoods, beech, and oak blanket the area, interspersed with miles of grape rows on the winding hills. Tourinform can also provide information about the rowing tours that take place from spring to autumn; they take you from Tokaj to Sárospatak (37 km/22 miles).

## Mátra Mountains & Gyöngyös

Out of Budpaest on Route 3 or alternatively, coming from Miskolc on the same route, take the turn-off for Gyöngyös. This small town is a starting point for numerous tours into the Mátra mountains, even more popular for winter skiers than its cousin farther north, Bánkút. A settlement at the very beginning of Hungarian history, in the ninth century, King Robert Károly gave it town status in 1334, primarily due to its success at producing fine wines. The southern slopes of the volcanic Mátra mountains are a rich bed for grapes, baked to perfection by the summer sun.

"White Sapphire" wines such as Riesling, Muscat Otthonel, Leányka, Sauvignon Blanc, and Pinot, have gained international fame, which the Turks, with far less sensitivity to their finer characteristics, fully enjoyed.

**Farkasmalyi**, a little village just outside of Gyöngyös, is equipped with ancient wine-press houses and cellars. It is an excellent place for wine tasting.

As we enter Gyöngyös, Mergres út (Route 24) changes its name to Apris 4 út, just after its intersection with Eger út. You will pass the **Alsóvárosi ferences templom (Lower City Franciscan Church)** to the left, built circa 1400, and "updated" with Baroque ornamentation in later centuries. It is set back on Baratók tér (Baratók Square) and houses a Gothic sanctuary, a medieval library, and wooden statues carved by József Habenstreit sometime between 1759-1760.

Inside, János Vak Bottyán lies buried, one of the legendary figures in Hungarian history. Second only to Rákóczi in the military campaigns of the revolution for independence (1703-1711), he was a commoner who had risen to rank in the Imperial forces, and then chose to fight for the cause when the revolution began. Also known as blind Bottyán, because he had lost one of his eyes while fighting the Turks, he won a series of stunning victories against the Imperial forces using the "Hussar" fighting tactics.

Continue on Apris 4 út to Kossuth Lajos út. Turn right on Kossuth Lajos út and look immediately to your left. **Orczy-kastély** (Orczy Castle), now the home of the **Mátra Museum**, sits behind park-like grounds and a

black iron fence. Before we enter the bright yellow museum note the black iron fence, which was reputedly made from the gun barrels of the nobles who rose up in rebellion during the time of the Napoleonic Wars. The stone lions over the entrance symbolize the town of Gyöngyös. But, what you don't see is intriguing. Alexander I, Czar of Russia, stayed here in 1814. Just one dot in a history book, but it leaves you wondering. I could find no historical connection for the visit. Was there an unknown Hungarian mistress in the Czar's life? The museum displays Europe's largest collection of eggs (37,000), a diorama on the fauna of the Mátra, a living colony of bees, and numerous insects, butterflies and reptiles of the region, plus exhibits on the prehisty of the region, including a perfectly preserved mammoth skeleton.

Now, heading back up Kossuth Lajos út, cross Route 24 and go to the intersection of Fö tér on the left and Petöfi Sándor u on the right. You can walk or drive. We pass the **Szent Bertalan**

**Templom** (Saint Bartholomew Church), at Bertalan út 3 on our left. Dated from the 14th century, it was remodeled later with a Baroque facelift and superb examples of goldsmithing. It houses the second-richest Catholic archive in the country and a unique look into the past. Did you ever wonder what it was like to go to school in 1690? Walk around to the other side of the church to see the 330-year-old grammar school, a protected monument.

Continue on Fö tér and find the    *Szent Bertalan Templom*
**Borok Haza**, 10 Fö tér, ☎ 36-37-302-226, a wine cellar offering numerous programs. Call in advance. As an alternate, if you want to explore the area for a "vintage" experience, call the **Matraalja Borut Egyesulet** (Matraalja Wine Route Society) ☎ 36-37-500-300, and they will arrange local contacts and personal tours, or contact the closest Tourinform office (see *Appendix*).

Now we have a choice. We can continue on Route 24, up to the Mátra Mountains. Our first stop is Mátrafüred, and our second stop is Mátraháza. Alternatively we can take the narrow-guage train from the Gyöngyös station. If you drive Route 24, keep your eye open for **Sasta tó** (Sasta Lake). The turn-off will lead you to the highest lake in the country, with panoramic views of the countryside, a few hostels and hotels, plus boating, fishing and hiking. If you take the train, it would be wise to use Mátrafüred as your hub town if you plan on staying in this area. For narrow-guage train information see *Adventures*.

## Mátrafüred

The Mátravasút is the narrow guage railroad of the Mátra Mountains. Mátrafüred is one of its stops, a connection to numerous mountain trails and tracks. It also invites a good neighborhood exploration. There are three unnamed castle ruins that dot the area; taking any of the trail paths to the

north will wind you at one or two of them. From here a good hike will take you to Mátraháza and the Kékes Mountain. It's not necessary to wear hiking boots for this one, except in rainy periods or winter, though you should at least wear tennis shoes.

## Mátraháza

Leaving Mátrafüred we go north for Mátraháza. Mátraháza does not have a train stop, but from here, walking or driving, you can negotiate your way to the tallest mountain in Hungary, the **Kékes** (1,014 m/3,326 feet). Park in Mátraháza, and walk up the trail to the tower. This

is one of the most far-ranging views in Hungary on a clear day. You have two possibilities for viewing – the enclosed, windowed deck, which has an espresso mini-bar, or the "crow's nest" view. If heights make you nervous, the crow's nest is not for you. However, the 360-degree view from this tower cannot be duplicated. You see the entire range of the Mátra and Zemplen mountains, over the Bükk, and, on a clear day, into distant Slovakia and the High Tatras.

Kékes Mountain provides some of the best skiing in Hungary. The winter sports center consists of a 900-foot and a 7,200-foot downhill, as well as a ski jump, and ski lifts. However, this is not alpine skiing. It is best for leisurely beginning and moderately advanced skiers. If you are looking for downhill challenges, you should head over to Bank or Slovakia.

Leaving the high Mátra mountains, and continuing north on Route 24, we wind through picturesque forest in a gradual up and down descent. We will pass the turn-off for Gallyatetõ (second-highest point in Hungary, with skiing, hotels, summer hiking and mountain climbing) and will instead continue on Route 24 until we arrive at Parádsasvár

## Parádsasvár

In 1735 sulphuric water was found in Parádsasvár. We do not know how or when, but word reached the surrounding communities that drinking the water could cure digestive diseases. The water of Parádsasvár has a characteristic sulphur smell and has become known as Parád Water. Because of the popularity of the water, commercial development ensued, leading to a "drinking hall" and subsequently to a bottling works in 1881. The Hungarian architect, Miklós Ybl, designed the Chinese pagoda-like structure adorned with majolica that covers the well.

Back in 1776, a glass factory was established here. It has since produced world-famous cut crystal. The glass factory is a living museum of the techniques that once produced the fabulous stained glass in the cathedrals of Europe, and which fostered in later years the Tiffany style of glass lamps that so graced the Victorian age

After you stop for a drink from the well, as you leave town, you will see the **Károly Museum, Mansion & Hotel** on your right. This is the only five star in the region. This castle-hotel includes three different buildings, each with its own atmosphere, and

*Károly Museum, Mansion & Hotel*

connected by an underground tunnels (see *Places to Stay*). The tunnels are used for water adventures and recreation.

## Parád & Parádfürdő

Passing through Parádsasvár on Route 24 we arrive at Parád and Parádfürdő. Through the years they have melded with one another and are basically indistinguishable today. While Parádsasvár had water that reputedly cured gastric ailments, while the waters of Parádfürdő could reputedly cure leg aches, swollen feet, and various inflammatory diseases. The waters have been used for medicinal purposes since the 17th century. Today, the state hospital in Parádfürdő has gained a reputation for the effective treatment of gynecological illnesses and certain inflammatory diseases, using the thermal waters from the well.

But the first thing we see on entering the town is the 200-year-old house known simply as the **Páloc** at 10 Sziget út. We are in the middle of Palóc culture and this house is an 18th-century Palóc house, untouched by the passing of the ages, complete with tools, home crafts, weaving, wooden stick fences, and a genuine thatched roof (the thatching is replaced at certain intervals, identical in method and composition to its original roof). The next two stops are studies in contrast to the Palóc house. The **Cifra istálló** (Fancy Stable) at 217 Kossuth Lajos út is made of red marble. Several Hungarian horse breeds are stabled here. The same stables were used for the horses of the Hapsburg nobility. In the associated workshop (221 Kossuth Lajos út), a collection of 325 different bottles of mineral water from 25 different countries invites a look-see, but merely for its oddity.

A short walk farther up takes us to Hársfa út, where we can go to No. 6 Hársfa út, the **Hungarian Coach Museum**, focussing on the luxury of gold and brass trim, velvet and leather, used in the coaches of the nobility in days past. Next, a break from our walking might be welcome at the outside terrace of the **Parádi Kisvendéglõ és Vendégház**, Kossuth út 234, ☎ 36-36-364-831, mobile 30-955-9925, specializing in Palóc meals, (about 3,000 HUF), and overnight accommodations. It's bare-bones, but offers a comfortable single room, with bed, bathroom, TV, and refrigerator. They are closed on Tuesdays Apr 1-Sept 30, and Mon-Tues, Mar 1 to 31.

Having completed our glimpse of Hungary's mountains, its Palóc culture, its revolutionary spirit and world-class wines, we can go back to Budapest, or head through Sirok to Eger and from Eger south to the Tisza Lake region.

# ■ Adventures

## Hiking

### Rákóczi Trail

This is one of those truly adventuresome trails that takes you by castles and offers some picturesque camera shots. You can backpack it, or just walk a quarter of the trail and head back. Travel the route of Ferenc Rákóczi II, the leader of the Hungarian revolt of 1703-1711, known as the Rákóczi Revolution, almost 100 years before the American Revolution. The 56-km/34-mile trail is marked by a red stripe. You start at Füzér and walk the trail to Sárospatak. If you don't stop to see anything (unrealistic), you can do this in a day. But, if you are really keen on learning and exploring, it will take two to three days, maybe even four. At Füzér you can visit the castle, dating from the days of Arpad, at the very dawn of the Hungarian nation. Following the waymarks, the path takes you through Gönc, and the ruins of the monastery and church from 1371, then the Gothic Catholic Church, which harbors the remains of Gáspár Károli, the first translator of the Bible into Hungarian. From there you can turn southeast to the Amadé Castle. Heading on to Regéc, its castle ruins once echoed with Rákóczi's footseps. Then, on to Sárospatak and one of the best-preserved castles in Hungary, the early-Baroque Rákóczi castle. Rákóczi lived here from 1694 to 1700, where no doubt the resolve to fight the Hapsburg Imperial throne erupted into the revolution only a few years later.

## The Metallurgist's Trail

The natural surroundings of three of Hungary's most famous industrial towns give us a glimpse of the Bükk and Zemplén Hills. Start at Salgótarján, at the end of Route 21, in the northern section of the country. Follow the trail with the blue stripe and the blue cross. From Salgótarján, it winds through the hills and around valleys and gulleys in the Marancs-Medves Hills and finally through Heves-Borsod County to the town of Ózd, up through the Upponyi and Bükk Hills to finally end at Diósgyör. In Salgótarján look for the Salgó castle atop basaltic peaks, and the underground mining museum. In Bárna stop to take in the view from Nagy-ko Peak, and then on your way you can bathe or fish at a lake created by a natural landslide, the Arló. You walk past the Upponyi Pass and the Lázbérc Reservoir (in Hungarian the Upponyi-szoros and Lázbérci víztároló), where you can take out your fishing rod again. Or, press on through the sights at Miskolc-Omassa and Felsohámor, and finally, at Miskolc-Lillafüred you can end your journey with the healing air of the caves, a curative agent for respiratory diseases.

A few helpful phone numbers for hikers in Northern Hungary:

- **Nógrád Megyei Közmuvelõdési és Turisztikai Intézet** (Nograd County Institute for Culture and Tourism), 3100 Salgótarján, Ruhagyári u. 9, ☎/fax 36-32-432-099, nmkti@elender.hu, www.nogradtour.hu.

- **Heves Megyei Természetbarát Szövetség** (Heves County Friends of Nature Association), 3300 Eger, Dobó tér 6/A, ☎ 36-36-312-888, fax 36-36-515-075, hmosport@mail.inext.hu.

- **Borsod-Abaúj-Zemplén Megyei Természetjáró Szövetség** (BAZ County Rambler's Association), 3501 Miskolc, Széchenyi u. 103. Calling hours, 4:30 to 6:30 pm, ☎ 36-46-353-511.

- **Zempléni Idegenforgalmi Szövetség** (Zemplén Tourist Association), 3980 Sátoraljaújhely, Rákóczi u. 18, ☎ 36-47-523-081.

# Cycling

While it may be said that you can get beautiful and wonderful views from almost any vantage in the mountainous part of Hungary, for a cyclist it can be a real performance tester. I know of no "easy" paths in the bicycle routes of Northern Hungary. That being said, it is possible to have a truly beautiful trip with only moderate difficulty by going from Eger north, toward Miskolc, to Aggtelek, back to Takaca, Encs, Gönc, Hollóháza, Sárospatak, and then back on a long winding route that ultimately takes you to the wine country of Tokaj –a good way to wrap up this seven- to eight-day journey. You can take it in segments, by choice. For instance, you may choose to simply go from Miskolc and cycle out through Lillafüred, then back to Miskolc. So we have broken the trip into daily "segments" from which you can pick and choose, depending on your logistics and time. Cyclists can use any of the forest tracks signed for biking in the national parks, but note that in the Bükk, signs for cyclists are painted on tree trunks, or other local landmarks. They use the same colors as those used by hikers (yellow, blue, green and red). The Bükk National Forest is patrolled by EPA officers on bicycles. Many of these men also speak some English. A train arrives at Eger, and a train also goes to Misckolc, and also to Tokaj and Sarospatak (check the MAV schedules as noted in the Budapest section). It is a beautiful tour, taking you through protected forest and through the Bükk range, the Aggtelek karst, and the Zemplén Hills.

Check with the **Bükk Mountain Biking Center**, as well as Tourinform, to make sure of your plans. Tourinform can also book lodging for you so that you have a bed and meals waiting for you at the different stopovers.

Day 1 (58 km): Eger Felsõtárkány, Répáshuta, Bükkszentkereszt, Miskolctapolca, Miskolc.

Day 2 (63 km): Miskolc, Diósgyör, Lillafüred, Mályinka, Dédestapolcsány, Uppony, Putnok.

Day 3 (60 km): Putnok, Kelemér, (Görmöszölõs, 2 km), Ragály, Aggtelek, Jósfavõ, Perkupa, Szalonna (Szendrõ, Rudabánya, 16 km).

Day 4 (60 km): Sazlonna-Rakaca, Krasznokvajda, Baktakék, Encs.

Day 5 (53 km): Encs, Abaújszántó, Boldogkõváralja, Vizsoly, Gönc, (Telkibánya four km).

Day 6 (59 km): Gönc, Abaújvár, Kéded, Hollóháza, (Füzer 3 km), Pállháza, Sátorajlaújhely.

Day 7 (54 km): Sátorajlaújhely, Sárospatak, Vámosújfalu (Tolcsva four km), Tarcal, Tokaj.

Another helpful association for cyclists is the **National Association of Cycle Users and Hungarian Cycle Club** (Kerékpárral Közlekedõk Szövetsége és Magyar Kerékpáros Klub) H-1054 Budapest, Vadász u.29, ☎ 36-30-922-9052, ☎/ fax 36-1-206-6223, bringa@kerosz.hu www.kerosz.hu.

## Mountain Biking

A good route for mountain biking is from Eger directly to Szilvásvárad, via Nagyvisnyó, Mályinka, Lillafüred, Nagymezõ, Olaszkapu, Gerennavár, and ending in Szilvásvárad. It takes you through varied steep descents and climbs, through woods and by cliffside views. Anything but a mountain bike is not suitable for the climb. However, reaching the heights, the view is stunning, rising up along the edge of the Bükk Plateau. This requires someone in really good physical condition, with a good bike and well-maintained brakes and gears. Do not attempt it otherwise.

Follow the directions leaving Miskolc in the itineraries, but, as you start to leave town, make sure that you look for the green bicycle signs, which will steer you just north of the main road. The bicycle path follows the north side of the river through Diósgyõr and Lillafüred toward Hámor and Újmasa. Stop to see the sights, including the St. Istvan caves and the "Palota" (Palace Hotel), then wind past the longest waterfall in Hungary, and perhaps stop to do some boating on Hamor Lake. Here, I recommend that you head back, unless you are looking for a difficult tour, because the hills and slopes can be treacherous if you are not in condition. An alternative route that takes you to Aggtelek, heading back to Miskolc, rides parallel to the river on the west. Take the road to Parasznya, and Radostyán, following in order through the towns of

Sajószentpéter, Kazincbarcika, Mucsony, Kurityán, Felsõnyárád, Zubogy, Ragály, Trizs, and end the trip at Aggtelek and/or Jósvafõ.

## On Water

 A number of rivers wind their way through Hungary from surrounding countries, along romantic riverbanks, by castles and through misty glades. Canoeing or boating in Hungary, simply because of its effort to preserve its past, is an experience unique in the world, and in many aspects, is a trip back in time as well as one in nature. However, as adventurous and wonderful as this is, it still often requires strength, stamina, skill, and at times courage, varying with the rivers. It is recommended that you travel with a guide. The Upper Tisza has the best broadwaters of Europe. The water runs swiftly in some parts,

but is generally only a moderately challenging run, and in some parts an easy beginner's excursion as well. At the same time, the wild waters of the Hernád and Bódva are only for a d v a n c e d kayakers and canoers. Usually  one- or two-seat kayaks or canoes are best. An experienced tour guide will also be able to guide you away from protected species, just enough so you don't disturb their habitat, yet close enough to get a picture that will serve a lifetime of memories.

A few canoe and kayak contact numbers:

- **Hanyi Istój**, Bt 3980 Sátoraljaújhely, Achimu út 42, ☎ 36-47-323-432, fax 36-47-324-771.
- **Kékcápák Kenukölcönzõ** (Blue Shark Canoe Rental) 3910 Tokaj, Malom út 11, ☎ 36-47-353-227.

- **Unió Vizitelep** (Unió Water Site), 3910 Tokaj, Bodrogkeresztúri út 5, ☎/fax 36-47-352-927 or 36-20-9576-569.
- **NATURA Sportiroda** (NATURA Sport Agency), 3561 Felsőzsolca, Szent István út 2, ☎ 36-46-383-087 or 36-60-483-863.

## The Bodrog

The Bodrog is a gentle, easy river to canoe and it is perfectly suited for beginners and family excursions. At the same time, its often mist-shrouded banks and romantic countryside is an absolute charm from the water. Running from Sátoraljaújhely, and squeezing itself in between the Hegyalja mountains and the Bodrogköz Hills, it winds down southward to join the Tisza at Tokaj. The length of the run is about 51 km/32 miles and no lifting over is necessary. Although this can easily be a one-day trip, it is probably better to take it slow, take in the country, and rest a day on the way down. There are several campsites and/or guest houses along the way.

## The Sajó River

The Sajó River crosses into Hungary at Sajópüspöki and snakes through valleys and ravines of Northern Hungary, for a total of 125 km/78 miles until it arrives at the town of Tiszaújváros. Lifting over is required at two places, and usually the number of days taken is three to four, assuming at least one complete rest day. This is for kayaks, canoes and boats.

## The Hernád

From Aaújvár this river runs between Zemplén and the Cserehát Hills, to join the Sajó at Sajóhidegvég. The 118.4-km/74-mile run requires some lifting over at four places. Water levels that are low will force the use of the Kesznyéten artificial canal after the Bocs barrage. The canal will take you through for 9.9 km/six miles until you arrive at the Sajó estuary. Though the canal part is shorter by 34.5 km/22 miles, it requires two more lift overs. This run usually takes three-five days, assuming one-two rest days.

## The Bódva

The Bódva runs between the Aggtelek Hills and Cserehát Hills, from Hidvégardó. At the village of Bóldva it joins the Sajó River. Its 56.1 km/35 miles will require lifting over at least five places, and depending on the season and rains, maybe more (two more in low water). This is usually a three-day tour with a one-day rest.

## The Zagyva

During medium water level the 104.4 km/65 miles from Hatvan to the Tisza Estuary at Szolnok will require at least three lift overs, sometimes more, depending on the conditions. It ends with a fabulous view of the broad Tisza preserve and its extraordinarily rich wildlife, harkening back to the time when America herself harbored numerous wondrous estuaries of waterlands and wildlife.

## Tisza

Although we might rightly include the Tisza River here, we have instead placed it in the Lake Tisza section of the book, through which it flows.

# On Horseback

As we noted previously, in general, horseback riding in Hungary is in the English style. Appropriate dress and training are required. You can get the dress and the training here, but the long tours are only recommended for experienced riders. And, while there are some "string-along" horseback riding tours, generally, a riding tour will require at least a moderate level of control and experience with horses. You can get training in Hungary at any number of stables, and then, under the guidance of your teachers, wander the country. The cost is half or less what it would be elsewhere. For any horseman, the Cifra Stables and the Cart Museum in Parád are a must see.

There are four notable herds in Northern Hungary, some of which are famous throughout the world. The Lipizaner herd in Szilvásvárad, the Furioso North-Star herd in Bekölce, the Hucul herd in the valley near Aggtelek, and the Kisbér Hungarian herd near Vanyarc.

It is no accident that the international Horseback Rally of 2000 was held in Hungary in Szilvásvárad, nor that the most beautiful horse, internationally recognized, was a Hungarian one from the herd in Bekölce.

The freedom and range of what you can do here on horseback far exceeds most countries in the world. So, it is a favorite spot for those interested in equine tourism. This is expected to continue for only a few more years, however, as private investors are increasingly fencing off the land.

Training in coach (team) driving, as they used to do on the wagon trains in the American West, and as they once did on royal carriages, can be had at Eger and Szilvásvárad. Numerous stables also train in horseback jumping and acrobatic horsemanship. Again, it is wise to book through the Hungarian Equine Association (see below) or through Tourinform.

Cross-country adventures can take you through protected lands, past castles, through villages in the outback, across streams, and up mountain trails, through woods and plains.

For the Northern Region the best adventures can be had with **Equus Ltd.**, Özgida u. 32, 1025 Budapest, ☎/fax 36-1-325-6349, www.equi.hu, or contact Márta Jókai, mobile ☎ 36-20-911-8275, equus@matavnet.hu. The ranch is in a low-lying mountain area outside of Hollókõ, but starting points for excursions can vary. Some tours can be done with accompanying horse-drawn carriage for the inexperienced, but a minimum number of riders is required. Check with Márta Jókai. It is the center for breeding 80 Kisbéri horses. These noble-looking creatures were bred for the legendary Hussar cavalry officers during the Austro-Hungarian monarchy. Highly intelligent and easy to ride, they are extremely reliable, stable, and an enduring partner on long trips. The average height is 16-17 hands. They are kept under the best conditions, with wide, healthy pastures. The leader of this stable is János Lóska, former member of the Hungarian Eventing team. Instruction is on an international level. The cross-country ride averages 40-50 km/25 to 30 miles a day, in English style. You will cross prairies and fields, ford streams, pass through forest glades, and witness the Hungarian countryside of the farmers and woodsmen. They will pick you up in Budapest and take you to the starting point, if it is at the ranch or elsewhere, and book all accommodations ahead in "stable" hotels where you will have good quality double bedrooms with bathroom, and all meals (genuine Hungarian, of course), with an option to purchase good quality wines as well. At the stable hotels, they will feed, water, and bed down the horses as required, so they'll be ready for you to leave in the morning.

The **Rákóczi riding trip** lasts eight days. The first day starts in Tokaj where you dine, visit a wine cellar and perhaps see a few sights in Tokaj, then, for the next seven days, you will ride cross-country. Picnic stops are coordinated to rest the horses as well as the riders (a support van and an extra horse are carefully coordinated to follow the route at select coordinates, with equipment and meals). You may ride through Sárospatak to the hills and castles of medieval and Renaissance Hungary. You will cross the Tisza River with your horses on a ferryboat, then ride over to the famous Bodrog River. Trailing along the Bodrog you hug the banks and turn into the mist-laden forest of Zemplen, where once the knights of Hungary rode their steeds. The trip ends at Kéked Castle. From there you are taken back to Budapest.

The **Mátra-Ipoly ride** starts at the horse farm on the first day. On the second day you head to Hollókõ where you tour the village, and then bed down for a night in a Páloc village. Afterwards, the tour winds past castles and villages across the countryside, and over to the Ipoly River, the border between Slovakia and Hungary, and the Börzöny Hills. These are one- and two-day excursions, then back to the ranch. On the eighth day you are transferred back to Budapest. Five people must be booked for this trip to take place, at €990 per person.

**The Way of the Legend/Eger** takes you from the ranch through Hollókõ, Mátraszele, Bekölce, and on to Szilvásvárad to visit the Lippizaner horses and ranch. Hungarian horsemen took many international prizes in the championships held in Szilvásvárad. You visit the carriage museum, the trout farm of Szilvásvárad, sample cuisine made with fresh trout, and tour the hills and the forests of Bükk and Aggtelek National Parks. On the last day, after riding in the morning, you take a coach tour to Eger for a historical tour, which includes the Szépasszonyvölgy (the wine cellars in the caves) where you sample Egri Bikavér (Bull's Blood).

Shorter rides and training can be arranged at the following stables (also check with the Hungarian Equestrian Tourism Association under *Budapest Adventures*):

**Fényes Major Kft.** it 3242 Parádsasvár, Kossuth út 1, ☎ 36-36-444-444. This place is pricey, but with a wide range of options, including jeep adventures, hot air ballooning, and hang gliding. The farm is also open for visitors Wed through Sun with a 500 HUF entrance fee. Children under 12 are free if accompanied by an adult. Groups require prior arrangements. They have a full agenda of programs, getting to know horses and the local animals, including the Hungarian Bogáncs, the peculiar matty-haired Hungarian sheep dog, donkeys, horses, foul, buffalo, grey cattle, goats, kids, and Racka sheep. Riding lessons on the ranch property are 3,000 HUF per hour. Simple riding inside a stabled enclosure is 2,500 HUF. Cross-country riding with a guide is 4,000 HUF per hour. Carriage riding with a driver to a maximum of four persons is 8,000 HUF per hour. It is located next to Route 24, about a 30 minute walk to Károly Castle. Surrounded by woods, they stable 10 horses, including two Lippizans and two Hungarian halfbreeds. By special arrangement, longer equine tours can be organized. Horse and cart trips can also be arranged to the Cifra Stable and Cart Museum, as can a combined walk to the Ilona Valley to see the waterfall. Jeep tours and occasional paint ball countryside competitions are other options. While at the ranch, special chef lunches may be incorporated in the visit. But, be aware that just about everything is an add-on. Keep track of expenses.

## Five Horseshoe Category

**János Lóska Private Stud Farm**, 2688 Banyarc – Sarlóspuszta, ☎ 36-32-484-064, 36-1-355-7608. János is president of the Hungarian Equestrian Tourism Association, and one of the founders of the Hungarian horseshoe certification system. His horses are some of the finest Kisberi horses in the country, and his tours some of the best.

**Stud Farm in Szilvásvásvárad**, 3348 Szilvásvásvárad, Fenyves út 4, ☎ 36-36-355-155.

**Mátyus Mansion**, Egedhegyi Lipicai Lovastanya Kft. (Lipizzan Equestrian Farm of Egedhegy Ltd.), 3300 Eger, Külterület, Noszvaj út, ☎ 36-36-312-804.

### Four Horseshoe Category

**Cifra Istálló** (Cifra Stable), 3240 Parádfürdő, Kossuth u., ☎ 36-36-4-387.

### Three Horseshoe Category

**Egeres-völgyi Lovastanya** (Horse Farm of Egers Valley), 3324 Felsőtárkány, Egeres-völgy, ☎ 36-36-434-740.

### Two Horseshoe Category

**Balogh Ligeti Lovas Club** (Balogh Ligeti Equestrian Club), 3530 Miskolc, Görgey út, ☎ 36-46-412-527.

**Csapó Sportistálló és Üdülőház** (Csapó Sports Stable and Boarding House), Gábor Csapó, 3343 Bekölce, Béke út 252, ☎ 36-36-485-648.

**Sziráki Baráti Kör és Lovasklub** (Szirák Friends Society and Equestrian Club), 3044 Szirák Kastély, ☎ 36-32-485-300.

### One Horseshoe Category

**Kudrin Lovasiskola** (Kudrin Riding School), 3910 Tokaj, Szabadság u. 27, ☎ 36-47-352-257.

**Tamarix Lovasiskola Kft.** (Tamarix Riding Yard/School), 3991 Vilyvitány, Somogyi Béla utca 33, ☎ 36-47-308-112 or 36-06-20-450-7199.

## Cave Adventures

Ranking at the top of our cave adventures is the Aggtelek-Jósvafő tour(s) in the Baradla Cave System, as we have already discussed, and the Anna Cave near the Szinva-patak (Szinva Stream), which is about 200 m/660 feet long. In the Aggtelek, Jósvafő, the Szeleta and the caves around Lillafüred, in order to maintain public safety and conservation as well, Hungary has allowed cave explorations, but only under professional guidance. Accordingly, it is best to check with Tourinform, and also with the following agencies. Otherwise, as noted in itineraries, the standard guided tours can be unique adventures in themselves.

Open every day, the public bath and cave adventures should not be missed at Miskolctapolca.

All cave exploration societies in Hungary are coordinated through the **Hungarian Karst and Cave Explorer Society** (Magyar Karszt és Barlangkutató Társulat, MKBT), 1027 Budapest 2nd District, Fö út 68, ☎ 36 1-201 9493. However, a number of local/regional organizations will probably give a quicker response for their particular area. Check these organizations:

**Aggtelek Nemzeti Park Igazgatósága** (Aggtelek National Park Directorate), 3758 Jósfavo, Tengerszem oldal 1, ☎/fax 36-48-350-006, info.amp@mail.matav.hu.

**Bükk Nemzeti Park Igazgatósága** (Bükk National Park Directorate), 3300 Eger, Sánc út 6, ☎ 36-36-411-581, fax 36-36-412-791, bukknp@ktm.x400gw.itb.hu.

**Sziklaorom Hegymászó és Barlangász Klub** (Rock Peak Rock Climbing and Cave Explorer Club), 3100 Salgótarján, Medves körut 94, ☎ 36-32-431-081 or 36-32-310-140.

**Miskolctapolcai Termál Barlangfürdő** (Miskolctapolca Thermal Bath), 3525 Miskolctapolca, Pazár István sétány, ☎/ fax 36-46-304-128 or 36-46-369-452, www.barlangfürdo.hu.

**Lillafüred Anna Mésztufa Barlang és Szent István Cseppkőbarlang** (Lillafüred Anna Lime Tuf Cave and Szt. István Stalagmite Cave), 3517 Lillafüred, Erzsébet sétány, ☎ 36-46-334-130.

## Rock Climbing

 As with caving, you need to have permission for the use of certain natural features in the land. However, the following locations are particularly suited for rock climbing, and so we will list them here.

The Bükk Hills are particularly noted for three main crags, the Dédes, Hámor, and Fehérkő.

### Dédes

On the edge of the Bükk National Park, the highest rockfaces in Hungary are laced with more than 50 different routes across the hard white limestone face. They range in difficulty from VI to VIII+. Although you need nuts and slings for some of the routes, almost all are bolted. A camping spot at the foot of the cliffs has water and basic facilities. Heading through Bélapátfalva and Szilvásvárad, at the second crossing after Nagyvisnyó, turn right. You will come to the children's camp, and parking spaces. From the children's camp follow the yellow waymarks to the cliff. It is about two km/1.2 miles.

## Hámor

We have already covered some aspects of these cliffs above. The cliffs rise from the low-lying Hámor Valley, solid limestone walls that overlook the road below. The faces are well developed, but appearances are deceptive from below. Most of the climbs are not for beginners, with face and overhang climbs, rating from V up through X. It is a simple drive from Miskolc toward Hámor, as the cliffs border both sides of the road outside of Hámor.

## Fehérkõ

Fehérkõ means white stone, referring to the white stone face of Jávor Hill, which is said to be a special type of climb. Its sharp edges and small holes have been compared to steep rock faces on the alps, or to shear cliffside escarpments  in the Tatras. Yet, it is baked constantly by the sun, due to its southern face, with major portions of the climb exuding a hot micro-climate during any scaling attempt. Climbs are VII to a "warm" X. Climbing is generally not possible from Nov into Feb. Driving from Miskolc toward Lillafüred, turn left just before the lake and after the village of Hámor. Follow the road all the way to the last stop for bus number 5. It will be posted with a sign and sometimes you will see a bus sitting there. Behind the stop you can see the snaking pathway up to the climbing face.

Contact the following for tours and guidance:

**Salgótarjáni Hegymászó Klub** (Salgótarján Mountain Climber Club), 3100 Salgótarján, Csokonai út 52/b, ☎ 36-32-440-314.

**Extreme Sport**, 3300 Eger, Dobó utca 21, ☎ 36-36-410-221.

**Adventure Club**, 3348 Szilvásvárad Kertalja út 9, ☎/fax 36-309-850-609 or 36-36-355-703, szalajka.fogado@axelero.hu. The adventure club is known for many different types of adventures and tours. It is best to e-mail as in most cases the telephone respondents do not speak enough English to communicate, though they do have translators for written correspondence.

# In the Air

As with caving, some adventures require special permission. Among these are paragliding. Available at Szilvásvárad and at the Kopasz Hill next to Tokaj, it is allowed in the presence of authorized trainers in most instances. You must check with the Tourinform office and/or one of the following organizations.

**Pipis-hegyi Repülotér** (Pipis Hill Airport), Gyöngyös, Pipis-hegy, ☎ 36-37-312-393.

**Egri Repüloklub** (Eger Flying Club), 3397 Maklár, Repülotér, ☎ 36-36-357-100.

**Egri Sárkányrepülo Klub** (Eger Hang Gliding Club), 3398 Nagytálya, Kossuth út 57, ☎ 36-30-9636-979, fax 36-36-336-20-208, apollo@mail.datanet.hu.

For motorized gliding, contact the Maklár airport at the top of the Vécsey Valley near Eger or the Pipis Hill airport.

# Skiing

Szilváskõ near Karancs-Medves has two ski lifts. The Nógrád part of Galyatető, at Mátraalmás, has the only ski run in Hungary suitable for international competition, but essentially, only two ski areas are popular in Hungary, at Bankut, and at Matra, and they are covered in the text under itineraries.

Northern Hungary

Further information and special itineraries can be planned and confirmed through one or more of these organizations. In all cases, you can also check with Tourinform.

**Nógrád Megyei Közmuvelodési és Turisztikai Intézet** (Nógrád County Institute for Culture and Tourism), 3100 Salgótarján, Ruhagyári út 9, ☎/fax 36-32-432-099 or 36-32-432-101, nmkti@elender.hu.

**Salgótarjáni Sí Club** (Salgótarjáni Sí Club), Gábor Janák, 3100 Salgótarján, Fö tér 1, ☎ 36-32-438-005.

**Magyar Sí Szövetség** (Hungarian Ski Association), 1143 Budapest, Stefánia út 2, ☎ 36-1-251-1222. Visit www.sielok. hu for information. The chart is in Hungarian, but it is simple to understand if you know the meanings of the columns. Helység means the place. Síipályák is the ski slope, length, etc. Sífelvonók is the ski lift. The last column is the telephone number. After you click for English, then switch your search to the locations and click on Magyarorszag (the Hungarian word for Hungary).

**Bánkút Sí Club** (Bánkút Ski Club), 3517 Miskolc-Lillafüred. The automated information line is ☎ 36-46-390-135 or 36-46-390-182.

## Bankut Ski Center

☎ 36-46-390-182. Length of runs, 800-900 m (2,400-2,700 feet); average drop, 130 m (390 feet); eight ski runs, eight adult lifts and one baby lift; snow machines and evening lighting. There is a 10-km/six-mile cross-country ski run. Difficulty of runs is marked in black (most difficult) to red (moderately difficult) to normal (blue), and in order from the easiest to the most difficult slope.

| Ski Run | Run Length | Drop | Color |
|---|---|---|---|
| Run 1 (A) | 600 m | 170 m | Black |
| Run 2 (B) | 500 m | 130 m | Black |
| Run 3 (C) | 300 m | 80 m | Red |
| Run 4 (D) | 200 m | 15 m | Red |
| Run 5 (E) | 150 m | 20 m | Blue |
| Run 6 (F) | 1,300 m | 150 m | Blue |
| Run 7 (H) | 180 m | 30 m | Blue |
| Run 8 (L) | 150m | 20m | Blue |

Train connections are available from Miskolc, Lillafüred, Szentlélek, and from the Bankut train station.

Services of Bankut Ski Center are bare by western standards, but are still adequate. It can accommodate 90 persons and has central heating as well as common restroom facilities. It was built in 1936 and costs 1,000 HUF per night for a private room or 700 HUF per night for a common room. Price of lodging includes a blanket and a cushion. Bedclothes are an extra 350 HUF. The prices are great, but it is a backpacker's hostel with Soviet-era service. You can bring your own blankets and quilts; your own slippers are a must. You are not allowed on the floors without slippers. Restaurant and parking are next to the building.

## Miscellaneous Adventures

### Car Derby & Auto Races

**XPA Motorsport Tolcsva Ring**, István Trembeczki, ☎ 36-47-584-003 or 36-47-384-245.

**Hor-völgye Autó-Motor Sport Egyesület** (Hor Valley Automobile and Motorcycle Sport Club), ☎ 36-49-334-2581.

### Bird-Watching

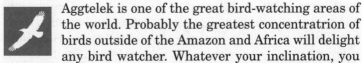 Aggtelek is one of the great bird-watching areas of the world. Probably the greatest concentratrion of birds outside of the Amazon and Africa will delight any bird watcher. Whatever your inclination, you cannot but be captivated watching thousands of birds take flight in one great flock across the sky. Try to time your trip with the arrival of the storks in the spring. Corvina's *A Guide to Bird Watching In Hungary* tells you the best places and permit requirements, if needed. Spring and autumn are the top seasons, but the best month is May. The **Hungarian Ornithological Society** is at Budapest XII, Költő út 21, ☎ 36-1-395-2605.

# Hunting

Hunting is possible, but it is strictly controlled. It must be done through the proper organizations. The best place to start is with **Mavad I Logodi**, út 22-24 ☎ 36-375-9611.

# Special Boat Trips

Between Sárospatak, Tokaj, and Tiszacseged, a number of boat trips are possible, often by special arrangement, which may include dinners and special sightseeing inside the Tisza reserve, or in the mountains of Northern Hungary. Contact **Gabor Palotas** at ☎ 06-30-500-3232.

# The Mountain Forest Train

The narrow-guage railroad, the Mátrai Erdei Vasutak (Mátra Forest Train), runs from Gyöngyös through Mátrafüred and a number of other points in the Mátra Mountains. A round-trip is about 560 HUF and a one-way ticket is 300 HUF to Mátrafüred. The Gyöngyös station is at 3200 Gyöngyös, Dobó út 1, ☎ 36-37-312-447, ☎/fax 36-37-312-453, www.matrahegy.hu (the website is Hungarian, but a little persistence can render much of it understandable). The line is almost 100 years old and the rail car that used to carry lumber down from the hills has been modified with open-air seating for tourists. There is also a closed passenger coach.

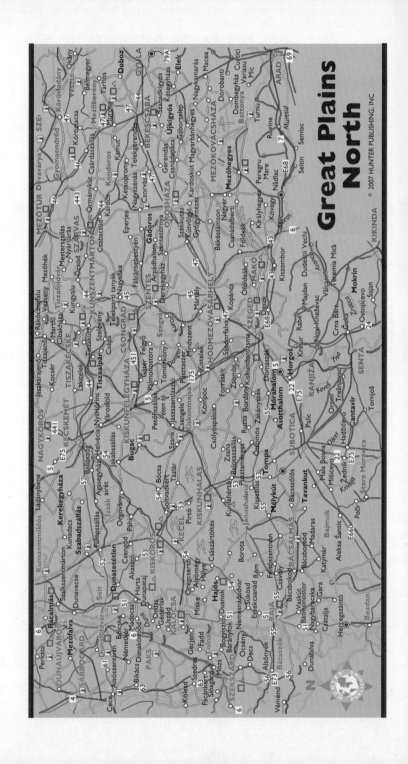

Great Plains North

© 2007 HUNTER PUBLISHING, INC

# The Great Plains

In the silence of the wind, sometimes you can hear a whisper from the ancient past. That is what they say on the plains of Hungary, where the panorama often stretches out to infinity, as

flat and wild as it was in the days of Árpád. The view is occasionally traversed by a stream or river, and in a few areas, near the Tisza, and to the far north, forest and bog. The region is bordered on the east by Ukraine and Romania, and on the west by the Tisza River. In some locations the structures and culture from the Middle Ages are still there. You may well see rare species of fowl and abundant small game; the area is popular for pheasant, hare, and deer hunting. The flat terrain is perfect for horses and cattle, and hence it is Hungary's major equine and cattle ranching area as well. Hungarian "goulash" originated here, as did the "bogac," the tripod-suspended cooking pot of the open plains. The Csikós shepherds, the cowboys of Hungary, whose horse riding skills have become legendary, also call this home. This combination of culture, history, and geography, has led to the Hortobágy National Park and its adjoining Tisza Reserve (see *Tisza* section) being designated as a UNESCO World Heritage Site.

## ■ Places to Stay

> The **Civis hotel chain** has a number of good quality accommodations throughout this region, all of which provide excellent support services for travelers. Check their website *www.civishotels.hu.*

## Four Star

★★**Hotel Aranybika**, €€, H-4025 Debrecen Piac út 11-15, ☎ 36-52-508-600, fax 36-52-421-834, www.civishotels.hu. Mar 25-Oct 31 (high season), doubles are €89. A part of the Civis hotel chain, its low-season average is €70 and includes buffet breakfast, pool, sauna, gym, and hydro massage. Spa services, offered in low-cost packages, include doctor's examinations, dental services (doctor, nursing, and dental staff at the hotel), slimming plans, life-style changes, curative and recuperative programs for various ailments, and beauty treatments. Built by the

| HOTEL PRICE CHART | |
|---|---|
| Double room without tax | |
| € | Under €80 |
| €€ | €81-€150 |
| €€€ | €151-€250 |
| €€€€ | Over €250 |

famed Alfréd Hajós at the turn of the century in Art Nouveau style, it rises castle-like in the center square of the city of Debrecen, next to the Reformed Great Church (see *Itineraries*). Rated four stars, it has a turn of the century five-star elegance. The Glass Restaurant is fabulously ornate, patterned after a king's dining hall, where gypsy musicians entertain nightly. Béla Bartók performed three of his famous

compositions inside its glass-lined rooms. The wine cellar, pub, and nightclub/dance club (nightly until 1 am), are widely known. The 24-hour front desk and the support staff have many English speakers. It is the best value in this class of hotel.

★★**Aquaticum Thermal & Wellness Hotel**, €€€€, 4032 Debrecen, Nagyerdei park 1, ☎ 36-52-514-111, fax 36-52-311-730, hotel@aquaticum.hu, www.aquaticum.hu. Doubles are €180 in low season and €200 in high season. A part of the Lido baths (see *Thermal Adventures*), lying in the heart of the

woods, the spa provides dozens of economical packages for lifestyle changes, beauty treatments, recuperation, and rejuvenation. Beauticians, therapists, doctors, and nurses, the 24-hour front desk, and the

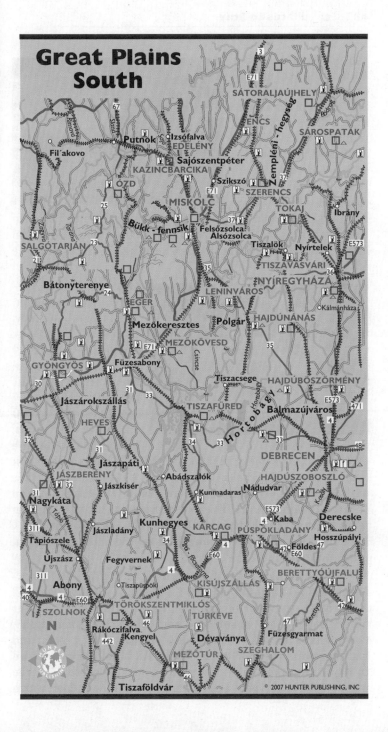

# Great Plains
# South

SÁTORALJAÚJHELY

ENCS

Putnok  Izsófalva
EDELÉNY
Fil'akovo  Sajószentpéter
KAZINCBARCIKA
ÓZD  Szikszó
MISKOLC
Bükk - fennsík  Felsőzsolca
Alsózsolca
SALGÓTARJÁN  Tiszalök  Nyírtelek
TISZAVASVÁRI
NYÍREGYHÁZA
Bátonyterenye  LENINVÁROS
EGER
Mezőkeresztes  Polgár  HAJDÚNÁNÁS
Kálmánháza
MEZŐKÖVESD
GYÖNGYÖS  Füzesabony
Tiszacsege  HAJDÚBÖSZÖRMÉNY
Jászárokszállás  TISZAFÜRED  Balmazújváros
HEVES
DEBRECEN
Jászapáti  Abádszalók  HAJDÚSZOBOSZLÓ
JÁSZBERÉNY  Jászkisér  Nádudvar
Kunmadaras
Nagykáta  Kaba  Derecske
Jászladány  Kunhegyes  PÜSPÖKLADÁNY  Hosszúpályi
Tápiószele  KARCAG  Földes
Újszász  Fegyvernek
Abony  Tiszapüspöki  KISÚJSZÁLLÁS  BERETTYÓÚJFALU
SZOLNOK  TÖRÖKSZENTMIKLÓS  TÚRKEVE
Rákóczifalva  Dévaványa  Füzesgyarmat
Kengyel  MEZŐTÚR  SZEGHALOM
Tiszaföldvár

Zempléni - hegység

SÁROSPATAK

SZERENCS

TOKAJ  Ibrány

Hortobágy

Berettyó

N

© 2007 HUNTER PUBLISHING, INC

support staff have many English speakers. In-room phone, SAT TV, air-conditioning, and mini-bar are room basics. Several different restaurants add spice to the cuisine. The Aqua Restaurant always has  live music and a Hungarian/international cuisine. The Régi Vigado restaurant with its earthenware oven, built to model an old Hungarian csárda (country restaurant), serves cuisine of the Hungarian plains.

 **Garden Hotel**, €€-€€€, 5000 Szolnok, Tiszaliget sétány, ☎ 36-56-520-530, fax 36-56-520-540, info@ gardenhotel.hu, www. gardenhotel.hu. 21,500 HUF per night/person plus 200 HUF tax per night. While a bit on the pricey side, it is right next to the thermal baths of Szolnok (see *Thermal Adventures*). In-house sauna/massages are extra. Rooms have in-room phone, cable TV, mini-bar, and Internet connections. The restaurant is superb, supplemented by a bar. Extras include tennis (courts next door), horseback riding, rowing, hang gliding, and fishing, arranged from the front desk.

★★★**Hortobágy Máta Club Hotel**, €€, 4071 Hortobágy-Máta, ☎ 36-52-369-020, fax 36-52-369-027, hortobágyhotel@ axelerol.hu, www.hortobagyhotel.hu. An affordable four-star hotel. Doubles are about €83 and cabins are about €168. Cabins have a full kitchen, cable TV, baths, living room, and bedrooms and they include a stable. All hotel rooms have an in-room mini-bar, cable TV, and a balcony/porch. A large indoor cold-water pool and a smaller shallow indoor warm water pool supplement the gym and sauna. The staf is English-speaking at the 24-hour front desk. Several restaurants serve Hungarian cuisine. At night, the bar provides music and a place to meet. The hotel has a huge equine complex, which includes a field for eventing, jumping, and an indoor equine stadium, making it a

center for horse shows and events. In addition, it is in walking

distance of the Nine-Hole Bridge (see *Itineraries*) and the Hortobagy Csárda. Travel packages emphasize the Plains culture, horseback riding, hunting, and fishing. There are also less active programs, such as pottery and bird watching. Csikós cowboys and their herds range over the surrounding area.

**Aranyhomok Hotel**, €-€€€, H-6000 Kecskemét, Kossuth tér 3, 36-76-503-730, fax 36-76-503-731, hotel@hotelaranyhomok.hu, www.hotelaranyhomok.hu. Newly remodeled in 2005, the basic facilities of the hotel spa are included in the

room rate, making it a high value for the money. The high-season rate is 21,250 HUF per night for two persons in an air-conditioned double with a balcony. Included are breakfast, cable TV with some English sta-

tions, mini-bar, tele-
phone, room service,
bath, and the use of the
sauna, indoor and out-
door pools, fitness
room, and steam bath.
You can try your luck at
the casino in the hotel.
The restaurant and bar
are both open from 7
am to 11 pm.

## Three Star

**Sóház Hotel**, €€, 5000
Szolnok, Sóház út 4, ☎ 36-
56-516-560, reserve@
sohazhotel.hu, www.
sohazhotel.hu. At 13,500
HUF per person/per night,
it does not offer a large
array of support services
and there is no in-house
restaurant. But it does offer
a small kitchen in each "apartment." So it is possible to fix
your own meals. Catered breakfast and room service is
offered by the hotel in association with several local restaurants, all within walking distance. Add to that a tennis court
and secured parking in the courtyard, a 24-hour front desk,
SAT TV, Internet connection, an in-room telephone, and a
shower/bathroom. All the rooms are-conditioned. The hotel is
in walking distance of most sites in the area, and you are next
to the Tisza River (ask for a river view).

★**Cívis Hotel Délibáb**, €€,
H-4200 Hajdúszoboszló,
József Attila út 4 ☎ 36-52-360-
366, fax 36-52-362-059,
delibab@civishotels.hu, www.
civishotels.hu. €66. This is
probably the deal in the three-
star category. Although com-

fortable, it is rated three instead of four stars because the rooms do not have air-conditioning, and it can get hot. But don't let that put you off. Individual rooms may have portable air. And everything is available for a spa vacation. Non-smoking rooms, in-room SAT TV, direct-dial phones, mini-bar are a mere introduction to the extraordinary savings at the hotel spa. The hotel medical department supports guests with individually tailored programs, in addition to the public Hajdúszoboszló spa, and provides physical examinations, massages, hydro-, electro-, and physical therapies in association with the Hajdúszoboszló main spa. There is also a sauna, solarium, hairdressers, manicures, pedicures, beauty parlor, room service and gift shop. The Restaurant Szoboszló has international and Hungarian cuisine with live gypsy music in the evenings, Restaurant Bocskai features an outdoor Mediterranean terrace and Restaurant Pávai-Vajna has a continental atmosphere along with a bar. There is also an automatic double-aisle bowling alley, darts, billiards, and the hotel's own thermal pool.

**The Trófea Vadászház**, €-€€, 4181 Nádudvar, Hajdúszoboszlói útfél, ☎ 36-54-525-535, fax 36-54-480-704, trofea@ nagisz.hu, www.hotels. hu/trofeavadaszhaz. At €32 to €40 per person per night, the lodge is at the

edge of the Hortobágy puszta (flat plains) on the outskirts of the town and surrounded with marsh and woods. Though built in the 1990s, with its thatched-roof design, it evokes an image of the Middle Ages. However, every room is air-conditioned and spacious, with its own bath, Internet connection, phone, color TV, minibar and queen-sized beds. Tours and personal excursions can be arranged from the 24-hour front desk, including horseback riding, hunting, fishing, and boating.  There is a bar and café, as well as a fine restaurant, serving international, Hungarian, and vegetarian cuisine. A favorite for birders, the hotel is in prime avian territory. There are six long-horned owl nests near the hotel. Can you find them? The room rate includes breakfast, sauna, and a fishing package.

 ★★**Hotel Mátyás Király**, €-€€, 4200 Hajdúszoboszló, Mátyás király sétány 17, ☎ 36-52-360-200, fax 36-52-361-974, matyashotel@ axelero.hu, www. matyashotel.hu. Low-season doubles for two people are 16,800 HUF and in high season about 19,000 HUF. Breakfast, thermal bath, the "bubbling bath," an outdoor summer swimming pool, sauna and the fitness room are included in the rate, plus hotel transfer. Although without air-conditioning, an astounding round of amenities makes up for it, including tours and excursions sponsored by the hotel itself. Folklore and karaoke regularly accompany meals in the restaurants (Renaissance, Span-

ish, Hungarian), in addition to garden parties and poolside entertainment. The foods can range from wellness-conscious meals to sumptuous calorie-riddled cakes by a superb kitchen staff. Cave baths, diving pool, indoor-outdoor swimming pool, Jacuzzi and solarium are supplemented with beauticians as well as a doctor, physical therapist, and nursing staff. With proven medicinal waters, the bath complex provides aromatherapy, and individually tailored skin, bone, and muscle treatments. Their wellness packages can cut costs down to less than €60 per day per person, including use of all their spa facilities.

## Less than Three Star

For this classification in particular, it is important to check with Tourinform (see *Appendix*). They verify facilities and can help find what is most suitable for your tastes and wallet. Many villages and farms open up special rooms, and some smaller places include a swimming pool, air-conditioning, and plenty of amenities that may compete with a highly rated hotel. Plus, you make friends with the locals.

### Lajosmizse

★**Tanyacsárda Restaurant, Horse Farm and Guest House**, €-€€, 6050 Lajosmizse, Bene 625, ☎ 36-76-356-250, or 36-76-356-802, fax 36-76-356-576, tanyacsarda@tanyacsarda.hu, www.tanyacsarda.hu (see also *Adventures* and *Places to Eat*). Tanyacsárda combines its own facilities with those of several other hotels (see website) to provide lodging for guests. At 11,600 HUF per double room per night at the csárda ranch itself, don't expect a bevy of amenities (add 1,500 HUF per person for breakfast), but do expect a Csikos cowboy atmosphere, with stables, horses, and horse shows (sometimes daily) that attract tour groups from all over the world. Add to that one of the finest restaurants in the area.

Accommodations are comfortable, and there is an English-friendly front desk.

# ■ Places to Eat

## Hortobágy

**Club Hotel**, 4071 Hortobágy-Máta, ☎ 36-52-369-020, fax 36-52-369-027, hortobagyhotel@axelero.hu, www.hortobagyhotel.hu (see also *Places to Stay*). There are show grounds for

| DINING PRICE CHART | |
|---|---|
| Price for an entrée, with tax | |
| € | Under $10 |
| €€ | $10-$25 |
| €€€ | Over $25 |

horseback competitions, superior stables, and a bevy of Csikós cowboys here. The cuisine in each of its restaurants is superb. An excellent stopover for a meal.

**Hortobágy Csárda**, €-€€, 4071 Hortobágy, Petõfi tér 1, ☎ 36-52-589-339, 36-52-589-144, fax 36-52-589-338. Inside an inn that has been there for over 300 years (see *Itineraries*), the csárda's menu is in English, but the food is pure Hun-

garian with an emphasis on the Puszta (Plains) of Hungary. An average entrée will be about 2,000 to 3,500 HUF. Enjoy its gypsy entertainment in the evenings, superb cuisine, and then walk over the famous nine-hole bridge next to the csárda as the sun sets on the Hungarian plains.

## Jászberény

**Aranysas Vendéglõ**, €, 5100 Jaszberény, Jákóhalmi út 11, ☎/fax 36-57-402-189. Open Sun-Thur, 10 am to 10 pm, and Fri-Sat, 10 am to 12 pm. The average cost of a meal is about 2,000 HUF. The cuisine and the atmosphere is like that of a Hungarian country csárda (old country inn), but with a touch of elegance.

# Karcag

Off Highway 4, south of Debrecen, on the western side of the Hortobágy National Park, is a hotel with an excellent restaurant. The **Hotel Fehér Holló**, €-€€, 5300 Karcag, Püspökladányi út 3-5, will cost about 2,400 HUF on average. They serve Hungarian as well as international food and are open daily from 10 am to 10 pm.

# Debrecen

**Aranybika Restaurant**, €-€€, in the Hotel Aranybika, H-4025 Debrecen, Piac út 11-15, ☎ 36-52-508-600, fax 36-52-421-834, www.civishotel.hu, will cost anywhere from 1,500 to about 3,500 HUF. Located in the Civis Grand Hotel in Debrecen, this restaurant should not be missed for good Hungarian cuisine and an elegant ambience. Live gypsy music adds to exquisite meal preparations. However, the word in this hotel is variety. The hotel also has a Gösser Beer-House, Tokaji Wine House, and a confectionary (see Places to Stay).

# Mezõtúr

**Gyöngyhalász Étterem**, 5400 Mezõtúr, Kossuth út 44, ☎ 36-56-352-330, €. Average cost of meal is about 1,800 HUF. Open 9 am-11 pm daily. Their specialty is Hungarian fish, although their menu is a complete cross-section of every kind of Hungarian dish. The quality is excellent, at a reasonable price.

## Szolnok

**Tisza Szállo és Gyógyfürdő** (on the website, click on Étterem), €€, reserve@hoteltisza.hu, www.hotltisza.hu, 5000 Szolnok, Verseghy park 2, ☎ 36-56-371-155, fax 36-56-421-520. The average cost of a meal is about 2,000 HUF for some of the finest cuisine in the Tisza lakes area. Open 7 am to 11 pm daily. The Hungarian and international offerings have won several awards from the Association of Hungarian Chefs and Confectioners. After a relaxing day in the hotel spa, dinner in the elegance of this restaurant is exquisite.

## Kecskemét

**Három Gúnár Restaurant**, €-€€, 6000 Kecskemét, Batthány út 1-7, ☎ 36-76-483-948, fax 36-76-481-253. With an average tab from 2,000 up to 4000 HUF, you can expect elegance. The pink and white entrance seems almost garish until you get inside, where a white and dark walnut air-conditioned interior and background stereo introduces you to an atmosphere of upscale leisure. The cuisine is Hungarian with a few international selections and a superb wine list. Goose has been a Hungarian specialty for centuries. The libatoros (goose) here includes leg of goose, filled goose breast, roasted goose liver, served with creamed mashed potatoes, stuffed baked apples, and steamed cabbage with a unique sweet flavor. The wine bar is superb, and you can bed down for the night in the hotel (good quality rooms with balcony).

## Lajosmizse

**Tanyacsárda Restaurant, Horse Farm and Guest House**, €-€€ 6050, Lajosmizse, Bene 625, ☎ 36-76-350-010, or 36-76-356-166, fax 36-76-356-576, tanyacsarda@

tanyacsarda.hu, www.
tanyacsarda.hu (see also
*Adventures* and *Places to
Stay*). Open daily from 11 am
to 10 pm. In addition to
numerous other awards, the
Tanyacsárda has been named
the best restaurant in the
country, and it is no wonder.
Try the cold-stuffed pike perch. Freshly caught pike perch fil-
lets, with their delicate white meat, are seasoned in white
pepper, nutmeg, and chopped parsley leaves, drenched in a
house gelatin and combined with quail eggs, shrimps and
olives. These are rolled in a house marinade with bay leaves
and simmered for an hour. Follow this with the divine
kecskemét apricot cream soup.

**Gerébi Kúria Hotel and Horse Yard**, 6050 Lajosmizse,
Alsólajos 224, ☎ 36-76-365-555, fax 36-76-356-045, gerebi@
gerebi.hu, www.gerebi.hu. Try the lad catching soup. It is one
of oldest recipes from the Hungarian Plains. The Gerébi is
known for its great food and horse shows, open-pit and
bogrács (Hungarian plains cooking pot) menus, and evening
outdoor cookouts.

# ■ Itineraries

## Jászberény

Wandering all the way from Iran in the 1200s, the
Jász tribe came to the banks of the Zagyva River, a
tributary of the Tisza, and said this is home. Thus
was born the town of Jászberény (www.jaszbereny.
hu). With time, a number of other towns would emerge as
well, developing a regional Hungarian culture with Iranian
roots. Any towns on the map that begin with Jász have their
roots in Jászberény. After Ottoman Leopold I sold the town to
the Knights of the Teutonic Order, whose taxation policies
were renowned, the citizens of Jászberény fell into serfdom.

But their independent spirit would not let this last rest. In a particularly poor crop year, they held an emergency meeting. All the "Jász" towns attended. Knowing that heavy taxation was about to descend upon their small shire, they collected 500,000 gold florins, a king's ransom for that time. They were going to try to buy off their new rulers with a lump sum payment and thus escape taxation. Empress Mother Theresa ended the sacrifice, however, when she restored the lands and semi-independence to the Iranian descendents. The Jászkúnság made the agreement with Empress Theresa in 1745, in which they also agreed to make the lump sum payment as a security pledge in place of their taxes, thus witnessing in hard cash that they were loyal to the Hapsburg Empire. They succeeded in paying the entire sum in 1751, thus insur-

ing a semi-auton-
omy that lasted for
the next 150 years.

Yet, despite the Ira-
nian heritage, the
Magyar roots are
strong here as well.
Local legend says
that Attila the Hun
was buried here.
How we love our
pagan roots – sev-

eral other Hungarian towns make the same claim. The center of town is the **Szentháromság tér (Trinity Square)**, bordered by a street that is called Lehel Vezér tér. In Trinity Square, where Lehel Vezér tér intersects with Nagytemplom street, the **Church of the Virgin Mary** dominates the intersection. Originally a 1300s Gothic structure, it was rebuilt after the Turks destroyed it. The reconstruction gave it the current Baroque façade. Its semi-Turkish Baroque spire, so typical of Hungary, is topped by a copy of the Hungarian crown. Also facing the square, the town hall was built in 1839.

Despite Jászberény's Iranian roots, it is unequivocally Magyar, as evidenced by the village **Museum**, which houses one of the artifact treasures of Hungary, the famed **Horn of Lehel**. Lehel was one of the great chieftains of the Magyars as they

*The Horn of Lehel*

led their raids into Europe. In one particularly desperate battle in Germany, Lehel was captured. The German emperor gave him a choice of any two ways to die. Lehel asked for his horn so that he could blow it in the final dramatic seconds of life. When they brought him his horn, he promptly struck the emperor with it, killing him instantly, and announced, even as the German knights closed around him, "Now you will be my slaves." The early Magyars believed that anyone they killed in battle in this life would be their slave in the after-life. The horn is in the Museum at 5 Táncsics M Street, ☎ 36-57-312-753, open 9 am to 4 pm, summer until 5 pm.

The time to visit this town is in the month of August, the harvest time, when fairs and events take place almost every day of the month. In the first week of August the notable **Folk Art Country Fair** (on Margit Island) will offer you plenty of souvenirs. Opening festivities include the "Csángó Procession" (in the main square), folk dancing in the streets, lutes, and violins, and bands, as well as villagers from throughout the region. After the parade, visit the **Camp of Hussars** (Hatvani road at Margit-Sziget Island), where you can see a duplicated encampment from the age of the famous Hussar cavalry, and see enactments of horseback fighting tactics. Within a few days of these events, Jászberény usually hosts the **International Honey Fair** and **Meeting of Bee-Keepers**. As the exact dates may vary, contact Tourinform in Jászberény (see *Appendix*).

The **Zoological and Botanical Garden** at 1 Fémnyomó street, www.jaszberenyzoo.hu is not just a zoo but also a large park with children's playground areas, a petting zoo, and huge habitat cages, where animals live in semi-natural surroundings, including lakes and streams. In a unique program, bears and wolves are kept in the same cage area. When they feed the animals they try to duplicate natural conditions, so the animals must actually use their natural instincts to find the food. The public is invited to watch. The feeding hours are on the website. Soft drink, ice cream, souvenir, and food vendors range across the huge territory.

The thermal spas are open to the public at the **Jásvíz Strand és termálfürdő** (open-air thermal bath), at 5 Hatvani út, ☎ 36-57-412-108, fax 36-57-412-612, open daily 9 am to 7 pm, or alternatively at the **Lehel Sport**

*Lehel Sport Kft*

**Kft**, Szabadidőközpont és termálfürdő, Kiserdei út 10, ☎ 36-57-415-245. Our next destination is south on Route 32 to Szolnok.

## Szolnok

At the junction of the Tisza and Zagyva, the town (www. szolnok.hu) has been at a river crossing for over 900 years and, as a result, many battles have been fought here. It has been totally destroyed and rebuilt five times. On Route 32 from Szolnok, make a right at Baross Gábor, and head straight to the train station. It is one of the most modern in all of Central or Eastern Europe. From the station we head down Baross Gábor út, toward the Tisza River, and make a right at Szapári út (where Baross Gábor út changes to Kossuth Lajos út). As you arrive at útja Templom, the street on your right, it changes to Sóház út on your left.

The yellow cream-colored **Szolnoki Galéria** (Szolnok Gallery), at Templom út 2, is a former synagogue, today a museum for Szolnok's artists and a concert hall most of the year. Before WWII there was a thriving community of Jews in

Szolnok, hence the monument, near the gallery. Built in the 1890s, the beautiful synagogue building was a demonstration of the wealth and influence of the community. The entire population of 2,500 was sent to death camps in WWII. There is no exact count of survivors. Some say 600, others say fewer. But of those few who returned, there was probably too much pain associated with the memory to make head counts. Besides, others now occupied their homes and businesses. There is a very small Jewish community in this town of 78,000 today. They do not keep a high profile.

Now head west on Sóház út. The **Tisza Park** adorns the shoreline in the next block on the right. The **Szigliget Theater** at Tisza Park 1, ☎ 36-56-342-633 or 36-56-423-770, is a combination of Art Nouveau and modern architecture. Theater performances are in Hungarian, not English, even if they advertise English classics.

Now go to the shoreline of the Tisza River and continue the walk east on the Tiszaparti sétány. Look to your left as you arrive at the Vershegy park. You will see the Gyógyfürdő (healing baths) in the Vershegy park 2, today the Neo-Baroque **Tisza Hotel and Medical Bath**, ☎ 36-56-510-810, fax 36-56-421-520, reserve@ hoteltisza.hu, www.hoteltisza.hu. These baths were once reserved for the nobility. They are reputed to cure gynecological, rheumatic, and digestive problems, and the water is used, not just for bathing, but for drinking as well.

If we continue our walk farther, but go one block from the shore onto Sóház út, near the intersection of Damjanich út and Sóház út we will find Kossuth Lajos tér, which spills across Kossuth Lajos út eastward to Szabadsag tér. The **János Damjanich Museum**, at Lajos Kossuth Square 4, has dioramas, paintings and historical material from the battle of

Szolnok in the 1848-49 Revolution, as well as a history of the Jász, Nagykun, and Szolnok counties. János Damjanich was the leader of the Hungarian patriots that defeated the forces of Imperial Austria on the plains outside Szolnok.

Now cross Kossuth Lajos út to Vershegy út, which takes us to Gutenberg tér (Gutenberg Square). At Gutenberg Square 4 we will find the **Szolnok Artist's Colony**, center for such great Hungarian artists as Béla Ivány, Grünwald, Vilmos Novák Aba, Pál Páczay, János Vaszary, and Adolf Fényes. Established in 1902, many of the works that emerged from the colony are at the Szolnok Gallery.

Leaving Szolnok, take Route 442 south to Route 4, head east to Route 46 in Törökszentmiklós, then south toward Mezõtúr.

## Mezõtúr

A composite of two towns, Mezõ and Túr, situated on the edge of the "Nagykunság" region, this town was already famous in medieval times for its potters and fairs. The history of the town's 500-year pottery tradition is shown in the **Túri Fazekas Múzeum**, turi.mezotur@museum.hu, at Bajcsy-Zsilinszky út 41, open 10-12 am and 3-5 pm daily. It is closed Monday. The pottery tradition is carried on today by the internationally renowned Béla Badár, whose works fill the rooms of the **Fazekas Artist and Memorial House** at Sugár út 28. To be a master potter, in ancient times you generally belonged to a guild, most often in a particular family. The secrets of the guild were passed from father to son. The traditions and methods were nearly destroyed by the Industrial Revolution, but in Mezõtúr the traditions have been revived. The Túri Fazekas Múzeum has pottery courses that use the ancient guild methods (many free) during the months of June and July. English is halting, but, you may want to give it a try.

Mezõtúr also has its public spa, **Strandfürdõ és Fedett uszoda** (lido and indoor swimming pool), 5400 Mezõtûr, Erzsébet Liget, ☎ 36-56-350-252, mezotur@tourinform.hu. The top floor of the indoor swimming pool building holds a display on Tamás Faragó, European and world water polo champion, and native son. The medicinal water that supplies the swimming pool and bath has a high content of salt, alkali hydrogen carbonate, iodine, and fluorine. They have treated locomotor, rheumatoid, gynecological, urological, and allergy related illnesses with its healing qualities. It is located on a six-acre park, with a lake and a sports center. The baths include indoor and outdoor pools, an adventure pool, a children's paddle pool, eateries and medical professionals.

From Highway 42 in the town center we now take the road that heads toward Túrkeve.

## Túrkeve

Passing through Túrkeve we can stop at the **Túrkeve Finta Múzeum**, 5420 Attila út 1, ☎ 36-56-361-183, open 9 am-12 am and 2 pm-5 pm daily, closed Monday. The permanent exhibitions of two great Hungarian sculptors, Sándor Finta, who worked with Rodin, and Gergely Finta, his brother, leads us to another connecting link to greater Europe and to America. Vince Korda's mementos and those of his brothers, Sándor Korda and Zoltán Korda, are on permanent exhibition. Vince Korda was an Oscar-winning director in 1940. Sándor Korda was the founder of the British film industry and Zoltán Korda was the American director of the *The Jungle Book*.

Visit in May during the annual **Shepherd Festival of Keve.** The festival brings together food, drink, (some fine wines of course), shepherds, and many Csikós cowboys from all over Hungary. Their music, dance, games and competitions celebrate the ancient arts of the shepherds. The unique National Sheep Shearing Competition and the National Shepherding Competition seek to find the best in the nation. The National Shepherding Competition pits the skills of the shepherds against each other in controlling a moving mass of animals in all kinds of situations. In some events, there is a cross-cultural inter-active approach. You can join in and learn how to do it yourself. The National Pastoral Singing Contest will bring together the best in folk music, and then there is the Shepherd's Ball. This is all capped with the Mutton Cooking Competition and a two-day folk arts and crafts fair. A folk funhouse for children runs in conjunction with the fair. Get information from Tourinform, or from the town Mayor's

Office, 5420 Túrkeve, Petõfi tér 1, ☎ 36-56-361-111, fax 36-56-361-030, turkeve@externet.hu.

Before you leave Túrkeve you may want to try the thermal spa at **Gyógy-és Strand-fürdõ (Health Spa and Lido)**, 5420 Túrkeve, Gyomai út 1, ☎ 36-56-361-313. The 72°C/161°F water is drawn from depths of over 7,000 feet, cooled, and then funneled into the baths. Alkali, hydrogen carbonate, iodine and sulphides turn the water into a curative stream. There is also a sauna, various massage treatments, a gym, and medical support personnel.

Leaving Túrkeve, we head north toward Kisújszállás, to the intersection of Route 4 and head northeast past Karcag to the town of Püspökladány, where we find the village of Újtelep on the north side of Route 4. Entering Újtelep we follow the road signs that take us to Nádudvar.

## Nádudvar

There are two main churches here, the Catholic Church and the Calvinist Church. In the 16th century almost the entire town converted to Calvinism, and it has been a home of Calvinism ever since. But its fame lies in its pottery, a tradition going back hundreds of years. The clay is taken from the local clay mine. When it is glazed it takes on a unique deep black color. The potter's guild has made good use of it. World-recognized works using floral patterns and a scoured gravel appearance have won prizes in numerous international exhibits. It's a good place to pick up an original, and to see the process in action at the workshop of Lajos Fazekas Jr., a master craftsman. He is at the **Potter's House**, Fõ út 159. In the town center, the **Baroque Calvin-**

ist Church was originally built in 1774, then rebuilt in 1878, whereas the early Classicist **Roman Catholic Church** was built in 1819.

Marsh lands, flat lands, and trails surround the town, offering some unusual adventuring possibilities. You can find guides and information at the **Trófea Vadászház**, 4181 Nádudvar, Hajdúszoboszlói útfél ☎ 36- 54-525-535 fax 36-54-480-704 trofea@nagisz.hu www. hotels.hu/trofeavadaszhaz (see *Places to Stay*).

Leaving the rural areas we now head to a more densely populated area, Hajdúszoboszló. We take the road back to Highway 4, and go east, or we can take the rural route, right from Nádudvar, heading east toward Debrecen, keeping our eyes open for the signs that read Hajdúszoboszló.

## Hajdúszoboszló

Prince István Bocskay of Transylvania gave large parts of the eastern Hortobagy plains to the Hajdúu people, who had fought valiantly against the Hapsburgs. The Hajdú established a number of towns, all with the prefix of "Hajdú." But the fame of Hajdúszoboszló has come from its thermal water, which has attracted people from throughout the world. The **Hajdúszoboszló Gyógyfürdõ (Hajdúszoboszló Healing Baths)** are at 4200 Hajdúszoboszló, Szent István Park 1-3, ☎ 36-52-558-558, fax 36-52-360-039, info@hajduszoboszlogyogyfurdo.hu, www. hajduszoboszlogyogyfurdo.hu. The spa's 75°C/167°F thermal waters boil up from 3,300 feet below ground with astounding curative properties. It is said that a two- to three-week stay has resulted in up to 90% improvement in various ambulatory, gynecological and skin disorders. An Iodine-salt steam rises from the water surface here, creating a unique micro-climate which is hostile to bacterial growth and marvelously healthy for the body. Couple that with 2,000 hours of sunshine a year, 62 acres surrounding the baths, rowboats, pedal boats, and the Aquapark. The newly built park includes adventure pools, children's pools, canals, a giant slide for the adventurous, a four-track racing slide, a crazy stream, and an even crazier 101-m/331-foot black hole (not for the clauustrophobic). This is complemented by hotels, eateries, grassy lounging areas, and entertainment (see *Thermal Adventures*).

The bathing tradition goes back hundreds of years. Even the 18th-century St. László church is decorated with frescoes showing the discovery of the medicinal waters. Also on the outskirts of town are the **Béke Medicinal Baths** at Mátyás Király út 10 (see *Thermal Adventures*), and several other three- and four-star spa hotels, all within three blocks of each other on Mátyás Király út.

There are two small museums in Hajdúszoboszló. The collection of the **István Bocskai Museum** includes a fairly complete village and ethnographic collection at Bocskai út 12, 14, and 21. And the **Potter's House** at Ady út 2 displays the black pottery of Nádudvar (see *Nádudvar*) and a collection of artifacts from the 19th and 20th centuries. Having finished these few sights, the temptation may be to head toward Debrecen, Hungary's second-largest city, to find lodging. But I urge you to follow the main road north out of town instead, until you intersect with Route 33, where you make a left and go to the town of Hortobágy.

# Hortobágy & Hortobágy National Park

The town of Hortobágy (www.hortobagy.hu) lies on the middle of the Hortobágy National Park (HNP, www.hnp.hu). The HNP is a World Heritage Site and one of the most fantastic bird nesting areas in the world (see also the *Tisza* section). It has Europe's largest protected grasslands. Its 14,000 square

*Western entrance to the Hortobágyi National Park*

km/5,405 square miles harbor vast plains, marshes and bird sanctuaries, dotted with fishponds, lakes, and streams. Towns in the Hortobágy protected zone are small collections of buildings, where a few people, descendents of shepherds and horsemen, live amidst a flat windswept landscape. Csikós herders traditionally did not build houses, but temporary shelters, as they moved with their herds from place to place. Various csárda (country inns) were located at various road stops, sometimes next to a bridge, a necessity because of the frequent flooding of the Tisza. When the Tisza was first dammed in the 1800s, its meandering stopped, and wide areas of the "Puszta" (wide flat alkaline grassland), began to dry out. With time, the government reopened channels and resurrected ancient lakebeds, to restore the ecosystem of the Hortobagy. Some of the ancient bridges remain, such as the **Nine-Hole Bridge** on Highway 33. When we arrive at the bridge, we are on the western end of the town of Hortobagy, or what we might call, simply, the old csárda way stop.

The 300-year-old csárda country inn rises, with its red roof and white plaster walls, next to the road at the head of the bridge, as it did when salt traders carried their cargo from Debrecen, heading for the bustling cities of the west. A few other whitewashed buildings are set back

*Nine-Hole Bridge*

from the road, hiding
the town from view.
Several souvenir
stands line Petőfi tér
(Petőfi Square), on the
south face of the
csárda. They sell wood
carvings, leather-laced
goods, handmade
whips, hats, smoking
pipes, urns, and jack-
ets from the Puszta
flatlands. In a stag-
gered line they lead
inevitably to the **Pas-**

**toral Museum**, set back on the eastern end of the square.
The museum building was once the coach house of the csárda.
Today, its memories are replayed with displays of the history
of the Csikós herders and the flora and fauna of the Puszta or
grassland. Stop in at the csárda (see *Places to Eat*). Although
the food is on the pricey side, the menu is the authentic shepherd food of the Puszta. The rich full-bodied flavors stay on
the palate for hours. But walking through the small village
behind Petőfi tér will take us to two public buildings, the **Old
Town Hall** (19th-century), and the **Hortobágy Gallery of
Art** (with paintings of the Puszta plains, its wildlife and its
culture).

Farther up the village main street is the **Hortobágy Puszta
Animal Park** (Pusztai Állatpark), a small hostel for native
species, the "kuvasz" dog, the domesticated buffalo, Hungarian grey cattle, Nóniusz horse, and dozens of breeds from the
heartlands of Hungary not seen anywhere else in the world.
From the fence line, Csikós herders sometimes work the
herds within camera distance. In the distance, via the trail
that winds from the back of the village, you can see the
**Hortobágy Máta Club Hotel** (see *Places to Stay*). You can
also reach it by driving from the csárda across the bridge to
the road at the right on the other side of the bridge. The
Hortobágy Máta Club is also the home of the state breeding
farms. Csikós herders, dressed in their traditional black hats,

blue baggy trousers and shirts, and black boots hold public shows on its grounds.

Plan your stay to coincide with the **Bridge Fair** on the 19th and 20th of August, when thousands of folk items are on sale, and there are games, food, drink, music, and folk dancing.

The **Hortobágy International Equestrian Days** are held here on the first weekend in July. Csikós sheepherders and cattlemen compete in drawing water, lassoing, herding the gigantic twisted-horned grey cattle, sheep, and herds of horses, using the stick and the long whip. There is ubiquitous food and wine.

This is a time to try the goulash, a product of the plains, or the slambuc (a dish of potatoes, pasta, and salt, for hard times). As you would expect, there is a goulash cook-off every year.

But these experiences are not the full story of the Hortobagy. Always, there is the wildlife of the air, even in the most remote areas. One birdwatcher claimed to have seen a flock of over 36,000 white cranes. As you travel the roads of the region, keep your eyes peeled for what appear to be huge bundles of sticks on chimneys and poles. These are stork nests. There are so many that their nests are often seen from the roadside, or as you walk village streets.

Having finished our exposure to the world of the Csikós on the Hortobagy, we can head back on 33 and take the road north to Balmazújváros and from there, continuing on the same road we veer eastward, toward Hajdúböszörmény.

## Hajdúböszörmény

Hajdúböszörmény was the capital of the hajdús footsoldiers of the 17th century. Hajdúböszörmény is built around the original ring defense system, centered at Bocskai tér, where once a ring road circled the protected inner settlement, fortified with an outer palisade and a system of fortified ditches. The Hajdúsagi museum is at Kossuth út 1. It borders Bocskai tér. It once hid a four-cell basement

*Hajdúböszörmény City Hall*

dungeon where Bandi Angyal, the hero of many local ballads, was once imprisoned. The Museum displays the Hajdú people's history up until their defeat in the Revolution of 1956.

Hajdúböszörmény's honey cake is legendary, perhaps due to the types of flowers the bees pollinate in the surrounding country. As with other Hungarian pastries, it is called sutemény (shoe-teh-main), and sold in most pastry shops. The local thermal baths reputedly bubble with healing waters. At less than 600 HUF per day, the **Városi Fürdő (City Baths)** are at Uzsok tér 1 and promote healing with natural sodium chloride, bromide, iodide and fluoride concentrations. The complex is in the town park, which includes sport pools, children's pools, a sauna, and eateries. After the baths, eat at the **Hajdú Hotel restaurant**, at Petőfi Sándor út 2, for excellent cuisine and wine, and then perhaps either bed down, or head for Debrecen (about eight miles), southeast on Route 35.

## Debrecen

Just as Budapest dominates the west, Debrecen (www. debrecen.hu), the second largest city in the country, dominates the east. It has always been a major regional center and acquired municipal status in the end of the 14th century. Sitting on the edge of the Hortobagy, it developed into a market town, and what we might call the Chicago stockyards of Hungary. From here, the long-horned grey cattle of the Hortobágy plains were gathered into vast herds and then driven to Prague and Vienna. Debrecen was also the center of Calvinist reform, and so powerful was the Protestant Revolution here that Debrecen came to be called "The Calvinist Rome." A 1552 royal proclamation allowed Protestants to settle here. Three years later the Turks invaded. Ironically, the Calvinists had less trouble from the Turks than from their Hapsburg Catholic brothers. Today there are plenty of events, restaurants, hangouts, promenades, baths, and festivals. Every year the great **Military Band Festival** brings military bands from the USA, Russia, Europe, and the Far East for a parade, and music competition (check with Tourinform on dates and times).

Kossuth Lajos declared independence from the Hapsburg Empire on April 14, 1849. It was on the steps of the **Calvinist Church**, which had been built only 28 years before, in 1821. The church is at the town square, Kossuth tér, its tall bright yellow spires topped with black domes faced with clocks. A church has always stood on this spot since the 13th century, built and rebuilt through the wars. For a few hundred HUF you can walk up the western spire for a camera's-eye view of the surrounding city. Afterward, walk across the square to Kálvin tér 16, the **Calvinist Reformed College**, which was founded by former professors and students from Krakow and Wittenberg in 1538. It houses one of the finest Protestant Biblical collections anywhere. The library museum also has a collection of 6,000 medallions and medals going back to 1831, and a 33,000-piece micro and macro crystal collection from throughout the world. An eclectic mixture of artifacts includes the briefcase of Kossuth Lajos (the leader of the Hungarian freedom movement), Kazinczy's rifle (Ferenc Kazinczy was the leader of the Hungarian language reform movement in the 19th century), and Csokonai's flute (Mihály Csokonai Vitéz was a 19th century poet). ☎ 36-52-414-774, ext 1923; open Tue-Sat 9 am to 5 pm and Sun 9 am to 1 pm. They are closed Monday.

The **Déri Museum** is at Déri tér 1 (off Hunyádi János út, on Bethlen, to Múzeum út, and Déri tér is off Múzeum út), open 10 am to 6 pm daily, except Monday, ☎ 36-52-322-207. Inside the Neo-Baroque domed structure is the richest cultural-historical collection of Hungary. The four statues in the entrance were done by Ference Medgyessy and won the Grand Prix in the Paris Exhibition in 1937. One of the greatest assemblages of paintings in Hungarian art is "The Trilogy" done by Mihály Munkácsy, which works on the themes of Christ before Pilate and Golgotha. Dioramas, paintings, specimens of minerals, birds, and animals are a cross-section of Eastern Hungary.

Tourinform and Aranybika Hotel (see *Places to Stay*), both front Kossuth Square, and they can direct you to the **Csokonai Theatre**, at Kossuth utca 10, several blocks up. You may want to take your car, down Péterfia út and then left at Kossuth út, two blocks. But for fun and excitement, and for a cross-section of natural history as well, head out to the **Great Forest** and the **Debrecen Zoo**. Take Simonyi út off of Hadházu út and head north. Spreading out over 2,672 acres, it harbors nearly 800 species of native plants and many "old forest" stands. Plan more than a day. The zoo, at Ady Endre út 1, has 1,400 different animals and 170 species from four different continents. Open 9 am to 9 pm daily, the entrance fee is 1000 HUF. ☎ 36-52-310-065. The zoo is bordered by an amusement park and has plenty of places to eat.

You should also take advantage of the **Aquaticum**, which attracts people from all over the world (see *Thermal Adventures*). It is in the Great Forest at Nagyerdei park 1, ☎ 36-52-514-182, fax 36-52-311-730 or 346-883, kozpont@aquaticum. hu, www.aquaticum. hu. It is part of the Aquaticum Thermal and Wellness Hotel, but you do not have to stay at the hotel to avail yourself of the public baths and adventure pools.

Festivals take place every week throughout the year. But several are gaining international prominence. Try the **Debrecen Flower Festival** and **Flower Week** every August, usually between the 15th and 20th. A huge gala parade brings bands, horse troupes, dancers, floats, and literally thousands of vendors and street performers. It is accompanied by concerts, fireworks, exhibitions, and dozens of open-air theatrical performances, many of them centered near the great church in Kossuth Square. But the parade marches all the way up to the Great Forest, where it enters a stadium. The rest of the night is devoted to a huge show. Appropriately, the **Borsodi Beer Fest** takes place at the same time, usually between Rózsa utca and City Hall. Jazz fans should try Debrecen during the second week of September. Organized since 1972, the **Debrecen Jazz Days** attract internationally known jazz stars. Their performances are capped with festivals of food and song.

Debrecen regularly hosts international sporting events. The 14th **European Hot-Air Balloon Championship** was held here during the 22nd though the 29th of May in 2005, accompanied by spectacular balloon-filled skies, and a chance to take a ride as well. The **Debrecen Marathon** is held the first or second week of April, and is a part of the Hungarian National championships, but it attracts spectators and participants from all over the globe, as does the **Male and Female Individual European Championship of Gymnastics**, which was held here in the first week of June in Fõnix Hall. Check with Tourinform for the scheduled events (see *Appendix*).

From Debrecen, head to Nyírbátor by taking Route 4 north, but before you leave the city take Route 471 to the northeast.

## Nyírbátor

The Turks left some buildings standing in Nyírbátor (www.nyirbator.hu). The result is evident in the 15th-century **Church of St. György** (Báthory út 24), with its harangtorony (belltower). It is a Gothic masterpiece. Originally a Catholic hall-church with Gothic vaulting over the nave, because of its magnificent acoustical qualities concerts are frequently held inside. The wooden **bell tower** (harangtorony) alongside the church is a superb example of medieval wood construction and craftsmanship. Not a single nail holds it together – only wooden pegs, spikes, and notched wood. The National Museum in Budapest now displays the superb Renaissance carved pew that was once here.

*Church of St. György*

A walk through town may also take you to the **Báthory István Museum** (Károlyi út 15), the old monastery of the Grey Friars. Its local history exhibition includes relics from the Renaissance and an exhibition on the noble families that once dominated the region.

Time your visit for the second Friday of July. Every year, it is the week of the **Winged Dragon Festival**, which attracts performers and artists from all over the world. Artists perform while folk festival cook-outs and other activities are being conducted in town. Fireworks, puppets, street-side vendors, water games, kite-flying contests, food and wine, attract thousands.

Depending on your time, you may now want to get a taste of the "far east" of Hungary. Head north on Route 471 for the region known as the Szabolcs-Szatmár-Bereg megye (Szabolcs-Szatmár-Bereg Counties).

We will continue and turn north and then east again with the road as it melds into 491, and drive east until we enter the village of Mátészalka. From Mátészalka we can take the road that leads north to Vásárosnamény, which hugs the north-eastern border with Ukraine.

# Szabolcs-Szatmár-Bereg Megye

Szabolcs-Szatmár-Bereg Megye (or County) is at the headwaters of the Tisza River. Set on a higher plateau than the flatlands of the Hortobagy, it is at the foot of the Carpathians. The peat-moss marshes surrounding Lakes Nyires, Bábtava, Zsid, and Bence contain eight species of peat moss, strawberries, cranberries, the round leaved sundew, cotton rush, willows, and the mysterious alder marshes. Thick green foliage and the flowers of the duckweed, lady fern, bearded shield-fern and water violet fill the alder marshes. The waters are crystal clear, but it seems you can't penetrate the deep black mirror finish. It gets its color from the thick black spongy bottom of the stream and lakebeds, an accumulation of rich soil and plant life. Csaronda means "black water," the name attached to the waters of the Szátmar-Bereg Plain. It requires a permit to visit some these areas (check with Tourinform, see *Appendix*). Significantly, the fresh hay fields of the villages have made this the last redoubt of the disappearing

*Corncrake*

**corncrake**, a bird that depends on the natural interconnection of the grasslands and forest with the haystacks and barns. About 100 of these nesting birds still survive. It is an area for canoeing on slow rivers, leisurely cycling, and horseback riding. Fishing is amply rewarded. There are 50 species of fish, and prize catches are not uncommon.

Most villages are within easy walking or bicycle distance of each other, each one with its own church. Some 55 churches still have hand-painted interiors from hundreds of years ago, 37 of which date to the Middle Ages. There are 17 wooden belfry towers, over 400 years old, that still chime. In many places thatched huts and old barns border small farm plots. Tourinform can arrange stays with villagers as well as with the traditional hotels and hostels. Souvenirs can often be purchased from the very people who made them, craftsmen who

The Great Plains

have learned their skills from their parents, for generations. And thermal baths sprout from the deep interior of the earth here as well.

## Vásárosnamény

Since Vásárosnamény is a regional center (www.vasaros-nameny.hu), you can get to all the towns in the region from here by bus or by train. The ticket manager's office at the railway station is open week-days from 5:15 am to 6:40 pm and Saturdays and Sundays 6 am to 5 pm. ☎ 36-45-470-745. Bus tickets are bought from the bus drivers. For additional help, contact Tourinform at 33 Szabadság tér, vasarosnameny@tourinform.hu, ☎ 36-45-570-206. Ask for Judit Babinecz.

Located at the junction of the Kraszna River and the Tisza River, Vásárosnamény is known for its free beach on the banks of the Tisza River, the Gergelyugornya, where inns, rental shops, and eateries can be found. Gergelyugornya is also known for its adventure baths, **The Atlantik**, atlantika@axelero.hu, www.atlantika.hu, at Gulácsi út 56, ☎ 36-45-570-112, fax 36-45-472-553. It is open May 15 to June 30, 9 am to 6 pm daily.

During the summer, singing, dancing, and disco programs are featured on the stage of **Gergelyugornya**. The town is a base for canoeing, hiking, and cycling northeastern Hungary, and as a springboard to Carpathian exploration. It is known for its nuts and fruits (notably the red namény apple), and most of the locals work either in agriculture or tourism. There is no cocktail circuit. Small taverns sit isolated amid the shuttered houses and the crickets at night. The four-towered **Tomcsánnyi Castle** remains (1729), looming ghost-like over the town and now closed due to its deteriorating condition. However, at 59 Jókai Mór út, **Miklós Eötvös** built a mansion-castle in 1720, today a listed monument, and also a museum displaying a typical 18th-century schoolhouse, complete with texts, desks, and classroom accessories.

Vásárosnamény is a modern Hungarian village, where cross-stitch embroidery is considered an art worth knowing. There are no factories. The work of the hands is extolled. Wonderful examples are at the **Bereg Museum** in the old Máthé Castle on 13 Rákóczi út, open weekdays 9 am to 4 pm and Sat, Sun, and holidays from 8 am to 4 pm. It is closed Mondays. Woodcarvings, hand chiseled pipes, hand-made clothing, artifacts, 18,000 archeological, 10,000 historical, and 12,000 ethnographic artifacts include coins, medallions, pottery, and some 3,500 examples of the Bereg embroidery art.

*Embroidery from Kalocsa*

The largest poplar in the entire Trans-Tisza region (the **Namény Poplar**) is by the huge pier on the bank of the Kraszna Bridge. It measures eight m/26 feet in circumference. Large forests of sycamore, poplar, maple, and ash, and a huge variety of birds and small mammals, makes this a popular area for hunting and for hiking. And, everywhere, as in the lower Tisza, there is an abundance of birds. Proof of that can be seen on the road between Vásárosamény and Jánd. It is bordered by Sand Martin Hill, home to the largest colony of sand martins in Europe. From our location here, the following villages can be easily reached.

**Tákos** is reached by heading out 41 east from Vásárosnamény. The Calvinist Church here is called the "barefoot Notre Dame." It is made of an unusual spackled mud and brick and was built circa 1760. Of the 58 painted coffers, none is identical, departing from the norm of church art. From Tákos, drive east on 41 to Beregsurány. From Beregsurány, head south to Tarpa.

**Tarpa's** 45-m/148-foot, 15th-century Calvinist church is visible from a distance. The church's bell tower was added in the 18th century. A testimony to its time, the wood shingle covered mill off Árpád út was formerly powered by horses. The **Ethnographic Museum**, a treasure of local folk art, is at 29 Kossuth út.

We can now go back to Tákos, then drive south through Tivadar and cross the Tisza River to the south bank town of Kisar. In Kisar, pick up the road heading east again, to Szatmárcseke.

## Szatmárcseke

One of the most unusual artifacts in all of Europe are found in Szatmárcseke. In the village cemetery there are 600 gravestone headboards, carved in wood, and shaped like boats. Did 600 people die on the river? Was this in menory of Noah's ark? No one knows exactly why, but

*Szatmárcseke village cemetery*

each headboard is very clearly carved like the prow of a boat facing up to the sky. Szatmárcseke is the birthplace and burial home of Ferenc Kölcsey (1790-1838). He composed the Hungarian National Anthem. A poet by occupation, he also made a lasting impression on the reform and spread of the Magyar language. At the **Kölcsey Memorial House**, at 46 Kölcsey Ferenc út, his home, life works, artifacts, and mementos are on display. He lived about 200 years ago, a period recalled in the **Regional House of Szatmárcseke**, at 4 Vasvári Pál út, where the original furnishings are still in their same places.

Szatmárcseke should be visited during the **International Plum Jam Making Contest** every August (check with Tourinform). The Szatmár plum is famous in Hungary for its exquisite body and flavor. It is cooked for 24 hours prior to packing or eating. Its distilled products are equally celebrated. During the festival you will no doubt encounter plum cider or sour prune soup. Also, the Hungarian fried bread, lángos, fried on the spot and covered in cheese or in several different dressings, is sold everywhere. And the Hungarian plum derivative that can wilt your socks, palinka is available. Carriage rides, folk dancing and music add to the mix.

**Palinka** *is to Hungary what saki is to Japan. The liqueur is famous in Central Europe, and it has a growing reputation in many parts of the world. Distilled from 100% fruit, without any added alcohol or artificial aromas, it is aged to a minimium 37.5% alcohol content. But its astounding smoothness is what makes it unique. It is often considered an excellent aperitif with Hungarian meat dishes.*

In the colder month of February, on the other hand, the **"Cinke" cooking contest** is indoors and offers a completely different flavor. When long winters ate up the food stores, inventive ladies had to make the most of plain flour and bare bones meals. Perhaps hundreds of years ago, no one knows for sure, a Cinke cooking contest developed in Szatmárcseke. While cold winds blew outside, they fanned their cooking fires and tried to outdo each other with their best simple bread and baking recipes. Cinke is a dough made of boiled potatoes and flour, then fried. Puliszka, a maize flour boiled in salt water, is another choice. Is the cooking plain? Try the different samples. They will amaze you.

Leaving Szatmárcseke, take the main road south, to Túristvándi

## Túristvándi

The 18th-century water-driven mill at Túristvándi still turns to the rhythm of the river's current and still grinds wheat. It works in conjunction with a system of sluices that regulate the water level of the River Túr. Along with the mill, the village has preserved the medieval guild arts. Bread-making, kneading the dough by hand, is still done by the villagers as it was hundreds of years ago. Dough-making, fruit-drying, and

food-processing demonstrations are on-going. So are fish soup competitions, made with the day's catch from the river. Check with Tourinform in Vásáros-namény or the Village and Agrotourism Organization of Szabolcs-Szatmár-Bereg County, 4400 Nyíregyháza, Hősök tere 5, ☎/fax 36-42-599-589, hanusz@ zeus.nyf.hu.

After visiting the villagers and seeing the area, perhaps staying for a few days, you can pack up and retrace your steps to Route 41 from Túristvándi, then go west toward Nyíregyháza. In Nyíregyháza, take Route 4 south, through Szolnok to Route 441 south toward Kecskemét. If you are bicycling, take 471 southeast through Debrecen where you can pick up the parallel roads to Route 4.

## Kecskemét

If you had been living in Kecskemét (www.rkk.hu and www. kecskemet.hu) in the 13th century, you would probably have been baptized into the Christian faith by Saint Nicholas of the Franciscan Catholic Church. And consider that Saint Nicholas would have given you a goat as a present for your baptism. Kecske means goat in Hungarian. However, the "mét" seems to be derived from a verb that means walking. And hence we have the town of the walking goat, or of walking the goats.

Kecskemét can be seen from a distance, not just because it rises from the flat sandy plains of the Alföld (Hungarian plains), but also because it is a city of church spires. It is one of those eclectic examples of different cultures and faiths that have melded into the Hungarian matrix. Catholic, Calvinist, Jewish, Evangelist, Greek Orthodox, and their splinters all find a home in Kecskemét, evidence of a religious tolerance that started in 1564 when the followers of the "old belief" agreed to abide peaceably with the followers of the "new belief." So began the foundations of Calvinism here. Yet, though it is a historically religious town, it has sustained a market economy for centuries, based on the buying and selling of livestock and the produce of the plains, so rich that it was able to pay off its medieval debts in cash in 1832.

The center of town, the main square is actually made up of five squares that border each other. Kossuth tér (Kossuth Square) sits in the middle, the heart of the old town. To the southeast is Deak tér, cut off from Kossuth tér by Csányi út. However, the other four squares spill over into each other, forming a large pedestrian park. From Kossuth tér you can walk into Szabadság tér to the west. On the other hand, Széchenyi tér is a short walk north, while Katona József tér is on the south. All the main sites of the city can be walked between these five squares. There are numerous restaurants and places to stay in the vicinity.

*Town Hall*

The center of the town, Kossuth tér, contains the **Town Hall**. It was built in 1893 by the designer of the Budapest Postal Bank Building (see *Itineraries* in the Budapest section), Ödön Lechner, in partnership with Gyula Pártos. The building is typical Lechner Art Nouveau with bright pink and purple majolica tiles, swirls and curves on the roofline and a façade with flowered colors and patterns. The carillon chimes a classical composer's composition every hour. Next to it is the spired **Nagytemplom (Great Church)**, 73 m/239 feet tall, the largest Rococo cathedral on the Puszta (the grassland plains). Climb its stairs for superb camera shots. Its gigantic bell can be heard for miles, and was once used by farmers to signal lunchtime. It still sets break time for thousands of city workers.

The Franciscan **Church of St Nicholas** (the goat giver), is the next one east of the Great Church. It is the oldest structure in Kesckemét, used by both Catholics and Protestants up until 1564, when they separated peacefully. Franciscans assumed control in 1647, and began remodeling, culminating in a new Baroque façade in 1799. An unknown 18th-century sculptor did the beautiful Calvary sculpture in the front. The tower was added in the early 1800s. Thus, its original 14th-century Gothic has long since given way to 18th- and 19th-century styles. The south side of

*Katona József Theatre*

Kossuth tér is bordered with Katona József tér, where the Neo-Baroque **Katona József Theatre** was built to the plans of Ferdinand Fellner and Hermann Helmer in 1896. It is still the venue of the best in Hungarian drama. It is fronted by Kecskemét's **Trinity Column**, a 1742 sandstone sculpture with Saints Elizabeth, Roch, Sebastian, and Stephen. The **Magyar fotográfiai múzeum (Hungarian Museum of Photography)**, www.fotomuzeum.hu, at Katona József tér 12, is a growing and eclectic collection of all the modern visual arts in Hungary.

Now, heading back to Kossuth tér, you can follow the southern edge of Katona József tér, which is bordered by Bajcsy-Zsilinski út, northeast to Kéttemplomköz út, and follow it back north in the direction of Kossuth tér. You will pass the former Franciscan Church Priori, built in 1736, but today the Zóltan Kodály Pedagogical School of Music, a branch of the Liszt Ferenc School of Music in Budapest. Occasionally you can take in a concert here in the old refectory or the cloister courtyard.

As you continue the walk, Kéttemplomköz út takes you in a straight line toward the early Baroque **Calvinist Church**, built in the 1680s. This is now in Szabadság tér. Curiously, the church is also a monument to religious tolerance. Under the direct control of the Sultan during the Turkish occupation, the town benefited from royal favoritism. The church was built during the Turkish occupation, even while villages burned, and the countryside and most of its religious structures in other locations were destroyed.

Directly across from the Calvinist Church is the **Calvinist New College**, built in 1912 in Art Nouveau style with Transylvanian reliefs across the façade. It is still used as a school but also holds the **Ráday Ecclesiastical Museum**, a repository of the regional Calvinist artistic treasures. Try the **Café Szabadság** in the square, for some coffee and cake, before continuing to the far eastern end, and its intersection with Rákóczi út.

*Cifrapalota*

The Art Nouveau **Cifrapalota** (Garish Palace), at Rákóczi út 1, with its flower-patterned multicolored ceramic façade, stands out like a child's fantasy. It was built to the design of Géza Márkus, obviously a pupil of Lechner. Originally meant to be an office, such a building demands more than office space, so, since the 1960s, it has been fittingly also home to the **Kecskemét Gallery of Fine Art** (10 am to 5 pm, Tue to Sat and Sun 1:30-5 pm. Entry is about 250 HUF). Directly across from it, at Rákóczi út 2, the **Museum of Science and Technology** (10 am to 5 pm, Tue to Sat and Sun 1:30 pm to 5 pm), has an entry fee of about 300 HUF. It is inside the Moorish-style former synagogue of Kecskemét, built between 1864 and 1871. The main square is the repository of numerous Art Nouveau buildings because Kecskemét has been leveled so many times, due to invasions and wars, that hardly anything was left standing from before the mid-19th century, except by luck and the Turkish Pasha's favoritism.

Kecskemét is also the repository of over 2,400 paintings and sculptures in the **Hungarian Native Artists Museum** at 11 Gáspár András utca (10 am to 5 pm, except Sun and Mon). The entry fee is 200 HUF. It shares the same building with the **Szórakaténusz Toy Museum and Workshop**, szorakatenusz@mail.datanet.hu (10 am to 12:30 pm and 1 to 5 pm daily). It is closed Monday. The entry fee is 300 HUF. Children under six are free). This is a gigantic exhibit of over 10,000 railway models, toys, and children's instruments from the early 20th century. They also conduct workshops in toy making.

Farther afield is the **Leskowsky Collection of Musical Instruments** at 6/A Zimay utca, ☎ 36-76-486-616. This private collection covers the world, including examples of just about every type of instrument imaginable, about 1,500 in total. However, the museum is not open without prior appointment. Tours are arranged for groups. Fee is 500 HUF and includes a musical performance.

But Kecskemét, like so much of Hungary, is also a city of the vine, and of fruit. In fact, not only are several fine wines produced in outlying vineyards, but its liqueurs have gained international fame. The Kecskemét Apricot Palinka is available at better restaurants (see *Places to Eat*). But the most local brew is perhaps the Unicum (see insert), a liqueur elixir for rejuvenation and health. Its factory exhibition is at Matkói út 2. Tour groups of at least 20 are allowed entrance. Check with Tourinform to find out if you can join one of the groups.

### THE STORY OF UNICUM

József Zwack was physician to the Imperial Court of Austria under Emperor Joseph II. He worked tirelessly to develop a rejuvenating formula from natural herbs that would alleviate the drinking maladies of the Emperor. Finally, after aging 40 different herbs in oak barrels for six months, Zwack thought he had discovered the secret. In 1790 he gave the first taste to the Emperor. Joseph II sipped the digestive elixir and proclaimed, "Das ist ein Unikum" (that is unique). The fame and popularity of the drink spread rapidly, first throughout the court, and then abroad. Its thrilling rejuvenative qualities soon became universally associated with its red label and white cross. Dr. Zwack formed a company in 1840, calling it J Zwack és Társa. It would turn into a dynasty that would outlast the Austro-Hungarian Empire. After the Dual Monarchy was formed in 1867, the Zwack firm became the Sole Purveyor to the Imperial Court. Upon his death in 1915, József's son,

Lajos, inherited the factory. The family went through two generations. Then came WW II and the factory was destroyed by bombing. One thing was left... the formula. As Russian forces fought their way into Hungary, Zwack Sr. risked his life. He hid the formula for Unicum inside his breast pocket, squeezed himself inside an upturned oak barrel on the back of a truck, and secretly fled his beloved country. His son, Peter Zwack, waited for him in America. A few years later the Russians tried to re-institute production, using the label (without the secret formula). They never succeeded.

With the fall of communism, Zwack returned to Hungary and restored the factory. He began production with the secret formula that had been hidden in his father's coat so many years before. A bitter drink, its rejuvenative qualities have remained. Today Peter Zwack is the Chairman of the Board, has seven children and four grandchildren, and directs a true success story. His company is profitable and growing, and his family has preserved a European tradition of over 200 years. www.zwack.hu.

Try to time your visit to Kecskemét with one of the many equine championships that are held in the local horse parade grounds. As an example, the Four-in-Hand (four-horse team driving) International Championships were held in Kecskemét in 2004. The Kecskemét office of Tourinform will have a schedule of most events.

## The Kiskunság National Park

Don't miss the Kiskunság National Park. Their offices are at 6000 Kecskemét, Liszt Ferenc út 19, at the Természet Háza, ☎ 36-76-482-611, fax 36-76-481-074, mailknp@knp.hu, www.knp.hu. Special tourist information, such as how to find a

personal guide through protected areas, is provided at
☎ 36-76-601-596 or 36-76-501-
594. They are open Tue to Fri 9
am to 4 pm and Sat 10 am to 2
pm. They have maps, and
sometimes tours and guides
(see *Adventures, Hiking &
Biking)*. This is also the ticket
office for the regular and nos-
talgia narrow guage trains that
travel through the park system, ☎ 36-76-504-308.

There are an incredible nine separate ecological regions in the
123,550 protected acres of the Kiskunság National Park.
Reeded lake lands, swamps, forests, salt lakes, grasslands,
bogs, sand dunes, wetlands, swamps, and marshes border
each other in a staggering variety of lowland environments.
As such, the area attracts scientists and environmentalists as
well as tourists. Careful planning and building has managed
to interlace study trails, lookouts, rest points, hiking routes
and specially marked horseback roads for horse-driven
coaches and/or horseback excursions (these require permits
and guides, obtainable through the park offices in Bugac and
some other towns in the park lands).

Leaving Kecskemét, take Highway 52 south toward the
Fülöpházi turnoff, but look for the 20 km mark on Highway
52. Near the marker there is a parking lot and the educational
building for the National Park. Park here and take the
**Báránypirositó educational track**. It is here that you will
find the **Fülöpházi sand dunes**, one of the most unusual
and most studied areas in all of Europe. Some vending
machines inside the educational building dispense softdrinks
and candies. When finished, head back on 52 and catch 54
going southeast.

## Bugac

On 54, drive past Jakabszállás until you arrive at the side-
road for Bugac. It is on your left. Head up to the Bugac
Pusztaháza (Bugac Puszta House). Probably the name comes

from the time when there was only one house here, a way-stop for the itinerant cowboys and sheep herders of the plains. Exactly 2.3 km/1.4 miles farther, you can have a meal at the **Bugac Csárda**. At the csárda, or country inn, you can also get information, tickets, and perhaps book yourself an overnight stay at one of the local ranches. The Bugac area of the Puszta plains is a special bio-reserve within the Kiskunság National Park. This 11,000-acre nature preserve is the most visited part of the park. Carriage rides hook up with village-style accommodations that allow you to taste the plains as a villager might have hundreds of years ago (with modern amenities). Walking trails, biking paths, and horseback excursions traverse fields where grey cattle and racka sheep graze in the open. Daily horse shows can entertain you, but try to coordinate your visit with the annual Puszta Bogrács Festival, an exciting time of horse races, carriage races, stunts, and the Puszta ötös – the Puszta Five,

where a rider stands on the rumps of two horses, guiding them and at the same time drives three ahead of him using only reigns). You can also get a slice of the lifestyle and history of the Csikós herdsmen in the tall cone-shaped **Bugacpuszta Herdsman's Museum**, open May 1 to October 31, 10 am to 5 pm, ☎ 36-76-372-688.

A small narrow-guage steam train that travels from Kecskemét to Bugac Puszta stops at Hittanya. If you get off at

Hittanya, you will
be at the head of
the Boróka-Bugac
educational track
(red cross and
stripes, and make
sure you checked
with the office in
Kecskemét before
you embark on the
trail). This is an
easy two-km walk,

posted with signboards, showing the animal husbandry,
plant, and animal life of the Lower-Plain (Alsó-Puszta) and
the Bugac Great Forest (Bugac Nagyerdő) in the Kiskunság
National Park. The trail walks past sand dunes, the open
grasslands and plains, and a stand of juniper trees, unusual
for this part of the world. It is a protected site, and harbors
numerous protected species of birds and small animals. The
lookout tower that overlooks the grove offers shade and excellent picture views. The trail ends at the Shepherd's Museum
(Pásztormúzeum) in Bugac, the tall unmistakable cone-like
structure on the outskirts of town. However, first head for the
Csárda (Karikas Csárda) across from the museum. There you
can get information, a guide if necessary.

Go back to Route 54, then veer back to Kecskemét where you
connect to Highway 5, and head south. You will eventually
come to the turnoff for Kistelek. This will put you on the road
to Ópusztaszer. Turn east.

## ★★Ópusztaszer

As you drive east, just before
you get to the town of
Ópusztaszer, a diminutive
sign stands by the side of the
road, and it says,
"Pusztaszermajor." There is
also a sign for the **Nemzeti
Történeti Emlékpark**

(National Historical Statue Park). Follow this road. It will take you to one of the most famous sites in Hungary, known and seen by every Hungarian. This exhibit extends through numerous different buildings and numerous village huts. Dioramas depict wildlife in the days of Àrpad, the ecosystem of the Danube and the plains, and the growth of the Hungarian people, from nomads to farmers to villagers. Virtually every phase of Hungarian history and every region of the country is covered in detail. But the greatest emphasis is on the glorious days of the Magyar warriors.

The Great Plains

The exhibit reaches its climax in a huge round building. Inside is one of the great historical-cultural paintings of the world. The cyclorama took Árpád Feszty and his team of artists two years to complete, from 1892 to 1894. Over 120 m/394 feet long and 15 m/49 feet wide, the dramatic Hungarian conquest of the Carpathian basin unfolds. Stretching around you, thousands of people, horsemen, carriage drivers, villagers, peasants, warriors and chieftens depict hundreds of different aspects of Hungarian culture. Charging horses raise the dust of battle as arrows fly and spearmen raise their lances, while peasants drive oxen over the dead and the dying in other parts of the valley. Àrpad and his chieftens, astride their steeds on a hill, look around them as the scenes unfold.

Why did they pick this town, on the far eastern border, for such a monument? Ópusztaszer was the site of what might be called the first Hungarian Parliament. The tribes gathered and voted on how to divide the conquered lands, who would be their leaders, and how they would be governed. Horseshows, many in Magyar dress, and folk and historical festivals are regular parts of the park's programs (see website). A few eateries and benches can provide rest stops on the over 120 acres of trails and historical exhibits. The admission fee, which includes a visit to the cyclorama, is 1,900 HUF. Contact: ONEP, 6767 Ópusztaszer, Szoborkert 68, ☎ 36-62-275-257 ext 103,104, or 105, fax 36-62-275-007, info@opusztaszer.hu, www.opusztaszer.hu. Plan for a full day and, if it's sunny, wear a cap because shade is sparse on some trails.

# ■ Adventures

## Hiking & Biking

Although most of the country is open to exploration, the **Hortobágy National Park** and the **Kiskunság National Park** are protected reserves. Check with the Park offices for trails and permits. Many require that you use a guide, and the park offices (see *Itineraries*) and Tourinform (see *Appendix*) can provide contacts for English-speaking guides. Kiskunság's excellent website (www.knpi.hu) has information about the primary hiking paths and educational study trails throughout Hungary, listed with appropriate contact addresses, phone numbers and directions.

## Egyuek-Pusztakócs

This marshland is sometimes mist-laden and foggy in the early morning, echoing with the occasionally call of a loon, or the distant sound of flapping wings as a bird takes off somewhere in the mist. Something is always flying in the high sky of the Hortobagy. The trail begins at the **Egyek Western Hortobagy National Park Visitor's Center** (Nyugati Fogadóházö, ☎ 36-52-378-054, 36-52-529-920, fax 36-52-529-940, hnp@hnp.datanet.hu), where you can get pamphlets and books, permits and information. The trail proceeds from there on the old "salt road," the same trail that once brought salt to Hungary from Transylvannia in the Middle Ages. The first stop, or as Hungarians dub it, the second station, is at the Fekete-rét (Black Marsh), where a half-mile stilt-supported walkway across the marshes takes you to a 30-foot-high observation tower. The third station on the trail is the Górés tanya (Górés Farm), a combination museum and rehabilitation center for injured birds, where they are nurtured to return to the wild. The Górés tanya is an ancient Hungarian farm of the Puszta, also converted into a museum, which includes the filagória halom (arbor mound), standing in the shadows next to the farm, one of the mysterious burial mounds of the ancient Cumanian people from the east, another one of the ancient tribes to travel into the Carpathian Basin.

*Hortobágy Fishpond*
*(Derek Moore)*

## Hortobágy-Halásztó

This is a fish pond, and you might not think there was anything special to such a plain body of water, except that this is the Hortobágy-Tisza area, and everything is done naturally. So this "pond" is not really a pond, but a series of lakes designed to integrate with the environment, including the bird- and other wildlife of the area. All the fish grown here are raised on their natural foods. The area is another bird-watcher's paradise. The observation stands along the way, together with your camera, can provide great pictures. ☎ 36-52-529-935.

## Spas & Baths

### Debrecen

See also *Aquaticum Thermal and Wellness Hotel* and *Grand Hotel Aranybika*, under *Places to Stay* – both of which are

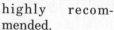 highly recommended.

**Aquaticum**, Nagyerdei park 1, ☎ 36-52-514-100 or fax 36-52-346-883, kozpont@ aquaticum.hu, www. aquaticum.hu. Open daily 6 am to 7 pm, the entry fee is 1,500 HUF for adults. The

first bathhouse in Debrecen was built in 1826 and, since then, it has flowered to become one of the finest medicinal and recreational spas in Europe. People come from everywhere for healing, relaxation, and fun. It is also an excellent medicinal spa. The medical staff employs 40 different types of therapies and cures. There are quiet healing centers and secluded, serene pools. But there are also the more popular public-use thermal baths. There are steam chambers and fountains, waterfalls and artificial caves, indoor and outdoor pools, artificial canals and streams, bubble chambers, whirlpool baths, rock climbing walls, underwater jets and above-water jet streams and mushroom showers. And in the Aquaticum Mediterranean, decorated with tropical plants and palms, is an indoor wonderland of water slides and showers, bridges and eateries.

### Jászberény

**Strand és Termálfürdő (Lido & Thermal Bath)**, 5100 Jászberény, Hatvani út 5, ☎ 36-57-412-108, is not a huge beach, as in so many other lidos in Hungary, but its five pools,

sauna, and solarium are enough when combined with other services there, including therapeutic gymnastics, mudpacks, underwater hydromassage, and a fitness room. The curative effects of the high-alkaline hydrogen carbonate water have been well documented in cases of some locomotor, osteological and gynecological diseases. Of course, as with any of these baths, there is no guarantee, but the rest and relaxation you will find here, coupled with extraordinarily low prices, are worth a lot.

Additional information is also available from **Tourinform Jászberény**, 5100 Jászberény, Lehel vezér tér 33, ☎ /fax 36-57-406-439 jaszbereny@tourinform.hu. Other services and accommodations are available from **Lehel Sport és Szabadidõ Kft (Lehel Sports and Leisure Non-Profit Company)**, 5100 Jászberény, Kiserdei sétány 10 ☎ 36-57-415-267.

## Hajdúszoboszló

**Hajdúszoboszlói Gyógy-fürdõ** (Hajdúszoboszló Health Spa), 4200 Hajdú-szoboszló, Szent István park 1-3, ☎ 36-52-360-344, fax 36-52-360-039, gyogy-fur@elender.hu, www.haj-duszoboszlogyogyfurdo.hu. Hajdúszoboszló is a watering place with a Mediterranean atmosphere, popular over more than 70 years for recuperation and relaxation, coupled with entertainment, food, and fun. It has been called the "Mecca of rheumatism patients." The lido is an 80-acre bath-park complex, surrounded by park-like grounds, with a rowing lake, giant slides, wave pool, Jacuzzi pools, beach volleyball courts, a 50-m/164-foot swimming pool, adventure currents and showers, waterfalls, and entertainment events during the summer. Its pools inside follow a Mediterranean motif, with a green glass roof that showers the room and its palm trees, tropical vegetation, and indoor waterfalls, with pastel greens and whites. Restaurants border the shore and a pirate ship and lighthouse sit astride the sandy beaches of the wave pool, sparking the imagination of the kids. Nine rides include the Black Hole and the Crazy River Twister. Programs for revitalization and healing use the thermal waters of the spa, which, at 73°C/163°F, come from a depth of 1,100 m/3,600 feet. These waters are particularly rich in trace minerals and elements – iodine, bromine, sodium chloride, hydrogen carbonate, as well as titanium, copper, zinc, silver, barium, and vanadium. Dozens of medical treatments are provided by the medical staff, which include acupuncture, inhalation therapies, a salt chamber, mud packs, Jacuzzi, light therapy, and massages. You may also contact **Tourinform at Hajdúszoboszló**, 4200 Hajdúszoboszló, Szilfákalja út 2, ☎/fax 36-52-558-928, hajduszoboszlo@ tourinform.hu.

Other services and accommodations at the Hajdúszoboszló thermal springs include:

- **Barátság Gyógyszálló** (Barátság Health Hotel), 4200 Hajdúszoboszló, Mátyás király sétány 19, ☎ 36-52-361-744.

- **Hunguest Hotel Béke Gyógyfürdője** (Health Spa of Hunguest Hotel Béke), 4200 Hajdúszoboszló, Mátyás király sétány 10, ☎ 36-52-362-748.

- **Hotel Silver Gyógyfürdője**, 4200 Hajdúszoboszló, Mátyás király sétány 25, ☎ 36-52-363-811.

- **Hotel Délibáb Gyógyfürdője** (Health Spa of Hotel Délibáb), 4200 Hajdúszoboszló, József Attila út 4, ☎ 36-52-360-366.

- **Hunguest Hotel Hőforrás Gyógyfürdője** (Health Spa of Hunguest Hotel Hőforrás), 4200 Hajdúszoboszló, Mátyás király sétány 21, ☎ 36-52-362-144.

- **Mátyás Király Hotel barlangfürdõje** (Cave Spa of King Matthias Hotel), 4200 Hajdúszoboszló, Mátyás király sétány 17, ☎ 36-52-360-200.
- **Thermal Hotel Victoria Gyógyfürdõje** (Health Spa of Thermal Hotel Victoria), 4200 Hajdúszoboszló, Debreceni útfél 6, ☎ 36-52-557-550, www.thermalhotelvictoria.hu.

## Hajdúnánás

**Városi Gyógyfürdõ** (Town Thermal Bath), 4080 Hajdúnánás, Fürdõ ut 7, ☎ 36-52-381-858. This small town also houses the **Rural House Museum**, with an exhibit of reedwork and straw weaving, an art dating back over a millennium on the Puszta (the grass-land plains). And, in the same town, there is also an ostrich farm. But the primary draw is the thermal bath. At 67°C/ 153°F, it comes from a depth of 1,019 m/3,342 feet, with sodium chloride, iodine and bromine plus other trace minerals. There are several campgrounds both in and around the baths, cabins, restaurants and boating on the Keleti-fõcsatorna (Eastern Canal), or on the small lake, which is on the Bath property. The Bath complex ranges across 37 acres, with open-air swimming and thermal pools of various sizes and temperature, a 50-m/164-foot water slide, plus adventure currents and underwater jets. The indoor bath includes two health pools, a sauna and aromatherapy chamber. Medical professionals service the public here as well, with services that include treatments for rheumatism using therapeutic gymnastics, massages, in-water massages and carbon dioxide baths. **Tourinform Hajdúnánás** will help in making arrangements, at 4080 Hajdúnánás, Köztársaság tér 6 or at Fürdõ út at the Baths during the high season. ☎ 36-52-382-076 or 36-52-239-014, hajdunanas@tourinform.hu.

## Hajdúböszömény

**Városi fürdő** (Town Bath), 4220 Hajdúböszörmény, Uzsok tér 1, ☎ 36-52-371-653. Sodium chloride, iodide, bromide, and flouride bubble up in the waters of the thermal baths here, with recuperative and curative effects that attract people from throughout Europe. The outside season here is June 1-September 1, while activities move indoors during the rest of the year. It has a beautiful 30-m/98-foot indoor pool styled after Roman baths, complete with Doric columns, thermal pools and a sauna for adults, a young children's pool and an adventure pool for the young.

**The Hajdú Hotel**, 4220 Hajdúböszömény, Petőfi Sándor út 2, ☎ 36-52-228-307, has both a quality restaurant (Hungarian with a good wine list) and rooms with bath, mini-bar, television, telephone and central heating.

## Cserkeszőlő

**Gyógy és Strand-fürdő** (Thermal Bath and Lido), 5465 Cserkeszőlő, Fürdő út 1/a, ☎ 36-56-568-465. Situated in the sunshine belt of Hungary, Cserkeszőlő has a population of 2,500, and exactly double that

capacity to receive tourists and visitors, for one primary reason – its thermal baths. Discovered in 1943, these waters come from 2,300 m/7,500 feet below the surface, running at 82°C/180°F and enriched from mother earth with iodide-ions, alkali chloride and hydrogen carbonate, again having qualities that make them both recuperative and healing. The waters have also been used for internal applications. Every year something new is added to the medicinal bath, from wave pools, adventure currents and mushroom showers, to quiet thermal baths set serenely aside for healing, using hydro-massage, Jacuzzis, massages, sauna, solarium, "Biotron" light therapy, and even dental services. There are weight reduction programs, wellness programs, healing programs, and beauty programs. While the licensed professionals do their healing magic, kids can play in the children's adventure pools, the playground, or run in the park grounds. Contact **Tourinform Cserkeszõlõ** at the entrance to the baths at 5465 Cserkeszõlõ, Fürdõ út 1/a, ☎ 36-56-568-465 fax 36-56-568-466.

## Canoes & Kayaks on Gentle Waters

 You are strongly advised to contact Tourinform (see *Appendix*) for appropriate information for guides and other contacts. Also see the Budapest section under *Adventures* for organizations that can help make your trip trouble-free.

### Canoe the Keleti Main Canal

This branches from the Tisza at the Tiszalök gate, then it ranges across the flatlands of the Hortobágy plains, winding through the reeds to join the Berettyó River. It is approxi-mately 110 km/66 miles from the gate to the town of Darvas, where the Keleti River intersects with the Berettyó. Four places require lifting over, and when you come to the Balmazújváros, you will have to use a pass authorized by the Hydrographic Office of Engineering of Tiszántúli. Check with Tourinform on coordinating details. The average speed of flow is about 13 km/eight miles per hour and both kayaks and canoes are allowed. The recommended number of days is about four-five with at least one added day for rest. The forms filed with the State Hydrographic Office must contain all stops, camp sites, and days when you will pass dam gates.

Accordingly, filling out the forms requires someone with an intimate knowledge of the river and its flood control system.

## Canoe The Kettös-Körös

This starts at the gentle eddies at the junction of Fekete- and Fehér-Körös. As you travel the waters of the Köröstarcsa at Sebes-Körös meld in. The water is regulated by the dam at Békés. It is a very gentle and leisurely trip of about 37 km/22 miles so it can be covered in one to two days. The average descent is negligible, and the river width averages about 50 m/164 feet. Since the drop is so gentle, the current is incredibly lazy, at 2.1 km/3.36 miles per hour. Its depth is a comparatively shallow two-3.5 m/six-10 feet. There are plenty of birds and natural sights along this run.

## Canoe the Berettyó

This run leaves Romania at Kismarja and runs to Nyírség and onward for 75 km/45 miles toward Körösök, where it joins the Sebes-Körös at Szeghalom. Nicely bordered by forests and the quiet of the northern Hungarian lower mountains; you may be able to see wildlife on the banks. No lifting over is required on this route, and you can figure about three days, with a day for rest. Either canoes or kayaks are fine.

## Canoe from the Keleti Main Canal through the Hortobágy-Berettyó Main Canal

Coming out of the Keleti Main Canal flood gates at Tiszavasvár, the waterway wanders through the Hortobágy Plain. It is surprising how much wildlife can be seen from the shore. After leaving Mezotúr the 160-km/96-mile run joins the Hármas-Körös River system. Four flood gates require lifting over. If the Tiszavasvár isn't open you will have to lift over there as well. This tour encompasses about five to six days and you need to add two to three days for rest.

## Canoe the Transylvania-Körösök

The main river drainage system of southeastern Hungary starts with the Sebes, Fekete, and the Fehér-Körös in the towering mountains of Transylvania, and winds down toward the Tisza, joining together as the Kettős-Körös and then the Hármas-Körös. Eventually the Hármas-Körös joins with the Tisza at Csongrád. This route has numerous campsites, parks and forests along its banks, and it also immerses you in the mystery of the Transylvania Mountains. Bird and animal life can be seen in numerous areas along the banks. This may take about a week, with an added three to four days of rest. It can be broken into several sub-tours. For instance, the junction of the Sebes and Kettős-Körös can be the start of a tour, following the river course until it unites with the Tisza. It is regulated by a barrage and navigation lock in Békésszentandrás and Bökény, snaking for 91 km/54 miles at a depth of about three to four m/nine to 12 feet. This sub-tour, by itself, is an extraordinarily mild canoe or kayak trip, running through the heart of the Körös-Maros National Park. By itself this takes four to six days with an added two to three days of rest.

## On Horseback

 The Great Plains are home to some great riding stables and a world heritage riding tradition for over a thousand years. As such, there are literally hundreds of riding possibilities in the flatlands and the rolling hills. Learn how to ride or, if you are more advanced, learn to drive teams of horses, or shoot a bow and arrow from the back of your horse. Dressage, jumping, carriage riding, and even hunting on horseback are all characteristics of the Hungarian plains. Check the Budapest chapter, pages 176 ff, to see how the horseshoe rating system works.

## COACH RACING

Everyone knows about horse races, but few are acquainted with coach races, a team competition with horses that requires extraordinary skill, discipline, patience, and years of development, far more than simply riding a single horse. But, although used for years, carriage (team) driving is a newcomer to the world competitive stage, standardized for the first time in 1970 with an international competition in Luzern. Queen Elizabeth entered her four-in-hand, but the race was won by the Hungarian Imre Abonyi. The coaches themselves are judged on their esthetic value, and then comes the race. Imre, the world champion, was succeeded by other Hungarians, László Kádár, Sándor Fülöp, and György Bárdos, each in turn winning various international and European championships. The tradition continues to this day, with Vilmos and Zoltán Zabar. When you see these Hungarian Csikós cowboys display their horsemanship, it is not just tricks. They are in fact training themselves and their horses to compete internationally, and so it would appear that the Hungarian dominance of this extraordinary sport will continue. As a German writer once wrote, "Horses are to Hungarians as national loyalty is to a Frenchman, as wine is to an Italian, and as a harem is to a Turk."

## Five Horseshoe Stables

**János Lóska's** stables, mentioned in Northern Hungary, extend all the way down through the Hortobagy, and are among the finest in the country. Call Marta, ☎ 36-20-911-8275 or e-mail her and mention this book, at jokaim@hu.inter.net, www.lovastura.hu. Although the web notes requirements for skilled riders, their cross-country tours may also include a horse-drawn carriage driven by a Hungarian horseman, so the entire family could go along. Ranging across streams and backlands, and on to the Hortobagy plains, the carriage is not allowed on some parts of the

Hortobagy plains for environmental reasons, but this is very small part of most of the tours. A support van may be used in these situations, until you can join in once again on the carriage where the park rules will allow it. Lodgings are in good quality hotels. Wine tasting evenings in the cellars of Tokaj, include meals in top Hungarian restaurants, and a final few days lounging in the warm pools of the **Hortobagy Club Hotel**, www.hortobagyhotel.hu (see *Places to Stay*). The hotel accommodations are in one of their excellent cottages, equipped with individual stables. You can rent a horse for your stay, but, due to the Hortobagy restrictions, it is much better to use János's stables, or one of the licensed guides listed below. Otherwise, you could find yourself in serious trouble.

**Fülöp Hajtó és Lovasiskola** (Fülöp Riding and Driving School), 6000 Kecskemét, Matkói út 58, ☎ 36-20-920-5118, fax 36-76-472-701, info@fulopfli.com. Sándor Fülöp, former team driving international champion takes a personal interest with his staff of highly qualified instructors. From begin-

ning through to advanced riders, they teach team driving or individual horseback riding, eventing, dressage, and jumping in English style. In the Magyar tradition, they work with some specialized stables to teach how to shoot a bow and arrow from horseback. A full-sized indoor riding track means bad weather doesn't stop you and there are horseback excursions into the country for experienced riders.

**Gerébi Kúria Hotel és Lovasudvar**, 6050 Lajosmizse, Alsólajos 224, ☎ 36-76-356-555, fax 36-76-356-045, gerebi@ gerebi.hu, www.gerebi. hu. Rated as a three-star hotel, with many of the rooms and bungalows air-conditioned, this will cost anywhere from a low 9,000 HUF (a double in high season) up to about 18,000 HUF (a double superior suite in high season). Horse activities can cost upwards from 1,500 HUF. However, they have everything here, from an outdoor swimming pool to a fine restaurant, gym, billiards, sauna, tennis courts, and equestrian activities ranging from carriage rides and horse riding competitions to local tours. The Gerébi stables also carry casualty insurance and accept credit cards.

**Pongrácz Major** (Pongrácz Farm – priority show facility), 6041 Kerekeg-yháza, Kunpuszta 76, ☎ 36-76-545-023, fax 36-76-371-240, pongracz-tanya@axelero.hu, www.pongracz-major.hu. Six km/3. 6 miles outside of

Kerekegyháza, this is a stable/hotel that combines wine tasting, full meals (including outdoor bogrács cooking fests as well as traditional Hungarian and international cuisine) and folk programs. They also have a 75-foot swimming pool, automated bowling alley, tennis court, squash court, billiards, table tennis, and Finnish sauna. However, the big plus here is that they are apparently the only stable in the country that combines their regular horse shows with the fabulous Csikós herders, who maneuver with authentic Hussar cavalry and mounted artillery. To experience this you must be part of

a tour group, or coordinate your stay with one of their visiting tour groups (contact Tourinform or the stable directly). Their local tours encompass the Kiskunság National Park areas. For those who can't ride, some tours are in horse-drawn carriages. Out of Pongrácz, for the intermediate to advanced riders, they also have longer endurance riding tours and events.

**Tanyacsárda** (Farm Inn), 6050 Lajosmizse, Bene 625, ☎ 36-76-356-166, fax 36-76-356-576. Contact: Cseko Anita, ☎ 36-36-958-9460, tanyacsárda@tanyacsárda.hu, www.tanyacsárda.hu. An excellent stable, it is also a prime restaurant (see *Places to Eat*). The Csárda often combines nighttime campfires, torch-light shows, bonfires, gypsy music and dance, barbecues Hungarian style, peasant weddings, and carriage and horseback riding in the National Park, and surroundings.

**Varga Stables and Guest House** (Priority Show Facility), 6041 Kerekegyháza, Kunpuszta 150, ☎ 36-76-371-030, fax 36-76-371-163, gyurgyik@axelero.hu. Down the road from the Pongrácz Farm, this 100-year-old thatched roof inn harks back to the turn of the 19th century, although it has been updated with modern facilities and a swimming pool. The food here is patterned after a Hungarian peasant kitchen, providing a unique culinary experience. Lessons for beginners through advanced may also include horse shows, hunting on horseback, and carriage rides. Insurance can be purchased here also.

**Bugaci Ménes** (Bugac Stud Farm – priority show facility suitable for international exhibiting and competitions), 6114 Bugac, Nagybugac Ménes, ☎/fax 36-76-575-028. Mentioned in *Itineraries*, above, this is located in the Kiskunság National Park. A tourist attraction for 30 years, it is both a breeding center for Hungarian horses, and a ranch with herds of Racka sheep and the Hungarian grey cattle. But the big attraction is their skillful Csikós herders, who regularly compete against each other in the Puszta Five and other equine events. Lodging is available, and so is horseback riding, carriage four-in-hand, hunting on horseback, jumping and cross-country horseback excursions. You can purchase insurance here as well.

**Bugac-Táltos Equestrian Guesthouse**, 6114 Bugac, Nagybugac 135, ☎ 36-76-372-633. The Táltos Equestrian Guesthouse is on the Great Plain in the Kiskunság National Park, 120 km/75 miles from Budapest in a 43-acre stand of forest and farmland. The building is thatched roof. Instructors show beginners the rudiments of horseback riding, or more advanced riders explore the beauty of the Bugac Puszta (grassland plains) on horseback with a qualified guide. Those who don't want to sit in the saddle can go out onto the Puszta or plains in a horse-drawn carriage. The guesthouse has a restaurant that serves traditional local specialties as well as some international dishes.

The following stables have been rated five horseshoes and are added upon the recommendation of the Hungarian Equestrian Tourism Association:

- **Hortobágy Máta Stud Farm**, 4071 Hortobágy, Czinege J. út 1, ☎ 36-52-589-369, fax 36-52-369-087, mataimenes@ hortobagyikht.hu. Contact: Varga Emese, ☎ 36-30-967-8006 (cell).

- **Nyíri Riding Park**, 6044 Kecsekmét, Belsõnyír 257, ☎ 36-76-482-154, fax 36-76-472-377. Contact: Polyák Irén, ☎ 36-30-279-2512 (cell).

- **Timpex Riding School**, 4400 Nyíregyháza Újmajor, ☎/ fax 36-42-408-420, timpex@elender.hu.

## Four Horseshoe Stables

**SZIL-KO Kft Nyíreségi Ménese és Lovásiskolája** (SZIL-KO Riding School), Nyíregyháza, Bem Jozsef út 22-23, ☎ 36-42-728-826, fax 36-42-728-823. Established in 1994, they have been gaining every year in reputation. You are advised to book ahead because they have numerous returning clients. Their specialty is teaching, aside from a complete range of horseback activities – carriage rides, cross-country, pony trekking, jumping, hunting on horseback, and exploring the plains. They serve fine cuisine in their restaurant. The rooms are comfortable, and the staff is internationally seasoned, receiving visitors from every part of the world. Their teachers have a methodology that has been honed for 30 years. They have regular

youth summer riding camps as well. Rather than Hungarian breeds, they use English thoroughbreds.

**Pegazus Riding School** (in the extreme east of the country), 5600 Békécsaba, Fényes Tanya 1025, ☎/fax 36-66-432-131, peazus@bekesnet.hu. Contact: Susánszky Pál, ☎ 36-30-228-5222 (cell).

**Akácos Farm**, 6042 Fülöpháza, II kerület 150, ☎ 36-76-717-952, fax 36-20-467-4137, kathrin@roida.de, www.akazienhof. org. Contact: Kaufmann Klaudia.

Dechy Stables, 6050 Lajosmizse, Mizse 339, ☎ 36-76-715-248, fax 36-76-715-253, info@dechy-tanya.hu, www.dechy-tanya. hu. Contact: Dechy István, ☎ 36-20-961-3309 (cell).

**El Bronco Western Ranch**, ☎ 36-76-722-752, fax 36-76-722-753, elbronco@axelero.hu, www.elbronco.hu, Contact Kurcsics Rita, ☎ 36-70-389-5712 or 36-70-389-5720 (cell).

# Lake Tisza

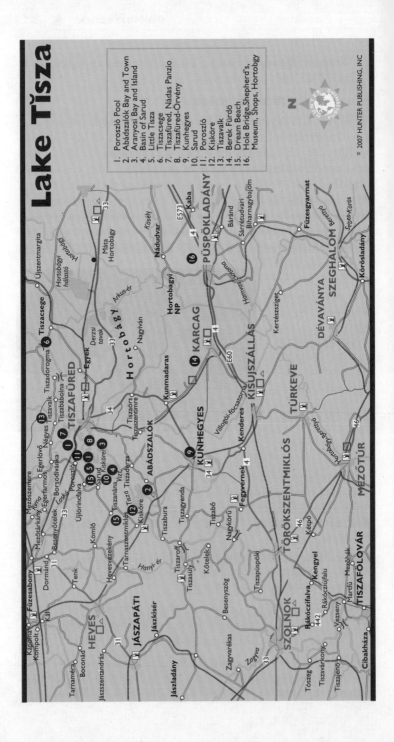

1. Poroszló Pool
2. Abádszalók Bay and Town
3. Aranyosi Bay and Island
4. Basin of Sarud
5. Little Tisza
6. Tiszacsege
7. Tiszafüred, Nádas Panzio
8. Tiszafüred-Örvény
9. Kunhegyes
10. Sarud
11. Poroszló
12. Kisköre
13. Tisztalk
14. Berek Fürdő
15. Dream Beach
16. Hole Bridge,Shepherd's, Museum, Shops, Hortobgy

© 2007 HUNTER PUBLISHING, INC

N

# Lake Tisza

The Tisza River shimmers in the sun as it enters its huge reservoir. It seems alive, brushed into movement by the wind, slapping the shore with its fingers, lined by reed forests

where hundreds of birds nest. Hundreds of cormorants and eagles perch atop branches rising out of the water in the vast expanse of the shallow lake, appearing as specks, watching boaters approach and then pass by. It is a primeval forest close enough to touch and experience, a water wonderland.

Yet, though naturally beautiful, the Tisza is artificially created. It is probably the first dam control system in the world (1970) to deliberately integrate a self-sustaining environmental area. The water is cleaned by millions of plants as it runs its course. It has resulted in the return of many once-disappearing species and has spawned a natural habitat for hundreds of different animals and birds, as well as 50 different kinds of fish. Integrated into the **Hortobágy National Park** (see *The Great Plains* chapter), it has been named a UNESCO World Heritage Site. Its 49 square miles make up the second-largest lake in Hungary. Yet, the shallows warm up quickly and draw hundreds of bathers to the silky warm water at the public beaches. Some deeper areas are set aside for watersports, jet skis, and motorboats. Protected areas are marked with safe passages for boaters, canoeists, and kayakers, who are catered to by shoreline shops, hotels and restaurants.

Sightseers can explore the largest yellow floating heart and the largest floating chestnut fields in Europe, mist-laden shorelines, inlets and quays filled with nesting birds, vine-covered forests, and miles of reeds, brushed into waves by the wind. Between the two dams there are 16 islands and 10 water channels, a paradise for nesting birds, especially concentrated in the reeds of the **Tiszavalk Pool**. Of the 380 native bird species in Hungary, 200 nest here.

## BIRD SONGS

When you hear a bird sing in the early morning, or listen as it says goodbye to the evening sun, it is actually putting together an astonishing complex of sounds. The sedge warbler, for instance, creates his call from 50 different sounds. But the absolute king of "warbling" is the marsh warbler, left. He listens to other birds, and then duplicates the calls of 40 different species. Just imagine the number of sounds he has mastered. If each species averaged 50 sounds, as with the sedge warbler, the marsh warbler would have mastered 2,000 different sounds!

And, then there are the thousands of migrating birds – the summer goose, lanner, the great winged bustard, largest of the birds in Europe, and the great herons, spreading their wide wings to land on their long thin legs in gigantic nests of moss, branches, reeds and grass. Making their homes here in the spring and autumn, tens of thousands of birds in a flock can rise at once to create a fantastic skyscape that rivals some of the great nesting areas of the tropics. As a result, the area has attracted birders from every part of the world, and it alone is a major aspect of the tourism of the area. The higher banks of the "living Tisza," the flowing natural course, as opposed to the dead backwaters and oxbows, are carpeted with a rich forest harking back to ancient times. Domestic poplar, wisteria, and wild grapes appear in dense patches. In fact, since the Tisza reservoir system was created, the habitats of the different forest patches are developing at an astonishing pace, untouched and often impassable! Willow beds are on the inner islands, white fen-land meadow types are interspersed between duckweed and, sometimes, huge expanses of water lilies.

The Tisza dead channels or oxbows add miles of swamp on the fringe of the main course. Although some of these were formed naturally, most were caused when the dam system cut them off from the direct flow of the river. They are cluttered with reeds and riverbank forests, a natural home for the black kite, the black stork, and the white-tailed eagle. The undisturbed and inaccessible channels harbor water plantain, marsh iris, and willow bushes, which hide the nests of the rarely seen whiskered tern and the water rail.

Outside of the nesting season, the reservoir system is open to visitors. However, the dykes may be walked, biked, or ridden on horseback anytime, sometimes giving dramatic glimpses of the wildlife. Not to be confined, the younger generation dives, water skis, sails, rows, and swims, while nightclubs ring with the latest music or, occasionally, gypsy music, as couples walk the shore beneath the stars and listen to the birds of the night.

Anglers find a paradise here. While many birds find their meals in the overflowing underwater life of the Tisza, it is the richest freshwater fishing ground in all of Europe. It attracts anglers from every coun-

*Pike caught by weekend tourist (HNTB)*

try of the EU. The lake is restocked monthly to make sure that the cycle continues unabated! In spring perch several feet long glide along in the shallows. May brings tench, September the great catfish (some as long as five feet), while October chill brings on the northern pike. Carp is fished year-round, caught in winter by ice fishing in selected areas of the lake. Fishing guides, tackle shops and numerous associations and tours cater to anglers from all countries.

*Water chestnuts blooming in Lake Tisza (HNTB)*

Environmentally, the lake is divided into three basic parts. The area north of Highway 33 is the **Bird Reservation** of Lake Tisza (known as Tiszavalk Pool). Since 1973 priority has been given to protection of its natural resources. Tours in this area must be with a licensed guide, and along specified routes (check with Tourinform offices in the area; see *Appendix*).

**Aranyosi Bay**, the **Basin of Sarud**, and the **Small Tisza** border Lake Tisza's deepest hole, the **Poroszló Pool**. These areas, protected since 1966 as part of the Hortobagy National Park, are laced with trails that allow individual as well as guided tourism, where there are heron and cormorant colonies and fields of giant white water lilies, and the "fairy veil" fringed water lily. The balance of the lake, primarily on the southern and eastern shore, is devoted to watersports. Astonishingly, the parts of the Tisza open to the public make it the only motorboating recreational lake in Europe. This includes parts of the Bay of Sarud, the Bay of Abádsalók, and the Basin of Tiszafüred.

### THE WATER CHESTNUT

Flourishing in Hungary's Tisza channels, water chestnuts are registered in Europe as a highly endangered species. Once they covered the riverbanks and low-lying waters of the continent. But its tuberous root was once a source of food for the poor. Many a family survived times of war and scarcity because they harvested its white nut-like pulp, fried it, or turned it into pasty flour for water chestnut pancakes.

# ■ Places to Stay

 Unlike many areas, a large percentage of the accommodations in the Tisza area will book only for a minimum of four days to a week. Demand allows this, as many sportsmen, bird-watchers and fun-seekers book for extended periods.

## Tiszafüred

 **Nádas Panzió**, Tiszafüred, Kismuhi út 2, €, ☎ 36 59 511 401 or 36-30-219-4886, fax 36-59-511-402, tiszafured@nadaspanzio.hu, www.nadaspanzio.hu. Requires booking a week minimum. Bungalows for four to six people with air-conditioning, pool, sauna, Jacuzzi. Or two air-conditioned apartments with four rooms, including a kitchen, can compete with some two star hotels. Meals can be supplemented with the wine cellar offerings. See the website for the latest prices, which run about 5,000 to 7,000 HUF per person per night, breakfast included – an excellent rate considering the amenities. Children under 12 receive a 25% discount, and under age four are free.

**Hotel Hableány**, Hableány Vigadó, Tiszafüred-Örvény, 5358 Tiszafüred-Örvény, Hunyadi út 2, €, ☎/fax 36-59-353-3333, tiszafured@ tourinform.hu, www. dunaweb.hu/~hableany-hotel. This hotel has a restaurant, sauna, solarium,

| HOTEL PRICE CHART | |
|---|---|
| Double room without tax | |
| € | Under €80 |
| €€ | €81-€150 |
| €€€ | €151-€250 |
| €€€€ | Over €250 |

and can offer massages. Prices run from 5,000 HUF per person per night for a room, to about 7,000 HUF for an apartment, depending on season, including breakfast. A laundromat and dry-cleaning services are available to guests. The air-conditioned sports center includes a pool table, bowling, table tennis, and several other table games. The restaurant is superb and will serve dietary and vegetarian food if necessary; it offers terrace dining facing the Tisza shore. Boat

excursions and fishing are just a walk away (pictures of fish caught by guests sit on the front desk) and horse carriage and horseback riding excursions can be arranged by the hotel. English is halting, but communication is not impossible. Practice your Hungarian phrases and bring along your guidebook.

**Horgászcentrum**, 5350 Tiszafüred, Kasfono út 12, €, ☎ 36-30-9659-824 and ☎/fax 36-59-353-443, tiszafured@ tourinform.hu, www.horgaszcentrum.hu. Requires a one-week minimum. A two-star accommodation with fishing and a boat tour center, which can arrange accommodations at several local hotels or provide packages and facilities of their own. Open from April 15 to Oct 31. A one-week package for four is 108,000 HUF, with six nights in doubles at the Lilaakác Guesthouse. Your stay will follow a program, as follows: Day 1, arrival and bed down. Day 2, boat excursion through the Tisza Lake Bird Sanctuary (this takes about 4½ hours). Day 3, fishing from the boat and from shore. An alternative for family members who don't fish is an afternoon of potterymaking Hungarian-

style, with kiln, foot-operated potter's wheel, and instruction at the local guild workshop. Day 4, fish soup in the morning, as Hungarians are wont to do, and then an afternoon on the beach. Day 5 is a three-hour wildlife watching excursion to another part of Lake Tisza. Day 6, you ride a trail (about 3½ hours) along the Tisza levee. The last day is departure.

## Berekfürdő

**Termal Hotel Pávai**, H-5309 Berekfürdő, Pávai Vajna Ferenc út 3, €, ☎ 36-59-519-111 or 36-59-519-222, fax 36-59-519-444, termalhotelpavai@ netelek.hu, www.termalhotelpavai.hu. At 6,400 HUF to about 8,000 HUF per night, you get far more than a room. It is a three-star wellness hotel, and the price includes an excellent breakfast, and use of the hydro-massage pool and sauna. You will have to use cash, as they only accept cards from the OTP bank of Hungary. Parking lot, high-quality restaurant, hotel taxi, TV, mini-bar, air-conditioning, baby sitter, laundry, sauna, massage, thermal spa, thermal bath, fishing, billiards, horseback riding, boating, mini-golf, indoor pool, computer connections, movie channel, room service, central safe, 24-hour front desk, and diabetic meals.

Lake Tisza

## Sarud

**Guest House**, 3386 Sarud, Akácfa út 4, €, ☎ 36-36-362-194 or 36-30-550-7142 , sarud-info@ sarudi-piheno.hu, www. sarudi-piheno.hu. This is a home, for an extraordinarily low cost; 3,200 HUF per person per night, children under  three, 1,000 HUF, three-six, 1,800 HUF. Located two km/1.2 miles from the Tisza, so a car is definitely advisable. Its relatively central location is within an hour of the Zemplen Hills, the Tisza, Hortobagy National Park, and southern Hungary. So it is a perfect location for families with younger children who want to keep control over the distance their little feet may wander, yet be in striking distance of the sites of eastern and northern Hungary. The atmosphere cannot be duplicated. There are two bedrooms and two bathrooms, a well-equipped American-style kitchen and a sauna (depending on usage, they may add a fee for it), a fireplace, and living room with a color SAT television. The huge lawn includes a garden pond, a barbecue, a swimming pool, and a place for kettle cooking Hungarian-style. Trailers and tents can be pitched on the lawn with prior permission.

## Poroszló

**Hotel Club Thermál Kastély**, 3388 Poroszló, €€, ☎ 36-36-453-003 or 36-36-30-634-1582, poroszlokastely@ axelero.hu, www.poroszlokastely.hu. The cost of 7,000 HUF for a double room with two people means that for, cost and quality, this is one of the best. It's especially good for families or for retirees. The entire facility is fenced in and grassed, with an outside picnic area and children's play area. Though the pool is on the small side, it is nicely kept up. But the facilities for the money are hard to duplicate.

The apartments are studios. The downstairs rooms all have a small kitchen including a refrigerator, dining table and chairs, a large color television, and a small living room with couch. Upstairs, the sleeping quarters offer privacy and although there is no air-conditioning, the upstairs roof windows open out. Mosquitoes can be a problem. The bathrooms are newly tiled. A disco rocks a couple of hundred yards down the street until 2 am. In the same direction the restaurant is about 120 yards. The lake is a long stroll; about a half-mile to the boat slips, where you can take excursions. To get here, from M3 take the turnoff for Füzesabony, then follow Route 33 toward Tiszafüred about 20 km/12 miles. They are just off the road.

★**Fûzfa Pihenõpark** (Fûzfa Recreational Park), 3388 Poroszló, Kossuth Lajos út 81, €, ☎/fax 36-36-353-738, 36-36-353-008 or 36-30-9352-117, www.fapihenopark.hu, postmaster@ertank.axelero.net. This recreational park has a hotel in a main building and a series of excellent cabins along a dead branch of the Tisza River. Facilities include swimming pool, sauna, tennis courts, table tennis, bowling lanes, and an outdoor spit. There is also an on-site restaurant. Add to that a playground and a wading pool for children. Every room has a bathroom, a color SAT TV and mini-bar. A t10-day (nine-night) package is 90,000 HUF per person, which includes breakfast, free use of the swimming pool, fitness room, billiard tables, free paddle-boats, and free rowboats on a small private fishing lake.

# Abádszalók

**Füzes Camping és Panzió**, 5241 Abádszalók, Strand út 2, €, ☎/fax 36-59-535-345, fuzes@fw.hu or abadszalok@tourinform.hu. The hotel offers a three-day package at 14,900 HUF including half-board, parking space, participation in the summer programs of Abádszalók, a visit to the village museum, and a visit to the doll museum for a small group. They have several categories of rooms, from basic apartments to camping sites. The website has a complete listing with photos. Double rooms, at 8,500 HUF per night, have a toilet, shower, beds and TV (small Hungarian black and white), with a small closet, desk and chair. The bungalows and apartments are in two classes. Those that have a kitchen are Class I. These start at about 10,500 HUF, ranging up to 11,500 HUF.

The other bungalows, of a lower class, are about half the price, but there is no kitchen and the facilities are bare-bones, at 5,000 HUF per night. Tent sites are 300 HUF plus about 1,300 HUF per person. Entrance to the strand and the pools, normally 700  HUF for adults, is free for all overnight guests. Open May 1 to October 31.

# ■ Places to Eat

**Ezüst Horgony Étterem** (Silver Anchor Restaurant), €-€€, 3384 Kisköre Tisza II, Ltp7/A, ☎ 36-36-358-589, fax 36-36-358-130, ehorgony@amoba-2000.hu. This is a family type restaurant that fronts the hotel of the same name. It offers good food and good prices, but its all Hungarian.

| DINING PRICE CHART | |
|---|---|
| Price for an entrée, with tax | |
| € | Under $10 |
| €€ | $10-$25 |
| €€€ | Over $25 |

**Tisza-tó Panzió Étterem** (Lake Tisza apartments and restaurant), €, 3384 Kisköre, Platán sor 56, ☎ 36-36-358-667, 36-36-358-668, 36-70-337-0429, fax 36-36-358-669. This is also an inn, with tennis courts and air-conditioning. It's a good value at about 10,000 HUF for a double.

Open May 1st to Sept 15 the restaurant's average entrée is about 1,000 HUF and side dishes are 250 to 450 HUF. The halászlé (fish soup), from freshly caught Tisza fish, is a meal in itself. At this writing they are constructing a thermal spa next door. They have English-speaking waiters and menus.

**Hotel Hableány**, Hableány Vigadó, €, Tiszafüred-Örvény, 5358 Tiszafüred-Örvény, Hunyadi út 2, ☎ 36-59-353-3333. The restaurant at this hotel is excellent, English is on the menu, and there is a summer terrace with delightful atmosphere near the riverbank. Average entrée is about 1,000 HUF.

# ■ Itineraries

## Tiszaújváros

From Miskolc (see *Northern Hungary*) take Route 3 (E71) southwest, toward Budapest, and get off at Nyékládháza, where you connect to Route 35, and press east toward the

Tisza River. The first major town on our way is Tiszaújváros (www.tiszaujvaros.hu), just before the junction of the Tisza and Sajó rivers.

One of the most modern thermal baths in the country here may be worth a stopover – **Tiszaújváros Spa and Swimming Pool**, Teleki blanka út 2, ☎ 36-49-544-322, termal@ tujvaros.hu, www.termal. tujvaros.hu. As you enter town from Miskolc, make a left at Béke út (after the Shell gas station). Follow it all the way to Teleki blanka út, where you make a right. The baths will be on your left, just before the stadium and the sports complex. The adventure bath and medicinal pools are equipped with the latest technology. If you want maps or further information, as you drive up Béke út, make a left at Széchenyi út. Tourinform is at the end of that block, before the next intersection. The Triathlon World Cup, as well as many popular canoe and boat races are organized in Tiszaújváros. As a result, the town has a number of hotels and hostels.

Our next stop takes us further east on Route 35. We go over the Tisza River, on through the town of Polgár. We make a right off of Route 35 after we pass through Polgár, and head south, passing though the town of Folyás, and past the Hortobagy National Park office on the right, until we meet the next major inter-  section, which takes us west to Tiszacsege.

# Tiszacsege

Tiszacsege's 81°C/177°F
thermal water rises from a
depth of 1,150 m/3,772 feet,
at the **Tiszacsege
gyógyfürdő** (Tiszacsege
Healing Baths). Here, as in
other parts of Hungary, the
waters, after cooling, were
found to have healing
affects, suitable for the
treatment of rheumatic and

muscular pains, and even for herpes. It is at Tiszacsege 4066,
at Bocskai út and Fürdő út 6. If language is a problem, contact
the Tourinform office at ☎/fax 36-52-588-036, tiszacsege@
tourinform.hu, There are indoor and outdoor pools, dressing
cabins and eateries. Entrance fee is 500 HUF and the cabins
are 400 HUF. You can also see a glimpse of local village folk
history at the **Cotter House**, at 4066 Tiszacsege Hajdú-
Bihar Óvoda utca 24, ☎ 36-52-373-432. The small boat slip
which is in the suburbs near the river is a launching point for
boating excursions to Tokaj and Kiskörös (see *Adventures*).
However, we can press south toward a connection with Route
33, where we head west to Tiszafüred.

# Tiszafüred

In addition to Tourinform, The Tisza Lake Regional Tourism
Project Office is at 5350 Tiszafüred, Kossuth tér 1,
rmitiszato@hungarytourism.hu, where you can also get information and support relating to Tiszafüred (www.tiszafured.
lap.hu).

They come from all over
Europe for the curative
waters of the 39°C/102°F
**Tiszafüred Thermal Baths**,
5350 Tiszafüred, Poroslói út 2,
☎/fax 36-59-352-366. E-mail
Tourinform at tiszafured@
tourinform.hu if you have a

Lake Tisza

difficult time communicating. The healing waters have been found effective in treating locomotor ailments, some gynecological diseases, and in recovery from neurological diseases that cause muscular paralysis or atrophy. On the other hand, the **strand** on the Tisza shore has grassy lawns, with open-air showers, a 24-hour grocery store, restaurants, and snack bars. As you come through Tiszafüred, Route 33 becomes Fö út, then Baross Gábor út, after which it makes a 90-degree turn west, and changes into Poroszlói út. Watch for the MOL gas station on your right, and the Penny grocery store on the left. Turn left and it will take you directly to the strand.

In 1877, the first village museum in Hungary was founded in Tiszaüred, at the behest of Roman Catholic priest Endre Taricky. Its continuation was a testimony to tolerance and cooperation. The society established to support the museum welcomed all, regardless of religion or affiliations, and so eventually, the Calvinist Béla Milesz joined in, paving the way for many different faiths and occupations. The museum became a monument that was blind to social inequalities. The **Kiss Pál Museum**, Taricky sétány 6, exhibits the Füred saddle of the Csikos shepherds, an eclectic collection of folk art, ecological oddities and historical artifacts of the Tisza Lake and the great plains.

The **Gáspár Nyúzó Pottery and House**, at 5350 Tiszafüred, Malom út 12 ☎ 36 59 253 106, open May 1 to Sept 9, Tue-Sat 9 am to 12 pm and 2 to 5 pm, represents over 100 years of the same family and its Nyúzó pottery. In the early 1800s, finely made pottery was in great demand. Gáspár Nyúzó Sr. developed a great following, but his son blossomed into a far greater craftsman, producing designs that were true works of art. But, as his reputation spread, so did the industrial revolution. Mass-produced items became more common, and Gáspár Nyúzó II, though extraordinarily talented, became a part of history. By 1910 he was forced to close up the pottery business, upon which the family and the home had been based for over a hundred years. Gáspár Nyúzó II went to work in a beer factory. The house is essentially the same, with the furniture as it was then, and even the last work that he molded with his hands is here.

Pottery gained fame in Hungary in the early 19th century. The Miska Jug earthenware is made by hand in the tradition of the Alföld. It is usually made with a Hussar figure on its face, with buttons and rich decorative trim on his clothing. Today the pottery tradition is carried on by the **Fazekasság (pottery) house** belonging to Nagyné Török Zsóka, at Szõlõsi út 27, where you can watch pottery being made in the old tradition, and buy souvenirs.

Now, we can go back east on Route 33 to Route 34 south. Route 34 south leads through the southern great plains area that borders the Tisza. At Kunmadaras, leave 34 and bear southeast toward Berekfürdõ (next stop), and Karcag.

## Berekfürdõ

Berekfürdõ springs out from the earth. Literally. Again, as in so many other places in Hungary, this is home to hot water from deep in the earth. It is popular for the treatment of locomotive diseases such as arthritis, osteoporosis of the spine and

some cardiovascular treatments as well. **Berek Spa** (Termál és Strandfürdõ, Berek tér 11, ☎ 36-59-519-029, fax 36-59-319-302) is a huge thermal bath complex with two covered swimming pools, and seven outdoor pools, waterfalls, eateries, green lawns for lounging, and a host of medical services. As a help, the **Berekfürdõ Tourinform** office is at the thermal

Lake Tisza

complex (see *Appendix*), berekfurdo@tourinform.hu. There are a number of fairly good hotels here as well.

It also hosts a glass factory, the origin of the unique Fátyol glass (gossamer or frosted glass), and its "veil-glass," decorated with delicate hairline clefts. However, to tour the factory you must have a guide, arranged through Tourinform (at the thermal baths). For atmosphere it is probably best to visit this place during the Berekfürdő Days open-air folk festival, from mid-June to the end of August. Now, however, we continue farther south to Karcag.

# Karcag

The Nagykunság region is southeast of Lake Tisza. It skirts the Hortobagy National Park and a flat land marked by its tumuli – conical or dome-shaped mounds of five-10 m/16-32 feet high. They are thought to have been ancient burial mounds of the nomadic Kun people, who settled here in the 13th century. The Kun's extraordinary reputation as warriors was, ironically, balanced by a sense of artistry, which showed in their fine furniture and unique skill in pottery making.

Visit the **Györffy István Nagykun Museum** at Kálvin út 4, ☎ 59-31-2087, karcagimuzeum@netquick.hu, to see the first-prize winner of the Brussels World Exhibition, the Miska Jug, and other examples of unique folk art, glazed black crockery, the bone lace, and the colorfully embroidered long black coat of the plains.

The **Regional House of the Naykunság**, the Nagykunsági Tájház, at Jokai út 6, is a traditional peasant house known as the Kun house, typical of 18th- through early 20th-century Cumanian culture. May 1 to Sept 30, 10 am to 2 pm, Tue-Sun.

Sándor Kántor, winner of international and national prizes for his superb pottery work is at the **Fazakasház** (Pottery House) at Erkel Ferenc út 1.

The **Szélmalmi Fogadoház Pub** is at the southern entrance of the Hortobágy National Park. Converted to a park entry building, it is a preserved 19th-century windmill, the only one left. May 1 to Sept 30, 10 am to 6 pm Mon-Fri. ☎ 36-59-313-200 or 36-59-503-224. Almost across the street from it, the

**Windmill Reception House,**Vágóhíd út 22, ☎ 36-59-400-064 is a preserved 19th-century windmill, the only one left standing of the 60 that once occupied the area.

The town's open-air spas and swimming pools are located at Forrás út 3, off Madarasi út on to Deák körút and then west on Forrás út.

# Kunhegyes

Why stop here, amidst the fields of sunflowers and wheat? Perhaps you can grab an expresso at one of the few chardas or cafés as you pass through town, or you may want to stop at the two- to three-star **Kunhegyes Sport Hotel**, with its sports facilites and pool (for a budget family or single, see *Places to Stay*).

This was the birth place of Gabor Sego (1895-1985). For most of us who may not be familiar with the name, he was formerly the Chairman of the Department of Mathematics at Stanford University until his retirement in 1960, and turned it into one of the finest mathematics departments in the world. All children in Hungary have annual mathematics problem-solving competitions, which they perform from their home, and which are sent into the national center for grading and processing. Sego benefited from this and eventually he authored unrivaled classics in the instruction of advanced mathematics. He was forced out of Hungary by antisemitic pressures and fled to America. His bust is in front of the town library.

On a contemporary note, the Kunhegyes Sport Hotel is also the center of the international Kun Cup competitions in basekball, soccer, handball, and volleyball. They are the largest tournament organizers in Hungary, and the largest private training camp for youth in the country. Perhaps your school class might give this a try, as their training camps are known throughout the world for low prices, outstanding facilites, and high-quality instruction. Leaving town now, we head north to Abádszalók.

## Abádszalók

Before venturing in the town I would strongly urge that you contact **Tourinform** to help you explore the literally hundreds of options and get your bearings here. Expect tons of people and crowded beaches. Abádszalók Bay (www. abadszalok.hu) is the recreation paradise of the Tisza southern shore, the home of power-boating, ski events, free ranging water acrobatics, giant slides and a jet ski course. The longest stretch of beach in the region is along Feltáró ut. Here you can rent sailing boats and surfboards, rowboats and excursion craft. The **Abádszalók Summer Festival** attracts the young crowd as well as younger families for its active nightlife and daytime fun. Dozens of bars, büfés, cafés and restaurants, tour agencies, hotels and hostels, each offer their own special programs to entertain and educate.

The beach alternates between grassy lawn and sand. Umbrellas and beach gear may be rented at many shops that line the strand. Water bobsled, parachuting, and hot air balloon fly-overs complement the thermal baths that are located here as well. The **Puppet Museum**, in the Village House at 41 Kiraly István út, is a reminder that you are in Hungary and not at a French beach resort. It displays 250 handmade puppets dressed in authentic folk costumes of the Carpathian basin, along with tools, furniture and crafts.

## Dream Beaches

This is the more settled and less developed side of the lake. Coming from Abádszalók, travel southward across the bottom of the lake and then west to pass the Vizügyi Repülotér (Vizügyi Airport), taking the first road to the right, which leads north toward Kiskore.

**Kiskore** (www.kiskore.hu) looks out on the Tisza, with a history of over 700 years of farming. Nevertheless, the oldest building in the village is only the Baroque Roman Catholic church built in 1777. Incredibly, pews are hand-carved oak, and the wooden Baroque pulpit is the original one. With the exception of mass, however, the church is closed. Mass is at 6 pm, Sun, Mon, Wed and Fri. The **Village Museum** is in a preserved house built in 1856. Everything in the house is from the period, including the loom in the middle of the main room, which you can try out, and the barn, which stores the horse carriages and the tools of the farm. Kossuth Lajos út 8, ☎ 36-358-023. Open from 10 am to 12 pm. May 1 to Sept 30. Closed Mondays.

Of course the main attraction is the shore, with its water slides, motorboats, row boats, kayaks, canoes, jet skis, swimming, beach soccer and an outdoor cinema. Restaurants are all within walking distance. The strand also has camping sites for tents, motorhomes, trailers, and motorbikers (rates are 400 HUF per day, with an added 400 HUF for electricity). Contact **Kisköre Strand Sétány**, ☎/fax 36-36-358-194, kiskore@agria.hu. Tickets to use the beach average 300 to 500 HUF for the day. For motorboats, skis and accessories, contact **Rabby Lajos** (Banana Joe), Kisköre, Szabadvizû Strand (the free beach), ☎ 36-30-242-6320.

Leaving Kisköre, our next stop to the north is **Tiszanána** (www.tiszanana.hu), situated by a wide stream, five km/three miles from the shoreline village of Dinnyéshát. The beach is cordoned off by barriers. Sunbathing terraces and grass are bordered by trails and a restaurant. The islands offshore from the strand can be reached with a hand-controlled ferry. Tent space can be rented (check with Tourinform, see *Appendix*). This area is home to a large Roma population, meaning gypsy bands and folk festivals. However, we continue on throuigh **Sarud**, widely known by local fishermen. The sand is particularly smooth and silky, making it popular for bathers as well.

The next stop to the north is **Poroszlo** (www.poroszlo.hu). The grassy sunbathing spots are complemented by ample shoreline rentals and facilities for families. The restaurants and csárdas here all carry fish specialties, Hungarian-style, and every one will delight you with its own selection of halászlé (Hungarian soup). Fish catches are abundant in the Poroszló Pool, the central part of the lake inhabited by huge quantities of predatory fish. So, as you would expect, anglers shops are plentiful here. A couple of places of interest may be worth a stop here as well. The **Tájház Village Museum** contains a collection of fishing implements from hundreds of

Lake Tisza

years ago, and chronicles the history of fishing in the area. The **Cathedral of the Great Plain** is a twin-towered Calvinist chapel with a capacity of 5,000 people, visible at great distances on the Puszta (the grassland plains).

## Tiszavalk

To the north of Highway 33, in the month of August, as the last days of summer wind down, in the northern villages of the lake you will see men harvesting the long bulrush reeds in the backwaters of the Tisza region (the Tiszavalki Basin). It has been this way for centuries. The dried plant is taken in sheaves, and then processed at home, either by "spinners" or by "weavers," producing baskets, bags, doormats, and small pieces of furniture out of the same material. Today the people of Tisvavalk live for their craft.

# ■ Adventures

## Hiking & Biking

**Middle Lake Excursion.** In this region you cannot get lost. Simply follow the dike system of the Tisza rivers, and cross over the bridges and passageways of the Tisza ring. It is the same for bike riding as it is for hiking. There are no significant slopes; the land is gentle and offers no resistance. Hiking the entire Tisza region replicates the way of life on the lakeside and bog 200 years ago. Hundreds of miles of pathways assure enjoyment.

One path about 74 km/46 miles long is excellent for both cyclists and hikers. Follow the bike signs that start at the shoreline and lead along the dykes, starting in Tiszafüred and heading southward toward Abádszalók, through Tiszabura, Pusztataksony, Kisköre, Tiszanána, Sarud, Újlőrincfalva, Poroszló, and then across the bridge back to Tiszafüred. This is an easy tour. Because of its ease and proximity to the primary sights, it can be combined with a day at the beach, and some beautiful views from the dikes. Because these are public roads, you are never far from a place to take a break or stay the night.

**Cycling the Upper Tisza.** Starting in Tokaj, you should allow three to four days to cover about 225 km/135 miles, riding through Taktabáj, Prügy,

Taktakenéz, Taktaharkány, Tikszalúc, Kesznyéten, Tiszaújváros, Tiszapalkonia, Oszlár, Hejõkürt, Mezõcsát, Ároktõ, Tiszadorogma, Tiszabábolna, Tiszavalk, Négyes, Borsodivánka, Poroszló, Tiszafüred, Tiszaszentimre, Kunmadars, Karcag, Kunhegyes, Tiszagyenda, Tiszaroff, Fegyvemek, Nagykörû and Törökszentmiklos. This excursion is on public roads, which sometimes can get busy, but on this route they are usually quiet.

## On Water

**Sport Boating Association of the Tisza**, contact Gyula Berényi, 2120 Dunakeszi, Németh László köz 4/C, ☎ /fax 36-27-345-655 or 36-60-341-859.

To take a cruise, try **Mahart Passnave Kft.**, Tiszacsegei Képviselete, 3534 Miskolc, Iván u. 18 I/4. Contact Kiss Lászlo, ☎ /fax 36-46-372-803. From May through October you can take a cruise that allows you to experience the wildlife of the lake and the river. The boat leaves Tiszacsege at 9 am and returns at 7 pm. Adults pay 5,800 HUF, children ages four-14, 4,300 HUF. The cost includes lunch, a stop at the lock of Kisköre, and a 1½- to two-hour side-excursion by motorboat from the Szabics Marina to the bird sanctuary and back. The boat can also be rented for special occasions.

To rent a catamaran, contact **Poroszló Nyárfa Camping**, 3388 Poroszló, Alsóréti út 16/a, ☎ 36-36-353-162 or 36-30-299-7762.

Boats, kayaks and cannoes can be rented at the marinas. Generally rowboats will run 1,500 to 2,500 HUF per day, motorboats 4,000 to 5,000 HUF per day plus gas. Boat trips with a guide usually consist of four people and average 4,000 to 7,700 HUF for two hours.

Fishing trips with a guide will cost an average of 3,500 HUF to 6,000 HUF per day plus gas. Hungary requires fishing licenses. Contact Tourinform (see *Appendix* for Tisza offices) to obtain referral phone numbers.

Tours by canoe, rowboat, motorboat, or kayak must be done along posted routes in the sanctuary areas. The rules are strictly enforced. Violations can lead to a hefty fine if not temporary imprisonment, so especially in this area you must follow the rules.

The following harbor marinas will provide boat rentals of all types and may also provide tour and fishing guides.

Lake Tisza

**Szalók Harbor**, 5241 Abádszalók, József A. Krt. 42, ☎ 36-59-445-174, fax 36-59-445-174.

**Tiszavirág Harbor**, 5243 Tiszaderzs, Pf. 4, ☎ 36-70-310-7189 or 36-70-262-6694.

**Katamarán Harbor**, 5350 Tiszafüred-Örvény, ☎ 36-30-952-7039.

**Szabics Harbor**, 5358 Tiszafüred-Örvény, ☎ 36-30-954-8620, fax 36-59-511-123, tiszafured@tourinfom.hu.

**Cormoran Harbor**, 5358 Tiszafüred-Örvény, Kormorán Harbor, ☎ 36-20-939-1979, fax 36-59-350-350, kormoran@mail.datanet.hu.

**Albatrosz Harbor**, 5350 Tiszafüred, Bán Zsigmond ut 67, ☎ 36-30-967-6037, fax 36-59 351-523.

**Dolphin Harbor**, 3588 Poroszló, ☎ 36-36-353-826.

**Tiszanána-Dinnyésháti Harbor**, 3385 Tiszanána, Fő ut 108/1, ☎ 36-36-366-429, fax 36-36-566-005, dinnyeshat@mail.datanet.hu.

## Spas & Baths

 The baths at **Berekfürdő**, with their waterfall, adventure pool, eateries and slides are much more than fun, and they almost seem magical. When the geologist Ferenc Pávai Vajna discovered an underground thermal spring in 1928, there appeared to be nothing special about it. Imré Mándoki opened up a strand with the newly drilled spring in 1929. But the numbers of people soon far exceeded the original estimates. The waters seemed to have marvelous properties for rejuvenation, and people returned again and again, often bringing others with them. By the mid-1930s the entire country had heard about it. Incredibly, tests later found a direct correlation between using the baths and healing of rheumatological and nervous disorders. Doctors and nurses now complement the regular staff there, as do wellness hotels at all levels of luxury. The **Berekfürdő Thermal and Open-Air Baths** are at at 5309 Berekfürdő, Berek tér 11 (see *Itineraries*).

**Tiszaújváros** is a lot of fun if you get there early but, as the day goes on in the summer months, expect the crowd to thicken. This is both a medical facility and a grand complex of pools, places to eat, slides, waves, waterfalls, and adventure pools. Separate medicinal baths are devoted to the cure of gout, nervous disorders, and rheumatic disabilities. Their facilities are also designed to receive the handicapped. Expect to pay around 1,000 HUF per person at the door. Once inside, there are places where you can eat. The medicinal baths, sauna, mud treatments, etc, all have individual fees. Take a family cabin for privacy, security, and peace of mind. Contact them at **Tiszaújváros Termálfürdő**, 3580 Tiszaújváros, Teleki Blanka út. 2, ☎ 36-49-544-570, fax 36-49-341-420, termal@tujvaros.hu and www.termal.tujvaros.hu (also see *Itineraries*).

# Horseback Riding

**Patkós Csárda Motel and Campground**, 5350 Tiszafüred-Egyk, ☎ 36-52-378-605 or fax 36-52-378-100, is at the "western gate" of the Hortobágy National Park, eight km/4.8 miles from Tiszafüred on Highway 33. The csárda has bungalows and apartments, with doubles, including a bathroom and TV in each room. The csárda is over 250 years old, still sporting thatched roofs. The accommodations are a bit close to the stables, but the restaurant serves Hungarian dishes, with gypsy music. A weekend special at this writing includes three days and two nights in three- to six-person groups, at 36,000 HUF. The package includes full board. Individually, meals will average about 5,000 HUF. Riding lessons can be had for 3,000 HUF per person. Though this place may be available for lodging, I do not recommend it, as the flies are horrible in the area (after all it is a farm). It is better to stay at the **Hableany Hotel** and then come to the ranch for a day excursion if you are not on a tour. The weekend program starts on Friday, with an assessment of your riding level, and then a short tour (six-eight km/three-five miles) of the Lake Tisza. Anyone interested can try team driving! On Saturday you ride through the Egyek-Pusztakócsi marshes (30 km/19 miles), visit the Csárda Museum, the Black Marsh Nature Trail, the Górés Farm for Predatory Birds Repatriation Center and the Jusztus Mangalica Pig Reserve. On Sunday you travel along the Tisza (30 km/19 miles), crossing creeks and viewing the natural wonders on horseback.

**Janos Loska**, 2688 Vanyarc-Sarlóspuszta, ☎/fax 36-32-484-064 and 36-20-455-7251 (cell), jloska@freemail.hu, www.lovastura.hu, or contact Márta Jokai, Özgida út 32, 1025

Lake Tisza

Budapest, ☎/fax 36-1-325-6349, 36-20-911-8275, jokaim@hu.
inter.net. This horseback tour operator offers transport, full
board, horses, and lodging for an entire week at €1,090 per
person. They can be relied on for a quality tour that will give
you a good feel for the Hungarian countryside, with excellent
cuisine and hospitality. The Hortobágy National Park riding
tour starts in Tiszafüred, heads through the Puszta (the
plains), and then goes north to Tokaj, where you visit the wine
cellars. The first day can include a transfer from Budapest to
Tisazafüred. You stay at the Hotel Hableány, which has wonderful views overlooking the river and absolutely great Hungarian food. The rooms are good, each with bathroom and TV.
On day two, you leave from the Gulyás Farm and move out to
the Puszta, the grassland plains. Days two through seven are
spent riding and picnicing, visiting csárdas across the Puszta.
Extras may include visiting the Shepherd Museum in
Hortobágy, a Csikós party on the Puszta, thermal baths and
swimming. You will see the typical Puszta animals, the racka
sheep, grey-cattle, nóniusz horses, curly hair pigs and hundreds of birds. One evening you will visit with shepherds as
they cook their typical Puszta food, Slambuc, over a campfire.

## In the Air

 **Hot-air ballon flights** start at Tiszacsege, at
Kossuth út 13, July 10 through August 15, including weekends. Special arrangements can be made
for other times of the year. Costs are 22,000 HUF
for adults; children under 12 are 18,000 HUF. Call **Szabó
Péter**, 1154 Budapest, Szerencs út 176, ☎ 36-30-949-4311,
szpeter.ballon@dpg.hu, www.extra.hu/ballonsport. Wear
warm clothing. You start at 6 am and drift in the sky until
about 6:30 pm. You can take photos of the lake and Puszta
habitats of Hungary, of farmers in their fields, and the horizon as the sun sets. The flight lasts about 50 minutes. At the
end of the flight you are presented with a certificate as a balloon flyer!

**Flights in small airplanes** (including photo shoots) over the
region can be made through **AERO-WASP**, Darazsac András,
5300 Karcag, Szövetkezet út 2/c, ☎/fax 36-59-400-194 or 36-
20-9256-990 (cell), http://aero-wasp.internettudakozo.hu/
indexen.htm.

# Appendix

## Star Ratings

### Official Hotel Ratings

Star ratings in Hungary are assigned by the Hotel Association of Hungary (HAH). Their website is www.hah.hu. Click on *Classification in Hungary* for a detailed explanation of the rating system. However, for a quick comparison, click on *Tourist Guide to Hotels Classification Hungary* after you click *Classification in Hungary*.

Generally, **five-star** hotels all have 24-hour room service, garage services, language facility in at least three foreign languages, 24-hour concierge, and air-conditioning in every room. They have butlers, a sophisticated service and staff, and are fairly luxurious. **Four-stars** have smaller rooms, and do not necessarily have air-conditioning in the rooms or a garage on the property. **Three-stars** have both private and shared bathrooms. They are required to have a 24-hour front desk manned by personnel who can speak at least two languages. Their services are not as broad, nor do they necessarily have a garage. They are required to have a front desk.

### Author Star Ratings

Attractions, restaurants, hotels and sites of all kinds have been rated by the author, a resident of Budapest. Blue stars may indicate unbelievable ambience, magnificent views, great entertainment, or the best food. Sites with special appeal are given **one star** (★). An attraction given **two stars** (★★) is outstanding. If it has **three stars** (★★★), don't miss it!

## Tourinform Offices

### Western Transdanubia

Bük
    9737 Eötvös u. 11.
    ☎ (94) 558-419, (94) 558-439, fax (94) 359-322
    buk@tourinform.hu, www.buk.hu
Celldömölk
    9500 Dr. Géfin L. tér 1.
    ☎/fax (95) 423-940
    celldomolk@tourinform.hu, www.celldomolk.hu
Fertőd
    9431 J. Haydn u. 3.
    ☎/fax (99) 370-544, ☎ (99) 370-182
    fertod@tourinform.hu, www.fertod.hu
Fertőszéplak
    9436 Nagy Lajos u. 43. (peak season)

☎ (99) 537-140, fax (99) 537-141
fertoszeplak@tourinform.hu, www.fertoszeplak.hu
Győr
    9021 Árpád u. 32.
    ☎/fax (96) 311-771, ☎ (96) 336-817
    gyor@tourinform.hu, www.gyor.hu
Kőszeg
    9730 Jurisics tér 7.
    ☎ (94) 563-120, ☎/fax (94) 563-121
    koszeg@tourinform.hu, www.koszeg.hu
Lenti
    8960 Táncsics M. u. 2/A.
    ☎ (92) 551-188, fax (92) 551-189
    lenti@tourinform.hu, www.lenti.hu
Mosonmagyaróvár
    9200 Kápolna tér 16.
    ☎/fax (96) 206-304
    mosonmagyarovar@tourinform.hu, www.mosonmagyarovar.hu
Nagykanizsa
    8800 Csengery u. 1-3.
    ☎ (93) 313-285, fax (93) 536-077
    nagykanizsa@tourinform.hu, tourinform.nagykanizsa.hu, www.
    nagykanizsa.hu
Őrség
    9941 Őriszentpéter, Siskaszer 26/A
    ☎ (94) 548-034, fax (94) 428-791
    orseg@tourinform.hu
Pannonhalma
    9090 Petőfi u. 25.
    ☎/fax (96) 471-733
    pannonhalma@tourinform.hu, www.pannonhalma.hu
Sárvár
    9600 Várkerület 33.
    ☎ (95) 520-178, (95) 520-181, fax (95) 520-179
    sarvar@tourinform.hu, www.sarvar.hu
Sopron
    9400 Liszt Ferenc u. 1.
    ☎ (99) 517-560, (99) 517-561, fax (99) 517-527
    sopron@tourinform.hu, www.sopron.hu
Szombathely
    9700 Kossuth Lajos u. 1-3.
    ☎ (94) 514-451, fax (94) 514-450
    szombathely@tourinform.hu, www.szombathely.hu
Zalaegerszeg
    8900 Széchenyi tér 4-6. Pf.: 506
    ☎ (92) 316-160, (92) 510-696, fax (92) 510-697
    zalaegerszeg@tourinform.hu, www.zalaegerszeg.hu

# Lake Balaton Region
Alsóörs
    8226 Strand sétány 1. (peak season)
    ☎/fax (87) 575-001
    alsoors@tourinform.hu, www.alsoors.hu
Badacsonytomaj
    8261 Park utca 6.
    ☎/fax (87) 431-046, ☎ (87) 531-013
    badacsonytomaj@tourinform.hu, www.badacsonytomaj.hu

Balatonalmádi
   8220 Városháza tér 4.
   ☎/fax (88) 594-080, ☎ (88) 594-081
   balatonalmadi@tourinform.hu, www.balatonalmadi.hu
Balatonboglár
   8630 Erzsébet u. 12-14.
   ☎/fax (85) 550-168
   balatonboglar@tourinform.hu, www.balatonboglar.hu
Balatonföldvár
   8623 Széchenyi Imre utca 2. (peak season)
   ☎ (84) 700-036, ☎/fax (84) 540-220
   8623 Kőröshegyi út 1. (off season)
   ☎ (84) 700-036, ☎/fax (84) 540-220
   balatonfoldvar@tourinform.hu, www.balatonfoldvar.hu
Balatonfüred
   8230 Petőfi u. 68.
   ☎ (87) 580-480, fax (87) 580-481
   balatonfured@tourinform.hu, www.balatonfured.hu
Balatonkenese
   8174 Táncsics Mihály u. 24.
   ☎/fax (88) 594-645
   balatonkenese@tourinform.hu, www.balatonkenese.hu
Balatonvilágos
   8171 Aligai út 1.
   ☎/fax (88) 446-034
   balatonvilagos@tourinform.hu, www.balatonvilagos.hu
Buzsák
   8695 Fő tér 1/a
   ☎ (85) 530-070
   buzsak@tourinform.hu, www.buzsak.hu
Fonyód
   8640 Ady Endre u. 1.
   ☎/fax (85) 560-313
   fonyod@tourinform.hu, www.fonyod.hu
Gyenesdiás
   8315 Kossuth L. u. 97.
   ☎/fax (83) 511-790
   gyenesdias@tourinform.hu, www.gyenesdias.hu
Keszthely
   8360 Kossuth L. u. 28.
   ☎/fax (83) 314-144, ☎ (83) 511-660, (83) 511-661
   keszthely@tourinform.hu, www.keszthely.hu
Révfülöp
   8253 Villa Filip tér 8/b
   ☎/fax (87) 563-091, ☎ (87) 463-194
   revfulop@tourinform.hu, www.revfulop.hu
Siófok
   8600 Víztorony, Pf.: 75.
   ☎/fax (84) 315-355, (84) 310-117
   siofok@tourinform.hu, www.siofok.hu
Tapolca
   8300 Fő tér 17.
   ☎ (87) 510-777, fax (87) 510-778
   tapolca@tourinform.hu, www.tapolca.hu
Tihany
   8237 Kossuth L. u. 20.

**Appendix**

☎/fax(87) 448-804, ☎ (87) 438-016
tihany@tourinform.hu, www.tihany.hu
Vonyarcvashegy
8314 Kossuth u. 42. (peak season)
☎ (83) 348-033, fax (83) 548-021
vonyarcvashegy@tourinform.hu
Zalakaros
8749 Gyógyfürdő tér 10.
☎/fax (93) 340-421
zalakaros@tourinform.hu, www.zalakaros.hu
Zamárdi
8621 Kossuth utca 16.
☎ (84) 345-291, (84) 545-052, (84) 545-053, fax (84) 345-290
zamardi@tourinform.hu, www.zamardi.hu

# Central Transdanubia

Bakonybél
8427 Fő u. 15.
☎/fax (88) 461-476
bakonybel@tourinform.hu, www.bakonybel.hu
Bakonyszombathely
2884 Kossuth u. 50.
☎ (34) 359-155, fax (34) 359-122
bakonyszombathely@tourinform.hu, www.bakonyszombathely.hu
Dunaújváros
2400 Vasmû út 10/a
☎/fax (25) 500-148, (25) 500-149
dunaujvaros@tourinform.hu, www.dunaujvaros.hu
Enying
8130 Kossuth u. 29.
☎ (22) 372-952, ☎/fax (22) 572-072
enying@tourinform.hu, www.enying.hu
Gárdony
2483 Szabadság út 16.
☎ (22) 570-078, ☎/fax (22) 570-077
gardony@tourinform.hu, www.gardony.hu
Komárom
2900 Igmándi út 2.
☎ (34) 540-590, ☎/fax (34) 540-591
komarom@tourimform.hu, www.komarom.hu
Pákozd
8095 Budai út 134.
☎ (22) 732-002, fax (22) 458-722
pakozd@tourinform.hu
Pápa
8500 Fő u. 5.
☎/fax (89) 311-535
papa@tourinform.hu, www.papa.hu
Sümeg
8330 Kossuth L. u. 15.
☎ (87) 550-276, ☎/fax (87) 550-275
sumeg@tourinform.hu, www.sumeg.hu
Székesfehérvár (megyei)
8000 Piac tér 12-14.
☎ (22) 312-818, fax (22) 502-772
fejer-m@tourinform.hu, www.tourinform.fejer.hu, www.szekesfehervar.hu

Székesfehérvár (városi)
   8000 Városház tér 1.
   ☎ (22) 537-261, ☎/fax (22) 340-330
   szekesfehervar@tourinform.hu, www.szekesfehervar.hu
Tata
   2890 Ady Endre út 9. Pf.: 218
   ☎/fax (34) 586-045, (34) 586-046
   tata@tourinform.hu, www.tata.hu, www.kembridge.hu/tourinform
Veszprém
   8200 Megyeház tér 1.
   ☎ (88) 545-045, (88) 545-047, (88) 545-048, (88) 545-049
   fax (88) 545-039
   veszprem-m@tourinform.hu, www.vpmegye.hu
Veszprém
   8200 Vár utca 4.
   ☎/fax (88) 404-548
   veszprem@tourinform.hu, www.veszpreminfo.hu, www.veszprem.hu
Zirc
   8420 József Attila u. 1.
   ☎ (88) 416-816, fax (88) 416-817
   zirc@tourinform.hu, www.zirc.hu

## Southern Transdanubia

Bóly
   7754 Erzsébet tér 1.
   ☎/fax (69) 368-100
   boly@tourinform.hu, www.boly.hu
Csurgó
   8840 Csokonai u. 24.
   ☎/fax (82) 571-046
   csurgo@tourinform.hu, www.csurgo.hu
Dombóvár
   7200 Hunyadi tér 27.
   ☎/fax (74) 466-053
   dombovar@tourinform.hu, www.dombovar.hu
Dunaföldvár
   7020 Rákóczi u. 2.
   ☎/fax (75) 341-176
   dunafoldvar@tourinform.hu, www.dunafoldvar.hu, www.dunasio.hu
Harkány
   7815 Kossuth u. 2/a
   ☎ (72) 479-624, fax (72) 479-989
   harkany@tourinform.hu, www.harkany.hu
Kaposvár
   7400 Csokonai u. 3.
   ☎/fax (82) 317-133, ☎ (82) 508-151
   somogy-m@tourinform.hu, www.somogytourism.hu
Kaposvár
   7400 Fő u. 8.
   ☎ (82) 512-921, (82) 512-922, fax (82) 320-404
   kaposvar@tourinform.hu, www.kaposvar.hu
Kárász
   7333 Petőfi u. 36.
   ☎/fax (72) 420-074
   karasz@tourinform.hu, www.szaszvar.hu
Magyarhertelend
   7394 Kossuth L. u. 46.

☎/fax (72) 521-001, ☎ (72) 521-002
magyarhertelend@tourinform.hu, www.magyarhertelend.hu
Mohács
 7700 Széchenyi tér 1.
 ☎ (69) 505-515, (69) 510-113, fax (69) 505-504
 mohacs@tourinform.hu, www.mohacs.hu
Nagyatád
 7500 Baross Gábor u. 2.
 ☎ (82) 553-012, fax (82) 553-013
 nagyatad@tourinform.hu, www.nagyatad.hu
Orfű
 7677 Széchenyi tér 1.
 ☎ (72) 598-115, (72) 598-116, fax (72) 598-119
 orfu@tourinform.hu, www.orfu.hu
Paks
 7030 Szent István tér 2.
 ☎ (75) 421-575, fax (75) 510-265
 paks@tourinform.hu, www.paks.hu
Pécs
 7621 Széchenyi tér 9.
 ☎ (72) 213-315, (72) 511-232, ☎/fax (72) 212-632
 baranya-m@tourinform.hu, www.pecs.hu
Pécsvárad
 7720 Kossuth Lajos u. 31.
 ☎/fax (72) 466-487
 pecsvarad@tourinform.hu, www.pecsvarad.hu
Siklós
 7800 Felszabadulás u. 3.
 ☎ (72) 579-090, fax (72) 579-091
 siklos@tourinform.hu, www.siklos.hu
Szekszárd
 7100 Bajcsy-Zsilinszky u. 7.
 ☎ (74) 418-907, fax (74) 412-082
 tolna-m@tourinform.hu, www.szekszard.hu
Szekszárd
 7100 Garay tér 18.
 ☎ (74) 511-263, ☎/fax (74) 511-264
 szekszard@tourinform.hu, www.szekszard.hu
Tamási
 7090 Szabadság u. 29.
 ☎/fax (74) 470-902
 tamasi@tourinform.hu, www.tamasi.hu

## Budapest Central Danubia

TOURINFORM HEAD OFFICE - POLICE INFO OFFICE
 Budapest
 1052 Deák tér (Sütő utca 2.)
 (Opening hours: every day 8 am-8 pm)
Budapest
 1061 Liszt Ferenc tér 11.
 ☎ (1) 322-4098, fax (1) 342-9390
 liszt@budapestinfo.hu
Budapest
 1062 Western Railway Station
 ☎/fax (1) 302-8580
 nyugati@budapestinfo.hu

Budapest (Buda Castle)
  1014 Szentháromság tér
  ☎ (1) 488-0475, fax (1) 488-0474
  var@budapestinfo.hu
Budapest
  1052 Városház u. 7.
  ☎ (1) 428-0377, (1) 428-0375, fax (1) 353-2956
  pest-m@tourinform.hu
Budapest
  Ferihegy Airport Terminal 2A and 2B
Cegléd
  2700 Kossuth tér 1.
  ☎ (53) 500-285, fax (53) 500-286
  cegled@tourinform.hu, www.cegled.hu
Gödöllő
  2100 Királyi Kastély
  ☎/fax (28) 415-402, (28) 415-403
  godollo@tourinform.hu, www.gkrte.hu, www.godollotourinform.hu
Ócsa
  2364 Bajcsy-Zsilinszky utca 2.
  ☎ (29) 578-750 ☎/fax (29) 578-751
  ocsa@tourinform.hu, www.ocsa.hu
Ráckeve
  2300 Kossuth L. u. 51.
  ☎/fax (24) 429-747
  rackeve@tourinform.hu, www.rackeve.hu, www.tourinform.rackeve.hu
Rétság
  2651 Rákóczi út 26.
  ☎ (35) 550-155, fax (35) 550-156
  retsag@tourinform.hu, www.retsag.hu
Szentendre
  2000 Dumtsa Jenő u. 22.
  ☎/fax (26) 317-965, (26) 317-966
  szentendre@tourinform.hu, www.szentendre.hu
Vác
  2600 Március 15. tér 16-18.
  ☎ (27) 316-160, fax (27) 316-464
  vac@tourinform.hu, www.vac.hu
Veresegyház
  2112 Fő út 35.
  ☎/fax (28) 558-036, ☎ (28) 558-035
  veresegyhaz@tourinform.hu, www.veresegyhaz.hu, www.veresikisterseg.
  hu
Zsámbék
  2072 Etyeki u. 2.
  ☎/fax (23) 342-318
  zsambek@tourinform.hu, www.zsambek.hu

## Southern Great Plains Region

Baja
  6500 Szentháromság tér 5.
  ☎ (79) 420-793, ☎/fax (79) 420-792
  baja@tourinform.hu, www.baja.hu
Békéscsaba
  5600 Szent István tér 9.
  ☎/fax (66) 441-261
  bekescsaba@tourinform.hu, www.bekescsaba.hu

Csongrád
6640 Szentháromság tér 8.
☎/fax (63) 570-325
csongrad@tourinform.hu, www.csongrad.hu

Gyomaendrőd
5500 Erzsébet liget 2.
☎ (66) 386-851, fax (66) 282-109
gyomaendrod@tourinform.hu, www.gyomaendrod.hu

Gyula
5700 Kossuth L. u. 7.
☎ (66) 561-681 ☎/fax (66) 561-680
bekes-m@tourinform.hu, www.gyula.hu

Hódmezővásárhely
6800 Szőnyi utca 1.
☎ (62) 249-350, fax (62) 530-140
hodmezovasarhely@tourinform.hu, www.hodmezovasarhely.hu

Kecskemét
6000 Kossuth tér 1.
☎/fax (76) 481-065
kecskemet@tourinform.hu, www.kecskemet.hu

Kiskőrös
6200 Petőfi tér 4/a.
☎ (78) 514-850, (78) 514-851, fax (78) 414-850
kiskoros@tourinform.hu

Kiskunfélegyháza
6100 Szent János tér 2.
☎ (76) 561-420, fax (76) 561-414
kiskunfelegyhaza@tourinform.hu

Kiskunmajsa
6120 Zárda u. 2.
☎/fax (77) 481-327
kiskunmajsa@tourinform.hu, www.kiskunmajsa.hu

Kistelek
6760 Kossuth u. 5-7.
☎ (62) 597-420, fax (62) 597-421
kistelek@tourinform.hu, www.kistelek.hu

Makó
6900 Széchenyi tér 10.
☎/fax (62) 210-708
mako@tourinform.hu, www.mako.hu

Mórahalom
6782 Röszkei u. 1.
☎/fax (62) 280-294
morahalom@tourinform.hu, www.morahalom.hu

Ópusztaszer
6767 Szoborkert 68.
☎ (62) 275-133/121m, fax (62) 275-007
opusztaszer@tourinform.hu, www.opusztaszer.hu

Orosháza
5904 Fasor u. 2/a.,
☎/fax (68) 414-422
oroshaza@tourinform.hu, www.oroshaza.hu

Pusztamérges
6785 Móra tér 4.
☎/fax (62) 286-702
pusztamerges@tourinform.hu

Ruzsa
  6786 Alkotmány tér 2.
  ☎/fax (62) 585-210
  ruzsa@tourinform.hu, www.ruzsa.hu
Szarvas
  5540 Kossuth tér 3.
  ☎/fax (66) 311-140, ☎ (66) 210-062
  szarvas@tourinform.hu, www.szarvas.hu
Szeged
  6722 Tábor u. 7/b.
  ☎ (62) 548-092, fax (62) 548-093
  csongrad-m@tourinform.hu, www.csongrad-megye.hu
Szeged
  6720 Dugonics tér 2.
  ☎/fax (62) 488-690 ☎ (62) 488-699
  szeged@tourinform.hu, www.szegedportal.hu, www.szeged.hu, www.
  szegedvaros.hu
Szeghalom
  5520 Szabadság tér 10-12.
  ☎/fax (66) 470-380
  szeghalom@tourinform.hu, www.szeghalom.hu
Tótkomlós
  5940 Marx u. 15.
  ☎/fax (68) 462-908
  totkomlos@tourinform.hu, www.totkomlos.hu

# Northern Great Plains

Berettyóújfalu
  4100 József Attila u. 35.
  ☎/fax (54) 400-718
  berettyoujfalu@tourinform.hu, www.berettyoujfalu.hu
Debrecen
  4026 Kálvin tér 2/A.
  ☎ (52) 534-544, fax (52) 534-545
  hajdu-m@tourinform.hu
Debrecen
  4024 Piac u. 20.
  ☎ (52) 412-250, (52) 316-419, fax (52) 535-323
  debrecen@tourinform.hu, www.debrecen.hu
Hajdúböszörmény
  4220 Kálvin tér 6.
  ☎/fax (52) 561-851, ☎ (52) 561-852
  hajduboszormeny@tourinform.hu, www.hajduboszormeny.hu
Hajdúnánás
  4080 Fürdő u. 7. (peak season)
  ☎/fax (52) 702-223
  4080 Köztársaság tér 6. (off season)
  ☎/fax (52) 382-076
  hajdunanas@tourinform.hu, www.hajdunanas.hu
Hajdúszoboszló
  4200 Szent István park 1-3.
  ☎/fax (52) 558-928, (52) 558-929
  hajduszoboszlo@tourinform.hu, www.hajduszoboszlo.hu
Hortobágy
  4071 Pásztormúzeum, Petőfi tér 1.
  ☎/fax (52) 589-321
  hortobagy@tourinform.hu, www.hortobagy.hu

Appendix

Jászapáti
　5130 Tompa M. u. 2.
　☎/fax (57) 441-008
　jaszapati@tourinform.hu, www.jaszapati.hu
Jászberény
　5100 Lehel vezér tér 33.
　☎/fax (57) 406-439, ☎ (57) 411-976/16
　jaszbereny@tourinform.hu, www.jaszbereny.hu
Kisújszállás
　5310 Rákóczi u. 3/a (peak season)
　☎ (59) 520-800, fax (59) 520-672
　kisujszallas@tourinform, www.kisujszallas.hu
Mezõtúr
　5400 Szabadság tér 17.
　☎/fax (56) 350-901, ☎ (56) 550-637
　mezotur@tourinform.hu, www.mezotur.hu
Nyíracsád
　4262 Petõfi tér 3.
　☎/fax (52) 207-271
　nyiracsad@tourinform.hu
Nyíregyháza
　4400 Országzászló tér 6.
　☎/fax (42) 504-647, (42) 504-648
　szabolcs-m@tourinform.hu, tourinform.szabolcs.net
Polgár
　4090 Hõsök útja 10.
　polgar@tourinform.hu
Sóstógyógyfürdõ
　4431 Nyíregyháza Sóstógyógyfürdõ, Víztorony (peak season)
　☎/fax (42) 411-193
　sostofurdo@tourinform.hu
Szolnok
　5000 Ságvári krt. 4.
　☎ (56) 420-704, fax (56) 341-441
　szolnok-m@tourinform.hu, www.szolnok.hu
Vásárosnamény
　4800 Szabadság tér 33.
　☎ (45) 570-206, fax (45) 570-207
　vasarosnameny@tourinform.hu, www.vasarosnameny.hu

# Lake Tisza Region

Abádszalók
　5241 Füzes Kemping, Strand út 2. (peak season)
　☎ (59) 535-346, fax (59) 535-345
　5241 Deák Ferenc u. 1/17. (off season)
　☎/fax (59) 357-376
　abadszalok@tourinform.hu, www.abadszalok.hu
Berekfürdõ
　5309 Berek tér 11. (peak season)
　☎ (59319-408, fax (59) 519-007
　berekfurdo@tourinform.hu, www.berekfurdo.hu
Karcag
　5300 Dózsa György u. 5-7.
　☎ (59) 503-224, ☎/fax (59) 503-225
　karcag@tourinform.hu, www.karcag.hu
Kisköre
　3384 Kossuth utca 8.

☎/fax (36) 358-023
kiskore@tourinform.hu, www.kiskore.hu
Nagykörû
5065 Kossuth tér 1. (peak season)
☎/fax (56) 494-822
nagykoru@tourinform.hu, www.nagykoru.hu
Tiszacsege
4066 Fõ út 38.
☎/fax (52) 588-036, (52) 588-037
tiszacsege@tourinform.hu, www.tiszacsege.hu
Tiszafüred
5350 Fürdõ u. 21.
☎/fax (59) 511-123, (59) 511-124
tiszafured@tourinform.hu, www.tiszafured.hu
Tiszaújváros
3580 Széchenyi út 27.
☎ (49) 540-238, (49) 540-239, fax (49) 540-122
tiszaujvaros@tourinform.hu, www.tiszaujvaros.hu

# Northern Hungary

Abaújszántó
3881 Szent István tér 4.
☎/fax (47) 330-053
abaujszanto@tourinform.hu, www.abaujszanto.hu
Aggtelek
3759 Baradla oldal 3.
☎ (48) 503-001, fax (48) 503-002
aggtelek@tourinform.hu, www.aggtelek.hu
Balassagyarmat
2660 Köztársaság tér 6.
☎ (35) 500-640, fax (35) 500-641
balassagyarmat@tourinform.hu, www.balassagyarmat.hu
Bátonyterenye
3070 Molnár S. u. 1-3.
batonyterenye@tourinform.hu, www.batonyterenye.hu
Dédestapolcsány
3643 Petõfi u. 24. (peak season)
☎/fax (48) 501-037
dedestapolcsany@tourinform.hu, www.dedestapolcsany.hu
Edelény
3780 István király út 63.
☎/fax (48) 342-999
edeleny@tourinform.hu, www.edeleny.hu
Eger
3300 Bajcsy-Zsilinszky u. 9. Pf: 263.
☎ (36) 517-715, fax (36) 518-815
eger@tourinform.hu, www.eger.hu
Encs
3860 Petõfi u. 20-22.
☎/fax (46) 587-390, ☎ (46) 587-389
encs@tourinform.hu, www.encs.hu
Gyöngyös
3200 Fõ tér 10.
☎/fax (37) 311-155
gyongyos@tourinform.hu, www.gyongyos.hu
Hollókõ
3176 Kossuth u. 68.

☎ (32) 579-011, ☎/fax (32) 579-010
holloko@tourinform.hu, www.holloko.hu
Kazár
  3127 Damjanich út 3.
  ☎/fax (32) 341-363
  kazar@tourinform.hu
Mezõkövesd
  3400 Szent László tér 23.
  ☎ (49) 500-285, fax (49) 500-286
  mezokovesd@tourinform.hu, www.mezokovesd.hu
Miskolc
  3525 Széchenyi u. 35.
  ☎/fax (46) 508-773
  borsod-m@tourinform.hu, www.kult-tura.hu
Miskolc
  3525 Városház tér 13.
  ☎ (46) 350-425, ☎/fax (46) 350-439, (46) 348-921
  miskolc@tourinform.hu, www.miskolc.hu
Salgótarján
  3100 Fõ tér 5.
  ☎ (32) 512-315, ☎/fax (32) 512-316
  salgotarjan@tourinform.hu, www.salgotarjan.hu
Sárospatak
  3950 Eötvös u. 6.
  ☎ (47) 315-316, ☎/fax (47) 511-441
  sarospatak@tourinform.hu, www.sarospatak.hu
Sátoraljaújhely
  3980 Kossuth tér 5.
  ☎/fax (47) 321-458
  satoraljaujhely@tourinform.hu, www.satoraljaujhely.hu
Szécsény
  3170 Ady Endre út 12.
  ☎/fax (32) 370-777
  szecseny@tourinform.hu, www.szecseny.hu
Tokaj
  3910 Serház u. 1.
  ☎ (47) 552-070, ☎/fax (47) 352-259
  tokaj@tourinform.hu, www.tokaj.hu

## World Heritage Sites

The following World Heritage Sites may also be viewed individually
on this web site: www.hungary.com. Click on attractions and, then,
unique attractions to make your selection.

**Budapest, the Banks of the Danube and the Buda Castle
Quarter**
One of the great restored monuments of the world, remains are still
there of the Roman city of Aquincum and the Gothic castle of Buda.
Secessionist and turn-of-the-century architecture overwhelms you
throughout this city, and touches virtually every period of Hungarian and Central European History. www.fsz.bme.hu/hungary/buda-
pest/budapest.html

**Hollokö**
Hollokö still remains as it was during the 17th and 18th centuries.

Although somewhat commercialized due to the huge number of visitors, the villagers have kept their culture, and the village has kept its ambience, so that it still attracts people from around the world to see a living example of rural life before the agricultural revolution of the 20th century. www.c3.hu/~holloko/

**Millenary Benedictine Monastery of Pannonhalma**
The school and Benedictine order are still here, since 996, over 1,000 years since they came to convert the Hungarians to Christianity. The first Hungarian school and the first written document in Hungarian came out of this monastery, not to mention its wide-ranging influence on all of Europe in the Middle Ages and the Renaissance. The monastery building dates from 1224. www.bences.hu/en

**Hortobágy National Park**
The Hortobágy Puszta is the site of numerous horseback adventures (See *Adventures*), ranging long horned grey cattle, and a grazing and wetlands history that extends back two millennia. It truly extends to a place that time forgot. Many of the Csikós cowboys still sleep with their horses and herds. www.nps.gov/badl/exp/hortobagy.htm

**Pécs (Sopianae) Early Christian Cemetery**
Here you descend into a remarkable series of decorated tombs, underground burial chambers from the fourth century in the cemetery of Sopianae (modern Pécs). The memorial chapels above invite you in with extraordinarily intricate murals of Christian art created a few hundred years after the time of Christ. There are also the remains of medieval and ancient Roman remains, since the town was settled by Rome in the second century AD, and became a regional capital by the fourth century AD.

**Caves of the Aggtelek Karst and Slovak Karst**
Twisting under the earth in fabulous variety and colorful formations, the over 700 caves of the Aggtelek and Slovak Karst are shared by Hungary and Slovakia. Underground lakes and rivers, ancient volcanic formations echo with rushing waters from distant caverns deep in the earth. 10 million years of life on earth are cross-sectioned in the caves. This site is shared with the Slovak Republic.

**The Tokaj Wine Region**
In 1737 this wine region was declared a natural protectorate of the king, the first such "ecological" decree in history. It is no wonder. The vines intermingle beneath the perfectly shaped volcanic Mt. Tokaj, bringing forth world-class wine grapes. The Ungvari Wine Cellar, Rakoczi Wine Cellar, Koporosi Cellars, Gomboshegyi Cellars, Oremus Cellars, and Tolcsva Wine Museum Cellars, all are here. Tokaj has survived as a jewel of the world wine-growing tradition, and filled with trails and adventures.

**Fertö-Neusiedlersee**
This is one of the unique wetland habitats of the world. Hundreds of thousands of birds regularly use Lake Fertö for nesting, resting, and feeding as they migrate between the southern and northern parts of

the globe. Egrets, great cranes, and thousands of species remind one of the great bird sanctuaries of Africa.

# Hungarian Pronunciation

Letters are pronounced the same way as in English, with the following exceptions.

A a – like the aw in awl, with the mouth slightly closed.

Á á – sounds like aah!

C c – like "tse" in tse tse fly.

Cs cs – like ch in couch.

Dz – like "ds" at the end of "beds."

Dzs dzs – like "j" in jam, but with a slight "d" sound, as in djam.

É é – like "a" in pay.

Gy gy – like "d" with an "ia" as in dia.

I i – like "i" in hip.

Í í – like "e" in see.

J j – like "y" in yank.

Ly ly – like "y" in yeah.

Ny ny – like the ni in onion.

O o – like the "o" in on.

Ó ó – like the "o" in tore.

Ö ö – like "er" in her.

Ő ő – like "ur" in turn, but stretch out the "ur" sound. Same as ö but longer.

S s – like "sh" in sheik.

Sz sz – like "s" in say.

Ty ty – like "t" plus "ye" as in yen but without the "n."

U u – like "u" in put.

Ú ú – like "oo" in spook.

Ü ü – like "ew" in mew, but with shorter length

Ű ű – like the "ew" of mew, but longer and with a slight "r" inflection, by rounding the lips.

Zs zs – like the "s" in pleasure.

# Hungarian Numbers

0 – nulla  (new-lah)

1 – egy (sounds like edgey)

2 – kettö (sounds like ketter)

3 – három (hah-roam)

4 – négy (nayj)

5 – öt (like urt)

6 – hat (sounds like hot)

7 – hét (sounds like hate)

8 – nyolc (sounds like nwolts)

9 – kilenc (sounds like keelents)

10 – tíz (sounds like tease)

20  – husz (sounds like whose)
30  – harminc (sounds like harmeents)
40  – negyven (sounds like nedgven)
50  – ötven (sounds like urtven)
60  – hatvan (sounds like hotvon)
70  – hetven
80  – nyolcvan (sounds like nwoltsvon)
90  – kilencven (sounds like keelentsven)
100  – szaz (sounds like sawz)
1,000  – ezer (sounds like ezair)
1,000,000 – millió

# Hungarian Phrases

| | |
|---|---|
| Here is my.....passport. | Itt van az útlevelem (Eet von ahzz oot-levelem).<br>When handing something over you can say simply, Tessék  (tesh-ake) |
| My name is____.<br>I am an American/Canadian/Australian/Englishman.<br>What is your name? | _____ a nevem.<br>Amerikai/Kanadai/Austrál/Angol vagyok<br>Mi az ön neve? (Mee awz urn neve) |
| Please write it down.<br><br>Please, how is this word spelled?<br>Do you know the English word? | Kérem, le tudná ezt írni? (Kay-rem le toodnaah ezt earnee)<br>Kérem, hogy írják? (Kay-rem, hoe-dgia eeryaahk?)<br>Ismeri az angol szót? (Eesh-merry  awz awn-goal soat?) |
| Hello. How are you? | Szervusz.  Hogy van? (Ser-voos    Hoadgi-van?<br>For good friends say: Servusz. Hogy vagy? (Ser-voos. Hoadgi-vawdgi?) |
| Good-bye. | Viszontlátásra! (Vee-soant-laah-taahsh-raw) |
| Please. | Kérem (Kay-rem) Roll the "r" slightly like the Spanish r. |
| Thank you. | Köszönöm. (Ker-sir-nerm) |
| Yes. | Igen. (Ee-gen) Hard "g." |
| No. | Nem. |
| I am fine, thank you. | Köszönöm, jól. (Ker-sir-nerm, yoal)<br>For good friends, say: Kösz, jól. (Curse, yoal) |
| Good morning. | Jó reggelt. (Yoa re-gelt) Hard "g" and roll the "r" as in Spanish |
| Good afternoon. Good day. | Jó napot. (Yoa nawpot) |
| Good evening. | Jó estét (Yoa esh-tate) Final "e" is silent |

| | |
|---|---|
| Good night, I must go to bed. | Dobrú noc, idem si l'ahnút'. (Dough-bruu nots idem si luh-nuut) Pronounce nuut as in loot |
| Excuse me. I have to leave. | Jó éjszakát. (Yoa aysaw-kaaht) |
| I am sorry. | Sajnálom. (Shaw-yee-naahl-om) Also used frequently as an apology is Bocsánat (Boech-aah-not) |
| I don't understand. I don't know. | Nem értem. (Nem air-tem) The "r" is rolled as in Spanish |
| Can you help me, please? | Kérem, meg tudná ezt ismételni? (Kayrem, meg toodnaw, ezt eesh-may-tell-nee?) |
| Do you speak English? I don't speak Hungarian (Czech, Slovakian). | Beszél anglul? (Bes-ail awn-goa-lool) Nem jól beszélek Magyarul (Csech, Szlovák). |
| What is this? What is that? | Mi ez? Mi az? (Me awz?) |
| I would like this/that, please. (pointing) | Kérem, ezt/azt Szeretnék. (Kayrem, ezt/ awzt seretnake) |
| How much (a) money (b) quantity? | a) Mennyibe kerül? (Menyebe kerule) b) Mennyi? (Men-nye) |
| Where am I? I want to go here. (Pointing to a place on a map) | Hol vagyok? (Hole vawdgiok) Ide megyek. (Eede medgiek) |
| Please, what bus/tram/ metro do I take? | Kérem, melyik busszal/vonattal/metroval menjek? (Kayrem, meyeek boos-sawl/ voanot-tawl/metro-vawl men-yek) |
| Where is the bustop/train station/metro station? | Hol van a buszmegálló/vasútállomás/ metróállomás? (Hole vawn aw boos-megaahlloe/vawshewt-aahl-oa-maash/ metro-aahloa-maash) |
| Please, I need a doctor. I need a dentist. | Orvost keresek (Or-voasht kereshek). Fogorvost keresek (Foa-g-or-voasht kereshek) |
| I need a policeman. | Rendört keresek (Rend-ert kereshek) |
| I need to call my embassy. | Hívnom kell a nagykövetséget. (Heevnom kell nadgy-ker-vet-shayg-et) |
| I need to call the hotel. | Hívnom kell a hotelt (Heevnom kell aw hotelt) |
| May I use your telephone to call? | Hívhatok az ön telefonján? (Heev-haw-toak awz urn telephonyaahn) |
| One ticket. Two or more tickets. One round-trip ticket. Return ticket. | Egy jegy. (Edgi yedgy) Jegyek. (Hold up fingers to indicate two, three, etc.) Retur jegy. (Retoor yedgi) |

| My son/daughter is____years old. | A fiam/lányam ____ éves. (Aw feeawm/ laahniawm____ayvesh) |
| It is just my wife and me. | Csak én és a feleségem. (Chalk ayn aysh aw feleshaygem) |
| It is my family. | A családom. (Aw chawlaahdom) |
| Excuse me, I am going to____ (point to map). | Bocsánat én _____megyek. (Boa-chaah- not ayn____ medgyek) |
| Do I get off at the next stop? | Leszállok a következö megállonál?(Less- aah-lloak aw kurvet-kezur meg gaahl- loanaahl) |
| What is the next stop? | Mi a következö megálló? (Mee aw kurvet- kezur meg gaahl-loa) |
| One person. | Egy ember. (Edgy em-bear) |
| Two persons. | Két ember. (Kate em-bear) |

# Index